TO ___Paula_____

FROM ___Joy DeKok_____

ON ___when we started the "When God_____
Doesn't Fix It"
Bible study___

May 1, 2020 → started reading (pg 1)

June 21, 2020 → completed reading

Give all your worries

and cares to God,

He cares

for He cares about you.

1 PETER 5:7

# HE cares

## NEW TESTAMENT
### with Psalms & Proverbs

**New Living Translation®**

SECOND EDITION

Tyndale House Publishers, Inc.
Carol Stream, Illinois

# contents

# foreword

NONE OF US expect that we will ever receive a bad report from a medical test. Somehow we manage to go about our daily lives blissfully denying the realities of our fallen, broken world. But many of us *do* actually receive frightening news about our health at some point, and at those moments, we need the reassuring truths of Scripture. We need comfort, encouragement, support, stability, and most of all, we need Hope.

When I was going through breast cancer treatment a few years ago, I found it difficult to read books on cancer or even long portions of Scripture. I was nauseated, weak, and mentally fuzzy. How I wish this marvelous version of the New Testament with practical and insightful comments by Lynn Eib had been available. I have read each section of the notes with tears in my eyes, overwhelmed by the genuine comfort and solace Lynn's words bring as she identifies with those who are ill. She strongly, yet tenderly—as only those who have walked the road of suffering can do—points the reader to the inner strengthening and peace that Jesus can give to those who trust Him completely.

Read the Word of God and the words of His dearly loved child Lynn and find what you need to survive and thrive on your own journey through the Valley of the Shadow.

*Kay Warren*
Breast cancer survivor, speaker, pastor's wife

# how not to be defeated
# by illness

*I*F, as best-selling author Rick Warren says, "The greatest insights in life are found at the center of pain," most of us probably would be satisfied with less insight if it would mean less pain, too! Suffering may be a great teacher, but it's one class we all would just as soon skip.

But that isn't always possible. While serious illness tends to strike the elderly most often, it's no respecter of persons. You may be young and athletic and yet still stricken. You may be middle-aged and follow all the recommended guidelines for healthy living, but still face a health crisis. And you may have a little child still filled with wide-eyed innocence and yet fighting for life. And even if you or your loved one has lived a long life, this may not be the way you imagined those golden years to be.

So here you are at the "center of pain"—maybe physical pain, probably emotional pain, and perhaps even spiritual pain. You're not interested in trite platitudes like: *Think positive. Things could be worse. God doesn't give you more than you can handle.*

**You need to know today that somebody really cares about your diagnosis and prognosis and more importantly has the power to do something about it.**

You've come to the right place.

*He Cares* is designed for those facing serious illness, even life-threatening illnesses. It's not just another book on the market giving advice to disease-fighting people. This book is unlike any other because it contains the very Word of God. If you've never read the Bible, you're going to be amazed that these words written thousands of years ago contain the answers to your deepest needs today. And you can expect to experience God's supernatural power in your life as He shows you how much He truly cares about you.

If you already know and love the Bible, you're going to appreciate that *He Cares* highlights Scriptures that speak to the special struggles of those facing a health crisis. You may know in your head that He cares, but you need to feel it in your heart.

* * *

That's the way I would describe how I felt in 1990 when I was diagnosed with advanced colon cancer at the age of thirty-six. I had a personal relationship with God for many years and even was married to a pastor, but my devastating diagnosis left me struggling to feel God's love for me.

"We found a tumor" were the four simple words that came from my doctor's lips and turned my world upside down on June 26, 1990. I can still picture my husband's ashen face as he stood at the end of my hospital gurney. This was his worst nightmare revisited as some twenty years earlier a doctor diagnosed his first wife with amyotrophic lateral sclerosis (Lou Gehrig's disease). She died while they were still newlyweds.

Although colon cancer is considered very curable in its early stages, I was not that fortunate. Mine had spread into several lymph nodes, making it a late stage 3 diagnosis and giving me about a 40 percent chance of survival.

Treatment at that time consisted of weekly chemotherapy for a year. I experienced just about every side effect possible, including strange ones like the air smelling so bad that I had to hold my nose to walk outside without getting sick! To top it off, I was extremely allergic to the main drug, which caused my nose to run, my eyes to water, and my feet and hands to swell and feel like they were on fire. Thankfully, my oncologist decided to stop the treatments after six months.

During my chemo treatments I counted hundreds of people in sixteen different states who were praying for me, so it was tough to understand why things were so difficult. I remember asking God one day, "Why aren't things going a little easier for me? Would it be too much to ask to feel normal again for just a couple of hours?" But I heard only silence from heaven.

Even though God didn't answer my question that day, I feel He has answered it in the intervening years. I now believe I was allowed to suffer so that I could encourage and support suffering people. It's a path I never would have chosen for myself, but one which has given my life more fulfillment and joy than anything else I've ever done.

In 1991 I founded the first of the three prayer support groups I still facilitate—two for cancer patients and one for those who have lost a loved one to cancer. Since 1996 my oncologist has employed me as a patient advocate, offering emotional and spiritual encouragement to cancer patients and their caregivers. I have watched time and again as suffering people *have* found the greatest insights in life at the center of their pain, because as author Ben Patterson explains in his book *Deepening Your Conversation with God*, "When you're well, you think you're in charge and when you're not, you know you aren't."

I also have learned more as a student of suffering at the University of Pain than I ever could have imagined. But when I was first diagnosed, that was hardly my objective.

I remember when I was in the hospital after my cancer surgery, a friend came into my room and told me God was going to teach me great things through this trial. I wanted to take the IV out of my arm, stab it into hers, and tell her, "You get into the bed and learn great things from God because I don't want to learn this way."

If you or someone you love has been diagnosed with a serious illness, I doubt you are rejoicing over the possibilities of what you can learn through suffering. But I hope you are praying and believing that God can touch you. Whoever you are. Right where you are.

**Whether you have a bunch of questions for God or you just would like to hear His comforting voice, you have the right tool in your hands.** The Word of God has the power to change your life unlike anything else you ever could read.

You even may discover there are some things that you (and many others) thought the Bible says, but it doesn't. There aren't any verses here or in the rest of the Old Testament that say, "God helps those who help themselves." (Ben Franklin apparently coined that phrase.) You also won't read, "Cleanliness is next to godliness" (twentieth-century American journalist Christopher Morley is credited with that quip). And don't look for the comfort of the verse "This, too, shall pass" because it's not in the Bible either. We don't know who first uttered those wise words, but Abraham Lincoln quoted them in one of his speeches as coming from an Eastern monarch.

On the other hand, some of what you read may surprise you, as it will run counter to much of what we hear in our culture. You'll see, among other things, that there are *not* many paths to God, but only one; the devil is real, but he doesn't wear red tights; it is possible to know for certain you're headed for heaven; and Jesus wasn't a mild-mannered, happy-go-lucky guy. Instead, He experienced a wide range of human emotions: sadness, anguish, hurt, frustration, disappointment, and loneliness, and he even got really angry at least a couple of times—yet He never sinned through any of these difficult moments.

\* \* \* \*

So what's the best way to read *He Cares* and experience its powerful message? There isn't a single right way, but we can suggest several possibilities.

You can turn to the book of Matthew and read straight through like you would any book. You might want to read one chapter a day and any accompanying inspirational boxes within the chapter. Or you might want to look at the book introductions and see which theme seems to fit your interest, and then start reading that book. You also could use the topical index on page A13 to find verses and thoughts on such topics as peace, worry, healing, or heaven. Or you could check out the four themes listed on page A15 and study one of those by finding the corresponding symbols throughout the text. And finally, you could do as many people do during difficult times: Start reading in the Psalms as they are filled with people calling for God to help them get through the troubling seasons of life.

However you choose to read *He Cares*, try to read it every day. It is necessary food and refreshment for the soul, because our souls can get malnourished, too. Reading *He Cares* also will feed your mind as you fill it with absolute truths and precious promises.

**If you don't want to be defeated by illness—no matter what it does or has done to you or your loved one—this is a book for you.** While there may be little we can do to choose whether we get a serious illness, we believe we can do a lot to choose whether we are its victims. We don't just mean by this whether we live or die, but how illness affects us in the deepest parts of who we are. We believe illness cannot conquer our spirit unless we choose to become its victim. And we also believe that beating disease can mean more than just a physical cure.

For quite a while in my life I was "beating" cancer. There was no sign of it in my body, but it was beating me. It was controlling my mind, my attitude, and my relationship with God. It was the first thing I thought about each day and the last thing each night. It was hard to enjoy holidays and special moments because I wondered if they would be my last.

But God gradually began to enlarge my picture of beating disease as He spoke to my heart: "Whether you live or die from this is up to Me, but *how* you live is up to you."

The pressure finally was off. I would do my part to physically combat my illness, but I would not judge whether I beat it by whether I was cured or not. I would beat it no matter what, because I would refuse to let it conquer me and control my life.

Certainly we beat disease when we are declared to be in remission or cured. However, we also beat it moment by moment when we allow God, not disease, to control our thoughts. We beat it hour by hour as we remember that God's power within us is greater than any serious illness. And we beat it day by day as we trust in God's strength and not disease's weakness.

**If you want to beat the grip serious illness can have on your life, you need a supernatural touch.**

We are praying for you to receive that touch as you read *He Cares*. We're asking and believing that the God of the universe will reveal Himself to you as never before. We're praying that you won't just know *about* Jesus like you do some other famous person, but that you'll know Him *personally* as your Friend. We're praying that you don't view the Holy Spirit as some kind of eerie ghost, but understand He's the real Spirit of God who can live inside you and help you become all you were meant to be (even better than any human "spiritual life coach"!). And we're praying most of all that you know and have received the cure for your soul (see page 486). If you have, you cannot lose your battle with illness. Either God will take the disease out of you, or He one day will take you out of the disease.

But *He Cares* is more than a guide to your future; it's how to find healing every day along your journey. It will help you draw closer to the One whose healing touch can reach your body, mind, and spirit.

So whether your heart is looking for a place to call home or your mind is searching for some answers to life's tough questions or your spirit is thirsting for some much-needed refreshment, you have found your answer: *He Cares* and He wants to show you just how much . . . starting right now.

*Lynn Eib*
Cancer survivor, journalist, cancer patient advocate

# helpful topics

*He Cares* is filled with encouragement, guidance, and answers for your heavy heart or your questioning mind. Listed here are some popular topics, which may be helpful to you as you walk this journey with a serious illness. Simply choose a topic and then turn to the pages listed for the related "inspirational boxes" and book introductions. This list is by no means an exhaustive one, but it will point you to places where God's Word can speak to your needs.

# A NOTE TO READERS

The *Holy Bible,* New Living Translation, was first published in 1996. It quickly became one of the most popular Bible translations in the English-speaking world. While the NLT's influence was rapidly growing, the Bible Translation Committee determined that an additional investment in scholarly review and text refinement could make it even better. So shortly after its initial publication, the committee began an eight-year process with the purpose of increasing the level of the NLT's precision without sacrificing its easy-to-understand quality. This second-generation text was completed in 2004 and is reflected in this edition of the New Living Translation.

The goal of any Bible translation is to convey the meaning and content of the ancient Hebrew, Aramaic, and Greek texts as accurately as possible to contemporary readers. The challenge for our translators was to create a text that would communicate as clearly and powerfully to today's readers as the original texts did to readers and listeners in the ancient biblical world. The resulting translation is easy to read and understand, while also accurately communicating the meaning and content of the original biblical texts. The NLT is a general-purpose text especially good for study, devotional reading, and reading aloud in worship services.

We believe that the New Living Translation—which combines the latest biblical scholarship with a clear, dynamic writing style—will communicate God's word powerfully to all who read it. We publish it with the prayer that God will use it to speak his timeless truth to the church and the world in a fresh, new way.

*The Publishers*
*July 2004*

# INTRODUCTION TO THE
## *New Living Translation*

*Translation Philosophy and Methodology*   English Bible translations tend to be governed by one of two general translation theories. The first theory has been called "formal-equivalence," "literal," or "word-for-word" translation. According to this theory, the translator attempts to render each word of the original language into English and seeks to preserve the original syntax and sentence structure as much as possible in translation. The second theory has been called "dynamic-equivalence," "functional-equivalence," or "thought-for-thought" translation. The goal of this translation theory is to produce in English the closest natural equivalent of the message expressed by the original-language text, both in meaning and in style.

Both of these translation theories have their strengths. A formal-equivalence translation preserves aspects of the original text—including ancient idioms, term consistency, and original-language syntax—that are valuable for scholars and professional study. It allows a reader to trace formal elements of the original-language text through the English translation. A dynamic-equivalence translation, on the other hand, focuses on translating the message of the original-language text. It ensures that the meaning of the text is readily apparent to the contemporary reader. This allows the message to come through with immediacy, without requiring the reader to struggle with foreign idioms and awkward syntax. It also facilitates serious study of the text's message and clarity in both devotional and public reading.

The pure application of either of these translation philosophies would create translations at opposite ends of the translation spectrum. But in reality, all translations contain a mixture of these two philosophies. A purely formal-equivalence translation would be unintelligible in English, and a purely dynamic-equivalence translation would risk being unfaithful to the original. That is why translations shaped by dynamic-equivalence theory are usually quite literal when the original text is relatively clear, and the translations shaped by formal-equivalence theory are sometimes quite dynamic when the original text is obscure.

The translators of the New Living Translation set out to render the message of the original texts of Scripture into clear, contemporary English. As they did so, they kept the concerns of both formal-equivalence and dynamic-equivalence in mind. On the one hand, they translated as simply and literally as possible when that approach yielded an accurate, clear, and natural English text. Many words and phrases were rendered literally and consistently into English, preserving essential literary and rhetorical devices, ancient metaphors, and word choices that give structure to the text and provide echoes of meaning from one passage to the next.

On the other hand, the translators rendered the message more dynamically when the literal rendering was hard to understand, was misleading, or yielded archaic or foreign wording. They clarified difficult metaphors and terms to aid in the reader's understanding. The translators first worked to understand the meaning of the words and phrases in the ancient context; then they rendered the message into clear, natural English. Their goal was to be both faithful to the ancient texts and eminently readable. The result is a translation that is both exegetically accurate and idiomatically powerful.

*Translation Process and Team*   To produce an accurate translation of the Bible into contemporary English, the translation team needed the skills necessary to enter into the thought patterns of the ancient authors and then to render their ideas, connotations, and effects into clear, contemporary English. To begin this process, qualified biblical scholars were needed to interpret the meaning of the original text and to check it against our base English translation. In order to guard against personal and theological biases, the scholars needed to represent a diverse group who would employ the best exegetical tools. Then to work alongside the scholars, skilled English stylists were needed to shape the text into clear, contemporary English.

With these concerns in mind, the Bible Translation Committee recruited teams of scholars that represented a broad spectrum of denominations, theological perspectives, and backgrounds within the worldwide evangelical community. (These scholars are listed at the end of this introduction.) Each book of the Bible was assigned to three different scholars with proven expertise in the book or group of books to be reviewed. Each of these scholars made a thorough review of the base translation and submitted suggested revisions to the appropriate Senior Translator. The Senior Translator then reviewed and summarized these suggestions and proposed a first-draft revision of the base text. This draft served as the basis for several additional phases of exegetical and stylistic committee review. Then the Bible Translation Committee jointly reviewed and approved every verse of the final translation.

The New Living Translation was first published in 1996. Shortly after its initial publication, the Bible Translation Committee began a process of further committee review and translation refinement. The purpose of this continued revision was to increase the level of precision without sacrificing the text's easy-to-understand quality. This second-edition text was completed in 2004, and this printing of the New Living Translation reflects the updated text.

*The Texts behind the New Living Translation*   The New Testament translators used the two standard editions of the Greek New Testament: the *Greek New Testament,* published by the United Bible Societies (UBS, fourth revised edition, 1993), and *Novum Testamentum Graece,* edited by Nestle and Aland (NA, twenty-seventh edition, 1993). These two editions, which have the same text but differ in punctuation and textual notes, represent, for the most part, the best in modern textual scholarship. However, in cases where strong textual or other scholarly evidence supported the decision, the translators sometimes chose to differ from the UBS and NA Greek texts and followed variant readings found in other ancient witnesses. Significant textual variants of this sort are always noted in the textual notes of the New Living Translation.

*Translation Issues*    The translators have made a conscious effort to provide a text that can be easily understood by the typical reader of modern English. To this end, we sought to use only vocabulary and language structures in common use today. We avoided using language likely to become quickly dated or that reflects only a narrow sub-dialect of English, with the goal of making the New Living Translation as broadly useful and timeless as possible.

But our concern for readability goes beyond the concerns of vocabulary and sentence structure. We are also concerned about historical and cultural barriers to understanding the Bible, and we have sought to translate terms shrouded in history and culture in ways that can be immediately understood. This includes using contemporary renderings for historical particulars like weights and measures, dates and times, as well as clarifying ancient imagery and sentence structures.

*Lexical Consistency in Terminology*    For the sake of clarity, we have translated certain original-language terms consistently, especially within synoptic passages and for commonly repeated rhetorical phrases, and within certain word categories such as divine names and technical terminology (e.g., liturgical, legal, cultural, zoological, and botanical terms). For theological terms, we have allowed a greater semantic range of acceptable English words or phrases for a single Hebrew or Greek word. We have avoided some theological terms that are not readily understood by many modern readers. For example, we avoided using words such as "justification," "sanctification," and "regeneration," which are carryovers from Latin translations. In place of these words, we have provided renderings such as "we are made right with God," "we are made holy," and "we are born anew."

*Textual Footnotes*    The New Living Translation provides several kinds of textual footnotes, all designated in the text with an asterisk:

- When for the sake of clarity the NLT renders a difficult or potentially confusing phrase dynamically, we often give the literal rendering in a textual footnote. This allows the reader to see the literal source of our dynamic rendering and how our translation relates to other more literal translations. For example, in Acts 2:42 we translated the literal "breaking of bread" (from the Greek) as "the Lord's Supper" to clarify that this verse refers to the ceremonial practice of the church rather than just an ordinary meal. Then we attached a footnote to "the Lord's Supper," which reads: "Greek *the breaking of bread*."
- Textual footnotes are also used to show alternative renderings, prefaced with the word "Or." For example, the footnote to the translation "wise men" at Matthew 2:1 says, "Or *royal astrologers;* Greek reads *magi*."
- When our translators follow a textual variant that differs significantly from our standard Greek texts (listed earlier), we document that difference with a footnote. We also footnote cases when the NLT excludes a passage that is included in the Greek text known as the *Textus Receptus* (and familiar to readers through its translation in the King James Version). In such cases, we offer a translation of the excluded text in a footnote, even though it is generally recognized as a later addition to the Greek text and not part of the original Greek New Testament.
- All Old Testament passages that are quoted in the New Testament are identified by a textual footnote at the New Testament location.
- Some textual footnotes provide cultural and historical information on places, things, and people in the Bible that may be obscure to modern readers. Such notes should aid the reader in understanding the message of the text. For example, in Acts 12:1, "King Herod" is named in this translation as "King Herod Agrippa" and is identified in a footnote as being "the nephew of Herod Antipas and a grandson of Herod the Great."
- One challenge we faced was how to translate accurately the ancient biblical text that was originally written in a context where male-oriented terms were used to refer to humanity generally. Often the original text, though using masculine nouns and pronouns, clearly intends that the message be applied to both men and women. A typical example is found in the New Testament letters, where the believers are called "brothers" (*adelphoi*). Yet it is clear from the content of these letters that they were addressed to all the believers—male and female. Thus, we have often translated this Greek word as "brothers and sisters" in order to represent the historical situation more accurately.

  We have also been sensitive to passages where the text applies generally to human beings or to the human condition. In some instances we have used plural pronouns (they, them) in place of the masculine singular (he, him). For example, a traditional rendering of Romans 3:28 is: "For we maintain that a man is justified by faith apart from the law." We have rendered it: "So we are made right with God through faith and not by obeying the law." A traditional rendering of Galatians 6:7 is: "Do not be deceived: God cannot be mocked. A man reaps what he sows." We have rendered it: "Don't be misled—you cannot mock the justice of God. You will always harvest what you plant."

As we submit this translation for publication, we recognize that any translation of the Scriptures is subject to limitations and imperfections. Anyone who has attempted to communicate the richness of God's Word into another language will realize it is impossible to make a perfect translation. Recognizing these limitations, we sought God's guidance and wisdom throughout this project. Now we pray that he will accept our efforts and use this translation for the benefit of the church and of all people.

We pray that the New Living Translation will overcome some of the barriers of history, culture, and language that have kept people from reading and understanding God's Word. We hope that readers unfamiliar with the Bible will find the words clear and easy to understand and that readers well versed in the Scriptures will gain a fresh perspective. We pray that readers will gain insight and wisdom for living, but most of all that they will meet the God of the Bible and be forever changed by knowing him.

# BIBLE TRANSLATION TEAM
## *New Living Translation*

### GOSPELS AND ACTS
Grant R. Osborne, Senior Translator
*Trinity Evangelical Divinity School*

### MATTHEW
Craig Blomberg, *Denver Seminary*
Donald A. Hagner, *Fuller Theological Seminary*
David Turner, *Grand Rapids Baptist Seminary*

### MARK
Robert Guelich (deceased), *Fuller Theological Seminary*
George Guthrie, *Union University*
Grant R. Osborne, *Trinity Evangelical Divinity School*

### LUKE
Darrell Bock, *Dallas Theological Seminary*
Scot McKnight, *North Park University*
Robert Stein, *The Southern Baptist Theological Seminary*

### JOHN
Gary M. Burge, *Wheaton College*
Philip W. Comfort, *Coastal Carolina University*
Marianne Meye Thompson, *Fuller Theological Seminary*

### ACTS
D. A. Carson, *Trinity Evangelical Divinity School*
William J. Larkin, *Columbia International University*
Roger Mohrlang, *Whitworth College*

### LETTERS AND REVELATION
Norman R. Ericson, Senior Translator
*Wheaton College*

### ROMANS, GALATIANS
Gerald Borchert, *Northern Baptist Theological Seminary*
Douglas J. Moo, *Wheaton College*
Thomas R. Schreiner, *The Southern Baptist Theological Seminary*

### 1 & 2 CORINTHIANS
Joseph Alexanian, *Trinity International University*
Linda Belleville, *North Park Theological Seminary*
Douglas A. Oss, *Central Bible College*
Robert Sloan, *Baylor University*

### EPHESIANS—PHILEMON
Harold W. Hoehner, *Dallas Theological Seminary*
Moises Silva, *Gordon-Conwell Theological Seminary*
Klyne Snodgrass, *North Park Theological Seminary*

### HEBREWS, JAMES, 1 & 2 PETER, JUDE
Peter Davids, *Schloss Mittersill Study Centre*
Norman R. Ericson, *Wheaton College*
William Lane (deceased), *Seattle Pacific University*
J. Ramsey Michaels, *S. W. Missouri State University*

### 1—3 JOHN, REVELATION
Greg Beale, *Wheaton College*
Robert Mounce, *Whitworth College*
M. Robert Mulholland Jr., *Asbury Theological Seminary*

### PSALMS AND PROVERBS
Tremper Longman III, Senior Translator
*Westmont College*

### PSALMS 1–75
Mark D. Futato, *Reformed Theological Seminary*
Douglas Green, *Westminster Theological Seminary*
Richard Pratt, *Reformed Theological Seminary*

### PSALMS 76–150
David M. Howard Jr., *Bethel Theological Seminary*
Raymond C. Ortlund Jr., *Trinity Evangelical Divinity School*
Willem VanGemeren, *Trinity Evangelical Divinity School*

### PROVERBS
Ted Hildebrandt, *Gordon College*
Richard Schultz, *Wheaton College*
Raymond C. Van Leeuwen, *Eastern College*

### BIBLE TRANSLATION COMMITTEE SCHOLARS
Daniel I. Block, *Wheaton College*
Barry J. Beitzel, *Trinity Evangelical Divinity School*
Tremper Longman III, *Westmont College*
John N. Oswalt, *Wesley Biblical Seminary*
Grant R. Osborne, *Trinity Evangelical Divinity School*
Norman R. Ericson, *Wheaton College*

### SPECIAL REVIEWERS
F. F. Bruce (deceased), *University of Manchester*
Kenneth N. Taylor (deceased), *Translator,* The Living Bible

### COORDINATING TEAM
Mark D. Taylor, *Director and Chief Stylist*
Ronald A. Beers, *Executive Director and Stylist*
Mark R. Norton, *Managing Editor and O.T. Coordinating Editor*
Philip W. Comfort, *N.T. Coordinating Editor*
Daniel W. Taylor, *Bethel University, Senior Stylist*

# reader's guide to margin symbols

*Highlighted Verses.* Scripture is filled with God's wisdom and truth. It clarifies who we are—gifted and creative beings made to have an ongoing relationship with God. It also explains how that vital relationship is broken by our own sins. It details God's work on our behalf, enabling us to receive His grace and salvation. And it reveals to us the person of Jesus Christ, Who has made our hope and healing possible.

Throughout this New Testament, you will find four different symbols sprinkled in the margins. They will help you to quickly find passages that relate to important New Testament themes.

 THE RAINBOW is a sign of hope first set in the sky for Noah when God promised He never again would flood the whole earth. This symbol leads you to verses about the security, peace, and comfort found in a relationship with God.

 LIGHTNING is not a force to be ignored as it has the power to injure or even kill. The power of evil should not be taken lightly either. Sin injures and kills our spiritual life with God. This symbol shows you verses about sin and its destructive power.

 THE CROSS is a timeless symbol of the greatest sacrifice ever made: Jesus' death for our life. This symbol directs you to verses which explain how the Cross changed history and how anyone can find forgiveness through Jesus Christ.

 THE PIERCED HAND reminds us that Jesus willingly allowed Himself to be nailed to the cross as payment for our sins. This symbol highlights for you verses about Jesus' nature and character, which prove He really is the Son of God and our Messiah.

# MATTHEW

*Seek the Kingdom of God above all else, and live righteously, and he will give you everything you need.*

MATTHEW 6:33

When healthcare professionals treat us, they give instructions that make it clear what we need to do—and not do—to get the desired physical results.

"If you take this drug, your symptoms will lessen."

"If you do these exercises, you'll improve."

"If you don't change your diet, you're in for trouble."

Sometimes we take the advice and sometimes we don't.

The Gospel of Matthew is very much a book of practical advice for living, except this advice doesn't just affect our physical bodies; it also influences our minds and eternal souls. It's a prescription for living and it comes from the very Son of God Himself—Jesus, the promised Jewish Messiah. Jesus told people that if they stopped going in the direction they were headed and went in the direction of the Kingdom of God instead, their lives would be transformed. Matthew took those words to heart and went from being a despised tax collector to becoming one who did miracles for others in Jesus' name.

Which direction are you headed in today? Toward the Kingdom of God or somewhere else? Toward living righteously or not? If you're not sure exactly what it means to seek and live this way, just keep reading and it will become very clear as you hear Jesus' teachings and you witness His life, death, and resurrection. Of course, if you already have *everything* you need in life, you don't have to keep reading!

1

## The Ancestors of Jesus the Messiah

**1** This is a record of the ancestors of Jesus the Messiah, a descendant of David* and of Abraham:

2 Abraham was the father of Isaac.
Isaac was the father of Jacob.
Jacob was the father of Judah and his brothers.
3 Judah was the father of Perez and Zerah (whose mother was Tamar).
Perez was the father of Hezron.
Hezron was the father of Ram.*
4 Ram was the father of Amminadab.
Amminadab was the father of Nahshon.
Nahshon was the father of Salmon.
5 Salmon was the father of Boaz (whose mother was Rahab).
Boaz was the father of Obed (whose mother was Ruth).
Obed was the father of Jesse.
6 Jesse was the father of King David.
David was the father of Solomon (whose mother was Bathsheba, the widow of Uriah).
7 Solomon was the father of Rehoboam.
Rehoboam was the father of Abijah.
Abijah was the father of Asa.*
8 Asa was the father of Jehoshaphat.
Jehoshaphat was the father of Jehoram.*
Jehoram was the father* of Uzziah.
9 Uzziah was the father of Jotham.
Jotham was the father of Ahaz.
Ahaz was the father of Hezekiah.
10 Hezekiah was the father of Manasseh.
Manasseh was the father of Amon.*
Amon was the father of Josiah.
11 Josiah was the father of Jehoiachin* and his brothers (born at the time of the exile to Babylon).

12 After the Babylonian exile:
Jehoiachin was the father of Shealtiel.
Shealtiel was the father of Zerubbabel.
13 Zerubbabel was the father of Abiud.

*14 generations each* [handwritten note in left margin]

Abiud was the father of Eliakim.
Eliakim was the father of Azor.
14 Azor was the father of Zadok.
Zadok was the father of Akim.
Akim was the father of Eliud.
15 Eliud was the father of Eleazar.
Eleazar was the father of Matthan.
Matthan was the father of Jacob.
16 Jacob was the father of Joseph, the husband of Mary.
Mary gave birth to Jesus, who is called the Messiah.

17All those listed above include fourteen generations from Abraham to David, fourteen from David to the Babylonian exile, and fourteen from the Babylonian exile to the Messiah.

## The Birth of Jesus the Messiah

18This is how Jesus the Messiah was born. His mother, Mary, was engaged to be married to Joseph. But before the marriage took place, while she was still a virgin, she became pregnant through the power of the Holy Spirit. 19Joseph, her fiancé, was a good man and did not want to disgrace her publicly, so he decided to break the engagement* quietly.

20As he considered this, an angel of the Lord appeared to him in a dream. "Joseph, son of David," the angel said, "do not be afraid to take Mary as your wife. For the child within her was conceived by the Holy Spirit. 21And she will have a son, and you are to name him Jesus,* for he will save his people from their sins."

22All of this occurred to fulfill the Lord's message through his prophet:

23 "Look! The virgin will conceive a child!
She will give birth to a son,
and they will call him Immanuel,*
which means 'God is with us.'"

---

**1:1** Greek *Jesus the Messiah, son of David.* **1:3** Greek *Aram,* a variant spelling of Ram; also in 1:4. See 1 Chr 2:9-10. **1:7** Greek *Asaph,* a variant spelling of Asa; also in 1:8. See 1 Chr 3:10. **1:8a** Greek *Joram,* a variant spelling of Jehoram; also in 1:8b. See 1 Kgs 22:50 and note at 1 Chr 3:11. **1:8b** Or *ancestor;* also in 1:11. **1:10** Greek *Amos,* a variant spelling of Amon; also in 1:10b. See 1 Kgs 3:14. **1:11** Greek *Jeconiah,* a variant spelling of Jehoiachin; also in 1:12. See 2 Kgs 24:6 and note at 1 Chr 3:16. **1:19** Greek *to divorce her.* **1:21** *Jesus* means "The LORD saves." **1:23** Isa 7:14; 8:8, 10 (Greek version).

24When Joseph woke up, he did as the angel of the Lord commanded and took Mary as his wife. 25But he did not have sexual relations with her until her son was born. And Joseph named him Jesus.

## Visitors from the East

**2** Jesus was born in Bethlehem in Judea, during the reign of King Herod. About that time some wise men* from eastern lands arrived in Jerusalem, asking, 2"Where is the newborn king of the Jews? We saw his star as it rose,* and we have come to worship him."

3King Herod was deeply disturbed when he heard this, as was everyone in Jerusalem. 4He called a meeting of the leading priests and teachers of religious law and asked, "Where is the Messiah supposed to be born?"

5"In Bethlehem in Judea," they said, "for this is what the prophet wrote:

6 'And you, O Bethlehem in the land
        of Judah,
    are not least among the ruling cities*
        of Judah,
    for a ruler will come from you
        who will be the shepherd for my
            people Israel.'*"

7Then Herod called for a private meeting with the wise men, and he learned from them the time when the star first appeared. 8Then he told them, "Go to Bethlehem and search carefully for the child. And when you find him, come back and tell me so that I can go and worship him, too!"

9After this interview the wise men went their way. And the star they had seen in the east guided them to Bethlehem. It went ahead of them and stopped over the place where the child was. 10When they saw the star, they were filled with joy! 11They entered the house and saw the child with his mother, Mary, and they bowed down and worshiped him. Then they opened their treasure chests and gave him gifts of gold, frankincense, and myrrh.

12When it was time to leave, they returned to their own country by another route, for God had warned them in a dream not to return to Herod.

## WATCHING you from a distance?
### READ MATTHEW 1:23

This verse, which actually is a quote from the Old Testament (Isaiah 7:14), blows away the notion described in a Bette Midler song that "God is watching us from a distance." It's a beautiful melody, but incorrect theology. God is not watching us from a distance. He sent His Son, Jesus, to earth to live as a human being so we could see what God is like, and so He could experience what we have to face. And after Jesus left this earth, He sent His Spirit to be with us. God is very near. If you are a believer, His Spirit lives inside you. If you are a seeker of spiritual truth, He is only a prayer away.

## The Escape to Egypt

13After the wise men were gone, an angel of the Lord appeared to Joseph in a dream. "Get up! Flee to Egypt with the child and his mother," the angel said. "Stay there until I tell you to return, because Herod is going to search for the child to kill him."

14That night Joseph left for Egypt with the child and Mary, his mother, 15and they stayed there until Herod's death. This fulfilled what the Lord had spoken through the prophet: "I called my Son out of Egypt."*

16Herod was furious when he realized that the wise men had outwitted him. He sent soldiers to kill all the boys in and around Bethlehem who were two years old and under, based on the wise men's report of the star's first appearance. 17Herod's brutal action fulfilled what God had spoken through the prophet Jeremiah:

18 "A cry was heard in Ramah—
        weeping and great mourning.
    Rachel weeps for her children,
        refusing to be comforted,
        for they are dead."*

## The Return to Nazareth

19When Herod died, an angel of the Lord appeared in a dream to Joseph in Egypt. 20"Get up!" the angel said. "Take the child and his

2:1 Or *royal astrologers;* Greek reads *magi;* also in 2:7, 16.   2:2 Or *star in the east.*   2:6a Greek *the rulers.*   2:6b Mic 5:2; 2 Sam 5:2.
2:15 Hos 11:1.   2:18 Jer 31:15.

mother back to the land of Israel, because those who were trying to kill the child are dead."

21 So Joseph got up and returned to the land of Israel with Jesus and his mother. 22 But when he learned that the new ruler of Judea was Herod's son Archelaus, he was afraid to go there. Then, after being warned in a dream, he left for the region of Galilee. 23 So the family went and lived in a town called Nazareth. This fulfilled what the prophets had said: "He will be called a Nazarene."

## John the Baptist Prepares the Way

**3** In those days John the Baptist came to the Judean wilderness and began preaching. His message was, 2 "Repent of your sins and turn to God, for the Kingdom of Heaven is near.*" 3 The prophet Isaiah was speaking about John when he said,

"He is a voice shouting in the wilderness,
'Prepare the way for the Lord's coming!
  Clear the road for him!'"*

4 John's clothes were woven from coarse camel hair, and he wore a leather belt around his waist. For food he ate locusts and wild honey. 5 People from Jerusalem and from all of Judea and all over the Jordan Valley went out to see and hear John. 6 And when they confessed their sins, he baptized them in the Jordan River.

7 But when he saw many Pharisees and Sadducees coming to watch him baptize,* he denounced them. "You brood of snakes!" he exclaimed. "Who warned you to flee God's coming wrath? 8 Prove by the way you live that you have repented of your sins and turned to God. 9 Don't just say to each other, 'We're safe, for we are descendants of Abraham.' That means nothing, for I tell you, God can create children of Abraham from these very stones. 10 Even now the ax of God's judgment is poised, ready to sever the roots of the trees. Yes, every tree that does not produce good fruit will be chopped down and thrown into the fire.

11 "I baptize with* water those who repent of their sins and turn to God. But someone is coming soon who is greater than I am—so much greater that I'm not worthy even to be his slave and carry his sandals. He will baptize you with the Holy Spirit and with fire.* 12 He is ready to separate the chaff from the wheat with his winnowing fork. Then he will clean up the threshing area, gathering the wheat into his barn but burning the chaff with never-ending fire."

## The Baptism of Jesus

13 Then Jesus went from Galilee to the Jordan River to be baptized by John. 14 But John tried to talk him out of it. "I am the one who needs to be baptized by you," he said, "so why are you coming to me?"

15 But Jesus said, "It should be done, for we must carry out all that God requires.*" So John agreed to baptize him.

16 After his baptism, as Jesus came up out of the water, the heavens were opened* and he saw the Spirit of God descending like a dove and settling on him. 17 And a voice from heaven said, "This is my dearly loved Son, who brings me great joy."

## The Temptation of Jesus

**4** Then Jesus was led by the Spirit into the wilderness to be tempted there by the devil. 2 For forty days and forty nights he fasted and became very hungry.

3 During that time the devil* came and said to him, "If you are the Son of God, tell these stones to become loaves of bread."

4 But Jesus told him, "No! The Scriptures say,

'People do not live by bread alone,
  but by every word that comes from the mouth of God.'*"

5 Then the devil took him to the holy city, Jerusalem, to the highest point of the Temple, 6 and said, "If you are the Son of God, jump off! For the Scriptures say,

'He will order his angels to protect you.
And they will hold you up with their hands
  so you won't even hurt your foot on a stone.'*"

3:2 Or has come, or is coming soon.   3:3 Isa 40:3 (Greek version).   3:7 Or coming to be baptized.   3:11a Or in.   3:11b Or in the Holy Spirit and in fire.   3:15 Or for we must fulfill all righteousness.   3:16 Some manuscripts read opened to him.   4:3 Greek the tempter.   4:4 Deut 8:3.   4:6 Ps 91:11-12.

⁷Jesus responded, "The Scriptures also say, 'You must not test the Lᴏʀᴅ your God.'*"

⁸Next the devil took him to the peak of a very high mountain and showed him all the kingdoms of the world and their glory. ⁹"I will give it all to you," he said, "if you will kneel down and worship me."

¹⁰"Get out of here, Satan," Jesus told him. "For the Scriptures say,

> 'You must worship the Lᴏʀᴅ your God
>     and serve only him.'*"

¹¹Then the devil went away, and angels came and took care of Jesus.

## The Ministry of Jesus Begins

¹²When Jesus heard that John had been arrested, he left Judea and returned to Galilee. ¹³He went first to Nazareth, then left there and moved to Capernaum, beside the Sea of Galilee, in the region of Zebulun and Naphtali. ¹⁴This fulfilled what God said through the prophet Isaiah:

¹⁵ "In the land of Zebulun and of Naphtali,
    beside the sea, beyond the Jordan
        River,
    in Galilee where so many Gentiles live,
¹⁶ the people who sat in darkness
        have seen a great light.
    And for those who lived in the land
        where death casts its shadow,
    a light has shined."*

¹⁷From then on Jesus began to preach, "Repent of your sins and turn to God, for the Kingdom of Heaven is near.*"

## The First Disciples

¹⁸One day as Jesus was walking along the shore of the Sea of Galilee, he saw two brothers—Simon, also called Peter, and Andrew—throwing a net into the water, for they fished for a living. ¹⁹Jesus called out to them, "Come, follow me, and I will show you how to fish for people!" ²⁰And they left their nets at once and followed him.

²¹A little farther up the shore he saw two other brothers, James and John, sitting in a boat with their father, Zebedee, repairing their nets. And he called them to come, too.

²²They immediately followed him, leaving the boat and their father behind.

## Crowds Follow Jesus

²³Jesus traveled throughout the region of Galilee, teaching in the synagogues and announcing the Good News about the Kingdom. And he healed every kind of disease and illness. ²⁴News about him spread as far as Syria, and people soon began bringing to him all who were sick. And whatever their sickness or disease, or if they were demon possessed or epileptic or paralyzed—he healed them all. ²⁵Large crowds followed him wherever he went—people from Galilee, the Ten Towns,* Jerusalem, from all over Judea, and from east of the Jordan River.

## The Sermon on the Mount

**5** One day as he saw the crowds gathering, Jesus went up on the mountainside and sat down. His disciples gathered around him, ²and he began to teach them.

### The Beatitudes

³"God blesses those who are poor and
        realize their need for him,*
    for the Kingdom of Heaven is theirs.
⁴ God blesses those who mourn,
    for they will be comforted.
⁵ God blesses those who are humble,
    for they will inherit the whole earth.
⁶ God blesses those who hunger and thirst
        for justice,*
    for they will be satisfied.
⁷ God blesses those who are merciful,
    for they will be shown mercy.
⁸ God blesses those whose hearts are pure,
    for they will see God.
⁹ God blesses those who work for peace,
    for they will be called the children
        of God.
¹⁰ God blesses those who are persecuted
        for doing right,
    for the Kingdom of Heaven is theirs.

¹¹"God blesses you when people mock you and persecute you and lie about you* and say all sorts of evil things against you because you are my followers. ¹²Be happy about it! Be

4:7 Deut 6:16.    4:10 Deut 6:13.    4:15-16 Isa 9:1-2 (Greek version).    4:17 Or has come, or is coming soon.    4:25 Greek Decapolis.
5:3 Greek poor in spirit.    5:6 Or for righteousness.    5:11 Some manuscripts omit and lie about you.

very glad! For a great reward awaits you in heaven. And remember, the ancient prophets were persecuted in the same way.

### Teaching about Salt and Light

13"You are the salt of the earth. But what good is salt if it has lost its flavor? Can you make it salty again? It will be thrown out and trampled underfoot as worthless.

14"You are the light of the world—like a city on a hilltop that cannot be hidden. 15No one lights a lamp and then puts it under a basket. Instead, a lamp is placed on a stand, where it gives light to everyone in the house. 16In the same way, let your good deeds shine out for all to see, so that everyone will praise your heavenly Father.

### Teaching about the Law

17"Don't misunderstand why I have come. I did not come to abolish the law of Moses or the writings of the prophets. No, I came to accomplish their purpose. 18I tell you the truth, until heaven and earth disappear, not even the smallest detail of God's law will disappear until its purpose is achieved. 19So if you ignore the least commandment and teach others to do the same, you will be called the least in the Kingdom of Heaven. But anyone who obeys God's laws and teaches them will be called great in the Kingdom of Heaven.

20"But I warn you—unless your righteousness is better than the righteousness of the teachers of religious law and the Pharisees, you will never enter the Kingdom of Heaven!

### Teaching about Anger

21"You have heard that our ancestors were told, 'You must not murder. If you commit murder, you are subject to judgment.'* 22But I say, if you are even angry with someone,* you are subject to judgment! If you call someone an idiot,* you are in danger of being brought before the court. And if you curse someone,* you are in danger of the fires of hell.*

23"So if you are presenting a sacrifice* at the altar in the Temple and you suddenly remember that someone has something against you, 24leave your sacrifice there at the altar. Go and be reconciled to that person. Then come and offer your sacrifice to God.

25"When you are on the way to court with your adversary, settle your differences quickly. Otherwise, your accuser may hand you over to the judge, who will hand you over to an officer, and you will be thrown into prison. 26And if that happens, you surely won't be free again until you have paid the last penny.*

**5:21** Exod 20:13; Deut 5:17.   **5:22a** Some manuscripts add *without cause.*   **5:22b** Greek uses an Aramaic term of contempt: *If you say to your brother, 'Raca.'*   **5:22c** Greek *if you say, 'You fool.'*   **5:22d** Greek *Gehenna;* also in 5:29, 30.   **5:23** Greek *gift;* also in 5:24.   **5:26** Greek *the last kodrantes* [i.e., quadrans].

## LIVING under a shadow
READ MATTHEW 4:16

Shadows fall *opposite* their light source. That's why your shadow is in front of you when the sun is behind you and vice versa. The way you're facing determines whether or not you can see your shadow easily. This physical truth has profound spiritual implications for us as we live under the shadow of illness. We have to keep facing the light in order not to see the shadow so easily.

Perhaps when you heard the diagnosis, you got out of position spiritually. You couldn't figure out how a loving God could allow this to happen. Maybe you even felt at times as if He didn't hear your prayers. We hope you will check today to see which way you're facing. This prophecy from Isaiah 9:2 shows us that Jesus is the great light. You know you're turned toward the light when you talk with Him, pouring out your heart to the One who hears, understands, and has the power to respond. Are you facing the right direction?

## Teaching about Adultery

27 "You have heard the commandment that says, ' You must not commit adultery.'* 28 But I say, anyone who even looks at a woman with lust has already committed adultery with her in his heart. 29 So if your eye—even your good eye*—causes you to lust, gouge it out and throw it away. It is better for you to lose one part of your body than for your whole body to be thrown into hell. 30 And if your hand— even your stronger hand*—causes you to sin, cut it off and throw it away. It is better for you to lose one part of your body than for your whole body to be thrown into hell.

## Teaching about Divorce

31 "You have heard the law that says, 'A man can divorce his wife by merely giving her a written notice of divorce.'* 32 But I say that a man who divorces his wife, unless she has been unfaithful, causes her to commit adultery. And anyone who marries a divorced woman also commits adultery.

## Teaching about Vows

33 "You have also heard that our ancestors were told, 'You must not break your vows; you must carry out the vows you make to the LORD.'* 34 But I say, do not make any vows! Do not say, 'By heaven!' because heaven is God's throne. 35 And do not say, 'By the earth!' because the earth is his footstool. And do not say, 'By Jerusalem!' for Jerusalem is the city of the great King. 36 Do not even say, 'By my head!' for you can't turn one hair white or black. 37 Just say a simple, 'Yes, I will,' or 'No, I won't.' Anything beyond this is from the evil one.

## Teaching about Revenge

38 "You have heard the law that says the punishment must match the injury: 'An eye for an eye, and a tooth for a tooth.'* 39 But I say, do not resist an evil person! If someone slaps you on the right cheek, offer the other cheek also. 40 If you are sued in court and your shirt is taken from you, give your coat, too. 41 If a soldier demands that you carry his gear for a mile,* carry it two miles. 42 Give to those who ask, and don't turn away from those who want to borrow.

## Teaching about Love for Enemies

43 "You have heard the law that says, 'Love your neighbor'* and hate your enemy. 44 But I say, love your enemies!* Pray for those who persecute you! 45 In that way, you will be acting as true children of your Father in heaven. For he gives his sunlight to both the evil and the good, and he sends rain on the just and the unjust alike. 46 If you love only those who love you, what reward is there for that? Even corrupt tax collectors do that much. 47 If you are kind only to your friends,* how are you different from anyone else? Even pagans do that. 48 But you are to be perfect, even as your Father in heaven is perfect.

## Teaching about Giving to the Needy

6 "Watch out! Don't do your good deeds publicly, to be admired by others, for you will lose the reward from your Father in heaven. 2 When you give to someone in need, don't do as the hypocrites do—blowing trumpets in the synagogues and streets to call attention to their acts of charity! I tell you the truth, they have received all the reward they will ever get. 3 But when you give to someone in need, don't let your left hand know what your right hand is doing. 4 Give your gifts in private, and your Father, who sees everything, will reward you.

## Teaching about Prayer and Fasting

5 "When you pray, don't be like the hypocrites who love to pray publicly on street corners and in the synagogues where everyone can see them. I tell you the truth, that is all the reward they will ever get. 6 But when you pray, go away by yourself, shut the door behind you, and pray to your Father in private. Then your Father, who sees everything, will reward you.

7 "When you pray, don't babble on and on as people of other religions do. They think their prayers are answered merely by repeating their words again and again. 8 Don't be

5:27 Exod 20:14; Deut 5:18.   5:29 Greek your right eye.   5:30 Greek your right hand.   5:31 Deut 24:1.   5:33 Num 30:2.
5:38 Greek the law that says: 'An eye for an eye and a tooth for a tooth.' Exod 21:24; Lev 24:20; Deut 19:21.   5:41 Greek milion [4,854 feet or 1,478 meters].   5:43 Lev 19:18.   5:44 Some manuscripts add Bless those who curse you. Do good to those who hate you. Compare Luke 6:27-28.   5:47 Greek your brothers.

like them, for your Father knows exactly what you need even before you ask him! 9 Pray like this:

> Our Father in heaven,
> may your name be kept holy.
> 10 May your Kingdom come soon.
> May your will be done on earth,
> as it is in heaven.
> 11 Give us today the food we need,*
> 12 and forgive us our sins,
> as we have forgiven those who sin against us.
> 13 And don't let us yield to temptation,*
> but rescue us from the evil one.*

14 "If you forgive those who sin against you, your heavenly Father will forgive you. 15 But if you refuse to forgive others, your Father will not forgive your sins.

16 "And when you fast, don't make it obvious, as the hypocrites do, for they try to look miserable and disheveled so people will admire them for their fasting. I tell you the truth, that is the only reward they will ever get. 17 But when you fast, comb your hair and wash your face. 18 Then no one will notice that you are fasting, except your Father, who knows what you do in private. And your Father, who sees everything, will reward you.

*Teaching about Money and Possessions*
19 "Don't store up treasures here on earth, where moths eat them and rust destroys them, and where thieves break in and steal. 20 Store your treasures in heaven, where moths and rust cannot destroy, and thieves do not break in and steal. 21 Wherever your treasure is, there the desires of your heart will also be.

22 "Your eye is a lamp that provides light for your body. When your eye is good, your whole body is filled with light. 23 But when your eye is bad, your whole body is filled with darkness. And if the light you think you have is actually darkness, how deep that darkness is!

24 "No one can serve two masters. For you will hate one and love the other; you will be devoted to one and despise the other. You cannot serve both God and money.

25 "That is why I tell you not to worry about everyday life—whether you have enough food and drink, or enough clothes to wear. Isn't life more than food, and your body more than clothing? 26 Look at the birds. They don't plant or harvest or store food in barns, for your heavenly Father feeds them. And aren't you far more valuable to him than they are? 27 Can all your worries add a single moment to your life?

28 "And why worry about your clothing? Look at the lilies of the field and how they grow. They don't work or make their clothing, 29 yet Solomon in all his glory was not dressed as beautifully as they are. 30 And if God cares so wonderfully for wildflowers that are here today and thrown into the fire tomorrow, he will certainly care for you. Why do you have so little faith?

31 "So don't worry about these things, saying, ' What will we eat? What will we drink? What will we wear?' 32 These things dominate the thoughts of unbelievers, but your heavenly Father already knows all your needs. 33 Seek the Kingdom of God* above all else, and live righteously, and he will give you everything you need.

34 "So don't worry about tomorrow, for tomorrow will bring its own worries. Today's trouble is enough for today.

*Do Not Judge Others*
7 "Do not judge others, and you will not be judged. 2 For you will be treated as you treat others.* The standard you use in judging is the standard by which you will be judged.*

3 "And why worry about a speck in your friend's eye* when you have a log in your own? 4 How can you think of saying to your friend,* 'Let me help you get rid of that speck in your eye,' when you can't see past the log in your own eye? 5 Hypocrite! First get rid of the log in your own eye; then you will see well enough to deal with the speck in your friend's eye.

6 "Don't waste what is holy on people who are unholy.* Don't throw your pearls to pigs! They will trample the pearls, then turn and attack you.

---

6:11 Or *Give us today our food for the day;* or *Give us today our food for tomorrow.*   6:13a Or *And keep us from being tested.*
6:13b Or *from evil.* Some manuscripts add *For yours is the kingdom and the power and the glory forever. Amen.*   6:33 Some manuscripts do not include *of God.*   7:2a Or *For God will judge you as you judge others.*   7:2b Or *The measure you give will be the measure you get back.*   7:3 Greek *your brother's eye;* also in 7:5.   7:4 Greek *your brother.*   7:6 Greek *Don't give the sacred to dogs.*

## Effective Prayer

7"Keep on asking, and you will receive what you ask for. Keep on seeking, and you will find. Keep on knocking, and the door will be opened to you. 8For everyone who asks receives. Everyone who seeks finds. And to everyone who knocks, the door will be opened.

9"You parents—if your children ask for a loaf of bread, do you give them a stone instead? 10Or if they ask for a fish, do you give them a snake? Of course not! 11So if you sinful people know how to give good gifts to your children, how much more will your heavenly Father give good gifts to those who ask him.

## The Golden Rule

12"Do to others whatever you would like them to do to you. This is the essence of all that is taught in the law and the prophets.

## The Narrow Gate

13"You can enter God's Kingdom only through the narrow gate. The highway to hell* is broad, and its gate is wide for the many who choose that way. 14But the gateway to life is very narrow and the road is difficult, and only a few ever find it.

## The Tree and Its Fruit

15"Beware of false prophets who come disguised as harmless sheep but are really vicious wolves. 16You can identify them by their fruit, that is, by the way they act. Can you pick grapes from thornbushes, or figs from thistles? 17A good tree produces good fruit, and a bad tree produces bad fruit. 18A good tree can't produce bad fruit, and a bad tree can't produce good fruit. 19So every tree that does not produce good fruit is chopped down and thrown into the fire. 20Yes, just as you can identify a tree by its fruit, so you can identify people by their actions.

## True Disciples

21"Not everyone who calls out to me, 'Lord! Lord!' will enter the Kingdom of Heaven. Only those who actually do the will of my Father in heaven will enter. 22On judgment day many will say to me, 'Lord! Lord! We prophe-

sied in your name and cast out demons in your name and performed many miracles in your name.' 23But I will reply, 'I never knew you. Get away from me, you who break God's laws.'

## Building on a Solid Foundation

24"Anyone who listens to my teaching and follows it is wise, like a person who builds a house on solid rock. 25Though the rain comes in torrents and the floodwaters rise and the winds beat against that house, it won't collapse because it is built on bedrock. 26But anyone who hears my teaching and doesn't obey it is foolish, like a person who builds a house on sand. 27When the rains and floods come and the winds beat against that house, it will collapse with a mighty crash."

28When Jesus had finished saying these things, the crowds were amazed at his teaching, 29for he taught with real authority—quite unlike their teachers of religious law.

## Jesus Heals a Man with Leprosy

8 Large crowds followed Jesus as he came down the mountainside. 2Suddenly, a man with leprosy approached him and knelt before him. "Lord," the man said, "if you are willing, you can heal me and make me clean."

3Jesus reached out and touched him. "I am willing," he said. "Be healed!" And instantly the leprosy disappeared. 4Then Jesus said to him, "Don't tell anyone about this. Instead, go to the priest and let him examine you. Take along the offering required in the law of Moses for those who have been healed of leprosy.* This will be a public testimony that you have been cleansed."

## The Faith of a Roman Officer

5When Jesus returned to Capernaum, a Roman officer* came and pleaded with him, 6"Lord, my young servant* lies in bed, paralyzed and in terrible pain."

7Jesus said, "I will come and heal him."

8But the officer said, "Lord, I am not worthy to have you come into my home. Just say the word from where you are, and my servant will be healed. 9I know this because

7:13 Greek *The road that leads to destruction.*  8:4 See Lev 14:2-32.  8:5 Greek *a centurion;* similarly in 8:8, 13.  8:6 Or *child;* also in 8:13.

I am under the authority of my superior officers, and I have authority over my soldiers. I only need to say, 'Go,' and they go, or 'Come,' and they come. And if I say to my slaves, 'Do this,' they do it."

10 When Jesus heard this, he was amazed. Turning to those who were following him, he said, "I tell you the truth, I haven't seen faith like this in all Israel! 11 And I tell you this, that many Gentiles will come from all over the world—from east and west—and sit down with Abraham, Isaac, and Jacob at the feast in the Kingdom of Heaven. 12 But many Israelites—those for whom the Kingdom was prepared—will be thrown into outer darkness, where there will be weeping and gnashing of teeth."

13 Then Jesus said to the Roman officer, "Go back home. Because you believed, it has happened." And the young servant was healed that same hour.

### Jesus Heals Many People

14 When Jesus arrived at Peter's house, Peter's mother-in-law was sick in bed with a high fever. 15 But when Jesus touched her hand, the fever left her. Then she got up and prepared a meal for him.

16 That evening many demon-possessed people were brought to Jesus. He cast out the evil spirits with a simple command, and he healed all the sick. 17 This fulfilled the word of the Lord through the prophet Isaiah, who said,

> "He took our sicknesses
> and removed our diseases."*

### The Cost of Following Jesus

18 When Jesus saw the crowd around him, he instructed his disciples to cross to the other side of the lake.

19 Then one of the teachers of religious law said to him, "Teacher, I will follow you wherever you go."

20 But Jesus replied, "Foxes have dens to live in, and birds have nests, but the Son of Man* has no place even to lay his head."

21 Another of his disciples said, "Lord, first let me return home and bury my father."

22 But Jesus told him, "Follow me now. Let the spiritually dead bury their own dead.*"

### Jesus Calms the Storm

23 Then Jesus got into the boat and started across the lake with his disciples. 24 Suddenly, a fierce storm struck the lake, with waves breaking into the boat. But Jesus was sleeping. 25 The disciples went and woke him up, shouting, "Lord, save us! We're going to drown!"

26 Jesus responded, "Why are you afraid?

8:17 Isa 53:4.   8:20 "Son of Man" is a title Jesus used for himself.   8:22 Greek *Let the dead bury their own dead.*

# WORRYwarts

READ MATTHEW 6:34

What are you worried about today? That your spouse will be widowed? That your children will grow up without you? That this next holiday will be your last? That you'll never feel normal again? You may even be worried that you worry so much! Holocaust survivor Corrie ten Boom wrote, "Worrying about tomorrow robs today of its joy." That is so true. Your mind will find peace when you can live in the present and not in the "what-ifs" of the future. People often suggest we take life "one day at a time," but there may be some days when we can only face one *hour* or one *minute* at a time!

When you hear the phrase "what-if" pop into your mind, that's a signal you're not living in the present and are probably getting ready to worry. Most of the things you'll worry about will *not* come true anyway, so why not memorize this short verse and meditate on it instead of any "what-ifs."

You have so little faith!" Then he got up and rebuked the wind and waves, and suddenly there was a great calm.

27 The disciples were amazed. "Who is this man?" they asked. "Even the winds and waves obey him!"

### Jesus Heals Two Demon-Possessed Men

28 When Jesus arrived on the other side of the lake, in the region of the Gadarenes,* two men who were possessed by demons met him. They lived in a cemetery and were so violent that no one could go through that area. 29 They began screaming at him, "Why are you interfering with us, Son of God? Have you come here to torture us before God's appointed time?"

30 There happened to be a large herd of pigs feeding in the distance. 31 So the demons begged, "If you cast us out, send us into that herd of pigs."

32 "All right, go!" Jesus commanded them. So the demons came out of the men and entered the pigs, and the whole herd plunged down the steep hillside into the lake and drowned in the water.

33 The herdsmen fled to the nearby town, telling everyone what happened to the demon-possessed men. 34 Then the entire town came out to meet Jesus, but they begged him to go away and leave them alone.

### Jesus Heals a Paralyzed Man

**9** Jesus climbed into a boat and went back across the lake to his own town. 2 Some people brought to him a paralyzed man on a mat. Seeing their faith, Jesus said to the paralyzed man, "Be encouraged, my child! Your sins are forgiven."

3 But some of the teachers of religious law said to themselves, "That's blasphemy! Does he think he's God?"

4 Jesus knew* what they were thinking, so he asked them, " Why do you have such evil thoughts in your hearts? 5 Is it easier to say ' Your sins are forgiven,' or 'Stand up and walk'? 6 So I will prove to you that the Son of Man* has the authority on earth to forgive sins." Then Jesus turned to the paralyzed man and said, "Stand up, pick up your mat, and go home!"

7 And the man jumped up and went home! 8 Fear swept through the crowd as they saw this happen. And they praised God for sending a man with such great authority.*

### Jesus Calls Matthew

9 As Jesus was walking along, he saw a man named Matthew sitting at his tax collector's booth. "Follow me and be my disciple," Jesus said to him. So Matthew got up and followed him.

10 Later, Matthew invited Jesus and his disciples to his home as dinner guests, along with many tax collectors and other disreputable sinners. 11 But when the Pharisees saw this, they asked his disciples, "Why does your teacher eat with such scum?*"

12 When Jesus heard this, he said, "Healthy people don't need a doctor—sick people do." 13 Then he added, "Now go and learn the meaning of this Scripture: 'I want you to show mercy, not offer sacrifices.'* For I have come to call not those who think they are righteous, but those who know they are sinners."

### A Discussion about Fasting

14 One day the disciples of John the Baptist came to Jesus and asked him, "Why don't your disciples fast* like we do and the Pharisees do?"

15 Jesus replied, "Do wedding guests mourn while celebrating with the groom? Of course not. But someday the groom will be taken away from them, and then they will fast.

16 "Besides, who would patch old clothing with new cloth? For the new patch would shrink and rip away from the old cloth, leaving an even bigger tear than before.

17 "And no one puts new wine into old wineskins. For the old skins would burst from the pressure, spilling the wine and ruining the skins. New wine is stored in new wineskins so that both are preserved."

### Jesus Heals in Response to Faith

18 As Jesus was saying this, the leader of a synagogue came and knelt before him. "My daughter has just died," he said, "but you can

---

8:28 Other manuscripts read *Gerasenes;* still others read *Gergesenes.* Compare Mark 5:1; Luke 8:26.   9:4 Some manuscripts read *saw.* 9:6 "Son of Man" is a title Jesus used for himself.   9:8 Greek *for giving such authority to human beings.*   9:11 Greek *with tax collectors and sinners?*   9:13 Hos 6:6 (Greek version).   9:14 Some manuscripts read *fast often.*

bring her back to life again if you just come and lay your hand on her."

19So Jesus and his disciples got up and went with him. 20Just then a woman who had suffered for twelve years with constant bleeding came up behind him. She touched the fringe of his robe, 21for she thought, "If I can just touch his robe, I will be healed."

22Jesus turned around, and when he saw her he said, "Daughter, be encouraged! Your faith has made you well." And the woman was healed at that moment.

23When Jesus arrived at the official's home, he saw the noisy crowd and heard the funeral music. 24"Get out!" he told them. " The girl isn't dead; she's only asleep." But the crowd laughed at him. 25After the crowd was put outside, however, Jesus went in and took the girl by the hand, and she stood up! 26The report of this miracle swept through the entire countryside.

## Jesus Heals the Blind

27After Jesus left the girl's home, two blind men followed along behind him, shouting, "Son of David, have mercy on us!"

28They went right into the house where he was staying, and Jesus asked them, "Do you believe I can make you see?"

"Yes, Lord," they told him, "we do."

29Then he touched their eyes and said, "Because of your faith, it will happen." 30Then their eyes were opened, and they could see! Jesus sternly warned them, "Don't tell anyone about this." 31But instead, they went out and spread his fame all over the region.

32When they left, a demon-possessed man who couldn't speak was brought to Jesus. 33So Jesus cast out the demon, and then the man began to speak. The crowds were amazed. "Nothing like this has ever happened in Israel!" they exclaimed.

34But the Pharisees said, "He can cast out demons because he is empowered by the prince of demons."

## The Need for Workers

35Jesus traveled through all the towns and villages of that area, teaching in the synagogues and announcing the Good News about the Kingdom. And he healed every kind of disease and illness. 36When he saw the crowds, he had compassion on them because they were confused and helpless, like sheep without a shepherd. 37He said to his disciples, "The harvest is great, but the workers are few. 38So pray to the Lord who is in charge of the harvest; ask him to send more workers into his fields."

## Jesus Sends Out the Twelve Apostles

**10** Jesus called his twelve disciples together and gave them authority to cast out evil* spirits and to heal every kind of disease and illness. 2Here are the names of the twelve apostles:

first, Simon (also called Peter),
then Andrew (Peter's brother),
James (son of Zebedee),
John (James's brother),
3 Philip,
Bartholomew,
Thomas,
Matthew (the tax collector),
James (son of Alphaeus),
Thaddaeus,*
4 Simon (the zealot*),
Judas Iscariot (who later betrayed him).

5Jesus sent out the twelve apostles with these instructions: "Don't go to the Gentiles or the Samaritans, 6but only to the people of Israel—God's lost sheep. 7Go and announce to them that the Kingdom of Heaven is near.* 8Heal the sick, raise the dead, cure those with leprosy, and cast out demons. Give as freely as you have received!

9"Don't take any money in your money belts—no gold, silver, or even copper coins. 10Don't carry a traveler's bag with a change of clothes and sandals or even a walking stick. Don't hesitate to accept hospitality, because those who work deserve to be fed.

11"Whenever you enter a city or village, search for a worthy person and stay in his home until you leave town. 12When you enter the home, give it your blessing. 13If it turns out to be a worthy home, let your blessing stand; if it is not, take back the blessing. 14If any household or town refuses to welcome

10:1 Greek *unclean.* 10:3 Other manuscripts read *Lebbaeus;* still others read *Lebbaeus who is called Thaddaeus.* 10:4 Greek *the Cananean,* an Aramaic term for Jewish nationalists. 10:7 Or *has come,* or *is coming soon.*

# CONFUSED and helpless

READ MATTHEW 9:35-36

Some animals are pretty smart. Dogs seem to have a sixth sense about finding their way home. Horses know how to follow the lead horse that looks out for the herd, and even pigs can be trained as indoor house pets. But sheep are another story. No offense to Shari Lewis's loveable puppet Lamb Chop, but <u>sheep are not real bright</u>. They get turned over on their backs and can't get themselves righted. (Maybe they originated the phrase "I've fallen, and I can't get up!") Sheep will follow one another to places where it's not safe for sheep to go—like off the edge of a cliff! They can't really help it; it's just their nature to get into ruts and lose perspective on their surroundings. So it's not exactly a compliment when the Bible says we are like sheep.

Do you feel confused or helpless today? Jesus feels compassion for you and, even more importantly, He is the Good Shepherd who knows exactly how to take care of your "sheepish" needs.

---

you or listen to your message, shake its dust from your feet as you leave. ¹⁵I tell you the truth, the wicked cities of Sodom and Gomorrah will be better off than such a town on the judgment day.

¹⁶"Look, I am sending you out as sheep among wolves. So be as shrewd as snakes and harmless as doves. ¹⁷But beware! For you will be handed over to the courts and will be flogged with whips in the synagogues. ¹⁸You will stand trial before governors and kings because you are my followers. But this will be your opportunity to tell the rulers and other unbelievers about me.* ¹⁹When you are arrested, don't worry about how to respond or what to say. God will give you the right words at the right time. ²⁰For it is not you who will be speaking—it will be the Spirit of your Father speaking through you.

²¹"A brother will betray his brother to death, a father will betray his own child, and children will rebel against their parents and cause them to be killed. ²²And all nations will hate you because you are my followers.* But everyone who endures to the end will be saved. ²³When you are persecuted in one town, flee to the next. I tell you the truth, the Son of Man* will return before you have reached all the towns of Israel.

²⁴"Students* are not greater than their teacher, and slaves are not greater than their master. ²⁵Students are to be like their teacher, and slaves are to be like their master. And since I, the master of the household, have been called the prince of demons,* the members of my household will be called by even worse names!

²⁶"But don't be afraid of those who threaten you. For the time is coming when everything that is covered will be revealed, and all that is secret will be made known to all. ²⁷What I tell you now in the darkness, shout abroad when daybreak comes. What I whisper in your ear, shout from the housetops for all to hear!

²⁸"Don't be afraid of those who want to kill your body; they cannot touch your soul. Fear only God, who can destroy both soul and body in hell.* ²⁹What is the price of two sparrows—one copper coin*? But not a single sparrow can fall to the ground without your Father knowing it. ³⁰And the very hairs on your head are all numbered. ³¹So don't be afraid; you are more valuable to God than a whole flock of sparrows.

³²"Everyone who acknowledges me publicly here on earth, I will also acknowledge before my Father in heaven. ³³But everyone

10:18 Or *But this will be your testimony against the rulers and other unbelievers.*  10:22 Greek *on account of my name.*
10:23 "Son of Man" is a title Jesus used for himself.  10:24 Or *Disciples.*  10:25 Greek *Beelzeboul;* other manuscripts read *Beezeboul;* Latin version reads *Beelzebub.*  10:28 Greek *Gehenna.*  10:29 Greek *one assarion* [i.e., one "as," a Roman coin equal to ¹⁄₁₆ of a denarius].

who denies me here on earth, I will also deny before my Father in heaven.

34 "Don't imagine that I came to bring peace to the earth! I came not to bring peace, but a sword.

35 'I have come to set a man against his
    father,
    a daughter against her mother,
    and a daughter-in-law against her
        mother-in-law.
36   Your enemies will be right in your
        own household!'*

37 "If you love your father or mother more than you love me, you are not worthy of being mine; or if you love your son or daughter more than me, you are not worthy of being mine. 38 If you refuse to take up your cross and follow me, you are not worthy of being mine. 39 If you cling to your life, you will lose it; but if you give up your life for me, you will find it.

40 "Anyone who receives you receives me, and anyone who receives me receives the Father who sent me. 41 If you receive a prophet as one who speaks for God,* you will be given the same reward as a prophet. And if you receive righteous people because of their righteousness, you will be given a reward like theirs. 42 And if you give even a cup of cold water to one of the least of my followers, you will surely be rewarded."

## Jesus and John the Baptist

**11** When Jesus had finished giving these instructions to his twelve disciples, he went out to teach and preach in towns throughout the region.

2 John the Baptist, who was in prison, heard about all the things the Messiah was doing. So he sent his disciples to ask Jesus, 3 "Are you the Messiah we've been expecting,* or should we keep looking for someone else?"

4 Jesus told them, "Go back to John and tell him what you have heard and seen—5 the blind see, the lame walk, the lepers are cured, the deaf hear, the dead are raised to life, and the Good News is being preached to the poor. 6 And tell him, 'God blesses those who do not turn away because of me.*' "

7 As John's disciples were leaving, Jesus began talking about him to the crowds. "What kind of man did you go into the wilderness to see? Was he a weak reed, swayed by every breath of wind? 8 Or were you expecting to see a man dressed in expensive clothes? No, people with expensive clothes live in palaces. 9 Were you looking for a prophet? Yes, and he is more than a prophet. 10 John is the man to whom the Scriptures refer when they say,

'Look, I am sending my messenger ahead
    of you,
    and he will prepare your way before
        you.'*

11 "I tell you the truth, of all who have ever lived, none is greater than John the Baptist. Yet even the least person in the Kingdom of Heaven is greater than he is! 12 And from the time John the Baptist began preaching until now, the Kingdom of Heaven has been forcefully advancing,* and violent people are attacking it. 13 For before John came, all the prophets and the law of Moses looked forward to this present time. 14 And if you are willing to accept what I say, he is Elijah, the one the prophets said would come.* 15 Anyone with ears to hear should listen and understand!

16 "To what can I compare this generation? It is like children playing a game in the public square. They complain to their friends,

17 'We played wedding songs,
    and you didn't dance,
so we played funeral songs,
    and you didn't mourn.'

18 For John didn't spend his time eating and drinking, and you say, 'He's possessed by a demon.' 19 The Son of Man,* on the other hand, feasts and drinks, and you say, 'He's a glutton and a drunkard, and a friend of tax collectors and other sinners!' But wisdom is shown to be right by its results."

## Judgment for the Unbelievers

20 Then Jesus began to denounce the towns where he had done so many of his miracles,

**10:35-36** Mic 7:6.   **10:41** Greek *receive a prophet in the name of a prophet.*   **11:3** Greek *Are you the one who is coming?*   **11:6** Or *who are not offended by me.*   **11:10** Mal 3:1.   **11:12** Or *the Kingdom of Heaven has suffered from violence.*   **11:14** See Mal 4:5.   **11:19** "Son of Man" is a title Jesus used for himself.

because they hadn't repented of their sins and turned to God. 21"What sorrow awaits you, Korazin and Bethsaida! For if the miracles I did in you had been done in wicked Tyre and Sidon, their people would have repented of their sins long ago, clothing themselves in burlap and throwing ashes on their heads to show their remorse. 22I tell you, Tyre and Sidon will be better off on judgment day than you.

23"And you people of Capernaum, will you be honored in heaven? No, you will go down to the place of the dead.* For if the miracles I did for you had been done in wicked Sodom, it would still be here today. 24I tell you, even Sodom will be better off on judgment day than you."

### Jesus' Prayer of Thanksgiving

25At that time Jesus prayed this prayer: "O Father, Lord of heaven and earth, thank you for hiding these things from those who think themselves wise and clever, and for revealing them to the childlike. 26Yes, Father, it pleased you to do it this way!

27"My Father has entrusted everything to me. No one truly knows the Son except the Father, and no one truly knows the Father except the Son and those to whom the Son chooses to reveal him."

28Then Jesus said, "Come to me, all of you who are weary and carry heavy burdens, and I will give you rest. 29Take my yoke upon you. Let me teach you, because I am humble and gentle at heart, and you will find rest for your souls. 30For my yoke is easy to bear, and the burden I give you is light."

### A Discussion about the Sabbath

**12** At about that time Jesus was walking through some grainfields on the Sabbath. His disciples were hungry, so they began breaking off some heads of grain and eating them. 2But some Pharisees saw them do it and protested, "Look, your disciples are breaking the law by harvesting grain on the Sabbath."

3Jesus said to them, "Haven't you read in the Scriptures what David did when he and his companions were hungry? 4He went into the house of God, and he and his compan-

ions broke the law by eating the sacred loaves of bread that only the priests are allowed to eat. 5And haven't you read in the law of Moses that the priests on duty in the Temple may work on the Sabbath? 6I tell you, there is one here who is even greater than the Temple! 7But you would not have condemned my innocent disciples if you knew the meaning of this Scripture: 'I want you to show mercy, not offer sacrifices.'* 8For the Son of Man* is Lord, even over the Sabbath!"

### Jesus Heals on the Sabbath

9Then Jesus went over to their synagogue, 10where he noticed a man with a deformed hand. The Pharisees asked Jesus, "Does the law permit a person to work by healing on the Sabbath?" (They were hoping he would say yes, so they could bring charges against him.)

11And he answered, "If you had a sheep that fell into a well on the Sabbath, wouldn't you work to pull it out? Of course you would. 12And how much more valuable is a person than a sheep! Yes, the law permits a person to do good on the Sabbath."

13Then he said to the man, "Hold out your hand." So the man held out his hand, and it was restored, just like the other one! 14Then the Pharisees called a meeting to plot how to kill Jesus.

### Jesus, God's Chosen Servant

15But Jesus knew what they were planning. So he left that area, and many people followed him. He healed all the sick among them, 16but he warned them not to reveal who he was. 17This fulfilled the prophecy of Isaiah concerning him:

18 "Look at my Servant, whom I have
         chosen.
    He is my Beloved, who pleases me.
    I will put my Spirit upon him,
         and he will proclaim justice to the
         nations.
19 He will not fight or shout
         or raise his voice in public.
20 He will not crush the weakest reed
         or put out a flickering candle.

---

**11:23** Greek *to Hades.*   **12:7** Hos 6:6 (Greek version).   **12:8** "Son of Man" is a title Jesus used for himself.

Finally he will cause justice to be victorious.
21 And his name will be the hope of all the world."*

## Jesus and the Prince of Demons

22 Then a demon-possessed man, who was blind and couldn't speak, was brought to Jesus. He healed the man so that he could both speak and see. 23 The crowd was amazed and asked, "Could it be that Jesus is the Son of David, the Messiah?"

24 But when the Pharisees heard about the miracle, they said, "No wonder he can cast out demons. He gets his power from Satan,* the prince of demons."

25 Jesus knew their thoughts and replied, "Any kingdom divided by civil war is doomed. A town or family splintered by feuding will fall apart. 26 And if Satan is casting out Satan, he is divided and fighting against himself. His own kingdom will not survive. 27 And if I am empowered by Satan, what about your own exorcists? They cast out demons, too, so they will condemn you for what you have said. 28 But if I am casting out demons by the Spirit of God, then the Kingdom of God has arrived among you. 29 For who is powerful enough to enter the house of a strong man like Satan and plunder his goods? Only someone even stronger—someone who could tie him up and then plunder his house.

30 "Anyone who isn't with me opposes me, and anyone who isn't working with me is actually working against me.

31 "So I tell you, every sin and blasphemy can be forgiven—except blasphemy against the Holy Spirit, which will never be forgiven. 32 Anyone who speaks against the Son of Man can be forgiven, but anyone who speaks against the Holy Spirit will never be forgiven, either in this world or in the world to come.

33 "A tree is identified by its fruit. If a tree is good, its fruit will be good. If a tree is bad, its fruit will be bad. 34 You brood of snakes! How could evil men like you speak what is good and right? For whatever is in your heart determines what you say. 35 A good person produces good things from the treasury of a good heart, and an evil person produces evil things from the treasury of an evil heart. 36 And I tell you this, you must give an account on judgment day for every idle word you speak. 37 The words you say will either acquit you or condemn you."

## The Sign of Jonah

38 One day some teachers of religious law and Pharisees came to Jesus and said, "Teacher, we want you to show us a miraculous sign to prove your authority."

**12:18-21** Isa 42:1-4 (Greek version for 42:4). **12:24** Greek *Beelzeboul;* also in 12:27. Other manuscripts read *Beezeboul;* Latin version reads *Beelzebub.*

# LAY your burdens down
READ MATTHEW 11:28-30

How heavy is the load you are carrying these days? Are your arms weary from trying to hold up your loved one? Is your back breaking from the weight of medical bills piling up? Is your mind exhausted from trying to keep track of all the appointments and medications?

Jesus has an exchange He'd like to make: your heavy burdens for His light one. Notice He doesn't promise to just take everything away so that we have *no* burdens. It's as if right now we're plowing through life as a single ox with a heavy yoke on our necks. When we give that big burden to Jesus, He comes alongside us, attaches His double yoke, and plows right with us. No wonder our burdens are so much lighter and we are so much less weary! You don't have to carry this heavy load by yourself. Get rid of your I-can-do-it-myself yoke and allow Jesus to lighten the load as you walk side by side through whatever lies ahead.

**39** But Jesus replied, "Only an evil, adulterous generation would demand a miraculous sign; but the only sign I will give them is the sign of the prophet Jonah. **40** For as Jonah was in the belly of the great fish for three days and three nights, so will the Son of Man be in the heart of the earth for three days and three nights.

**41** "The people of Nineveh will stand up against this generation on judgment day and condemn it, for they repented of their sins at the preaching of Jonah. Now someone greater than Jonah is here—but you refuse to repent. **42** The queen of Sheba* will also stand up against this generation on judgment day and condemn it, for she came from a distant land to hear the wisdom of Solomon. Now someone greater than Solomon is here—but you refuse to listen.

**43** "When an evil* spirit leaves a person, it goes into the desert, seeking rest but finding none. **44** Then it says, 'I will return to the person I came from.' So it returns and finds its former home empty, swept, and in order. **45** Then the spirit finds seven other spirits more evil than itself, and they all enter the person and live there. And so that person is worse off than before. That will be the experience of this evil generation."

### The True Family of Jesus

**46** As Jesus was speaking to the crowd, his mother and brothers stood outside, asking to speak to him. **47** Someone told Jesus, "Your mother and your brothers are outside, and they want to speak to you."*

**48** Jesus asked, "Who is my mother? Who are my brothers?" **49** Then he pointed to his disciples and said, "Look, these are my mother and brothers. **50** Anyone who does the will of my Father in heaven is my brother and sister and mother!"

### Parable of the Farmer Scattering Seed

**13** Later that same day Jesus left the house and sat beside the lake. **2** A large crowd soon gathered around him, so he got into a boat. Then he sat there and taught as the people stood on the shore. **3** He told many stories in the form of parables, such as this one:

"Listen! A farmer went out to plant some seeds. **4** As he scattered them across his field, some seeds fell on a footpath, and the birds came and ate them. **5** Other seeds fell on shallow soil with underlying rock. The seeds sprouted quickly because the soil was shallow. **6** But the plants soon wilted under the hot sun, and since they didn't have deep roots, they died. **7** Other seeds fell among thorns that grew up and choked out the tender plants. **8** Still other seeds fell on fertile soil, and they produced a crop that was thirty, sixty, and even a hundred times as much as had been planted! **9** Anyone with ears to hear should listen and understand."

**10** His disciples came and asked him, "Why do you use parables when you talk to the people?"

**11** He replied, "You are permitted to understand the secrets* of the Kingdom of Heaven, but others are not. **12** To those who listen to my teaching, more understanding will be given, and they will have an abundance of knowledge. But for those who are not listening, even what little understanding they have will be taken away from them. **13** That is why I use these parables,

For they look, but they don't really see.
They hear, but they don't really listen
or understand.

**14** This fulfills the prophecy of Isaiah that says,

'When you hear what I say,
you will not understand.
When you see what I do,
you will not comprehend.
**15** For the hearts of these people are hardened,
and their ears cannot hear,
and they have closed their eyes—
so their eyes cannot see,
and their ears cannot hear,
and their hearts cannot understand,
and they cannot turn to me
and let me heal them.'*

**12:42** Greek *The queen of the south.*   **12:43** Greek *unclean.*   **12:47** Some manuscripts do not include verse 47. Compare Mark 3:32 and Luke 8:20.   **13:11** Greek *the mysteries.*   **13:14-15** Isa 6:9-10 (Greek version).

16"But blessed are your eyes, because they see; and your ears, because they hear. 17I tell you the truth, many prophets and righteous people longed to see what you see, but they didn't see it. And they longed to hear what you hear, but they didn't hear it.

18"Now listen to the explanation of the parable about the farmer planting seeds: 19The seed that fell on the footpath represents those who hear the message about the Kingdom and don't understand it. Then the evil one comes and snatches away the seed that was planted in their hearts. 20The seed on the rocky soil represents those who hear the message and immediately receive it with joy. 21But since they don't have deep roots, they don't last long. They fall away as soon as they have problems or are persecuted for believing God's word. 22The seed that fell among the thorns represents those who hear God's word, but all too quickly the message is crowded out by the worries of this life and the lure of wealth, so no fruit is produced. 23The seed that fell on good soil represents those who truly hear and understand God's word and produce a harvest of thirty, sixty, or even a hundred times as much as had been planted!"

## Parable of the Wheat and Weeds

24Here is another story Jesus told: " The Kingdom of Heaven is like a farmer who planted good seed in his field. 25But that night as the workers slept, his enemy came and planted weeds among the wheat, then slipped away. 26When the crop began to grow and produce grain, the weeds also grew.

27"The farmer's workers went to him and said, 'Sir, the field where you planted that good seed is full of weeds! Where did they come from?'

28"'An enemy has done this!' the farmer exclaimed.

"'Should we pull out the weeds?' they asked.

29"'No,' he replied, 'you'll uproot the wheat if you do. 30Let both grow together until the harvest. Then I will tell the harvesters to sort out the weeds, tie them into bun-

dles, and burn them, and to put the wheat in the barn.' "

## Parable of the Mustard Seed

31Here is another illustration Jesus used: "The Kingdom of Heaven is like a mustard seed planted in a field. 32It is the smallest of all seeds, but it becomes the largest of garden plants; it grows into a tree, and birds come and make nests in its branches."

## Parable of the Yeast

33Jesus also used this illustration: " The Kingdom of Heaven is like the yeast a woman used in making bread. Even though she put only a little yeast in three measures of flour, it permeated every part of the dough."

34Jesus always used stories and illustrations like these when speaking to the crowds. In fact, he never spoke to them without using such parables. 35This fulfilled what God had spoken through the prophet:

"I will speak to you in parables.
I will explain things hidden
since the creation of the world.*"

## Parable of the Wheat and Weeds Explained

36Then, leaving the crowds outside, Jesus went into the house. His disciples said, "Please explain to us the story of the weeds in the field."

37Jesus replied, " The Son of Man* is the farmer who plants the good seed. 38The field is the world, and the good seed represents the people of the Kingdom. The weeds are the people who belong to the evil one. 39The enemy who planted the weeds among the wheat is the devil. The harvest is the end of the world,* and the harvesters are the angels.

40"Just as the weeds are sorted out and burned in the fire, so it will be at the end of the world. 41The Son of Man will send his angels, and they will remove from his Kingdom everything that causes sin and all who do evil. 42And the angels will throw them into the fiery furnace, where there will be weeping and gnashing of teeth. 43Then the righteous will shine like the sun in their Father's Kingdom. Anyone with ears to hear should listen and understand!

**13:35** Some manuscripts do not include *of the world*. Ps 78:2. **13:37** "Son of Man" is a title Jesus used for himself. **13:39** Or *the age;* also in 13:40, 49.

## Parables of the Hidden Treasure and the Pearl

44"The Kingdom of Heaven is like a treasure that a man discovered hidden in a field. In his excitement, he hid it again and sold everything he owned to get enough money to buy the field.

45"Again, the Kingdom of Heaven is like a merchant on the lookout for choice pearls. 46When he discovered a pearl of great value, he sold everything he owned and bought it!

## Parable of the Fishing Net

47"Again, the Kingdom of Heaven is like a fishing net that was thrown into the water and caught fish of every kind. 48When the net was full, they dragged it up onto the shore, sat down, and sorted the good fish into crates, but threw the bad ones away. 49That is the way it will be at the end of the world. The angels will come and separate the wicked people from the righteous, 50throwing the wicked into the fiery furnace, where there will be weeping and gnashing of teeth. 51Do you understand all these things?"

"Yes," they said, "we do."

52Then he added, "Every teacher of religious law who becomes a disciple in the Kingdom of Heaven is like a homeowner who brings from his storeroom new gems of truth as well as old."

## Jesus Rejected at Nazareth

53When Jesus had finished telling these stories and illustrations, he left that part of the country. 54He returned to Nazareth, his hometown. When he taught there in the synagogue, everyone was amazed and said, "Where does he get this wisdom and the power to do miracles?" 55Then they scoffed, "He's just the carpenter's son, and we know Mary, his mother, and his brothers—James, Joseph,* Simon, and Judas. 56All his sisters live right here among us. Where did he learn all these things?" 57And they were deeply offended and refused to believe in him.

Then Jesus told them, "A prophet is honored everywhere except in his own home-town and among his own family." 58And so he did only a few miracles there because of their unbelief.

## The Death of John the Baptist

**14** When Herod Antipas, the ruler of Galilee,* heard about Jesus, 2he said to his advisers, "This must be John the Baptist raised from the dead! That is why he can do such miracles."

3For Herod had arrested and imprisoned John as a favor to his wife Herodias (the former wife of Herod's brother Philip). 4John had been telling Herod, "It is against God's law for you to marry her." 5Herod wanted to kill John, but he was afraid of a riot, because all the people believed John was a prophet.

6But at a birthday party for Herod, Herodias's daughter performed a dance that greatly pleased him, 7so he promised with a vow to give her anything she wanted. 8At her mother's urging, the girl said, "I want the head of John the Baptist on a tray!" 9Then the king regretted what he had said; but because of the vow he had made in front of his guests, he issued the necessary orders. 10So John was beheaded in the prison, 11and his head was brought on a tray and given to the girl, who took it to her mother. 12Later, John's disciples came for his body and buried it. Then they went and told Jesus what had happened.

## Jesus Feeds Five Thousand

13As soon as Jesus heard the news, he left in a boat to a remote area to be alone. But the crowds heard where he was headed and followed on foot from many towns. 14Jesus saw the huge crowd as he stepped from the boat, and he had compassion on them and healed their sick.

15That evening the disciples came to him and said, "This is a remote place, and it's already getting late. Send the crowds away so they can go to the villages and buy food for themselves."

16But Jesus said, " That isn't necessary—you feed them."

17"But we have only five loaves of bread and two fish!" they answered.

13:55 Other manuscripts read *Joses;* still others read *John.*   14:1 Greek *Herod the tetrarch.* Herod Antipas was a son of King Herod and was ruler over Galilee.

¹⁸"Bring them here," he said. ¹⁹Then he told the people to sit down on the grass. Jesus took the five loaves and two fish, looked up toward heaven, and blessed them. Then, breaking the loaves into pieces, he gave the bread to the disciples, who distributed it to the people. ²⁰They all ate as much as they wanted, and afterward, the disciples picked up twelve baskets of leftovers. ²¹About 5,000 men were fed that day, in addition to all the women and children!

## Jesus Walks on Water

²²Immediately after this, Jesus insisted that his disciples get back into the boat and cross to the other side of the lake, while he sent the people home. ²³After sending them home, he went up into the hills by himself to pray. Night fell while he was there alone.

²⁴Meanwhile, the disciples were in trouble far away from land, for a strong wind had risen, and they were fighting heavy waves. ²⁵About three o'clock in the morning* Jesus came toward them, walking on the water. ²⁶When the disciples saw him walking on the water, they were terrified. In their fear, they cried out, "It's a ghost!"

²⁷But Jesus spoke to them at once. "Don't be afraid," he said. "Take courage. I am here!*"

²⁸Then Peter called to him, "Lord, if it's really you, tell me to come to you, walking on the water."

²⁹"Yes, come," Jesus said.

So Peter went over the side of the boat and walked on the water toward Jesus. ³⁰But when he saw the strong* wind and the waves, he was terrified and began to sink. "Save me, Lord!" he shouted.

³¹Jesus immediately reached out and grabbed him. "You have so little faith," Jesus said. "Why did you doubt me?"

³²When they climbed back into the boat, the wind stopped. ³³Then the disciples worshiped him. "You really are the Son of God!" they exclaimed.

³⁴After they had crossed the lake, they landed at Gennesaret. ³⁵When the people recognized Jesus, the news of his arrival spread quickly throughout the whole area,

and soon people were bringing all their sick to be healed. ³⁶They begged him to let the sick touch at least the fringe of his robe, and all who touched him were healed.

## Jesus Teaches about Inner Purity

**15** Some Pharisees and teachers of religious law now arrived from Jerusalem to see Jesus. They asked him, ²"Why do your disciples disobey our age-old tradition? For they ignore our tradition of ceremonial hand washing before they eat."

³Jesus replied, "And why do you, by your traditions, violate the direct commandments of God? ⁴For instance, God says, 'Honor your father and mother,'* and 'Anyone who speaks disrespectfully of father or mother must be put to death.'* ⁵But you say it is all right for people to say to their parents, 'Sorry, I can't help you. For I have vowed to give to God what I would have given to you.' ⁶In this way, you say they don't need to honor their parents.* And so you cancel the word of God for the sake of your own tradition. ⁷You hypocrites! Isaiah was right when he prophesied about you, for he wrote,

⁸ 'These people honor me with
their lips,
but their hearts are far from me.
⁹ Their worship is a farce,
for they teach man-made ideas as
commands from God.'* "

¹⁰Then Jesus called to the crowd to come and hear. "Listen," he said, "and try to understand. ¹¹It's not what goes into your mouth that defiles you; you are defiled by the words that come out of your mouth."

¹²Then the disciples came to him and asked, "Do you realize you offended the Pharisees by what you just said?"

¹³Jesus replied, "Every plant not planted by my heavenly Father will be uprooted, ¹⁴so ignore them. They are blind guides leading the blind, and if one blind person guides another, they will both fall into a ditch."

¹⁵Then Peter said to Jesus, "Explain to us the parable that says people aren't defiled by what they eat."

---

14:25 Greek *In the fourth watch of the night.* 14:27 Or *The 'I Am' is here;* Greek reads *I am.* See Exod 3:14. 14:30 Some manuscripts do not include *strong.* 15:4a Exod 20:12; Deut 5:16. 15:4b Exod 21:17 (Greek version); Lev 20:9 (Greek version). 15:6 Greek *their father;* other manuscripts read *their father or their mother.* 15:8-9 Isa 29:13 (Greek version).

# HOW to walk on water
READ MATTHEW 14:22-33

If you were a disciple watching Jesus walking on the water, what would you have done? Been afraid or, like Peter, wished to walk on water, too? Now remember this was no calm lake on a bright, sunny day that Peter stepped onto. It was the middle of the night, a strong wind was whipping, and the boat was fighting heavy waves. It took some courage on Peter's part to get out of that boat. And it paid off as he walked on *top* of the water toward Jesus. But Peter's triumph quickly turned to trouble as he became terrified and started sinking. Did Peter sink because the wind got stronger or the waves got higher? No, <u>because he took his eyes off Jesus and looked at his circumstances instead.</u>

Don't look at the "waves" below you or the "wind" above you today. Instead, as the old hymn says, "Turn your eyes upon Jesus, Look full in His wonderful face, And the things of earth will grow strangely dim In the light of His glory and grace."

---

16"Don't you understand yet?" Jesus asked. 17"Anything you eat passes through the stomach and then goes into the sewer. 18 But the words you speak come from the heart—that's what defiles you. 19For from the heart come evil thoughts, murder, adultery, all sexual immorality, theft, lying, and slander. 20These are what defile you. Eating with unwashed hands will never defile you."

### The Faith of a Gentile Woman
21 Then Jesus left Galilee and went north to the region of Tyre and Sidon. 22A Gentile* woman who lived there came to him, pleading, "Have mercy on me, O Lord, Son of David! For my daughter is possessed by a demon that torments her severely."

23 But Jesus gave her no reply, not even a word. Then his disciples urged him to send her away. "Tell her to go away," they said. "She is bothering us with all her begging."

24 Then Jesus said to the woman, "I was sent only to help God's lost sheep—the people of Israel."

25 But she came and worshiped him, pleading again, "Lord, help me!"

26Jesus responded, "It isn't right to take food from the children and throw it to the dogs."

27 She replied, "That's true, Lord, but even

dogs are allowed to eat the scraps that fall beneath their masters' table."

28"Dear woman," Jesus said to her, "your faith is great. Your request is granted." And her daughter was instantly healed.

### Jesus Heals Many People
29Jesus returned to the Sea of Galilee and climbed a hill and sat down. 30A vast crowd brought to him people who were lame, blind, crippled, those who couldn't speak, and many others. They laid them before Jesus, and he healed them all. 31The crowd was amazed! Those who hadn't been able to speak were talking, the crippled were made well, the lame were walking, and the blind could see again! And they praised the God of Israel.

### Jesus Feeds Four Thousand
32Then Jesus called his disciples and told them, "I feel sorry for these people. They have been here with me for three days, and they have nothing left to eat. I don't want to send them away hungry, or they will faint along the way."

33The disciples replied, "Where would we get enough food here in the wilderness for such a huge crowd?"

34Jesus asked, "How much bread do you have?"

**15:22** Greek *Canaanite*.

They replied, "Seven loaves, and a few small fish."

35 So Jesus told all the people to sit down on the ground. 36 Then he took the seven loaves and the fish, thanked God for them, and broke them into pieces. He gave them to the disciples, who distributed the food to the crowd.

37 They all ate as much as they wanted. Afterward, the disciples picked up seven large baskets of leftover food. 38 There were 4,000 men who were fed that day, in addition to all the women and children. 39 Then Jesus sent the people home, and he got into a boat and crossed over to the region of Magadan.

## Leaders Demand a Miraculous Sign

**16** One day the Pharisees and Sadducees came to test Jesus, demanding that he show them a miraculous sign from heaven to prove his authority.

2 He replied, " You know the saying, 'Red sky at night means fair weather tomorrow; 3 red sky in the morning means foul weather all day.' You know how to interpret the weather signs in the sky, but you don't know how to interpret the signs of the times!* 4 Only an evil, adulterous generation would demand a miraculous sign, but the only sign I will give them is the sign of the prophet Jonah.*" Then Jesus left them and went away.

## Yeast of the Pharisees and Sadducees

5 Later, after they crossed to the other side of the lake, the disciples discovered they had forgotten to bring any bread. 6 " Watch out!" Jesus warned them. "Beware of the yeast of the Pharisees and Sadducees."

7 At this they began to argue with each other because they hadn't brought any bread. 8 Jesus knew what they were saying, so he said, " You have so little faith! Why are you arguing with each other about having no bread? 9 Don't you understand even yet? Don't you remember the 5,000 I fed with five loaves, and the baskets of leftovers you picked up? 10 Or the 4,000 I fed with seven

loaves, and the large baskets of leftovers you picked up? 11 Why can't you understand that I'm not talking about bread? So again I say, 'Beware of the yeast of the Pharisees and Sadducees.'"

12 Then at last they understood that he wasn't speaking about the yeast in bread, but about the deceptive teaching of the Pharisees and Sadducees.

## Peter's Declaration about Jesus

13 When Jesus came to the region of Caesarea Philippi, he asked his disciples, " Who do people say that the Son of Man is?"*

14 "Well," they replied, "some say John the Baptist, some say Elijah, and others say Jeremiah or one of the other prophets."

15 Then he asked them, "But who do you say I am?"

16 Simon Peter answered, "You are the Messiah,* the Son of the living God."

17 Jesus replied, " You are blessed, Simon son of John,* because my Father in heaven has revealed this to you. You did not learn this from any human being. 18 Now I say to you that you are Peter (which means 'rock'),* and upon this rock I will build my church, and all the powers of hell* will not conquer it. 19 And I will give you the keys of the Kingdom of Heaven. Whatever you forbid* on earth will be forbidden in heaven, and whatever you permit* on earth will be permitted in heaven."

20 Then he sternly warned the disciples not to tell anyone that he was the Messiah.

## Jesus Predicts His Death

21 From then on Jesus* began to tell his disciples plainly that it was necessary for him to go to Jerusalem, and that he would suffer many terrible things at the hands of the elders, the leading priests, and the teachers of religious law. He would be killed, but on the third day he would be raised from the dead.

22 But Peter took him aside and began to reprimand him* for saying such things. "Heaven forbid, Lord," he said. "This will never happen to you!"

**16:2-3** Several manuscripts do not include any of the words in 16:2-3 after *He replied.*   **16:4** Greek *the sign of Jonah.*   **16:13** "Son of Man" is a title Jesus used for himself.   **16:16** Or *the Christ. Messiah* (a Hebrew term) and *Christ* (a Greek term) both mean "the anointed one."   **16:17** Greek *Simon bar-Jonah;* see John 1:42; 21:15-17.   **16:18a** Greek *that you are Peter.*   **16:18b** Greek *and the gates of Hades.*   **16:19a** Or *bind,* or *lock.*   **16:19b** Or *loose,* or *open.*   **16:21** Some manuscripts read *Jesus the Messiah.*   **16:22** Or *began to correct him.*

23 Jesus turned to Peter and said, "Get away from me, Satan! You are a dangerous trap to me. You are seeing things merely from a human point of view, not from God's."

24 Then Jesus said to his disciples, "If any of you wants to be my follower, you must turn from your selfish ways, take up your cross, and follow me. 25 If you try to hang on to your life, you will lose it. But if you give up your life for my sake, you will save it. 26 And what do you benefit if you gain the whole world but lose your own soul?* Is anything worth more than your soul? 27 For the Son of Man will come with his angels in the glory of his Father and will judge all people according to their deeds. 28 And I tell you the truth, some standing here right now will not die before they see the Son of Man coming in his Kingdom."

## The Transfiguration

**17** Six days later Jesus took Peter and the two brothers, James and John, and led them up a high mountain to be alone. 2 As the men watched, Jesus' appearance was transformed so that his face shone like the sun, and his clothes became as white as light. 3 Suddenly, Moses and Elijah appeared and began talking with Jesus.

4 Peter exclaimed, "Lord, it's wonderful for us to be here! If you want, I'll make three shelters as memorials*—one for you, one for Moses, and one for Elijah."

5 But even as he spoke, a bright cloud overshadowed them, and a voice from the cloud said, "This is my dearly loved Son, who brings me great joy. Listen to him." 6 The disciples were terrified and fell face down on the ground.

7 Then Jesus came over and touched them. "Get up," he said. "Don't be afraid." 8 And when they looked up, Moses and Elijah were gone, and they saw only Jesus.

9 As they went back down the mountain, Jesus commanded them, "Don't tell anyone what you have seen until the Son of Man* has been raised from the dead."

10 Then his disciples asked him, "Why do the teachers of religious law insist that Elijah must return before the Messiah comes?*"

11 Jesus replied, "Elijah is indeed coming first to get everything ready. 12 But I tell you, Elijah has already come, but he wasn't recognized, and they chose to abuse him. And in the same way they will also make the Son of Man suffer." 13 Then the disciples realized he was talking about John the Baptist.

## Jesus Heals a Demon-Possessed Boy

14 At the foot of the mountain, a large crowd was waiting for them. A man came and knelt before Jesus and said, 15 "Lord, have mercy on my son. He has seizures and suffers terribly. He often falls into the fire or into the water. 16 So I brought him to your disciples, but they couldn't heal him."

17 Jesus said, "You faithless and corrupt people! How long must I be with you? How long must I put up with you? Bring the boy here to me." 18 Then Jesus rebuked the demon in the boy, and it left him. From that moment the boy was well.

19 Afterward the disciples asked Jesus privately, "Why couldn't we cast out that demon?"

20 "You don't have enough faith," Jesus told them. "I tell you the truth, if you had faith even as small as a mustard seed, you could say to this mountain, 'Move from here to there,' and it would move. Nothing would be impossible.*"

## Jesus Again Predicts His Death

22 After they gathered again in Galilee, Jesus told them, "The Son of Man is going to be betrayed into the hands of his enemies. 23 He will be killed, but on the third day he will be raised from the dead." And the disciples were filled with grief.

## Payment of the Temple Tax

24 On their arrival in Capernaum, the collectors of the Temple tax* came to Peter and asked him, "Doesn't your teacher pay the Temple tax?"

25 "Yes, he does," Peter replied. Then he went into the house.

But before he had a chance to speak, Jesus asked him, "What do you think, Peter?* Do

---

**16:26** Or *your self?* also in 16:26b.   **17:4** Greek *three tabernacles.*   **17:9** "Son of Man" is a title Jesus used for himself.   **17:10** Greek *that Elijah must come first?*   **17:20** Some manuscripts add verse 21, *But this kind of demon won't leave except by prayer and fasting.* Compare Mark 9:29.   **17:24** Greek *the two-drachma (tax);* also in 17:24b. See Exod 30:13-16; Neh 10:32-33.   **17:25a** Greek *Simon?*

# FAITH enough

IT'S VERY CLEAR from Matthew and the other Gospels that Jesus was a healer. We don't know the exact number of people He healed, but it certainly was in the thousands as on many occasions the Gospel writers tell us He healed "multitudes." We don't know all the afflictions that were healed, but they included leprosy, a deformed hand, swollen limbs, hemorrhaging, blindness, deafness, lameness, paralysis, seizures, a severed ear, and even death.

It's tempting to believe all these people were healed by their faith, but we don't know that for sure. We do know, however, that they all were healed by Jesus.

We're not just playing with words here.

There are about forty different descriptions of healings in the four Gospels (many are described in more than one Gospel), but faith is said to play an explicit part only in a little more than a third of them. In more than half of those healings, it's the faith of *another* person, not the afflicted person, that is mentioned. Faith is not even mentioned at all in the *majority* of Jesus' healings. Only on two occasions (Matthew 8:10 and 15:28) does Jesus remark about someone having a lot of faith before He heals that person's loved one.

The common factor in all Jesus' healing miracles is Jesus Himself—not necessarily the faith of the sick person.

*God is sovereign. The choice of whether or not we are healed on this earth now is not ours, but His.*

It's true that a lack of faith can limit healing, as Matthew explains in 13:58 concerning Jesus' hometown of Nazareth ("And so he did only a few miracles there because of their unbelief.") But apparently in spite of this unbelief, or lack of faith, Jesus chose to do *some* miracles there.

Think about it. If the power to be healed came from having enough faith or just the right kind of faith, we could conjure up our own healing. (If we're honest, we all must admit we've known people with great faith who were *not* healed here on earth.) While faith in God can help unleash His healing power and our ability to receive a miracle, we also must accept that God can choose to heal us because of our faith or *in spite of* our lack of faith.

As pastor and author Larry Keefauver explains: "Be careful to note that our faith is not *in faith*. Just believing hard enough, long enough or strong

# for a miracle

enough will not strengthen you or effect your healing. Holding on to your miracle or your healing will not cause your healing to manifest *now*."[1]

In his book *When God Doesn't Heal Now,* Keefauver does a wonderful job of tackling the aching question of why some pray and get physical healing and others don't. He's a strong believer in such miracles and has personally witnessed many, but ultimately accepts that <u>sometimes God heals believers in the here and now and sometimes He heals them in eternity</u>. He also acknowledges that there are no easy answers.

"If you have trusted human reason or wisdom to help you understand why you are sick or when you will be healed, you may have found yourself to be frustrated or even angry with God," Keefauver explains.

"**If we try to reason *when* God will heal, then we will be forced to create myths to answer.** Reasoning about *when God heals* forces the creation of myths such as

- God will heal *when* my faith is great enough.
- God will heal *when* my prayers or the prayers of others are righteous, powerful, and effective.
- God will heal *when* He is finished punishing me.
- God will heal *when* the right person touches me."[2]

Are you believing any of these myths about your healing or your loved one's?

We believe the Bible teaches God is sovereign—supreme, independent, autonomous—and also not bound by our concept of time. So the choice of whether or not we are healed on this earth now is not ours, but His.

So if it's all up to God and not us or our faith, does it matter what we do or say?

Yes, it does—because God has chosen to allow us to work *with* Him in fulfilling His purposes for our lives.

"We cannot control or manipulate our sovereign God," Keefauver explains. "Faith, prayer, repentance, and claiming the promises of God do not force Him to act. But God has sovereignly chosen in His mercy and compassion to risk relationship with us in time and space. He has chosen to respond as He wills to faith, prayer, repentance, and acting upon His promises."

So keep on having faith, keep on praying, keep on turning away from sin, and keep on believing God's promises. Just leave the healing up to God, because if you're a believer, you *will* be healed. Either in the here and now . . . or in eternity.

[1] Larry Keefauver, *When God Doesn't Heal Now* (Nashville: Thomas Nelson Publishers, 2000), 39.    [2] Ibid., 104–105.

kings tax their own people or the people they have conquered?*"

26"They tax the people they have conquered," Peter replied.

" Well, then," Jesus said, "the citizens are free! 27However, we don't want to offend them, so go down to the lake and throw in a line. Open the mouth of the first fish you catch, and you will find a large silver coin.* Take it and pay the tax for both of us."

## The Greatest in the Kingdom

**18** About that time the disciples came to Jesus and asked, "Who is greatest in the Kingdom of Heaven?"

2Jesus called a little child to him and put the child among them. 3Then he said, "I tell you the truth, unless you turn from your sins and become like little children, you will never get into the Kingdom of Heaven. 4So anyone who becomes as humble as this little child is the greatest in the Kingdom of Heaven.

5"And anyone who welcomes a little child like this on my behalf* is welcoming me. 6But if you cause one of these little ones who trusts in me to fall into sin, it would be better for you to have a large millstone tied around your neck and be drowned in the depths of the sea.

7"What sorrow awaits the world, because it tempts people to sin. Temptations are inevitable, but what sorrow awaits the person who does the tempting. 8So if your hand or foot causes you to sin, cut it off and throw it away. It's better to enter eternal life with only one hand or one foot than to be thrown into eternal fire with both of your hands and feet. 9And if your eye causes you to sin, gouge it out and throw it away. It's better to enter eternal life with only one eye than to have two eyes and be thrown into the fire of hell.*

10"Beware that you don't look down on any of these little ones. For I tell you that in heaven their angels are always in the presence of my heavenly Father.*

## Parable of the Lost Sheep

12"If a man has a hundred sheep and one of them wanders away, what will he do? Won't he leave the ninety-nine others on the hills and go out to search for the one that is lost? 13And if he finds it, I tell you the truth, he will rejoice over it more than over the ninety-nine that didn't wander away! 14In the same way, it is not my heavenly Father's will that even one of these little ones should perish.

## Correcting Another Believer

15"If another believer* sins against you,* go privately and point out the offense. If the other person listens and confesses it, you have won that person back. 16But if you are unsuccessful, take one or two others with you

17:25b Greek *their sons or others?*   17:27 Greek *a stater* [a Greek coin equivalent to four drachmas].   18:5 Greek *in my name*.
18:9 Greek *the Gehenna of fire*.   18:10 Some manuscripts add verse 11, *And the Son of Man came to save those who are lost.* Compare Luke 19:10.   18:15a Greek *If your brother.*   18:15b Some manuscripts do not include *against you*.

# PRETENDING to be a doctor

READ MATTHEW 16:13-17

What if your physician lied or was crazy and claimed to be a doctor but really wasn't—would you still think he or she was a great person? Hardly. Yet some people want to dismiss Jesus' claims to be the Son of God and call Him simply a great moral teacher.

The late British author C. S. Lewis in his book *Mere Christianity* explains why this is not an option for us: "A man who was merely a man and said the sort of things Jesus said would not be a great moral teacher. . . . You must make your choice. Either this man was, and is, the Son of God; or else a madman or something worse. You can shut Him up for a fool, you can spit at Him and kill Him as a demon; or you can fall at His feet and call Him Lord and God. But let us not come with any patronizing nonsense about His being a great human teacher. He has not left that open to us. He did not intend to."

and go back again, so that everything you say may be confirmed by two or three witnesses. ¹⁷If the person still refuses to listen, take your case to the church. Then if he or she won't accept the church's decision, treat that person as a pagan or a corrupt tax collector.

¹⁸"I tell you the truth, whatever you forbid* on earth will be forbidden in heaven, and whatever you permit* on earth will be permitted in heaven.

¹⁹"I also tell you this: If two of you agree here on earth concerning anything you ask, my Father in heaven will do it for you. ²⁰For where two or three gather together as my followers,* I am there among them."

## Parable of the Unforgiving Debtor

²¹Then Peter came to him and asked, "Lord, how often should I forgive someone* who sins against me? Seven times?"

²²"No, not seven times," Jesus replied, "but seventy times seven!*

²³"Therefore, the Kingdom of Heaven can be compared to a king who decided to bring his accounts up to date with servants who had borrowed money from him. ²⁴In the process, one of his debtors was brought in who owed him millions of dollars.* ²⁵He couldn't pay, so his master ordered that he be sold—along with his wife, his children, and everything he owned—to pay the debt.

²⁶"But the man fell down before his master and begged him, 'Please, be patient with me, and I will pay it all.' ²⁷Then his master was filled with pity for him, and he released him and forgave his debt.

²⁸"But when the man left the king, he went to a fellow servant who owed him a few thousand dollars.* He grabbed him by the throat and demanded instant payment.

²⁹"His fellow servant fell down before him and begged for a little more time. 'Be patient with me, and I will pay it,' he pleaded. ³⁰But his creditor wouldn't wait. He had the man arrested and put in prison until the debt could be paid in full.

³¹"When some of the other servants saw this, they were very upset. They went to the king and told him everything that had happened. ³²Then the king called in the man he had forgiven and said, 'You evil servant! I forgave you that tremendous debt because you pleaded with me. ³³Shouldn't you have mercy on your fellow servant, just as I had mercy on you?' ³⁴Then the angry king sent the man to prison to be tortured until he had paid his entire debt.

³⁵"That's what my heavenly Father will do to you if you refuse to forgive your brothers and sisters* from your heart."

## Discussion about Divorce and Marriage

**19** When Jesus had finished saying these things, he left Galilee and went down to the region of Judea east of the Jordan River. ²Large crowds followed him there, and he healed their sick.

³Some Pharisees came and tried to trap him with this question: "Should a man be allowed to divorce his wife for just any reason?"

⁴"Haven't you read the Scriptures?" Jesus replied. "They record that from the beginning 'God made them male and female.'* ⁵And he said, 'This explains why a man leaves his father and mother and is joined to his wife, and the two are united into one.'* ⁶Since they are no longer two but one, let no one split apart what God has joined together."

⁷"Then why did Moses say in the law that a man could give his wife a written notice of divorce and send her away?"* they asked.

⁸Jesus replied, "Moses permitted divorce only as a concession to your hard hearts, but it was not what God had originally intended. ⁹And I tell you this, whoever divorces his wife and marries someone else commits adultery—unless his wife has been unfaithful.*"

¹⁰Jesus' disciples then said to him, "If this is the case, it is better not to marry!"

¹¹"Not everyone can accept this statement," Jesus said. "Only those whom God helps. ¹²Some are born as eunuchs, some have been made eunuchs by others, and some choose not to marry* for the sake of the Kingdom of Heaven. Let anyone accept this who can."

**18:18a** Or *bind,* or *lock.*　**18:18b** Or *loose,* or *open.*　**18:20** Greek *gather together in my name.*　**18:21** Greek *my brother.*
**18:22** Or *seventy-seven times.*　**18:24** Greek *10,000 talents* [375 tons or 340 metric tons of silver].　**18:28** Greek *100 denarii.* A denarius was equivalent to a laborer's full day's wage.　**18:35** Greek *your brother.*　**19:4** Gen 1:27; 5:2.　**19:5** Gen 2:24.　**19:7** See Deut 24:1.　**19:9** Some manuscripts add *And anyone who marries a divorced woman commits adultery.* Compare Matt 5:32.
**19:12** Greek *and some make themselves eunuchs.*

## Jesus Blesses the Children

13One day some parents brought their children to Jesus so he could lay his hands on them and pray for them. But the disciples scolded the parents for bothering him. 14But Jesus said, "Let the children come to me. Don't stop them! For the Kingdom of Heaven belongs to those who are like these children." 15And he placed his hands on their heads and blessed them before he left.

## The Rich Man

16Someone came to Jesus with this question: "Teacher,* what good deed must I do to have eternal life?"

17"Why ask me about what is good?" Jesus replied. " There is only One who is good. But to answer your question—if you want to receive eternal life, keep* the commandments."

18"Which ones?" the man asked.

And Jesus replied: " ' You must not murder. You must not commit adultery. You must not steal. You must not testify falsely. 19Honor your father and mother. Love your neighbor as yourself.'* "

20"I've obeyed all these commandments," the young man replied. "What else must I do?"

21Jesus told him, "If you want to be perfect, go and sell all your possessions and give the money to the poor, and you will have treasure in heaven. Then come, follow me."

22But when the young man heard this, he went away sad, for he had many possessions.

23Then Jesus said to his disciples, "I tell you the truth, it is very hard for a rich person to enter the Kingdom of Heaven. 24I'll say it again—it is easier for a camel to go through the eye of a needle than for a rich person to enter the Kingdom of God!"

25The disciples were astounded. "Then who in the world can be saved?" they asked.

26Jesus looked at them intently and said, "Humanly speaking, it is impossible. But with God everything is possible."

27Then Peter said to him, "We've given up everything to follow you. What will we get?"

28Jesus replied, "I assure you that when the world is made new* and the Son of Man* sits upon his glorious throne, you who have been my followers will also sit on twelve thrones, judging the twelve tribes of Israel. 29And everyone who has given up houses or brothers or sisters or father or mother or children or property, for my sake, will receive a hundred times as much in return and will inherit eternal life. 30But many who are the greatest now will be least important then, and those who seem least important now will be the greatest then.*

## Parable of the Vineyard Workers

**20** "For the Kingdom of Heaven is like the landowner who went out early one morning to hire workers for his vineyard. 2He agreed to pay the normal daily wage* and sent them out to work.

3"At nine o'clock in the morning he was passing through the marketplace and saw some people standing around doing nothing. 4So he hired them, telling them he would pay them whatever was right at the end of the day. 5So they went to work in the vineyard. At noon and again at three o'clock he did the same thing.

6"At five o'clock that afternoon he was in town again and saw some more people standing around. He asked them, ' Why haven't you been working today?'

7"They replied, 'Because no one hired us.'

"The landowner told them, ' Then go out and join the others in my vineyard.'

8"That evening he told the foreman to call the workers in and pay them, beginning with the last workers first. 9When those hired at five o'clock were paid, each received a full day's wage. 10When those hired first came to get their pay, they assumed they would receive more. But they, too, were paid a day's wage. 11When they received their pay, they protested to the owner, 12'Those people worked only one hour, and yet you've paid them just as much as you paid us who worked all day in the scorching heat.'

13"He answered one of them, 'Friend, I haven't been unfair! Didn't you agree to work all day for the usual wage? 14Take your money and go. I wanted to pay this last worker the

19:16 Some manuscripts read Good Teacher.   19:17 Some manuscripts read continue to keep.   19:18-19 Exod 20:12-16; Deut 5:16-20; Lev 19:18.   19:28a Or in the regeneration.   19:28b "Son of Man" is a title Jesus used for himself.   19:30 Greek But many who are first will be last; and the last, first.   20:2 Greek a denarius, the payment for a full day's labor; similarly in 20:9, 10, 13.

same as you. 15Is it against the law for me to do what I want with my money? Should you be jealous because I am kind to others?'

16"So those who are last now will be first then, and those who are first will be last."

## Jesus Again Predicts His Death

17As Jesus was going up to Jerusalem, he took the twelve disciples aside privately and told them what was going to happen to him. 18"Listen," he said, "we're going up to Jerusalem, where the Son of Man* will be betrayed to the leading priests and the teachers of religious law. They will sentence him to die. 19Then they will hand him over to the Romans* to be mocked, flogged with a whip, and crucified. But on the third day he will be raised from the dead."

## Jesus Teaches about Serving Others

20Then the mother of James and John, the sons of Zebedee, came to Jesus with her sons. She knelt respectfully to ask a favor. 21"What is your request?" he asked.

She replied, "In your Kingdom, please let my two sons sit in places of honor next to you, one on your right and the other on your left."

22But Jesus answered by saying to them, "You don't know what you are asking! Are you able to drink from the bitter cup of suffering I am about to drink?"

"Oh yes," they replied, "we are able!"

23Jesus told them, "You will indeed drink from my bitter cup. But I have no right to say who will sit on my right or my left. My Father has prepared those places for the ones he has chosen."

24When the ten other disciples heard what James and John had asked, they were indignant. 25But Jesus called them together and said, "You know that the rulers in this world lord it over their people, and officials flaunt their authority over those under them. 26But among you it will be different. Whoever wants to be a leader among you must be your servant, 27and whoever wants to be first among you must become your slave. 28For even the Son of Man came not to be served but to serve others and to give his life as a ransom for many."

## LAST will be first
READ MATTHEW 20:1-16

Sometimes people facing a health crisis think about turning to God but feel badly about doing so because they've pretty much ignored Him most of their lives. Their thoughts go something like this: *I don't want to give my life to Him now because it seems like I'm only doing it because I need something.* Or maybe even: *It doesn't seem right to go running to God now that I don't have much time left.*

But this story makes it clear how Jesus feels about those who have served Him for a long time and those who only can serve Him a short time. He treats them all the same. No more excuses— why not begin serving Him today?

## Jesus Heals Two Blind Men

29As Jesus and the disciples left the town of Jericho, a large crowd followed behind. 30Two blind men were sitting beside the road. When they heard that Jesus was coming that way, they began shouting, "Lord, Son of David, have mercy on us!"

31"Be quiet!" the crowd yelled at them.

But they only shouted louder, "Lord, Son of David, have mercy on us!"

32When Jesus heard them, he stopped and called, "What do you want me to do for you?"

33"Lord," they said, "we want to see!" 34Jesus felt sorry for them and touched their eyes. Instantly they could see! Then they followed him.

## Jesus' Triumphant Entry

**21** As Jesus and the disciples approached Jerusalem, they came to the town of Bethphage on the Mount of Olives. Jesus sent two of them on ahead. 2"Go into the village over there," he said. "As soon as you enter it, you will see a donkey tied there, with its colt beside it. Untie them and bring them to me. 3If anyone asks what you are doing, just say, 'The Lord needs them,' and he will immediately let you take them."

4This took place to fulfill the prophecy that said,

20:18 "Son of Man" is a title Jesus used for himself.   20:19 Greek *the Gentiles*.

5 "Tell the people of Israel,*
  'Look, your King is coming to you.
He is humble, riding on a donkey—
    riding on a donkey's colt.'"*

6 The two disciples did as Jesus commanded. 7 They brought the donkey and the colt to him and threw their garments over the colt, and he sat on it.*

8 Most of the crowd spread their garments on the road ahead of him, and others cut branches from the trees and spread them on the road. 9 Jesus was in the center of the procession, and the people all around him were shouting,

"Praise God* for the Son of David!
  Blessings on the one who comes in the
    name of the LORD!
  Praise God in highest heaven!"*

10 The entire city of Jerusalem was in an uproar as he entered. "Who is this?" they asked.

11 And the crowds replied, "It's Jesus, the prophet from Nazareth in Galilee."

## Jesus Clears the Temple

12 Jesus entered the Temple and began to drive out all the people buying and selling animals for sacrifice. He knocked over the tables of the money changers and the chairs of those selling doves. 13 He said to them, "The Scriptures declare, 'My Temple will be called a house of prayer,' but you have turned it into a den of thieves!"*

14 The blind and the lame came to him in the Temple, and he healed them. 15 The leading priests and the teachers of religious law saw these wonderful miracles and heard even the children in the Temple shouting, "Praise God for the Son of David."

But the leaders were indignant. 16 They asked Jesus, "Do you hear what these children are saying?"

"Yes," Jesus replied. "Haven't you ever read the Scriptures? For they say, ' You have taught children and infants to give you praise.'* "

17 Then he returned to Bethany, where he stayed overnight.

## Jesus Curses the Fig Tree

18 In the morning, as Jesus was returning to Jerusalem, he was hungry, 19 and he noticed a fig tree beside the road. He went over to see if there were any figs, but there were only leaves. Then he said to it, "May you never bear fruit again!" And immediately the fig tree withered up.

20 The disciples were amazed when they saw this and asked, "How did the fig tree wither so quickly?"

21 Then Jesus told them, "I tell you the truth, if you have faith and don't doubt, you can do things like this and much more. You can even say to this mountain, 'May you be lifted up and thrown into the sea,' and it will happen. 22 You can pray for anything, and if you have faith, you will receive it."

## The Authority of Jesus Challenged

23 When Jesus returned to the Temple and began teaching, the leading priests and elders came up to him. They demanded, "By what authority are you doing all these things? Who gave you the right?"

24 "I'll tell you by what authority I do these things if you answer one question," Jesus replied. 25 "Did John's authority to baptize come from heaven, or was it merely human?"

They talked it over among themselves. "If we say it was from heaven, he will ask us why we didn't believe John. 26 But if we say it was merely human, we'll be mobbed because the people believe John was a prophet." 27 So they finally replied, "We don't know."

And Jesus responded, " Then I won't tell you by what authority I do these things.

## Parable of the Two Sons

28 "But what do you think about this? A man with two sons told the older boy, 'Son, go out and work in the vineyard today.' 29 The son answered, 'No, I won't go,' but later he changed his mind and went anyway. 30 Then the father told the other son, ' You go,' and he said, ' Yes, sir, I will.' But he didn't go.

31 "Which of the two obeyed his father?"
They replied, "The first."*

21:5a Greek *Tell the daughter of Zion.* Isa 62:11.   21:5b Zech 9:9.   21:7 Greek *over them, and he sat on them.*   21:9a Greek *Hosanna,* an exclamation of praise that literally means "save now"; also in 21:9b, 15.   21:9b Pss 118:25-26; 148:1.   21:13 Isa 56:7; Jer 7:11.   21:16 Ps 8:2.   21:29-31 Other manuscripts read *"The second."* In still other manuscripts the first son says "Yes" but does nothing, the second son says "No" but then repents and goes, and the answer to Jesus' question is that the second son obeyed his father.

Then Jesus explained his meaning: "I tell you the truth, corrupt tax collectors and prostitutes will get into the Kingdom of God before you do. 32For John the Baptist came and showed you the right way to live, but you didn't believe him, while tax collectors and prostitutes did. And even when you saw this happening, you refused to believe him and repent of your sins.

### Parable of the Evil Farmers

33"Now listen to another story. A certain landowner planted a vineyard, built a wall around it, dug a pit for pressing out the grape juice, and built a lookout tower. Then he leased the vineyard to tenant farmers and moved to another country. 34At the time of the grape harvest, he sent his servants to collect his share of the crop. 35But the farmers grabbed his servants, beat one, killed one, and stoned another. 36So the landowner sent a larger group of his servants to collect for him, but the results were the same.

37"Finally, the owner sent his son, thinking, 'Surely they will respect my son.'

38"But when the tenant farmers saw his son coming, they said to one another, 'Here comes the heir to this estate. Come on, let's kill him and get the estate for ourselves!' 39So they grabbed him, dragged him out of the vineyard, and murdered him.

40"When the owner of the vineyard returns," Jesus asked, "what do you think he will do to those farmers?"

41The religious leaders replied, "He will put the wicked men to a horrible death and lease the vineyard to others who will give him his share of the crop after each harvest."

42Then Jesus asked them, "Didn't you ever read this in the Scriptures?

' The stone that the builders rejected
    has now become the cornerstone.
This is the LORD's doing,
    and it is wonderful to see.'*

43I tell you, the Kingdom of God will be taken away from you and given to a nation that will produce the proper fruit. 44Anyone who stumbles over that stone will be broken to pieces, and it will crush anyone it falls on.*"

45When the leading priests and Pharisees heard this parable, they realized he was telling the story against them—they were the wicked farmers. 46They wanted to arrest him, but they were afraid of the crowds, who considered Jesus to be a prophet.

### Parable of the Great Feast

**22** Jesus also told them other parables. He said, 2" The Kingdom of Heaven can be illustrated by the story of a king who prepared a great wedding feast for his son. 3When the banquet was ready, he sent his servants to notify those who were invited. But they all refused to come!

4"So he sent other servants to tell them, 'The feast has been prepared. The bulls and fattened cattle have been killed, and everything is ready. Come to the banquet!' 5But the guests he had invited ignored them and went their own way, one to his farm, another to his business. 6Others seized his messengers and insulted them and killed them.

7"The king was furious, and he sent out his army to destroy the murderers and burn their town. 8And he said to his servants, 'The wedding feast is ready, and the guests I invited aren't worthy of the honor. 9Now go out to the street corners and invite everyone you see.' 10 So the servants brought in everyone they could find, good and bad alike, and the banquet hall was filled with guests.

11"But when the king came in to meet the guests, he noticed a man who wasn't wearing the proper clothes for a wedding. 12'Friend,' he asked, 'how is it that you are here without wedding clothes?' But the man had no reply. 13Then the king said to his aides, 'Bind his hands and feet and throw him into the outer darkness, where there will be weeping and gnashing of teeth.'

14"For many are called, but few are chosen."

### Taxes for Caesar

15Then the Pharisees met together to plot how to trap Jesus into saying something for which he could be arrested. 16They sent some of their disciples, along with the supporters of Herod, to meet with him.

21:42 Ps 118:22-23.    21:44 This verse is omitted in some early manuscripts. Compare Luke 20:18.

"Teacher," they said, "we know how honest you are. You teach the way of God truthfully. You are impartial and don't play favorites. 17Now tell us what you think about this: Is it right to pay taxes to Caesar or not?"

18But Jesus knew their evil motives. " You hypocrites!" he said. " Why are you trying to trap me? 19Here, show me the coin used for the tax." When they handed him a Roman coin,* 20he asked, " Whose picture and title are stamped on it?"

21"Caesar's," they replied.

"Well, then," he said, "give to Caesar what belongs to Caesar, and give to God what belongs to God."

22His reply amazed them, and they went away.

### Discussion about Resurrection

23That same day Jesus was approached by some Sadducees—religious leaders who say there is no resurrection from the dead. They posed this question: 24"Teacher, Moses said, 'If a man dies without children, his brother should marry the widow and have a child who will carry on the brother's name.'* 25Well, suppose there were seven brothers. The oldest one married and then died without children, so his brother married the widow. 26But the second brother also died, and the third brother married her. This con-

tinued with all seven of them. 27Last of all, the woman also died. 28So tell us, whose wife will she be in the resurrection? For all seven were married to her."

29Jesus replied, "Your mistake is that you don't know the Scriptures, and you don't know the power of God. 30For when the dead rise, they will neither marry nor be given in marriage. In this respect they will be like the angels in heaven.

31"But now, as to whether there will be a resurrection of the dead—haven't you ever read about this in the Scriptures? Long after Abraham, Isaac, and Jacob had died, God said,* 32'I am the God of Abraham, the God of Isaac, and the God of Jacob.'* So he is the God of the living, not the dead."

33When the crowds heard him, they were astounded at his teaching.

### The Most Important Commandment

34But when the Pharisees heard that he had silenced the Sadducees with his reply, they met together to question him again. 35One of them, an expert in religious law, tried to trap him with this question: 36"Teacher, which is the most important commandment in the law of Moses?"

37Jesus replied, " 'You must love the LORD your God with all your heart, all your soul, and all your mind.'* 38This is the first and

22:19 Greek *a denarius*.   22:24 Deut 25:5-6.   22:31 Greek *read about this? God said*.   22:32 Exod 3:6.   22:37 Deut 6:5.

## SAFE beneath the wings
READ MATTHEW 23:37

What a curious verse this is as Jesus likens himself to a mother hen! If you've ever seen a mother hen spread her wings and gather her little chicks to safety as danger was approaching, you have the picture of what Jesus portrays here. As He looked over the city of Jerusalem, Jesus knew He was the answer to the longings of Jewish hearts, but the people didn't want to hear it. Like a protective, loving parent, the Lord wished He could draw them close to His heart and keep them safe, but they wouldn't let Him. He warned them that they wouldn't have such a chance again for a long, long time.

Can you feel those imaginary wings over you today—protecting you, shielding you, and drawing you close? Have you trusted Jesus enough to let Him truly cover you? He longs to do that for you. Don't miss your chance today to be hidden safely in Jesus' arms.

greatest commandment. ³⁹A second is equally important: 'Love your neighbor as yourself.'* ⁴⁰The entire law and all the demands of the prophets are based on these two commandments."

### Whose Son Is the Messiah?

⁴¹Then, surrounded by the Pharisees, Jesus asked them a question: ⁴²"What do you think about the Messiah? Whose son is he?"

They replied, "He is the son of David."

⁴³Jesus responded, " Then why does David, speaking under the inspiration of the Spirit, call the Messiah 'my Lord'? For David said,

⁴⁴'The LORD said to my Lord,

Sit in the place of honor at my right hand
    until I humble your enemies beneath
    your feet.'*

⁴⁵Since David called the Messiah 'my Lord,' how can the Messiah be his son?"

⁴⁶No one could answer him. And after that, no one dared to ask him any more questions.

### Jesus Criticizes the Religious Leaders

**23** Then Jesus said to the crowds and to his disciples, ²" The teachers of religious law and the Pharisees are the official interpreters of the law of Moses.* ³So practice and obey whatever they tell you, but don't follow their example. For they don't practice what they teach. ⁴They crush people with unbearable religious demands and never lift a finger to ease the burden.

⁵"Everything they do is for show. On their arms they wear extra wide prayer boxes with Scripture verses inside, and they wear robes with extra long tassels.* ⁶And they love to sit at the head table at banquets and in the seats of honor in the synagogues. ⁷They love to receive respectful greetings as they walk in the marketplaces, and to be called 'Rabbi.'*

⁸"Don't let anyone call you 'Rabbi,' for you have only one teacher, and all of you are equal as brothers and sisters.* ⁹And don't address anyone here on earth as 'Father,' for only God

in heaven is your spiritual Father. ¹⁰And don't let anyone call you 'Teacher,' for you have only one teacher, the Messiah. ¹¹The greatest among you must be a servant. ¹²But those who exalt themselves will be humbled, and those who humble themselves will be exalted.

¹³"What sorrow awaits you teachers of religious law and you Pharisees. Hypocrites! For you shut the door of the Kingdom of Heaven in people's faces. You won't go in yourselves, and you don't let others enter either.*

¹⁵"What sorrow awaits you teachers of religious law and you Pharisees. Hypocrites! For you cross land and sea to make one convert, and then you turn that person into twice the child of hell* you yourselves are!

¹⁶"Blind guides! What sorrow awaits you! For you say that it means nothing to swear 'by God's Temple,' but that it is binding to swear 'by the gold in the Temple.' ¹⁷Blind fools! Which is more important—the gold or the Temple that makes the gold sacred? ¹⁸And you say that to swear 'by the altar' is not binding, but to swear 'by the gifts on the altar' is binding. ¹⁹How blind! For which is more important—the gift on the altar or the altar that makes the gift sacred? ²⁰When you swear 'by the altar,' you are swearing by it and by everything on it. ²¹And when you swear 'by the Temple,' you are swearing by it and by God, who lives in it. ²²And when you swear 'by heaven,' you are swearing by the throne of God and by God, who sits on the throne.

²³"What sorrow awaits you teachers of religious law and you Pharisees. Hypocrites! For you are careful to tithe even the tiniest income from your herb gardens,* but you ignore the more important aspects of the law—justice, mercy, and faith. You should tithe, yes, but do not neglect the more important things. ²⁴Blind guides! You strain your water so you won't accidentally swallow a gnat, but you swallow a camel!*

²⁵"What sorrow awaits you teachers of religious law and you Pharisees. Hypocrites! For you are so careful to clean the outside of

---

**22:39** Lev 19:18.   **22:44** Ps 110:1.   **23:2** Greek *and the Pharisees sit in the seat of Moses.*   **23:5** Greek *They enlarge their phylacteries and lengthen their tassels.*   **23:7** *Rabbi*, from Aramaic, means "master" or "teacher."   **23:8** Greek *brothers.*   **23:13** Some manuscripts add verse 14, *What sorrow awaits you teachers of religious law and you Pharisees. Hypocrites! You shamelessly cheat widows out of their property and then pretend to be pious by making long prayers in public. Because of this, you will be severely punished.* Compare Mark 12:40 and Luke 20:47.   **23:15** Greek *of Gehenna;* also in 23:33.   **23:23** Greek *tithe the mint, the dill, and the cumin.*   **23:24** See Lev 11:4, 23, where gnats and camels are both forbidden as food.

the cup and the dish, but inside you are filthy—full of greed and self-indulgence! 26You blind Pharisee! First wash the inside of the cup and the dish,* and then the outside will become clean, too.

27"What sorrow awaits you teachers of religious law and you Pharisees. Hypocrites! For you are like whitewashed tombs—beautiful on the outside but filled on the inside with dead people's bones and all sorts of impurity. 28Outwardly you look like righteous people, but inwardly your hearts are filled with hypocrisy and lawlessness.

29"What sorrow awaits you teachers of religious law and you Pharisees. Hypocrites! For you build tombs for the prophets your ancestors killed, and you decorate the monuments of the godly people your ancestors destroyed. 30Then you say, 'If we had lived in the days of our ancestors, we would never have joined them in killing the prophets.'

31"But in saying that, you testify against yourselves that you are indeed the descendants of those who murdered the prophets. 32Go ahead and finish what your ancestors started. 33Snakes! Sons of vipers! How will you escape the judgment of hell?

34"Therefore, I am sending you prophets and wise men and teachers of religious law. But you will kill some by crucifixion, and you will flog others with whips in your synagogues, chasing them from city to city. 35As a result, you will be held responsible for the murder of all godly people of all time—from the murder of righteous Abel to the murder of Zechariah son of Barachiah, whom you killed in the Temple between the sanctuary and the altar. 36I tell you the truth, this judgment will fall on this very generation.

## Jesus Grieves over Jerusalem

37"O Jerusalem, Jerusalem, the city that kills the prophets and stones God's messengers! How often I have wanted to gather your children together as a hen protects her chicks beneath her wings, but you wouldn't let me. 38And now, look, your house is abandoned and desolate.* 39For I tell you this, you will never see me again un-

til you say, 'Blessings on the one who comes in the name of the LORD!'* "

## Jesus Foretells the Future

**24** As Jesus was leaving the Temple grounds, his disciples pointed out to him the various Temple buildings. 2But he responded, "Do you see all these buildings? I tell you the truth, they will be completely demolished. Not one stone will be left on top of another!"

3Later, Jesus sat on the Mount of Olives. His disciples came to him privately and said, "Tell us, when will all this happen? What sign will signal your return and the end of the world?*"

4Jesus told them, "Don't let anyone mislead you, 5for many will come in my name, claiming, 'I am the Messiah.' They will deceive many. 6And you will hear of wars and threats of wars, but don't panic. Yes, these things must take place, but the end won't follow immediately. 7Nation will go to war against nation, and kingdom against kingdom. There will be famines and earthquakes in many parts of the world. 8But all this is only the first of the birth pains, with more to come.

9"Then you will be arrested, persecuted, and killed. You will be hated all over the world because you are my followers.* 10And many will turn away from me and betray and hate each other. 11And many false prophets will appear and will deceive many people. 12Sin will be rampant everywhere, and the love of many will grow cold. 13But the one who endures to the end will be saved. 14And the Good News about the Kingdom will be preached throughout the whole world, so that all nations* will hear it; and then the end will come.

15"The day is coming when you will see what Daniel the prophet spoke about—the sacrilegious object that causes desecration* standing in the Holy Place." (Reader, pay attention!) 16"Then those in Judea must flee to the hills. 17A person out on the deck of a roof must not go down into the house to pack. 18A person out in the field must not return even to get a coat. 19How terrible it

---

23:26 Some manuscripts do not include *and the dish.*   23:38 Some manuscripts do not include *and desolate.*   23:39 Ps 118:26.
24:3 Or *the age?*   24:9 Greek *on account of my name.*   24:14 Or *all peoples.*   24:15 Greek *the abomination of desolation.* See Dan 9:27; 11:31; 12:11.

will be for pregnant women and for nursing mothers in those days. ²⁰And pray that your flight will not be in winter or on the Sabbath. ²¹For there will be greater anguish than at any time since the world began. And it will never be so great again. ²²In fact, unless that time of calamity is shortened, not a single person will survive. But it will be shortened for the sake of God's chosen ones.

²³"Then if anyone tells you, 'Look, here is the Messiah,' or ' There he is,' don't believe it. ²⁴For false messiahs and false prophets will rise up and perform great signs and wonders so as to deceive, if possible, even God's chosen ones. ²⁵See, I have warned you about this ahead of time.

²⁶"So if someone tells you, 'Look, the Messiah is out in the desert,' don't bother to go and look. Or, 'Look, he is hiding here,' don't believe it! ²⁷For as the lightning flashes in the east and shines to the west, so it will be when the Son of Man* comes. ²⁸Just as the gathering of vultures shows there is a carcass nearby, so these signs indicate that the end is near.*

²⁹"Immediately after the anguish of those days,

the sun will be darkened,
    the moon will give no light,
the stars will fall from the sky,
    and the powers in the heavens will
        be shaken.*

³⁰And then at last, the sign that the Son of Man is coming will appear in the heavens, and there will be deep mourning among all the peoples of the earth. And they will see the Son of Man coming on the clouds of heaven with power and great glory.* ³¹And he will send out his angels with the mighty blast of a trumpet, and they will gather his chosen ones from all over the world*—from the farthest ends of the earth and heaven.

³²"Now learn a lesson from the fig tree. When its branches bud and its leaves begin to sprout, you know that summer is near. ³³In the same way, when you see all these things, you can know his return is very near, right at the door. ³⁴I tell you the truth, this generation* will not pass from the scene until all these things take place. ³⁵Heaven and earth will disappear, but my words will never disappear.

³⁶"However, no one knows the day or hour when these things will happen, not even the angels in heaven or the Son himself.* Only the Father knows.

³⁷"When the Son of Man returns, it will be like it was in Noah's day. ³⁸In those days before the flood, the people were enjoying banquets and parties and weddings right up to the time Noah entered his boat. ³⁹People didn't realize what was going to happen until the flood came and swept them all away. That is the way it will be when the Son of Man comes.

⁴⁰"Two men will be working together in the field; one will be taken, the other left. ⁴¹Two women will be grinding flour at the mill; one will be taken, the other left.

⁴²"So you, too, must keep watch! For you don't know what day your Lord is coming. ⁴³Understand this: If a homeowner knew exactly when a burglar was coming, he would keep watch and not permit his house to be broken into. ⁴⁴You also must be ready all the time, for the Son of Man will come when least expected.

⁴⁵"A faithful, sensible servant is one to whom the master can give the responsibility of managing his other household servants and feeding them. ⁴⁶If the master returns and finds that the servant has done a good job, there will be a reward. ⁴⁷I tell you the truth, the master will put that servant in charge of all he owns. ⁴⁸But what if the servant is evil and thinks, 'My master won't be back for a while,' ⁴⁹and he begins beating the other servants, partying, and getting drunk? ⁵⁰The master will return unannounced and unexpected, ⁵¹and he will cut the servant to pieces and assign him a place with the hypocrites. In that place there will be weeping and gnashing of teeth.

### Parable of the Ten Bridesmaids

**25** "Then the Kingdom of Heaven will be like ten bridesmaids* who took their lamps and went to meet the

---

24:27 "Son of Man" is a title Jesus used for himself.   24:28 Greek *Wherever the carcass is, the vultures gather.*   24:29 See Isa 13:10; 34:4; Joel 2:10.   24:30 See Dan 7:13.   24:31 Greek *from the four winds.*   24:34 Or *this age,* or *this nation.*   24:36 Some manuscripts do not include *or the Son himself.*   25:1 Or *virgins;* also in 25:7, 11.

bridegroom. ²Five of them were foolish, and five were wise. ³The five who were foolish didn't take enough olive oil for their lamps, ⁴but the other five were wise enough to take along extra oil. ⁵When the bridegroom was delayed, they all became drowsy and fell asleep.

⁶"At midnight they were roused by the shout, 'Look, the bridegroom is coming! Come out and meet him!'

⁷"All the bridesmaids got up and prepared their lamps. ⁸Then the five foolish ones asked the others, 'Please give us some of your oil because our lamps are going out.'

⁹"But the others replied, ' We don't have enough for all of us. Go to a shop and buy some for yourselves.'

¹⁰"But while they were gone to buy oil, the bridegroom came. Then those who were ready went in with him to the marriage feast, and the door was locked. ¹¹Later, when the other five bridesmaids returned, they stood outside, calling, 'Lord! Lord! Open the door for us!'

¹²"But he called back, 'Believe me, I don't know you!'

¹³"So you, too, must keep watch! For you do not know the day or hour of my return.

## Parable of the Three Servants

¹⁴"Again, the Kingdom of Heaven can be illustrated by the story of a man going on a long trip. He called together his servants and entrusted his money to them while he was gone. ¹⁵He gave five bags of silver* to one, two bags of silver to another, and one bag of silver to the last—dividing it in proportion to their abilities. He then left on his trip.

¹⁶"The servant who received the five bags of silver began to invest the money and earned five more. ¹⁷The servant with two bags of silver also went to work and earned two more. ¹⁸But the servant who received the one bag of silver dug a hole in the ground and hid the master's money.

¹⁹"After a long time their master returned from his trip and called them to give an account of how they had used his money. ²⁰The servant to whom he had entrusted the five bags of silver came forward with five more and said, 'Master, you gave me five bags of silver to invest, and I have earned five more.'

²¹"The master was full of praise. ' Well done, my good and faithful servant. You have been faithful in handling this small amount, so now I will give you many more responsibilities. Let's celebrate together!*'

²²"The servant who had received the two bags of silver came forward and said, 'Master, you gave me two bags of silver to invest, and I have earned two more.'

²³"The master said, 'Well done, my good and faithful servant. You have been faithful in handling this small amount, so now I will give you many more responsibilities. Let's celebrate together!'

²⁴"Then the servant with the one bag of silver came and said, 'Master, I knew you were a harsh man, harvesting crops you didn't plant and gathering crops you didn't cultivate. ²⁵I was afraid I would lose your money, so I hid it in the earth. Look, here is your money back.'

²⁶"But the master replied, 'You wicked and lazy servant! If you knew I harvested crops I didn't plant and gathered crops I didn't cultivate, ²⁷why didn't you deposit my money in the bank? At least I could have gotten some interest on it.'

²⁸"Then he ordered, 'Take the money from this servant, and give it to the one with the ten bags of silver. ²⁹To those who use well what they are given, even more will be given, and they will have an abundance. But from those who do nothing, even what little they have will be taken away. ³⁰Now throw this useless servant into outer darkness, where there will be weeping and gnashing of teeth.'

## The Final Judgment

³¹"But when the Son of Man* comes in his glory, and all the angels with him, then he will sit upon his glorious throne. ³²All the nations* will be gathered in his presence, and he will separate the people as a shepherd separates the sheep from the goats. ³³He will place the sheep at his right hand and the goats at his left.

---

**25:15** Greek *talents;* also throughout the story. A talent is equal to 75 pounds or 34 kilograms. **25:21** Greek *Enter into the joy of your master* (or *your Lord*); also in 25:23. **25:31** "Son of Man" is a title Jesus used for himself. **25:32** Or *peoples.*

# NOTICING the little things

READ MATTHEW 25:31-40

What wonderful encouragement these verses are for caregivers! Jesus says that He sees all the "little" things you do for others, that He will reward those good deeds, and that every time you perform one of these actions, you really are doing it for Him!

When you took off work to go to the doctor with your loved one, you did it for Jesus.

When you spent all that time juicing those fruits and veggies for just the right blender drink, you did it for Jesus.

When you got up in the middle of the night to get more pain medicine, you did it for Jesus. When you rubbed a back, cooled a brow, cleaned up a mess, and sat through another long test, you did it for Jesus.

Whether or not you got any appreciation from your loved one here and now, Jesus saw your kindness and He will bless you for it.

**34** "Then the King will say to those on his right, 'Come, you who are blessed by my Father, inherit the Kingdom prepared for you from the creation of the world. **35** For I was hungry, and you fed me. I was thirsty, and you gave me a drink. I was a stranger, and you invited me into your home. **36** I was naked, and you gave me clothing. I was sick, and you cared for me. I was in prison, and you visited me.'

**37** "Then these righteous ones will reply, 'Lord, when did we ever see you hungry and feed you? Or thirsty and give you something to drink? **38** Or a stranger and show you hospitality? Or naked and give you clothing? **39** When did we ever see you sick or in prison and visit you?'

**40** "And the King will say, 'I tell you the truth, when you did it to one of the least of these my brothers and sisters,* you were doing it to me!'

**41** "Then the King will turn to those on the left and say, 'Away with you, you cursed ones, into the eternal fire prepared for the devil and his demons.* **42** For I was hungry, and you didn't feed me. I was thirsty, and you didn't give me a drink. **43** I was a stranger, and you didn't invite me into your home. I was naked, and you didn't give me clothing. I was sick and in prison, and you didn't visit me.'

**44** "Then they will reply, 'Lord, when did we ever see you hungry or thirsty or a stranger or naked or sick or in prison, and not help you?'

**45** "And he will answer, 'I tell you the truth, when you refused to help the least of these my brothers and sisters, you were refusing to help me.'

**46** "And they will go away into eternal punishment, but the righteous will go into eternal life."

## The Plot to Kill Jesus

**26** When Jesus had finished saying all these things, he said to his disciples, **2** "As you know, Passover begins in two days, and the Son of Man* will be handed over to be crucified."

**3** At that same time the leading priests and elders were meeting at the residence of Caiaphas, the high priest, **4** plotting how to capture Jesus secretly and kill him. **5** "But not during the Passover celebration," they agreed, "or the people may riot."

## Jesus Anointed at Bethany

**6** Meanwhile, Jesus was in Bethany at the home of Simon, a man who had previously had leprosy. **7** While he was eating,* a woman came in with a beautiful alabaster jar of expensive perfume and poured it over his head.

25:40 Greek *my brothers.*   25:41 Greek *his angels.*   26:2 "Son of Man" is a title Jesus used for himself.   26:7 Or *reclining.*

8The disciples were indignant when they saw this. "What a waste!" they said. 9"It could have been sold for a high price and the money given to the poor."

10But Jesus, aware of this, replied, "Why criticize this woman for doing such a good thing to me? 11You will always have the poor among you, but you will not always have me. 12She has poured this perfume on me to prepare my body for burial. 13I tell you the truth, wherever the Good News is preached throughout the world, this woman's deed will be remembered and discussed."

## Judas Agrees to Betray Jesus

14Then Judas Iscariot, one of the twelve disciples, went to the leading priests 15and asked, "How much will you pay me to betray Jesus to you?" And they gave him thirty pieces of silver. 16From that time on, Judas began looking for an opportunity to betray Jesus.

## The Last Supper

17On the first day of the Festival of Unleavened Bread, the disciples came to Jesus and asked, "Where do you want us to prepare the Passover meal for you?"

18"As you go into the city," he told them, "you will see a certain man. Tell him, 'The Teacher says: My time has come, and I will eat the Passover meal with my disciples at your house.'" 19So the disciples did as Jesus told them and prepared the Passover meal there.

20When it was evening, Jesus sat down at the table* with the twelve disciples.* 21While they were eating, he said, "I tell you the truth, one of you will betray me."

22Greatly distressed, each one asked in turn, "Am I the one, Lord?"

23He replied, "One of you who has just eaten from this bowl with me will betray me. 24For the Son of Man must die, as the Scriptures declared long ago. But how terrible it will be for the one who betrays him. It would be far better for that man if he had never been born!"

25Judas, the one who would betray him, also asked, "Rabbi, am I the one?"

And Jesus told him, "You have said it."

26As they were eating, Jesus took some bread and blessed it. Then he broke it in pieces and gave it to the disciples, saying, "Take this and eat it, for this is my body."

27And he took a cup of wine and gave thanks to God for it. He gave it to them and said, "Each of you drink from it, 28for this is my blood, which confirms the covenant* between God and his people. It is poured out as a sacrifice to forgive the sins of many. 29Mark my words—I will not drink wine again until the day I drink it new with you in my Father's Kingdom."

30Then they sang a hymn and went out to the Mount of Olives.

## Jesus Predicts Peter's Denial

31On the way, Jesus told them, "Tonight all of you will desert me. For the Scriptures say,

'God will strike* the Shepherd,
     and the sheep of the flock will be
        scattered.'

32But after I have been raised from the dead, I will go ahead of you to Galilee and meet you there."

33Peter declared, "Even if everyone else deserts you, I will never desert you."

34Jesus replied, "I tell you the truth, Peter—this very night, before the rooster crows, you will deny three times that you even know me."

35"No!" Peter insisted. "Even if I have to die with you, I will never deny you!" And all the other disciples vowed the same.

## Jesus Prays in Gethsemane

36Then Jesus went with them to the olive grove called Gethsemane, and he said, "Sit here while I go over there to pray." 37He took Peter and Zebedee's two sons, James and John, and he became anguished and distressed. 38He told them, "My soul is crushed with grief to the point of death. Stay here and keep watch with me."

39He went on a little farther and bowed with his face to the ground, praying, "My Father! If it is possible, let this cup of suffering be taken away from me. Yet I want your will to be done, not mine."

40Then he returned to the disciples and

---

26:20a Or Jesus reclined.    26:20b Some manuscripts read the Twelve.    26:28 Some manuscripts read the new covenant.
26:31 Greek I will strike. Zech 13:7.

found them asleep. He said to Peter, "Couldn't you watch with me even one hour? ⁴¹Keep watch and pray, so that you will not give in to temptation. For the spirit is willing, but the body is weak!"

⁴²Then Jesus left them a second time and prayed, "My Father! If this cup cannot be taken away* unless I drink it, your will be done." ⁴³When he returned to them again, he found them sleeping, for they couldn't keep their eyes open.

⁴⁴So he went to pray a third time, saying the same things again. ⁴⁵Then he came to the disciples and said, "Go ahead and sleep. Have your rest. But look—the time has come. The Son of Man is betrayed into the hands of sinners. ⁴⁶Up, let's be going. Look, my betrayer is here!"

### Jesus Is Betrayed and Arrested

⁴⁷And even as Jesus said this, Judas, one of the twelve disciples, arrived with a crowd of men armed with swords and clubs. They had been sent by the leading priests and elders of the people. ⁴⁸The traitor, Judas, had given them a prearranged signal: "You will know which one to arrest when I greet him with a kiss." ⁴⁹So Judas came straight to Jesus. "Greetings, Rabbi!" he exclaimed and gave him the kiss.

⁵⁰Jesus said, "My friend, go ahead and do what you have come for."

Then the others grabbed Jesus and arrested him. ⁵¹But one of the men with Jesus pulled out his sword and struck the high priest's slave, slashing off his ear.

⁵²"Put away your sword," Jesus told him. "Those who use the sword will die by the sword. ⁵³Don't you realize that I could ask my Father for thousands* of angels to protect us, and he would send them instantly? ⁵⁴But if I did, how would the Scriptures be fulfilled that describe what must happen now?"

⁵⁵Then Jesus said to the crowd, "Am I some dangerous revolutionary, that you come with swords and clubs to arrest me? Why didn't you arrest me in the Temple? I was there teaching every day. ⁵⁶But this is all happening to fulfill the words of the prophets as recorded in the Scriptures." At that point, all the disciples deserted him and fled.

### Jesus before the Council

⁵⁷Then the people who had arrested Jesus led him to the home of Caiaphas, the high priest, where the teachers of religious law and the elders had gathered. ⁵⁸Meanwhile, Peter followed him at a distance and came to the high priest's courtyard. He went in and sat with the guards and waited to see how it would all end.

⁵⁹Inside, the leading priests and the entire high council* were trying to find witnesses who would lie about Jesus, so they could put him to death. ⁶⁰But even though they found many who agreed to give false witness, they could not use anyone's testimony. Finally, two men came forward ⁶¹who declared, "This man said, 'I am able to destroy the Temple of God and rebuild it in three days.'"

⁶²Then the high priest stood up and said to Jesus, "Well, aren't you going to answer these charges? What do you have to say for yourself?" ⁶³But Jesus remained silent. Then the high priest said to him, "I demand in the name of the living God—tell us if you are the Messiah, the Son of God."

⁶⁴Jesus replied, "You have said it. And in the future you will see the Son of Man seated in the place of power at God's right hand* and coming on the clouds of heaven."*

⁶⁵Then the high priest tore his clothing to show his horror and said, "Blasphemy! Why do we need other witnesses? You have all heard his blasphemy. ⁶⁶What is your verdict?"

"Guilty!" they shouted. "He deserves to die!"

⁶⁷Then they began to spit in Jesus' face and beat him with their fists. And some slapped him, ⁶⁸jeering, "Prophesy to us, you Messiah! Who hit you that time?"

### Peter Denies Jesus

⁶⁹Meanwhile, Peter was sitting outside in the courtyard. A servant girl came over and said to him, "You were one of those with Jesus the Galilean."

⁷⁰But Peter denied it in front of everyone.

---

26:42 Greek *If this cannot pass.*    26:53 Greek *twelve legions.*    26:59 Greek *the Sanhedrin.*    26:64a Greek *seated at the right hand of the power.* See Ps 110:1.    26:64b See Dan 7:13.

"I don't know what you're talking about," he said.

71 Later, out by the gate, another servant girl noticed him and said to those standing around, "This man was with Jesus of Nazareth.*"

72 Again Peter denied it, this time with an oath. "I don't even know the man," he said.

73 A little later some of the other bystanders came over to Peter and said, "You must be one of them; we can tell by your Galilean accent."

74 Peter swore, "A curse on me if I'm lying—I don't know the man!" And immediately the rooster crowed.

75 Suddenly, Jesus' words flashed through Peter's mind: "Before the rooster crows, you will deny three times that you even know me." And he went away, weeping bitterly.

## Judas Hangs Himself

**27** Very early in the morning the leading priests and the elders met again to lay plans for putting Jesus to death. 2 Then they bound him, led him away, and took him to Pilate, the Roman governor.

3 When Judas, who had betrayed him, realized that Jesus had been condemned to die, he was filled with remorse. So he took the thirty pieces of silver back to the leading priests and the elders. 4 "I have sinned," he declared, "for I have betrayed an innocent man."

"What do we care?" they retorted. "That's your problem."

5 Then Judas threw the silver coins down in the Temple and went out and hanged himself.

6 The leading priests picked up the coins. "It wouldn't be right to put this money in the Temple treasury," they said, "since it was payment for murder."* 7 After some discussion they finally decided to buy the potter's field, and they made it into a cemetery for foreigners. 8 That is why the field is still called the Field of Blood. 9 This fulfilled the prophecy of Jeremiah that says,

"They took* the thirty pieces of silver—
   the price at which he was valued by the
   people of Israel,

10 and purchased the potter's field,
   as the LORD directed.*"

### Jesus' Trial before Pilate

11 Now Jesus was standing before Pilate, the Roman governor. "Are you the king of the Jews?" the governor asked him.

Jesus replied, "You have said it."

12 But when the leading priests and the elders made their accusations against him, Jesus remained silent. 13 "Don't you hear all these charges they are bringing against you?" Pilate demanded. 14 But Jesus made no response to any of the charges, much to the governor's surprise.

15 Now it was the governor's custom each year during the Passover celebration to release one prisoner to the crowd—anyone they wanted. 16 This year there was a notorious prisoner, a man named Barabbas.* 17 As the crowds gathered before Pilate's house that morning, he asked them, "Which one do you want me to release to you—Barabbas, or Jesus who is called the Messiah?" 18 (He knew very well that the religious leaders had arrested Jesus out of envy.)

19 Just then, as Pilate was sitting on the judgment seat, his wife sent him this message: "Leave that innocent man alone. I suffered through a terrible nightmare about him last night."

20 Meanwhile, the leading priests and the elders persuaded the crowd to ask for Barabbas to be released and for Jesus to be put to death. 21 So the governor asked again, "Which of these two do you want me to release to you?"

The crowd shouted back, "Barabbas!"

22 Pilate responded, "Then what should I do with Jesus who is called the Messiah?"

They shouted back, "Crucify him!"

23 "Why?" Pilate demanded. "What crime has he committed?"

But the mob roared even louder, "Crucify him!"

24 Pilate saw that he wasn't getting anywhere and that a riot was developing. So he sent for a bowl of water and washed his hands before the crowd, saying, "I am inno-

26:71 Or Jesus the Nazarene.    27:6 Greek since it is the price for blood.    27:9 Or I took.    27:9-10 Greek as the LORD directed me.
Zech 11:12-13; Jer 32:6-9.    27:16 Some manuscripts read Jesus Barabbas; also in 27:17.

cent of this man's blood. The responsibility is yours!"

25And all the people yelled back, "We will take responsibility for his death—we and our children!"*

26So Pilate released Barabbas to them. He ordered Jesus flogged with a lead-tipped whip, then turned him over to the Roman soldiers to be crucified.

### The Soldiers Mock Jesus

27Some of the governor's soldiers took Jesus into their headquarters* and called out the entire regiment. 28They stripped him and put a scarlet robe on him. 29They wove thorn branches into a crown and put it on his head, and they placed a reed stick in his right hand as a scepter. Then they knelt before him in mockery and taunted, "Hail! King of the Jews!" 30And they spit on him and grabbed the stick and struck him on the head with it. 31When they were finally tired of mocking him, they took off the robe and put his own clothes on him again. Then they led him away to be crucified.

### The Crucifixion

32Along the way, they came across a man named Simon, who was from Cyrene,* and the soldiers forced him to carry Jesus' cross. 33And they went out to a place called Golgotha (which means "Place of the Skull"). 34The soldiers gave him wine mixed with bitter gall, but when he had tasted it, he refused to drink it.

35After they had nailed him to the cross, the soldiers gambled for his clothes by throwing dice.* 36Then they sat around and kept guard as he hung there. 37A sign was fastened to the cross above Jesus' head, announcing the charge against him. It read: "This is Jesus, the King of the Jews." 38Two revolutionaries* were crucified with him, one on his right and one on his left.

39The people passing by shouted abuse, shaking their heads in mockery. 40"Look at you now!" they yelled at him. "You said you were going to destroy the Temple and re-

## IMMUNE to pain
READ MATTHEW 27:27-50

It's always reassuring to find someone who has experienced what we have: had the same surgery, taken the same drugs, or been hampered with the same annoying symptoms. It's those "kindred spirits" who seem to better understand our pain.

Can you imagine worshipping a God who was immune to pain? What if He never felt a slap, never knew the pang of betrayal, never was in misery with no relief in sight? Such a God never could sympathize with our weaknesses and understand our pain.

The torturous mocking of Jesus and His agonizing crucifixion make it clear that our God is not immune to pain: He understands exactly what we feel.

build it in three days. Well then, if you are the Son of God, save yourself and come down from the cross!"

41The leading priests, the teachers of religious law, and the elders also mocked Jesus. 42"He saved others," they scoffed, "but he can't save himself! So he is the King of Israel, is he? Let him come down from the cross right now, and we will believe in him! 43He trusted God, so let God rescue him now if he wants him! For he said, 'I am the Son of God.'" 44Even the revolutionaries who were crucified with him ridiculed him in the same way.

### The Death of Jesus

45At noon, darkness fell across the whole land until three o'clock. 46At about three o'clock, Jesus called out with a loud voice, "Eli, Eli,* lema sabachthani?" which means "My God, my God, why have you abandoned me?"*

47Some of the bystanders misunderstood and thought he was calling for the prophet Elijah. 48One of them ran and filled a sponge with sour wine, holding it up to him on a reed stick so he could drink. 49But the rest said, "Wait! Let's see whether Elijah comes to save him."*

50Then Jesus shouted out again, and he

27:25 Greek "His blood be on us and on our children."   27:27 Or into the Praetorium.   27:32 Cyrene was a city in northern Africa.
27:35 Greek by casting lots. A few late manuscripts add This fulfilled the word of the prophet: "They divided my garments among
themselves and cast lots for my robe." See Ps 22:18.   27:38 Or criminals; also in 27:44.   27:46a Some manuscripts read Eloi, Eloi.
27:46b Ps 22:1.   27:49 Some manuscripts add And another took a spear and pierced his side, and out flowed water and blood.
Compare John 19:34.

released his spirit. [51]At that moment <u>the curtain in the sanctuary of the Temple was torn in two, from top to bottom.</u> The earth shook, rocks split apart, [52]and tombs opened. The bodies of many godly men and women who had died were raised from the dead. [53]They left the cemetery after Jesus' resurrection, went into the holy city of Jerusalem, and appeared to many people.

[54]The Roman officer* and the other soldiers at the crucifixion were terrified by the earthquake and all that had happened. They said, "This man truly was the Son of God!"

[55]And many women who had come from Galilee with Jesus to care for him were watching from a distance. [56]Among them were Mary Magdalene, Mary (the mother of James and Joseph), and the mother of James and John, the sons of Zebedee.

### The Burial of Jesus

[57]As evening approached, Joseph, a rich man from Arimathea who had become a follower of Jesus, [58]went to Pilate and asked for Jesus' body. And Pilate issued an order to release it to him. [59]Joseph took the body and wrapped it in a long sheet of clean linen cloth. [60]He placed it in his own new tomb, which had been carved out of the rock. Then he rolled a great stone across the entrance and left. [61]Both Mary Magdalene and the other Mary were sitting across from the tomb and watching.

### The Guard at the Tomb

[62]The next day, on the Sabbath,* the leading priests and Pharisees went to see Pilate. [63]They told him, "Sir, we remember what that deceiver once said while he was still alive: 'After three days I will rise from the dead.' [64]So we request that you seal the tomb until the third day. This will prevent his disciples from coming and stealing his body and then telling everyone he was raised from the dead! If that happens, we'll be worse off than we were at first."

[65]Pilate replied, "Take guards and secure it the best you can." [66]So they sealed the tomb and posted guards to protect it.

### The Resurrection

**28** Early on Sunday morning,* as the new day was dawning, Mary Magdalene and the other Mary went out to visit the tomb.

[2]Suddenly there was a great earthquake! For an angel of the Lord came down from heaven, rolled aside the stone, and sat on it. [3]His face shone like lightning, and his clothing was as white as snow. [4]The guards shook with fear when they saw him, and they fell into a dead faint.

[5]Then the angel spoke to the women. "Don't be afraid!" he said. "I know you are looking for Jesus, who was crucified. [6]He isn't here! He is risen from the dead, just as he said would happen. Come, see where his body was lying. [7]And now, go quickly and tell his disciples that he has risen from the dead, and he is going ahead of you to Galilee. You will see him there. Remember what I have told you."

[8]The women ran quickly from the tomb. They were very frightened but also filled with great joy, and they rushed to give the disciples the angel's message. [9]And as they went, Jesus met them and greeted them. And they ran to him, grasped his feet, and worshiped him. [10]Then Jesus said to them, "Don't be afraid! Go tell my brothers to leave for Galilee, and they will see me there."

### The Report of the Guard

[11]As the women were on their way, some of the guards went into the city and told the leading priests what had happened. [12]A meeting with the elders was called, and they decided to give the soldiers a large bribe. [13]They told the soldiers, "You must say, 'Jesus' disciples came during the night while we were sleeping, and they stole his body.' [14]If the governor hears about it, we'll stand up for you so you won't get in trouble." [15]So the guards accepted the bribe and said what they were told to say. Their story spread widely among the Jews, and they still tell it today.

### The Great Commission

[16]Then the eleven disciples left for Galilee, going to the mountain where Jesus had

---

27:54 Greek *The centurion.*   27:62 Or *On the next day, which is after the Preparation.*   28:1 Greek *After the Sabbath, on the first day of the week.*

told them to go. ¹⁷When they saw him, they worshiped him—but some of them doubted!

¹⁸Jesus came and told his disciples, "I have been given all authority in heaven and on earth. ¹⁹Therefore, go and make disciples of all the nations,* baptizing them in the name of the Father and the Son and the Holy Spirit. ²⁰Teach these new disciples to obey all the commands I have given you. And be sure of this: I am with you always, even to the end of the age."

**28:19** Or *all peoples.*

# FINDING the right attitude

It's often said that there are two kinds of people in life: optimists and pessimists. You probably think we're going to tell you to be an optimist, but we're not.

We have found that the best attitude for someone facing a life-threatening illness is neither total optimism (*without a doubt, I'm going to be cured*) nor total pessimism (*without a doubt, I'm going to die*), but realism (*without a doubt, I have a life-threatening illness and I may or may not get better, so I will plan for both*).

When we insist we are going to be cured, we set ourselves up for a terrible defeat if it doesn't happen. On the other hand, if we insist our situation is hopeless, we are defeated before we start. We believe it's best to be realistic and make plans to be financially, emotionally, and spiritually ready to depart this life. That's not giving up. It's coming to grips with our own mortality, so we can really live fully without fear of death.

**We believe there's a difference between total optimism and a positive attitude.** Total optimism says: "I'm absolutely, positively going to be cured." A positive attitude says: "I hope and pray and even expect that I'm going to be cured; but even if I'm not, I will not be defeated."

A totally optimistic attitude insists lemons will get sweeter. A positive attitude adds some sweetener and makes lemonade out of the lemons.

Author Chuck Swindoll has a wonderful description of the power of a positive attitude:

> "Words can never adequately convey the incredible impact of our attitude toward life. The longer I live the more convinced I am that life is 10 percent what happens to us and 90 percent how we respond to it. I believe the single most significant decision I can make on a day-to-day basis is my choice of attitude. It is more important than my past, my education, my bankroll, my successes or failures, fame or pain, what other people think of me or say about me, my circumstances, or my position. Attitude keeps me going or cripples my progress. It alone fuels my fire or assaults my hope. When my attitudes are right, there's no barrier too high, no valley too deep, no dream too extreme, no challenge too great for me."[1]

We pray your heart finds the right attitude—a positive, realistic attitude.

[1] Charles R. Swindoll, *Strengthening Your Grip* (Nashville: W Publishing Group, formerly Word Publishing, 1982), 206–207.

# MARK

*Jesus healed many people who were sick with various diseases, and he cast out many demons.*

MARK 1:34

*Webster's* dictionary defines a miracle as an "extraordinary event manifesting divine intervention in human affairs."

If you are praying for a miracle today, you've come to the right book. Miracles helped define who Jesus was. This book's author, John Mark, focuses more on Jesus' amazing actions than on His words. (Mark most likely got his information about Jesus from the apostle Peter, and he was also a traveling companion of the apostle Paul.)

As you read about the astonishing works Jesus did, make sure you notice the *different ways* Jesus healed people (touching them, speaking to them, and even spitting on them!) and the *different kinds* of healing He brought (healthy bodies, sane minds, forgiven souls). Physical healings are absolutely wonderful and we pray you or your loved one gets such a touch from God. But they are not the *only* way God heals and sometimes not even the *best* way.

Think about it: All the people you will read about Jesus healing in the Gospels eventually died. Those with *only* a temporary physical healing missed out on the best healing—a permanent spiritual healing of their souls.

The Bible tells us God is Yahweh-Rapha, the One who heals. Don't ever doubt it. But don't ever limit Him to just one way to heal. God even can heal you so much on the *inside* that it truly doesn't matter to you if He heals you on the *outside*! Now that would be a miracle!

*God's ways aren't our ways*

### John the Baptist Prepares the Way

**1** This is the Good News about Jesus the Messiah, the Son of God.* It began ²just as the prophet Isaiah had written:

"Look, I am sending my messenger ahead of you,
and he will prepare your way.*
³ He is a voice shouting in the wilderness,
'Prepare the way for the LORD's coming!
Clear the road for him!'*"

⁴This messenger was John the Baptist. He was in the wilderness and preached that people should be baptized to show that they had repented of their sins and turned to God to be forgiven. ⁵All of Judea, including all the people of Jerusalem, went out to see and hear John. And when they confessed their sins, he baptized them in the Jordan River. ⁶His clothes were woven from coarse camel hair, and he wore a leather belt around his waist. For food he ate locusts and wild honey.

⁷John announced: "Someone is coming soon who is greater than I am—so much greater that I'm not even worthy to stoop down like a slave and untie the straps of his sandals. ⁸I baptize you with* water, but he will baptize you with the Holy Spirit!"

### The Baptism and Temptation of Jesus

⁹One day Jesus came from Nazareth in Galilee, and John baptized him in the Jordan River. ¹⁰As Jesus came up out of the water, he saw the heavens splitting apart and the Holy Spirit descending on him* like a dove. ¹¹And a voice from heaven said, "You are my dearly loved Son, and you bring me great joy."

¹²The Spirit then compelled Jesus to go into the wilderness, ¹³where he was tempted by Satan for forty days. He was out among the wild animals, and angels took care of him.

¹⁴Later on, after John was arrested, Jesus went into Galilee, where he preached God's Good News.* ¹⁵"The time promised by God has come at last!" he announced. "The Kingdom of God is near! Repent of your sins and believe the Good News!"

*command!*

### The First Disciples

¹⁶One day as Jesus was walking along the shore of the Sea of Galilee, he saw Simon*

1:1 Some manuscripts do not include *the Son of God.* 1:2 Mal 3:1. 1:3 Isa 40:3 (Greek version). 1:8 Or *in;* also in 1:8b. 1:10 Or *toward him,* or *into him.* 1:14 Some manuscripts read *the Good News of the Kingdom of God.* 1:16 *Simon* is called "Peter" in 3:16 and thereafter.

## CLOSE doesn't count

READ MARK 1:14-15

Isn't it irritating when someone only does something "halfway"? They take two tubes of your blood, but should have taken four. They have the results of the scan, but forget to fax them to your doctor. They submit the insurance claim, but write down the wrong reimbursement code.

All of these situations are incredibly annoying, but not life-threatening.

In these verses Jesus tells His listeners two things they need to do: "Repent of your sins and believe the Good News!" Unfortunately, many people then—and now—want to follow this teaching halfway. They definitely want to believe the Good News that God loves them so much He sent His only Son to die for their sins. But that first part is a little tougher. It's not quite as easy to "repent"—not just feel sorry for our sins, but actually name them, seek forgiveness, and by God's strength turn away from them.

Have you embraced both parts of Jesus' command? It's not only irritating to only halfway obey Him—it's life-threatening.

and his brother <u>Andrew</u> throwing a net into the water, for they fished for a living. 17Jesus called out to them, "Come, follow me, and I will show you how to fish for people!" 18And they left their nets at once and followed him.

19A little farther up the shore Jesus saw Zebedee's sons, <u>James</u> and <u>John</u>, in a boat repairing their nets. 20He called them at once, and they also followed him, leaving their father, Zebedee, in the boat with the hired men.

## Jesus Casts Out an Evil Spirit

21Jesus and his companions went to the town of Capernaum. When the Sabbath day came, he went into the synagogue and began to teach. 22The people were amazed at his teaching, for <u>he taught with real authority</u>—quite unlike the teachers of religious law.

23Suddenly, a man in the synagogue who was possessed by an evil* spirit began shouting, 24"Why are you interfering with us, Jesus of Nazareth? Have you come to destroy us? I know who you are—the Holy One sent from God!"

25Jesus cut him short. "Be quiet! Come out of the man," he ordered. 26At that, the evil spirit screamed, threw the man into a convulsion, and then came out of him.

27Amazement gripped the audience, and they began to discuss what had happened. "What sort of new teaching is this?" they asked excitedly. "It has such authority! Even evil spirits obey his orders!" 28The news about Jesus spread quickly throughout the entire region of Galilee.

## Jesus Heals Many People

29After Jesus left the synagogue with James and John, they went to Simon and Andrew's home. 30Now Simon's mother-in-law was sick in bed with a high fever. They told Jesus about her right away. 31So he went to her bedside, took her by the hand, and helped her sit up. Then the fever left her, and she prepared a meal for them.

32That evening after sunset, many sick and demon-possessed people were brought to Jesus. 33The whole town gathered at the door to watch. 34So Jesus healed many people who were sick with various diseases, and he cast out many demons. But because the demons knew who he was, he did not allow them to speak.

## Jesus Preaches in Galilee

35Before daybreak the next morning, Jesus got up and went out to an isolated place to pray. 36Later Simon and the others went out to find him. 37When they found him, they said, "Everyone is looking for you."

38But Jesus replied, "We must go on to other towns as well, and I will preach to them, too. That is why I came." 39So he traveled throughout the region of Galilee, preaching in the synagogues and casting out demons.

## Jesus Heals a Man with Leprosy

40A man with leprosy came and knelt in front of Jesus, begging to be healed. "If you are willing, you can heal me and make me clean," he said.

41Moved with compassion,* Jesus reached out and touched him. "I am willing," he said. "Be healed!" 42Instantly the leprosy disappeared, and the man was healed. 43Then Jesus sent him on his way with a stern warning: 44"Don't tell anyone about this. Instead, go to the priest and let him examine you. Take along the offering required in the law of Moses for those who have been healed of leprosy.* This will be a public testimony that you have been cleansed."

45But the man went and spread the word, proclaiming to everyone what had happened. As a result, large crowds soon surrounded Jesus, and he couldn't publicly enter a town anywhere. He had to stay out in the secluded places, but people from everywhere kept coming to him.

## Jesus Heals a Paralyzed Man

**2** When Jesus returned to Capernaum several days later, the news spread quickly that he was back home. 2Soon the house where he was staying was so packed with visitors that there was no more room, even outside the door. While he was preaching God's word to them, 3four men arrived

**1:23** Greek *unclean;* also in 1:26, 27.   **1:41** Some manuscripts read *Moved with anger.*   **1:44** See Lev 14:2-32.

carrying a paralyzed man on a mat. 4They couldn't bring him to Jesus because of the crowd, so they dug a hole through the roof above his head. Then they lowered the man on his mat, right down in front of Jesus. 5 Seeing their faith, Jesus said to the paralyzed man, "My child, your sins are forgiven."

6But some of the teachers of religious law who were sitting there thought to themselves, 7"What is he saying? This is blasphemy! Only God can forgive sins!"

8Jesus knew immediately what they were thinking, so he asked them, "Why do you question this in your hearts? 9Is it easier to say to the paralyzed man 'Your sins are forgiven,' or 'Stand up, pick up your mat, and walk'? 10So I will prove to you that the Son of Man* has the authority on earth to forgive sins." Then Jesus turned to the paralyzed man and said, 11"Stand up, pick up your mat, and go home!"

12And the man jumped up, grabbed his mat, and walked out through the stunned onlookers. They were all amazed and praised God, exclaiming, "We've never seen anything like this before!"

### Jesus Calls Levi (Matthew)

13Then Jesus went out to the lakeshore again and taught the crowds that were coming to him. 14As he walked along, he saw Levi son of Alphaeus sitting at his tax collector's booth. "Follow me and be my disciple," Jesus said to him. So Levi got up and followed him.

15Later, Levi invited Jesus and his disciples to his home as dinner guests, along with many tax collectors and other disreputable sinners. (There were many people of this kind among Jesus' followers.) 16But when the teachers of religious law who were Pharisees* saw him eating with tax collectors and other sinners, they asked his disciples, "Why does he eat with such scum?*"

17 When Jesus heard this, he told them, "Healthy people don't need a doctor—sick people do. I have come to call not those who think they are righteous, but those who know they are sinners."

### A Discussion about Fasting

18Once when John's disciples and the Pharisees were fasting, some people came to Jesus and asked, "Why don't your disciples fast like John's disciples and the Pharisees do?"

19Jesus replied, "Do wedding guests fast while celebrating with the groom? Of course not. They can't fast while the groom is with them. 20But someday the groom will be taken away from them, and then they will fast.

21"Besides, who would patch old clothing with new cloth? For the new patch would shrink and rip away from the old cloth, leaving an even bigger tear than before.

22"And no one puts new wine into old wineskins. For the wine would burst the wineskins, and the wine and the skins would both be lost. New wine calls for new wineskins."

### A Discussion about the Sabbath

23One Sabbath day as Jesus was walking through some grainfields, his disciples began breaking off heads of grain to eat. 24But the Pharisees said to Jesus, "Look, why are they breaking the law by harvesting grain on the Sabbath?"

25Jesus said to them, "Haven't you ever read in the Scriptures what David did when he and his companions were hungry? 26He went into the house of God (during the days when Abiathar was high priest) and broke the law by eating the sacred loaves of bread that only the priests are allowed to eat. He also gave some to his companions."

27Then Jesus said to them, "The Sabbath was made to meet the needs of people, and not people to meet the requirements of the Sabbath. 28So the Son of Man is Lord, even over the Sabbath!"

### Jesus Heals on the Sabbath

3 Jesus went into the synagogue again and noticed a man with a deformed hand. 2Since it was the Sabbath, Jesus' enemies watched him closely. If he healed the man's hand, they planned to accuse him of working on the Sabbath.

2:10 "Son of Man" is a title Jesus used for himself.   2:16a Greek *the scribes of the Pharisees.*   2:16b Greek *with tax collectors and sinners?*

49

³Jesus said to the man with the deformed hand, "Come and stand in front of everyone." ⁴Then he turned to his critics and asked, "Does the law permit good deeds on the Sabbath, or is it a day for doing evil? Is this a day to save life or to destroy it?" But they wouldn't answer him.

⁵He looked around at them angrily and was deeply saddened by their hard hearts. Then he said to the man, "Hold out your hand." So the man held out his hand, and it was restored! ⁶At once the Pharisees went away and met with the supporters of Herod to plot how to kill Jesus.

## Crowds Follow Jesus

⁷Jesus went out to the lake with his disciples, and a large crowd followed him. They came from all over Galilee, Judea, ⁸Jerusalem, Idumea, from east of the Jordan River, and even from as far north as Tyre and Sidon. The news about his miracles had spread far and wide, and vast numbers of people came to see him.

⁹Jesus instructed his disciples to have a boat ready so the crowd would not crush him. ¹⁰He had healed many people that day, so all the sick people eagerly pushed forward to touch him. ¹¹And whenever those possessed by evil* spirits caught sight of him, the spirits would throw them to the ground in front of him shrieking, "You are the Son of God!" ¹²But Jesus sternly commanded the spirits not to reveal who he was.

## Jesus Chooses the Twelve Apostles

¹³Afterward Jesus went up on a mountain and called out the ones he wanted to go with him. And they came to him. ¹⁴Then he appointed twelve of them and called them his apostles.* They were to accompany him, and he would send them out to preach, ¹⁵giving them authority to cast out demons. ¹⁶These are the twelve he chose:

Simon (whom he named Peter),
¹⁷James and John (the sons of Zebedee, but Jesus nicknamed them "Sons of Thunder"*),

## A LITTLE HELP from my friends
READ MARK 2:1-12

Most of us never realize how many—or how few—friends we have until a health crisis hits and we need a little help from them to get by. Sometimes people we didn't even realize cared about us step forward with offers of help. Other times, friends we were sure we could count on are strangely silent.

Who wouldn't love the friends in this story? Instead of giving up, they made a hole in the tiled roof and lowered their paralyzed friend right down to Jesus!

Would your friends go all out for you? If so, thank God for them. Would you do anything for a needy friend? If so, ask God to give you that opportunity.

¹⁸Andrew,
Philip,
Bartholomew,
Matthew,
Thomas,
James (son of Alphaeus),
Thaddaeus,
Simon (the zealot*),
¹⁹Judas Iscariot (who later betrayed him).

## Jesus and the Prince of Demons

²⁰One time Jesus entered a house, and the crowds began to gather again. Soon he and his disciples couldn't even find time to eat. ²¹When his family heard what was happening, they tried to take him away. "He's out of his mind," they said.

²²But the teachers of religious law who had arrived from Jerusalem said, "He's possessed by Satan,* the prince of demons. That's where he gets the power to cast out demons."

²³Jesus called them over and responded with an illustration. "How can Satan cast out Satan?" he asked. ²⁴"A kingdom divided by civil war will collapse. ²⁵Similarly, a family splintered by feuding will fall apart. ²⁶And if Satan is divided and fights against himself, how can he stand? He would never survive. ²⁷Let me illustrate this further. Who is powerful enough to enter the house of a

3:11 Greek unclean; also in 3:30.   3:14 Some manuscripts do not include and called them his apostles.   3:17 Greek whom he named Boanerges, which means Sons of Thunder.   3:18 Greek the Cananean, an Aramaic term for Jewish nationalists.   3:22 Greek Beelzeboul; other manuscripts read Beezeboul; Latin version reads Beelzebub.

strong man like Satan and plunder his goods? Only someone even stronger—someone who could tie him up and then plunder his house.

28"I tell you the truth, all sin and blasphemy can be forgiven, 29but anyone who blasphemes the Holy Spirit will never be forgiven. This is a sin with eternal consequences." 30He told them this because they were saying, "He's possessed by an evil spirit."

### The True Family of Jesus

31Then Jesus' mother and brothers came to see him. They stood outside and sent word for him to come out and talk with them. 32There was a crowd sitting around Jesus, and someone said, "Your mother and your brothers* are outside asking for you."

33Jesus replied, "Who is my mother? Who are my brothers?" 34Then he looked at those around him and said, "Look, these are my mother and brothers. 35Anyone who does God's will is my brother and sister and mother."

### Parable of the Farmer Scattering Seed

4 Once again Jesus began teaching by the lakeshore. A very large crowd soon gathered around him, so he got into a boat. Then he sat in the boat while all the people remained on the shore. 2He taught them by telling many stories in the form of parables, such as this one:

3"Listen! A farmer went out to plant some seed. 4As he scattered it across his field, some of the seed fell on a footpath, and the birds came and ate it. 5Other seed fell on shallow soil with underlying rock. The seed sprouted quickly because the soil was shallow. 6But the plant soon wilted under the hot sun, and since it didn't have deep roots, it died. 7Other seed fell among thorns that grew up and choked out the tender plants so they produced no grain. 8Still other seeds fell on fertile soil, and they sprouted, grew, and produced a crop that was thirty, sixty, and even a hundred times as much as had been planted!" 9Then he said, "Anyone with ears to hear should listen and understand."

10Later, when Jesus was alone with the twelve disciples and with the others who were gathered around, they asked him what the parables meant.

11He replied, "You are permitted to understand the secret* of the Kingdom of God. But I use parables for everything I say to outsiders, 12so that the Scriptures might be fulfilled:

'When they see what I do,
    they will learn nothing.
When they hear what I say,
    they will not understand.
Otherwise, they will turn to me
    and be forgiven.'* "

13Then Jesus said to them, "If you can't understand the meaning of this parable, how will you understand all the other parables? 14The farmer plants seed by taking God's word to others. 15The seed that fell on the footpath represents those who hear the message, only to have Satan come at once and take it away. 16The seed on the rocky soil represents those who hear the message and immediately receive it with joy. 17But since they don't have deep roots, they don't last long. They fall away as soon as they have problems or are persecuted for believing God's word. 18The seed that fell among the thorns represents others who hear God's word, 19but all too quickly the message is crowded out by the worries of this life, the lure of wealth, and the desire for other things, so no fruit is produced. 20And the seed that fell on good soil represents those who hear and accept God's word and produce a harvest of thirty, sixty, or even a hundred times as much as had been planted!"

### Parable of the Lamp

21Then Jesus asked them, "Would anyone light a lamp and then put it under a basket or under a bed? Of course not! A lamp is placed on a stand, where its light will shine. 22For everything that is hidden will eventually be brought into the open, and every secret will be brought to light. 23Anyone with ears to hear should listen and understand."

24Then he added, "Pay close attention to what you hear. The closer you listen, the

3:32 Some manuscripts add *and sisters.*   4:11 Greek *mystery.*   4:12 Isa 6:9-10 (Greek version).

more understanding you will be given*—and you will receive even more. 25 To those who listen to my teaching, more understanding will be given. But for those who are not listening, even what little understanding they have will be taken away from them."

### Parable of the Growing Seed

26 Jesus also said, "The Kingdom of God is like a farmer who scatters seed on the ground. 27 Night and day, while he's asleep or awake, the seed sprouts and grows, but he does not understand how it happens. 28 The earth produces the crops on its own. First a leaf blade pushes through, then the heads of wheat are formed, and finally the grain ripens. 29 And as soon as the grain is ready, the farmer comes and harvests it with a sickle, for the harvest time has come."

### Parable of the Mustard Seed

30 Jesus said, "How can I describe the Kingdom of God? What story should I use to illustrate it? 31 It is like a mustard seed planted in the ground. It is the smallest of all seeds, 32 but it becomes the largest of all garden plants; it grows long branches, and birds can make nests in its shade."

33 Jesus used many similar stories and illustrations to teach the people as much as they could understand. 34 In fact, in his public ministry he never taught without using parables; but afterward, when he was alone with his disciples, he explained everything to them.

### Jesus Calms the Storm

35 As evening came, Jesus said to his disciples, "Let's cross to the other side of the lake." 36 So they took Jesus in the boat and started out, leaving the crowds behind (although other boats followed). 37 But soon a fierce storm came up. High waves were breaking into the boat, and it began to fill with water.

38 Jesus was sleeping at the back of the boat with his head on a cushion. The disciples woke him up, shouting, "Teacher, don't you care that we're going to drown?"

39 When Jesus woke up, he rebuked the wind and said to the waves, "Silence! Be still!" Suddenly the wind stopped, and there was a great calm. 40 Then he asked them, "Why are you afraid? Do you still have no faith?"

41 The disciples were absolutely terrified. "Who is this man?" they asked each other. "Even the wind and waves obey him!"

### Jesus Heals a Demon-Possessed Man

5 So they arrived at the other side of the lake, in the region of the Gerasenes.* 2 When Jesus climbed out of the boat, a man possessed by an evil* spirit came out from a cemetery to meet him. 3 This man lived among the burial caves and could no longer be restrained, even with a chain. 4 Whenever he was put into chains and shackles—as he often was—he snapped the chains from his wrists and smashed the shackles. No one was strong enough to subdue him. 5 Day and night he wandered among the burial caves and in the hills, howling and cutting himself with sharp stones.

6 When Jesus was still some distance away, the man saw him, ran to meet him, and bowed low before him. 7 With a shriek, he screamed, "Why are you interfering with me, Jesus, Son of the Most High God? In the name of God, I beg you, don't torture me!" 8 For Jesus had already said to the spirit, "Come out of the man, you evil spirit."

9 Then Jesus demanded, "What is your name?"

And he replied, "My name is Legion, because there are many of us inside this man." 10 Then the evil spirits begged him again and again not to send them to some distant place.

11 There happened to be a large herd of pigs feeding on the hillside nearby. 12 "Send us into those pigs," the spirits begged. "Let us enter them."

13 So Jesus gave them permission. The evil spirits came out of the man and entered the pigs, and the entire herd of 2,000 pigs plunged down the steep hillside into the lake and drowned in the water.

14 The herdsmen fled to the nearby town and the surrounding countryside, spreading

4:24 Or *The measure you give will be the measure you get back.*   5:1 Other manuscripts read *Gadarenes;* still others read *Gergesenes.*
See Matt 8:28; Luke 8:26.   5:2 Greek *unclean;* also in 5:8, 13.

the news as they ran. People rushed out to see what had happened. [15]A crowd soon gathered around Jesus, and they saw the man who had been possessed by the legion of demons. He was sitting there fully clothed and perfectly sane, and they were all afraid. [16]Then those who had seen what happened told the others about the demon-possessed man and the pigs. [17]And the crowd began pleading with Jesus to go away and leave them alone.

[18]As Jesus was getting into the boat, the man who had been demon possessed begged to go with him. [19]But Jesus said, "No, go home to your family, and tell them everything the Lord has done for you and how merciful he has been." [20]So the man started off to visit the Ten Towns* of that region and began to proclaim the great things Jesus had done for him; and everyone was amazed at what he told them.

### Jesus Heals in Response to Faith

[21]Jesus got into the boat again and went back to the other side of the lake, where a large crowd gathered around him on the shore. [22]Then a leader of the local synagogue, whose name was Jairus, arrived. When he saw Jesus, he fell at his feet, [23]pleading fervently with him. "My little daughter is dying," he said. "Please come and lay your hands on her; heal her so she can live."

[24]Jesus went with him, and all the people followed, crowding around him. [25]A woman in the crowd had suffered for twelve years with constant bleeding. [26]She had suffered a great deal from many doctors, and over the years she had spent everything she had to pay them, but she had gotten no better. In fact, she had gotten worse. [27]She had heard about Jesus, so she came up behind him through the crowd and touched his robe. [28]For she thought to herself, "If I can just touch his robe, I will be healed." [29]Immediately the bleeding stopped, and she could feel in her body that she had been healed of her terrible condition.

[30]Jesus realized at once that healing power had gone out from him, so he turned around in the crowd and asked, "Who touched my robe?"

[31]His disciples said to him, "Look at this crowd pressing around you. How can you ask, 'Who touched me?'"

[32]But he kept on looking around to see who had done it. [33]Then the frightened woman, trembling at the realization of what had happened to her, came and fell to her knees in front of him and told him what she had done. [34]And he said to her, "Daughter, your faith has made you well. Go in peace. Your suffering is over."

[35]While he was still speaking to her, messengers arrived from the home of Jairus, the leader of the synagogue. They told him, "Your daughter is dead. There's no use troubling the Teacher now."

[36]But Jesus overheard* them and said to Jairus, "Don't be afraid. Just have faith."

[37]Then Jesus stopped the crowd and wouldn't let anyone go with him except Peter, James, and John (the brother of James). [38]When they came to the home of the synagogue leader, Jesus saw much commotion and weeping and wailing. [39]He went inside and asked, "Why all this commotion and weeping? The child isn't dead; she's only asleep."

[40]The crowd laughed at him. But he made them all leave, and he took the girl's father and mother and his three disciples into the room where the girl was lying. [41]Holding her hand, he said to her, "*Talitha koum*," which means "Little girl, get up!" [42]And the girl, who was twelve years old, immediately stood up and walked around! They were overwhelmed and totally amazed. [43]Jesus gave them strict orders not to tell anyone what had happened, and then he told them to give her something to eat.

### Jesus Rejected at Nazareth

**6** Jesus left that part of the country and returned with his disciples to Nazareth, his hometown. [2]The next Sabbath he began teaching in the synagogue, and many who heard him were amazed. They asked, "Where did he get all this wisdom and the power to perform such miracles?" [3]Then they scoffed, "He's just a carpenter, the son of Mary* and the brother of James, Joseph,*

---

**5:20** Greek *Decapolis.*   **5:36** Or *ignored.*   **6:3a** Some manuscripts read *He's just the son of the carpenter and of Mary.*   **6:3b** Most manuscripts read *Joses;* see Matt 13:55.

Judas, and Simon. And his sisters live right here among us." They were deeply offended and refused to believe in him.

⁴Then Jesus told them, "A prophet is honored everywhere except in his own hometown and among his relatives and his own family." ⁵And because of their unbelief, he couldn't do any miracles among them except to place his hands on a few sick people and heal them. ⁶And he was amazed at their unbelief.

## Jesus Sends Out the Twelve Disciples

Then Jesus went from village to village, teaching the people. ⁷And he called his twelve disciples together and began sending them out two by two, giving them authority to cast out evil* spirits. ⁸He told them to take nothing for their journey except a walking stick—no food, no traveler's bag, no money.* ⁹He allowed them to wear sandals but not to take a change of clothes.

¹⁰"Wherever you go," he said, "stay in the same house until you leave town. ¹¹But if any place refuses to welcome you or listen to you, shake its dust from your feet as you leave to show that you have abandoned those people to their fate."

¹²So the disciples went out, telling everyone they met to repent of their sins and turn to God. ¹³And they cast out many demons and healed many sick people, anointing them with olive oil.

## The Death of John the Baptist

¹⁴Herod Antipas, the king, soon heard about Jesus, because everyone was talking about him. Some were saying,* "This must be John the Baptist raised from the dead. That is why he can do such miracles." ¹⁵Others said, "He's the prophet Elijah." Still others said, "He's a prophet like the other great prophets of the past."

¹⁶When Herod heard about Jesus, he said, "John, the man I beheaded, has come back from the dead."

¹⁷For Herod had sent soldiers to arrest and imprison John as a favor to Herodias. She had been his brother Philip's wife, but Herod had married her. ¹⁸John had been

6:7 Greek *unclean.*   6:8 Greek *no copper coins in their money belts.*   6:14 Some manuscripts read *He was saying.*
6:22 Some manuscripts read *the daughter of Herodias herself.*

telling Herod, "It is against God's law for you to marry your brother's wife." ¹⁹So Herodias bore a grudge against John and wanted to kill him. But without Herod's approval she was powerless, ²⁰for Herod respected John; and knowing that he was a good and holy man, he protected him. Herod was greatly disturbed whenever he talked with John, but even so, he liked to listen to him.

²¹Herodias's chance finally came on Herod's birthday. He gave a party for his high government officials, army officers, and the leading citizens of Galilee. ²²Then his daughter, also named Herodias,* came in and performed a dance that greatly pleased Herod and his guests. "Ask me for anything you like," the king said to the girl, "and I will give it to you." ²³He even vowed, "I will give you whatever you ask, up to half my kingdom!"

²⁴She went out and asked her mother, "What should I ask for?"

Her mother told her, "Ask for the head of John the Baptist!"

²⁵So the girl hurried back to the king and told him, "I want the head of John the Baptist, right now, on a tray!"

²⁶Then the king deeply regretted what he had said; but because of the vows he had made in front of his guests, he couldn't refuse her. ²⁷So he immediately sent an executioner to the prison to cut off John's head and bring it to him. The soldier beheaded John in the prison, ²⁸brought his

## ARE YOU the right dirt?

READ MARK 4:1-10, 13-20

You probably know the details of your medical situation—what your blood count is or what your breathing capacity is or when your last flare-up was. But do you know the condition of your soil?

Jesus says our hearts are like soil and His truth is like a seed planted there. Sometimes our soil is so rocky that when problems come along—like illness—our love for God grows weak. Other times, our soil is so thorny that all the worries—health, financial, and otherwise—choke out our closeness with God.

How open is your heart to God today? Is your soil ready to receive whatever He has for you? Let Him pour His brand of "miracle-grow" on you!

head on a tray, and gave it to the girl, who took it to her mother. ²⁹When John's disciples heard what had happened, they came to get his body and buried it in a tomb.

## Jesus Feeds Five Thousand

³⁰The apostles returned to Jesus from their ministry tour and told him all they had done and taught. ³¹Then Jesus said, "Let's go off by ourselves to a quiet place and rest awhile." He said this because there were so many people coming and going that Jesus and his apostles didn't even have time to eat.

³²So they left by boat for a quiet place, where they could be alone. ³³But many people recognized them and saw them leaving, and people from many towns ran ahead along the shore and got there ahead of them. ³⁴Jesus saw the huge crowd as he stepped from the boat, and he had compassion on them because they were like sheep without a shepherd. So he began teaching them many things.

³⁵Late in the afternoon his disciples came to him and said, "This is a remote place, and it's already getting late. ³⁶Send the crowds away so they can go to the nearby farms and villages and buy something to eat."

³⁷But Jesus said, "You feed them."

"With what?" they asked. "We'd have to work for months to earn enough money* to buy food for all these people!"

³⁸"How much bread do you have?" he asked. "Go and find out."

They came back and reported, "We have five loaves of bread and two fish."

³⁹Then Jesus told the disciples to have the people sit down in groups on the green grass. ⁴⁰So they sat down in groups of fifty or a hundred.

⁴¹Jesus took the five loaves and two fish, looked up toward heaven, and blessed them. Then, breaking the loaves into pieces, he kept giving the bread to the disciples so they could distribute it to the people. He also divided the fish for everyone to share. ⁴²They all ate as much as they wanted, ⁴³and afterward, the disciples picked up twelve baskets of leftover bread and fish. ⁴⁴A total of 5,000 men and their families were fed from those loaves!

## Jesus Walks on Water

⁴⁵Immediately after this, Jesus insisted that his disciples get back into the boat and head across the lake to Bethsaida, while he sent the people home. ⁴⁶After telling everyone good-bye, he went up into the hills by himself to pray.

⁴⁷Late that night, the disciples were in their boat in the middle of the lake, and Jesus was alone on land. ⁴⁸He saw that they were in serious trouble, rowing hard and struggling against the wind and waves. About three o'clock in the morning* Jesus came toward them, walking on the water. He intended to go past them, ⁴⁹but when they saw him walking on the water, they cried out in terror, thinking he was a ghost. ⁵⁰They were all terrified when they saw him.

But Jesus spoke to them at once. "Don't be afraid," he said. "Take courage! I am here!*" ⁵¹Then he climbed into the boat, and the wind stopped. They were totally amazed, ⁵²for they still didn't understand the significance of the miracle of the loaves. Their hearts were too hard to take it in.

⁵³After they had crossed the lake, they landed at Gennesaret. They brought the boat to shore ⁵⁴and climbed out. The people recognized Jesus at once, ⁵⁵and they ran throughout the whole area, carrying sick people on mats to wherever they heard he was. ⁵⁶Wherever he went—in villages, cities, or the countryside—they brought the sick out to the marketplaces. They begged him to let the sick touch at least the fringe of his robe, and all who touched him were healed.

## Jesus Teaches about Inner Purity

**7** One day some Pharisees and teachers of religious law arrived from Jerusalem to see Jesus. ²They noticed that some of his disciples failed to follow the Jewish ritual of hand washing before eating. ³(The Jews, especially the Pharisees, do not eat until they have poured water over their cupped hands,* as required by their ancient traditions. ⁴Similarly, they don't eat anything from the market until they immerse their

**6:37** Greek *It would take 200 denarii.* A denarius was equivalent to a laborer's full day's wage.   **6:48** Greek *About the fourth watch of the night.*   **6:50** Or *The 'I Aᴍ' is here;* Greek reads *I am.* See Exod 3:14.   **7:3** Greek *have washed with the fist.*

hands* in water. This is but one of many traditions they have clung to—such as their ceremonial washing of cups, pitchers, and kettles.*)

5 So the Pharisees and teachers of religious law asked him, "Why don't your disciples follow our age-old tradition? They eat without first performing the hand-washing ceremony."

6 Jesus replied, "You hypocrites! Isaiah was right when he prophesied about you, for he wrote,

'These people honor me with their lips,
    but their hearts are far from me.
7 Their worship is a farce,
    for they teach man-made ideas as
        commands from God.'*

8 For you ignore God's law and substitute your own tradition."

9 Then he said, "You skillfully sidestep God's law in order to hold on to your own tradition. 10 For instance, Moses gave you this law from God: 'Honor your father and mother,'* and 'Anyone who speaks disrespectfully of father or mother must be put to death.'* 11 But you say it is all right for people to say to their parents, 'Sorry, I can't help you. For I have vowed to give to God what I would have given to you.'* 12 In this way, you let them disregard their needy parents. 13 And so you cancel the word of God in order to hand down your own tradition. And this is only one example among many others."

14 Then Jesus called to the crowd to come and hear. "All of you listen," he said, "and try to understand. 15 It's not what goes into your body that defiles you; you are defiled by what comes from your heart.*"

17 Then Jesus went into a house to get away from the crowd, and his disciples asked him what he meant by the parable he had just used. 18 "Don't you understand either?" he asked. "Can't you see that the food you put into your body cannot defile you? 19 Food doesn't go into your heart, but only passes through the stomach and then goes into the sewer." (By saying this, he declared that every kind of food is acceptable in God's eyes.)

20 And then he added, "It is what comes from inside that defiles you. 21 For from within, out of a person's heart, come evil thoughts, sexual immorality, theft, murder, 22 adultery, greed, wickedness, deceit, lustful desires, envy, slander, pride, and foolishness. 23 All these vile things come from within; they are what defile you."

### The Faith of a Gentile Woman

24 Then Jesus left Galilee and went north to the region of Tyre.* He didn't want anyone to know which house he was staying in, but he couldn't keep it a secret. 25 Right away a woman who had heard about him came and fell at his feet. Her little girl was possessed by an evil* spirit, 26 and she begged him to cast out the demon from her daughter.

Since she was a Gentile, born in Syrian Phoenicia, 27 Jesus told her, "First I should feed the children—my own family, the Jews.* It isn't right to take food from the children and throw it to the dogs."

28 She replied, "That's true, Lord, but even the dogs under the table are allowed to eat the scraps from the children's plates."

29 "Good answer!" he said. "Now go home, for the demon has left your daughter." 30 And when she arrived home, she found her little girl lying quietly in bed, and the demon was gone.

### Jesus Heals a Deaf Man

31 Jesus left Tyre and went up to Sidon before going back to the Sea of Galilee and the region of the Ten Towns.* 32 A deaf man with a speech impediment was brought to him, and the people begged Jesus to lay his hands on the man to heal him.

33 Jesus led him away from the crowd so they could be alone. He put his fingers into the man's ears. Then, spitting on his own fingers, he touched the man's tongue. 34 Looking up to heaven, he sighed and said, "*Ephphatha*," which means, "Be opened!" 35 Instantly the man could hear perfectly,

7:4a Some manuscripts read *sprinkle themselves*.   7:4b Some manuscripts add *and dining couches*.   7:7 Isa 29:13 (Greek version).
7:10a Exod 20:12; Deut 5:16.   7:10b Exod 21:17 (Greek version); Lev 20:9 (Greek version).   7:11 Greek *'What I would have given
to you is Corban' (that is, a gift)*.   7:15 Some manuscripts add verse 16, *Anyone with ears to hear should listen and understand.*
Compare 4:9, 23.   7:24 Some manuscripts add *and Sidon*.   7:25 Greek *unclean*.   7:27 Greek *Let the children eat first.*   7:31 Greek
*Decapolis*.

and his tongue was freed so he could speak plainly!

36 Jesus told the crowd not to tell anyone, but the more he told them not to, the more they spread the news. 37 They were completely amazed and said again and again, "Everything he does is wonderful. He even makes the deaf to hear and gives speech to those who cannot speak."

### Jesus Feeds Four Thousand

**8** About this time another large crowd had gathered, and the people ran out of food again. Jesus called his disciples and told them, 2 "I feel sorry for these people. They have been here with me for three days, and they have nothing left to eat. 3 If I send them home hungry, they will faint along the way. For some of them have come a long distance."

4 His disciples replied, "How are we supposed to find enough food to feed them out here in the wilderness?"

5 Jesus asked, "How much bread do you have?"

"Seven loaves," they replied.

6 So Jesus told all the people to sit down on the ground. Then he took the seven loaves, thanked God for them, and broke them into pieces. He gave them to his disciples, who distributed the bread to the crowd. 7 A few small fish were found, too, so Jesus also blessed these and told the disciples to distribute them.

8 They ate as much as they wanted. Afterward, the disciples picked up seven large baskets of leftover food. 9 There were about 4,000 people in the crowd that day, and Jesus sent them home after they had eaten. 10 Immediately after this, he got into a boat with his disciples and crossed over to the region of Dalmanutha.

### Pharisees Demand a Miraculous Sign

11 When the Pharisees heard that Jesus had arrived, they came and started to argue with him. Testing him, they demanded that he show them a miraculous sign from heaven to prove his authority.

12 When he heard this, he sighed deeply in his spirit and said, "Why do these people keep demanding a miraculous sign? I tell you the truth, I will not give this generation any such sign." 13 So he got back into the boat and left them, and he crossed to the other side of the lake.

### Yeast of the Pharisees and Herod

14 But the disciples had forgotten to bring any food. They had only one loaf of bread with them in the boat. 15 As they were crossing the lake, Jesus warned them, "Watch out! Beware of the yeast of the Pharisees and of Herod."

16 At this they began to argue with each other because they hadn't brought any bread. 17 Jesus knew what they were saying, so he said, "Why are you arguing about having no bread? Don't you know or understand even yet? Are your hearts too hard to take it in? 18 'You have eyes—can't you see? You have ears—can't you hear?'* Don't you remember anything at all? 19 When I fed the 5,000 with five loaves of bread, how many baskets of leftovers did you pick up afterward?"

"Twelve," they said.

20 "And when I fed the 4,000 with seven loaves, how many large baskets of leftovers did you pick up?"

"Seven," they said.

21 "Don't you understand yet?" he asked them.

### Jesus Heals a Blind Man

22 When they arrived at Bethsaida, some people brought a blind man to Jesus, and they begged him to touch the man and heal him. 23 Jesus took the blind man by the hand and led him out of the village. Then, spitting on the man's eyes, he laid his hands on him and asked, "Can you see anything now?"

24 The man looked around. "Yes," he said, "I see people, but I can't see them very clearly. They look like trees walking around."

25 Then Jesus placed his hands on the man's eyes again, and his eyes were opened. His sight was completely restored, and he could see everything clearly. 26 Jesus sent him away, saying, "Don't go back into the village on your way home."

**8:18** Jer 5:21.

*Moses represents the Law; Elijah the prophets*

### Peter's Declaration about Jesus

27 Jesus and his disciples left Galilee and went up to the villages near Caesarea Philippi. As they were walking along, he asked them, "Who do people say I am?"

28 "Well," they replied, "some say John the Baptist, some say Elijah, and others say you are one of the other prophets."

29 Then he asked them, "But who do you say I am?"

Peter replied, "You are the Messiah.*"

30 But Jesus warned them not to tell anyone about him.

### Jesus Predicts His Death

31 Then Jesus began to tell them that the Son of Man* must suffer many terrible things and be rejected by the elders, the leading priests, and the teachers of religious law. He would be killed, but three days later he would rise from the dead. 32 As he talked about this openly with his disciples, Peter took him aside and began to reprimand him for saying such things.*

33 Jesus turned around and looked at his disciples, then reprimanded Peter. "Get away from me, Satan!" he said. "You are seeing things merely from a human point of view, not from God's."

34 Then, calling the crowd to join his disciples, he said, "If any of you wants to be my follower, you must turn from your selfish ways, take up your cross, and follow me. 35 If you try to hang on to your life, you will lose it. But if you give up your life for my sake and for the sake of the Good News, you will save it. 36 And what do you benefit if you gain the whole world but lose your own soul?* 37 Is anything worth more than your soul? 38 If anyone is ashamed of me and my message in these adulterous and sinful days, the Son of Man will be ashamed of that person when he returns in the glory of his Father with the holy angels."

**9** Jesus went on to say, "I tell you the truth, some standing here right now will not die before they see the Kingdom of God arrive in great power!"

### The Transfiguration

2 Six days later Jesus took Peter, James, and John, and led them up a high mountain to be alone. As the men watched, Jesus' appearance was transformed, 3 and his clothes became dazzling white, far whiter than any earthly bleach could ever make them. 4 Then Elijah and Moses appeared and began talking with Jesus.

5 Peter exclaimed, "Rabbi, it's wonderful for us to be here! Let's make three shelters as memorials*—one for you, one for Moses, and one for Elijah." 6 He said this because he didn't really know what else to say, for they were all terrified.

7 Then a cloud overshadowed them, and a voice from the cloud said, "This is my dearly loved Son. Listen to him." 8 Suddenly, when they looked around, Moses and Elijah were gone, and they saw only Jesus with them.

9 As they went back down the mountain, he told them not to tell anyone what they had seen until the Son of Man* had risen from the dead. 10 So they kept it to themselves, but they often asked each other what he meant by "rising from the dead."

11 Then they asked him, "Why do the teachers of religious law insist that Elijah must return before the Messiah comes?*"

12 Jesus responded, "Elijah is indeed coming first to get everything ready. Yet why do the Scriptures say that the Son of Man must suffer greatly and be treated with utter contempt? 13 But I tell you, Elijah has already come, and they chose to abuse him, just as the Scriptures predicted."

### Jesus Heals a Demon-Possessed Boy

14 When they returned to the other disciples, they saw a large crowd surrounding them, and some teachers of religious law were arguing with them. 15 When the crowd saw Jesus, they were overwhelmed with awe, and they ran to greet him.

16 "What is all this arguing about?" Jesus asked.

17 One of the men in the crowd spoke up and said, "Teacher, I brought my son so you could heal him. He is possessed by an evil

8:29 Or *the Christ. Messiah* (a Hebrew term) and *Christ* (a Greek term) both mean "the anointed one." 8:31 "Son of Man" is a title Jesus used for himself. 8:32 Or *began to correct him.* 8:36 Or *your self?* also in 8:37. 9:5 Greek *three tabernacles.* 9:9 "Son of Man" is a title Jesus used for himself. 9:11 Greek *that Elijah must come first?*

spirit that won't let him talk. ¹⁸And whenever this spirit seizes him, it throws him violently to the ground. Then he foams at the mouth and grinds his teeth and becomes rigid.* So I asked your disciples to cast out the evil spirit, but they couldn't do it."

¹⁹Jesus said to them,* "You faithless people! How long must I be with you? How long must I put up with you? Bring the boy to me."

²⁰So they brought the boy. But when the evil spirit saw Jesus, it threw the child into a violent convulsion, and he fell to the ground, writhing and foaming at the mouth.

²¹"How long has this been happening?" Jesus asked the boy's father.

He replied, "Since he was a little boy. ²²The spirit often throws him into the fire or into water, trying to kill him. Have mercy on us and help us, if you can."

²³"What do you mean, 'If I can'?" Jesus asked. "Anything is possible if a person believes."

²⁴The father instantly cried out, "I do believe, but help me overcome my unbelief!"

²⁵When Jesus saw that the crowd of onlookers was growing, he rebuked the evil* spirit. "Listen, you spirit that makes this boy unable to hear and speak," he said. "I command you to come out of this child and never enter him again!"

²⁶Then the spirit screamed and threw the boy into another violent convulsion and left him. The boy appeared to be dead. A murmur ran through the crowd as people said, "He's dead." ²⁷But Jesus took him by the hand and helped him to his feet, and he stood up.

²⁸Afterward, when Jesus was alone in the house with his disciples, they asked him, "Why couldn't we cast out that evil spirit?"

²⁹Jesus replied, "This kind can be cast out only by prayer.*"

### Jesus Again Predicts His Death

³⁰Leaving that region, they traveled through Galilee. Jesus didn't want anyone to know he was there, ³¹for he wanted to spend more time with his disciples and teach them. He said to them, "The Son of Man is going to be betrayed into the hands of his enemies. He will be killed, but three days later he will rise from the dead." ³²They didn't understand what he was saying, however, and they were afraid to ask him what he meant.

### The Greatest in the Kingdom

³³After they arrived at Capernaum and settled in a house, Jesus asked his disciples, "What were you discussing out on the road?" ³⁴But they didn't answer, because they had been arguing about which of them was the greatest. ³⁵He sat down, called the

---

9:18 Or *becomes weak.*   9:19 Or *said to his disciples.*   9:25 Greek *unclean.*   9:29 Some manuscripts read *by prayer and fasting.*

## HERE'S MUD in your eye

READ MARK 8:22-25

If you were standing face-to-face with Jesus hoping for a healing, how would you expect Him to deliver a miracle? By a gentle touch? With strong words? How about with mud or spit!

When Jesus encountered the blind man at Bethsaida, He spit in his eyes and then laid His hands on him. In Mark 7:33-34, Jesus put His fingers in a deaf man's ears, spit on His own fingers before touching the man's tongue, and then commanded his ears to be opened. In John 9:6, Jesus spit on the ground, made some mud from the saliva, and placed it on the blind man's eyes. In each case, the person was fully restored.

Don't you love how God has so many ways to heal? Sometimes His ways don't seem logical to us. We don't presume to know the reasons why Jesus healed each person in such different ways, but we trust He knew each one and how to meet their needs.

He knows just the touch you need today.

twelve disciples over to him, and said, "Whoever wants to be first must take last place and be the servant of everyone else."

36Then he put a little child among them. Taking the child in his arms, he said to them, 37"Anyone who welcomes a little child like this on my behalf* welcomes me, and anyone who welcomes me welcomes not only me but also my Father who sent me."

### Using the Name of Jesus

38John said to Jesus, "Teacher, we saw someone using your name to cast out demons, but we told him to stop because he wasn't in our group."

39"Don't stop him!" Jesus said. "No one who performs a miracle in my name will soon be able to speak evil of me. 40Anyone who is not against us is for us. 41If anyone gives you even a cup of water because you belong to the Messiah, I tell you the truth, that person will surely be rewarded.

42"But if you cause one of these little ones who trusts in me to fall into sin, it would be better for you to be thrown into the sea with a large millstone hung around your neck. 43If your hand causes you to sin, cut it off. It's better to enter eternal life with only one hand than to go into the unquenchable fires of hell* with two hands.* 45If your foot causes you to sin, cut it off. It's better to enter eternal life with only one foot than to be thrown into hell with two feet.* 47And if your eye causes you to sin, gouge it out. It's better to enter the Kingdom of God with only one eye than to have two eyes and be thrown into hell, 48'where the maggots never die and the fire never goes out.'*

49"For everyone will be tested with fire.* 50Salt is good for seasoning. But if it loses its flavor, how do you make it salty again? You must have the qualities of salt among yourselves and live in peace with each other."

### Discussion about Divorce and Marriage

**10** Then Jesus left Capernaum and went down to the region of Judea and into the area east of the Jordan River. Once again crowds gathered around him, and as usual he was teaching them.

2Some Pharisees came and tried to trap him with this question: "Should a man be allowed to divorce his wife?"

3Jesus answered them with a question: "What did Moses say in the law about divorce?"

4"Well, he permitted it," they replied. "He said a man can give his wife a written notice of divorce and send her away."*

5But Jesus responded, "He wrote this commandment only as a concession to your hard hearts. 6But 'God made them male and female'* from the beginning of creation. 7'This explains why a man leaves his father and mother and is joined to his wife,* 8and the two are united into one.'* Since they are no longer two but one, 9let no one split apart what God has joined together."

10Later, when he was alone with his disciples in the house, they brought up the subject again. 11He told them, "Whoever divorces his wife and marries someone else commits adultery against her. 12And if a woman divorces her husband and marries someone else, she commits adultery."

### Jesus Blesses the Children

13One day some parents brought their children to Jesus so he could touch and bless them. But the disciples scolded the parents for bothering him.

14When Jesus saw what was happening, he was angry with his disciples. He said to them, "Let the children come to me. Don't stop them! For the Kingdom of God belongs to those who are like these children. 15I tell you the truth, anyone who doesn't receive the Kingdom of God like a child will never enter it." 16Then he took the children in his arms and placed his hands on their heads and blessed them.

### The Rich Man

17As Jesus was starting out on his way to Jerusalem, a man came running up to him, knelt down, and asked, "Good Teacher, what must I do to inherit eternal life?"

---

9:37 Greek *in my name.*   9:43a Greek *Gehenna;* also in 9:45, 47.   9:43b Some manuscripts add verse 44, '*where the maggots never die and the fire never goes out.*' See 9:48.   9:45 Some manuscripts add verse 46, '*where the maggots never die and the fire never goes out.*' See 9:48.   9:48 Isa 66:24.   9:49 Greek *salted with fire;* other manuscripts add *and every sacrifice will be salted with salt.* 10:4 See Deut 24:1.   10:6 Gen 1:27; 5:2.   10:7 Some manuscripts do not include *and is joined to his wife.*   10:7-8 Gen 2:24.

¹⁸"Why do you call me good?" Jesus asked. "Only God is truly good. ¹⁹But to answer your question, you know the commandments: 'You must not murder. You must not commit adultery. You must not steal. You must not testify falsely. You must not cheat anyone. Honor your father and mother.'* "

²⁰"Teacher," the man replied, "I've obeyed all these commandments since I was young."

²¹Looking at the man, Jesus felt genuine love for him. "There is still one thing you haven't done," he told him. "Go and sell all your possessions and give the money to the poor, and you will have treasure in heaven. Then come, follow me."

²²At this the man's face fell, and he went away sad, for he had many possessions.

²³Jesus looked around and said to his disciples, "How hard it is for the rich to enter the Kingdom of God!" ²⁴This amazed them. But Jesus said again, "Dear children, it is very hard* to enter the Kingdom of God. ²⁵In fact, it is easier for a camel to go through the eye of a needle than for a rich person to enter the Kingdom of God!"

²⁶The disciples were astounded. "Then who in the world can be saved?" they asked.

²⁷Jesus looked at them intently and said, "Humanly speaking, it is impossible. But not with God. Everything is possible with God."

²⁸Then Peter began to speak up. "We've given up everything to follow you," he said.

²⁹"Yes," Jesus replied, "and I assure you that everyone who has given up house or brothers or sisters or mother or father or children or property, for my sake and for the Good News, ³⁰will receive now in return a hundred times as many houses, brothers, sisters, mothers, children, and property—along with persecution. And in the world to come that person will have eternal life. ³¹But many who are the greatest now will be least important then, and those who seem least important now will be the greatest then.*"

### Jesus Again Predicts His Death

³²They were now on the way up to Jerusalem, and Jesus was walking ahead of them. The disciples were filled with awe, and the people following behind were overwhelmed with fear. Taking the twelve disciples aside, Jesus once more began to describe everything that was about to happen to him. ³³"Listen," he said, "we're going up to Jerusalem, where the Son of Man* will be betrayed to the leading priests and the teachers of religious law. They will sentence him to die and hand him over to the Romans.* ³⁴They will mock him, spit on him, flog him with a whip, and kill him, but after three days he will rise again."

### Jesus Teaches about Serving Others

³⁵Then James and John, the sons of Zebedee, came over and spoke to him. "Teacher," they said, "we want you to do us a favor."

³⁶"What is your request?" he asked.

³⁷They replied, "When you sit on your glorious throne, we want to sit in places of honor next to you, one on your right and the other on your left."

³⁸But Jesus said to them, "You don't know what you are asking! Are you able to drink from the bitter cup of suffering I am about to drink? Are you able to be baptized with the baptism of suffering I must be baptized with?"

³⁹"Oh yes," they replied, "we are able!"

Then Jesus told them, "You will indeed drink from my bitter cup and be baptized with my baptism of suffering. ⁴⁰But I have no right to say who will sit on my right or my left. God has prepared those places for the ones he has chosen."

⁴¹When the ten other disciples heard what James and John had asked, they were indignant. ⁴²So Jesus called them together and said, "You know that the rulers in this world lord it over their people, and officials flaunt their authority over those under them. ⁴³But among you it will be different. Whoever wants to be a leader among you must be your servant, ⁴⁴and whoever wants to be first among you must be the slave of everyone else. ⁴⁵For even the Son of Man came not to be served but to serve others and to give his life as a ransom for many."

### Jesus Heals Blind Bartimaeus

⁴⁶Then they reached Jericho, and as Jesus and his disciples left town, a large crowd fol-

**10:19** Exod 20:12-16; Deut 5:16-20.   **10:24** Some manuscripts read *very hard for those who trust in riches.*   **10:31** Greek *But many who are first will be last; and the last, first.*   **10:33a** "Son of Man" is a title Jesus used for himself.   **10:33b** Greek *the Gentiles.*

lowed him. A blind beggar named Bartimaeus (son of Timaeus) was sitting beside the road. ⁴⁷When Bartimaeus heard that Jesus of Nazareth was nearby, he began to shout, "Jesus, Son of David, have mercy on me!"

⁴⁸"Be quiet!" many of the people yelled at him.

But he only shouted louder, "Son of David, have mercy on me!"

⁴⁹When Jesus heard him, he stopped and said, "Tell him to come here."

So they called the blind man. "Cheer up," they said. "Come on, he's calling you!" ⁵⁰Bartimaeus threw aside his coat, jumped up, and came to Jesus.

⁵¹"What do you want me to do for you?" Jesus asked.

"My rabbi,*" the blind man said, "I want to see!"

⁵²And Jesus said to him, "Go, for your faith has healed you." Instantly the man could see, and he followed Jesus down the road.*

## Jesus' Triumphant Entry

**11** As Jesus and his disciples approached Jerusalem, they came to the towns of Bethphage and Bethany on the Mount of Olives. Jesus sent two of them on ahead. ²"Go into that village over there," he told them. "As soon as you enter it, you will see a young donkey tied there that no one has ever ridden. Untie it and bring it here. ³If anyone asks, 'What are you doing?' just say, 'The Lord needs it and will return it soon.' "

⁴The two disciples left and found the colt standing in the street, tied outside the front door. ⁵As they were untying it, some bystanders demanded, "What are you doing, untying that colt?" ⁶They said what Jesus had told them to say, and they were permitted to take it. ⁷Then they brought the colt to Jesus and threw their garments over it, and he sat on it.

⁸Many in the crowd spread their garments on the road ahead of him, and others spread leafy branches they had cut in the fields. ⁹Jesus was in the center of the procession, and the people all around him were shouting,

"Praise God!*
　Blessings on the one who comes in the
　　name of the Lord!
¹⁰Blessings on the coming Kingdom of our
　　ancestor David!
　Praise God in highest heaven!"*

¹¹So Jesus came to Jerusalem and went into the Temple. After looking around carefully at everything, he left because it was late in the afternoon. Then he returned to Bethany with the twelve disciples.

## Jesus Curses the Fig Tree

¹²The next morning as they were leaving Bethany, Jesus was hungry. ¹³He noticed a fig tree in full leaf a little way off, so he went over to see if he could find any figs. But there were only leaves because it was too early in the season for fruit. ¹⁴Then Jesus said to the tree, "May no one ever eat your fruit again!" And the disciples heard him say it.

## Jesus Clears the Temple

¹⁵When they arrived back in Jerusalem, Jesus entered the Temple and began to drive out the people buying and selling animals for sacrifices. He knocked over the tables of the money changers and the chairs of those selling doves, ¹⁶and he stopped everyone from using the Temple as a marketplace.*

10:51 Greek uses the Hebrew term *Rabboni.*　10:52 Or *on the way.*　11:9 Greek *Hosanna,* an exclamation of praise that literally means "save now"; also in 11:10.　11:9-10 Pss 118:25-26; 148:1.　11:16 Or *from carrying merchandise through the Temple.*

17He said to them, "The Scriptures declare, 'My Temple will be called a house of prayer for all nations,' but you have turned it into a den of thieves."*

18When the leading priests and teachers of religious law heard what Jesus had done, they began planning how to kill him. But they were afraid of him because the people were so amazed at his teaching.

19That evening Jesus and the disciples left* the city.

20The next morning as they passed by the fig tree he had cursed, the disciples noticed it had withered from the roots up. 21 Peter remembered what Jesus had said to the tree on the previous day and exclaimed, "Look, Rabbi! The fig tree you cursed has withered and died!"

22Then Jesus said to the disciples, "Have faith in God. 23I tell you the truth, you can say to this mountain, 'May you be lifted up and thrown into the sea,' and it will happen. But you must really believe it will happen and have no doubt in your heart. 24I tell you, you can pray for anything, and if you believe that you've received it, it will be yours. 25But when you are praying, first forgive anyone you are holding a grudge against, so that your Father in heaven will forgive your sins, too.*"

### The Authority of Jesus Challenged

27Again they entered Jerusalem. As Jesus was walking through the Temple area, the leading priests, the teachers of religious law, and the elders came up to him. 28They demanded, "By what authority are you doing all these things? Who gave you the right to do them?"

29"I'll tell you by what authority I do these things if you answer one question," Jesus replied. 30"Did John's authority to baptize come from heaven, or was it merely human? Answer me!"

31They talked it over among themselves. "If we say it was from heaven, he will ask why we didn't believe John. 32But do we dare say it was merely human?" For they were afraid of what the people would do, because everyone believed that John was a prophet. 33So they finally replied, "We don't know."

And Jesus responded, "Then I won't tell you by what authority I do these things."

### Parable of the Evil Farmers

**12** Then Jesus began teaching them with stories: "A man planted a vineyard. He built a wall around it, dug a pit for pressing out the grape juice, and built a lookout tower. Then he leased the vineyard to tenant farmers and moved to another country. 2At the time of the grape harvest, he sent one of his servants to collect his share of the crop. 3But the farmers grabbed the servant, beat him up, and sent him back empty-handed. 4The owner then sent another servant, but they insulted him and beat him over the head. 5The next servant he sent was killed. Others he sent were either beaten or killed, 6until there was only one left—his son whom he loved dearly. The owner finally sent him, thinking, 'Surely they will respect my son.'

7"But the tenant farmers said to one another, 'Here comes the heir to this estate. Let's kill him and get the estate for ourselves!' 8So they grabbed him and murdered him and threw his body out of the vineyard.

9"What do you suppose the owner of the vineyard will do?" Jesus asked. "I'll tell you—he will come and kill those farmers and lease the vineyard to others. 10Didn't you ever read this in the Scriptures?

'The stone that the builders rejected
    has now become the cornerstone.
11 This is the LORD's doing,
    and it is wonderful to see.'* "

12The religious leaders* wanted to arrest Jesus because they realized he was telling the story against them—they were the wicked farmers. But they were afraid of the crowd, so they left him and went away.

### Taxes for Caesar

13Later the leaders sent some Pharisees and supporters of Herod to trap Jesus into saying something for which he could be arrested. 14"Teacher," they said, "we know how honest you are. You are impartial and don't play favorites. You teach the way of God truthfully. Now tell us—is it right to pay taxes to Caesar

11:17 Isa 56:7; Jer 7:11.   11:19 Greek they left; other manuscripts read he left.   11:25 Some manuscripts add verse 26, But if you refuse to forgive, your Father in heaven will not forgive your sins. Compare Matt 6:15.   12:10-11 Ps 118:22-23.   12:12 Greek They.

or not? [15]Should we pay them, or shouldn't we?"

Jesus saw through their hypocrisy and said, "Why are you trying to trap me? Show me a Roman coin,* and I'll tell you." [16]When they handed it to him, he asked, "Whose picture and title are stamped on it?"

"Caesar's," they replied.

[17]"Well, then," Jesus said, "give to Caesar what belongs to Caesar, and give to God what belongs to God."

His reply completely amazed them.

## Discussion about Resurrection
[18]Then Jesus was approached by some Sadducees—religious leaders who say there is no resurrection from the dead. They posed this question: [19]"Teacher, Moses gave us a law that if a man dies, leaving a wife without children, his brother should marry the widow and have a child who will carry on the brother's name.* [20]Well, suppose there were seven brothers. The oldest one married and then died without children. [21]So the second brother married the widow, but he also died without children. Then the third brother married her. [22]This continued with all seven of them, and still there were no children. Last of all, the woman also died. [23]So tell us, whose wife will she be in the resurrection? For all seven were married to her."

[24]Jesus replied, "Your mistake is that you don't know the Scriptures, and you don't know the power of God. [25]For when the dead rise, they will neither marry nor be given in marriage. In this respect they will be like the angels in heaven.

[26]"But now, as to whether the dead will be raised—haven't you ever read about this in the writings of Moses, in the story of the burning bush? Long after Abraham, Isaac, and Jacob had died, God said to Moses,* 'I am the God of Abraham, the God of Isaac, and the God of Jacob.'* [27]So he is the God of the living, not the dead. You have made a serious error."

## The Most Important Commandment
[28]One of the teachers of religious law was standing there listening to the debate. He realized that Jesus had answered well, so he asked, "Of all the commandments, which is the most important?"

[29]Jesus replied, "The most important commandment is this: 'Listen, O Israel! The LORD our God is the one and only LORD. [30]And you must love the LORD your God with all your heart, all your soul, all your mind, and all your strength.'* [31]The second is equally important: 'Love your neighbor as yourself.'* No other commandment is greater than these."

[32]The teacher of religious law replied, "Well said, Teacher. You have spoken the truth by saying that there is only one God and no other. [33]And I know it is important to love him with all my heart and all my understanding and all my strength, and to love my neighbor as myself. This is more important than to offer all of the burnt offerings and sacrifices required in the law."

[34]Realizing how much the man understood, Jesus said to him, "You are not far from the Kingdom of God." And after that, no one dared to ask him any more questions.

## Whose Son Is the Messiah?
[35]Later, as Jesus was teaching the people in the Temple, he asked, " Why do the teachers of religious law claim that the Messiah is the son of David? [36]For David himself, speaking under the inspiration of the Holy Spirit, said,

'The LORD said to my Lord,
Sit in the place of honor at my right
      hand
   until I humble your enemies beneath
      your feet.'*

[37]Since David himself called the Messiah 'my Lord,' how can the Messiah be his son?" The large crowd listened to him with great delight.

[38]Jesus also taught: "Beware of these teachers of religious law! For they like to parade around in flowing robes and receive respectful greetings as they walk in the marketplaces. [39]And how they love the seats of honor in the synagogues and the head table at banquets. [40]Yet they shamelessly cheat widows out of their property and then pretend to be pious by making long prayers in

12:15 Greek a denarius.    12:19 See Deut 25:5-6.    12:26a Greek in the story of the bush? God said to him.    12:26b Exod 3:6.
12:29-30 Deut 6:4-5.    12:31 Lev 19:18.    12:36 Ps 110:1.

public. Because of this, they will be more severely punished."

### The Widow's Offering

⁴¹Jesus sat down near the collection box in the Temple and watched as the crowds dropped in their money. Many rich people put in large amounts. ⁴²Then a poor widow came and dropped in two small coins.*

⁴³Jesus called his disciples to him and said, "I tell you the truth, this poor widow has given more than all the others who are making contributions. ⁴⁴For they gave a tiny part of their surplus, but she, poor as she is, has given everything she had to live on."

### Jesus Foretells the Future

**13** As Jesus was leaving the Temple that day, one of his disciples said, "Teacher, look at these magnificent buildings! Look at the impressive stones in the walls."

²Jesus replied, "Yes, look at these great buildings. But they will be completely demolished. Not one stone will be left on top of another!"

³Later, Jesus sat on the Mount of Olives across the valley from the Temple. Peter, James, John, and Andrew came to him privately and asked him, ⁴"Tell us, when will all this happen? What sign will show us that these things are about to be fulfilled?"

⁵Jesus replied, "Don't let anyone mislead you, ⁶for many will come in my name, claiming, 'I am the Messiah.'* They will deceive many. ⁷And you will hear of wars and threats of wars, but don't panic. Yes, these things must take place, but the end won't follow immediately. ⁸Nation will go to war against nation, and kingdom against kingdom. There will be earthquakes in many parts of the world, as well as famines. But this is only the first of the birth pains, with more to come.

⁹"When these things begin to happen, watch out! You will be handed over to the local councils and beaten in the synagogues. You will stand trial before governors and kings because you are my followers. But this will be your opportunity to tell them about me.* ¹⁰For the Good News must first be preached to all nations.* ¹¹But when you are arrested and stand trial, don't worry in advance about what to say. Just say what God tells you at that time, for it is not you who will be speaking, but the Holy Spirit.

¹²"A brother will betray his brother to death, a father will betray his own child, and children will rebel against their parents and cause them to be killed. ¹³And everyone will hate you because you are my followers.* But the one who endures to the end will be saved.

¹⁴"The day is coming when you will see the sacrilegious object that causes desecration* standing where he* should not be." (Reader, pay attention!) "Then those in Judea must flee to the hills. ¹⁵A person out on the deck of a roof must not go down into the house to pack. ¹⁶A person out in the field must not return even to get a coat. ¹⁷How terrible it will be for pregnant women and for nursing mothers in those days. ¹⁸And pray that your flight will not be in winter. ¹⁹For there will be greater anguish in those days than at any time since God created the world. And it will never be so great again. ²⁰In fact, unless the Lord shortens that time of calamity, not a single person will survive. But for the sake of his chosen ones he has shortened those days.

²¹"Then if anyone tells you, 'Look, here is the Messiah,' or 'There he is,' don't believe it. ²²For false messiahs and false prophets will rise up and perform signs and wonders so as to deceive, if possible, even God's chosen ones. ²³Watch out! I have warned you about this ahead of time!

²⁴"At that time, after the anguish of those days,

> the sun will be darkened,
>     the moon will give no light,
> ²⁵the stars will fall from the sky,
>     and the powers in the heavens will
>     be shaken.*

²⁶Then everyone will see the Son of Man* coming on the clouds with great power and glory.* ²⁷And he will send out his angels to gather his chosen ones from all over the

**12:42** Greek *two lepta, which is a kodrantes* [i.e., a quadrans]. **13:6** Greek *claiming, 'I am.'* **13:9** Or *But this will be your testimony against them.* **13:10** Or *all peoples.* **13:13** Greek *on account of my name.* **13:14a** Greek *the abomination of desolation.* See Dan 9:27; 11:31; 12:11. **13:14b** Or *it.* **13:24-25** See Isa 13:10; 34:4; Joel 2:10. **13:26a** "Son of Man" is a title Jesus used for himself. **13:26b** See Dan 7:13.

world*—from the farthest ends of the earth and heaven.

28 "Now learn a lesson from the fig tree. When its branches bud and its leaves begin to sprout, you know that summer is near. 29 In the same way, when you see all these things taking place, you can know that his return is very near, right at the door. 30 I tell you the truth, this generation* will not pass from the scene before all these things take place. 31 Heaven and earth will disappear, but my words will never disappear.

32 "However, no one knows the day or hour when these things will happen, not even the angels in heaven or the Son himself. Only the Father knows. 33 And since you don't know when that time will come, be on guard! Stay alert*!

34 "The coming of the Son of Man can be illustrated by the story of a man going on a long trip. When he left home, he gave each of his slaves instructions about the work they were to do, and he told the gatekeeper to watch for his return. 35 You, too, must keep watch! For you don't know when the master of the household will return—in the evening, at midnight, before dawn, or at daybreak. 36 Don't let him find you sleeping when he arrives without warning. 37 I say to you what I say to everyone: Watch for him!"

## Jesus Anointed at Bethany

**14** It was now two days before Passover and the Festival of Unleavened Bread. The leading priests and the teachers of religious law were still looking for an opportunity to capture Jesus secretly and kill him. 2 "But not during the Passover celebration," they agreed, "or the people may riot."

3 Meanwhile, Jesus was in Bethany at the home of Simon, a man who had previously had leprosy. While he was eating,* a woman came in with a beautiful alabaster jar of expensive perfume made from essence of nard. She broke open the jar and poured the perfume over his head.

4 Some of those at the table were indignant. "Why waste such expensive perfume?" they asked. 5 "It could have been sold for a year's wages* and the money given to the poor!" So they scolded her harshly.

6 But Jesus replied, "Leave her alone. Why criticize her for doing such a good thing to me? 7 You will always have the poor among you, and you can help them whenever you want to. But you will not always have me. 8 She has done what she could and has anointed my body for burial ahead of time. 9 I tell you the truth, wherever the Good News is preached throughout the world, this woman's deed will be remembered and discussed."

## Judas Agrees to Betray Jesus

10 Then Judas Iscariot, one of the twelve disciples, went to the leading priests to arrange to betray Jesus to them. 11 They were delighted when they heard why he had come, and they promised to give him money. So he began looking for an opportunity to betray Jesus.

## The Last Supper

12 On the first day of the Festival of Unleavened Bread, when the Passover lamb is sacrificed, Jesus' disciples asked him, "Where do you want us to go to prepare the Passover meal for you?"

13 So Jesus sent two of them into Jerusalem with these instructions: "As you go into the city, a man carrying a pitcher of water will meet you. Follow him. 14 At the house he enters, say to the owner, 'The Teacher asks: Where is the guest room where I can eat the Passover meal with my disciples?' 15 He will take you upstairs to a large room that is already set up. That is where you should prepare our meal." 16 So the two disciples went into the city and found everything just as Jesus had said, and they prepared the Passover meal there.

17 In the evening Jesus arrived with the twelve disciples.* 18 As they were at the table* eating, Jesus said, "I tell you the truth, one of you eating with me here will betray me."

19 Greatly distressed, each one asked in turn, "Am I the one?"

20 He replied, "It is one of you twelve who

---

**13:27** Greek *from the four winds.*   **13:30** Or *this age,* or *this nation.*   **13:33** Some manuscripts add *and pray.*   **14:3** Or *reclining.*
**14:5** Greek *for 300 denarii.* A denarius was equivalent to a laborer's full day's wage.   **14:17** Greek *the Twelve.*   **14:18** Or *As they reclined.*

is eating from this bowl with me. ²¹For the Son of Man* must die, as the Scriptures declared long ago. But how terrible it will be for the one who betrays him. It would be far better for that man if he had never been born!"

²²As they were eating, Jesus took some bread and blessed it. Then he broke it in pieces and gave it to the disciples, saying, "Take it, for this is my body."

²³And he took a cup of wine and gave thanks to God for it. He gave it to them, and they all drank from it. **²⁴**And he said to them, "This is my blood, which confirms the covenant* between God and his people. It is poured out as a sacrifice for many. ²⁵I tell you the truth, I will not drink wine again until the day I drink it new in the Kingdom of God."

²⁶Then they sang a hymn and went out to the Mount of Olives.

### Jesus Predicts Peter's Denial

²⁷On the way, Jesus told them, "All of you will desert me. For the Scriptures say,

'God will strike* the Shepherd,
and the sheep will be scattered.'

²⁸But after I am raised from the dead, I will go ahead of you to Galilee and meet you there."

²⁹Peter said to him, "Even if everyone else deserts you, I never will."

³⁰Jesus replied, "I tell you the truth, Peter—this very night, <u>before the rooster crows twice, you will deny three times that you even know me.</u>"

³¹"No!" Peter declared emphatically. "Even if I have to die with you, I will never deny you!" And all the others vowed the same.

### Jesus Prays in Gethsemane

³²They went to the olive grove called Gethsemane, and Jesus said, "Sit here while I go and pray." ³³He took Peter, James, and John with him, and he became deeply troubled and distressed. ³⁴He told them, "My soul is crushed with grief to the point of death. Stay here and keep watch with me."

³⁵He went on a little farther and fell to the ground. He prayed that, if it were possible, the awful hour awaiting him might pass him by. ³⁶"Abba, Father,"* he cried out, "everything is possible for you. Please take this cup of suffering away from me. <u>Yet I want your will to be done, not mine.</u>"

³⁷Then he returned and found the disciples asleep. He said to Peter, "Simon, are you asleep? Couldn't you watch with me even one hour? ³⁸Keep watch and pray, so that you will not give in to temptation. For the spirit is willing, but the body is weak."

**14:21** "Son of Man" is a title Jesus used for himself.   **14:24** Some manuscripts read *the new covenant*.   **14:27** Greek *I will strike*. Zech 13:7.   **14:36** *Abba* is an Aramaic term for "father."

## WHEN God says no
READ MARK 14:32-42

It's hard to accept when God says "no" to our prayers. It's the reply we never want to hear. *If He really cares, why doesn't He do what I ask of Him? God has the power to take this away, so why won't He?*

When God says "no," it doesn't have to mean something is wrong with you or your prayers. After all, He said "no" to His only Son.

Jesus, who lived a life perfectly pleasing to God, prayed for hours in the garden. Mark says He was "deeply troubled," "distressed," and "crushed with grief." He cried out to His Father, who can do anything, and asked that "this cup of suffering" might be taken away. But God said "no" and Jesus was betrayed, arrested, and crucified.

Why? Because the Father didn't love His Son? No, because God had a better plan. He would take His Son's suffering and use it for our salvation. His pain would be our gain. <u>Believe God loves you and has a plan even when He says "no."</u>

[39] Then Jesus left them again and prayed the same prayer as before. [40] When he returned to them again, he found them sleeping, for they couldn't keep their eyes open. And they didn't know what to say.

[41] When he returned to them the third time, he said, "Go ahead and sleep. Have your rest. But no—the time has come. The Son of Man is betrayed into the hands of sinners. [42] Up, let's be going. Look, my betrayer is here!"

## Jesus Is Betrayed and Arrested

[43] And immediately, even as Jesus said this, Judas, one of the twelve disciples, arrived with a crowd of men armed with swords and clubs. They had been sent by the leading priests, the teachers of religious law, and the elders. [44] The traitor, Judas, had given them a prearranged signal: "You will know which one to arrest when I greet him with a kiss. Then you can take him away under guard." [45] As soon as they arrived, Judas walked up to Jesus. "Rabbi!" he exclaimed, and gave him the kiss.

[46] Then the others grabbed Jesus and arrested him. [47] But one of the men with Jesus pulled out his sword and struck the high priest's slave, slashing off his ear.

[48] Jesus asked them, "Am I some dangerous revolutionary, that you come with swords and clubs to arrest me? [49] Why didn't you arrest me in the Temple? I was there among you teaching every day. But these things are happening to fulfill what the Scriptures say about me."

[50] Then all his disciples deserted him and ran away. [51] One young man following behind was clothed only in a long linen shirt. When the mob tried to grab him, [52] he slipped out of his shirt and ran away naked.

## Jesus before the Council

[53] They took Jesus to the high priest's home where the leading priests, the elders, and the teachers of religious law had gathered. [54] Meanwhile, Peter followed him at a distance and went right into the high priest's courtyard. There he sat with the guards, warming himself by the fire.

[55] Inside, the leading priests and the entire high council* were trying to find evidence against Jesus, so they could put him to death. But they couldn't find any. [56] Many false witnesses spoke against him, but they contradicted each other. [57] Finally, some men stood up and gave this false testimony: [58] "We heard him say, 'I will destroy this Temple made with human hands, and in three days I will build another, made without human hands.' " [59] But even then they didn't get their stories straight!

[60] Then the high priest stood up before the others and asked Jesus, "Well, aren't you going to answer these charges? What do you have to say for yourself?" [61] But Jesus was silent and made no reply. Then the high priest asked him, "Are you the Messiah, the Son of the Blessed One?"

[62] Jesus said, "I Am.* And you will see the Son of Man seated in the place of power at God's right hand* and coming on the clouds of heaven.*"

[63] Then the high priest tore his clothing to show his horror and said, "Why do we need other witnesses? [64] You have all heard his blasphemy. What is your verdict?"

"Guilty!" they all cried. "He deserves to die!"

[65] Then some of them began to spit at him, and they blindfolded him and beat him with their fists. "Prophesy to us," they jeered. And the guards slapped him as they took him away.

## Peter Denies Jesus

[66] Meanwhile, Peter was in the courtyard below. One of the servant girls who worked for the high priest came by [67] and noticed Peter warming himself at the fire. She looked at him closely and said, "You were one of those with Jesus of Nazareth.*"

[68] But Peter denied it. "I don't know what you're talking about," he said, and he went out into the entryway. Just then, a rooster crowed.*

[69] When the servant girl saw him standing

14:55 Greek *the Sanhedrin.* 14:62a Or *The 'I Am' is here;* or *I am the Lord.* See Exod 3:14. 14:62b Greek *at the right hand of the power.* See Ps 110:1. 14:62c See Dan 7:13. 14:67 Or *Jesus the Nazarene.* 14:68 Some manuscripts do not include *Just then, a rooster crowed.*

there, she began telling the others, "This man is definitely one of them!" 70But Peter denied it again.

A little later some of the other bystanders confronted Peter and said, "You must be one of them, because you are a Galilean."

71Peter swore, "A curse on me if I'm lying— I don't know this man you're talking about!" 72And immediately the rooster crowed the second time.

Suddenly, Jesus' words flashed through Peter's mind: "Before the rooster crows twice, you will deny three times that you even know me." And he broke down and wept.

## Jesus' Trial before Pilate

**15** Very early in the morning the leading priests, the elders, and the teachers of religious law—the entire high council*— met to discuss their next step. They bound Jesus, led him away, and took him to Pilate, the Roman governor.

2Pilate asked Jesus, "Are you the king of the Jews?"

Jesus replied, "You have said it."

3Then the leading priests kept accusing him of many crimes, 4and Pilate asked him, "Aren't you going to answer them? What about all these charges they are bringing against you?" 5But Jesus said nothing, much to Pilate's surprise.

6Now it was the governor's custom each year during the Passover celebration to re-lease one prisoner—anyone the people re-quested. 7One of the prisoners at that time was Barabbas, a revolutionary who had com-mitted murder in an uprising. 8The crowd went to Pilate and asked him to release a prisoner as usual.

9"Would you like me to release to you this 'King of the Jews'?" Pilate asked. 10(For he realized by now that the leading priests had arrested Jesus out of envy.) 11But at this point the leading priests stirred up the crowd to demand the release of Barabbas in-stead of Jesus. 12Pilate asked them, "Then what should I do with this man you call the king of the Jews?"

13They shouted back, "Crucify him!"

14"Why?" Pilate demanded. "What crime has he committed?"

But the mob roared even louder, "Crucify him!"

15So to pacify the crowd, Pilate released Barabbas to them. He ordered Jesus flogged with a lead-tipped whip, then turned him over to the Roman soldiers to be crucified.

## The Soldiers Mock Jesus

16The soldiers took Jesus into the courtyard of the governor's headquarters (called the Praetorium) and called out the entire regi-ment. 17They dressed him in a purple robe, and they wove thorn branches into a crown and put it on his head. 18Then they saluted him and taunted, "Hail! King of the Jews!" 19And they struck him on the head with a reed stick, spit on him, and dropped to their knees in mock worship. 20When they were finally tired of mocking him, they took off the purple robe and put his own clothes on him again. Then they led him away to be crucified.

## The Crucifixion

21A passerby named Simon, who was from Cyrene,* was coming in from the country-side just then, and the soldiers forced him to carry Jesus' cross. (Simon was the father of Alexander and Rufus.) 22And they brought Jesus to a place called Golgotha (which means "Place of the Skull"). 23They offered him wine drugged with myrrh, but he re-fused it.

24Then the soldiers nailed him to the cross. They divided his clothes and threw dice* to decide who would get each piece. 25It was nine o'clock in the morning when they crucified him. 26A sign was fastened to the cross, announcing the charge against him. It read, "The King of the Jews." 27Two revolutionaries* were crucified with him, one on his right and one on his left.*

29The people passing by shouted abuse, shaking their heads in mockery. "Ha! Look at you now!" they yelled at him. "You said you were going to destroy the Temple and re-

---

**15:1** Greek *the Sanhedrin;* also in 15:43.    **15:21** *Cyrene* was a city in northern Africa.    **15:24** Greek *cast lots.* See Ps 22:18.
**15:27a** Or *Two criminals.*    **15:27b** Some manuscripts add verse 28, *And the Scripture was fulfilled that said, "He was counted among those who were rebels."* See Isa 53:12; also compare Luke 22:37.

build it in three days. ³⁰Well then, save yourself and come down from the cross!"

³¹The leading priests and teachers of religious law also mocked Jesus. "He saved others," they scoffed, "but he can't save himself! ³²Let this Messiah, this King of Israel, come down from the cross so we can see it and believe him!" Even the men who were crucified with Jesus ridiculed him.

### The Death of Jesus

³³At noon, darkness fell across the whole land until three o'clock. ³⁴Then at three o'clock Jesus called out with a loud voice, "Eloi, Eloi, lema sabachthani?" which means "My God, my God, why have you abandoned me?"*

³⁵Some of the bystanders misunderstood and thought he was calling for the prophet Elijah. ³⁶One of them ran and filled a sponge with sour wine, holding it up to him on a reed stick so he could drink. "Wait!" he said. "Let's see whether Elijah comes to take him down!"

³⁷Then Jesus uttered another loud cry and breathed his last. ³⁸And the curtain in the sanctuary of the Temple was torn in two, from top to bottom.

³⁹When the Roman officer* who stood facing him* saw how he had died, he exclaimed, "This man truly was the Son of God!"

⁴⁰Some women were there, watching from a distance, including Mary Magdalene, Mary (the mother of James the younger and of Joseph*), and Salome. ⁴¹They had been followers of Jesus and had cared for him while he was in Galilee. Many other women who had come with him to Jerusalem were also there.

### The Burial of Jesus

⁴²This all happened on Friday, the day of preparation,* the day before the Sabbath. As evening approached, ⁴³Joseph of Arimathea took a risk and went to Pilate and asked for Jesus' body. (Joseph was an honored member of the high council, and he was waiting for the Kingdom of God to come.) ⁴⁴Pilate couldn't believe that Jesus was already dead, so he called for the Roman officer and asked if he had died yet. ⁴⁵The officer confirmed that Jesus was dead, so Pilate told Joseph he could have the body. ⁴⁶Joseph bought a long sheet of linen cloth. Then he took Jesus' body down from the cross, wrapped it in the cloth, and laid it in a tomb that had been carved out of the rock. Then he rolled a stone in front of the entrance. ⁴⁷Mary Magdalene and Mary the mother of Joseph saw where Jesus' body was laid.

### The Resurrection

**16** Saturday evening, when the Sabbath ended, Mary Magdalene, Mary the mother of James, and Salome went out and purchased burial spices so they could anoint Jesus' body. ²Very early on Sunday morning,* just at sunrise, they went to the tomb. ³On the way they were asking each other, "Who will roll away the stone for us from the entrance to the tomb?" ⁴But as they arrived, they looked up and saw that the stone, which was very large, had already been rolled aside.

⁵When they entered the tomb, they saw a young man clothed in a white robe sitting on the right side. The women were shocked, ⁶but the angel said, "Don't be alarmed. You are looking for Jesus of Nazareth,* who was crucified. He isn't here! He is risen from the dead! Look, this is where they laid his body. ⁷Now go and tell his disciples, including Peter, that Jesus is going ahead of you to Galilee. You will see him there, just as he told you before he died."

⁸The women fled from the tomb, trembling and bewildered, and they said nothing to anyone because they were too frightened.*

### [Shorter Ending of Mark]

Then they briefly reported all this to Peter and his companions. Afterward Jesus himself sent them out from east to west with the sacred and unfailing message of salvation that gives eternal life. Amen.

**15:34** Ps 22:1.   **15:39a** Greek *the centurion;* similarly in 15:44, 45.   **15:39b** Some manuscripts add *heard his cry and.* **15:40** Greek *Joses;* also in 15:47. See Matt 27:56.   **15:42** Greek *It was the day of preparation.*   **16:2** Greek *on the first day of the week;* also in 16:9.   **16:6** Or *Jesus the Nazarene.*   **16:8** The most reliable early manuscripts of the Gospel of Mark end at verse 8. Other manuscripts include various endings to the Gospel. A few include both the "shorter ending" and the "longer ending." The majority of manuscripts include the "longer ending" immediately after verse 8.

*[Longer Ending of Mark]*

⁹After Jesus rose from the dead early on Sunday morning, the first person who saw him was Mary Magdalene, the woman from whom he had cast out seven demons. ¹⁰She went to the disciples, who were grieving and weeping, and told them what had happened. ¹¹But when she told them that Jesus was alive and she had seen him, they didn't believe her.

¹²Afterward he appeared in a different form to two of his followers who were walking from Jerusalem into the country. ¹³They rushed back to tell the others, but no one believed them.

¹⁴Still later he appeared to the eleven disciples as they were eating together. He rebuked them for their stubborn unbelief because they refused to believe those who had seen him after he had been raised from the dead.*

¹⁵And then he told them, "Go into all the world and preach the Good News to everyone. ¹⁶Anyone who believes and is baptized will be saved. But anyone who refuses to believe will be condemned. ¹⁷These miraculous signs will accompany those who believe: They will cast out demons in my name, and they will speak in new languages.* ¹⁸They will be able to handle snakes with safety, and if they drink anything poisonous, it won't hurt them. They will be able to place their hands on the sick, and they will be healed."

¹⁹When the Lord Jesus had finished talking with them, he was taken up into heaven and sat down in the place of honor at God's right hand. ²⁰And the disciples went everywhere and preached, and the Lord worked through them, confirming what they said by many miraculous signs.

**16:14** Some early manuscripts add: *And they excused themselves, saying, "This age of lawlessness and unbelief is under Satan, who does not permit God's truth and power to conquer the evil (unclean) spirits. Therefore, reveal your justice now." This is what they said to Christ. And Christ replied to them, "The period of years of Satan's power has been fulfilled, but other dreadful things will happen soon. And I was handed over to death for those who have sinned, so that they may return to the truth and sin no more, and so they may inherit the spiritual, incorruptible, and righteous glory in heaven."* **16:17** Or *new tongues;* some manuscripts omit *new.*

# LUKE

> *Jesus answered them, "Healthy people don't need a doctor—sick people do."*
>
> LUKE 5:31

The doctor-patient relationship is so crucial when we're dealing with a serious illness. We need to have confidence in our physicians and yet not just blindly accept every suggestion they make. A really good physician won't feel threatened if we seek a second opinion, and the best doctors always are open to learning something new. The worst doctors are those who casually dismiss our worries and believe in their own minds that they know it all. Once in a while, we get really blessed by meeting a physician who understands we are more than just a physical body and who wants to care for our minds as well as our spirits.

The writer of this Gospel must have been that kind of a physician. Luke was a Gentile doctor and a traveling companion of Paul in the book of Acts. As an educated man, he examined all the evidence about Jesus and wrote this account to show how He was both fully man and fully God—the Great Physician, who can heal a body in an instant and heal a soul for all eternity.

This Gospel records many healings of sick bodies and troubled minds as Jesus fulfilled David's words in Psalm 103:3: "He forgives all my sins and heals all my diseases." Jesus' healings also showed He is truly divine because in Exodus 15:26 God declares: "I am the LORD who heals you."

Whatever your relationship with your earthly physician, as you read the Gospel of Luke, we pray that your relationship with the Great Physician will become very real and very powerful.

## Introduction

**1** Many people have set out to write accounts about the events that have been fulfilled among us. ²They used the eyewitness reports circulating among us from the early disciples.* ³Having carefully investigated everything from the beginning, I also have decided to write a careful account for you, most honorable Theophilus, ⁴so you can be certain of the truth of everything you were taught.

## The Birth of ⌐John the Baptist¬ Foretold

⁵When Herod was king of Judea, there was a Jewish priest named Zechariah. He was a member of the priestly order of Abijah, and his wife, Elizabeth, was also from the priestly line of Aaron. ⁶Zechariah and Elizabeth were righteous in God's eyes, careful to obey all of the Lord's commandments and regulations. ⁷They had no children because Elizabeth was unable to conceive, and they were both very old.

⁸One day Zechariah was serving God in the Temple, for his order was on duty that week. ⁹As was the custom of the priests, he was chosen by lot to enter the sanctuary of the Lord and burn incense. ¹⁰While the incense was being burned, a great crowd stood outside, praying.

¹¹While Zechariah was in the sanctuary, an angel of the Lord appeared to him, standing to the right of the incense altar. ¹²Zechariah was shaken and overwhelmed with fear when he saw him. ¹³But the angel said, "Don't be afraid, Zechariah! God has heard your prayer. Your wife, Elizabeth, will give you a son, and you are to name him John. ¹⁴You will have great joy and gladness, and many will rejoice at his birth, ¹⁵for he will be great in the eyes of the Lord. He must never touch wine or other alcoholic drinks. He will be filled with the Holy Spirit, even before his birth.* ¹⁶And he will turn many Israelites to the Lord their God. ¹⁷He will be a man with

the spirit and power of Elijah. He will prepare the people for the coming of the Lord. He will turn the hearts of the fathers to their children,* and he will cause those who are rebellious to accept the wisdom of the godly."

¹⁸Zechariah said to the angel, "How can I be sure this will happen? I'm an old man now, and my wife is also well along in years."

¹⁹Then the angel said, "I am Gabriel! I stand in the very presence of God. It was he who sent me to bring you this good news! ²⁰But now, since you didn't believe what I said, you will be silent and unable to speak until the child is born. For my words will certainly be fulfilled at the proper time."

²¹Meanwhile, the people were waiting for Zechariah to come out of the sanctuary, wondering why he was taking so long. ²²When he finally did come out, he couldn't speak to them. Then they realized from his gestures and his silence that he must have seen a vision in the sanctuary.

²³When Zechariah's week of service in the Temple was over, he returned home. ²⁴Soon afterward his wife, Elizabeth, became pregnant and went into seclusion for five months. ²⁵"How kind the Lord is!" she exclaimed. "He has taken away my disgrace of having no children."

## The Birth of Jesus Foretold

²⁶In the sixth month of Elizabeth's pregnancy, God sent the angel Gabriel to Nazareth, a village in Galilee, ²⁷to a virgin named Mary. She was engaged to be married to a man named Joseph, a descendant of King David. **28**Gabriel appeared to her and said, "Greetings, favored woman! The Lord is with you!*"

²⁹Confused and disturbed, Mary tried to think what the angel could mean. ³⁰"Don't be afraid, Mary," the angel told her, "for you have found favor with God! ³¹You will conceive and give birth to a son, and you will

1:2 Greek *from those who from the beginning were servants of the word.*   1:15 Or *even from birth.*   1:17 See Mal 4:5-6.
1:28 Some manuscripts add *Blessed are you among women.*

name him Jesus. [32]He will be very great and will be called the Son of the Most High. The Lord God will give him the throne of his ancestor David. [33]And he will reign over Israel* forever; his Kingdom will never end!"

[34]Mary asked the angel, "But how can this happen? I am a virgin."

[35]The angel replied, "The Holy Spirit will come upon you, and the power of the Most High will overshadow you. So the baby to be born will be holy, and he will be called the Son of God. [36]What's more, your relative Elizabeth has become pregnant in her old age! People used to say she was barren, but she's now in her sixth month. [37]For nothing is impossible with God.*"

[38]Mary responded, "I am the Lord's servant. May everything you have said about me come true." And then the angel left her.

### Mary Visits Elizabeth

[39]A few days later Mary hurried to the hill country of Judea, to the town [40]where Zechariah lived. She entered the house and greeted Elizabeth. [41]At the sound of Mary's greeting, Elizabeth's child leaped within her, and Elizabeth was filled with the Holy Spirit.

[42]Elizabeth gave a glad cry and exclaimed to Mary, "God has blessed you above all women, and your child is blessed. [43]Why am I so honored, that the mother of my Lord should visit me? [44]When I heard your greeting, the baby in my womb jumped for joy. [45]You are blessed because you believed that the Lord would do what he said."

### The Magnificat: Mary's Song of Praise

[46]Mary responded,

"Oh, how my soul praises the Lord.
[47]    How my spirit rejoices in God my
        Savior!
[48]For he took notice of his lowly servant
        girl,
        and from now on all generations will
        call me blessed.
[49]For the Mighty One is holy,
        and he has done great things for me.
[50]He shows mercy from generation to
        generation
        to all who fear him.

[51]His mighty arm has done tremendous
        things!
    He has scattered the proud and
        haughty ones.
[52]He has brought down princes from their
        thrones
    and exalted the humble.
[53]He has filled the hungry with good things
    and sent the rich away with empty
        hands.
[54]He has helped his servant Israel
    and remembered to be merciful.
[55]For he made this promise to our
        ancestors,
    to Abraham and his children forever."

[56]Mary stayed with Elizabeth about three months and then went back to her own home.

### The Birth of John the Baptist

[57]When it was time for Elizabeth's baby to be born, she gave birth to a son. [58]And when her neighbors and relatives heard that the Lord had been very merciful to her, everyone rejoiced with her.

[59]When the baby was eight days old, they all came for the circumcision ceremony. They wanted to name him Zechariah, after his father. [60]But Elizabeth said, "No! His name is John!"

[61]"What?" they exclaimed. "There is no one in all your family by that name." [62]So they used gestures to ask the baby's father what he wanted to name him. [63]He motioned for a writing tablet, and to everyone's surprise he wrote, "His name is John." [64]Instantly Zechariah could speak again, and he began praising God.

[65]Awe fell upon the whole neighborhood, and the news of what had happened spread throughout the Judean hills. [66]Everyone who heard about it reflected on these events and asked, "What will this child turn out to be?" For the hand of the Lord was surely upon him in a special way.

### Zechariah's Prophecy

[67]Then his father, Zechariah, was filled with the Holy Spirit and gave this prophecy:

**1:33** Greek *over the house of Jacob.*   **1:37** Some manuscripts read *For the word of God will never fail.*

68 "Praise the Lord, the God of Israel,
  because he has visited and redeemed
    his people.
69 He has sent us a mighty Savior*
  from the royal line of his servant David,
70 just as he promised
  through his holy prophets long ago.
71 Now we will be saved from our enemies
  and from all who hate us.
72 He has been merciful to our ancestors
  by remembering his sacred covenant—
73 the covenant he swore with an oath
  to our ancestor Abraham.
74 We have been rescued from our enemies
  so we can serve God without fear,
75 in holiness and righteousness
  for as long as we live.

76 "And you, my little son,
  will be called the prophet of the
    Most High,
  because you will prepare the way for
    the Lord.
77 You will tell his people how to find
    salvation
  through forgiveness of their sins.
78 Because of God's tender mercy,
  the morning light from heaven is about
    to break upon us,*
79 to give light to those who sit in darkness
  and in the shadow of death,
  and to guide us to the path of peace."

80 John grew up and became strong in spirit. And he lived in the wilderness until he began his public ministry to Israel.

## The Birth of Jesus

2 At that time the Roman emperor, Augustus, decreed that a census should be taken throughout the Roman Empire. 2(This was the first census taken when Quirinius was governor of Syria.) 3All returned to their own ancestral towns to register for this census. 4And because Joseph was a descendant of King David, he had to go to Bethlehem in Judea, David's ancient home. He traveled there from the village of Nazareth in Galilee. 5He took with him Mary, his fiancée, who was now obviously pregnant. 6And while they were there, the time came for her baby to be born. 7She gave birth to her first child, a son. She wrapped him snugly in strips of cloth and laid him in a manger, because there was no lodging available for them.

## The Shepherds and Angels

8That night there were shepherds staying in the fields nearby, guarding their flocks of sheep. 9Suddenly, an angel of the Lord appeared among them, and the radiance of the Lord's glory surrounded them. They were terrified, 10but the angel reassured them. "Don't be afraid!" he said. "I bring you good news that will bring great joy to all people. 11The Savior—yes, the Messiah, the Lord—has been born today in Bethlehem, the city of David! 12And you will recognize him by this sign: You will find a baby wrapped snugly in strips of cloth, lying in a manger."

13Suddenly, the angel was joined by a vast host of others—the armies of heaven—praising God and saying,

14 "Glory to God in highest heaven,
  and peace on earth to those with
    whom God is pleased."

15When the angels had returned to heaven, the shepherds said to each other, "Let's go to Bethlehem! Let's see this thing that has happened, which the Lord has told us about."

16They hurried to the village and found Mary and Joseph. And there was the baby, lying in the manger. 17After seeing him, the shepherds told everyone what had happened and what the angel had said to them about this child. 18All who heard the shepherds' story were astonished, 19but Mary kept all these things in her heart and thought about them often. 20The shepherds went back to their flocks, glorifying and praising God for all they had heard and seen. It was just as the angel had told them.

## Jesus Is Presented in the Temple

21Eight days later, when the baby was circumcised, he was named Jesus, the name given him by the angel even before he was conceived.

1:69 Greek *has raised up a horn of salvation for us.*   1:78 Or *the Morning Light from Heaven is about to visit us.*

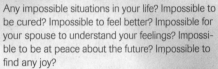

22Then it was time for their purification offering, as required by the law of Moses after the birth of a child; so his parents took him to Jerusalem to present him to the Lord. 23The law of the Lord says, "If a woman's first child is a boy, he must be dedicated to the LORD."* 24So they offered the sacrifice required in the law of the Lord—"either a pair of turtledoves or two young pigeons."*

### The Prophecy of Simeon

25At that time there was a man in Jerusalem named Simeon. He was righteous and devout and was eagerly waiting for the Messiah to come and rescue Israel. The Holy Spirit was upon him 26and had revealed to him that he would not die until he had seen the Lord's Messiah. 27That day the Spirit led him to the Temple. So when Mary and Joseph came to present the baby Jesus to the Lord as the law required, 28Simeon was there. He took the child in his arms and praised God, saying,

29"Sovereign Lord, now let your servant die in peace,
   as you have promised.
30I have seen your salvation,
31   which you have prepared for all people.
32He is a light to reveal God to the nations,
   and he is the glory of your people Israel!"

33Jesus' parents were amazed at what was being said about him. 34Then Simeon blessed them, and he said to Mary, the baby's mother, "This child is destined to cause many in Israel to fall, but he will be a joy to many others. He has been sent as a sign from God, but many will oppose him. 35As a result, the deepest thoughts of many hearts will be revealed. And a sword will pierce your very soul."

### The Prophecy of Anna

36Anna, a prophet, was also there in the Temple. She was the daughter of Phanuel from the tribe of Asher, and she was very old. Her husband died when they had been married only seven years. 37Then she lived as a widow to the age of eighty-four.* She never left the Temple but stayed there day

## IMPOSSIBLE situations
READ LUKE 1:37

Any impossible situations in your life? Impossible to be cured? Impossible to feel better? Impossible for your spouse to understand your feelings? Impossible to be at peace about the future? Impossible to find any joy?

Don't run out ahead of God by trying to deal with all the endless negative possibilities facing you down the road. Never forget we have a God who loves to do the improbable and specializes in the impossible: things like healing "hopeless cases," filling us with peace instead of worry, and turning heavy hearts into hearts of joy.

Ask the God of the improbable and even the impossible to meet your deepest needs. "For nothing is impossible with God."

and night, worshiping God with fasting and prayer. 38She came along just as Simeon was talking with Mary and Joseph, and she began praising God. She talked about the child to everyone who had been waiting expectantly for God to rescue Jerusalem.

39When Jesus' parents had fulfilled all the requirements of the law of the Lord, they returned home to Nazareth in Galilee. 40There the child grew up healthy and strong. He was filled with wisdom, and God's favor was on him.

### Jesus Speaks with the Teachers

41Every year Jesus' parents went to Jerusalem for the Passover festival. 42When Jesus was twelve years old, they attended the festival as usual. 43After the celebration was over, they started home to Nazareth, but Jesus stayed behind in Jerusalem. His parents didn't miss him at first, 44because they assumed he was among the other travelers. But when he didn't show up that evening, they started looking for him among their relatives and friends.

45When they couldn't find him, they went back to Jerusalem to search for him there. 46Three days later they finally discovered him in the Temple, sitting among the religious teachers, listening to them and asking questions. 47All who heard him were amazed at his understanding and his answers.

2:23 Exod 13:2.   2:24 Lev 12:8.   2:37 Or She had been a widow for eighty-four years.

**48**His parents didn't know what to think. "Son," his mother said to him, "why have you done this to us? Your father and I have been frantic, searching for you everywhere."

**49**"But why did you need to search?" he asked. "Didn't you know that I must be in my Father's house?"* **50**But they didn't understand what he meant.

**51**Then he returned to Nazareth with them and was obedient to them. And his mother stored all these things in her heart.

**52**Jesus grew in wisdom and in stature and in favor with God and all the people.

### John the Baptist Prepares the Way

**3** It was now the fifteenth year of the reign of Tiberius, the Roman emperor. Pontius Pilate was governor over Judea; Herod Antipas was ruler* over Galilee; his brother Philip was ruler* over Iturea and Traconitis; Lysanias was ruler over Abilene. **2**Annas and Caiaphas were the high priests. At this time a message from God came to John son of Zechariah, who was living in the wilderness. **3**Then John went from place to place on both sides of the Jordan River, preaching that people should be baptized to show that they had repented of their sins and turned to God to be forgiven. **4**Isaiah had spoken of John when he said,

"He is a voice shouting in the wilderness,
'Prepare the way for the LORD's coming!
　Clear the road for him!
**5** The valleys will be filled,
　and the mountains and hills made
　　level.
The curves will be straightened,
　and the rough places made smooth.
**6** And then all people will see
　the salvation sent from God.'"*

**7**When the crowds came to John for baptism, he said, "You brood of snakes! Who warned you to flee God's coming wrath? **8**Prove by the way you live that you have repented of your sins and turned to God. Don't just say to each other, 'We're safe, for we are descendants of Abraham.' That means nothing, for I tell you, God can create children of Abraham from these very stones. **9**Even now the ax of God's judgment is poised, ready to sever the roots of the trees. Yes, every tree that does not produce good fruit will be chopped down and thrown into the fire."

**10**The crowds asked, "What should we do?"

**11**John replied, "If you have two shirts, give one to the poor. If you have food, share it with those who are hungry."

**12**Even corrupt tax collectors came to be baptized and asked, "Teacher, what should we do?"

**13**He replied, "Collect no more taxes than the government requires."

**14**"What should we do?" asked some soldiers.

John replied, "Don't extort money or make false accusations. And be content with your pay."

**15**Everyone was expecting the Messiah to come soon, and they were eager to know whether John might be the Messiah. **16**John answered their questions by saying, "I baptize you with* water; but someone is coming soon who is greater than I am—so much greater that I'm not even worthy to be his slave and untie the straps of his sandals. He will baptize you with the Holy Spirit and with fire.* **17**He is ready to separate the chaff from the wheat with his winnowing fork. Then he will clean up the threshing area, gathering the wheat into his barn but burning the chaff with never-ending fire." **18**John used many such warnings as he announced the Good News to the people.

**19**John also publicly criticized Herod Antipas, the ruler of Galilee,* for marrying Herodias, his brother's wife, and for many other wrongs he had done. **20**So Herod put John in prison, adding this sin to his many others.

### The Baptism of Jesus

**21**One day when the crowds were being baptized, Jesus himself was baptized. As he was praying, the heavens opened, **22**and the Holy Spirit, in bodily form, descended on him like a dove. And a voice from heaven said, "You are my dearly loved Son, and you bring me great joy.*"

---

**2:49** Or *"Didn't you realize that I should be involved with my Father's affairs?"*　**3:1a** Greek *Herod was tetrarch.* Herod Antipas was a son of King Herod.　**3:1b** Greek *tetrarch;* also in 3:1c.　**3:4-6** Isa 40:3-5 (Greek version).　**3:16a** Or *in.*　**3:16b** Or *in the Holy Spirit and in fire.*　**3:19** Greek *Herod the tetrarch.*　**3:22** Some manuscripts read *my Son, and today I have become your Father.*

## The Ancestors of Jesus

23 Jesus was about thirty years old when he began his public ministry.

Jesus was known as the son of Joseph.
Joseph was the son of Heli.
24 Heli was the son of Matthat.
Matthat was the son of Levi.
Levi was the son of Melki.
Melki was the son of Jannai.
Jannai was the son of Joseph.
25 Joseph was the son of Mattathias.
Mattathias was the son of Amos.
Amos was the son of Nahum.
Nahum was the son of Esli.
Esli was the son of Naggai.
26 Naggai was the son of Maath.
Maath was the son of Mattathias.
Mattathias was the son of Semein.
Semein was the son of Josech.
Josech was the son of Joda.
27 Joda was the son of Joanan.
Joanan was the son of Rhesa.
Rhesa was the son of Zerubbabel.
Zerubbabel was the son of Shealtiel.
Shealtiel was the son of Neri.
28 Neri was the son of Melki.
Melki was the son of Addi.
Addi was the son of Cosam.
Cosam was the son of Elmadam.
Elmadam was the son of Er.
29 Er was the son of Joshua.
Joshua was the son of Eliezer.
Eliezer was the son of Jorim.
Jorim was the son of Matthat.
Matthat was the son of Levi.
30 Levi was the son of Simeon.
Simeon was the son of Judah.
Judah was the son of Joseph.
Joseph was the son of Jonam.
Jonam was the son of Eliakim.
31 Eliakim was the son of Melea.
Melea was the son of Menna.
Menna was the son of Mattatha.
Mattatha was the son of Nathan.
Nathan was the son of David.
32 David was the son of Jesse.
Jesse was the son of Obed.
Obed was the son of Boaz.
Boaz was the son of Salmon.*
Salmon was the son of Nahshon.
33 Nahshon was the son of
Amminadab.
Amminadab was the son of Admin.
Admin was the son of Arni.*
Arni was the son of Hezron.
Hezron was the son of Perez.
Perez was the son of Judah.
34 Judah was the son of Jacob.
Jacob was the son of Isaac.
Isaac was the son of Abraham.
Abraham was the son of Terah.
Terah was the son of Nahor.
35 Nahor was the son of Serug.
Serug was the son of Reu.
Reu was the son of Peleg.
Peleg was the son of Eber.
Eber was the son of Shelah.
36 Shelah was the son of Cainan.
Cainan was the son of Arphaxad.
Arphaxad was the son of Shem.
Shem was the son of Noah.
Noah was the son of Lamech.
37 Lamech was the son of Methuselah.
Methuselah was the son of Enoch.
Enoch was the son of Jared.
Jared was the son of Mahalalel.
Mahalalel was the son of Kenan.
38 Kenan was the son of Enosh.*
Enosh was the son of Seth.
Seth was the son of Adam.
Adam was the son of God.

## The Temptation of Jesus

4 Then Jesus, full of the Holy Spirit, returned from the Jordan River. He was led by the Spirit in the wilderness,* 2where he was tempted by the devil for forty days. Jesus ate nothing all that time and became very hungry.

3 Then the devil said to him, "If you are the Son of God, tell this stone to become a loaf of bread."

4 But Jesus told him, "No! The Scriptures say, 'People do not live by bread alone.'*"

5 Then the devil took him up and revealed to him all the kingdoms of the world in a moment of time. 6"I will give you the glory

---

**3:32** Greek *Sala*, a variant spelling of Salmon; also in 3:32b. See Ruth 4:22.   **3:33** Some manuscripts read *Amminadab was the son of Aram. Arni* and *Aram* are alternate spellings of Ram. See 1 Chr 2:9-10.   **3:38** Greek *Enos*, a variant spelling of Enosh; also in 3:38b. See Gen 5:6.   **4:1** Some manuscripts read *into the wilderness*.   **4:4** Deut 8:3.

of these kingdoms and authority over them," the devil said, "because they are mine to give to anyone I please. ⁷I will give it all to you if you will worship me."

⁸Jesus replied, "The Scriptures say,

'You must worship the LORD your God
and serve only him.'* "

⁹Then the devil took him to Jerusalem, to the highest point of the Temple, and said, "If you are the Son of God, jump off! ¹⁰For the Scriptures say,

'He will order his angels to protect and
    guard you.
¹¹ And they will hold you up with their
    hands
    so you won't even hurt your foot
    on a stone.'*"

¹²Jesus responded, "The Scriptures also say,' You must not test the LORD your God.'* "

¹³When the devil had finished tempting Jesus, he left him until the next opportunity came.

## Jesus Rejected at Nazareth

¹⁴Then Jesus returned to Galilee, filled with the Holy Spirit's power. Reports about him spread quickly through the whole region. ¹⁵He taught regularly in their synagogues and was praised by everyone.

¹⁶When he came to the village of Nazareth, his boyhood home, he went as usual to the synagogue on the Sabbath and stood up to read the Scriptures. ¹⁷The scroll of Isaiah the prophet was handed to him. He unrolled the scroll and found the place where this was written:

¹⁸"The Spirit of the LORD is upon me,
    for he has anointed me to bring Good
        News to the poor.
He has sent me to proclaim that captives
    will be released,
    that the blind will see,
that the oppressed will be set free,
¹⁹    and that the time of the LORD's favor
        has come.*"

²⁰He rolled up the scroll, handed it back to the attendant, and sat down. All eyes in the synagogue looked at him intently. ²¹Then he began to speak to them. " The Scripture you've just heard has been fulfilled this very day!"

²²Everyone spoke well of him and was amazed by the gracious words that came from his lips. "How can this be?" they asked. "Isn't this Joseph's son?"

²³Then he said, " You will undoubtedly quote me this proverb: 'Physician, heal yourself'—meaning, 'Do miracles here in your hometown like those you did in Capernaum.' ²⁴But I tell you the truth, no prophet is accepted in his own hometown.

²⁵"Certainly there were many needy widows in Israel in Elijah's time, when the heavens were closed for three and a half years, and a severe famine devastated the land. ²⁶Yet Elijah was not sent to any of them. He was sent instead to a foreigner—a widow of Zarephath in the land of Sidon. ²⁷And there were many lepers in Israel in the time of the prophet Elisha, but the only one healed was Naaman, a Syrian."

²⁸When they heard this, the people in the synagogue were furious. ²⁹Jumping up, they mobbed him and forced him to the edge of the hill on which the town was built. They intended to push him over the cliff, ³⁰but he passed right through the crowd and went on his way.

## Jesus Casts Out a Demon

³¹Then Jesus went to Capernaum, a town in Galilee, and taught there in the synagogue every Sabbath day. ³²There, too, the people were amazed at his teaching, for he spoke with authority.

³³Once when he was in the synagogue, a man possessed by a demon—an evil* spirit—began shouting at Jesus, ³⁴"Go away! Why are you interfering with us, Jesus of Nazareth? Have you come to destroy us? I know who you are—the Holy One sent from God!"

³⁵Jesus cut him short. "Be quiet! Come out of the man," he ordered. At that, the demon threw the man to the floor as the crowd watched; then it came out of him without hurting him further.

4:8 Deut 6:13.   4:10-11 Ps 91:11-12.   4:12 Deut 6:16.   4:18-19 Or *and to proclaim the acceptable year of the LORD.* Isa 61:1-2 (Greek version); 58:6.   4:33 Greek *unclean;* also in 4:36.

³⁶Amazed, the people exclaimed, "What authority and power this man's words possess! Even evil spirits obey him, and they flee at his command!" ³⁷The news about Jesus spread through every village in the entire region.

## Jesus Heals Many People

³⁸After leaving the synagogue that day, Jesus went to Simon's home, where he found Simon's mother-in-law very sick with a high fever. "Please heal her," everyone begged. ³⁹Standing at her bedside, he rebuked the fever, and it left her. And she got up at once and prepared a meal for them.

⁴⁰As the sun went down that evening, people throughout the village brought sick family members to Jesus. No matter what their diseases were, the touch of his hand healed every one. ⁴¹Many were possessed by demons; and the demons came out at his command, shouting, "You are the Son of God!" But because they knew he was the Messiah, he rebuked them and refused to let them speak.

## Jesus Continues to Preach

⁴²Early the next morning Jesus went out to an isolated place. The crowds searched everywhere for him, and when they finally found him, they begged him not to leave them. ⁴³But he replied, "I must preach the Good News of the Kingdom of God in other towns, too, because that is why I was sent." ⁴⁴So he continued to travel around, preaching in synagogues throughout Judea.*

## The First Disciples

**5** One day as Jesus was preaching on the shore of the Sea of Galilee,* great crowds pressed in on him to listen to the word of God. ²He noticed two empty boats at the water's edge, for the fishermen had left them and were washing their nets. ³Stepping into one of the boats, Jesus asked Simon,* its owner, to push it out into the water. So he sat in the boat and taught the crowds from there.

⁴When he had finished speaking, he said to Simon, "Now go out where it is deeper, and let down your nets to catch some fish."

⁵"Master," Simon replied, "we worked hard all last night and didn't catch a thing. But if you say so, I'll let the nets down again." ⁶And this time their nets were so full of fish they began to tear! ⁷A shout for help brought their partners in the other boat, and soon both boats were filled with fish and on the verge of sinking.

⁸When Simon Peter realized what had happened, he fell to his knees before Jesus and said, "Oh, Lord, please leave me—I'm too much of a sinner to be around you." ⁹For he was awestruck by the number of fish they had caught, as were the others with him. ¹⁰His partners, James and John, the sons of Zebedee, were also amazed.

Jesus replied to Simon, "Don't be afraid! From now on you'll be fishing for people!" ¹¹And as soon as they landed, they left everything and followed Jesus.

## Jesus Heals a Man with Leprosy

¹²In one of the villages, Jesus met a man with an advanced case of leprosy. When the man saw Jesus, he bowed with his face to the ground, begging to be healed. "Lord," he said, "if you are willing, you can heal me and make me clean."

¹³Jesus reached out and touched him. "I am willing," he said. "Be healed!" And instantly the leprosy disappeared. ¹⁴Then Jesus instructed him not to tell anyone what had happened. He said, "Go to the priest and let him examine you. Take along the offering required in the law of Moses for those who have been healed of leprosy.* This will be a public testimony that you have been cleansed."

¹⁵But despite Jesus' instructions, the report of his power spread even faster, and vast crowds came to hear him preach and to be healed of their diseases. ¹⁶But Jesus often withdrew to the wilderness for prayer.

## Jesus Heals a Paralyzed Man

¹⁷One day while Jesus was teaching, some Pharisees and teachers of religious law were sitting nearby. (It seemed that these men showed up from every village in all Galilee and Judea, as well as from Jerusalem.) And

**4:44** Some manuscripts read *Galilee.*   **5:1** Greek *Lake Gennesaret,* another name for the Sea of Galilee.   **5:3** *Simon* is called "Peter" in 6:14 and thereafter.   **5:14** See Lev 14:2-32.

the Lord's healing power was strongly with Jesus.

18Some men came carrying a paralyzed man on a sleeping mat. They tried to take him inside to Jesus, 19but they couldn't reach him because of the crowd. So they went up to the roof and took off some tiles. Then they lowered the sick man on his mat down into the crowd, right in front of Jesus. 20Seeing their faith, Jesus said to the man, "Young man, your sins are forgiven."

21But the Pharisees and teachers of religious law said to themselves, "Who does he think he is? That's blasphemy! Only God can forgive sins!"

22Jesus knew what they were thinking, so he asked them, "Why do you question this in your hearts? 23Is it easier to say 'Your sins are forgiven,' or 'Stand up and walk'? 24So I will prove to you that the Son of Man* has the authority on earth to forgive sins." Then Jesus turned to the paralyzed man and said, "Stand up, pick up your mat, and go home!"

25And immediately, as everyone watched, the man jumped up, picked up his mat, and went home praising God. 26Everyone was gripped with great wonder and awe, and they praised God, exclaiming, "We have seen amazing things today!"

### Jesus Calls Levi (Matthew)

27Later, as Jesus left the town, he saw a tax collector named Levi sitting at his tax collector's booth. "Follow me and be my disciple," Jesus said to him. 28So Levi got up, left everything, and followed him.

29Later, Levi held a banquet in his home with Jesus as the guest of honor. Many of Levi's fellow tax collectors and other guests also ate with them. 30But the Pharisees and their teachers of religious law complained bitterly to Jesus' disciples, "Why do you eat and drink with such scum?*"

31Jesus answered them, "Healthy people don't need a doctor—sick people do. 32I have come to call not those who think they are righteous, but those who know they are sinners and need to repent."

### A Discussion about Fasting

33One day some people said to Jesus, "John the Baptist's disciples fast and pray regularly, and so do the disciples of the Pharisees. Why are your disciples always eating and drinking?"

34Jesus responded, "Do wedding guests fast while celebrating with the groom? Of course not. 35But someday the groom will be taken away from them, and then they will fast."

5:24 "Son of Man" is a title Jesus used for himself.    5:30 Greek *with tax collectors and sinners?*

# EDGE of a cliff

READ LUKE 4:16-30

Ever hear a sermon where the congregation jumped up, chased the pastor to the edge of town, and wanted to push him off a cliff? That's just what happened to Jesus after His first "sermon" in His hometown of Nazareth. He read a messianic prophecy from Isaiah 61 and announced He had just fulfilled that Scripture. Jesus angered the synagogue crowd by telling them He wouldn't be doing as many miracles in His hometown because they hadn't accepted Him as a true prophet.

Here we have a picture of Jesus doing just what God wanted Him to and yet something really bad happened to Him. So much for the notion that if we live for God troubles won't come our way! It *is* possible to be doing everything "right" and still have things go wrong. You may have a "right," close relationship with God . . . and yet troubles are chasing you to the edge of a cliff.

Be encouraged: Just as He did for Jesus and as the gospel song promises, "God will make a way where there seems to be no way."

36Then Jesus gave them this illustration: "No one tears a piece of cloth from a new garment and uses it to patch an old garment. For then the new garment would be ruined, and the new patch wouldn't even match the old garment.

37"And no one puts new wine into old wineskins. For the new wine would burst the wineskins, spilling the wine and ruining the skins. 38New wine must be stored in new wineskins. 39But no one who drinks the old wine seems to want the new wine. 'The old is just fine,' they say."

## A Discussion about the Sabbath

**6** One Sabbath day as Jesus was walking through some grainfields, his disciples broke off heads of grain, rubbed off the husks in their hands, and ate the grain. 2But some Pharisees said, "Why are you breaking the law by harvesting grain on the Sabbath?"

3Jesus replied, "Haven't you read in the Scriptures what David did when he and his companions were hungry? 4He went into the house of God and broke the law by eating the sacred loaves of bread that only the priests can eat. He also gave some to his companions." 5And Jesus added, "The Son of Man* is Lord, even over the Sabbath."

## Jesus Heals on the Sabbath

6On another Sabbath day, a man with a deformed right hand was in the synagogue while Jesus was teaching. 7The teachers of religious law and the Pharisees watched Jesus closely. If he healed the man's hand, they planned to accuse him of working on the Sabbath.

8But Jesus knew their thoughts. He said to the man with the deformed hand, "Come and stand in front of everyone." So the man came forward. 9Then Jesus said to his critics, "I have a question for you. Does the law permit good deeds on the Sabbath, or is it a day for doing evil? Is this a day to save life or to destroy it?"

10He looked around at them one by one and then said to the man, "Hold out your hand." So the man held out his hand, and it was restored! 11At this, the enemies of Jesus were wild with rage and began to discuss what to do with him.

## Jesus Chooses the Twelve Apostles

12One day soon afterward Jesus went up on a mountain to pray, and he prayed to God all night. 13At daybreak he called together all of his disciples and chose twelve of them to be apostles. Here are their names:

14 Simon (whom he named Peter),
    Andrew (Peter's brother),
    James,
    John,
    Philip,
    Bartholomew,
15 Matthew,
    Thomas,
    James (son of Alphaeus),
    Simon (who was called the zealot),
16 Judas (son of James),
    Judas Iscariot (who later betrayed him).

## Crowds Follow Jesus

17When they came down from the mountain, the disciples stood with Jesus on a large, level area, surrounded by many of his followers and by the crowds. There were people from all over Judea and from Jerusalem and from as far north as the seacoasts of Tyre and Sidon. 18They had come to hear him and to be healed of their diseases; and those troubled by evil* spirits were healed. 19Everyone tried to touch him, because healing power went out from him, and he healed everyone.

## The Beatitudes

20Then Jesus turned to his disciples and said,

"God blesses you who are poor,
    for the Kingdom of God is yours.
21 God blesses you who are hungry now,
    for you will be satisfied.
God blesses you who weep now,
    for in due time you will laugh.

22What blessings await you when people hate you and exclude you and mock you and curse you as evil because you follow the Son of Man. 23When that happens, be happy! Yes, leap for joy! For a great reward awaits

6:5 "Son of Man" is a title Jesus used for himself.    6:18 Greek unclean.

you in heaven. And remember, their ancestors treated the ancient prophets that same way.

### Sorrows Foretold

24 "What sorrow awaits you who are rich,
> for you have your only happiness now.
25 What sorrow awaits you who are fat and
> prosperous now,
> for a time of awful hunger awaits you.
> What sorrow awaits you who laugh now,
> for your laughing will turn to
> mourning and sorrow.
26 What sorrow awaits you who are praised
> by the crowds,
> for their ancestors also praised false
> prophets.

### Love for Enemies

27 "But to you who are willing to listen, I say, love your enemies! Do good to those who hate you. 28 Bless those who curse you. Pray for those who hurt you. 29 If someone slaps you on one cheek, offer the other cheek also. If someone demands your coat, offer your shirt also. 30 Give to anyone who asks; and when things are taken away from you, don't try to get them back. 31 Do to others as you would like them to do to you.

32 "If you love only those who love you, why should you get credit for that? Even sinners love those who love them! 33 And if you do good only to those who do good to you, why should you get credit? Even sinners do that much! 34 And if you lend money only to those who can repay you, why should you get credit? Even sinners will lend to other sinners for a full return.

35 "Love your enemies! Do good to them. Lend to them without expecting to be repaid. Then your reward from heaven will be very great, and you will truly be acting as children of the Most High, for he is kind to those who are unthankful and wicked. 36 You must be compassionate, just as your Father is compassionate.

### Do Not Judge Others

37 "Do not judge others, and you will not be judged. Do not condemn others, or it will all come back against you. Forgive others, and you will be forgiven. 38 Give, and you will receive. Your gift will return to you in full—pressed down, shaken together to make room for more, running over, and poured into your lap. The amount you give will determine the amount you get back.*"

39 Then Jesus gave the following illustration: "Can one blind person lead another? Won't they both fall into a ditch? 40 Students* are not greater than their teacher. But the student who is fully trained will become like the teacher.

41 "And why worry about a speck in your friend's eye* when you have a log in your own? 42 How can you think of saying, 'Friend,* let me help you get rid of that speck in your eye,' when you can't see past the log in your own eye? Hypocrite! First get rid of the log in your own eye; then you will see well enough to deal with the speck in your friend's eye.

### The Tree and Its Fruit

43 "A good tree can't produce bad fruit, and a bad tree can't produce good fruit. 44 A tree is identified by its fruit. Figs are never gathered from thornbushes, and grapes are not picked from bramble bushes. 45 A good person produces good things from the treasury of a good heart, and an evil person produces evil things from the treasury of an evil heart. What you say flows from what is in your heart.

### Building on a Solid Foundation

46 "So why do you keep calling me 'Lord, Lord!' when you don't do what I say? 47 I will show you what it's like when someone comes to me, listens to my teaching, and then follows it. 48 It is like a person building a house who digs deep and lays the foundation on solid rock. When the floodwaters rise and break against that house, it stands firm because it is well built. 49 But anyone who hears and doesn't obey is like a person who builds a house without a foundation. When the floods sweep down against that house, it will collapse into a heap of ruins."

**6:38** Or *The measure you give will be the measure you get back.*   **6:40** Or *Disciples.*   **6:41** Greek *your brother's eye;* also in 6:42.
**6:42** Greek *Brother.*

## The Faith of a Roman Officer

**7** When Jesus had finished saying all this to the people, he returned to Capernaum. ²At that time the highly valued slave of a Roman officer* was sick and near death. ³When the officer heard about Jesus, he sent some respected Jewish elders to ask him to come and heal his slave. ⁴So they earnestly begged Jesus to help the man. "If anyone deserves your help, he does," they said, ⁵"for he loves the Jewish people and even built a synagogue for us."

⁶So Jesus went with them. But just before they arrived at the house, the officer sent some friends to say, "Lord, don't trouble yourself by coming to my home, for I am not worthy of such an honor. ⁷I am not even worthy to come and meet you. Just say the word from where you are, and my servant will be healed. ⁸I know this because I am under the authority of my superior officers, and I have authority over my soldiers. I only need to say, 'Go,' and they go, or 'Come,' and they come. And if I say to my slaves, 'Do this,' they do it."

⁹When Jesus heard this, he was amazed. Turning to the crowd that was following him, he said, "I tell you, I haven't seen faith like this in all Israel!" ¹⁰And when the officer's friends returned to his house, they found the slave completely healed.

## Jesus Raises a Widow's Son

¹¹Soon afterward Jesus went with his disciples to the village of Nain, and a large crowd followed him. ¹²A funeral procession was coming out as he approached the village gate. The young man who had died was a widow's only son, and a large crowd from the village was with her. ¹³When the Lord saw her, his heart overflowed with compassion. "Don't cry!" he said. ¹⁴Then he walked over to the coffin and touched it, and the bearers stopped. " Young man," he said, "I tell you, get up." ¹⁵Then the dead boy sat up and began to talk! And Jesus gave him back to his mother.

¹⁶Great fear swept the crowd, and they praised God, saying, "A mighty prophet has risen among us," and "God has visited his

people today." ¹⁷And the news about Jesus spread throughout Judea and the surrounding countryside.

## Jesus and John the Baptist

¹⁸The disciples of John the Baptist told John about everything Jesus was doing. So John called for two of his disciples, ¹⁹and he sent them to the Lord to ask him, "Are you the Messiah we've been expecting,* or should we keep looking for someone else?"

²⁰John's two disciples found Jesus and said to him, "John the Baptist sent us to ask, 'Are you the Messiah we've been expecting, or should we keep looking for someone else?'"

²¹At that very time, Jesus cured many people of their diseases, illnesses, and evil spirits, and he restored sight to many who were blind. ²²Then he told John's disciples, "Go back to John and tell him what you have seen and heard—the blind see, the lame walk, the lepers are cured, the deaf hear, the dead are raised to life, and the Good News is being preached to the poor. ²³And tell him, 'God blesses those who do not turn away because of me.*'"

²⁴After John's disciples left, Jesus began talking about him to the crowds. " What kind of man did you go into the wilderness to see? Was he a weak reed, swayed by every breath of wind? ²⁵Or were you expecting to see a man dressed in expensive clothes? No, people who wear beautiful clothes and live in luxury are found in palaces. ²⁶Were you looking for a prophet? Yes, and he is more than a prophet. ²⁷John is the man to whom the Scriptures refer when they say,

'Look, I am sending my messenger ahead of you,
    and he will prepare your way before you.'*

²⁸I tell you, of all who have ever lived, none is greater than John. Yet even the least person in the Kingdom of God is greater than he is!"

²⁹When they heard this, all the people—even the tax collectors—agreed that God's way was right,* for they had been baptized by John. ³⁰But the Pharisees and experts in

---

7:2 Greek *a centurion;* similarly in 7:6.   7:19 Greek *Are you the one who is coming?* Also in 7:20.   7:23 Or *who are not offended by me.*   7:27 Mal 3:1.   7:29 Or *praised God for his justice.*

religious law rejected God's plan for them, for they had refused John's baptism.

31"To what can I compare the people of this generation?" Jesus asked. "How can I describe them? 32They are like children playing a game in the public square. They complain to their friends,

'We played wedding songs,
    and you didn't dance,
so we played funeral songs,
    and you didn't weep.'

33For John the Baptist didn't spend his time eating bread or drinking wine, and you say, 'He's possessed by a demon.' 34The Son of Man,* on the other hand, feasts and drinks, and you say, 'He's a glutton and a drunkard, and a friend of tax collectors and other sinners!' 35But wisdom is shown to be right by the lives of those who follow it.*"

### Jesus Anointed by a Sinful Woman

36One of the Pharisees asked Jesus to have dinner with him, so Jesus went to his home and sat down to eat.* 37When a certain immoral woman from that city heard he was eating there, she brought a beautiful alabaster jar filled with expensive perfume. 38Then she knelt behind him at his feet, weeping. Her tears fell on his feet, and she wiped them off with her hair. Then she kept kissing his feet and putting perfume on them.

39When the Pharisee who had invited him saw this, he said to himself, "If this man were a prophet, he would know what kind of woman is touching him. She's a sinner!"

40Then Jesus answered his thoughts. "Simon," he said to the Pharisee, "I have something to say to you."

"Go ahead, Teacher," Simon replied.

41Then Jesus told him this story: "A man loaned money to two people—500 pieces of silver* to one and 50 pieces to the other. 42But neither of them could repay him, so he kindly forgave them both, canceling their debts. Who do you suppose loved him more after that?"

43Simon answered, "I suppose the one for whom he canceled the larger debt."

"That's right," Jesus said. 44Then he turned to the woman and said to Simon, "Look at this woman kneeling here. When I entered your home, you didn't offer me water to wash the dust from my feet, but she has washed them with her tears and wiped them with her hair. 45You didn't greet me with a kiss, but from the time I first came in, she has not stopped kissing my feet. 46You neglected the courtesy of olive oil to anoint my head, but she has anointed my feet with rare perfume.

47"I tell you, her sins—and they are many— have been forgiven, so she has shown me much love. But a person who is forgiven little shows only little love." 48Then Jesus said to the woman, "Your sins are forgiven."

49The men at the table said among themselves, "Who is this man, that he goes around forgiving sins?"

50And Jesus said to the woman, "Your faith has saved you; go in peace."

### Women Who Followed Jesus

**8** Soon afterward Jesus began a tour of the nearby towns and villages, preaching and announcing the Good News about the Kingdom of God. He took his twelve disciples with him, 2along with some women who had been cured of evil spirits and diseases. Among them were Mary Magdalene, from whom he had cast out seven demons; 3Joanna, the wife of Chuza, Herod's business manager; Susanna; and many others who were contributing their own resources to support Jesus and his disciples.

### Parable of the Farmer Scattering Seed

4One day Jesus told a story in the form of a parable to a large crowd that had gathered from many towns to hear him: 5"A farmer went out to plant his seed. As he scattered it across his field, some seed fell on a footpath, where it was stepped on, and the birds ate it. 6Other seed fell among rocks. It began to grow, but the plant soon wilted and died for lack of moisture. 7Other seed fell among thorns that grew up with it and choked out the tender plants. 8Still other seed fell on fertile soil. This seed grew and produced a

---

7:34 "Son of Man" is a title Jesus used for himself.    7:35 Or *But wisdom is justified by all her children.*    7:36 Or *and reclined.*
7:41 Greek *500 denarii.* A denarius was equivalent to a laborer's full day's wage.

# TOUCH of faith

READ LUKE 8:43-48

Can you imagine the uproar if Jesus walked into Sloan-Kettering, Johns Hopkins, the Mayo Clinic, or any other large medical center today? There would be a real "feeding frenzy" of sick patients wanting to get close to Him.

That's the way it was when He walked through Galilee, too. Crowds surrounded Him, pressing up against Him. But this touch was different. Someone *deliberately* reached out and touched the holiest part of His robe—the Jewish *tzitzit*, or fringes, at the corner of observant men's garments, spoken of in Numbers 15:37-41. It was against the Jewish law for this woman to touch a male stranger. She also was bleeding and, therefore, ritually impure. But she was desperate. (Mark 5:26 says she had spent all her money on physicians who couldn't cure her.) So she crept up behind the Messiah, reached out, and felt the fringes. Instantly she was healed as her touch of faith released His power.

Go ahead—reach out to Jesus, touch the holiest part of His robe, and wait for His powerful response.

---

crop that was a hundred times as much as had been planted!" When he had said this, he called out, "Anyone with ears to hear should listen and understand."

⁹His disciples asked him what this parable meant. ¹⁰He replied, " You are permitted to understand the secrets* of the Kingdom of God. But I use parables to teach the others so that the Scriptures might be fulfilled:

'When they look, they won't really
    see.
When they hear, they won't
    understand.'*

¹¹"This is the meaning of the parable: The seed is God's word. ¹²The seeds that fell on the footpath represent those who hear the message, only to have the devil come and take it away from their hearts and prevent them from believing and being saved. ¹³The seeds on the rocky soil represent those who hear the message and receive it with joy. But since they don't have deep roots, they believe for a while, then they fall away when they face temptation. ¹⁴The seeds that fell among the thorns represent those who hear the message, but all too quickly the message is crowded out by the cares and riches and pleasures of this life. And so they never grow into maturity. ¹⁵And the seeds that fell on the good soil

represent honest, good-hearted people who hear God's word, cling to it, and patiently produce a huge harvest.

### Parable of the Lamp

¹⁶"No one lights a lamp and then covers it with a bowl or hides it under a bed. A lamp is placed on a stand, where its light can be seen by all who enter the house. ¹⁷For all that is secret will eventually be brought into the open, and everything that is concealed will be brought to light and made known to all.

¹⁸"So pay attention to how you hear. To those who listen to my teaching, more understanding will be given. But for those who are not listening, even what they think they understand will be taken away from them."

### The True Family of Jesus

¹⁹Then Jesus' mother and brothers came to see him, but they couldn't get to him because of the crowd. ²⁰Someone told Jesus, " Your mother and your brothers are outside, and they want to see you."

²¹Jesus replied, "My mother and my brothers are all those who hear God's word and obey it."

### Jesus Calms the Storm

²²One day Jesus said to his disciples, "Let's cross to the other side of the lake." So they

8:10a Greek *mysteries.*    8:10b Isa 6:9 (Greek version).

got into a boat and started out. 23As they sailed across, Jesus settled down for a nap. But soon a fierce storm came down on the lake. The boat was filling with water, and they were in real danger.

24The disciples went and woke him up, shouting, "Master, Master, we're going to drown!"

When Jesus woke up, he rebuked the wind and the raging waves. Suddenly the storm stopped and all was calm. 25Then he asked them, " Where is your faith?"

The disciples were terrified and amazed. "Who is this man?" they asked each other. "When he gives a command, even the wind and waves obey him!"

### Jesus Heals a Demon-Possessed Man

26So they arrived in the region of the Gerasenes,* across the lake from Galilee. 27As Jesus was climbing out of the boat, a man who was possessed by demons came out to meet him. For a long time he had been homeless and naked, living in a cemetery outside the town.

28As soon as he saw Jesus, he shrieked and fell down in front of him. Then he screamed, "Why are you interfering with me, Jesus, Son of the Most High God? Please, I beg you, don't torture me!" 29For Jesus had already commanded the evil* spirit to come out of him. This spirit had often taken control of the man. Even when he was placed under guard and put in chains and shackles, he simply broke them and rushed out into the wilderness, completely under the demon's power.

30Jesus demanded," What is your name?"

"Legion," he replied, for he was filled with many demons. 31The demons kept begging Jesus not to send them into the bottomless pit.*

· 32There happened to be a large herd of pigs feeding on the hillside nearby, and the demons begged him to let them enter into the pigs.

So Jesus gave them permission. 33Then the demons came out of the man and entered the pigs, and the entire herd plunged down the steep hillside into the lake and drowned.

34When the herdsmen saw it, they fled to the nearby town and the surrounding countryside, spreading the news as they ran. 35People rushed out to see what had happened. A crowd soon gathered around Jesus, and they saw the man who had been freed from the demons. He was sitting at Jesus' feet, fully clothed and perfectly sane, and they were all afraid. 36Then those who had seen what happened told the others how the demon-possessed man had been healed. 37And all the people in the region of the Gerasenes begged Jesus to go away and leave them alone, for a great wave of fear swept over them.

So Jesus returned to the boat and left, crossing back to the other side of the lake. 38The man who had been freed from the demons begged to go with him. But Jesus sent him home, saying, 39"No, go back to your family, and tell them everything God has done for you." So he went all through the town proclaiming the great things Jesus had done for him.

### Jesus Heals in Response to Faith

40On the other side of the lake the crowds welcomed Jesus, because they had been waiting for him. 41Then a man named Jairus, a leader of the local synagogue, came and fell at Jesus' feet, pleading with him to come home with him. 42His only daughter,* who was about twelve years old, was dying.

As Jesus went with him, he was surrounded by the crowds. 43A woman in the crowd had suffered for twelve years with constant bleeding,* and she could find no cure. 44Coming up behind Jesus, she touched the fringe of his robe. Immediately, the bleeding stopped.

45" Who touched me?" Jesus asked.

Everyone denied it, and Peter said, "Master, this whole crowd is pressing up against you."

46But Jesus said, "Someone deliberately touched me, for I felt healing power go out from me." 47When the woman realized that she could not stay hidden, she began to tremble and fell to her knees in front of him. The whole crowd heard her explain why she had touched him and that she had been im-

8:26 Other manuscripts read *Gadarenes;* still others read *Gergesenes;* also in 8:37. See Matt 8:28; Mark 5:1.  8:29 Greek *unclean.* 8:31 Or *the abyss,* or *the underworld.*  8:42 Or *His only child, a daughter.*  8:43 Some manuscripts add *having spent everything she had on doctors.*

mediately healed. [48]"Daughter," he said to her, "your faith has made you well. Go in peace."

[49]While he was still speaking to her, a messenger arrived from the home of Jairus, the leader of the synagogue. He told him, "Your daughter is dead. There's no use troubling the Teacher now."

[50]But when Jesus heard what had happened, he said to Jairus, "Don't be afraid. Just have faith, and she will be healed."

[51]When they arrived at the house, Jesus wouldn't let anyone go in with him except Peter, John, James, and the little girl's father and mother. [52]The house was filled with people weeping and wailing, but he said, "Stop the weeping! She isn't dead; she's only asleep."

[53]But the crowd laughed at him because they all knew she had died. [54]Then Jesus took her by the hand and said in a loud voice, "My child, get up!" [55]And at that moment her life* returned, and she immediately stood up! Then Jesus told them to give her something to eat. [56]Her parents were overwhelmed, but Jesus insisted that they not tell anyone what had happened.

## Jesus Sends Out the Twelve Disciples

**9** One day Jesus called together his twelve disciples* and gave them power and authority to cast out all demons and to heal all diseases. [2]Then he sent them out to tell everyone about the Kingdom of God and to heal the sick. [3]"Take nothing for your journey," he instructed them. "Don't take a walking stick, a traveler's bag, food, money,* or even a change of clothes. [4]Wherever you go, stay in the same house until you leave town. [5]And if a town refuses to welcome you, shake its dust from your feet as you leave to show that you have abandoned those people to their fate."

[6]So they began their circuit of the villages, preaching the Good News and healing the sick.

## Herod's Confusion

[7]When Herod Antipas, the ruler of Galilee,* heard about everything Jesus was doing, he was puzzled. Some were saying that John the Baptist had been raised from the dead. [8]Others thought Jesus was Elijah or one of the other prophets risen from the dead.

[9]"I beheaded John," Herod said, "so who is this man about whom I hear such stories?" And he kept trying to see him.

## Jesus Feeds Five Thousand

[10]When the apostles returned, they told Jesus everything they had done. Then he slipped quietly away with them toward the town of Bethsaida. [11]But the crowds found out where he was going, and they followed him. He welcomed them and taught them about the Kingdom of God, and he healed those who were sick.

[12]Late in the afternoon the twelve disciples came to him and said, "Send the crowds away to the nearby villages and farms, so they can find food and lodging for the night. There is nothing to eat here in this remote place."

[13]But Jesus said, " You feed them."

"But we have only five loaves of bread and two fish," they answered. "Or are you expecting us to go and buy enough food for this whole crowd?" [14]For there were about 5,000 men there.

Jesus replied, "Tell them to sit down in groups of about fifty each." [15]So the people all sat down. [16]Jesus took the five loaves and two fish, looked up toward heaven, and blessed them. Then, breaking the loaves into pieces, he kept giving the bread and fish to the disciples so they could distribute it to the people. [17]They all ate as much as they wanted, and afterward, the disciples picked up twelve baskets of leftovers!

## Peter's Declaration about Jesus

[18]One day Jesus left the crowds to pray alone. Only his disciples were with him, and he asked them, " Who do people say I am?"

[19]"Well," they replied, "some say John the Baptist, some say Elijah, and others say you are one of the other ancient prophets risen from the dead."

[20]Then he asked them, "But who do you say I am?"

---

**8:55** Or *her spirit.*   **9:1** Greek *the Twelve;* other manuscripts read *the twelve apostles.*   **9:3** Or *silver coins.*   **9:7** Greek *Herod the tetrarch.* Herod Antipas was a son of King Herod and was ruler over Galilee.

Peter replied, "You are the Messiah* sent from God!"

## Jesus Predicts His Death

21 Jesus warned his disciples not to tell anyone who he was. 22 "The Son of Man* must suffer many terrible things," he said. "He will be rejected by the elders, the leading priests, and the teachers of religious law. He will be killed, but on the third day he will be raised from the dead."

23 Then he said to the crowd, "If any of you wants to be my follower, you must turn from your selfish ways, take up your cross daily, and follow me. 24 If you try to hang on to your life, you will lose it. But if you give up your life for my sake, you will save it. 25 And what do you benefit if you gain the whole world but are yourself lost or destroyed? 26 If anyone is ashamed of me and my message, the Son of Man will be ashamed of that person when he returns in his glory and in the glory of the Father and the holy angels. 27 I tell you the truth, some standing here right now will not die before they see the Kingdom of God."

## The Transfiguration

28 About eight days later Jesus took Peter, John, and James up on a mountain to pray. 29 And as he was praying, the appearance of his face was transformed, and his clothes became dazzling white. 30 Suddenly, two men, Moses and Elijah, appeared and began talking with Jesus. 31 They were glorious to see. And they were speaking about his exodus from this world, which was about to be fulfilled in Jerusalem.

32 Peter and the others had fallen asleep. When they woke up, they saw Jesus' glory and the two men standing with him. 33 As Moses and Elijah were starting to leave, Peter, not even knowing what he was saying, blurted out, "Master, it's wonderful for us to be here! Let's make three shelters as memorials*—one for you, one for Moses, and one for Elijah." 34 But even as he was saying this, a cloud overshadowed them, and terror gripped them as the cloud covered them.

35 Then a voice from the cloud said, "This is my Son, my Chosen One.* Listen to him." 36 When the voice finished, Jesus was there alone. They didn't tell anyone at that time what they had seen.

## Jesus Heals a Demon-Possessed Boy

37 The next day, after they had come down the mountain, a large crowd met Jesus. 38 A man in the crowd called out to him, "Teacher, I beg you to look at my son, my only child. 39 An evil spirit keeps seizing him, making him scream. It throws him into convulsions so that he foams at the mouth. It batters him and hardly ever leaves him alone. 40 I begged your disciples to cast out the spirit, but they couldn't do it."

41 Jesus said, "You faithless and corrupt people! How long must I be with you and put up with you?" Then he said to the man, "Bring your son here."

42 As the boy came forward, the demon knocked him to the ground and threw him into a violent convulsion. But Jesus rebuked the evil* spirit and healed the boy. Then he gave him back to his father. 43 Awe gripped the people as they saw this majestic display of God's power.

## Jesus Again Predicts His Death

While everyone was marveling at everything he was doing, Jesus said to his disciples, 44 "Listen to me and remember what I say. The Son of Man is going to be betrayed into the hands of his enemies." 45 But they didn't know what he meant. Its significance was hidden from them, so they couldn't understand it, and they were afraid to ask him about it.

## The Greatest in the Kingdom

46 Then his disciples began arguing about which of them was the greatest. 47 But Jesus knew their thoughts, so he brought a little child to his side. 48 Then he said to them, "Anyone who welcomes a little child like this on my behalf* welcomes me, and anyone who welcomes me also welcomes my Father

9:20 Or the Christ. Messiah (a Hebrew term) and Christ (a Greek term) both mean "the anointed one." 9:22 "Son of Man" is a title Jesus used for himself. 9:33 Greek three tabernacles. 9:35 Some manuscripts read This is my dearly loved Son. 9:42 Greek unclean. 9:48 Greek in my name.

who sent me. Whoever is the least among you is the greatest."

## Using the Name of Jesus

⁴⁹John said to Jesus, "Master, we saw someone using your name to cast out demons, but we told him to stop because he isn't in our group."

⁵⁰But Jesus said, "Don't stop him! Anyone who is not against you is for you."

## Opposition from Samaritans

⁵¹As the time drew near for him to ascend to heaven, Jesus resolutely set out for Jerusalem. ⁵²He sent messengers ahead to a Samaritan village to prepare for his arrival. ⁵³But the people of the village did not welcome Jesus because he was on his way to Jerusalem. ⁵⁴When James and John saw this, they said to Jesus, "Lord, should we call down fire from heaven to burn them up*?" ⁵⁵But Jesus turned and rebuked them.* ⁵⁶So they went on to another village.

## The Cost of Following Jesus

⁵⁷As they were walking along, someone said to Jesus, "I will follow you wherever you go."

⁵⁸But Jesus replied, "Foxes have dens to live in, and birds have nests, but the Son of Man has no place even to lay his head."

⁵⁹He said to another person, "Come, follow me."

The man agreed, but he said, "Lord, first let me return home and bury my father."

⁶⁰But Jesus told him, "Let the spiritually dead bury their own dead!* Your duty is to go and preach about the Kingdom of God."

⁶¹Another said, "Yes, Lord, I will follow you, but first let me say good-bye to my family."

⁶²But Jesus told him, "Anyone who puts a hand to the plow and then looks back is not fit for the Kingdom of God."

## Jesus Sends Out His Disciples

**10** The Lord now chose seventy-two* other disciples and sent them ahead in pairs to all the towns and places he planned to visit. ²These were his instructions to them: " The harvest is great, but the workers are few. So pray to the Lord who is in charge of the harvest; ask him to send more workers into his fields. ³Now go, and remember that I am sending you out as lambs among wolves. ⁴Don't take any money with you, nor a traveler's bag, nor an extra pair of sandals. And don't stop to greet anyone on the road.

⁵"Whenever you enter someone's home, first say, 'May God's peace be on this house.' ⁶If those who live there are peaceful, the blessing will stand; if they are not, the blessing will return to you. ⁷Don't move around from home to home. Stay in one place, eating and drinking what they provide. Don't hesitate to accept hospitality, because those who work deserve their pay.

⁸"If you enter a town and it welcomes you, eat whatever is set before you. ⁹Heal the sick, and tell them, 'The Kingdom of God is near you now.' ¹⁰But if a town refuses to welcome you, go out into its streets and say, ¹¹' We wipe even the dust of your town from our feet to show that we have abandoned you to your fate. And know this—the Kingdom of God is near!' ¹²I assure you, even wicked Sodom will be better off than such a town on judgment day.

¹³" What sorrow awaits you, Korazin and Bethsaida! For if the miracles I did in you had been done in wicked Tyre and Sidon, their people would have repented of their sins long ago, clothing themselves in burlap and throwing ashes on their heads to show their remorse. ¹⁴Yes, Tyre and Sidon will be better off on judgment day than you. ¹⁵And you people of Capernaum, will you be honored in heaven? No, you will go down to the place of the dead.*"

¹⁶Then he said to the disciples, "Anyone who accepts your message is also accepting me. And anyone who rejects you is rejecting me. And anyone who rejects me is rejecting God, who sent me."

¹⁷When the seventy-two disciples returned, they joyfully reported to him, "Lord, even the demons obey us when we use your name!"

¹⁸"Yes," he told them, "I saw Satan fall

---

9:54 Some manuscripts add *as Elijah did.*　　9:55 Some manuscripts add an expanded conclusion to verse 55 and an additional sentence in verse 56: *And he said, "You don't realize what your hearts are like.* ⁵⁶*For the Son of Man has not come to destroy people's lives, but to save them."*　　9:60 Greek *Let the dead bury their own dead.*　　10:1 Some manuscripts read *seventy;* also in 10:17.
**10:15** Greek *to Hades.*

from heaven like lightning! ¹⁹Look, I have given you authority over all the power of the enemy, and you can walk among snakes and scorpions and crush them. Nothing will injure you. ²⁰But don't rejoice because evil spirits obey you; rejoice because your names are registered in heaven."

## Jesus' Prayer of Thanksgiving

²¹At that same time Jesus was filled with the joy of the Holy Spirit, and he said, "O Father, Lord of heaven and earth, thank you for hiding these things from those who think themselves wise and clever, and for revealing them to the childlike. Yes, Father, it pleased you to do it this way.

²²"My Father has entrusted everything to me. No one truly knows the Son except the Father, and no one truly knows the Father except the Son and those to whom the Son chooses to reveal him."

²³Then when they were alone, he turned to the disciples and said, "Blessed are the eyes that see what you have seen. ²⁴I tell you, many prophets and kings longed to see what you see, but they didn't see it. And they longed to hear what you hear, but they didn't hear it."

## The Most Important Commandment

²⁵One day an expert in religious law stood up to test Jesus by asking him this question:

10:27 Deut 6:5; Lev 19:18.   10:32 Greek *A Levite.*

"Teacher, what should I do to inherit eternal life?"

²⁶Jesus replied, "What does the law of Moses say? How do you read it?"

²⁷The man answered, "'You must love the Lord your God with all your heart, all your soul, all your strength, and all your mind.' And, 'Love your neighbor as yourself.'"*

²⁸"Right!" Jesus told him. "Do this and you will live!"

²⁹The man wanted to justify his actions, so he asked Jesus, "And who is my neighbor?"

## Parable of the Good Samaritan

³⁰Jesus replied with a story: "A Jewish man was traveling on a trip from Jerusalem to Jericho, and he was attacked by bandits. They stripped him of his clothes, beat him up, and left him half dead beside the road.

³¹"By chance a priest came along. But when he saw the man lying there, he crossed to the other side of the road and passed him by. ³²A Temple assistant* walked over and looked at him lying there, but he also passed by on the other side.

³³"Then a despised Samaritan came along, and when he saw the man, he felt compassion for him. ³⁴Going over to him, the Samaritan soothed his wounds with olive oil and wine and bandaged them. Then

# TOP of the list

READ LUKE 10:38-42

A lot of us have a "Martha" personality. We get caught up in our to-do lists and rush around trying to get everything done. This can be especially difficult if illness slows us down or treatments for it chew up a big chunk of time. But don't let your organizational skills and efficient handling of situations distract you from the most important thing to be done each day.

Martha complained that her sister Mary was "just" sitting there, but that really doesn't describe her actions. Yes, Mary was sitting still, but she was doing that so she could hear from Jesus.

No matter what is on your to-do list today, take time to sit at Jesus' feet and learn from Him. Read His Word and slow down long enough for Him to speak to your heart and renew your weary spirit. In fact, do like gospel musician Mark Cable says; at the top of today's to-do list, write these words: "Be like Jesus."

he put the man on his own donkey and took him to an inn, where he took care of him. 35 The next day he handed the innkeeper two silver coins,* telling him, ' Take care of this man. If his bill runs higher than this, I'll pay you the next time I'm here.'

36 "Now which of these three would you say was a neighbor to the man who was attacked by bandits?" Jesus asked.

37 The man replied, "The one who showed him mercy."

Then Jesus said, " Yes, now go and do the same."

## Jesus Visits Martha and Mary

38 As Jesus and the disciples continued on their way to Jerusalem, they came to a certain village where a woman named Martha welcomed him into her home. 39 Her sister, Mary, sat at the Lord's feet, listening to what he taught. 40 But Martha was distracted by the big dinner she was preparing. She came to Jesus and said, "Lord, doesn't it seem unfair to you that my sister just sits here while I do all the work? Tell her to come and help me."

41 But the Lord said to her, "My dear Martha, you are worried and upset over all these details! 42 There is only one thing worth being concerned about. Mary has discovered it, and it will not be taken away from her."

## Teaching about Prayer

**11** Once Jesus was in a certain place praying. As he finished, one of his disciples came to him and said, "Lord, teach us to pray, just as John taught his disciples."

2 Jesus said, "This is how you should pray:*

"Father, may your name be kept holy.
    May your Kingdom come soon.
3 Give us each day the food we need,*
4 and forgive us our sins,
    as we forgive those who sin against us.
And don't let us yield to temptation.*"

5 Then, teaching them more about prayer, he used this story: "Suppose you went to a friend's house at midnight, wanting to borrow three loaves of bread. You say to him, 6 'A friend of mine has just arrived for a visit, and I have nothing for him to eat.' 7 And suppose he calls out from his bedroom, 'Don't bother me. The door is locked for the night, and my family and I are all in bed. I can't help you.' 8 But I tell you this—though he won't do it for friendship's sake, if you keep knocking long enough, he will get up and give you whatever you need because of your shameless persistence.*

9 "And so I tell you, keep on asking, and you will receive what you ask for. Keep on seeking, and you will find. Keep on knocking, and the door will be opened to you. 10 For everyone who asks, receives. Everyone who seeks, finds. And to everyone who knocks, the door will be opened.

11 "You fathers—if your children ask* for a fish, do you give them a snake instead? 12 Or if they ask for an egg, do you give them a scorpion? Of course not! 13 So if you sinful people know how to give good gifts to your children, how much more will your heavenly Father give the Holy Spirit to those who ask him."

## Jesus and the Prince of Demons

14 One day Jesus cast out a demon from a man who couldn't speak, and when the demon was gone, the man began to speak. The crowds were amazed, 15 but some of them said, "No wonder he can cast out demons. He gets his power from Satan,* the prince of demons." 16 Others, trying to test Jesus, demanded that he show them a miraculous sign from heaven to prove his authority.

17 He knew their thoughts, so he said, "Any kingdom divided by civil war is doomed. A family splintered by feuding will fall apart. 18 You say I am empowered by Satan. But if Satan is divided and fighting against himself, how can his kingdom survive? 19 And if I am empowered by Satan, what about your own exorcists? They cast out demons, too, so they will condemn you for what you have

---

10:35 Greek *two denarii.* A denarius was equivalent to a laborer's full day's wage.   **11:2** Some manuscripts add additional phrases from the Lord's Prayer as it reads in Matt 6:9-13.   **11:3** Or *Give us each day our food for the day;* or *Give us each day our food for tomorrow.*   **11:4** Or *And keep us from being tested.*   **11:8** Or *in order to avoid shame,* or *so his reputation won't be damaged.*
**11:11** Some manuscripts add *for bread, do you give them a stone? Or [if they ask].*   **11:15** Greek *Beelzeboul;* also in 11:18, 19. Other manuscripts read *Beezeboul;* Latin version reads *Beelzebub.*

said. 20But if I am casting out demons by the power of God,* then the Kingdom of God has arrived among you. 21For when a strong man like Satan is fully armed and guards his palace, his possessions are safe—22until someone even stronger attacks and overpowers him, strips him of his weapons, and carries off his belongings.

23"Anyone who isn't with me opposes me, and anyone who isn't working with me is actually working against me.

24"When an evil* spirit leaves a person, it goes into the desert, searching for rest. But when it finds none, it says, 'I will return to the person I came from.' 25So it returns and finds that its former home is all swept and in order. 26Then the spirit finds seven other spirits more evil than itself, and they all enter the person and live there. And so that person is worse off than before."

27As he was speaking, a woman in the crowd called out, "God bless your mother—the womb from which you came, and the breasts that nursed you!"

28Jesus replied, "But even more blessed are all who hear the word of God and put it into practice."

## The Sign of Jonah

29As the crowd pressed in on Jesus, he said, "This evil generation keeps asking me to show them a miraculous sign. But the only sign I will give them is the sign of Jonah. 30What happened to him was a sign to the people of Nineveh that God had sent him. What happens to the Son of Man* will be a sign to these people that he was sent by God.

31"The queen of Sheba* will stand up against this generation on judgment day and condemn it, for she came from a distant land to hear the wisdom of Solomon. Now someone greater than Solomon is here—but you refuse to listen. 32The people of Nineveh will also stand up against this generation on judgment day and condemn it, for they repented of their sins at the preaching of Jonah. Now someone greater than Jonah is here—but you refuse to repent.

## Receiving the Light

33"No one lights a lamp and then hides it or puts it under a basket.* Instead, a lamp is placed on a stand, where its light can be seen by all who enter the house.

34"Your eye is a lamp that provides light for your body. When your eye is good, your whole body is filled with light. But when it is bad, your body is filled with darkness. 35Make sure that the light you think you have is not actually darkness. 36If you are filled with light, with no dark corners, then your whole life will be radiant, as though a floodlight were filling you with light."

## Jesus Criticizes the Religious Leaders

37As Jesus was speaking, one of the Pharisees invited him home for a meal. So he went in and took his place at the table.* 38His host was amazed to see that he sat down to eat without first performing the hand-washing ceremony required by Jewish custom. 39Then the Lord said to him, "You Pharisees are so careful to clean the outside of the cup and the dish, but inside you are filthy—full of greed and wickedness! 40Fools! Didn't God make the inside as well as the outside? 41So clean the inside by giving gifts to the poor, and you will be clean all over.

42"What sorrow awaits you Pharisees! For you are careful to tithe even the tiniest income from your herb gardens,* but you ignore justice and the love of God. You should tithe, yes, but do not neglect the more important things.

43"What sorrow awaits you Pharisees! For you love to sit in the seats of honor in the synagogues and receive respectful greetings as you walk in the marketplaces. 44Yes, what sorrow awaits you! For you are like hidden graves in a field. People walk over them without knowing the corruption they are stepping on."

45"Teacher," said an expert in religious law, "you have insulted us, too, in what you just said."

46"Yes," said Jesus, "what sorrow also awaits you experts in religious law! For you crush people with unbearable religious de-

11:20 Greek *by the finger of God.* 11:24 Greek *unclean.* 11:30 "Son of Man" is a title Jesus used for himself. 11:31 Greek *The queen of the south.* 11:33 Some manuscripts omit *or puts it under a basket.* 11:37 Or *and reclined.* 11:42 Greek *tithe the mint, the rue, and every herb.*

mands, and you never lift a finger to ease the burden. ⁴⁷What sorrow awaits you! For you build monuments for the prophets your own ancestors killed long ago. ⁴⁸But in fact, you stand as witnesses who agree with what your ancestors did. They killed the prophets, and you join in their crime by building the monuments! ⁴⁹This is what God in his wisdom said about you:* 'I will send prophets and apostles to them, but they will kill some and persecute the others.'

⁵⁰"As a result, this generation will be held responsible for the murder of all God's prophets from the creation of the world— ⁵¹from the murder of Abel to the murder of Zechariah, who was killed between the altar and the sanctuary. Yes, it will certainly be charged against this generation.

⁵²"What sorrow awaits you experts in religious law! For you remove the key to knowledge from the people. You don't enter the Kingdom yourselves, and you prevent others from entering."

⁵³As Jesus was leaving, the teachers of religious law and the Pharisees became hostile and tried to provoke him with many questions. ⁵⁴They wanted to trap him into saying something they could use against him.

### A Warning against Hypocrisy

**12** Meanwhile, the crowds grew until thousands were milling about and stepping on each other. Jesus turned first to his disciples and warned them, "Beware of the yeast of the Pharisees—their hypocrisy. ²The time is coming when everything that is covered up will be revealed, and all that is secret will be made known to all. ³Whatever you have said in the dark will be heard in the light, and what you have whispered behind closed doors will be shouted from the housetops for all to hear!

⁴"Dear friends, don't be afraid of those who want to kill your body; they cannot do any more to you after that. ⁵But I'll tell you whom to fear. Fear God, who has the power to kill you and then throw you into hell.* Yes, he's the one to fear.

⁶" What is the price of five sparrows—two copper coins*? Yet God does not forget a single one of them. ⁷And the very hairs on your head are all numbered. So don't be afraid; you are more valuable to God than a whole flock of sparrows.

⁸"I tell you the truth, everyone who acknowledges me publicly here on earth, the Son of Man* will also acknowledge in the presence of God's angels. ⁹But anyone who denies me here on earth will be denied before God's angels. ¹⁰Anyone who speaks against the Son of Man can be forgiven, but anyone who blasphemes the Holy Spirit will not be forgiven.

¹¹"And when you are brought to trial in the synagogues and before rulers and authorities, don't worry about how to defend yourself or what to say, ¹²for the Holy Spirit will teach you at that time what needs to be said."

### Parable of the Rich Fool

¹³Then someone called from the crowd, "Teacher, please tell my brother to divide our father's estate with me."

¹⁴Jesus replied, "Friend, who made me a judge over you to decide such things as that?" ¹⁵Then he said, "Beware! Guard against every kind of greed. Life is not measured by how much you own."

¹⁶Then he told them a story: "A rich man had a fertile farm that produced fine crops. ¹⁷He said to himself, 'What should I do? I don't have room for all my crops.' ¹⁸Then he said, 'I know! I'll tear down my barns and build bigger ones. Then I'll have room enough to store all my wheat and other goods. ¹⁹And I'll sit back and say to myself, "My friend, you have enough stored away for years to come. Now take it easy! Eat, drink, and be merry!"'

²⁰"But God said to him, 'You fool! You will die this very night. Then who will get everything you worked for?'

²¹"Yes, a person is a fool to store up earthly wealth but not have a rich relationship with God."

### Teaching about Money and Possessions

²²Then, turning to his disciples, Jesus said, "That is why I tell you not to worry about everyday life—whether you have enough

11:49 Greek Therefore, the wisdom of God said. 12:5 Greek Gehenna. 12:6 Greek two assaria [Roman coins equal to ¹⁄₁₆ of a denarius]. 12:8 "Son of Man" is a title Jesus used for himself.

food to eat or enough clothes to wear. ²³For life is more than food, and your body more than clothing. ²⁴Look at the ravens. They don't plant or harvest or store food in barns, for God feeds them. And you are far more valuable to him than any birds! ²⁵Can all your worries add a single moment to your life? ²⁶And if worry can't accomplish a little thing like that, what's the use of worrying over bigger things?

²⁷"Look at the lilies and how they grow. They don't work or make their clothing, yet Solomon in all his glory was not dressed as beautifully as they are. ²⁸And if God cares so wonderfully for flowers that are here today and thrown into the fire tomorrow, he will certainly care for you. Why do you have so little faith?

²⁹"And don't be concerned about what to eat and what to drink. Don't worry about such things. ³⁰These things dominate the thoughts of unbelievers all over the world, but your Father already knows your needs. ³¹Seek the Kingdom of God above all else, and he will give you everything you need.

³²"So don't be afraid, little flock. For it gives your Father great happiness to give you the Kingdom.

³³"Sell your possessions and give to those in need. This will store up treasure for you in heaven! And the purses of heaven never get old or develop holes. Your treasure will be safe; no thief can steal it and no moth can destroy it. ³⁴Wherever your treasure is, there the desires of your heart will also be.

### Be Ready for the Lord's Coming

³⁵"Be dressed for service and keep your lamps burning, ³⁶as though you were waiting for your master to return from the wedding feast. Then you will be ready to open the door and let him in the moment he arrives and knocks. ³⁷The servants who are ready and waiting for his return will be rewarded. I tell you the truth, he himself will seat them, put on an apron, and serve them as they sit and eat! ³⁸He may come in the middle of the night or just before dawn.* But whenever he comes, he will reward the servants who are ready.

³⁹"Understand this: If a homeowner knew exactly when a burglar was coming, he would not permit his house to be broken into. ⁴⁰You also must be ready all the time, for the Son of Man will come when least expected."

⁴¹Peter asked, "Lord, is that illustration just for us or for everyone?"

⁴²And the Lord replied, "A faithful, sensible servant is one to whom the master can give the responsibility of managing his other household servants and feeding them. ⁴³If the master returns and finds that the servant has done a good job, there will be a reward. ⁴⁴I tell you the truth, the master will put that servant in charge of all he owns. ⁴⁵But what if the servant thinks, 'My master won't be back for a while,' and he begins beating the other servants, partying, and getting drunk? ⁴⁶The master will return unannounced and unexpected, and he will cut the servant in pieces and banish him with the unfaithful.

⁴⁷"And a servant who knows what the master wants, but isn't prepared and doesn't carry out those instructions, will be severely punished. ⁴⁸But someone who does not know, and then does something wrong, will be punished only lightly. When someone has been given much, much will be required in return; and when someone has been entrusted with much, even more will be required.

### Jesus Causes Division

⁴⁹"I have come to set the world on fire, and I wish it were already burning! ⁵⁰I have a terrible baptism of suffering ahead of me, and I am under a heavy burden until it is accomplished. ⁵¹Do you think I have come to bring peace to the earth? No, I have come to divide people against each other! ⁵²From now on families will be split apart, three in favor of me, and two against—or two in favor and three against.

⁵³'Father will be divided against son
   and son against father;
mother against daughter
   and daughter against mother;
and mother-in-law against daughter-
   in-law
   and daughter-in-law against mother-
   in-law.'* "

12:38 Greek *in the second or third watch.*    12:53 Mic 7:6.

54Then Jesus turned to the crowd and said, "When you see clouds beginning to form in the west, you say, 'Here comes a shower.' And you are right. 55When the south wind blows, you say, 'Today will be a scorcher.' And it is. 56You fools! You know how to interpret the weather signs of the earth and sky, but you don't know how to interpret the present times.

57"Why can't you decide for yourselves what is right? 58When you are on the way to court with your accuser, try to settle the matter before you get there. Otherwise, your accuser may drag you before the judge, who will hand you over to an officer, who will throw you into prison. 59And if that happens, you won't be free again until you have paid the very last penny.*"

## A Call to Repentance

**13** About this time Jesus was informed that Pilate had murdered some people from Galilee as they were offering sacrifices at the Temple. 2"Do you think those Galileans were worse sinners than all the other people from Galilee?" Jesus asked. "Is that why they suffered? 3Not at all! And you will perish, too, unless you repent of your sins and turn to God. 4And what about the eighteen people who died when the tower in Siloam fell on them? Were they the worst sinners in Jerusalem? 5No, and I tell you again that unless you repent, you will perish, too."

## Parable of the Barren Fig Tree

6Then Jesus told this story: "A man planted a fig tree in his garden and came again and again to see if there was any fruit on it, but he was always disappointed. 7Finally, he said to his gardener, 'I've waited three years, and there hasn't been a single fig! Cut it down. It's just taking up space in the garden.'

8"The gardener answered, 'Sir, give it one more chance. Leave it another year, and I'll give it special attention and plenty of fertilizer. 9If we get figs next year, fine. If not, then you can cut it down.'"

## Jesus Heals on the Sabbath

10One Sabbath day as Jesus was teaching in a synagogue, 11he saw a woman who had

been crippled by an evil spirit. She had been bent double for eighteen years and was unable to stand up straight. 12When Jesus saw her, he called her over and said, "Dear woman, you are healed of your sickness!" 13Then he touched her, and instantly she could stand straight. How she praised God!

14But the leader in charge of the synagogue was indignant that Jesus had healed her on the Sabbath day. "There are six days of the week for working," he said to the crowd. "Come on those days to be healed, not on the Sabbath."

15But the Lord replied, "You hypocrites! Each of you works on the Sabbath day! Don't you untie your ox or your donkey from its stall on the Sabbath and lead it out for water? 16This dear woman, a daughter of Abraham, has been held in bondage by Satan for eighteen years. Isn't it right that she be released, even on the Sabbath?"

17This shamed his enemies, but all the people rejoiced at the wonderful things he did.

## Parable of the Mustard Seed

18Then Jesus said, "What is the Kingdom of God like? How can I illustrate it? 19It is like a tiny mustard seed that a man planted in a garden; it grows and becomes a tree, and the birds make nests in its branches."

## Parable of the Yeast

20He also asked, "What else is the Kingdom of God like? 21It is like the yeast a woman used in making bread. Even though she put only a little yeast in three measures of flour, it permeated every part of the dough."

## The Narrow Door

22Jesus went through the towns and villages, teaching as he went, always pressing on toward Jerusalem. 23Someone asked him, "Lord, will only a few be saved?"

He replied, 24"Work hard to enter the narrow door to God's Kingdom, for many will try to enter but will fail. 25When the master of the house has locked the door, it will be too late. You will stand outside knocking and pleading, 'Lord, open the door for us!'

12:59 Greek last lepton [the smallest Jewish coin].

But he will reply, 'I don't know you or where you come from.' 26 Then you will say, 'But we ate and drank with you, and you taught in our streets.' 27 And he will reply, 'I tell you, I don't know you or where you come from. Get away from me, all you who do evil.'

28 "There will be weeping and gnashing of teeth, for you will see Abraham, Isaac, Jacob, and all the prophets in the Kingdom of God, but you will be thrown out. 29 And people will come from all over the world—from east and west, north and south—to take their places in the Kingdom of God. 30 And note this: Some who seem least important now will be the greatest then, and some who are the greatest now will be least important then.*"

### Jesus Grieves over Jerusalem

31 At that time some Pharisees said to him, "Get away from here if you want to live! Herod Antipas wants to kill you!"

32 Jesus replied, "Go tell that fox that I will keep on casting out demons and healing people today and tomorrow; and the third day I will accomplish my purpose. 33 Yes, today, tomorrow, and the next day I must proceed on my way. For it wouldn't do for a prophet of God to be killed except in Jerusalem!

34 "O Jerusalem, Jerusalem, the city that kills the prophets and stones God's messengers! How often I have wanted to gather your children together as a hen protects her chicks beneath her wings, but you wouldn't let me. 35 And now, look, your house is abandoned. And you will never see me again until you say, 'Blessings on the one who comes in the name of the Lord!'* "

### Jesus Heals on the Sabbath

**14** One Sabbath day Jesus went to eat dinner in the home of a leader of the Pharisees, and the people were watching him closely. 2 There was a man there whose arms and legs were swollen.* 3 Jesus asked the Pharisees and experts in religious law, "Is it permitted in the law to heal people on the Sabbath day, or not?" 4 When they refused to answer, Jesus touched the sick man and healed him and sent him away. 5 Then he turned to them and said, "Which of you doesn't work on the Sabbath? If your son* or your cow falls into a pit, don't you rush to get him out?" 6 Again they could not answer.

### Jesus Teaches about Humility

7 When Jesus noticed that all who had come to the dinner were trying to sit in the seats of honor near the head of the table, he gave them this advice: 8 " When you are invited to a wedding feast, don't sit in the seat of honor. What if someone who is more distinguished than you has also been invited? 9 The host will come and say, 'Give this person your seat.' Then you will be embarrassed, and you will have to take whatever seat is left at the foot of the table!

10 "Instead, take the lowest place at the foot of the table. Then when your host sees you, he will come and say, 'Friend, we have a better place for you!' Then you will be honored in front of all the other guests. 11 For those who exalt themselves will be humbled, and those who humble themselves will be exalted."

12 Then he turned to his host. "When you put on a luncheon or a banquet," he said, "don't invite your friends, brothers, relatives, and rich neighbors. For they will invite you back, and that will be your only reward. 13 Instead, invite the poor, the crippled, the lame, and the blind. 14 Then at the resurrection of the righteous, God will reward you for inviting those who could not repay you."

### Parable of the Great Feast

15 Hearing this, a man sitting at the table with Jesus exclaimed, "What a blessing it will be to attend a banquet* in the Kingdom of God!"

16 Jesus replied with this story: "A man prepared a great feast and sent out many invitations. 17 When the banquet was ready, he sent his servant to tell the guests, 'Come, the banquet is ready.' 18 But they all began making excuses. One said, 'I have just bought a field and must inspect it. Please excuse me.' 19 Another said, 'I have just bought five pairs of oxen, and I want to try them out. Please excuse me.' 20 Another said, 'I now have a wife, so I can't come.'

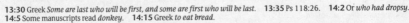

13:30 Greek *Some are last who will be first, and some are first who will be last.*   13:35 Ps 118:26.   14:2 Or *who had dropsy.*
14:5 Some manuscripts read *donkey.*   14:15 Greek *to eat bread.*

²¹"The servant returned and told his master what they had said. His master was furious and said, 'Go quickly into the streets and alleys of the town and invite the poor, the crippled, the blind, and the lame.' ²²After the servant had done this, he reported, ' There is still room for more.' ²³So his master said, 'Go out into the country lanes and behind the hedges and urge anyone you find to come, so that the house will be full. ²⁴For none of those I first invited will get even the smallest taste of my banquet.' "

### The Cost of Being a Disciple

²⁵A large crowd was following Jesus. He turned around and said to them, ²⁶"If you want to be my disciple, you must hate everyone else by comparison—your father and mother, wife and children, brothers and sisters—yes, even your own life. Otherwise, you cannot be my disciple. ²⁷And if you do not carry your own cross and follow me, you cannot be my disciple.

²⁸"But don't begin until you count the cost. For who would begin construction of a building without first calculating the cost to see if there is enough money to finish it? ²⁹Otherwise, you might complete only the foundation before running out of money, and then everyone would laugh at you. ³⁰They would say, ' There's the person who started that building and couldn't afford to finish it!'

³¹"Or what king would go to war against another king without first sitting down with his counselors to discuss whether his army of 10,000 could defeat the 20,000 soldiers marching against him? ³²And if he can't, he will send a delegation to discuss terms of peace while the enemy is still far away. ³³So you cannot become my disciple without giving up everything you own.

³⁴"Salt is good for seasoning. But if it loses its flavor, how do you make it salty again? ³⁵Flavorless salt is good neither for the soil nor for the manure pile. It is thrown away. Anyone with ears to hear should listen and understand!"

### Parable of the Lost Sheep

**15** Tax collectors and other notorious sinners often came to listen to Jesus teach. ²This made the Pharisees and teachers of religious law complain that he was associating with such sinful people—even eating with them!

³So Jesus told them this story: ⁴"If a man has a hundred sheep and one of them gets lost, what will he do? Won't he leave the ninety-nine others in the wilderness and go to search for the one that is lost until he finds it? ⁵And when he has found it, he will joyfully carry it home on his shoulders. ⁶When he arrives, he will call together his friends and neighbors, saying, 'Rejoice with me because I have found my lost sheep.' ⁷In the same way, there is more joy in heaven over one lost sinner who repents and returns to God than over ninety-nine others who are righteous and haven't strayed away!

### Parable of the Lost Coin

⁸"Or suppose a woman has ten silver coins* and loses one. Won't she light a lamp and sweep the entire house and search carefully until she finds it? ⁹And when she finds it, she will call in her friends and neighbors and say, 'Rejoice with me because I have found my lost coin.' ¹⁰In the same way, there is joy in the presence of God's angels when even one sinner repents."

### Parable of the Lost Son

¹¹To illustrate the point further, Jesus told them this story: "A man had two sons. ¹²The younger son told his father, 'I want my share of your estate now before you die.' So his father agreed to divide his wealth between his sons.

¹³"A few days later this younger son packed all his belongings and moved to a distant land, and there he wasted all his money in wild living. ¹⁴About the time his money ran out, a great famine swept over the land, and he began to starve. ¹⁵He persuaded a local farmer to hire him, and the man sent him into his fields to feed the pigs. ¹⁶The young man became so hungry that even the pods he was feeding the pigs

15:8 Greek *ten drachmas.* A drachma was the equivalent of a full day's wage.

looked good to him. But no one gave him anything.

<sup>17</sup>"When he finally came to his senses, he said to himself, 'At home even the hired servants have food enough to spare, and here I am dying of hunger! <sup>18</sup>I will go home to my father and say, "Father, I have sinned against both heaven and you, <sup>19</sup>and I am no longer worthy of being called your son. Please take me on as a hired servant."'

<sup>20</sup>"So he returned home to his father. And while he was still a long way off, his father saw him coming. Filled with love and compassion, he ran to his son, embraced him, and kissed him. <sup>21</sup>His son said to him, 'Father, I have sinned against both heaven and you, and I am no longer worthy of being called your son.*'

<sup>22</sup>"But his father said to the servants, 'Quick! Bring the finest robe in the house and put it on him. Get a ring for his finger and sandals for his feet. <sup>23</sup>And kill the calf we have been fattening. We must celebrate with a feast, <sup>24</sup>for this son of mine was dead and has now returned to life. He was lost, but now he is found.' So the party began.

<sup>25</sup>"Meanwhile, the older son was in the fields working. When he returned home, he heard music and dancing in the house, <sup>26</sup>and he asked one of the servants what was going on. <sup>27</sup>'Your brother is back,' he was told, 'and your father has killed the fattened calf. We are celebrating because of his safe return.'

<sup>28</sup>"The older brother was angry and wouldn't go in. His father came out and begged him, <sup>29</sup>but he replied, 'All these years I've slaved for you and never once refused to do a single thing you told me to. And in all that time you never gave me even one young goat for a feast with my friends. <sup>30</sup>Yet when this son of yours comes back after squandering your money on prostitutes, you celebrate by killing the fattened calf!'

<sup>31</sup>"His father said to him, 'Look, dear son, you have always stayed by me, and everything I have is yours. <sup>32</sup>We had to celebrate this happy day. For your brother was dead and has come back to life! He was lost, but now he is found!'"

## Parable of the Shrewd Manager

**16** Jesus told this story to his disciples: " There was a certain rich man who had a manager handling his affairs. One day a report came that the manager was wasting his employer's money. <sup>2</sup>So the employer called him in and said, ' What's this I hear about you? Get your report in order, because you are going to be fired.'

<sup>3</sup>"The manager thought to himself, 'Now what? My boss has fired me. I don't have the strength to dig ditches, and I'm too proud to beg. <sup>4</sup>Ah, I know how to ensure that I'll have plenty of friends who will give me a home when I am fired.'

<sup>5</sup>"So he invited each person who owed money to his employer to come and discuss the situation. He asked the first one, 'How much do you owe him?' <sup>6</sup>The man replied, 'I owe him 800 gallons of olive oil.' So the manager told him, ' Take the bill and quickly change it to 400 gallons.*'

<sup>7</sup>"'And how much do you owe my employer?' he asked the next man. 'I owe him 1,000 bushels of wheat,' was the reply. 'Here,' the manager said, 'take the bill and change it to 800 bushels.*'

<sup>8</sup>" The rich man had to admire the dishonest rascal for being so shrewd. And it is true that the children of this world are more shrewd in dealing with the world around them than are the children of the light. <sup>9</sup>Here's the lesson: Use your worldly resources to benefit others and make friends. Then, when your earthly possessions are gone, they will welcome you to an eternal home.*

<sup>10</sup>"If you are faithful in little things, you will be faithful in large ones. But if you are dishonest in little things, you won't be honest with greater responsibilities. <sup>11</sup>And if you are untrustworthy about worldly wealth, who will trust you with the true riches of heaven? <sup>12</sup>And if you are not faithful with other people's things, why should you be trusted with things of your own?

<sup>13</sup>"No one can serve two masters. For you will hate one and love the other; you will be devoted to one and despise the other. You cannot serve both God and money."

---

**15:21** Some manuscripts add *Please take me on as a hired servant.* **16:9** Or *you will be welcomed into eternal homes.* **16:6** Greek *100 baths . . . 50 [baths].* **16:7** Greek *100 korous . . . 80 [korous].*

# HIGH cost of drugs
READ LUKE 12:6-7

There's a debate raging in the medical insurance world today and it seems likely to only get more heated. As new drugs come on the market, the insurance industry is balking at paying for these incredibly expensive treatments (some of the new classes of anti-cancer treatments cost $60,000 a year!) because they cannot cure patients, but only modestly extend their lives. Patients are excited to hear about these new treatments—only to discover their insurance company will pay only a percentage of the costs, and there's no way they can afford the rest themselves.

The bottom-line question has become: <u>How much is a life worth?</u>

Jesus says that even a little sparrow, which could be bought for two cents, is valuable enough to God that He never forgets a single one. We, on the other hand, are so valuable to Him that our very hairs are numbered. (This might be easy if you've recently had chemo!) There's no price tag He would put on our lives—<u>we are priceless to Him.</u>

---

<sup>14</sup>The Pharisees, who dearly loved their money, heard all this and scoffed at him. <sup>15</sup>Then he said to them, " You like to appear righteous in public, but God knows your hearts. What this world honors is detestable in the sight of God.

<sup>16</sup>"Until John the Baptist, the law of Moses and the messages of the prophets were your guides. But now the Good News of the Kingdom of God is preached, and everyone is eager to get in.* <sup>17</sup>But that doesn't mean that the law has lost its force. It is easier for heaven and earth to disappear than for the smallest point of God's law to be overturned.

<sup>18</sup>"For example, a man who divorces his wife and marries someone else commits adultery. And anyone who marries a woman divorced from her husband commits adultery."

## Parable of the Rich Man and Lazarus
<sup>19</sup>Jesus said, "There was a certain rich man who was splendidly clothed in purple and fine linen and who lived each day in luxury. <sup>20</sup>At his gate lay a poor man named Lazarus who was covered with sores. <sup>21</sup>As Lazarus lay there longing for scraps from the rich man's table, the dogs would come and lick his open sores.

<sup>22</sup>"Finally, the poor man died and was carried by the angels to be with Abraham.* The rich man also died and was buried, <sup>23</sup>and his soul went to the place of the dead.* There, in torment, he saw Abraham in the far distance with Lazarus at his side.

<sup>24</sup>"The rich man shouted, 'Father Abraham, have some pity! Send Lazarus over here to dip the tip of his finger in water and cool my tongue. I am in anguish in these flames.'

<sup>25</sup>"But Abraham said to him, 'Son, remember that during your lifetime you had everything you wanted, and Lazarus had nothing. So now he is here being comforted, and you are in anguish. <sup>26</sup>And besides, there is a great chasm separating us. No one can cross over to you from here, and no one can cross over to us from there.'

<sup>27</sup>"Then the rich man said, 'Please, Father Abraham, at least send him to my father's home. <sup>28</sup>For I have five brothers, and I want him to warn them so they don't end up in this place of torment.'

<sup>29</sup>"But Abraham said, 'Moses and the prophets have warned them. Your brothers can read what they wrote.'

<sup>30</sup>"The rich man replied, 'No, Father Abraham! But if someone is sent to them from the dead, then they will repent of their sins and turn to God.'

<sup>31</sup>"But Abraham said, 'If they won't listen to Moses and the prophets, they won't listen even if someone rises from the dead.' "

**16:16** Or *everyone is urged to enter in.*   **16:22** Greek *into Abraham's bosom.*   **16:23** Greek *to Hades.*

## Teachings about Forgiveness and Faith

**17** ¹One day Jesus said to his disciples, "There will always be temptations to sin, but what sorrow awaits the person who does the tempting! ²It would be better to be thrown into the sea with a millstone hung around your neck than to cause one of these little ones to fall into sin. ³So watch yourselves!

"If another believer* sins, rebuke that person; then if there is repentance, forgive. ⁴Even if that person wrongs you seven times a day and each time turns again and asks forgiveness, you must forgive."

⁵The apostles said to the Lord, "Show us how to increase our faith."

⁶The Lord answered, "If you had faith even as small as a mustard seed, you could say to this mulberry tree, 'May you be uprooted and thrown into the sea,' and it would obey you!

⁷"When a servant comes in from plowing or taking care of sheep, does his master say, 'Come in and eat with me'? ⁸No, he says, 'Prepare my meal, put on your apron, and serve me while I eat. Then you can eat later.' ⁹And does the master thank the servant for doing what he was told to do? Of course not. ¹⁰In the same way, when you obey me you should say, 'We are unworthy servants who have simply done our duty.'"

## Ten Healed of Leprosy

¹¹As Jesus continued on toward Jerusalem, he reached the border between Galilee and Samaria. ¹²As he entered a village there, ten lepers stood at a distance, ¹³crying out, "Jesus, Master, have mercy on us!"

¹⁴He looked at them and said, "Go show yourselves to the priests."* And as they went, they were cleansed of their leprosy.

¹⁵One of them, when he saw that he was healed, came back to Jesus, shouting, "Praise God!" ¹⁶He fell to the ground at Jesus' feet, thanking him for what he had done. This man was a Samaritan.

¹⁷Jesus asked, "Didn't I heal ten men? Where are the other nine? ¹⁸Has no one returned to give glory to God except this foreigner?" ¹⁹And Jesus said to the man, "Stand up and go. Your faith has healed you.*"

## The Coming of the Kingdom

²⁰One day the Pharisees asked Jesus, "When will the Kingdom of God come?"

Jesus replied, "The Kingdom of God can't be detected by visible signs.* ²¹You won't be able to say, 'Here it is!' or 'It's over there!' For the Kingdom of God is already among you.*"

²²Then he said to his disciples, "The time is coming when you will long to see the day when the Son of Man returns,* but you won't see it. ²³People will tell you, 'Look, there is the Son of Man,' or 'Here he is,' but don't go out and follow them. ²⁴For as the lightning flashes and lights up the sky from one end to the other, so it will be on the day when the Son of Man comes. ²⁵But first the Son of Man must suffer terribly* and be rejected by this generation.

²⁶"When the Son of Man returns, it will be like it was in Noah's day. ²⁷In those days, the people enjoyed banquets and parties and weddings right up to the time Noah entered his boat and the flood came and destroyed them all.

²⁸"And the world will be as it was in the days of Lot. People went about their daily business—eating and drinking, buying and selling, farming and building—²⁹until the morning Lot left Sodom. Then fire and burning sulfur rained down from heaven and destroyed them all. ³⁰Yes, it will be 'business as usual' right up to the day when the Son of Man is revealed. ³¹On that day a person out on the deck of a roof must not go down into the house to pack. A person out in the field must not return home. ³²Remember what happened to Lot's wife! ³³If you cling to your life, you will lose it, and if you let your life go, you will save it. ³⁴That night two people will be asleep in one bed; one will be taken, the other left. ³⁵Two women will be grinding flour together at the mill; one will be taken, the other left.*"

³⁷"Where will this happen, Lord?"* the disciples asked.

17:3 Greek *If your brother.*    17:14 See Lev 14:2-32.    17:19 Or *Your faith has saved you.*    17:20 Or *by your speculations.*
17:21 Or *is within you,* or *is in your grasp.*    17:22 Or *long for even one day with the Son of Man.* "Son of Man" is a title Jesus used for himself.    17:25 Or *suffer many things.*    17:35 Some manuscripts add verse 36, *Two men will be working in the field; one will be taken, the other left.* Compare Matt 24:40.    17:37a Greek *"Where, Lord?"*

Jesus replied, "Just as the gathering of vultures shows there is a carcass nearby, so these signs indicate that the end is near."*

## Parable of the Persistent Widow

**18** One day Jesus told his disciples a story to show that they should always pray and never give up. ²"There was a judge in a certain city," he said, "who neither feared God nor cared about people. ³A widow of that city came to him repeatedly, saying, 'Give me justice in this dispute with my enemy.' ⁴The judge ignored her for a while, but finally he said to himself, 'I don't fear God or care about people, ⁵but this woman is driving me crazy. I'm going to see that she gets justice, because she is wearing me out with her constant requests!'"

⁶Then the Lord said, "Learn a lesson from this unjust judge. ⁷Even he rendered a just decision in the end. So don't you think God will surely give justice to his chosen people who cry out to him day and night? Will he keep putting them off? ⁸I tell you, he will grant justice to them quickly! But when the Son of Man* returns, how many will he find on the earth who have faith?"

## Parable of the Pharisee and Tax Collector

⁹Then Jesus told this story to some who had great confidence in their own righteousness and scorned everyone else: ¹⁰"Two men went to the Temple to pray. One was a Pharisee, and the other was a despised tax collector. ¹¹The Pharisee stood by himself and prayed this prayer*: 'I thank you, God, that I am not a sinner like everyone else. For I don't cheat, I don't sin, and I don't commit adultery. I'm certainly not like that tax collector! ¹²I fast twice a week, and I give you a tenth of my income.'

¹³"But the tax collector stood at a distance and dared not even lift his eyes to heaven as he prayed. Instead, he beat his chest in sorrow, saying, 'O God, be merciful to me, for I am a sinner.' ¹⁴I tell you, this sinner, not the Pharisee, returned home justified before God. For those who exalt themselves will be humbled, and those who humble themselves will be exalted."

## Jesus Blesses the Children

¹⁵One day some parents brought their little children to Jesus so he could touch and bless them. But when the disciples saw this, they scolded the parents for bothering him.

¹⁶Then Jesus called for the children and said to the disciples, "Let the children come to me. Don't stop them! For the Kingdom of God belongs to those who are like these children. ¹⁷I tell you the truth, anyone who doesn't receive the Kingdom of God like a child will never enter it."

## The Rich Man

¹⁸Once a religious leader asked Jesus this question: "Good Teacher, what should I do to inherit eternal life?"

¹⁹"Why do you call me good?" Jesus asked him. "Only God is truly good. ²⁰But to answer your question, you know the commandments: 'You must not commit adultery. You must not murder. You must not steal. You must not testify falsely. Honor your father and mother.'* "

²¹The man replied, "I've obeyed all these commandments since I was young."

²²When Jesus heard his answer, he said, "There is still one thing you haven't done. Sell all your possessions and give the money to the poor, and you will have treasure in heaven. Then come, follow me."

²³But when the man heard this he became very sad, for he was very rich.

**24**When Jesus saw this,* he said, "How hard it is for the rich to enter the Kingdom of God! ²⁵In fact, it is easier for a camel to go through the eye of a needle than for a rich person to enter the Kingdom of God!"

²⁶Those who heard this said, "Then who in the world can be saved?"

²⁷He replied, "What is impossible for people is possible with God."

²⁸Peter said, "We've left our homes to follow you."

**29**"Yes," Jesus replied, "and I assure you that everyone who has given up house or

17:37b Greek *"Wherever the carcass is, the vultures gather."*   18:8 "Son of Man" is a title Jesus used for himself.   18:11 Some manuscripts read *stood and prayed this prayer to himself.*   18:20 Exod 20:12-16; Deut 5:16-20.   18:24 Some manuscripts read *When Jesus saw how sad the man was.*

wife or brothers or parents or children, for the sake of the Kingdom of God, 30 will be repaid many times over in this life, and will have eternal life in the world to come."

### Jesus Again Predicts His Death

31 Taking the twelve disciples aside, Jesus said, "Listen, we're going up to Jerusalem, where all the predictions of the prophets concerning the Son of Man will come true. 32 He will be handed over to the Romans,* and he will be mocked, treated shamefully, and spit upon. 33 They will flog him with a whip and kill him, but on the third day he will rise again."

34 But they didn't understand any of this. The significance of his words was hidden from them, and they failed to grasp what he was talking about.

### Jesus Heals a Blind Beggar

35 As Jesus approached Jericho, a blind beggar was sitting beside the road. 36 When he heard the noise of a crowd going past, he asked what was happening. 37 They told him that Jesus the Nazarene* was going by. 38 So he began shouting, "Jesus, Son of David, have mercy on me!"

39 "Be quiet!" the people in front yelled at him.

But he only shouted louder, "Son of David, have mercy on me!"

18:32 Greek the Gentiles.    18:37 Or Jesus of Nazareth.

40 When Jesus heard him, he stopped and ordered that the man be brought to him. As the man came near, Jesus asked him, 41 "What do you want me to do for you?"

"Lord," he said, "I want to see!"

42 And Jesus said, "All right, receive your sight! Your faith has healed you." 43 Instantly the man could see, and he followed Jesus, praising God. And all who saw it praised God, too.

### Jesus and Zacchaeus

**19** Jesus entered Jericho and made his way through the town. 2 There was a man there named Zacchaeus. He was the chief tax collector in the region, and he had become very rich. 3 He tried to get a look at Jesus, but he was too short to see over the crowd. 4 So he ran ahead and climbed a sycamore-fig tree beside the road, for Jesus was going to pass that way.

5 When Jesus came by, he looked up at Zacchaeus and called him by name. "Zacchaeus!" he said. "Quick, come down! I must be a guest in your home today."

6 Zacchaeus quickly climbed down and took Jesus to his house in great excitement and joy. 7 But the people were displeased. "He has gone to be the guest of a notorious sinner," they grumbled.

8 Meanwhile, Zacchaeus stood before the

---

*Sheep, Coin, Son*

## LOST and found

READ LUKE 15:1-32

We all fit into one of two categories in life: Either we're lost or we should be searching to rescue the lost. It doesn't matter whether we're sick or well—those are the two choices. Jesus tells three parables (stories) about a lost sheep, a lost coin, and a lost son to illustrate how much lost people matter to God.

If you still are lost, God is on an all-out search to find you and bring you home. He's pulling out all the stops, sending people to show you the way, even handing you a copy of *He Cares* to reveal His love for you. And when you find your way back home to Him, there will be incredible rejoicing over you.

If you've already found a relationship with God, your mission is like Jesus' mission to "seek and save the lost." Never miss an opportunity to show lost people they matter to God. Let them see that in spite of the trials you face, you have found a living hope.

Lord and said, "I will give half my wealth to the poor, Lord, and if I have cheated people on their taxes, I will give them back four times as much!"

**9** Jesus responded, "Salvation has come to this home today, for this man has shown himself to be a true son of Abraham. **10** For the Son of Man* came to seek and save those who are lost."

### Parable of the Ten Servants

**11** The crowd was listening to everything Jesus said. And because he was nearing Jerusalem, he told them a story to correct the impression that the Kingdom of God would begin right away. **12** He said, "A nobleman was called away to a distant empire to be crowned king and then return. **13** Before he left, he called together ten of his servants and divided among them ten pounds of silver,* saying, 'Invest this for me while I am gone.' **14** But his people hated him and sent a delegation after him to say, ' We do not want him to be our king.'

**15** "After he was crowned king, he returned and called in the servants to whom he had given the money. He wanted to find out what their profits were. **16** The first servant reported, 'Master, I invested your money and made ten times the original amount!'

**17** " ' Well done!' the king exclaimed. 'You are a good servant. You have been faithful with the little I entrusted to you, so you will be governor of ten cities as your reward.'

**18** " The next servant reported, 'Master, I invested your money and made five times the original amount.'

**19** " ' Well done!' the king said. ' You will be governor over five cities.'

**20** "But the third servant brought back only the original amount of money and said, 'Master, I hid your money and kept it safe. **21** I was afraid because you are a hard man to deal with, taking what isn't yours and harvesting crops you didn't plant.'

**22** " 'You wicked servant!' the king roared. 'Your own words condemn you. If you knew that I'm a hard man who takes what isn't mine and harvests crops I didn't plant, **23** why

didn't you deposit my money in the bank? At least I could have gotten some interest on it.'

**24** " Then, turning to the others standing nearby, the king ordered, ' Take the money from this servant, and give it to the one who has ten pounds.'

**25** " 'But, master,' they said, 'he already has ten pounds!'

**26** " ' Yes,' the king replied, 'and to those who use well what they are given, even more will be given. But from those who do nothing, even what little they have will be taken away. **27** And as for these enemies of mine who didn't want me to be their king—bring them in and execute them right here in front of me.' "

### Jesus' Triumphant Entry

**28** After telling this story, Jesus went on toward Jerusalem, walking ahead of his disciples. **29** As he came to the towns of Bethphage and Bethany on the Mount of Olives, he sent two disciples ahead. **30** "Go into that village over there," he told them. "As you enter it, you will see a young donkey tied there that no one has ever ridden. Untie it and bring it here. **31** If anyone asks, ' Why are you untying that colt?' just say, ' The Lord needs it.' "

**32** So they went and found the colt, just as Jesus had said. **33** And sure enough, as they were untying it, the owners asked them, "Why are you untying that colt?"

**34** And the disciples simply replied, "The Lord needs it." **35** So they brought the colt to Jesus and threw their garments over it for him to ride on.

**36** As he rode along, the crowds spread out their garments on the road ahead of him. **37** When he reached the place where the road started down the Mount of Olives, all of his followers began to shout and sing as they walked along, praising God for all the wonderful miracles they had seen.

**38** "Blessings on the King who comes in the
name of the Lord!
Peace in heaven, and glory in highest
heaven!"*

**39** But some of the Pharisees among the crowd said, "Teacher, rebuke your followers for saying things like that!"

---

19:10 "Son of Man" is a title Jesus used for himself.    19:13 Greek *ten minas;* one mina was worth about three months' wages.
19:38 Pss 118:26; 148:1.

⁴⁰He replied, "If they kept quiet, the stones along the road would burst into cheers!"

## Jesus Weeps over Jerusalem
⁴¹But as he came closer to Jerusalem and saw the city ahead, he began to weep. ⁴²"How I wish today that you of all people would understand the way to peace. But now it is too late, and peace is hidden from your eyes. ⁴³Before long your enemies will build ramparts against your walls and encircle you and close in on you from every side. ⁴⁴They will crush you into the ground, and your children with you. Your enemies will not leave a single stone in place, because you did not accept your opportunity for salvation."

## Jesus Clears the Temple
⁴⁵Then Jesus entered the Temple and began to drive out the people selling animals for sacrifices. ⁴⁶He said to them, "The Scriptures declare, 'My Temple will be a house of prayer,' but you have turned it into a den of thieves."*

⁴⁷After that, he taught daily in the Temple, but the leading priests, the teachers of religious law, and the other leaders of the people began planning how to kill him. ⁴⁸But they could think of nothing, because all the people hung on every word he said.

## The Authority of Jesus Challenged
**20** One day as Jesus was teaching the people and preaching the Good News in the Temple, the leading priests, the teachers of religious law, and the elders came up to him. ²They demanded, "By what authority are you doing all these things? Who gave you the right?"

³"Let me ask you a question first," he replied. ⁴"Did John's authority to baptize come from heaven, or was it merely human?"

⁵They talked it over among themselves. "If we say it was from heaven, he will ask why we didn't believe John. ⁶But if we say it was merely human, the people will stone us because they are convinced John was a prophet." ⁷So they finally replied that they didn't know.

⁸And Jesus responded, "Then I won't tell you by what authority I do these things."

## Parable of the Evil Farmers
⁹Now Jesus turned to the people again and told them this story: "A man planted a vineyard, leased it to tenant farmers, and moved to another country to live for several years. ¹⁰At the time of the grape harvest, he sent one of his servants to collect his share of the crop. But the farmers attacked the servant, beat him up, and sent him back empty-handed. ¹¹So the owner sent another servant, but they also insulted him, beat him up, and sent him away empty-handed. ¹²A third man was sent, and they wounded him and chased him away.

¹³" 'What will I do?' the owner asked himself. 'I know! I'll send my cherished son. Surely they will respect him.'

¹⁴"But when the tenant farmers saw his son, they said to each other, 'Here comes the heir to this estate. Let's kill him and get the estate for ourselves!' ¹⁵So they dragged him out of the vineyard and murdered him.

"What do you suppose the owner of the vineyard will do to them?" Jesus asked. ¹⁶"I'll tell you—he will come and kill those farmers and lease the vineyard to others."

"How terrible that such a thing should ever happen," his listeners protested.

¹⁷Jesus looked at them and said, " Then what does this Scripture mean?

'The stone that the builders rejected
has now become the cornerstone.'*

¹⁸Everyone who stumbles over that stone will be broken to pieces, and it will crush anyone it falls on."

¹⁹The teachers of religious law and the leading priests wanted to arrest Jesus immediately because they realized he was telling the story against them—they were the wicked farmers. But they were afraid of the people's reaction.

## Taxes for Caesar
²⁰Watching for their opportunity, the leaders sent spies pretending to be honest men. They tried to get Jesus to say something that could be reported to the Roman governor so

19:46 Isa 56:7; Jer 7:11.   20:17 Ps 118:22.

he would arrest Jesus. 21"Teacher," they said, "we know that you speak and teach what is right and are not influenced by what others think. You teach the way of God truthfully. 22Now tell us—is it right for us to pay taxes to Caesar or not?"

23He saw through their trickery and said, 24"Show me a Roman coin.* Whose picture and title are stamped on it?"

"Caesar's," they replied.

25"Well then," he said, "give to Caesar what belongs to Caesar, and give to God what belongs to God."

26So they failed to trap him by what he said in front of the people. Instead, they were amazed by his answer, and they became silent.

## Discussion about Resurrection

27Then Jesus was approached by some Sadducees—religious leaders who say there is no resurrection from the dead. 28They posed this question: "Teacher, Moses gave us a law that if a man dies, leaving a wife but no children, his brother should marry the widow and have a child who will carry on the brother's name.* 29Well, suppose there were seven brothers. The oldest one married and then died without children. 30So the second brother married the widow, but he also died. 31Then the third brother married her. This continued with all seven of them, who died without children. 32Finally, the woman also died. 33So tell us, whose wife will she be in the resurrection? For all seven were married to her!"

34Jesus replied, "Marriage is for people here on earth. 35But in the age to come, those worthy of being raised from the dead will neither marry nor be given in marriage. 36And they will never die again. In this respect they will be like angels. They are children of God and children of the resurrection.

37"But now, as to whether the dead will be raised—even Moses proved this when he wrote about the burning bush. Long after Abraham, Isaac, and Jacob had died, he referred to the Lord* as 'the God of Abraham, the God of Isaac, and the God of Jacob.'*

38So he is the God of the living, not the dead, for they are all alive to him."

39"Well said, Teacher!" remarked some of the teachers of religious law who were standing there. 40And then no one dared to ask him any more questions.

## Whose Son Is the Messiah?

41Then Jesus presented them with a question. " Why is it," he asked, "that the Messiah is said to be the son of David? 42For David himself wrote in the book of Psalms:

'The Lord said to my Lord,
   Sit in the place of honor at my right
     hand
43until I humble your enemies,
   making them a footstool under your
     feet.'*

44Since David called the Messiah 'Lord,' how can the Messiah be his son?"

45Then, with the crowds listening, he turned to his disciples and said, 46"Beware of these teachers of religious law! For they like to parade around in flowing robes and love to receive respectful greetings as they walk in the marketplaces. And how they love the seats of honor in the synagogues and the head table at banquets. 47Yet they shamelessly cheat widows out of their property and then pretend to be pious by making long prayers in public. Because of this, they will be severely punished."

## The Widow's Offering

**21** While Jesus was in the Temple, he watched the rich people dropping their gifts in the collection box. 2Then a poor widow came by and dropped in two small coins.*

3"I tell you the truth," Jesus said, "this poor widow has given more than all the rest of them. 4For they have given a tiny part of their surplus, but she, poor as she is, has given everything she has."

## Jesus Foretells the Future

5Some of his disciples began talking about the majestic stonework of the Temple and the memorial decorations on the walls. But

---

**20:24** Greek *a denarius.*   **20:28** See Deut 25:5-6.   **20:37a** Greek *when he wrote about the bush. He referred to the Lord.*
**20:37b** Exod 3:6.   **20:42-43** Ps 110:1.   **21:2** Greek *two lepta* [the smallest of Jewish coins].

Jesus said, 6 " The time is coming when all these things will be completely demolished. Not one stone will be left on top of another!"

7 "Teacher," they asked, "when will all this happen? What sign will show us that these things are about to take place?"

8 He replied, "Don't let anyone mislead you, for many will come in my name, claiming, 'I am the Messiah,'* and saying, 'The time has come!' But don't believe them. 9 And when you hear of wars and insurrections, don't panic. Yes, these things must take place first, but the end won't follow immediately." 10 Then he added, "Nation will go to war against nation, and kingdom against kingdom. 11 There will be great earthquakes, and there will be famines and plagues in many lands, and there will be terrifying things and great miraculous signs from heaven.

12 "But before all this occurs, there will be a time of great persecution. You will be dragged into synagogues and prisons, and you will stand trial before kings and governors because you are my followers. 13 But this will be your opportunity to tell them about me.* 14 So don't worry in advance about how to answer the charges against you, 15 for I will give you the right words and such wisdom that none of your opponents will be able to reply or refute you! 16 Even those closest to you—your parents, brothers, relatives, and friends—will betray you. They will even kill some of you. 17 And everyone will hate you because you are my followers.* 18 But not a hair of your head will perish! 19 By standing firm, you will win your souls.

20 "And when you see Jerusalem surrounded by armies, then you will know that the time of its destruction has arrived. 21 Then those in Judea must flee to the hills. Those in Jerusalem must get out, and those out in the country should not return to the city. 22 For those will be days of God's vengeance, and the prophetic words of the Scriptures will be fulfilled. 23 How terrible it will be for pregnant women and for nursing mothers in those days. For there will be disaster in the land and great anger against this people. 24 They will be killed by the sword or sent away as captives to all the nations of the world. And Jerusalem will be trampled down by the Gentiles until the period of the Gentiles comes to an end.

25 "And there will be strange signs in the sun, moon, and stars. And here on earth the nations will be in turmoil, perplexed by the roaring seas and strange tides. 26 People will be terrified at what they see coming upon the earth, for the powers in the heavens will be shaken. 27 Then everyone will see the Son of Man* coming on a cloud with power and great glory.* 28 So when all these things begin to happen, stand and look up, for your salvation is near!"

29 Then he gave them this illustration: "Notice the fig tree, or any other tree. 30 When the leaves come out, you know without being told that summer is near. 31 In the same way, when you see all these things taking place, you can know that the Kingdom of God is near. 32 I tell you the truth, this generation will not pass from the scene until all these things have taken place. 33 Heaven and earth will disappear, but my words will never disappear.

34 "Watch out! Don't let your hearts be dulled by carousing and drunkenness, and by the worries of this life. Don't let that day catch you unaware, 35 like a trap. For that day will come upon everyone living on the earth. 36 Keep alert at all times. And pray that you might be strong enough to escape these coming horrors and stand before the Son of Man."

37 Every day Jesus went to the Temple to teach, and each evening he returned to spend the night on the Mount of Olives. 38 The crowds gathered at the Temple early each morning to hear him.

## Judas Agrees to Betray Jesus

**22** The Festival of Unleavened Bread, which is also called Passover, was approaching. 2 The leading priests and teachers of religious law were plotting how to kill Jesus, but they were afraid of the people's reaction.

3 Then Satan entered into Judas Iscariot, who was one of the twelve disciples, 4 and he

---

21:8 Greek *claiming, 'I am.'*    21:13 Or *This will be your testimony against them.*    21:17 Greek *on account of my name.*
21:27a "Son of Man" is a title Jesus used for himself.    21:27b See Dan 7:13.

went to the leading priests and captains of the Temple guard to discuss the best way to betray Jesus to them. [5]They were delighted, and they promised to give him money. [6]So he agreed and began looking for an opportunity to betray Jesus so they could arrest him when the crowds weren't around.

### The Last Supper

[7]Now the Festival of Unleavened Bread arrived, when the Passover lamb is sacrificed. [8]Jesus sent Peter and John ahead and said, "Go and prepare the Passover meal, so we can eat it together."

[9]"Where do you want us to prepare it?" they asked him.

[10]He replied, "As soon as you enter Jerusalem, a man carrying a pitcher of water will meet you. Follow him. At the house he enters, [11]say to the owner, 'The Teacher asks: Where is the guest room where I can eat the Passover meal with my disciples?' [12]He will take you upstairs to a large room that is already set up. That is where you should prepare our meal." [13]They went off to the city and found everything just as Jesus had said, and they prepared the Passover meal there.

[14]When the time came, Jesus and the apostles sat down together at the table.* [15]Jesus said, "I have been very eager to eat this Passover meal with you before my suffering begins. [16]For I tell you now that I won't eat this meal again until its meaning is fulfilled in the Kingdom of God."

[17]Then he took a cup of wine and gave thanks to God for it. Then he said, "Take this and share it among yourselves. [18]For I will not drink wine again until the Kingdom of God has come."

[19]He took some bread and gave thanks to God for it. Then he broke it in pieces and gave it to the disciples, saying, "This is my body, which is given for you. Do this to remember me."

[20]After supper he took another cup of wine and said, "This cup is the new covenant between God and his people—an agreement confirmed with my blood, which is poured out as a sacrifice for you.* [21]"But here at this table, sitting among us

as a friend, is the man who will betray me. [22]For it has been determined that the Son of Man* must die. But what sorrow awaits the one who betrays him." [23]The disciples began to ask each other which of them would ever do such a thing.

[24]Then they began to argue among themselves about who would be the greatest among them. [25]Jesus told them, "In this world the kings and great men lord it over their people, yet they are called 'friends of the people.' [26]But among you it will be different. Those who are the greatest among you should take the lowest rank, and the leader should be like a servant. [27]Who is more important, the one who sits at the table or the one who serves? The one who sits at the table, of course. But not here! For I am among you as one who serves.

[28]"You have stayed with me in my time of trial. [29]And just as my Father has granted me a Kingdom, I now grant you the right [30]to eat and drink at my table in my Kingdom. And you will sit on thrones, judging the twelve tribes of Israel.

### Jesus Predicts Peter's Denial

[31]"Simon, Simon, Satan has asked to sift each of you like wheat. [32]But I have pleaded in prayer for you, Simon, that your faith should not fail. So when you have repented

## ATTITUDE of gratitude
READ LUKE 17:11-19

Do your pleas to God last longer than your praises?

Developing an attitude of gratitude is important during a health crisis. We can get so wrapped up praying for all the "big" things we want God to do that we may miss a lot of the important "little" things He's doing each day. Why not take a calendar and write down one thing every day for which you can praise God that day? (No fair writing the same thing down every day!) Some days you may want to fill the whole square with praises; other days it may take some thought. Either way, return at the end of each day to give glory to God.

22:14 Or *reclined together.*   22:19-20 Some manuscripts omit 22:19b-20, *which is given for you . . . which is poured out as a sacrifice for you.*   22:22 "Son of Man" is a title Jesus used for himself.

and turned to me again, strengthen your brothers."

33 Peter said, "Lord, I am ready to go to prison with you, and even to die with you."

34 But Jesus said, "Peter, let me tell you something. Before the rooster crows tomorrow morning, you will deny three times that you even know me."

35 Then Jesus asked them, " When I sent you out to preach the Good News and you did not have money, a traveler's bag, or extra clothing, did you need anything?"

"No," they replied.

36 "But now," he said, "take your money and a traveler's bag. And if you don't have a sword, sell your cloak and buy one! 37 For the time has come for this prophecy about me to be fulfilled: 'He was counted among the rebels.'* Yes, everything written about me by the prophets will come true."

38 "Look, Lord," they replied, "we have two swords among us."

"That's enough," he said.

### Jesus Prays on the Mount of Olives

39 Then, accompanied by the disciples, Jesus left the upstairs room and went as usual to the Mount of Olives. 40 There he told them, "Pray that you will not give in to temptation."

41 He walked away, about a stone's throw, and knelt down and prayed, 42 "Father, if you are willing, please take this cup of suffering away from me. Yet I want your will to be done, not mine." 43 Then an angel from heaven appeared and strengthened him. 44 He prayed more fervently, and he was in such agony of spirit that his sweat fell to the ground like great drops of blood.*

45 At last he stood up again and returned to the disciples, only to find them asleep, exhausted from grief. 46 "Why are you sleeping?" he asked them. "Get up and pray, so that you will not give in to temptation."

### Jesus Is Betrayed and Arrested

47 But even as Jesus said this, a crowd approached, led by Judas, one of the twelve disciples. Judas walked over to Jesus to greet him with a kiss. 48 But Jesus said, "Judas, would you betray the Son of Man with a kiss?"

49 When the other disciples saw what was about to happen, they exclaimed, "Lord, should we fight? We brought the swords!" 50 And one of them struck at the high priest's slave, slashing off his right ear.

51 But Jesus said, "No more of this." And he touched the man's ear and healed him.

52 Then Jesus spoke to the leading priests, the captains of the Temple guard, and the elders who had come for him. "Am I some dangerous revolutionary," he asked, "that you come with swords and clubs to arrest me? 53 Why didn't you arrest me in the Temple? I was there every day. But this is your moment, the time when the power of darkness reigns."

### Peter Denies Jesus

54 So they arrested him and led him to the high priest's home. And Peter followed at a distance. 55 The guards lit a fire in the middle of the courtyard and sat around it, and Peter joined them there. 56 A servant girl noticed him in the firelight and began staring at him. Finally she said, "This man was one of Jesus' followers!"

57 But Peter denied it. "Woman," he said, "I don't even know him!"

58 After a while someone else looked at him and said, "You must be one of them!"

"No, man, I'm not!" Peter retorted.

59 About an hour later someone else in-

---

## PRAYERS that prepare

READ LUKE 22:31-34, 54-62

Who's praying for you today? Your relatives? Your friends? Your coworkers or neighbors? How about Jesus?

He does pray for us. Here He tells Peter that He has "pleaded in prayer" for him. Because Jesus is all-knowing, He knows Peter will let Him down, so even *before* Peter denies Him, Jesus prays about the situation. He prays Peter will confess his sin, turn his heart back to Him, and that he eventually will be spiritually strong enough to strengthen others. Talk about a prayer that prepared Peter for the future!

How wonderful to know that Jesus sees around the bend in the road and is praying for what you'll need.

---

22:37 Isa 53:12. **22:43-44** Verses 43 and 44 are not included in many ancient manuscripts.

sisted, "This must be one of them, because he is a Galilean, too."

⁶⁰But Peter said, "Man, I don't know what you are talking about." And immediately, while he was still speaking, the rooster crowed.

⁶¹At that moment the Lord turned and looked at Peter. Suddenly, the Lord's words flashed through Peter's mind: "Before the rooster crows tomorrow morning, you will deny three times that you even know me." ⁶²And Peter left the courtyard, weeping bitterly.

⁶³The guards in charge of Jesus began mocking and beating him. ⁶⁴They blindfolded him and said, "Prophesy to us! Who hit you that time?" ⁶⁵And they hurled all sorts of terrible insults at him.

### Jesus before the Council
⁶⁶At daybreak all the elders of the people assembled, including the leading priests and the teachers of religious law. Jesus was led before this high council,* ⁶⁷and they said, "Tell us, are you the Messiah?"

But he replied, "If I tell you, you won't believe me. ⁶⁸And if I ask you a question, you won't answer. ⁶⁹But from now on the Son of Man will be seated in the place of power at God's right hand.*"

⁷⁰They all shouted, "So, are you claiming to be the Son of God?"

And he replied, "You say that I am."

⁷¹"Why do we need other witnesses?" they said. "We ourselves heard him say it."

### Jesus' Trial before Pilate
**23** Then the entire council took Jesus to Pilate, the Roman governor. ²They began to state their case: "This man has been leading our people astray by telling them not to pay their taxes to the Roman government and by claiming he is the Messiah, a king."

³So Pilate asked him, "Are you the king of the Jews?"

Jesus replied, "You have said it."

⁴Pilate turned to the leading priests and to the crowd and said, "I find nothing wrong with this man!"

⁵Then they became insistent. "But he is causing riots by his teaching wherever he goes—all over Judea, from Galilee to Jerusalem!"

⁶"Oh, is he a Galilean?" Pilate asked. ⁷When they said that he was, Pilate sent him to Herod Antipas, because Galilee was under Herod's jurisdiction, and Herod happened to be in Jerusalem at the time.

⁸Herod was delighted at the opportunity to see Jesus, because he had heard about him and had been hoping for a long time to see him perform a miracle. ⁹He asked Jesus question after question, but Jesus refused to answer. ¹⁰Meanwhile, the leading priests and the teachers of religious law stood there shouting their accusations. ¹¹Then Herod and his soldiers began mocking and ridiculing Jesus. Finally, they put a royal robe on him and sent him back to Pilate. ¹²(Herod and Pilate, who had been enemies before, became friends that day.)

¹³Then Pilate called together the leading priests and other religious leaders, along with the people, ¹⁴and he announced his verdict. "You brought this man to me, accusing him of leading a revolt. I have examined him thoroughly on this point in your presence and find him innocent. ¹⁵Herod came to the same conclusion and sent him back to us. Nothing this man has done calls for the death penalty. ¹⁶So I will have him flogged, and then I will release him."*

¹⁸Then a mighty roar rose from the crowd, and with one voice they shouted, "Kill him, and release Barabbas to us!" ¹⁹(Barabbas was in prison for taking part in an insurrection in Jerusalem against the government, and for murder.) ²⁰Pilate argued with them, because he wanted to release Jesus. ²¹But they kept shouting, "Crucify him! Crucify him!"

²²For the third time he demanded, "Why? What crime has he committed? I have found no reason to sentence him to death. So I will have him flogged, and then I will release him."

²³But the mob shouted louder and louder, demanding that Jesus be crucified, and their voices prevailed. ²⁴So Pilate sentenced Jesus to die as they demanded. ²⁵As they had

**22:66** Greek *before their Sanhedrin.*    **22:69** See Ps 110:1.    **23:16** Some manuscripts add verse 17, *Now it was necessary for him to release one prisoner to them during the Passover celebration.* Compare Matt 27:15; Mark 15:6; John 18:39.

requested, he released Barabbas, the man in prison for insurrection and murder. But he turned Jesus over to them to do as they wished.

## The Crucifixion

26As they led Jesus away, a man named Simon, who was from Cyrene,* happened to be coming in from the countryside. The soldiers seized him and put the cross on him and made him carry it behind Jesus. 27A large crowd trailed behind, including many grief-stricken women. 28But Jesus turned and said to them, "Daughters of Jerusalem, don't weep for me, but weep for yourselves and for your children. 29For the days are coming when they will say, 'Fortunate indeed are the women who are childless, the wombs that have not borne a child and the breasts that have never nursed.' 30People will beg the mountains, 'Fall on us,' and plead with the hills, 'Bury us.'* 31For if these things are done when the tree is green, what will happen when it is dry?*"

32Two others, both criminals, were led out to be executed with him. 33When they came to a place called The Skull,* they nailed him to the cross. And the criminals were also crucified—one on his right and one on his left.

34Jesus said, "Father, forgive them, for they don't know what they are doing."* And the soldiers gambled for his clothes by throwing dice.*

35The crowd watched and the leaders scoffed. "He saved others," they said, "let him save himself if he is really God's Messiah, the Chosen One." 36The soldiers mocked him, too, by offering him a drink of sour wine. 37They called out to him, "If you are the King of the Jews, save yourself!" 38A sign was fastened to the cross above him with these words: "This is the King of the Jews."

39One of the criminals hanging beside him scoffed, "So you're the Messiah, are you? Prove it by saving yourself—and us, too, while you're at it!"

40But the other criminal protested, "Don't you fear God even when you have been sentenced to die? 41We deserve to die for our crimes, but this man hasn't done anything wrong." 42Then he said, "Jesus, remember me when you come into your Kingdom."

43And Jesus replied, "I assure you, today you will be with me in paradise."

## The Death of Jesus

44By this time it was noon, and darkness fell across the whole land until three o'clock. 45The light from the sun was gone. And suddenly, the curtain in the sanctuary of the Temple was torn down the middle. 46Then Jesus shouted, "Father, I entrust my spirit into your hands!"* And with those words he breathed his last.

47When the Roman officer* overseeing the execution saw what had happened, he worshiped God and said, "Surely this man was innocent.*" 48And when all the crowd that came to see the crucifixion saw what had happened, they went home in deep sorrow.* 49But Jesus' friends, including the women who had followed him from Galilee, stood at a distance watching.

## The Burial of Jesus

50Now there was a good and righteous man named Joseph. He was a member of the Jewish high council, 51but he had not agreed with the decision and actions of the other religious leaders. He was from the town of Arimathea in Judea, and he was waiting for the Kingdom of God to come. 52He went to Pilate and asked for Jesus' body. 53Then he took the body down from the cross and wrapped it in a long sheet of linen cloth and laid it in a new tomb that had been carved out of rock. 54This was done late on Friday afternoon, the day of preparation,* as the Sabbath was about to begin.

55As his body was taken away, the women from Galilee followed and saw the tomb where his body was placed. 56Then they went home and prepared spices and ointments to anoint his body. But by the time they were finished the Sabbath had begun, so they rested as required by the law.

23:26 Cyrene was a city in northern Africa. 23:30 Hos 10:8. 23:31 Or If these things are done to me, the living tree, what will happen to you, the dry tree? 23:33 Sometimes rendered Calvary, which comes from the Latin word for "skull." 23:34a This sentence is not included in many ancient manuscripts. 23:34b Greek by casting lots. See Ps 22:18. 23:46 Ps 31:5. 23:47a Greek the centurion. 23:47b Or righteous. 23:48 Greek went home beating their breasts. 23:54 Greek It was the day of preparation.

## The Resurrection

**24** But very early on Sunday morning* the women went to the tomb, taking the spices they had prepared. ²They found that the stone had been rolled away from the entrance. ³So they went in, but they didn't find the body of the Lord Jesus. ⁴As they stood there puzzled, two men suddenly appeared to them, clothed in dazzling robes.

⁵The women were terrified and bowed with their faces to the ground. Then the men asked, "Why are you looking among the dead for someone who is alive? ⁶He isn't here! He is risen from the dead! Remember what he told you back in Galilee, ⁷that the Son of Man* must be betrayed into the hands of sinful men and be crucified, and that he would rise again on the third day."

⁸Then they remembered that he had said this. ⁹So they rushed back from the tomb to tell his eleven disciples—and everyone else—what had happened. ¹⁰It was Mary Magdalene, Joanna, Mary the mother of James, and several other women who told the apostles what had happened. ¹¹But the story sounded like nonsense to the men, so they didn't believe it. ¹²However, Peter jumped up and ran to the tomb to look. Stooping, he peered in and saw the empty linen wrappings; then he went home again, wondering what had happened.

## The Walk to Emmaus

¹³That same day two of Jesus' followers were walking to the village of Emmaus, seven miles* from Jerusalem. ¹⁴As they walked along they were talking about everything that had happened. ¹⁵As they talked and discussed these things, Jesus himself suddenly came and began walking with them. ¹⁶But God kept them from recognizing him.

¹⁷He asked them, "What are you discussing so intently as you walk along?"

They stopped short, sadness written across their faces. ¹⁸Then one of them, Cleopas, replied, "You must be the only person in Jerusalem who hasn't heard about all the things that have happened there the last few days."

¹⁹"What things?" Jesus asked.

## NOT at all expected
READ LUKE 24:1-12

Once again God does the unexpected. When the women go to Jesus' tomb, they find it empty. Not at all what they expected. The angel reminds them of Jesus' resurrection prediction, so they run to tell the Good News to His disciples. But it was not what the disciples expected either; in fact, "the story sounded like nonsense to the men, so they didn't believe it."

Sometimes we miss God's working in our lives because it's not the way we expected it to happen. It doesn't fit in with our ideas. But don't miss this fact: the same power that raised Jesus from the dead is at work in your life, too. Expect God to do the unexpected.

"The things that happened to Jesus, the man from Nazareth," they said. "He was a prophet who did powerful miracles, and he was a mighty teacher in the eyes of God and all the people. ²⁰But our leading priests and other religious leaders handed him over to be condemned to death, and they crucified him. ²¹We had hoped he was the Messiah who had come to rescue Israel. This all happened three days ago.

²²"Then some women from our group of his followers were at his tomb early this morning, and they came back with an amazing report. ²³They said his body was missing, and they had seen angels who told them Jesus is alive! ²⁴Some of our men ran out to see, and sure enough, his body was gone, just as the women had said."

²⁵Then Jesus said to them, "You foolish people! You find it so hard to believe all that the prophets wrote in the Scriptures. ²⁶Wasn't it clearly predicted that the Messiah would have to suffer all these things before entering his glory?" ²⁷Then Jesus took them through the writings of Moses and all the prophets, explaining from all the Scriptures the things concerning himself.

²⁸By this time they were nearing Emmaus and the end of their journey. Jesus acted as if he were going on, ²⁹but they begged him, "Stay the night with us, since it is getting

24:1 Greek *But on the first day of the week, very early in the morning.*   24:7 "Son of Man" is a title Jesus used for himself.
24:13 Greek *60 stadia* [11.1 kilometers].

late." So he went home with them. [30]As they sat down to eat,* he took the bread and blessed it. Then he broke it and gave it to them. [31]Suddenly, their eyes were opened, and they recognized him. And at that moment he disappeared!

[32]They said to each other, "Didn't our hearts burn within us as he talked with us on the road and explained the Scriptures to us?" [33]And within the hour they were on their way back to Jerusalem. There they found the eleven disciples and the others who had gathered with them, [34]who said, "The Lord has really risen! He appeared to Peter.*"

## Jesus Appears to the Disciples

[35]Then the two from Emmaus told their story of how Jesus had appeared to them as they were walking along the road, and how they had recognized him as he was breaking the bread. [36]And just as they were telling about it, Jesus himself was suddenly standing there among them. "Peace be with you," he said. [37]But the whole group was startled and frightened, thinking they were seeing a ghost!

[38]"Why are you frightened?" he asked. "Why are your hearts filled with doubt? [39]Look at my hands. Look at my feet. You can see that it's really me. Touch me and make sure that I am not a ghost, because ghosts don't have bodies, as you see that I do." [40]As he spoke, he showed them his hands and his feet.

[41]Still they stood there in disbelief, filled with joy and wonder. Then he asked them, "Do you have anything here to eat?" [42]They gave him a piece of broiled fish, [43]and he ate it as they watched.

[44]Then he said, " When I was with you before, I told you that everything written about me in the law of Moses and the prophets and in the Psalms must be fulfilled." [45]Then he opened their minds to understand the Scriptures. [46]And he said, "Yes, it was written long ago that the Messiah would suffer and die and rise from the dead on the third day. [47]It was also written that this message would be proclaimed in the authority of his name to all the nations,* beginning in Jerusalem: 'There is forgiveness of sins for all who repent.' [48]You are witnesses of all these things.

[49]"And now I will send the Holy Spirit, just as my Father promised. But stay here in the city until the Holy Spirit comes and fills you with power from heaven."

## The Ascension

[50]Then Jesus led them to Bethany, and lifting his hands to heaven, he blessed them. [51]While he was blessing them, he left them and was taken up to heaven.* [52]So they worshiped him and then returned to Jerusalem filled with great joy. [53]And they spent all of their time in the Temple, praising God.

**24:30** Or *As they reclined.*    **24:34** Greek *Simon.*    **24:47** Or *all peoples.*    **24:51** Some manuscripts do not include *and was taken up to heaven.*

# JOHN

*"There is no greater love than to lay down one's life for one's friends."*

JOHN 15:13

Illness has a way of showing us who our true friends really are. Some people we were sure would be there for us seem to disappear without a word, and others we never dreamed would show up come around and offer gestures to make life much easier. Close friends and best friends take on a much deeper meaning when we walk together during trials.

This book was written by one of Jesus' closest earthly friends: John, "the disciple Jesus loved." During the hard times of Jesus' life, John was there—at their last Passover meal together the night before His death; in the Garden of Gethsemane as Jesus struggled in prayer about His impending crucifixion; and even at the foot of the cross when most of Jesus' followers had deserted Him. As He was dying, Jesus asked John to take care of His mother.

No wonder the Gospel of John gives us such a rich and intimate picture of the Son of God. Jesus and John were friends. Close friends. They walked a difficult journey together, and while John may have felt that at times he let down his Rabbi (he fell asleep when Jesus asked him to stay awake and pray!), he also knew Jesus had never let him down. More importantly, John reminds us in this book that Jesus wants to be a friend to each of us: the light in our darkness, the living water for our thirsty souls, and the very bread of life that gives us strength for each day. Now that's a true friend.

## Prologue: Christ, the Eternal Word

**1** ¹In the beginning the Word already existed.

The Word was with God,
and the Word was God.
²He existed in the beginning with God.
³God created everything through him,
and nothing was created except
through him.
⁴The Word gave life to everything that was
created,*
and his life brought light to
everyone.
⁵The light shines in the darkness,
and the darkness can never
extinguish it.*

⁶God sent a man, John the Baptist,* ⁷to tell about the light so that everyone might believe because of his testimony. ⁸John himself was not the light; he was simply a witness to tell about the light. ⁹The one who is the true light, who gives light to everyone, was coming into the world.

¹⁰He came into the very world he created, but the world didn't recognize him. ¹¹He came to his own people, and even they rejected him. ¹²But to all who believed him and accepted him, he gave the right to become children of God. ¹³They are reborn—not with a physical birth resulting from human passion or plan, but a birth that comes from God.

¹⁴So the Word became human* and made his home among us. He was full of unfailing love and faithfulness.* And we have seen his glory, the glory of the Father's one and only Son.

¹⁵John testified about him when he shouted to the crowds, "This is the one I was talking about when I said, 'Someone is coming after me who is far greater than I am, for he existed long before me.'"

¹⁶From his abundance we have all received one gracious blessing after another.* ¹⁷For the law was given through Moses, but God's unfailing love and faithfulness came through Jesus Christ. ¹⁸No one has ever seen God. But the unique One, who is himself God,* is near to the Father's heart. He has revealed God to us.

## The Testimony of John the Baptist

¹⁹This was John's testimony when the Jewish leaders sent priests and Temple assistants*

**1:3-4** Or *and nothing that was created was created except through him. The Word gave life to everything.* **1:5** Or *and the darkness has not understood it.* **1:6** Greek *a man named John.* **1:14a** Greek *became flesh.* **1:14b** Or *grace and truth; also in 1:17.* **1:16** Or *received the grace of Christ rather than the grace of the law;* Greek reads *received grace upon grace.* **1:18** Some manuscripts read *But the one and only Son.* **1:19** Greek *and Levites.*

# THE first miracle

READ JOHN 2:1-11

If you were performing your very first miracle, what would you do? Leap a tall building? Run faster than a speeding bullet? How about turn some plain old water into fine wine? That's what Jesus chose to do as His first miracle while attending a wedding feast. While it might not seem like a super-hero feat to us, it probably was pretty important to the bride and groom that day. How embarrassing it would have been to run out of wine before the celebration was over. And how marvelous it must have been for the water-turned-into-wine to taste so good that guests were sure the best beverages had been saved for last.

Among the many things this miracle demonstrates, it shows that Jesus cares about the small things we care about.

He cares about your prayers to celebrate another birthday. He cares about your hopes to go on a special trip. He cares about your dreams to see your child married. He cares about your longings to hold a new grandbaby. He truly cares.

from Jerusalem to ask John, "Who are you?" [20]He came right out and said, "I am not the Messiah."

[21]"Well then, who are you?" they asked. "Are you Elijah?"

"No," he replied.

"Are you the Prophet we are expecting?"* "No."

[22]"Then who are you? We need an answer for those who sent us. What do you have to say about yourself?"

[23]John replied in the words of the prophet Isaiah:

"I am a voice shouting in the
  wilderness,
    'Clear the way for the LORD's coming!'"*

[24]Then the Pharisees who had been sent [25]asked him, "If you aren't the Messiah or Elijah or the Prophet, what right do you have to baptize?"

[26]John told them, "I baptize with* water, but right here in the crowd is someone you do not recognize. [27]Though his ministry follows mine, I'm not even worthy to be his slave and untie the straps of his sandal."

[28]This encounter took place in Bethany, an area east of the Jordan River, where John was baptizing.

### Jesus, the Lamb of God

[29]The next day John saw Jesus coming toward him and said, "Look! The Lamb of God who takes away the sin of the world! [30]He is the one I was talking about when I said, 'A man is coming after me who is far greater than I am, for he existed long before me.' [31]I did not recognize him as the Messiah, but I have been baptizing with water so that he might be revealed to Israel."

[32]Then John testified, "I saw the Holy Spirit descending like a dove from heaven and resting upon him. [33]I didn't know he was the one, but when God sent me to baptize with water, he told me, 'The one on whom you see the Spirit descend and rest is the one who will baptize with the Holy Spirit.' [34]I saw this happen to Jesus, so I testify that he is the Chosen One of God.*"

### The First Disciples

[35]The following day John was again standing with two of his disciples. [36]As Jesus walked by, John looked at him and declared, "Look! There is the Lamb of God!" [37]When John's two disciples heard this, they followed Jesus.

[38]Jesus looked around and saw them following. "What do you want?" he asked them.

They replied, "Rabbi" (which means "Teacher"), "where are you staying?"

[39]"Come and see," he said. It was about four o'clock in the afternoon when they went with him to the place where he was staying, and they remained with him the rest of the day.

[40]Andrew, Simon Peter's brother, was one of these men who heard what John said and then followed Jesus. [41]Andrew went to find his brother, Simon, and told him, "We have found the Messiah" (which means "Christ"*).

[42]Then Andrew brought Simon to meet Jesus. Looking intently at Simon, Jesus said, "Your name is Simon, son of John—but you will be called Cephas" (which means "Peter"*).

[43]The next day Jesus decided to go to Galilee. He found Philip and said to him, "Come, follow me." [44]Philip was from Bethsaida, Andrew and Peter's hometown.

[45]Philip went to look for Nathanael and told him, "We have found the very person Moses* and the prophets wrote about! His name is Jesus, the son of Joseph from Nazareth."

[46]"Nazareth!" exclaimed Nathanael. "Can anything good come from Nazareth?"

"Come and see for yourself," Philip replied.

[47]As they approached, Jesus said, "Now here is a genuine son of Israel—a man of complete integrity."

[48]"How do you know about me?" Nathanael asked.

Jesus replied, "I could see you under the fig tree before Philip found you."

[49]Then Nathanael exclaimed, "Rabbi, you are the Son of God—the King of Israel!"

[50]Jesus asked him, "Do you believe this

1:21 Greek *Are you the Prophet?* See Deut 18:15, 18; Mal 4:5-6.   1:23 Isa 40:3.   1:26 Or *in;* also in 1:31, 33.   1:34 Some manuscripts read *the Son of God.*   1:41 *Messiah* (a Hebrew term) and *Christ* (a Greek term) both mean "the anointed one."   1:42 The names *Cephas* (from Aramaic) and *Peter* (from Greek) both mean "rock."   1:45 Greek *Moses in the law.*

just because I told you I had seen you under the fig tree? You will see greater things than this." ⁵¹Then he said, "I tell you the truth, you will all see heaven open and the angels of God going up and down on the Son of Man, the one who is the stairway between heaven and earth.*"

## The Wedding at Cana

2 The next day* there was a wedding celebration in the village of Cana in Galilee. Jesus' mother was there, ²and Jesus and his disciples were also invited to the celebration. ³The wine supply ran out during the festivities, so Jesus' mother told him, "They have no more wine."

⁴"Dear woman, that's not our problem," Jesus replied. "My time has not yet come."

⁵But his mother told the servants, "Do whatever he tells you."

⁶Standing nearby were six stone water jars, used for Jewish ceremonial washing. Each could hold twenty to thirty gallons.* ⁷Jesus told the servants, "Fill the jars with water." When the jars had been filled, ⁸he said, "Now dip some out, and take it to the master of ceremonies." So the servants followed his instructions.

⁹When the master of ceremonies tasted the water that was now wine, not knowing where it had come from (though, of course, the servants knew), he called the bridegroom over. ¹⁰"A host always serves the best wine first," he said. "Then, when everyone has had a lot to drink, he brings out the less expensive wine. But you have kept the best until now!"

¹¹This miraculous sign at Cana in Galilee was the <u>first time Jesus revealed his glory.</u> And his disciples believed in him.

¹²After the wedding he went to Capernaum for a few days with his mother, his brothers, and his disciples.

## Jesus Clears the Temple

¹³It was nearly time for the Jewish Passover celebration, so Jesus went to Jerusalem. ¹⁴In the Temple area he saw merchants selling cattle, sheep, and doves for sacrifices; he also saw dealers at tables exchanging foreign money. ¹⁵Jesus made a whip from some ropes and chased them all out of the Temple. He drove out the sheep and cattle, scattered the money changers' coins over the floor, and turned over their tables. ¹⁶Then, going over to the people who sold doves, he told them, "Get these things out of here. Stop turning my Father's house into a marketplace!"

¹⁷Then his disciples remembered this prophecy from the Scriptures: "Passion for God's house will consume me."*

¹⁸But the Jewish leaders demanded, "What are you doing? If God gave you authority to do this, show us a miraculous sign to prove it."

¹⁹"All right," Jesus replied. "Destroy this temple, and in three days I will raise it up."

²⁰"What!" they exclaimed. "It has taken forty-six years to build this Temple, and you can rebuild it in three days?" ²¹But when Jesus said <u>"this temple,"</u> he meant his <u>own body.</u> ²²After he was raised from the dead, his disciples remembered he had said this, and they believed both the Scriptures and what Jesus had said.

## Jesus and Nicodemus

²³Because of the miraculous signs Jesus did in Jerusalem at the Passover celebration, many began to trust in him. ²⁴But Jesus didn't trust them, because he knew human nature. ²⁵No one needed to tell him what mankind is really like.

3 There was a man named Nicodemus, a Jewish religious leader who was a Pharisee. ²After dark one evening, he came to speak with Jesus. "Rabbi," he said, "we all know that God has sent you to teach us. Your miraculous signs are evidence that God is with you."

³Jesus replied, "I tell you the truth, unless you are born again,* you cannot see the Kingdom of God."

⁴"What do you mean?" exclaimed Nicodemus. "How can an old man go back into his mother's womb and be born again?"

⁵Jesus replied, "I assure you, no one can

# TWICE born

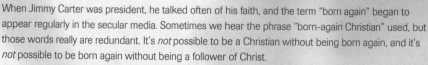

READ JOHN 3:1-8

When Jimmy Carter was president, he talked often of his faith, and the term "born again" began to appear regularly in the secular media. Sometimes we hear the phrase "born-again Christian" used, but those words really are redundant. It's *not* possible to be a Christian without being born again, and it's *not* possible to be born again without being a follower of Christ.

Jesus' declaration that Nicodemus had to be "born again" shocked him just as it does some folks today. *You mean there's no other way to get to heaven?* Absolutely none, Jesus says. Only humans give physical birth to humans, and only the Holy Spirit gives spiritual rebirth.

If your illness is taking you on a spiritual journey, make sure you end up at the right destination: Only the Spirit of God can give you new life and the absolute assurance of heaven. Just as we don't become a car by sitting in a garage, we don't become a Christian by sitting in a church building. We each must be born again.

enter the Kingdom of God without being born of water and the Spirit.* ⁶Humans can reproduce only human life, but the Holy Spirit gives birth to spiritual life.* ⁷So don't be surprised when I say, 'You* must be born again.' ⁸The wind blows wherever it wants. Just as you can hear the wind but can't tell where it comes from or where it is going, so you can't explain how people are born of the Spirit."

⁹"How are these things possible?" Nicodemus asked.

¹⁰Jesus replied, " You are a respected Jewish teacher, and yet you don't understand these things? ¹¹I assure you, we tell you what we know and have seen, and yet you won't believe our testimony. ¹²But if you don't believe me when I tell you about earthly things, how can you possibly believe if I tell you about heavenly things? ¹³No one has ever gone to heaven and returned. But the Son of Man* has come down from heaven. ¹⁴And as Moses lifted up the bronze snake on a pole in the wilderness, so the Son of Man must be lifted up, ¹⁵so that everyone who believes in him will have eternal life.*

¹⁶"For God loved the world so much that he gave his one and only Son, so that every-

one who believes in him will not perish but have eternal life. ¹⁷God sent his Son into the world not to judge the world, but to save the world through him.

¹⁸"There is no judgment against anyone who believes in him. But anyone who does not believe in him has already been judged for not believing in God's one and only Son. ¹⁹And the judgment is based on this fact: God's light came into the world, but people loved the darkness more than the light, for their actions were evil. ²⁰All who do evil hate the light and refuse to go near it for fear their sins will be exposed. ²¹But those who do what is right come to the light so others can see that they are doing what God wants.*"

## John the Baptist Exalts Jesus

²²Then Jesus and his disciples left Jerusalem and went into the Judean countryside. Jesus spent some time with them there, baptizing people.

²³At this time John the Baptist was baptizing at Aenon, near Salim, because there was plenty of water there; and people kept coming to him for baptism. ²⁴(This was before John was thrown into prison.) ²⁵A debate broke out between John's disciples and a certain Jew*

3:5 Or *and spirit.* The Greek word for *Spirit* can also be translated *wind;* see 3:8.   3:6 Greek *what is born of the Spirit is spirit.*
3:7 The Greek word for *you* is plural; also in 3:12.   3:13 Some manuscripts add *who lives in heaven.* "Son of Man" is a title Jesus used for himself.   3:15 Or *everyone who believes will have eternal life in him.*   3:21 Or *can see God at work in what he is doing.*
3:25 Some manuscripts read *some Jews.*

over ceremonial cleansing. 26So John's disciples came to him and said, "Rabbi, the man you met on the other side of the Jordan River, the one you identified as the Messiah, is also baptizing people. And everybody is going to him instead of coming to us."

27John replied, "No one can receive anything unless God gives it from heaven. 28You yourselves know how plainly I told you, 'I am not the Messiah. I am only here to prepare the way for him.' 29It is the bridegroom who marries the bride, and the best man is simply glad to stand with him and hear his vows. Therefore, I am filled with joy at his success. 30He must become greater and greater, and I must become less and less.

31"He has come from above and is greater than anyone else. We are of the earth, and we speak of earthly things, but he has come from heaven and is greater than anyone else.* 32He testifies about what he has seen and heard, but how few believe what he tells them! 33Anyone who accepts his testimony can affirm that God is true. 34For he is sent by God. He speaks God's words, for God gives him the Spirit without limit. 35The Father loves his Son and has put everything into his hands. 36And anyone who believes in God's Son has eternal life. Anyone who doesn't obey the Son will never experience eternal life but remains under God's angry judgment."

## Jesus and the Samaritan Woman

4 Jesus* knew the Pharisees had heard that he was baptizing and making more disciples than John 2(though Jesus himself didn't baptize them—his disciples did). 3So he left Judea and returned to Galilee.

4He had to go through Samaria on the way. 5Eventually he came to the Samaritan village of Sychar, near the field that Jacob gave to his son Joseph. 6Jacob's well was there; and Jesus, tired from the long walk, sat wearily beside the well about noontime. 7Soon a Samaritan woman came to draw water, and Jesus said to her, "Please give me a drink." 8He was alone at the time because his disciples had gone into the village to buy some food.

9The woman was surprised, for Jews refuse to have anything to do with Samari-

tans.* She said to Jesus, "You are a Jew, and I am a Samaritan woman. Why are you asking me for a drink?"

10Jesus replied, "If you only knew the gift God has for you and who you are speaking to, you would ask me, and I would give you living water."

11"But sir, you don't have a rope or a bucket," she said, "and this well is very deep. Where would you get this living water? 12And besides, do you think you're greater than our ancestor Jacob, who gave us this well? How can you offer better water than he and his sons and his animals enjoyed?"

13Jesus replied, "Anyone who drinks this water will soon become thirsty again. 14But those who drink the water I give will never be thirsty again. It becomes a fresh, bubbling spring within them, giving them eternal life."

15"Please, sir," the woman said, "give me this water! Then I'll never be thirsty again, and I won't have to come here to get water."

16"Go and get your husband," Jesus told her.

17"I don't have a husband," the woman replied.

Jesus said, "You're right! You don't have a husband—18for you have had five husbands, and you aren't even married to the man you're living with now. You certainly spoke the truth!"

19"Sir," the woman said, "you must be a prophet. 20So tell me, why is it that you Jews insist that Jerusalem is the only place of worship, while we Samaritans claim it is here at Mount Gerizim,* where our ancestors worshiped?"

21Jesus replied, "Believe me, dear woman, the time is coming when it will no longer matter whether you worship the Father on this mountain or in Jerusalem. 22You Samaritans know very little about the one you worship, while we Jews know all about him, for salvation comes through the Jews. 23But the time is coming—indeed it's here now—when true worshipers will worship the Father in spirit and in truth. The Father is looking for those who will worship him that way. 24For God is Spirit, so those who worship him must worship in spirit and in truth."

3:31 Some manuscripts omit *and is greater than anyone else.*   4:1 Some manuscripts read *The Lord.*   4:9 Some manuscripts omit this sentence.   4:20 Greek *on this mountain.*

25 The woman said, "I know the Messiah is coming—the one who is called Christ. When he comes, he will explain everything to us."

26 Then Jesus told her, "I AM the Messiah!"*

27 Just then his disciples came back. They were shocked to find him talking to a woman, but none of them had the nerve to ask, "What do you want with her?" or "Why are you talking to her?" 28 The woman left her water jar beside the well and ran back to the village, telling everyone, 29 "Come and see a man who told me everything I ever did! Could he possibly be the Messiah?" 30 So the people came streaming from the village to see him.

31 Meanwhile, the disciples were urging Jesus, "Rabbi, eat something."

32 But Jesus replied, "I have a kind of food you know nothing about."

33 "Did someone bring him food while we were gone?" the disciples asked each other.

34 Then Jesus explained: "My nourishment comes from doing the will of God, who sent me, and from finishing his work. 35 You know the saying, 'Four months between planting and harvest.' But I say, wake up and look around. The fields are already ripe* for harvest. 36 The harvesters are paid good wages, and the fruit they harvest is people brought to eternal life. What joy awaits both the planter and the harvester alike! 37 You know the saying, 'One plants and another harvests.' And it's true. 38 I sent you to harvest where you didn't plant; others had already done the work, and now you will get to gather the harvest."

## Many Samaritans Believe

39 Many Samaritans from the village believed in Jesus because the woman had said, "He told me everything I ever did!" 40 When they came out to see him, they begged him to stay in their village. So he stayed for two days, 41 long enough for many more to hear his message and believe. 42 Then they said to the woman, "Now we believe, not just because of what you told us, but because we have heard him ourselves. Now we know that he is indeed the Savior of the world."

## Jesus Heals an Official's Son

43 At the end of the two days, Jesus went on to Galilee. 44 He himself had said that a prophet is not honored in his own hometown. 45 Yet the Galileans welcomed him, for they had been in Jerusalem at the Passover celebration and had seen everything he did there.

46 As he traveled through Galilee, he came to Cana, where he had turned the water into wine. There was a government official in nearby Capernaum whose son was very sick. 47 When he heard that Jesus had come from Judea to Galilee, he went and begged Jesus to come to Capernaum to heal his son, who was about to die.

48 Jesus asked, "Will you never believe in me unless you see miraculous signs and wonders?"

49 The official pleaded, "Lord, please come now before my little boy dies."

50 Then Jesus told him, "Go back home. Your son will live!" And the man believed what Jesus said and started home.

51 While the man was on his way, some of his servants met him with the news that his son was alive and well. 52 He asked them when the boy had begun to get better, and they replied, "Yesterday afternoon at one o'clock his fever suddenly disappeared!" 53 Then the father realized that that was the very time Jesus had told him, "Your son will live." And he and his entire household believed in Jesus. 54 This was the second miraculous sign Jesus did in Galilee after coming from Judea.

#2

## Jesus Heals a Lame Man

5 Afterward Jesus returned to Jerusalem for one of the Jewish holy days. 2 Inside the city, near the Sheep Gate, was the pool of Bethesda,* with five covered porches. 3 Crowds of sick people—blind, lame, or paralyzed—lay on the porches.* 5 One of the men lying there had been sick for thirty-eight

4:26 Or "The 'I AM' is here"; or "I am the LORD"; Greek reads "I am, the one speaking to you." See Exod 3:14.    4:35 Greek white.
5:2 Other manuscripts read Beth-zatha; still others read Bethsaida.    5:3 Some manuscripts add an expanded conclusion to verse 3 and all of verse 4: waiting for a certain movement of the water, *for an angel of the Lord came from time to time and stirred up the water. And the first person to step in after the water was stirred was healed of whatever disease he had.

years. ⁶When Jesus saw him and knew he had been ill for a long time, he asked him, " Would you like to get well?"

⁷"I can't, sir," the sick man said, "for I have no one to put me into the pool when the water bubbles up. Someone else always gets there ahead of me."

⁸Jesus told him, "Stand up, pick up your mat, and walk!"

⁹Instantly, the man was healed! He rolled up his sleeping mat and began walking! But this miracle happened on the Sabbath, ¹⁰so the Jewish leaders objected. They said to the man who was cured, "You can't work on the Sabbath! The law doesn't allow you to carry that sleeping mat!"

¹¹But he replied, "The man who healed me told me, 'Pick up your mat and walk.'"

¹²"Who said such a thing as that?" they demanded.

¹³The man didn't know, for Jesus had disappeared into the crowd. ¹⁴But afterward Jesus found him in the Temple and told him, "Now you are well; so stop sinning, or something even worse may happen to you." ¹⁵Then the man went and told the Jewish leaders that it was Jesus who had healed him.

### Jesus Claims to Be the Son of God

¹⁶So the Jewish leaders began harassing* Jesus for breaking the Sabbath rules. ¹⁷But Jesus replied, "My Father is always working, and so am I." ¹⁸So the Jewish leaders tried all the harder to find a way to kill him. For he not only broke the Sabbath, he called God his Father, thereby making himself equal with God.

¹⁹So Jesus explained, "I tell you the truth, the Son can do nothing by himself. He does only what he sees the Father doing. Whatever the Father does, the Son also does. ²⁰For the Father loves the Son and shows him everything he is doing. In fact, the Father will show him how to do even greater works than healing this man. Then you will truly be astonished. ²¹For just as the Father gives life to those he raises from the dead, so the Son gives life to anyone he wants. ²²In addition, the Father judges no one. Instead, he has given the Son absolute authority to judge, ²³so that everyone will honor the Son, just as

they honor the Father. Anyone who does not honor the Son is certainly not honoring the Father who sent him.

²⁴"I tell you the truth, those who listen to my message and believe in God who sent me have eternal life. They will never be condemned for their sins, but they have already passed from death into life.

²⁵"And I assure you that the time is coming, indeed it's here now, when the dead will hear my voice—the voice of the Son of God. And those who listen will live. ²⁶The Father has life in himself, and he has granted that same life-giving power to his Son. ²⁷And he has given him authority to judge everyone because he is the Son of Man.* ²⁸Don't be so surprised! Indeed, the time is coming when all the dead in their graves will hear the voice of God's Son, ²⁹and they will rise again. Those who have done good will rise to experience eternal life, and those who have continued in evil will rise to experience judgment. ³⁰I can do nothing on my own. I judge as God tells me. Therefore, my judgment is just, because I carry out the will of the one who sent me, not my own will.

### Witnesses to Jesus

³¹"If I were to testify on my own behalf, my testimony would not be valid. ³²But someone else is also testifying about me, and I assure you that everything he says about me is true. ³³In fact, you sent investigators to listen to John the Baptist, and his testimony about me was true. ³⁴Of course, I have no need of human witnesses, but I say these things so you might be saved. ³⁵John was like a burning and shining lamp, and you were excited for a while about his message. ³⁶But I have a greater witness than John—my teachings and my miracles. The Father gave me these works to accomplish, and they prove that he sent me. ³⁷And the Father who sent me has testified about me himself. You have never heard his voice or seen him face to face, ³⁸and you do not have his message in your hearts, because you do not believe me—the one he sent to you.

³⁹" You search the Scriptures because you

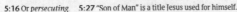

5:16 Or persecuting.    5:27 "Son of Man" is a title Jesus used for himself.

think they give you eternal life. But the Scriptures point to me! 40Yet you refuse to come to me to receive this life.

41"Your approval means nothing to me, 42because I know you don't have God's love within you. 43For I have come to you in my Father's name, and you have rejected me. Yet if others come in their own name, you gladly welcome them. 44No wonder you can't believe! For you gladly honor each other, but you don't care about the honor that comes from the one who alone is God.*

45"Yet it isn't I who will accuse you before the Father. Moses will accuse you! Yes, Moses, in whom you put your hopes. 46If you really believed Moses, you would believe me, because he wrote about me. 47But since you don't believe what he wrote, how will you believe what I say?"

### Jesus Feeds Five Thousand

**6** After this, Jesus crossed over to the far side of the Sea of Galilee, also known as the Sea of Tiberias. 2A huge crowd kept following him wherever he went, because they saw his miraculous signs as he healed the sick. 3Then Jesus climbed a hill and sat down with his disciples around him. 4(It was nearly time for the Jewish Passover celebration.) 5Jesus soon saw a huge crowd of people coming to look for him. Turning to Philip, he asked, "Where can we buy bread to feed all these people?" 6He was testing Philip, for he already knew what he was going to do.

7Philip replied, "Even if we worked for months, we wouldn't have enough money* to feed them!"

8Then Andrew, Simon Peter's brother, spoke up. 9"There's a young boy here with five barley loaves and two fish. But what good is that with this huge crowd?"

10"Tell everyone to sit down," Jesus said. So they all sat down on the grassy slopes. (The men alone numbered about 5,000.) 11Then Jesus took the loaves, gave thanks to God, and distributed them to the people. Afterward he did the same with the fish. And they all ate as much as they wanted. 12After everyone was full, Jesus told his disciples,

## STAIRWAY to heaven
READ JOHN 3:16, 36

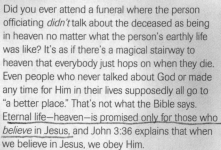

Did you ever attend a funeral where the person officiating *didn't* talk about the deceased as being in heaven no matter what the person's earthly life was like? It's as if there's a magical stairway to heaven that everybody just hops on when they die. Even people who never talked about God or made any time for Him in their lives supposedly all go to "a better place." That's not what the Bible says. Eternal life—heaven—is promised only for those who *believe* in Jesus, and John 3:36 explains that when we believe in Jesus, we obey Him.

Gallup polls show that most people think they're going to heaven. Are you sure you know the way to get there?

"Now gather the leftovers, so that nothing is wasted." 13So they picked up the pieces and filled twelve baskets with scraps left by the people who had eaten from the five barley loaves.

14When the people saw him* do this miraculous sign, they exclaimed, "Surely, he is the Prophet we have been expecting!"* 15When Jesus saw that they were ready to force him to be their king, he slipped away into the hills by himself.

### Jesus Walks on Water

16That evening Jesus' disciples went down to the shore to wait for him. 17But as darkness fell and Jesus still hadn't come back, they got into the boat and headed across the lake toward Capernaum. 18Soon a gale swept down upon them, and the sea grew very rough. 19They had rowed three or four miles* when suddenly they saw Jesus walking on the water toward the boat. They were terrified, 20but he called out to them, "Don't be afraid. I am here!*" 21Then they were eager to let him in the boat, and immediately they arrived at their destination!

### Jesus, the Bread of Life

22The next day the crowd that had stayed on the far shore saw that the disciples had

5:44 Some manuscripts read *from the only One.*   6:7 Greek *Two hundred denarii would not be enough.* A denarius was equivalent to a laborer's full day's wage.   6:14a Some manuscripts read *Jesus.*   6:14b See Deut 18:15, 18; Mal 4:5-6.   6:19 Greek *25 or 30 stadia* [4.6 or 5.5 kilometers].   6:20 Or *The 'I Am' is here;* Greek reads *I am.* See Exod 3:14.

taken the only boat, and they realized Jesus had not gone with them. 23 Several boats from Tiberias landed near the place where the Lord had blessed the bread and the people had eaten. 24 So when the crowd saw that neither Jesus nor his disciples were there, they got into the boats and went across to Capernaum to look for him. 25 They found him on the other side of the lake and asked, "Rabbi, when did you get here?"

26 Jesus replied, "I tell you the truth, you want to be with me because I fed you, not because you understood the miraculous signs. 27 But don't be so concerned about perishable things like food. Spend your energy seeking the eternal life that the Son of Man* can give you. For God the Father has given me the seal of his approval."

28 They replied, "We want to perform God's works, too. What should we do?"

29 Jesus told them, "This is the only work God wants from you: Believe in the one he has sent."

30 They answered, "Show us a miraculous sign if you want us to believe in you. What can you do? 31 After all, our ancestors ate manna while they journeyed through the wilderness! The Scriptures say, 'Moses gave them bread from heaven to eat.'*"

32 Jesus said, "I tell you the truth, Moses didn't give you bread from heaven. My Father did. And now he offers you the true bread from heaven. 33 The true bread of God is the one who comes down from heaven and gives life to the world."

34 "Sir," they said, "give us that bread every day."

35 Jesus replied, "I am the bread of life. Whoever comes to me will never be hungry again. Whoever believes in me will never be thirsty. 36 But you haven't believed in me even though you have seen me. 37 However, those the Father has given me will come to me, and I will never reject them. 38 For I have come down from heaven to do the will of God who sent me, not to do my own will. 39 And this is the will of God, that I should not lose even one of all those he has given me, but that I should raise them up at the last day. 40 For it is my Father's will that all

who see his Son and believe in him should have eternal life. I will raise them up at the last day."

41 Then the people* began to murmur in disagreement because he had said, "I am the bread that came down from heaven." 42 They said, "Isn't this Jesus, the son of Joseph? We know his father and mother. How can he say, 'I came down from heaven'?"

43 But Jesus replied, "Stop complaining about what I said. 44 For no one can come to me unless the Father who sent me draws them to me, and at the last day I will raise them up. 45 As it is written in the Scriptures,* 'They will all be taught by God.' Everyone who listens to the Father and learns from him comes to me. 46 (Not that anyone has ever seen the Father; only I, who was sent from God, have seen him.)

47 "I tell you the truth, anyone who believes has eternal life. 48 Yes, I am the bread of life! 49 Your ancestors ate manna in the wilderness, but they all died. 50 Anyone who eats the bread from heaven, however, will never die. 51 I am the living bread that came down from heaven. Anyone who eats this bread will live forever; and this bread, which I will offer so the world may live, is my flesh."

52 Then the people began arguing with each other about what he meant. "How can this man give us his flesh to eat?" they asked.

53 So Jesus said again, "I tell you the truth, unless you eat the flesh of the Son of Man and drink his blood, you cannot have eternal life within you. 54 But anyone who eats my flesh and drinks my blood has eternal life, and I will raise that person at the last day. 55 For my flesh is true food, and my blood is true drink. 56 Anyone who eats my flesh and drinks my blood remains in me, and I in him. 57 I live because of the living Father who sent me; in the same way, anyone who feeds on me will live because of me. 58 I am the true bread that came down from heaven. Anyone who eats this bread will not die as your ancestors did (even though they ate the manna) but will live forever."

59 He said these things while he was teaching in the synagogue in Capernaum.

---

6:27 "Son of Man" is a title Jesus used for himself.   6:31 Exod 16:4; Ps 78:24.   6:41 Greek *Jewish people;* also in 6:52.   6:45 Greek *in the prophets.* Isa 54:13.

## Many Disciples Desert Jesus

⁶⁰Many of his disciples said, "This is very hard to understand. How can anyone accept it?"

⁶¹Jesus was aware that his disciples were complaining, so he said to them, "Does this offend you? ⁶²Then what will you think if you see the Son of Man ascend to heaven again? ⁶³The Spirit alone gives eternal life. Human effort accomplishes nothing. And the very words I have spoken to you are spirit and life. ⁶⁴But some of you do not believe me." (For Jesus knew from the beginning which ones didn't believe, and he knew who would betray him.) ⁶⁵Then he said, "That is why I said that people can't come to me unless the Father gives them to me."

⁶⁶At this point many of his disciples turned away and deserted him. ⁶⁷Then Jesus turned to the Twelve and asked, "Are you also going to leave?"

⁶⁸Simon Peter replied, "Lord, to whom would we go? You have the words that give eternal life. ⁶⁹We believe, and we know you are the Holy One of God.*"

⁷⁰Then Jesus said, "I chose the twelve of you, but one is a devil." ⁷¹He was speaking of Judas, son of Simon Iscariot, one of the Twelve, who would later betray him.

## Jesus and His Brothers

**7** After this, Jesus traveled around Galilee. He wanted to stay out of Judea, where the Jewish leaders were plotting his death. ²But soon it was time for the Jewish Festival of Shelters, ³and Jesus' brothers said to him, "Leave here and go to Judea, where your followers can see your miracles! ⁴You can't become famous if you hide like this! If you can do such wonderful things, show yourself to the world!" ⁵For even his brothers didn't believe in him.

⁶Jesus replied, "Now is not the right time for me to go, but you can go anytime. ⁷The world can't hate you, but it does hate me because I accuse it of doing evil. ⁸You go on. I'm not going* to this festival, because my time has not yet come." ⁹After saying these things, Jesus remained in Galilee.

## Jesus Teaches Openly at the Temple

¹⁰But after his brothers left for the festival, Jesus also went, though secretly, staying out of public view. ¹¹The Jewish leaders tried to find him at the festival and kept asking if anyone had seen him. ¹²There was a lot of grumbling about him among the crowds. Some argued, "He's a good man," but others said, "He's nothing but a fraud who deceives the people." ¹³But no one had the courage to speak favorably about him in public, for they were afraid of getting in trouble with the Jewish leaders.

¹⁴Then, midway through the festival, Jesus went up to the Temple and began to teach. ¹⁵The people* were surprised when they heard him. "How does he know so much when he hasn't been trained?" they asked.

¹⁶So Jesus told them, "My message is not my own; it comes from God who sent me. ¹⁷Anyone who wants to do the will of God will know whether my teaching is from God or is merely my own. ¹⁸Those who speak for themselves want glory only for themselves, but a person who seeks to honor the one who sent him speaks truth, not lies. ¹⁹Moses gave you the law, but none of you obeys it! In fact, you are trying to kill me."

²⁰The crowd replied, "You're demon possessed! Who's trying to kill you?"

²¹Jesus replied, "I did one miracle on the Sabbath, and you were amazed. ²²But you work on the Sabbath, too, when you obey Moses' law of circumcision. (Actually, this tradition of circumcision began with the patriarchs, long before the law of Moses.) ²³For if the correct time for circumcising your son falls on the Sabbath, you go ahead and do it so as not to break the law of Moses. So why should you be angry with me for healing a man on the Sabbath? ²⁴Look beneath the surface so you can judge correctly."

## Is Jesus the Messiah?

²⁵Some of the people who lived in Jerusalem started to ask each other, "Isn't this the man they are trying to kill? ²⁶But here he is, speaking in public, and they say nothing to him. Could our leaders possibly believe that

6:69 Other manuscripts read *you are the Christ, the Holy One of God;* still others read *you are the Christ, the Son of God;* and still others read *you are the Christ, the Son of the living God.*   7:8 Some manuscripts read *not yet going.*   7:15 Greek *Jewish people.*

he is the Messiah? 27But how could he be? For we know where this man comes from. When the Messiah comes, he will simply appear; no one will know where he comes from."

28While Jesus was teaching in the Temple, he called out, "Yes, you know me, and you know where I come from. But I'm not here on my own. The one who sent me is true, and you don't know him. 29But I know him because I come from him, and he sent me to you." 30Then the leaders tried to arrest him; but no one laid a hand on him, because his time* had not yet come.

31Many among the crowds at the Temple believed in him. "After all," they said, "would you expect the Messiah to do more miraculous signs than this man has done?"

32When the Pharisees heard that the crowds were whispering such things, they and the leading priests sent Temple guards to arrest Jesus. 33But Jesus told them, "I will be with you only a little longer. Then I will return to the one who sent me. 34You will search for me but not find me. And you cannot go where I am going."

35The Jewish leaders were puzzled by this statement. "Where is he planning to go?" they asked. "Is he thinking of leaving the country and going to the Jews in other lands?* Maybe he will even teach the Greeks! 36What does he mean when he says, 'You will search for me but not find me,' and 'You cannot go where I am going'?"

## Jesus Promises Living Water

37On the last day, the climax of the festival, Jesus stood and shouted to the crowds, "Anyone who is thirsty may come to me! 38Anyone who believes in me may come and drink! For the Scriptures declare, 'Rivers of living water will flow from his heart.'"* 39(When he said "living water," he was speaking of the Spirit, who would be given to everyone believing in him. But the Spirit had not yet been given,* because Jesus had not yet entered into his glory.)

## Division and Unbelief

40When the crowds heard him say this, some of them declared, "Surely this man is the Prophet we've been expecting."* 41Others said, "He is the Messiah." Still others said, "But he can't be! Will the Messiah come from Galilee? 42For the Scriptures clearly state that the Messiah will be born of the royal line of David, in Bethlehem, the village where King David was born."* 43So the crowd was divided about him. 44Some even

7:30 Greek *his hour.*   7:35 Or *the Jews who live among the Greeks?*   7:37-38 Or *"Let anyone who is thirsty come to me and drink.* 38*For the Scriptures declare, 'Rivers of living water will flow from the heart of anyone who believes in me.'"*   7:39 Some manuscripts read *But as yet there was no Spirit.* Still others read *But as yet there was no Holy Spirit.*   7:40 See Deut 18:15, 18; Mal 4:5-6. 7:42 See Mic 5:2.

---

# TRUTH or fiction?

READ JOHN 8:32

What is feeding your mind these days? Is it the obituaries as you look to see if anyone you know has died? Is it the news of the latest celebrity who has cancer? Or is it the awesome truth that God really does love you and His plans for your life always are good?

Is your mind filled with the truth that the God who created this universe simply by speaking words is a lot more powerful than any possibly misguided cells within your body and a lot more trustworthy than any statistics in a medical journal?

One way to find the light while in the shadow of illness is to compare God's truth to each and every detail of our circumstances. What are you believing about your past, present, or future that isn't 100 percent true? Look around the corners of your mind for thoughts that are making you anxious or fearful, and replace them with God's truth. When we live by the truth of God's Word, we will be set free to really live.

wanted him arrested, but no one laid a hand on him.

45 When the Temple guards returned without having arrested Jesus, the leading priests and Pharisees demanded, "Why didn't you bring him in?"

46 "We have never heard anyone speak like this!" the guards responded.

47 "Have you been led astray, too?" the Pharisees mocked. 48 "Is there a single one of us rulers or Pharisees who believes in him? 49 This foolish crowd follows him, but they are ignorant of the law. God's curse is on them!"

50 Then Nicodemus, the leader who had met with Jesus earlier, spoke up. 51 "Is it legal to convict a man before he is given a hearing?" he asked.

52 They replied, "Are you from Galilee, too? Search the Scriptures and see for yourself—no prophet ever comes* from Galilee!"

---

[The most ancient Greek manuscripts do not include John 7:53–8:11.]

53 Then the meeting broke up, and everybody went home.

### A Woman Caught in Adultery

**8** Jesus returned to the Mount of Olives, 2 but early the next morning he was back again at the Temple. A crowd soon gathered, and he sat down and taught them. 3 As he was speaking, the teachers of religious law and the Pharisees brought a woman who had been caught in the act of adultery. They put her in front of the crowd.

4 "Teacher," they said to Jesus, "this woman was caught in the act of adultery. 5 The law of Moses says to stone her. What do you say?"

6 They were trying to trap him into saying something they could use against him, but Jesus stooped down and wrote in the dust with his finger. 7 They kept demanding an answer, so he stood up again and said, "All right, but let the one who has never sinned throw the first stone!" 8 Then he stooped down again and wrote in the dust.

9 When the accusers heard this, they slipped away one by one, beginning with the oldest, until only Jesus was left in the middle of the crowd with the woman. 10 Then Jesus stood up again and said to the woman, "Where are your accusers? Didn't even one of them condemn you?"

11 "No, Lord," she said.

And Jesus said, "Neither do I. Go and sin no more."

---

### Jesus, the Light of the World

12 Jesus spoke to the people once more and said, "I am the light of the world. If you follow me, you won't have to walk in darkness, because you will have the light that leads to life."

13 The Pharisees replied, "You are making those claims about yourself! Such testimony is not valid."

14 Jesus told them, " These claims are valid even though I make them about myself. For I know where I came from and where I am going, but you don't know this about me. 15 You judge me by human standards, but I do not judge anyone. 16 And if I did, my judgment would be correct in every respect because I am not alone. The Father* who sent me is with me. 17 Your own law says that if two people agree about something, their witness is accepted as fact.* 18 I am one witness, and my Father who sent me is the other."

19 "Where is your father?" they asked.

Jesus answered, "Since you don't know who I am, you don't know who my Father is. If you knew me, you would also know my Father." 20 Jesus made these statements while he was teaching in the section of the Temple known as the Treasury. But he was not arrested, because his time* had not yet come.

### The Unbelieving People Warned

21 Later Jesus said to them again, "I am going away. You will search for me but will die in your sin. You cannot come where I am going."

22 The people* asked, "Is he planning to commit suicide? What does he mean, 'You cannot come where I am going'?"

23 Jesus continued, " You are from below;

---

7:52 Some manuscripts read the prophet does not come.   8:16 Some manuscripts read The One.   8:17 See Deut 19:15.   8:20 Greek his hour.   8:22 Greek Jewish people; also in 8:31, 48, 52, 57.

I am from above. You belong to this world; I do not. 24 That is why I said that you will die in your sins; for unless you believe that I Am who I claim to be,* you will die in your sins."

25 "Who are you?" they demanded.

Jesus replied, "The one I have always claimed to be.* 26 I have much to say about you and much to condemn, but I won't. For I say only what I have heard from the one who sent me, and he is completely truthful." 27 But they still didn't understand that he was talking about his Father.

28 So Jesus said, " When you have lifted up the Son of Man on the cross, then you will understand that I Am he.* I do nothing on my own but say only what the Father taught me. 29 And the one who sent me is with me— he has not deserted me. For I always do what pleases him." 30 Then many who heard him say these things believed in him.

### Jesus and Abraham

31 Jesus said to the people who believed in him, " You are truly my disciples if you remain faithful to my teachings. 32 And you will know the truth, and the truth will set you free."

33 "But we are descendants of Abraham," they said. "We have never been slaves to anyone. What do you mean, 'You will be set free'?"

34 Jesus replied, "I tell you the truth, everyone who sins is a slave of sin. 35 A slave is not a permanent member of the family, but a son is part of the family forever. 36 So if the Son sets you free, you are truly free. 37 Yes, I realize that you are descendants of Abraham. And yet some of you are trying to kill me because there's no room in your hearts for my message. 38 I am telling you what I saw when I was with my Father. But you are following the advice of your father."

39 "Our father is Abraham!" they declared.

"No," Jesus replied, "for if you were really the children of Abraham, you would follow his example.* 40 Instead, you are trying to kill me because I told you the truth, which I heard from God. Abraham never did such a

thing. 41 No, you are imitating your real father."

They replied, "We aren't illegitimate children! God himself is our true Father."

42 Jesus told them, "If God were your Father, you would love me, because I have come to you from God. I am not here on my own, but he sent me. 43 Why can't you understand what I am saying? It's because you can't even hear me! 44 For you are the children of your father the devil, and you love to do the evil things he does. He was a murderer from the beginning. He has always hated the truth, because there is no truth in him. When he lies, it is consistent with his character; for he is a liar and the father of lies. 45 So when I tell the truth, you just naturally don't believe me! 46 Which of you can truthfully accuse me of sin? And since I am telling you the truth, why don't you believe me? 47 Anyone who belongs to God listens gladly to the words of God. But you don't listen because you don't belong to God."

48 The people retorted, "You Samaritan devil! Didn't we say all along that you were possessed by a demon?"

49 "No," Jesus said, "I have no demon in me. For I honor my Father—and you dishonor me. 50 And though I have no wish to glorify myself, God is going to glorify me. He is the true judge. 51 I tell you the truth, anyone who obeys my teaching will never die!"

52 The people said, "Now we know you are possessed by a demon. Even Abraham and the prophets died, but you say, 'Anyone who obeys my teaching will never die!' 53 Are you greater than our father Abraham? He died, and so did the prophets. Who do you think you are?"

54 Jesus answered, "If I want glory for myself, it doesn't count. But it is my Father who will glorify me. You say, 'He is our God,*' 55 but you don't even know him. I know him. If I said otherwise, I would be as great a liar as you! But I do know him and obey him. 56 Your father Abraham rejoiced as he looked forward to my coming. He saw it and was glad."

8:24 Greek *unless you believe that I am.* See Exod 3:14.   8:25 Or *Why do I speak to you at all?*   8:28 Greek *When you have lifted up the Son of Man, then you will know that I am.* "Son of Man" is a title Jesus used for himself.   8:39 Some manuscripts read *if you are really the children of Abraham, follow his example.*   8:54 Some manuscripts read *your God.*

57The people said, "You aren't even fifty years old. How can you say you have seen Abraham?*"

58Jesus answered, "I tell you the truth, before Abraham was even born, I AM!*" 59At that point they picked up stones to throw at him. But Jesus was hidden from them and left the Temple.

## Jesus Heals a Man Born Blind

9 As Jesus was walking along, he saw a man who had been blind from birth. 2"Rabbi," his disciples asked him, "why was this man born blind? Was it because of his own sins or his parents' sins?"

3"It was not because of his sins or his parents' sins," Jesus answered. " This happened so the power of God could be seen in him. 4We must quickly carry out the tasks assigned us by the one who sent us.* The night is coming, and then no one can work. 5But while I am here in the world, I am the light of the world."

6Then he spit on the ground, made mud with the saliva, and spread the mud over the blind man's eyes. 7He told him, "Go wash yourself in the pool of Siloam" (Siloam means "sent"). So the man went and washed and came back seeing!

8His neighbors and others who knew him as a blind beggar asked each other, "Isn't this the man who used to sit and beg?" 9Some said he was, and others said, "No, he just looks like him!"

But the beggar kept saying, "Yes, I am the same one!"

10They asked, "Who healed you? What happened?"

11He told them, "The man they call Jesus made mud and spread it over my eyes and told me, 'Go to the pool of Siloam and wash yourself.' So I went and washed, and now I can see!"

12"Where is he now?" they asked.

"I don't know," he replied.

13Then they took the man who had been blind to the Pharisees, 14because it was on the Sabbath that Jesus had made the mud and healed him. 15The Pharisees asked the man all about it. So he told them, "He put the mud over my eyes, and when I washed it away, I could see!"

16Some of the Pharisees said, "This man Jesus is not from God, for he is working on the Sabbath." Others said, "But how could an ordinary sinner do such miraculous signs?" So there was a deep division of opinion among them.

17Then the Pharisees again questioned the man who had been blind and demanded, "What's your opinion about this man who healed you?"

The man replied, "I think he must be a prophet."

18The Jewish leaders still refused to believe the man had been blind and could now see, so they called in his parents. 19They asked them, "Is this your son? Was he born blind? If so, how can he now see?"

20His parents replied, "We know this is our son and that he was born blind, 21but we don't know how he can see or who healed him. Ask him. He is old enough to speak for himself." 22His parents said this because they were afraid of the Jewish leaders, who had announced that anyone saying Jesus was the Messiah would be expelled from the synagogue. 23That's why they said, "He is old enough. Ask him."

24So for the second time they called in the man who had been blind and told him, "God should get the glory for this,* because we know this man Jesus is a sinner."

25"I don't know whether he is a sinner," the man replied. "But I know this: I was blind, and now I can see!"

26"But what did he do?" they asked. "How did he heal you?"

27"Look!" the man exclaimed. "I told you once. Didn't you listen? Why do you want to hear it again? Do you want to become his disciples, too?"

28Then they cursed him and said, "You are his disciple, but we are disciples of Moses! 29We know God spoke to Moses, but we don't even know where this man comes from."

30"Why, that's very strange!" the man replied. "He healed my eyes, and yet you don't

8:57 Some manuscripts read *How can you say Abraham has seen you?*    8:58 Or *before Abraham was even born, I have always been alive;* Greek reads *before Abraham was, I am.* See Exod 3:14.    9:4 Other manuscripts read *I must quickly carry out the tasks assigned me by the one who sent me;* still others read *We must quickly carry out the tasks assigned us by the one who sent me.*    9:24 Or *Give glory to God, not to Jesus;* Greek reads *Give glory to God.*

know where he comes from? <sup>31</sup>We know that God doesn't listen to sinners, but he is ready to hear those who worship him and do his will. <sup>32</sup>Ever since the world began, no one has been able to open the eyes of someone born blind. <sup>33</sup>If this man were not from God, he couldn't have done it."

<sup>34</sup>"You were born a total sinner!" they answered. "Are you trying to teach us?" And they threw him out of the synagogue.

## Spiritual Blindness

<sup>35</sup>When Jesus heard what had happened, he found the man and asked, "Do you believe in the Son of Man?*"

<sup>36</sup>The man answered, "Who is he, sir? I want to believe in him."

<sup>37</sup>"You have seen him," Jesus said, "and he is speaking to you!"

<sup>38</sup>"Yes, Lord, I believe!" the man said. And he worshiped Jesus.

<sup>39</sup>Then Jesus told him,* "I entered this world to render judgment—to give sight to the blind and to show those who think they see* that they are blind."

<sup>40</sup>Some Pharisees who were standing nearby heard him and asked, "Are you saying we're blind?"

<sup>41</sup>"If you were blind, you wouldn't be guilty," Jesus replied. "But you remain guilty because you claim you can see.

## The Good Shepherd and His Sheep

**10** "I tell you the truth, anyone who sneaks over the wall of a sheepfold, rather than going through the gate, must surely be a thief and a robber! <sup>2</sup>But the one who enters through the gate is the shepherd of the sheep. <sup>3</sup>The gatekeeper opens the gate for him, and the sheep recognize his voice and come to him. He calls his own sheep by name and leads them out. <sup>4</sup>After he has gathered his own flock, he walks ahead of them, and they follow him because they know his voice. <sup>5</sup>They won't follow a stranger; they will run from him because they don't know his voice."

<sup>6</sup>Those who heard Jesus use this illustration didn't understand what he meant, <sup>7</sup>so he

explained it to them: "I tell you the truth, I am the gate for the sheep. <sup>8</sup>All who came before me* were thieves and robbers. But the true sheep did not listen to them. <sup>9</sup>Yes, I am the gate. Those who come in through me will be saved.* They will come and go freely and will find good pastures. <sup>10</sup>The thief's purpose is to steal and kill and destroy. My purpose is to give them a rich and satisfying life.

<sup>11</sup>"I am the good shepherd. The good shepherd sacrifices his life for the sheep. <sup>12</sup>A hired hand will run when he sees a wolf coming. He will abandon the sheep because they don't belong to him and he isn't their shepherd. And so the wolf attacks them and scatters the flock. <sup>13</sup>The hired hand runs away because he's working only for the money and doesn't really care about the sheep.

<sup>14</sup>"I am the good shepherd; I know my own sheep, and they know me, <sup>15</sup>just as my Father knows me and I know the Father. So I sacrifice my life for the sheep. <sup>16</sup>I have other sheep, too, that are not in this sheepfold. I must bring them also. They will listen to my voice, and there will be one flock with one shepherd.

<sup>17</sup>"The Father loves me because I sacrifice my life so I may take it back again. <sup>18</sup>No one can take my life from me. I sacrifice it voluntarily. For I have the authority to lay it down when I want to and also to take it up again. For this is what my Father has commanded."

<sup>19</sup>When he said these things, the people* were again divided in their opinions about him. <sup>20</sup>Some said, "He's demon possessed and out of his mind. Why listen to a man like that?" <sup>21</sup>Others said, "This doesn't sound like a man possessed by a demon! Can a demon open the eyes of the blind?"

## Jesus Claims to Be the Son of God

<sup>22</sup>It was now winter, and Jesus was in Jerusalem at the time of Hanukkah, the Festival of Dedication. <sup>23</sup>He was in the Temple, walking through the section known as Solomon's Colonnade. <sup>24</sup>The people surrounded him and asked, "How long are you going to keep us in suspense? If you are the Messiah, tell us plainly."

**9:35** Some manuscripts read *the Son of God?* "Son of Man" is a title Jesus used for himself.   **9:38-39a** Some manuscripts do not include *"Yes, Lord, I believe!" the man said. And he worshiped Jesus. Then Jesus told him.*   **9:39b** Greek *those who see.*   **10:8** Some manuscripts do not include *before me.*   **10:9** Or *will find safety.*   **10:19** Greek *Jewish people;* also in 10:24, 31.

# WHY me?

READ JOHN 9:1-25

When something bad happens to us or someone we love, it's pretty instinctive to ask questions. *Why did this happen? What did I do wrong?*

When Jesus' disciples encountered a man blind since birth, they wondered if it was his parents' sin or his that resulted in his suffering. Jesus dismissed both reasons and said it happened "so the power of God could be seen in him."

Have you asked: *Why me? Why us?*

Perhaps it has happened so that the power of God can be seen in you.

In 1989 former major league pitcher Dave Dravecky made an incredible comeback from his bout of suffering when he resumed pitching after having a large cancerous tumor removed from his pitching arm. But during his second outing, his arm broke. As he lay on the pitcher's mound in agony, he didn't ask, *Why me?* Instead he asked a question that unleashed the power of God in his life like it never had been seen before. He asked *What now, God?* Make that your question today.

---

²⁵Jesus replied, "I have already told you, and you don't believe me. The proof is the work I do in my Father's name. ²⁶But you don't believe me because you are not my sheep. **²⁷**My sheep listen to my voice; I know them, and they follow me. ²⁸I give them eternal life, and they will never perish. No one can snatch them away from me, ²⁹for my Father has given them to me, and he is more powerful than anyone else.* No one can snatch them from the Father's hand. **³⁰**The Father and I are one."

³¹Once again the people picked up stones to kill him. ³²Jesus said, "At my Father's direction I have done many good works. For which one are you going to stone me?"

³³They replied, "We're stoning you not for any good work, but for blasphemy! You, a mere man, claim to be God."

³⁴Jesus replied, "It is written in your own Scriptures* that God said to certain leaders of the people, 'I say, you are gods!'* ³⁵And you know that the Scriptures cannot be altered. So if those people who received God's message were called 'gods,' ³⁶why do you call it blasphemy when I say, 'I am the Son of God'? After all, the Father set me apart and sent me into the world. ³⁷Don't believe me unless I carry out my Father's work. ³⁸But if

I do his work, believe in the evidence of the miraculous works I have done, even if you don't believe me. Then you will know and understand that the Father is in me, and I am in the Father."

³⁹Once again they tried to arrest him, but he got away and left them. ⁴⁰He went beyond the Jordan River near the place where John was first baptizing and stayed there awhile. ⁴¹And many followed him. "John didn't perform miraculous signs," they remarked to one another, "but everything he said about this man has come true." ⁴²And many who were there believed in Jesus.

### The Raising of Lazarus

**11** A man named Lazarus was sick. He lived in Bethany with his sisters, Mary and Martha. ²This is the Mary who later poured the expensive perfume on the Lord's feet and wiped them with her hair.* Her brother, Lazarus, was sick. ³So the two sisters sent a message to Jesus telling him, "Lord, your dear friend is very sick."

⁴But when Jesus heard about it he said, "Lazarus's sickness will not end in death. No, it happened for the glory of God so that the Son of God will receive glory from this." ⁵So although Jesus loved Martha, Mary, and

---

**10:29** Other manuscripts read *for what my Father has given me is more powerful than anything;* still others read *for regarding that which my Father has given me, he is greater than all.* **10:34a** Greek *your own law.* **10:34b** Ps 82:6. **11:2** This incident is recorded in chapter 12.

Lazarus, 6he stayed where he was for the next two days. 7Finally, he said to his disciples, "Let's go back to Judea."

8But his disciples objected. "Rabbi," they said, "only a few days ago the people* in Judea were trying to stone you. Are you going there again?"

9Jesus replied, "There are twelve hours of daylight every day. During the day people can walk safely. They can see because they have the light of this world. 10But at night there is danger of stumbling because they have no light." 11Then he said, "Our friend Lazarus has fallen asleep, but now I will go and wake him up."

12The disciples said, "Lord, if he is sleeping, he will soon get better!" 13They thought Jesus meant Lazarus was simply sleeping, but Jesus meant Lazarus had died.

14So he told them plainly, "Lazarus is dead. 15And for your sakes, I'm glad I wasn't there, for now you will really believe. Come, let's go see him."

16Thomas, nicknamed the Twin,* said to his fellow disciples, "Let's go, too—and die with Jesus."

17When Jesus arrived at Bethany, he was told that Lazarus had already been in his grave for four days. 18Bethany was only a few miles* down the road from Jerusalem, 19and many of the people had come to console Martha and Mary in their loss. 20When Martha got word that Jesus was coming, she went to meet him. But Mary stayed in the house. 21Martha said to Jesus, "Lord, if only you had been here, my brother would not have died. 22But even now I know that God will give you whatever you ask."

23Jesus told her, "Your brother will rise again."

24"Yes," Martha said, "he will rise when everyone else rises, at the last day."

25Jesus told her, "I am the resurrection and the life.* Anyone who believes in me will live, even after dying. 26Everyone who lives in me and believes in me will never ever die. Do you believe this, Martha?"

27"Yes, Lord," she told him. "I have always believed you are the Messiah, the Son of God, the one who has come into the world

from God." 28Then she returned to Mary. She called Mary aside from the mourners and told her, "The Teacher is here and wants to see you." 29So Mary immediately went to him.

30Jesus had stayed outside the village, at the place where Martha met him. 31When the people who were at the house consoling Mary saw her leave so hastily, they assumed she was going to Lazarus's grave to weep. So they followed her there. 32When Mary arrived and saw Jesus, she fell at his feet and said, "Lord, if only you had been here, my brother would not have died."

33When Jesus saw her weeping and saw the other people wailing with her, a deep anger welled up within him,* and he was deeply troubled. 34"Where have you put him?" he asked them.

They told him, "Lord, come and see." 35Then Jesus wept. 36The people who were standing nearby said, "See how much he loved him!" 37But some said, "This man healed a blind man. Couldn't he have kept Lazarus from dying?"

38Jesus was still angry as he arrived at the tomb, a cave with a stone rolled across its entrance. 39"Roll the stone aside," Jesus told them.

But Martha, the dead man's sister, protested, "Lord, he has been dead for four days. The smell will be terrible."

40Jesus responded, "Didn't I tell you that you would see God's glory if you believe?" 41So they rolled the stone aside. Then Jesus looked up to heaven and said, "Father, thank you for hearing me. 42You always hear me, but I said it out loud for the sake of all these people standing here, so that they will believe you sent me." 43Then Jesus shouted, "Lazarus, come out!" 44And the dead man came out, his hands and feet bound in graveclothes, his face wrapped in a headcloth. Jesus told them, "Unwrap him and let him go!"

### The Plot to Kill Jesus

45Many of the people who were with Mary believed in Jesus when they saw this happen. 46But some went to the Pharisees and

11:8 Greek Jewish people; also in 11:19, 31, 33, 36, 45, 54.    11:16 Greek Thomas, who was called Didymus.    11:18 Greek was about 15 stadia [about 2.8 kilometers].    11:25 Some manuscripts do not include and the life.    11:33 Or he was angry in his spirit.

told them what Jesus had done. 47Then the leading priests and Pharisees called the high council* together. "What are we going to do?" they asked each other. "This man certainly performs many miraculous signs. 48If we allow him to go on like this, soon everyone will believe in him. Then the Roman army will come and destroy both our Temple* and our nation."

49Caiaphas, who was high priest at that time,* said, "You don't know what you're talking about! 50You don't realize that it's better for you that one man should die for the people than for the whole nation to be destroyed."

51He did not say this on his own; as high priest at that time he was led to prophesy that Jesus would die for the entire nation. 52And not only for that nation, but to bring together and unite all the children of God scattered around the world.

53So from that time on, the Jewish leaders began to plot Jesus' death. 54As a result, Jesus stopped his public ministry among the people and left Jerusalem. He went to a place near the wilderness, to the village of Ephraim, and stayed there with his disciples.

55It was now almost time for the Jewish Passover celebration, and many people from all over the country arrived in Jerusalem several days early so they could go through the purification ceremony before Passover began. 56They kept looking for Jesus, but as they stood around in the Temple, they said to each other, "What do you think? He won't come for Passover, will he?" 57Meanwhile, the leading priests and Pharisees had publicly ordered that anyone seeing Jesus must report it immediately so they could arrest him.

## Jesus Anointed at Bethany

**12** Six days before the Passover celebration began, Jesus arrived in Bethany, the home of Lazarus—the man he had raised from the dead. 2A dinner was prepared in Jesus' honor. Martha served, and

Lazarus was among those who ate* with him. 3Then Mary took a twelve-ounce jar* of expensive perfume made from essence of nard, and she anointed Jesus' feet with it, wiping his feet with her hair. The house was filled with the fragrance.

4But Judas Iscariot, the disciple who would soon betray him, said, 5"That perfume was worth a year's wages.* It should have been sold and the money given to the poor." 6Not that he cared for the poor—he was a thief, and since he was in charge of the disciples' money, he often stole some for himself.

7Jesus replied, "Leave her alone. She did this in preparation for my burial. 8You will always have the poor among you, but you will not always have me."

9When all the people* heard of Jesus' arrival, they flocked to see him and also to see Lazarus, the man Jesus had raised from the dead. 10Then the leading priests decided to kill Lazarus, too, 11for it was because of him that many of the people had deserted them* and believed in Jesus.

## Jesus' Triumphant Entry

12The next day, the news that Jesus was on the way to Jerusalem swept through the city. A large crowd of Passover visitors 13took palm branches and went down the road to meet him. They shouted,

11:47 Greek the Sanhedrin.    11:48 Or our position; Greek reads our place.    11:49 Greek that year; also in 11:51.    12:2 Or who reclined.    12:3 Greek took 1 litra [327 grams].    12:5 Greek worth 300 denarii. A denarius was equivalent to a laborer's full day's wage.    12:9 Greek Jewish people; also in 12:11.    12:11 Or had deserted their traditions; Greek reads had deserted.

## THE LANGUAGE of tears
READ JOHN 11:17-44

Did you know that John 11:35 is the shortest verse in the Bible? Jesus was standing at the grave of His friend Lazarus, surrounded by Lazarus's weeping sisters and other wailing friends, and He began to cry. He could have said, "Don't worry, be happy!" After all, He knew He was going to raise Lazarus from the dead. But He didn't make any such positive-thinking comments. He wept.

He did it because He felt His friends' sadness and to show us that weeping is not a sign of weakness. Tears are a gift from God to express our deepest feelings. If the very Son of God can cry, you can, too.

"Praise God!*
Blessings on the one who comes in the
     name of the Lord!
Hail to the King of Israel!"*

14 Jesus found a young donkey and rode on it,
fulfilling the prophecy that said:

15 "Don't be afraid, people of Jerusalem.*
Look, your King is coming,
     riding on a donkey's colt."*

16 His disciples didn't understand at the
time that this was a fulfillment of prophecy.
But after Jesus entered into his glory, they remembered what had happened and realized
that these things had been written about
him.

17 Many in the crowd had seen Jesus call
Lazarus from the tomb, raising him from the
dead, and they were telling others* about it.
18 That was the reason so many went out to
meet him—because they had heard about
this miraculous sign. 19 Then the Pharisees
said to each other, "There's nothing we can
do. Look, everyone* has gone after him!"

## Jesus Predicts His Death

20 Some Greeks who had come to Jerusalem
for the Passover celebration 21 paid a visit to
Philip, who was from Bethsaida in Galilee.
They said, "Sir, we want to meet Jesus."
22 Philip told Andrew about it, and they went
together to ask Jesus.

23 Jesus replied, "Now the time has come
for the Son of Man* to enter into his glory.
24 I tell you the truth, unless a kernel of
wheat is planted in the soil and dies, it remains alone. But its death will produce
many new kernels—a plentiful harvest of
new lives. 25 Those who love their life in this
world will lose it. Those who care nothing
for their life in this world will keep it for
eternity. 26 Anyone who wants to be my disciple must follow me, because my servants
must be where I am. And the Father will
honor anyone who serves me.

27 "Now my soul is deeply troubled. Should
I pray, 'Father, save me from this hour'? But
this is the very reason I came! 28 Father, bring
glory to your name."

Then a voice spoke from heaven, saying,
"I have already brought glory to my name,
and I will do so again." 29 When the crowd
heard the voice, some thought it was thunder, while others declared an angel had spoken to him.

30 Then Jesus told them, " The voice was
for your benefit, not mine. 31 The time for
judging this world has come, when Satan,
the ruler of this world, will be cast out.
32 And when I am lifted up from the earth, I
will draw everyone to myself." 33 He said this
to indicate how he was going to die.

34 The crowd responded, "We understood
from Scripture* that the Messiah would live
forever. How can you say the Son of Man will
die? Just who is this Son of Man, anyway?"

35 Jesus replied, "My light will shine for
you just a little longer. Walk in the light
while you can, so the darkness will not overtake you. Those who walk in the darkness
cannot see where they are going. 36 Put your
trust in the light while there is still time;
then you will become children of the light."

After saying these things, Jesus went away
and was hidden from them.

## The Unbelief of the People

37 But despite all the miraculous signs Jesus
had done, most of the people still did not believe in him. 38 This is exactly what Isaiah the
prophet had predicted:

"Lord, who has believed our message?
     To whom has the Lord revealed his
          powerful arm?"*

39 But the people couldn't believe, for as Isaiah also said,

40 "The Lord has blinded their eyes
     and hardened their hearts—
so that their eyes cannot see,
     and their hearts cannot understand,
and they cannot turn to me
     and have me heal them."*

41 Isaiah was referring to Jesus when he said
this, because he saw the future and spoke of
the Messiah's glory. 42 Many people did believe in him, however, including some of the

12:13a Greek Hosanna, an exclamation of praise adapted from a Hebrew expression that means "save now."    12:13b Ps 118:25-26;
Zeph 3:15.    12:15a Greek daughter of Zion.    12:15b Zech 9:9.    12:17 Greek were testifying.    12:19 Greek the world.
12:23 "Son of Man" is a title Jesus used for himself.    12:34 Greek from the law.    12:38 Isa 53:1.    12:40 Isa 6:10.

Jewish leaders. But they wouldn't admit it for fear that the Pharisees would expel them from the synagogue. 43For they loved human praise more than the praise of God.

44Jesus shouted to the crowds, "If you trust me, you are trusting not only me, but also God who sent me. 45For when you see me, you are seeing the one who sent me. 46I have come as a light to shine in this dark world, so that all who put their trust in me will no longer remain in the dark. 47I will not judge those who hear me but don't obey me, for I have come to save the world and not to judge it. 48But all who reject me and my message will be judged on the day of judgment by the truth I have spoken. 49I don't speak on my own authority. The Father who sent me has commanded me what to say and how to say it. 50And I know his commands lead to eternal life; so I say whatever the Father tells me to say."

## Jesus Washes His Disciples' Feet

**13** Before the Passover celebration, Jesus knew that his hour had come to leave this world and return to his Father. He had loved his disciples during his ministry on earth, and now he loved them to the very end.* 2It was time for supper, and the devil had already prompted Judas,* son of Simon Iscariot, to betray Jesus. 3Jesus knew that the Father had given him authority over everything and that he had come from God and would return to God. 4So he got up from the table, took off his robe, wrapped a towel around his waist, 5and poured water into a basin. Then he began to wash the disciples' feet, drying them with the towel he had around him.

6When Jesus came to Simon Peter, Peter said to him, "Lord, are you going to wash my feet?"

7Jesus replied, " You don't understand now what I am doing, but someday you will."

8"No," Peter protested, "you will never ever wash my feet!"

Jesus replied, "Unless I wash you, you won't belong to me."

9Simon Peter exclaimed, "Then wash my hands and head as well, Lord, not just my feet!"

10Jesus replied, "A person who has bathed all over does not need to wash, except for the feet,* to be entirely clean. And you disciples are clean, but not all of you." 11For Jesus knew who would betray him. That is what he meant when he said, "Not all of you are clean."

12After washing their feet, he put on his robe again and sat down and asked, "Do you understand what I was doing? 13You call me 'Teacher' and 'Lord,' and you are right, because that's what I am. 14And since I, your Lord and Teacher, have washed your feet, you ought to wash each other's feet. 15I have given you an example to follow. Do as I have done to you. 16I tell you the truth, slaves are not greater than their master. Nor is the messenger more important than the one who sends the message. 17Now that you know these things, God will bless you for doing them.

## Jesus Predicts His Betrayal

18"I am not saying these things to all of you; I know the ones I have chosen. But this fulfills the Scripture that says, 'The one who eats my food has turned against me.'* 19I tell you this beforehand, so that when it happens you will believe that I AM the Messiah.* 20I tell you the truth, anyone who welcomes my messenger is welcoming me, and anyone who welcomes me is welcoming the Father who sent me."

21Now Jesus was deeply troubled,* and he exclaimed, "I tell you the truth, one of you will betray me!"

22The disciples looked at each other, wondering whom he could mean. 23The disciple Jesus loved was sitting next to Jesus at the table.* 24Simon Peter motioned to him to ask, "Who's he talking about?" 25So that disciple leaned over to Jesus and asked, "Lord, who is it?"

26Jesus responded, "It is the one to whom I give the bread I dip in the bowl." And when he had dipped it, he gave it to Judas, son of Simon Iscariot. 27When Judas had eaten the bread, Satan entered into him. Then Jesus told him, "Hurry and do what you're going to

# LEAVE the light on

READ JOHN 14:1-4

There's a motel chain that promises late-night arriving guests: "We'll leave the light on." It's comforting to know when we're headed for a new destination that someone is expecting us and has made the necessary arrangements for our arrival.

Here, Jesus wants to comfort His disciples concerning the longest journey any of them will ever make—the journey to heaven. He assures them there's plenty of room in His Father's house and that He personally has prepared their places. And the very best assurance He gives is that when the time is right, He will come and get them and take them home. This knowledge, He says, should keep their hearts from being troubled about the final journey we all must face.

Someday—maybe soon, maybe not—if you're a believer, Jesus will come for you. He's got room for you—a specially prepared place for you. But He doesn't need to leave the light on . . . after all, He is the Light of the World (John 8:12).

---

do." 28None of the others at the table knew what Jesus meant. 29Since Judas was their treasurer, some thought Jesus was telling him to go and pay for the food or to give some money to the poor. 30So Judas left at once, going out into the night.

## Jesus Predicts Peter's Denial

31As soon as Judas left the room, Jesus said, "The time has come for the Son of Man* to enter into his glory, and God will be glorified because of him. 32And since God receives glory because of the Son,* he will soon give glory to the Son. 33Dear children, I will be with you only a little longer. And as I told the Jewish leaders, you will search for me, but you can't come where I am going. 34So now I am giving you a new commandment: Love each other. Just as I have loved you, you should love each other. 35Your love for one another will prove to the world that you are my disciples."

36Simon Peter asked, "Lord, where are you going?"

And Jesus replied, " You can't go with me now, but you will follow me later."

37"But why can't I come now, Lord?" he asked. "I'm ready to die for you."

38Jesus answered, "Die for me? I tell you the truth, Peter—before the rooster crows tomorrow morning, you will deny three times that you even know me.

## Jesus, the Way to the Father

**14** "Don't let your hearts be troubled. Trust in God, and trust also in me. 2There is more than enough room in my Father's home.* If this were not so, would I have told you that I am going to prepare a place for you?* 3When everything is ready, I will come and get you, so that you will always be with me where I am. 4And you know the way to where I am going."

5"No, we don't know, Lord," Thomas said. "We have no idea where you are going, so how can we know the way?"

6Jesus told him, "I am the way, the truth, and the life. No one can come to the Father except through me. 7If you had really known me, you would know who my Father is.* From now on, you do know him and have seen him!"

8Philip said, "Lord, show us the Father, and we will be satisfied."

9Jesus replied, "Have I been with you all

---

13:31 "Son of Man" is a title Jesus used for himself.   13:32 Some manuscripts omit *And since God receives glory because of the Son.*
14:2a Or *There are many rooms in my Father's house.*   14:2b Or *If this were not so, I would have told you that I am going to prepare a place for you.* Some manuscripts read *If this were not so, I would have told you. I am going to prepare a place for you.*   14:7 Some manuscripts read *If you have really known me, you will know who my Father is.*

this time, Philip, and yet you still don't know who I am? Anyone who has seen me has seen the Father! So why are you asking me to show him to you? ¹⁰Don't you believe that I am in the Father and the Father is in me? The words I speak are not my own, but my Father who lives in me does his work through me. ¹¹Just believe that I am in the Father and the Father is in me. Or at least believe because of the work you have seen me do.

¹²"I tell you the truth, anyone who believes in me will do the same works I have done, and even greater works, because I am going to be with the Father. ¹³You can ask for anything in my name, and I will do it, so that the Son can bring glory to the Father. ¹⁴Yes, ask me for anything in my name, and I will do it!

### Jesus Promises the Holy Spirit

¹⁵"If you love me, obey* my commandments. ¹⁶And I will ask the Father, and he will give you another Advocate,* who will never leave you. ¹⁷He is the Holy Spirit, who leads into all truth. The world cannot receive him, because it isn't looking for him and doesn't recognize him. But you know him, because he lives with you now and later will be in you.* ¹⁸No, I will not abandon you as orphans—I will come to you. ¹⁹Soon the world will no longer see me, but you will see me. Since I live, you also will live. ²⁰When I am raised to life again, you will know that I am in my Father, and you are in me, and I am in you. ²¹Those who accept my commandments and obey them are the ones who love me. And because they love me, my Father will love them. And I will love them and reveal myself to each of them."

²²Judas (not Judas Iscariot, but the other disciple with that name) said to him, "Lord, why are you going to reveal yourself only to us and not to the world at large?"

²³Jesus replied, "All who love me will do what I say. My Father will love them, and we will come and make our home with each of them. ²⁴Anyone who doesn't love me will not obey me. And remember, my words are not my own. What I am telling you is from the Father who sent me. ²⁵I am telling you these things now while I am still with you.

²⁶But when the Father sends the Advocate as my representative—that is, the Holy Spirit—he will teach you everything and will remind you of everything I have told you.

²⁷"I am leaving you with a gift—peace of mind and heart. And the peace I give is a gift the world cannot give. So don't be troubled or afraid. ²⁸Remember what I told you: I am going away, but I will come back to you again. If you really loved me, you would be happy that I am going to the Father, who is greater than I am. ²⁹I have told you these things before they happen so that when they do happen, you will believe.

³⁰"I don't have much more time to talk to you, because the ruler of this world approaches. He has no power over me, ³¹but I will do what the Father requires of me, so that the world will know that I love the Father. Come, let's be going.

### Jesus, the True Vine

**15** "I am the true grapevine, and my Father is the gardener. ²He cuts off every branch of mine that doesn't produce fruit, and he prunes the branches that do bear fruit so they will produce even more. ³You have already been pruned and purified by the message I have given you. ⁴Remain in me, and I will remain in you. For a branch cannot produce fruit if it is severed from the vine, and you cannot be fruitful unless you remain in me.

⁵"Yes, I am the vine; you are the branches. Those who remain in me, and I in them, will produce much fruit. For apart from me you can do nothing. ⁶Anyone who does not remain in me is thrown away like a useless branch and withers. Such branches are gathered into a pile to be burned. ⁷But if you remain in me and my words remain in you, you may ask for anything you want, and it will be granted! ⁸When you produce much fruit, you are my true disciples. This brings great glory to my Father.

⁹"I have loved you even as the Father has loved me. Remain in my love. ¹⁰When you obey my commandments, you remain in my love, just as I obey my Father's commandments and remain in his love. ¹¹I have told

---

**14:15** Other manuscripts read *you will obey;* still others read *you should obey.*  **14:16** Or *Comforter,* or *Encourager,* or *Counselor.* Greek reads *Paraclete;* also in 14:26.  **14:17** Some manuscripts read *and is in you.*

you these things so that you will be filled with my joy. Yes, your joy will overflow! ¹²This is my commandment: Love each other in the same way I have loved you. ¹³There is no greater love than to lay down one's life for one's friends. ¹⁴You are my friends if you do what I command. ¹⁵I no longer call you slaves, because a master doesn't confide in his slaves. Now you are my friends, since I have told you everything the Father told me. ¹⁶You didn't choose me. I chose you. I appointed you to go and produce lasting fruit, so that the Father will give you whatever you ask for, using my name. ¹⁷This is my command: Love each other.

## The World's Hatred

¹⁸"If the world hates you, remember that it hated me first. ¹⁹The world would love you as one of its own if you belonged to it, but you are no longer part of the world. I chose you to come out of the world, so it hates you. ²⁰Do you remember what I told you? 'A slave is not greater than the master.' Since they persecuted me, naturally they will persecute you. And if they had listened to me, they would listen to you. ²¹They will do all this to you because of me, for they have rejected the One who sent me. ²²They would not be guilty if I had not come and spoken to them. But now they have no excuse for their sin. ²³Anyone who hates me also hates my Father. ²⁴If I hadn't done such miraculous signs among them that no one else could do, they would not be guilty. But as it is, they have seen everything I did, yet they still hate me and my Father. ²⁵This fulfills what is written in their Scriptures*: 'They hated me without cause.'

²⁶"But I will send you the Advocate*—the Spirit of truth. He will come to you from the Father and will testify all about me. ²⁷And you must also testify about me because you have been with me from the beginning of my ministry.

**16** "I have told you these things so that you won't abandon your faith. ²For you will be expelled from the synagogues, and the time is coming when those who kill

you will think they are doing a holy service for God. ³This is because they have never known the Father or me. ⁴Yes, I'm telling you these things now, so that when they happen, you will remember my warning. I didn't tell you earlier because I was going to be with you for a while longer.

## The Work of the Holy Spirit

⁵"But now I am going away to the One who sent me, and not one of you is asking where I am going. ⁶Instead, you grieve because of what I've told you. ⁷But in fact, it is best for you that I go away, because if I don't, the Advocate* won't come. If I do go away, then I will send him to you. ⁸And when he comes, he will convict the world of its sin, and of God's righteousness, and of the coming judgment. ⁹The world's sin is that it refuses to believe in me. ¹⁰Righteousness is available because I go to the Father, and you will see me no more. ¹¹Judgment will come because the ruler of this world has already been judged.

¹²"There is so much more I want to tell you, but you can't bear it now. ¹³When the Spirit of truth comes, he will guide you into all truth. He will not speak on his own but will tell you what he has heard. He will tell you about the future. ¹⁴He will bring me glory by telling you whatever he receives from me. ¹⁵All that belongs to the Father is mine; this is why I said, 'The Spirit will tell you whatever he receives from me.'

## Sadness Will Be Turned to Joy

¹⁶"In a little while you won't see me anymore. But a little while after that, you will see me again."

¹⁷Some of the disciples asked each other, "What does he mean when he says, 'In a little while you won't see me, but then you will see me,' and 'I am going to the Father'? ¹⁸And what does he mean by 'a little while'? We don't understand."

¹⁹Jesus realized they wanted to ask him about it, so he said, "Are you asking yourselves what I meant? I said in a little while you won't see me, but a little while after that you will see me again. ²⁰I tell you the truth, you will weep and mourn over what is

---

**15:25** Greek *in their law.* Pss 35:19; 69:4.   **15:26** Or *Comforter,* or *Encourager,* or *Counselor.* Greek reads *Paraclete.*   **16:7** Or *Comforter,* or *Encourager,* or *Counselor.* Greek reads *Paraclete.*

going to happen to me, but the world will rejoice. You will grieve, but your grief will suddenly turn to wonderful joy. 21 It will be like a woman suffering the pains of labor. When her child is born, her anguish gives way to joy because she has brought a new baby into the world. 22 So you have sorrow now, but I will see you again; then you will rejoice, and no one can rob you of that joy. 23 At that time you won't need to ask me for anything. I tell you the truth, you will ask the Father directly, and he will grant your request because you use my name. 24 You haven't done this before. Ask, using my name, and you will receive, and you will have abundant joy.

25 "I have spoken of these matters in figures of speech, but soon I will stop speaking figuratively and will tell you plainly all about the Father. 26 Then you will ask in my name. I'm not saying I will ask the Father on your behalf, 27 for the Father himself loves you dearly because you love me and believe that I came from God.* 28 Yes, I came from the Father into the world, and now I will leave the world and return to the Father."

29 Then his disciples said, "At last you are speaking plainly and not figuratively. 30 Now we understand that you know everything, and there's no need to question you. From this we believe that you came from God."

31 Jesus asked, "Do you finally believe? 32 But the time is coming—indeed it's here now—when you will be scattered, each one going his own way, leaving me alone. Yet I am not alone because the Father is with me. 33 I have told you all this so that you may have peace in me. Here on earth you will have many trials and sorrows. But take heart, because I have overcome the world."

## The Prayer of Jesus

**17** After saying all these things, Jesus looked up to heaven and said, "Father, the hour has come. Glorify your Son so he can give glory back to you. 2 For you have given him authority over everyone. He gives eternal life to each one you have given him. 3 And this is the way to have eternal life—to know you, the only true God, and Jesus Christ, the one you sent to earth. 4 I brought glory to you here on earth by completing the work you gave me to do. 5 Now, Father, bring me into the glory we shared before the world began.

6 "I have revealed you* to the ones you gave me from this world. They were always yours. You gave them to me, and they have kept your word. 7 Now they know that everything I have is a gift from you, 8 for I have passed on to them the message you gave me. They accepted it and know that I came from you, and they believe you sent me.

**16:27** Some manuscripts read *from the Father.*   **17:6** Greek *have revealed your name;* also in 17:26.

# DEEPLY at peace
READ JOHN 16:33

If Jesus couldn't promise His disciples they wouldn't experience trials, we certainly can't offer you such a promise. We *will* experience difficulties in this world, including the breakdown of our physical bodies. But we promise you—more importantly, Jesus the Messiah promises you—we can face these difficulties with unshakable assurance, remaining deeply at peace. Why? Because Jesus has overcome the world by overcoming the power of death in our lives. Jesus already has beaten cancer and heart disease and AIDS and every other illness that strikes us on this earth.

His kind of peace isn't just the absence of striving; it's the presence of something much more. Another Bible called *The Message* paraphrases this verse this way: "I've told you all this so that trusting me, you will be unshakable and assured, deeply at peace. In this godless world you will continue to experience difficulties. But take heart! I've conquered the world."

Ask Him today to give you His deep peace.

9"My prayer is not for the world, but for those you have given me, because they belong to you. 10All who are mine belong to you, and you have given them to me, so they bring me glory. 11Now I am departing from the world; they are staying in this world, but I am coming to you. Holy Father, you have given me your name;* now protect them by the power of your name so that they will be united just as we are. 12During my time here, I protected them by the power of the name you gave me.* I guarded them so that not one was lost, except the one headed for destruction, as the Scriptures foretold.

13"Now I am coming to you. I told them many things while I was with them in this world so they would be filled with my joy. 14I have given them your word. And the world hates them because they do not belong to the world, just as I do not belong to the world. 15I'm not asking you to take them out of the world, but to keep them safe from the evil one. 16They do not belong to this world any more than I do. 17Make them holy by your truth; teach them your word, which is truth. 18Just as you sent me into the world, I am sending them into the world. 19And I give myself as a holy sacrifice for them so they can be made holy by your truth.

20"I am praying not only for these disciples but also for all who will ever believe in me through their message. 21I pray that they will all be one, just as you and I are one—as you are in me, Father, and I am in you. And may they be in us so that the world will believe you sent me.

22"I have given them the glory you gave me, so they may be one as we are one. 23I am in them and you are in me. May they experience such perfect unity that the world will know that you sent me and that you love them as much as you love me. 24Father, I want these whom you have given me to be with me where I am. Then they can see all the glory you gave me because you loved me even before the world began!

25"O righteous Father, the world doesn't know you, but I do; and these disciples know you sent me. 26I have revealed you to them,

and I will continue to do so. Then your love for me will be in them, and I will be in them."

## Jesus Is Betrayed and Arrested

**18** After saying these things, Jesus crossed the Kidron Valley with his disciples and entered a grove of olive trees. 2Judas, the betrayer, knew this place, because Jesus had often gone there with his disciples. 3The leading priests and Pharisees had given Judas a contingent of Roman soldiers and Temple guards to accompany him. Now with blazing torches, lanterns, and weapons, they arrived at the olive grove.

4Jesus fully realized all that was going to happen to him, so he stepped forward to meet them. " Who are you looking for?" he asked.

5"Jesus the Nazarene,"* they replied.

"I Am he,"* Jesus said. (Judas, who betrayed him, was standing with them.) 6As Jesus said "I Am he," they all drew back and fell to the ground! 7Once more he asked them, " Who are you looking for?"

And again they replied, "Jesus the Nazarene."

8"I told you that I Am he," Jesus said. "And since I am the one you want, let these others go." 9He did this to fulfill his own statement: "I did not lose a single one of those you have given me."*

10Then Simon Peter drew a sword and slashed off the right ear of Malchus, the high priest's slave. 11But Jesus said to Peter, "Put your sword back into its sheath. Shall I not drink from the cup of suffering the Father has given me?"

## Jesus at the High Priest's House

12So the soldiers, their commanding officer, and the Temple guards arrested Jesus and tied him up. 13First they took him to Annas, the father-in-law of Caiaphas, the high priest at that time.* 14Caiaphas was the one who had told the other Jewish leaders, "It's better that one man should die for the people."

## Peter's First Denial

15Simon Peter followed Jesus, as did another of the disciples. That other disciple was ac-

**17:11** Some manuscripts read *you have given me these [disciples]. the power of your name.* **18:5a** Or *Jesus of Nazareth;* also in 18:7. **18:5b** Or *"The 'I Am' is here";* or *"I am the Lord";* Greek reads *I am;* also in 18:6, 8. See Exod 3:14. **18:9** See John 6:39 and 17:12. **17:12** Some manuscripts read *I protected those you gave me, by* **18:13** Greek *that year.*

quainted with the high priest, so he was allowed to enter the high priest's courtyard with Jesus. 16Peter had to stay outside the gate. Then the disciple who knew the high priest spoke to the woman watching at the gate, and she let Peter in. 17The woman asked Peter, "You're not one of that man's disciples, are you?"

"No," he said, "I am not."

18Because it was cold, the household servants and the guards had made a charcoal fire. They stood around it, warming themselves, and Peter stood with them, warming himself.

### The High Priest Questions Jesus

19Inside, the high priest began asking Jesus about his followers and what he had been teaching them. 20Jesus replied, "Everyone knows what I teach. I have preached regularly in the synagogues and the Temple, where the people* gather. I have not spoken in secret. 21Why are you asking me this question? Ask those who heard me. They know what I said."

22Then one of the Temple guards standing nearby slapped Jesus across the face. "Is that the way to answer the high priest?" he demanded.

23Jesus replied, "If I said anything wrong, you must prove it. But if I'm speaking the truth, why are you beating me?"

24Then Annas bound Jesus and sent him to Caiaphas, the high priest.

### Peter's Second and Third Denials

25Meanwhile, as Simon Peter was standing by the fire warming himself, they asked him again, "You're not one of his disciples, are you?"

He denied it, saying, "No, I am not."

26But one of the household slaves of the high priest, a relative of the man whose ear Peter had cut off, asked, "Didn't I see you out there in the olive grove with Jesus?" 27Again Peter denied it. And immediately a rooster crowed.

### Jesus' Trial before Pilate

28Jesus' trial before Caiaphas ended in the early hours of the morning. Then he was taken to the headquarters of the Roman governor.* His accusers didn't go inside because it would defile them, and they wouldn't be allowed to celebrate the Passover. 29So Pilate, the governor, went out to them and asked, "What is your charge against this man?"

30"We wouldn't have handed him over to you if he weren't a criminal!" they retorted.

31"Then take him away and judge him by your own law," Pilate told them.

"Only the Romans are permitted to execute someone," the Jewish leaders replied. 32(This fulfilled Jesus' prediction about the way he would die.*)

33Then Pilate went back into his headquarters and called for Jesus to be brought to him. "Are you the king of the Jews?" he asked him.

34Jesus replied, "Is this your own question, or did others tell you about me?"

35"Am I a Jew?" Pilate retorted. "Your own people and their leading priests brought you to me for trial. Why? What have you done?"

36Jesus answered, "My Kingdom is not an earthly kingdom. If it were, my followers would fight to keep me from being handed over to the Jewish leaders. But my Kingdom is not of this world."

37Pilate said, "So you are a king?"

Jesus responded, "You say I am a king. Actually, I was born and came into the world to testify to the truth. All who love the truth recognize that what I say is true."

38"What is truth?" Pilate asked. Then he went out again to the people and told them, "He is not guilty of any crime. 39But you have a custom of asking me to release one prisoner each year at Passover. Would you like me to release this 'King of the Jews'?"

40But they shouted back, "No! Not this man. We want Barabbas!" (Barabbas was a revolutionary.)

### Jesus Sentenced to Death

**19** Then Pilate had Jesus flogged with a lead-tipped whip. 2The soldiers wove a crown of thorns and put it on his head, and they put a purple robe on him.

18:20 Greek *Jewish people;* also in 18:38.   18:28 Greek *to the Praetorium;* also in 18:33.   18:32 See John 12:32-33.

3"Hail! King of the Jews!" they mocked, as they slapped him across the face.

4Pilate went outside again and said to the people, "I am going to bring him out to you now, but understand clearly that I find him not guilty." 5Then Jesus came out wearing the crown of thorns and the purple robe. And Pilate said, "Look, here is the man!"

6When they saw him, the leading priests and Temple guards began shouting, "Crucify him! Crucify him!"

"Take him yourselves and crucify him," Pilate said. "I find him not guilty."

7The Jewish leaders replied, "By our law he ought to die because he called himself the Son of God."

8When Pilate heard this, he was more frightened than ever. 9He took Jesus back into the headquarters* again and asked him, "Where are you from?" But Jesus gave no answer. 10"Why don't you talk to me?" Pilate demanded. "Don't you realize that I have the power to release you or crucify you?"

11Then Jesus said, "You would have no power over me at all unless it were given to you from above. So the one who handed me over to you has the greater sin."

12Then Pilate tried to release him, but the Jewish leaders shouted, "If you release this man, you are no 'friend of Caesar.'* Anyone who declares himself a king is a rebel against Caesar."

13When they said this, Pilate brought Jesus out to them again. Then Pilate sat down on the judgment seat on the platform that is called the Stone Pavement (in Hebrew, *Gabbatha*). 14It was now about noon on the day of preparation for the Passover. And Pilate said to the people,* "Look, here is your king!"

15"Away with him," they yelled. "Away with him! Crucify him!"

"What? Crucify your king?" Pilate asked.

"We have no king but Caesar," the leading priests shouted back.

16Then Pilate turned Jesus over to them to be crucified.

## The Crucifixion

So they took Jesus away. 17Carrying the cross by himself, he went to the place called Place of the Skull (in Hebrew, *Golgotha*). 18There they nailed him to the cross. Two others were crucified with him, one on either side, with Jesus between them. 19And Pilate posted a sign over him that read, "Jesus of Nazareth,* the King of the Jews." 20The place where Jesus was crucified was near the city, and the sign was written in Hebrew, Latin, and Greek, so that many people could read it.

21Then the leading priests objected and said to Pilate, "Change it from 'The King of the Jews' to 'He said, I am King of the Jews.'"

22Pilate replied, "No, what I have written, I have written."

23When the soldiers had crucified Jesus, they divided his clothes among the four of them. They also took his robe, but it was seamless, woven in one piece from top to bottom. 24So they said, "Rather than tearing it apart, let's throw dice* for it." This fulfilled the Scripture that says, "They divided my garments among themselves and threw dice for my clothing."* So that is what they did.

25Standing near the cross were Jesus' mother, and his mother's sister, Mary (the wife of Clopas), and Mary Magdalene. 26When Jesus saw his mother standing there beside the disciple he loved, he said to her, "Dear woman, here is your son." 27And he said to this disciple, "Here is your mother." And from then on this disciple took her into his home.

## The Death of Jesus

28Jesus knew that his mission was now finished, and to fulfill Scripture he said, "I am thirsty."* 29A jar of sour wine was sitting there, so they soaked a sponge in it, put it on a hyssop branch, and held it up to his lips. 30When Jesus had tasted it, he said, "It is finished!" Then he bowed his head and released his spirit.

31It was the day of preparation, and the Jewish leaders didn't want the bodies hanging there the next day, which was the Sabbath (and a very special Sabbath, because it was the Passover). So they asked Pilate to hasten their deaths by ordering that their

**19:9** Greek *the Praetorium.*    **19:12** "Friend of Caesar" is a technical term that refers to an ally of the emperor.    **19:14** Greek *Jewish people;* also in 19:20.    **19:19** Or *Jesus the Nazarene.*    **19:24a** Greek *cast lots.*    **19:24b** Ps 22:18.    **19:28** See Pss 22:15; 69:21.

legs be broken. Then their bodies could be taken down. [32] So the soldiers came and broke the legs of the two men crucified with Jesus. [33] But when they came to Jesus, they saw that he was already dead, so they didn't break his legs. [34] One of the soldiers, however, pierced his side with a spear, and immediately blood and water flowed out. [35] (This report is from an eyewitness giving an accurate account. He speaks the truth so that you also can believe.*) [36] These things happened in fulfillment of the Scriptures that say, "Not one of his bones will be broken,"* [37] and "They will look on the one they pierced."*

### The Burial of Jesus

[38] Afterward Joseph of Arimathea, who had been a secret disciple of Jesus (because he feared the Jewish leaders), asked Pilate for permission to take down Jesus' body. When Pilate gave permission, Joseph came and took the body away. [39] With him came Nicodemus, the man who had come to Jesus at night. He brought seventy-five pounds* of perfumed ointment made from myrrh and aloes. [40] Following Jewish burial custom, they wrapped Jesus' body with the spices in long sheets of linen cloth. [41] The place of crucifixion was near a garden, where there was a new tomb, never used before. [42] And so, because it was the day of preparation for the Jewish Passover* and since the tomb was close at hand, they laid Jesus there.

### The Resurrection

**20** Early on Sunday morning,* while it was still dark, Mary Magdalene came to the tomb and found that the stone had been rolled away from the entrance. [2] She ran and found Simon Peter and the other disciple, the one whom Jesus loved. She said, "They have taken the Lord's body out of the tomb, and we don't know where they have put him!"

[3] Peter and the other disciple started out for the tomb. [4] They were both running, but the other disciple outran Peter and reached the tomb first. [5] He stooped and looked in and saw the linen wrappings lying there, but he didn't go in. [6] Then Simon Peter arrived and went inside. He also noticed the linen wrappings lying there, [7] while the cloth that had covered Jesus' head was folded up and lying apart from the other wrappings. [8] Then the disciple who had reached the tomb first also went in, and he saw and believed—[9] for until then they still hadn't understood the Scriptures that said Jesus must rise from the dead. [10] Then they went home.

### Jesus Appears to Mary Magdalene

[11] Mary was standing outside the tomb crying, and as she wept, she stooped and looked in. [12] She saw two white-robed angels, one sitting at the head and the other at the foot of the place where the body of Jesus had been lying. [13] "Dear woman, why are you crying?" the angels asked her.

"Because they have taken away my Lord," she replied, "and I don't know where they have put him."

[14] She turned to leave and saw someone standing there. It was Jesus, but she didn't recognize him. [15] "Dear woman, why are you crying?" Jesus asked her. "Who are you looking for?"

She thought he was the gardener. "Sir," she said, "if you have taken him away, tell me where you have put him, and I will go and get him."

[16] "Mary!" Jesus said.

She turned to him and cried out, "Rabboni!" (which is Hebrew for "Teacher").

[17] "Don't cling to me," Jesus said, "for I haven't yet ascended to the Father. But go find my brothers and tell them, 'I am ascending to my Father and your Father, to my God and your God.' "

[18] Mary Magdalene found the disciples and told them, "I have seen the Lord!" Then she gave them his message.

### Jesus Appears to His Disciples

[19] That Sunday evening* the disciples were meeting behind locked doors because they were afraid of the Jewish leaders. Suddenly,

---

**19:35** Some manuscripts read *can continue to believe.*   **19:36** Exod 12:46; Num 9:12; Ps 34:20.   **19:37** Zech 12:10.   **19:39** Greek *100 litras* [32.7 kilograms].   **19:42** Greek *because of the Jewish day of preparation.*   **20:1** Greek *On the first day of the week.*
**20:19** Greek *In the evening of that day, the first day of the week.*

Jesus was standing there among them! "Peace be with you," he said. 20As he spoke, he showed them the wounds in his hands and his side. They were filled with joy when they saw the Lord! 21Again he said, "Peace be with you. As the Father has sent me, so I am sending you." 22Then he breathed on them and said, "Receive the Holy Spirit. 23If you forgive anyone's sins, they are forgiven. If you do not forgive them, they are not forgiven."

### Jesus Appears to Thomas

24One of the twelve disciples, Thomas (nicknamed the Twin),* was not with the others when Jesus came. 25They told him, "We have seen the Lord!"

But he replied, "I won't believe it unless I see the nail wounds in his hands, put my fingers into them, and place my hand into the wound in his side."

26Eight days later the disciples were together again, and this time Thomas was with them. The doors were locked; but suddenly, as before, Jesus was standing among them. "Peace be with you," he said. 27Then he said to Thomas, "Put your finger here, and look at my hands. Put your hand into the wound in my side. Don't be faithless any longer. Believe!"

28"My Lord and my God!" Thomas exclaimed.

29Then Jesus told him, "You believe because you have seen me. Blessed are those who believe without seeing me."

### Purpose of the Book

30The disciples saw Jesus do many other miraculous signs in addition to the ones recorded in this book. 31But these are written so that you may continue to believe* that Jesus is the Messiah, the Son of God, and that by believing in him you will have life by the power of his name.

### Epilogue: Jesus Appears to Seven Disciples

**21** Later, Jesus appeared again to the disciples beside the Sea of Galilee.* This is how it happened. 2Several of the disciples were there—Simon Peter, Thomas (nicknamed the Twin),* Nathanael from Cana in Galilee, the sons of Zebedee, and two other disciples.

3Simon Peter said, "I'm going fishing."

"We'll come, too," they all said. So they went out in the boat, but they caught nothing all night.

4At dawn Jesus was standing on the beach, but the disciples couldn't see who he was. 5He called out, "Fellows,* have you caught any fish?"

"No," they replied.

6Then he said, "Throw out your net on the right-hand side of the boat, and you'll get some!" So they did, and they couldn't haul in the net because there were so many fish in it.

7Then the disciple Jesus loved said to Peter, "It's the Lord!" When Simon Peter heard that it was the Lord, he put on his tunic (for he had stripped for work), jumped into the water, and headed to shore. 8The others stayed with the boat and pulled the loaded net to the shore, for they were only about a hundred yards* from shore. 9When they got there, they found breakfast waiting for them—fish cooking over a charcoal fire, and some bread.

10"Bring some of the fish you've just caught," Jesus said. 11So Simon Peter went aboard and dragged the net to the shore. There were 153 large fish, and yet the net hadn't torn.

12"Now come and have some breakfast!" Jesus said. None of the disciples dared to ask him, "Who are you?" They knew it was the Lord. 13Then Jesus served them the bread and the fish. 14This was the third time Jesus had appeared to his disciples since he had been raised from the dead.

15After breakfast Jesus asked Simon Peter, "Simon son of John, do you love me more than these?*"

"Yes, Lord," Peter replied, "you know I love you."

"Then feed my lambs," Jesus told him.

16Jesus repeated the question: "Simon son of John, do you love me?"

---

20:24 Greek *Thomas, who was called Didymus.* 20:31 Some manuscripts read *that you may believe.* 21:1 Greek *Sea of Tiberias,* another name for the Sea of Galilee. 21:2 Greek *Thomas, who was called Didymus.* 21:5 Greek *Children.* 21:8 Greek *200 cubits* [90 meters]. 21:15 Or *more than these others do?*

# GOING up?

READ JOHN 20:30-31

If you died today, do you know for certain where you'd spend eternity? That's not a morbid question—it's really the kindest, most caring thing to ask someone. After all, we tell people about life's fleeting pleasures: the best restaurants, the most beautiful golf courses, and the most fun vacation spots. Why not ask if they know where they are going to live forever?

When many people are asked that question about their eternal destiny, they answer that they "hope" they are going to heaven or they "think" they are going to get there. But John explains here that he has written down the life story of his close friend Jesus so that we can believe in Him as the Messiah and "have life by the power of his name."

When we say we know for sure we are going to heaven, it is not because of confidence in ourselves, but because of confidence in our relationship with Jesus. If He is our Lord and Savior, we can know for certain which way we're headed.

---

"Yes, Lord," Peter said, "you know I love you."

"Then take care of my sheep," Jesus said.

17A third time he asked him, "Simon son of John, do you love me?"

Peter was hurt that Jesus asked the question a third time. He said, "Lord, you know everything. You know that I love you."

Jesus said, " Then feed my sheep.

18"I tell you the truth, when you were young, you were able to do as you liked; you dressed yourself and went wherever you wanted to go. But when you are old, you will stretch out your hands, and others* will dress you and take you where you don't want to go."

19Jesus said this to let him know by what kind of death he would glorify God. Then Jesus told him, "Follow me."

20Peter turned around and saw behind them the disciple Jesus loved—the one who had leaned over to Jesus during supper and asked, "Lord, who will betray you?" 21Peter asked Jesus, "What about him, Lord?"

22Jesus replied, "If I want him to remain alive until I return, what is that to you? As for you, follow me." 23So the rumor spread among the community of believers* that this disciple wouldn't die. But that isn't what Jesus said at all. He only said, "If I want him to remain alive until I return, what is that to you?"

24This disciple is the one who testifies to these events and has recorded them here. And we know that his account of these things is accurate.

25Jesus also did many other things. If they were all written down, I suppose the whole world could not contain the books that would be written.

**21:18** Some manuscripts read *and another one.*   **21:23** Greek *the brothers.*

# BECOMING the "ideal patient"

Are you or your loved one an ideal patient?

We're not asking whether you do everything the doctors tell you to do. We're not referring to whether your disease is easily treatable. And we're not talking about whether you have the right personality.

What we do mean is this: **Do you have the right blend of realism and faith as you live wondering when and if your disease or your loved one's will be cured?**

If you haven't already reached "ideal" status, we pray we can inspire you to achieve it. If you're already there, we pray we can encourage you that it's definitely the best place to stay.

We think that an ideal patient is one who believes firmly in the power of prayer and has no doubt that God can answer with a miracle. Such a patient prays for complete physical healing, absolutely believing that God *can* do it and feverishly praying that He *will* do it. But this ideal patient also recognizes that God is sovereign—He is absolute, unlimited, independent, and has supreme authority over us and everything else in the world.

Such an ideal patient understands that when we give our lives to Jesus, we give up our rights and give Him the right to do whatever pleases Him with our lives. When we're "ideal," we pray and believe for a physical miracle, but never *demand* it as the only answer to our prayers.

Some people might say that our faith is decreased if we don't absolutely "expect" a miracle, but we think it takes even more faith to continue to trust God, stand on His promises, and cling to hope when we *aren't* healed.

It is *not* a lack of faith to accept whatever God's will is for us. It's a true sign of faith to trust Him no matter what happens—or doesn't happen—in this lifetime. We pray you will be an ideal patient: trusting God as you pray for His physical healing touch to come and trusting Him still if it doesn't.

To believe in someone
  is to have faith
    in God's ability as the Potter
      and in that person's willingness
        to be the clay.

We believe in *you*.

# ACTS

*When Simon saw that the Spirit was given when the apostles laid their hands on people, he offered them money to buy this power.*

ACTS 8:18

How much would you be willing to pay for a cure for yourself or your loved one?

Be very wary of medical promises without data and studies to back them up. It's very easy to make outlandish claims, and desperate people easily can fall prey to get-healed-quick schemes. If you look long and hard enough, you can find someone somewhere who wants to sell you the "answer" to your problem. Good luck in getting a written, money-back guarantee.

In the book of Acts, also written by Dr. Luke, we meet a man named Simon who was on the lookout for ways to make a buck. He had astounded people with his magic, which now looked pretty paltry in comparison to the amazing miracles the disciples were performing as the early church was established and the gospel spread throughout the region. When Simon saw the apostles' power, he offered money to buy it. He probably planned to charge others to receive the power from him.

But Simon was way off base. Oh, the power he saw was very real, but it wasn't available for any price. The power of the Holy Spirit was a gift to all who believed in Jesus—Jew or Gentile. It's the same power available to us believers today. It's not just for those who belong to a certain church or pray using certain words. The Holy Spirit lives inside each true believer and fills us with a supernatural power to be all God created us to be. And this power doesn't cost a cent.

### The Promise of the Holy Spirit

**1** In my first book* I told you, Theophilus, about everything Jesus began to do and teach ²until the day he was taken up to heaven after giving his chosen apostles further instructions through the Holy Spirit. ³During the forty days after his crucifixion, he appeared to the apostles from time to time, and he proved to them in many ways that he was actually alive. And he talked to them about the Kingdom of God.

⁴Once when he was eating with them, he commanded them, "Do not leave Jerusalem until the Father sends you the gift he promised, as I told you before. ⁵John baptized with* water, but in just a few days you will be baptized with the Holy Spirit."

### The Ascension of Jesus

⁶So when the apostles were with Jesus, they kept asking him, "Lord, has the time come for you to free Israel and restore our kingdom?"

⁷He replied, "The Father alone has the authority to set those dates and times, and they are not for you to know. ⁸But you will receive power when the Holy Spirit comes upon you. And you will be my witnesses, telling people about me everywhere—in Jerusalem, throughout Judea, in Samaria, and to the ends of the earth."

⁹After saying this, he was taken up into a cloud while they were watching, and they could no longer see him. ¹⁰As they strained to see him rising into heaven, two white-robed men suddenly stood among them. ¹¹"Men of Galilee," they said, "why are you standing here staring into heaven? Jesus has been taken from you into heaven, but someday he will return from heaven in the same way you saw him go!"

### Matthias Replaces Judas

¹²Then the apostles returned to Jerusalem from the Mount of Olives, a distance of half a mile.* ¹³When they arrived, they went to the upstairs room of the house where they were staying.

Here are the names of those who were present: Peter, John, James, Andrew, Philip, Thomas, Bartholomew, Matthew, James (son of Alphaeus), Simon (the Zealot), and Judas (son of James). ¹⁴They all met together and were constantly united in prayer, along with Mary the mother of Jesus, several other women, and the brothers of Jesus.

¹⁵During this time, when about 120 believers* were together in one place, Peter stood up and addressed them. ¹⁶"Brothers," he said, "the Scriptures had to be fulfilled concerning Judas, who guided those who arrested Jesus. This was predicted long ago by the Holy Spirit, speaking through King David. ¹⁷Judas was one of us and shared in the ministry with us."

¹⁸(Judas had bought a field with the money he received for his treachery. Falling headfirst there, his body split open, spilling out all his intestines. ¹⁹The news of his death spread to all the people of Jerusalem, and they gave the place the Aramaic name *Akeldama,* which means "Field of Blood.")

²⁰Peter continued, "This was written in the book of Psalms, where it says, 'Let his home become desolate, with no one living in it.' It also says, 'Let someone else take his position.'*

²¹"So now we must choose a replacement for Judas from among the men who were with us the entire time we were traveling with the Lord Jesus—²²from the time he was baptized by John until the day he was taken from us. Whoever is chosen will join us as a witness of Jesus' resurrection."

²³So they nominated two men: Joseph called Barsabbas (also known as Justus) and Matthias. ²⁴Then they all prayed, "O Lord, you know every heart. Show us which of these men you have chosen ²⁵as an apostle to replace Judas in this ministry, for he has

**1:1** The reference is to the Gospel of Luke.   **1:5** Or *in;* also in 1:5b.   **1:12** Greek *a Sabbath day's journey.*   **1:15** Greek *brothers.*
**1:20** Pss 69:25; 109:8.

deserted us and gone where he belongs." 26Then they cast lots, and Matthias was selected to become an apostle with the other eleven.

## The Holy Spirit Comes

2 On the day of Pentecost* all the believers were meeting together in one place. 2Suddenly, there was a sound from heaven like the roaring of a mighty windstorm, and it filled the house where they were sitting. 3Then, what looked like flames or tongues of fire appeared and settled on each of them. 4And everyone present was filled with the Holy Spirit and began speaking in other languages,* as the Holy Spirit gave them this ability.

5At that time there were devout Jews from every nation living in Jerusalem. 6When they heard the loud noise, everyone came running, and they were bewildered to hear their own languages being spoken by the believers.

7They were completely amazed. "How can this be?" they exclaimed. "These people are all from Galilee, 8and yet we hear them speaking in our own native languages! 9Here we are—Parthians, Medes, Elamites, people from Mesopotamia, Judea, Cappadocia, Pontus, the province of Asia, 10Phrygia, Pamphylia, Egypt, and the areas of Libya around Cyrene, visitors from Rome 11(both Jews and converts to Juda-ism), Cretans, and Arabs. And we all hear these people speaking in our own languages about the wonderful things God has done!" 12They stood there amazed and perplexed. "What can this mean?" they asked each other.

13But others in the crowd ridiculed them, saying, "They're just drunk, that's all!"

## Peter Preaches to the Crowd

14Then Peter stepped forward with the eleven other apostles and shouted to the crowd, "Listen carefully, all of you, fellow Jews and residents of Jerusalem! Make no mistake about this. 15These people are not drunk, as some of you are assuming. Nine o'clock in the morning is much too early for that. 16No, what you see was predicted long ago by the prophet Joel:

17 'In the last days,' God says,
     'I will pour out my Spirit upon
          all people.
     Your sons and daughters will prophesy.
          Your young men will see visions,
          and your old men will dream dreams.
18 In those days I will pour out my Spirit
          even on my servants—men and
               women alike—
          and they will prophesy.
19 And I will cause wonders in the heavens
          above

2:1 The Festival of Pentecost came 50 days after Passover (when Jesus was crucified).   2:4 Or in other tongues.

# DRUNK at 9 a.m.?

READ ACTS 2:1-13

Some people like surprises and others hate to be caught off-guard. Nobody likes to be surprised by illness or the continued, unwelcome surprises a health crisis can bring. But whether or not you like surprises, God often is a God of surprises.

Consider this scene in Jerusalem as the believers waited together for the gift God had promised in Acts 1:4. They probably were pretty surprised when a windstorm filled the house and flames of fire settled on each of them. There's no doubt the nearby crowd of Jews was surprised when they heard their native languages being spoken by the believers who hadn't learned them. These Jews tried to explain away the surprise by saying all the believers were drunk. But it was only 9 a.m. and the surprise couldn't be explained away so easily.

Along your journey with serious illness, God may surprise you. He may show up in ways you couldn't foresee or at times you hadn't figured. Don't be alarmed—if we always knew His next move, He wouldn't be God, would He?

and signs on the earth below—
blood and fire and clouds of smoke.
20 The sun will become dark,
and the moon will turn blood red
before that great and glorious day of
the LORD arrives.
21 But everyone who calls on the name of
the LORD
will be saved.'*

22 "People of Israel, listen! God publicly endorsed Jesus the Nazarene* by doing powerful miracles, wonders, and signs through him, as you well know. 23 But God knew what would happen, and his prearranged plan was carried out when Jesus was betrayed. With the help of lawless Gentiles, you nailed him to a cross and killed him. 24 But God released him from the horrors of death and raised him back to life, for death could not keep him in its grip. 25 King David said this about him:

'I see that the LORD is always with me.
I will not be shaken, for he is right
beside me.
26 No wonder my heart is glad,
and my tongue shouts his praises!
My body rests in hope.
27 For you will not leave my soul among
the dead*
or allow your Holy One to rot in the
grave.
28 You have shown me the way of life,
and you will fill me with the joy
of your presence.'*

29 "Dear brothers, think about this! You can be sure that the patriarch David wasn't referring to himself, for he died and was buried, and his tomb is still here among us. 30 But he was a prophet, and he knew God had promised with an oath that one of David's own descendants would sit on his throne. 31 David was looking into the future and speaking of the Messiah's resurrection. He was saying that God would not leave him among the dead or allow his body to rot in the grave.
32 "God raised Jesus from the dead, and we are all witnesses of this. 33 Now he is exalted to the place of highest honor in heaven, at God's right hand. And the Father, as he had promised, gave him the Holy Spirit to pour out upon us, just as you see and hear today. 34 For David himself never ascended into heaven, yet he said,

'The LORD said to my Lord,
"Sit in the place of honor at my right
hand
35 until I humble your enemies,
making them a footstool under your
feet."'*

36 "So let everyone in Israel know for certain that God has made this Jesus, whom you crucified, to be both Lord and Messiah!"
37 Peter's words pierced their hearts, and they said to him and to the other apostles, "Brothers, what should we do?"
38 Peter replied, "Each of you must repent of your sins and turn to God, and be baptized in the name of Jesus Christ for the forgiveness of your sins. Then you will receive the gift of the Holy Spirit. 39 This promise is to you, and to your children, and even to the Gentiles*—all who have been called by the Lord our God." 40 Then Peter continued preaching for a long time, strongly urging all his listeners, "Save yourselves from this crooked generation!"
41 Those who believed what Peter said were baptized and added to the church that day—about 3,000 in all.

### The Believers Form a Community
42 All the believers devoted themselves to the apostles' teaching, and to fellowship, and to sharing in meals (including the Lord's Supper*), and to prayer.
43 A deep sense of awe came over them all, and the apostles performed many miraculous signs and wonders. 44 And all the believers met together in one place and shared everything they had. 45 They sold their property and possessions and shared the money with those in need. 46 They worshiped together at the Temple each day, met in homes for the Lord's Supper, and shared their meals with great joy and generosity*—47 all

2:17-21 Joel 2:28-32.   2:22 Or *Jesus of Nazareth.*   2:27 Greek *in Hades;* also in 2:31.   2:25-28 Ps 16:8-11 (Greek version).
2:34-35 Ps 110:1.   2:39 Or *and to people far in the future;* Greek reads *and to those far away.*   2:42 Greek *the breaking of bread;*
also in 2:46.   2:46 Or *and sincere hearts.*

the while praising God and enjoying the goodwill of all the people. And each day the Lord added to their fellowship those who were being saved.

## Peter Heals a Crippled Beggar

3 Peter and John went to the Temple one afternoon to take part in the three o'clock prayer service. ²As they approached the Temple, a man lame from birth was being carried in. Each day he was put beside the Temple gate, the one called the Beautiful Gate, so he could beg from the people going into the Temple. ³When he saw Peter and John about to enter, he asked them for some money.

⁴Peter and John looked at him intently, and Peter said, "Look at us!" ⁵The lame man looked at them eagerly, expecting some money. ⁶But Peter said, "I don't have any silver or gold for you. But I'll give you what I have. In the name of Jesus Christ the Nazarene,* get up and* walk!"

⁷Then Peter took the lame man by the right hand and helped him up. And as he did, the man's feet and ankles were instantly healed and strengthened. ⁸He jumped up, stood on his feet, and began to walk! Then, walking, leaping, and praising God, he went into the Temple with them.

⁹All the people saw him walking and heard him praising God. ¹⁰When they realized he was the lame beggar they had seen so often at the Beautiful Gate, they were absolutely astounded! ¹¹They all rushed out in amazement to Solomon's Colonnade, where the man was holding tightly to Peter and John.

## Peter Preaches in the Temple

¹²Peter saw his opportunity and addressed the crowd. "People of Israel," he said, "what is so surprising about this? And why stare at us as though we had made this man walk by our own power or godliness? ¹³For it is the God of Abraham, Isaac, and Jacob—the God of all our ancestors—who has brought glory to his servant Jesus by doing this. This is the same Jesus whom you handed over and rejected before Pilate, despite Pilate's decision

to release him. ¹⁴You rejected this holy, righteous one and instead demanded the release of a murderer. ¹⁵You killed the author of life, but God raised him from the dead. And we are witnesses of this fact!

¹⁶"Through faith in the name of Jesus, this man was healed—and you know how crippled he was before. Faith in Jesus' name has healed him before your very eyes.

¹⁷"Friends,* I realize that what you and your leaders did to Jesus was done in ignorance. ¹⁸But God was fulfilling what all the prophets had foretold about the Messiah—that he must suffer these things. ¹⁹Now repent of your sins and turn to God, so that your sins may be wiped away. ²⁰Then times of refreshment will come from the presence of the Lord, and he will again send you Jesus, your appointed Messiah. ²¹For he must remain in heaven until the time for the final restoration of all things, as God promised long ago through his holy prophets. ²²Moses said, 'The LORD your God will raise up for you a Prophet like me from among your own people. Listen carefully to everything he tells you.'* ²³Then Moses said, 'Anyone who will not listen to that Prophet will be completely cut off from God's people.'*

²⁴"Starting with Samuel, every prophet spoke about what is happening today. ²⁵You are the children of those prophets, and you are included in the covenant God promised to your ancestors. For God said to Abraham, 'Through your descendants* all the families on earth will be blessed.' ²⁶When God raised up his servant, Jesus, he sent him first to you people of Israel, to bless you by turning each of you back from your sinful ways."

## Peter and John before the Council

4 While Peter and John were speaking to the people, they were confronted by the priests, the captain of the Temple guard, and some of the Sadducees. ²These leaders were very disturbed that Peter and John were teaching the people that through Jesus there is a resurrection of the dead. ³They arrested them and, since it was already evening, put them in jail until morning. ⁴But many of the people who heard their message believed it,

3:6a Or *Jesus Christ of Nazareth.*   3:6b Some manuscripts omit *get up and.*   3:17 Greek *Brothers.*   3:22 Deut 18:15.   3:23 Deut 18:19; Lev 23:29.   3:25 Greek *your seed;* see Gen 12:3; 22:18.

so the number of believers now totaled about 5,000 men, not counting women and children.*

5 The next day the council of all the rulers and elders and teachers of religious law met in Jerusalem. 6 Annas the high priest was there, along with Caiaphas, John, Alexander, and other relatives of the high priest. 7 They brought in the two disciples and demanded, "By what power, or in whose name, have you done this?"

8 Then Peter, filled with the Holy Spirit, said to them, "Rulers and elders of our people, 9 are we being questioned today because we've done a good deed for a crippled man? Do you want to know how he was healed? 10 Let me clearly state to all of you and to all the people of Israel that he was healed by the powerful name of Jesus Christ the Nazarene,* the man you crucified but whom God raised from the dead. 11 For Jesus is the one referred to in the Scriptures, where it says,

'The stone that you builders rejected
    has now become the cornerstone.'*

12 There is salvation in no one else! God has given no other name under heaven by which we must be saved."

13 The members of the council were amazed when they saw the boldness of Peter and John, for they could see that they were ordinary men with no special training in the Scriptures. They also recognized them as men who had been with Jesus. 14 But since they could see the man who had been healed standing right there among them, there was nothing the council could say. 15 So they ordered Peter and John out of the council chamber* and conferred among themselves.

16 "What should we do with these men?" they asked each other. "We can't deny that they have performed a miraculous sign, and everybody in Jerusalem knows about it. 17 But to keep them from spreading their propaganda any further, we must warn them not to speak to anyone in Jesus' name again." 18 So they called the apostles back in and commanded them never again to speak or teach in the name of Jesus.

19 But Peter and John replied, "Do you think God wants us to obey you rather than him? 20 We cannot stop telling about everything we have seen and heard."

21 The council then threatened them further, but they finally let them go because they didn't know how to punish them without starting a riot. For everyone was praising God 22 for this miraculous sign—the healing of a man who had been lame for more than forty years.

### The Believers Pray for Courage

23 As soon as they were freed, Peter and John returned to the other believers and told them what the leading priests and elders had said. 24 When they heard the report, all the believers lifted their voices together in prayer to God: "O Sovereign Lord, Creator of heaven and earth, the sea, and everything in them— 25 you spoke long ago by the Holy Spirit through our ancestor David, your servant, saying,

'Why were the nations so angry?
    Why did they waste their time with
        futile plans?
26 The kings of the earth prepared for
        battle;
    the rulers gathered together
against the LORD
    and against his Messiah.'*

27 "In fact, this has happened here in this very city! For Herod Antipas, Pontius Pilate

---

## BUDDY, can you spare a dime?

READ ACTS 3:1-11

The crippled man didn't have high expectations as he sat begging. Had Peter tossed him a coin, he would have been quite happy. But Peter wanted to give him much more than pocket change. He wanted him to *be changed*. So, he touched him, healed him, and filled him with praise for God. It was far more than the man ever dreamed.

God wants to do more in your life than you can ask or imagine. Ask Him for what's on your heart, but always trust that He knows your greatest needs better than you do and has the power to make you whole in every sense of the word.

---

4:4 Greek *5,000 adult males.* 4:10 Or *Jesus Christ of Nazareth.* 4:11 Ps 118:22. 4:15 Greek *the Sanhedrin.* 4:25-26 Or *his anointed one;* or *his Christ.* Ps 2:1-2.

the governor, the Gentiles, and the people of Israel were all united against Jesus, your holy servant, whom you anointed. 28But everything they did was determined beforehand according to your will. 29And now, O Lord, hear their threats, and give us, your servants, great boldness in preaching your word. 30Stretch out your hand with healing power; may miraculous signs and wonders be done through the name of your holy servant Jesus."

31After this prayer, the meeting place shook, and they were all filled with the Holy Spirit. Then they preached the word of God with boldness.

## The Believers Share Their Possessions

32All the believers were united in heart and mind. And they felt that what they owned was not their own, so they shared everything they had. 33The apostles testified powerfully to the resurrection of the Lord Jesus, and God's great blessing was upon them all. 34There were no needy people among them, because those who owned land or houses would sell them 35and bring the money to the apostles to give to those in need.

36For instance, there was Joseph, the one the apostles nicknamed Barnabas (which means "Son of Encouragement"). He was from the tribe of Levi and came from the island of Cyprus. 37He sold a field he owned and brought the money to the apostles.

## Ananias and Sapphira

5 But there was a certain man named Ananias who, with his wife, Sapphira, sold some property. 2He brought part of the money to the apostles, claiming it was the full amount. With his wife's consent, he kept the rest.

3Then Peter said, "Ananias, why have you let Satan fill your heart? You lied to the Holy Spirit, and you kept some of the money for yourself. 4The property was yours to sell or not sell, as you wished. And after selling it, the money was also yours to give away. How could you do a thing like this? You weren't lying to us but to God!"

5As soon as Ananias heard these words, he fell to the floor and died. Everyone who heard about it was terrified. 6Then some

young men got up, wrapped him in a sheet, and took him out and buried him.

7About three hours later his wife came in, not knowing what had happened. 8Peter asked her, "Was this the price you and your husband received for your land?"

"Yes," she replied, "that was the price."

9And Peter said, "How could the two of you even think of conspiring to test the Spirit of the Lord like this? The young men who buried your husband are just outside the door, and they will carry you out, too."

10Instantly, she fell to the floor and died. When the young men came in and saw that she was dead, they carried her out and buried her beside her husband. 11Great fear gripped the entire church and everyone else who heard what had happened.

## The Apostles Heal Many

12The apostles were performing many miraculous signs and wonders among the people. And all the believers were meeting regularly at the Temple in the area known as Solomon's Colonnade. 13But no one else dared to join them, even though all the people had high regard for them. 14Yet more and more people believed and were brought to the Lord—crowds of both men and women. 15As a result of the apostles' work, sick people were brought out into the streets on beds and mats so that Peter's shadow might fall across some of them as he went by. 16Crowds came from the villages around Jerusalem, bringing their sick and those possessed by evil* spirits, and they were all healed.

## The Apostles Meet Opposition

17The high priest and his officials, who were Sadducees, were filled with jealousy. 18They arrested the apostles and put them in the public jail. 19But an angel of the Lord came at night, opened the gates of the jail, and brought them out. Then he told them, 20"Go to the Temple and give the people this message of life!"

21So at daybreak the apostles entered the Temple, as they were told, and immediately began teaching.

When the high priest and his officials arrived, they convened the high council*—the

5:16 Greek unclean.   5:21 Greek Sanhedrin; also in 5:27, 41.

full assembly of the elders of Israel. Then they sent for the apostles to be brought from the jail for trial. 22But when the Temple guards went to the jail, the men were gone. So they returned to the council and reported, 23"The jail was securely locked, with the guards standing outside, but when we opened the gates, no one was there!"

24When the captain of the Temple guard and the leading priests heard this, they were perplexed, wondering where it would all end. 25Then someone arrived with startling news: "The men you put in jail are standing in the Temple, teaching the people!"

26The captain went with his Temple guards and arrested the apostles, but without violence, for they were afraid the people would stone them. 27Then they brought the apostles before the high council, where the high priest confronted them. 28"Didn't we tell you never again to teach in this man's name?" he demanded. "Instead, you have filled all Jerusalem with your teaching about him, and you want to make us responsible for his death!"

29But Peter and the apostles replied, "We must obey God rather than any human authority. 30The God of our ancestors raised Jesus from the dead after you killed him by hanging him on a cross.* 31Then God put him in the place of honor at his right hand as Prince and Savior. He did this so the people of Israel would repent of their sins and be forgiven. 32We are witnesses of these things and so is the Holy Spirit, who is given by God to those who obey him."

33When they heard this, the high council was furious and decided to kill them. 34But one member, a Pharisee named Gamaliel, who was an expert in religious law and respected by all the people, stood up and ordered that the men be sent outside the council chamber for a while. 35Then he said to his colleagues, "Men of Israel, take care what you are planning to do to these men! 36Some time ago there was that fellow Theudas, who pretended to be someone great. About 400 others joined him, but he was killed, and all his followers went their various ways. The whole movement came to nothing. 37After him, at the time of the census, there was Judas of Galilee. He got people

to follow him, but he was killed, too, and all his followers were scattered.

38"So my advice is, leave these men alone. Let them go. If they are planning and doing these things merely on their own, it will soon be overthrown. 39But if it is from God, you will not be able to overthrow them. You may even find yourselves fighting against God!"

40The others accepted his advice. They called in the apostles and had them flogged. Then they ordered them never again to speak in the name of Jesus, and they let them go.

41The apostles left the high council rejoicing that God had counted them worthy to suffer disgrace for the name of Jesus.* 42And every day, in the Temple and from house to house, they continued to teach and preach this message: "Jesus is the Messiah."

### Seven Men Chosen to Serve

6 But as the believers* rapidly multiplied, there were rumblings of discontent. The Greek-speaking believers complained about the Hebrew-speaking believers, saying that their widows were being discriminated against in the daily distribution of food.

2So the Twelve called a meeting of all the believers. They said, "We apostles should spend our time teaching the word of God, not running a food program. 3And so, brothers, select seven men who are well respected and are full of the Spirit and wisdom. We will give them this responsibility. 4Then we apostles can spend our time in prayer and teaching the word."

5Everyone liked this idea, and they chose the following: Stephen (a man full of faith and the Holy Spirit), Philip, Procorus, Nicanor, Timon, Parmenas, and Nicolas of Antioch (an earlier convert to the Jewish faith). 6These seven were presented to the apostles, who prayed for them as they laid their hands on them.

7So God's message continued to spread. The number of believers greatly increased in Jerusalem, and many of the Jewish priests were converted, too.

### Stephen Is Arrested

8Stephen, a man full of God's grace and power, performed amazing miracles and

5:30 Greek on a tree.    5:41 Greek for the name.    6:1 Greek disciples; also in 6:2, 7.

signs among the people. 9 But one day some men from the Synagogue of Freed Slaves, as it was called, started to debate with him. They were Jews from Cyrene, Alexandria, Cilicia, and the province of Asia. 10 None of them could stand against the wisdom and the Spirit with which Stephen spoke.

11 So they persuaded some men to lie about Stephen, saying, "We heard him blaspheme Moses, and even God." 12 This roused the people, the elders, and the teachers of religious law. So they arrested Stephen and brought him before the high council.*

13 The lying witnesses said, "This man is always speaking against the holy Temple and against the law of Moses. 14 We have heard him say that this Jesus of Nazareth* will destroy the Temple and change the customs Moses handed down to us."

15 At this point everyone in the high council stared at Stephen, because his face became as bright as an angel's.

## Stephen Addresses the Council

7 Then the high priest asked Stephen, "Are these accusations true?"

2 This was Stephen's reply: "Brothers and fathers, listen to me. Our glorious God appeared to our ancestor Abraham in Mesopotamia before he settled in Haran.* 3 God told him, 'Leave your native land and your relatives, and come into the land that I will show you.'* 4 So Abraham left the land of the Chaldeans and lived in Haran until his father died. Then God brought him here to the land where you now live.

5 "But God gave him no inheritance here, not even one square foot of land. God did promise, however, that eventually the whole land would belong to Abraham and his descendants—even though he had no children yet. 6 God also told him that his descendants would live in a foreign land, where they would be oppressed as slaves for 400 years. 7 'But I will punish the nation that enslaves them,' God said, 'and in the end they will come out and worship me here in this place.'*

8 "God also gave Abraham the covenant of circumcision at that time. So when Abraham became the father of Isaac, he circumcised him on the eighth day. And the practice was continued when Isaac became the father of Jacob, and when Jacob became the father of the twelve patriarchs of the Israelite nation.

9 "These patriarchs were jealous of their brother Joseph, and they sold him to be a slave in Egypt. But God was with him 10 and rescued him from all his troubles. And God gave him favor before Pharaoh, king of Egypt. God also gave Joseph unusual wisdom, so that Pharaoh appointed him governor over all of Egypt and put him in charge of the palace.

11 "But a famine came upon Egypt and Canaan. There was great misery, and our ancestors ran out of food. 12 Jacob heard that there was still grain in Egypt, so he sent his sons—our ancestors—to buy some. 13 The second time they went, Joseph revealed his identity to his brothers,* and they were introduced to Pharaoh. 14 Then Joseph sent for his father, Jacob, and all his relatives to come to Egypt, seventy-five persons in all. 15 So Jacob went to Egypt. He died there, as did our ancestors. 16 Their bodies were taken to Shechem and buried in the tomb Abraham had bought for a certain price from Hamor's sons in Shechem.

17 "As the time drew near when God would fulfill his promise to Abraham, the number of our people in Egypt greatly increased. 18 But then a new king came to the throne of Egypt who knew nothing about Joseph. 19 This king exploited our people and oppressed them, forcing parents to abandon their newborn babies so they would die.

20 "At that time Moses was born—a beautiful child in God's eyes. His parents cared for him at home for three months. 21 When they had to abandon him, Pharaoh's daughter adopted him and raised him as her own son. 22 Moses was taught all the wisdom of the Egyptians, and he was powerful in both speech and action.

23 "One day when Moses was forty years old, he decided to visit his relatives, the

6:12 Greek Sanhedrin; also in 6:15.   6:14 Or Jesus the Nazarene.   7:2 Mesopotamia was the region now called Iraq. Haran was a city in what is now called Syria.   7:3 Gen 12:1.   7:5-7 Gen 12:7; 15:13-14; Exod 3:12.   7:13 Other manuscripts read Joseph was recognized by his brothers.

people of Israel. ²⁴He saw an Egyptian mistreating an Israelite. So Moses came to the man's defense and avenged him, killing the Egyptian. ²⁵Moses assumed his fellow Israelites would realize that God had sent him to rescue them, but they didn't.

²⁶"The next day he visited them again and saw two men of Israel fighting. He tried to be a peacemaker. 'Men,' he said, 'you are brothers. Why are you fighting each other?'

²⁷"But the man in the wrong pushed Moses aside. 'Who made you a ruler and judge over us?' he asked. ²⁸'Are you going to kill me as you killed that Egyptian yesterday?' ²⁹When Moses heard that, he fled the country and lived as a foreigner in the land of Midian. There his two sons were born.

³⁰"Forty years later, in the desert near Mount Sinai, an angel appeared to Moses in the flame of a burning bush. ³¹When Moses saw it, he was amazed at the sight. As he went to take a closer look, the voice of the LORD called out to him, ³²'I am the God of your ancestors—the God of Abraham, Isaac, and Jacob.' Moses shook with terror and did not dare to look.

³³"Then the LORD said to him, 'Take off your sandals, for you are standing on holy ground. ³⁴I have certainly seen the oppression of my people in Egypt. I have heard their groans and have come down to rescue them. Now go, for I am sending you back to Egypt.'*

³⁵"So God sent back the same man his people had previously rejected when they demanded, 'Who made you a ruler and judge over us?' Through the angel who appeared to him in the burning bush, God sent Moses to be their ruler and savior. ³⁶And by means of many wonders and miraculous signs, he led them out of Egypt, through the Red Sea, and through the wilderness for forty years.

³⁷"Moses himself told the people of Israel, 'God will raise up for you a Prophet like me from among your own people.'* ³⁸Moses was with our ancestors, the assembly of God's people in the wilderness, when the angel spoke to him at Mount Sinai. And there Moses received life-giving words to pass on to us.*

³⁹"But our ancestors refused to listen to Moses. They rejected him and wanted to return to Egypt. ⁴⁰They told Aaron, 'Make us some gods who can lead us, for we don't know what has become of this Moses, who brought us out of Egypt.' ⁴¹So they made an idol shaped like a calf, and they sacrificed to it and celebrated over this thing they had made. ⁴²Then God turned away from them and abandoned them to serve the stars of heaven as their gods! In the book of the prophets it is written,

'Was it to me you were bringing
   sacrifices and offerings
during those forty years in the
   wilderness, Israel?
⁴³No, you carried your pagan gods—
   the shrine of Molech,
   the star of your god Rephan,
   and the images you made to worship
     them.
So I will send you into exile
   as far away as Babylon.'*

⁴⁴"Our ancestors carried the Tabernacle* with them through the wilderness. It was constructed according to the plan God had shown to Moses. ⁴⁵Years later, when Joshua led our ancestors in battle against the nations that God drove out of this land, the Tabernacle was taken with them into their new territory. And it stayed there until the time of King David.

⁴⁶"David found favor with God and asked for the privilege of building a permanent Temple for the God of Jacob.* ⁴⁷But it was Solomon who actually built it. ⁴⁸However, the Most High doesn't live in temples made by human hands. As the prophet says,

⁴⁹'Heaven is my throne,
   and the earth is my footstool.
Could you build me a temple as good
   as that?'
   asks the LORD.
'Could you build me such a resting place?
⁵⁰   Didn't my hands make both heaven
     and earth?'*

⁵¹"You stubborn people! You are heathen* at heart and deaf to the truth. Must you forever resist the Holy Spirit? That's what your ancestors did, and so do you! ⁵²Name one

7:31-34 Exod 3:5-10.   7:37 Deut 18:15.   7:38 Some manuscripts read *to you.*   7:42-43 Amos 5:25-27 (Greek version).
7:44 Greek *the tent of witness.*   7:46 Some manuscripts read *the house of Jacob.*   7:49-50 Isa 66:1-2.   7:51 Greek *uncircumcised.*

# SPONTANEOUS remissions

READ ACTS 5:12-16

The medical community calls them "spontaneous remissions." Somebody is given a death sentence but doesn't die. A patient is told there is no chance for a cure, yet the symptoms mysteriously disappear. We've all heard of those unexplained, remarkable recoveries for which science can take no credit.

The Bible calls them miracles and the book of Acts is full of them. In these verses we read about sick and demon-possessed people being healed just by Peter's shadow falling on them as he walked by! We know from grade-school science that a shadow is caused by the absence of light when an opaque object has absorbed the light. Shadows, of course, have no medical power to heal. But Peter (the opaque object) had absorbed the Light of the World (Jesus Christ) and through him God chose to perform miracles. Luke, the Gentile physician writing this account, would never have called them "spontaneous remissions"; he knew exactly who deserved the credit.

prophet your ancestors didn't persecute! They even killed the ones who predicted the coming of the Righteous One—the Messiah whom you betrayed and murdered. 53 You deliberately disobeyed God's law, even though you received it from the hands of angels."

54 The Jewish leaders were infuriated by Stephen's accusation, and they shook their fists at him in rage.* 55 But Stephen, full of the Holy Spirit, gazed steadily into heaven and saw the glory of God, and he saw Jesus standing in the place of honor at God's right hand. 56 And he told them, "Look, I see the heavens opened and the Son of Man standing in the place of honor at God's right hand!"

57 Then they put their hands over their ears and began shouting. They rushed at him 58 and dragged him out of the city and began to stone him. His accusers took off their coats and laid them at the feet of a young man named Saul.*

59 As they stoned him, Stephen prayed, "Lord Jesus, receive my spirit." 60 He fell to his knees, shouting, "Lord, don't charge them with this sin!" And with that, he died.

**8** Saul was one of the witnesses, and he agreed completely with the killing of Stephen.

### Persecution Scatters the Believers

A great wave of persecution began that day, sweeping over the church in Jerusalem; and all the believers except the apostles were scattered through the regions of Judea and Samaria. 2 (Some devout men came and buried Stephen with great mourning.) 3 But Saul was going everywhere to destroy the church. He went from house to house, dragging out both men and women to throw them into prison.

### Philip Preaches in Samaria

4 But the believers who were scattered preached the Good News about Jesus wherever they went. 5 Philip, for example, went to the city of Samaria and told the people there about the Messiah. 6 Crowds listened intently to Philip because they were eager to hear his message and see the miraculous signs he did. 7 Many evil* spirits were cast out, screaming as they left their victims. And many who had been paralyzed or lame were healed. 8 So there was great joy in that city.

9 A man named Simon had been a sorcerer there for many years, amazing the people of Samaria and claiming to be someone great. 10 Everyone, from the least to the greatest, often spoke of him as "the Great One—the Power of God." 11 They listened closely to him

7:54 Greek *they were grinding their teeth against him.*   7:58 *Saul* is later called Paul; see 13:9.   8:7 Greek *unclean.*

because for a long time he had astounded them with his magic.

¹²But now the people believed Philip's message of Good News concerning the Kingdom of God and the name of Jesus Christ. As a result, many men and women were baptized. ¹³Then Simon himself believed and was baptized. He began following Philip wherever he went, and he was amazed by the signs and great miracles Philip performed.

¹⁴When the apostles in Jerusalem heard that the people of Samaria had accepted God's message, they sent Peter and John there. ¹⁵As soon as they arrived, they prayed for these new believers to receive the Holy Spirit. ¹⁶The Holy Spirit had not yet come upon any of them, for they had only been baptized in the name of the Lord Jesus. ¹⁷Then Peter and John laid their hands upon these believers, and they received the Holy Spirit.

¹⁸When Simon saw that the Spirit was given when the apostles laid their hands on people, he offered them money to buy this power. ¹⁹"Let me have this power, too," he exclaimed, "so that when I lay my hands on people, they will receive the Holy Spirit!"

²⁰But Peter replied, "May your money be destroyed with you for thinking God's gift can be bought! ²¹You can have no part in this, for your heart is not right with God. ²²Repent of your wickedness and pray to the Lord. Perhaps he will forgive your evil thoughts, ²³for I can see that you are full of bitter jealousy and are held captive by sin."

²⁴"Pray to the Lord for me," Simon exclaimed, "that these terrible things you've said won't happen to me!"

²⁵After testifying and preaching the word of the Lord in Samaria, Peter and John returned to Jerusalem. And they stopped in many Samaritan villages along the way to preach the Good News.

## Philip and the Ethiopian Eunuch

²⁶As for Philip, an angel of the Lord said to him, "Go south* down the desert road that runs from Jerusalem to Gaza." ²⁷So he started out, and he met the treasurer of Ethiopia, a eunuch of great authority under the Kandake, the queen of Ethiopia. The eunuch

had gone to Jerusalem to worship, ²⁸and he was now returning. Seated in his carriage, he was reading aloud from the book of the prophet Isaiah.

²⁹The Holy Spirit said to Philip, "Go over and walk along beside the carriage."

³⁰Philip ran over and heard the man reading from the prophet Isaiah. Philip asked, "Do you understand what you are reading?"

³¹The man replied, "How can I, unless someone instructs me?" And he urged Philip to come up into the carriage and sit with him. ³²The passage of Scripture he had been reading was this:

"He was led like a sheep to the
    slaughter.
And as a lamb is silent before the
    shearers,
he did not open his mouth.
³³He was humiliated and received no
    justice.
Who can speak of his descendants?
For his life was taken from the
    earth."*

³⁴The eunuch asked Philip, "Tell me, was the prophet talking about himself or someone else?" ³⁵So beginning with this same Scripture, Philip told him the Good News about Jesus.

³⁶As they rode along, they came to some water, and the eunuch said, "Look! There's some water! Why can't I be baptized?"* ³⁸He ordered the carriage to stop, and they went down into the water, and Philip baptized him.

³⁹When they came up out of the water, the Spirit of the Lord snatched Philip away. The eunuch never saw him again but went on his way rejoicing. ⁴⁰Meanwhile, Philip found himself farther north at the town of Azotus. He preached the Good News there and in every town along the way until he came to Caesarea.

## Saul's Conversion

**9** Meanwhile, Saul was uttering threats with every breath and was eager to kill the Lord's followers.* So he went to the high priest. ²He requested letters addressed to

---

**8:26** Or *Go at noon.*    **8:32-33** Isa 53:7-8 (Greek version).    **8:36** Some manuscripts add verse 37, *"You can," Philip answered, "if you believe with all your heart." And the eunuch replied, "I believe that Jesus Christ is the Son of God."*    **9:1** Greek *disciples.*

the synagogues in Damascus, asking for their cooperation in the arrest of any followers of the Way he found there. He wanted to bring them—both men and women—back to Jerusalem in chains.

³As he was approaching Damascus on this mission, a light from heaven suddenly shone down around him. ⁴He fell to the ground and heard a voice saying to him, "Saul! Saul! Why are you persecuting me?"

⁵"Who are you, lord?" Saul asked.

And the voice replied, "I am Jesus, the one you are persecuting! ⁶Now get up and go into the city, and you will be told what you must do."

⁷The men with Saul stood speechless, for they heard the sound of someone's voice but saw no one! ⁸Saul picked himself up off the ground, but when he opened his eyes he was blind. So his companions led him by the hand to Damascus. ⁹He remained there blind for three days and did not eat or drink.

¹⁰Now there was a believer* in Damascus named Ananias. The Lord spoke to him in a vision, calling, "Ananias!"

"Yes, Lord!" he replied.

¹¹The Lord said, "Go over to Straight Street, to the house of Judas. When you get there, ask for a man from Tarsus named Saul. He is praying to me right now. ¹²I have shown him a vision of a man named Ananias coming in and laying hands on him so he can see again."

¹³"But Lord," exclaimed Ananias, "I've heard many people talk about the terrible things this man has done to the believers* in Jerusalem! ¹⁴And he is authorized by the leading priests to arrest everyone who calls upon your name."

¹⁵But the Lord said, "Go, for Saul is my chosen instrument to take my message to the Gentiles and to kings, as well as to the people of Israel. ¹⁶And I will show him how much he must suffer for my name's sake."

¹⁷So Ananias went and found Saul. He laid his hands on him and said, "Brother Saul, the Lord Jesus, who appeared to you on the road, has sent me so that you might regain your sight and be filled with the Holy Spirit." ¹⁸Instantly something like scales fell from Saul's eyes, and he regained his sight. Then he got up and was baptized. ¹⁹Afterward he ate some food and regained his strength.

### Saul in Damascus and Jerusalem

Saul stayed with the believers* in Damascus for a few days. ²⁰And immediately he began preaching about Jesus in the synagogues, saying, "He is indeed the Son of God!"

²¹All who heard him were amazed. "Isn't this the same man who caused such devastation among Jesus' followers in Jerusalem?" they asked. "And didn't he come here to arrest them and take them in chains to the leading priests?"

²²Saul's preaching became more and more powerful, and the Jews in Damascus couldn't refute his proofs that Jesus was indeed the Messiah. ²³After a while some of the Jews plotted together to kill him. ²⁴They were watching for him day and night at the city gate so they could murder him, but Saul was told about their plot. ²⁵So during the night, some of the other believers* lowered him in a large basket through an opening in the city wall.

²⁶When Saul arrived in Jerusalem, he tried to meet with the believers, but they were all afraid of him. They did not believe he had truly become a believer! ²⁷Then Barnabas brought him to the apostles and told them how Saul had seen the Lord on the way to Damascus and how the Lord had spoken to Saul. He also told them that Saul had preached boldly in the name of Jesus in Damascus.

²⁸So Saul stayed with the apostles and went all around Jerusalem with them, preaching boldly in the name of the Lord. ²⁹He debated with some Greek-speaking Jews, but they tried to murder him. ³⁰When the believers* heard about this, they took him down to Caesarea and sent him away to Tarsus, his hometown.

³¹The church then had peace throughout Judea, Galilee, and Samaria, and it became stronger as the believers lived in the fear of the Lord. And with the encouragement of the Holy Spirit, it also grew in numbers.

9:10 Greek *disciple;* also in 9:26, 36.    9:13 Greek *God's holy people;* also in 9:32, 41.    9:19 Greek *disciples;* also in 9:26, 38. 9:25 Greek *his disciples.*    9:30 Greek *brothers.*

## Peter Heals Aeneas and Raises Dorcas

32 Meanwhile, Peter traveled from place to place, and he came down to visit the believers in the town of Lydda. 33 There he met a man named Aeneas, who had been paralyzed and bedridden for eight years. 34 Peter said to him, "Aeneas, Jesus Christ heals you! Get up, and roll up your sleeping mat!" And he was healed instantly. 35 Then the whole population of Lydda and Sharon saw Aeneas walking around, and they turned to the Lord.

36 There was a believer in Joppa named Tabitha (which in Greek is Dorcas*). She was always doing kind things for others and helping the poor. 37 About this time she became ill and died. Her body was washed for burial and laid in an upstairs room. 38 But the believers had heard that Peter was nearby at Lydda, so they sent two men to beg him, "Please come as soon as possible!"

39 So Peter returned with them; and as soon as he arrived, they took him to the upstairs room. The room was filled with widows who were weeping and showing him the coats and other clothes Dorcas had made for them. 40 But Peter asked them all to leave the room; then he knelt and prayed. Turning to the body he said, "Get up, Tabitha." And she opened her eyes! When she saw Peter, she sat up! 41 He gave her his hand and helped her up. Then he called in the widows and all the believers, and he presented her to them alive.

42 The news spread through the whole town, and many believed in the Lord. 43 And Peter stayed a long time in Joppa, living with Simon, a tanner of hides.

## Cornelius Calls for Peter

10 In Caesarea there lived a Roman army officer* named Cornelius, who was a captain of the Italian Regiment. 2 He was a devout, God-fearing man, as was everyone in his household. He gave generously to the poor and prayed regularly to God. 3 One afternoon about three o'clock, he had a vision in which he saw an angel of God coming toward him. "Cornelius!" the angel said.

4 Cornelius stared at him in terror. "What is it, sir?" he asked the angel.

And the angel replied, "Your prayers and gifts to the poor have been received by God as an offering! 5 Now send some men to Joppa, and summon a man named Simon Peter. 6 He is staying with Simon, a tanner who lives near the seashore."

7 As soon as the angel was gone, Cornelius called two of his household servants and a devout soldier, one of his personal attendants. 8 He told them what had happened and sent them off to Joppa.

9:36 The names *Tabitha* in Aramaic and *Dorcas* in Greek both mean "gazelle." 10:1 Greek *a centurion;* similarly in 10:22.

# INCOMPLETE "miracles"

READ ACTS 9:32-35

You may have heard of a healing theology that says you have been healed even if you still have symptoms and that you need to "believe and confess" your healing until the symptoms go away. The book of Acts doesn't describe any such "delayed" healings. Every time someone is healed in these twenty-eight chapters, it happens instantly as it does here for the paralyzed and bedridden Aeneas. Never once does one of the disciples tell someone he or she is healed, but still will be sick with symptoms for a while. Never once is it suggested that a healing is partial and our continued prayers and faith will make it complete.

Certainly all healing—whether through a physician's hand or a medicine's power—ultimately is from God and in that sense healing can take time. But if we're talking bona fide, setting-aside-the-laws-of-nature miracles, they happen in an instant and the healing is complete right then and there. If you're miraculously healed, you'll be the first to know.

## Peter Visits Cornelius

9 The next day as Cornelius's messengers were nearing the town, Peter went up on the flat roof to pray. It was about noon, 10 and he was hungry. But while a meal was being prepared, he fell into a trance. 11 He saw the sky open, and something like a large sheet was let down by its four corners. 12 In the sheet were all sorts of animals, reptiles, and birds. 13 Then a voice said to him, "Get up, Peter; kill and eat them."

14 "No, Lord," Peter declared. "I have never eaten anything that our Jewish laws have declared impure and unclean.*"

15 But the voice spoke again: "Do not call something unclean if God has made it clean." 16 The same vision was repeated three times. Then the sheet was suddenly pulled up to heaven.

17 Peter was very perplexed. What could the vision mean? Just then the men sent by Cornelius found Simon's house. Standing outside the gate, 18 they asked if a man named Simon Peter was staying there.

19 Meanwhile, as Peter was puzzling over the vision, the Holy Spirit said to him, "Three men have come looking for you. 20 Get up, go downstairs, and go with them without hesitation. Don't worry, for I have sent them."

21 So Peter went down and said, "I'm the man you are looking for. Why have you come?"

22 They said, "We were sent by Cornelius, a Roman officer. He is a devout and God-fearing man, well respected by all the Jews. A holy angel instructed him to summon you to his house so that he can hear your message." 23 So Peter invited the men to stay for the night. The next day he went with them, accompanied by some of the brothers from Joppa.

24 They arrived in Caesarea the following day. Cornelius was waiting for them and had called together his relatives and close friends. 25 As Peter entered his home, Cornelius fell at his feet and worshiped him. 26 But Peter pulled him up and said, "Stand up! I'm a human being just like you!" 27 So they talked together and went inside, where many others were assembled.

28 Peter told them, "You know it is against our laws for a Jewish man to enter a Gentile home like this or to associate with you. But God has shown me that I should no longer think of anyone as impure or unclean. 29 So I came without objection as soon as I was sent for. Now tell me why you sent for me."

30 Cornelius replied, "Four days ago I was praying in my house about this same time, three o'clock in the afternoon. Suddenly, a man in dazzling clothes was standing in front of me. 31 He told me, 'Cornelius, your prayer has been heard, and your gifts to the poor have been noticed by God! 32 Now send messengers to Joppa, and summon a man named Simon Peter. He is staying in the home of Simon, a tanner who lives near the seashore.' 33 So I sent for you at once, and it was good of you to come. Now we are all here, waiting before God to hear the message the Lord has given you."

## The Gentiles Hear the Good News

34 Then Peter replied, "I see very clearly that God shows no favoritism. 35 In every nation he accepts those who fear him and do what is right. 36 This is the message of Good News for the people of Israel—that there is peace with God through Jesus Christ, who is Lord of all. 37 You know what happened throughout Judea, beginning in Galilee, after John began preaching his message of baptism. 38 And you know that God anointed Jesus of Nazareth with the Holy Spirit and with power. Then Jesus went around doing good and healing all who were oppressed by the devil, for God was with him.

39 "And we apostles are witnesses of all he did throughout Judea and in Jerusalem. They put him to death by hanging him on a cross,* 40 but God raised him to life on the third day. Then God allowed him to appear, 41 not to the general public,* but to us whom God had chosen in advance to be his witnesses. We were those who ate and drank with him after he rose from the dead. 42 And he ordered us to preach everywhere and to testify that Jesus is the one appointed by God to be the judge of all—the living and the dead. 43 He is the one all the prophets testified about, saying that everyone who believes in him will have their sins forgiven through his name."

10:14 Greek *anything common and unclean.*    10:39 Greek *on a tree.*    10:41 Greek *the people.*

## The Gentiles Receive the Holy Spirit

⁴⁴Even as Peter was saying these things, the Holy Spirit fell upon all who were listening to the message. ⁴⁵The Jewish believers* who came with Peter were amazed that the gift of the Holy Spirit had been poured out on the Gentiles, too. ⁴⁶For they heard them speaking in tongues and praising God.

Then Peter asked, ⁴⁷"Can anyone object to their being baptized, now that they have received the Holy Spirit just as we did?" ⁴⁸So he gave orders for them to be baptized in the name of Jesus Christ. Afterward Cornelius asked him to stay with them for several days.

### Peter Explains His Actions

**11** Soon the news reached the apostles and other believers* in Judea that the Gentiles had received the word of God. ²But when Peter arrived back in Jerusalem, the Jewish believers* criticized him. ³"You entered the home of Gentiles* and even ate with them!" they said.

⁴Then Peter told them exactly what had happened. ⁵"I was in the town of Joppa," he said, "and while I was praying, I went into a trance and saw a vision. Something like a large sheet was let down by its four corners from the sky. And it came right down to me. ⁶When I looked inside the sheet, I saw all sorts of small animals, wild animals, reptiles, and birds. ⁷And I heard a voice say, 'Get up, Peter; kill and eat them.'

⁸"'No, Lord,' I replied. 'I have never eaten anything that our Jewish laws have declared impure or unclean.*'

⁹"But the voice from heaven spoke again: 'Do not call something unclean if God has made it clean.' ¹⁰This happened three times before the sheet and all it contained was pulled back up to heaven.

¹¹"Just then three men who had been sent from Caesarea arrived at the house where we were staying. ¹²The Holy Spirit told me to go with them and not to worry that they were Gentiles. These six brothers here accompanied me, and we soon entered the home of the man who had sent for us. ¹³He told us how an angel had appeared to him in his home and had told him, 'Send messengers to Joppa, and summon a man named Simon Peter. ¹⁴He will tell you how you and everyone in your household can be saved!'

¹⁵"As I began to speak," Peter continued, "the Holy Spirit fell on them, just as he fell on us at the beginning. ¹⁶Then I thought of the Lord's words when he said, 'John baptized with* water, but you will be baptized with the Holy Spirit.' ¹⁷And since God gave these Gentiles the same gift he gave us when we believed in the Lord Jesus Christ, who was I to stand in God's way?"

¹⁸When the others heard this, they stopped objecting and began praising God. They said, "We can see that God has also given the Gentiles the privilege of repenting of their sins and receiving eternal life."

### The Church in Antioch of Syria

¹⁹Meanwhile, the believers who had been scattered during the persecution after Stephen's death traveled as far as Phoenicia, Cyprus, and Antioch of Syria. They preached the word of God, but only to Jews. ²⁰However, some of the believers who went to Antioch from Cyprus and Cyrene began preaching to the Gentiles* about the Lord Jesus. ²¹The power of the Lord was with them, and a large number of these Gentiles believed and turned to the Lord.

²²When the church at Jerusalem heard what had happened, they sent Barnabas to Antioch. ²³When he arrived and saw this evidence of God's blessing, he was filled with joy, and he encouraged the believers to stay true to the Lord. ²⁴Barnabas was a good man, full of the Holy Spirit and strong in faith. And many people were brought to the Lord.

²⁵Then Barnabas went on to Tarsus to look for Saul. ²⁶When he found him, he brought him back to Antioch. Both of them stayed there with the church for a full year, teaching large crowds of people. (It was at Antioch that the believers* were first called Christians.)

²⁷During this time some prophets traveled from Jerusalem to Antioch. ²⁸One of them named Agabus stood up in one of the meetings and predicted by the Spirit that a

10:45 Greek *The faithful ones of the circumcision.* 11:1 Greek *brothers.* 11:2 Greek *those of the circumcision.* 11:3 Greek *of uncircumcised men.* 11:8 Greek *anything common or unclean.* 11:16 Or *in;* also in 11:16b. 11:20 Greek *the Hellenists* (i.e., those who speak Greek); other manuscripts read *the Greeks.* 11:26 Greek *disciples;* also in 11:29.

great famine was coming upon the entire Roman world. (This was fulfilled during the reign of Claudius.) 29So the believers in Antioch decided to send relief to the brothers and sisters* in Judea, everyone giving as much as they could. 30This they did, entrusting their gifts to Barnabas and Saul to take to the elders of the church in Jerusalem.

## James Is Killed and Peter Is Imprisoned

**12** About that time King Herod Agrippa* began to persecute some believers in the church. 2He had the apostle James (John's brother) killed with a sword. 3When Herod saw how much this pleased the Jewish people, he also arrested Peter. (This took place during the Passover celebration.*) 4Then he imprisoned him, placing him under the guard of four squads of four soldiers each. Herod intended to bring Peter out for public trial after the Passover. 5But while Peter was in prison, the church prayed very earnestly for him.

## Peter's Miraculous Escape from Prison

6The night before Peter was to be placed on trial, he was asleep, fastened with two chains between two soldiers. Others stood guard at the prison gate. 7Suddenly, there was a bright light in the cell, and an angel of the Lord stood before Peter. The angel struck him on the side to awaken him and said, "Quick! Get up!" And the chains fell off his wrists. 8Then the angel told him, "Get dressed and put on your sandals." And he did. "Now put on your coat and follow me," the angel ordered.

9So Peter left the cell, following the angel. But all the time he thought it was a vision. He didn't realize it was actually happening. 10They passed the first and second guard posts and came to the iron gate leading to the city, and this opened for them all by itself. So they passed through and started walking down the street, and then the angel suddenly left him.

11Peter finally came to his senses. "It's really true!" he said. "The Lord has sent his angel and saved me from Herod and from what the Jewish leaders* had planned to do to me!"

12When he realized this, he went to the home of Mary, the mother of John Mark, where many were gathered for prayer. 13He knocked at the door in the gate, and a servant girl named Rhoda came to open it. 14When she recognized Peter's voice, she was so overjoyed that, instead of opening the door, she ran back inside and told everyone, "Peter is standing at the door!"

15"You're out of your mind!" they said. When she insisted, they decided, "It must be his angel."

16Meanwhile, Peter continued knocking. When they finally opened the door and saw him, they were amazed. 17He motioned for them to quiet down and told them how the Lord had led him out of prison. "Tell James and the other brothers what happened," he said. And then he went to another place.

18At dawn there was a great commotion among the soldiers about what had happened to Peter. 19Herod Agrippa ordered a thorough search for him. When he couldn't be found, Herod interrogated the guards and sentenced them to death. Afterward Herod left Judea to stay in Caesarea for a while.

## The Death of Herod Agrippa

20Now Herod was very angry with the people of Tyre and Sidon. So they sent a delegation to make peace with him because their cities were dependent upon Herod's country for food. The delegates won the support of Blastus, Herod's personal assistant, 21and an appointment with Herod was granted. When the day arrived, Herod put on his royal robes, sat on his throne, and made a speech to them. 22The people gave him a great ovation, shouting, "It's the voice of a god, not of a man!"

23Instantly, an angel of the Lord struck Herod with a sickness, because he accepted the people's worship instead of giving the glory to God. So he was consumed with worms and died.

24Meanwhile, the word of God continued to spread, and there were many new believers.

25When Barnabas and Saul had finished

11:29 Greek *the brothers.*    12:1 Greek *Herod the king.* He was the nephew of Herod Antipas and a grandson of Herod the Great.
12:3 Greek *the days of unleavened bread.*    12:11 Or *the Jewish people.*

their mission to Jerusalem, they returned,* taking John Mark with them.

### Barnabas and Saul Are Commissioned

**13** Among the prophets and teachers of the church at Antioch of Syria were Barnabas, Simeon (called "the black man"*), Lucius (from Cyrene), Manaen (the childhood companion of King Herod Antipas*), and Saul. ²One day as these men were worshiping the Lord and fasting, the Holy Spirit said, "Dedicate Barnabas and Saul for the special work to which I have called them." ³So after more fasting and prayer, the men laid their hands on them and sent them on their way.

### Paul's First Missionary Journey

⁴So Barnabas and Saul were sent out by the Holy Spirit. They went down to the seaport of Seleucia and then sailed for the island of Cyprus. ⁵There, in the town of Salamis, they went to the Jewish synagogues and preached the word of God. John Mark went with them as their assistant.

⁶Afterward they traveled from town to town across the entire island until finally they reached Paphos, where they met a Jewish sorcerer, a false prophet named Bar-Jesus. ⁷He had attached himself to the governor, Sergius Paulus, who was an intelligent man. The governor invited Barnabas and Saul to visit him, for he wanted to hear the word of God. ⁸But Elymas, the sorcerer (as his name means in Greek), interfered and urged the governor to pay no attention to what Barnabas and Saul said. He was trying to keep the governor from believing.

⁹Saul, also known as Paul, was filled with the Holy Spirit, and he looked the sorcerer in the eye. ¹⁰Then he said, "You son of the devil, full of every sort of deceit and fraud, and enemy of all that is good! Will you never stop perverting the true ways of the Lord? ¹¹Watch now, for the Lord has laid his hand of punishment upon you, and you will be struck blind. You will not see the sunlight for some time." Instantly mist and darkness came over the man's eyes, and he began groping around begging for someone to take his hand and lead him.

¹²When the governor saw what had happened, he became a believer, for he was astonished at the teaching about the Lord.

### Paul Preaches in Antioch of Pisidia

¹³Paul and his companions then left Paphos by ship for Pamphylia, landing at the port town of Perga. There John Mark left them and returned to Jerusalem. ¹⁴But Paul and Barnabas traveled inland to Antioch of Pisidia.*

On the Sabbath they went to the synagogue for the services. ¹⁵After the usual readings from the books of Moses* and the prophets, those in charge of the service sent them this message: "Brothers, if you have any word of encouragement for the people, come and give it."

¹⁶So Paul stood, lifted his hand to quiet them, and started speaking. "Men of Israel," he said, "and you God-fearing Gentiles, listen to me.

¹⁷"The God of this nation of Israel chose our ancestors and made them multiply and grow strong during their stay in Egypt. Then with a powerful arm he led them out of their slavery. ¹⁸He put up with them* through forty years of wandering in the wilderness. ¹⁹Then he destroyed seven nations in Canaan and gave their land to Israel as an inheritance. ²⁰All this took about 450 years.

"After that, God gave them judges to rule until the time of Samuel the prophet. ²¹Then the people begged for a king, and God gave them Saul son of Kish, a man of the tribe of Benjamin, who reigned for forty years. ²²But God removed Saul and replaced him with David, a man about whom God said, 'I have found David son of Jesse, a man after my own heart. He will do everything I want him to do.'*

²³"And it is one of King David's descendants, Jesus, who is God's promised Savior of Israel! ²⁴Before he came, John the Baptist preached that all the people of Israel needed to repent of their sins and turn to God and be

12:25 Or *mission, they returned to Jerusalem.* Other manuscripts read *mission, they returned from Jerusalem;* still others read *mission, they returned from Jerusalem to Antioch.*   13:1a Greek *who was called Niger.*   13:1b Greek *Herod the tetrarch.*   13:13-14 *Pamphylia* and *Pisidia* were districts in what is now Turkey.   13:15 Greek *from the law.*   13:18 Some manuscripts read *He cared for them;* compare Deut 1:31.   13:22 1 Sam 13:14.

baptized. <sup>25</sup>As John was finishing his ministry he asked, 'Do you think I am the Messiah? No, I am not! But he is coming soon—and I'm not even worthy to be his slave and untie the sandals on his feet.'

<sup>26</sup>"Brothers—you sons of Abraham, and also you God-fearing Gentiles—this message of salvation has been sent to us! <sup>27</sup>The people in Jerusalem and their leaders did not recognize Jesus as the one the prophets had spoken about. Instead, they condemned him, and in doing this they fulfilled the prophets' words that are read every Sabbath. <sup>28</sup>They found no legal reason to execute him, but they asked Pilate to have him killed anyway.

<sup>29</sup>"When they had done all that the prophecies said about him, they took him down from the cross* and placed him in a tomb. <sup>30</sup>But God raised him from the dead! <sup>31</sup>And over a period of many days he appeared to those who had gone with him from Galilee to Jerusalem. They are now his witnesses to the people of Israel.

<sup>32</sup>"And now we are here to bring you this Good News. The promise was made to our ancestors, <sup>33</sup>and God has now fulfilled it for us, their descendants, by raising Jesus. This is what the second psalm says about Jesus:

'You are my Son.
Today I have become your Father.*'

<sup>34</sup>For God had promised to raise him from the dead, not leaving him to rot in the grave. He said, 'I will give you the sacred blessings I promised to David.'* <sup>35</sup>Another psalm explains it more fully: 'You will not allow your Holy One to rot in the grave.'* <sup>36</sup>This is not a reference to David, for after David had done the will of God in his own generation, he died and was buried with his ancestors, and his body decayed. <sup>37</sup>No, it was a reference to someone else—someone whom God raised and whose body did not decay.

<sup>38</sup>*"Brothers, listen! We are here to proclaim that through this man Jesus there is forgiveness for your sins. <sup>39</sup>Everyone who believes in him is declared right with God—something the law of Moses could never do.

## FAITH enough for a miracle
READ ACTS 12:1-17

Apparently it doesn't always take a lot of faith to get a miracle. Here Peter is imprisoned and his friends are praying, no doubt for him. When Peter is miraculously released from jail, he goes to the home of the prayer meeting and knocks on the door. The servant girl is so overjoyed to hear his voice that she runs and tells the others that he is at the door. The praying friends tell her she's crazy until she finally convinces them to see for themselves. Of course, they do see Peter and they are "amazed." Take heart that God can and will answer even your prayers of "little" faith.

<sup>40</sup>Be careful! Don't let the prophets' words apply to you. For they said,

<sup>41</sup> 'Look, you mockers,
be amazed and die!
For I am doing something in your
own day,
something you wouldn't believe
even if someone told you about it.'*"

<sup>42</sup>As Paul and Barnabas left the synagogue that day, the people begged them to speak about these things again the next week. <sup>43</sup>Many Jews and devout converts to Judaism followed Paul and Barnabas, and the two men urged them to continue to rely on the grace of God.

### Paul Turns to the Gentiles
<sup>44</sup>The following week almost the entire city turned out to hear them preach the word of the Lord. <sup>45</sup>But when some of the Jews saw the crowds, they were jealous; so they slandered Paul and argued against whatever he said.

<sup>46</sup>Then Paul and Barnabas spoke out boldly and declared, "It was necessary that we first preach the word of God to you Jews. But since you have rejected it and judged yourselves unworthy of eternal life, we will offer it to the Gentiles. <sup>47</sup>For the Lord gave us this command when he said,

13:29 Greek *from the tree.*   13:33 Or *Today I reveal you as my Son.* Ps 2:7.   13:34 Isa 55:3.   13:35 Ps 16:10.   13:38 English translations divide verses 38 and 39 in various ways.   13:41 Hab 1:5 (Greek version).

'I have made you a light to the Gentiles,
to bring salvation to the farthest
corners of the earth.'*"

48When the Gentiles heard this, they were very glad and thanked the Lord for his message; and all who were chosen for eternal life became believers. 49So the Lord's message spread throughout that region.

50Then the Jews stirred up the influential religious women and the leaders of the city, and they incited a mob against Paul and Barnabas and ran them out of town. 51So they shook the dust from their feet as a sign of rejection and went to the town of Iconium. 52And the believers* were filled with joy and with the Holy Spirit.

## Paul and Barnabas in Iconium

**14** The same thing happened in Iconium.* Paul and Barnabas went to the Jewish synagogue and preached with such power that a great number of both Jews and Greeks became believers. 2Some of the Jews, however, spurned God's message and poisoned the minds of the Gentiles against Paul and Barnabas. 3But the apostles stayed there a long time, preaching boldly about the grace of the Lord. And the Lord proved their message was true by giving them power to do miraculous signs and wonders. 4But the people of the town were divided in their opinion about them. Some sided with the Jews, and some with the apostles.

5Then a mob of Gentiles and Jews, along with their leaders, decided to attack and stone them. 6When the apostles learned of it, they fled to the region of Lycaonia—to the towns of Lystra and Derbe and the surrounding area. 7And there they preached the Good News.

## Paul and Barnabas in Lystra and Derbe

8While they were at Lystra, Paul and Barnabas came upon a man with crippled feet. He had been that way from birth, so he had never walked. He was sitting 9and listening as Paul preached. Looking straight at him, Paul realized he had faith to be healed. 10So Paul called to him in a loud voice, "Stand up!" And the man jumped to his feet and started walking.

11When the crowd saw what Paul had done, they shouted in their local dialect, "These men are gods in human form!" 12They decided that Barnabas was the Greek god Zeus and that Paul was Hermes, since he was the chief speaker. 13Now the temple of Zeus was located just outside the town. So the priest of the temple and the crowd brought bulls and wreaths of flowers to the town gates, and they prepared to offer sacrifices to the apostles.

14But when the apostles Barnabas and Paul heard what was happening, they tore their clothing in dismay and ran out among the people, shouting, 15"Friends,* why are you doing this? We are merely human beings—just like you! We have come to bring you the Good News that you should turn from these worthless things and turn to the living God, who made heaven and earth, the sea, and everything in them. 16In the past he permitted all the nations to go their own ways, 17but he never left them without evidence of himself and his goodness. For instance, he sends you rain and good crops and gives you food and joyful hearts." 18But even with these words, Paul and Barnabas could scarcely restrain the people from sacrificing to them.

19Then some Jews arrived from Antioch and Iconium and won the crowds to their side. They stoned Paul and dragged him out of town, thinking he was dead. 20But as the believers* gathered around him, he got up and went back into the town. The next day he left with Barnabas for Derbe.

## Paul and Barnabas Return to Antioch of Syria

21After preaching the Good News in Derbe and making many disciples, Paul and Barnabas returned to Lystra, Iconium, and Antioch of Pisidia, 22where they strengthened the believers. They encouraged them to continue in the faith, reminding them that we must suffer many hardships to enter the Kingdom of God. 23Paul and Barnabas also appointed elders in every church. With prayer and fasting, they turned the elders over to the care of the Lord, in whom they had put their trust.

13:47 Isa 49:6.   13:52 Greek *the disciples*.   14:1 *Iconium*, as well as *Lystra* and *Derbe* (14:6), were towns in what is now Turkey.
14:15 Greek *Men*.   14:20 Greek *disciples*; also in 14:22, 28.

24 Then they traveled back through Pisidia to Pamphylia. 25 They preached the word in Perga, then went down to Attalia.

26 Finally, they returned by ship to Antioch of Syria, where their journey had begun. The believers there had entrusted them to the grace of God to do the work they had now completed. 27 Upon arriving in Antioch, they called the church together and reported everything God had done through them and how he had opened the door of faith to the Gentiles, too. 28 And they stayed there with the believers for a long time.

## The Council at Jerusalem

**15** While Paul and Barnabas were at Antioch of Syria, some men from Judea arrived and began to teach the believers*: "Unless you are circumcised as required by the law of Moses, you cannot be saved." 2 Paul and Barnabas disagreed with them, arguing vehemently. Finally, the church decided to send Paul and Barnabas to Jerusalem, accompanied by some local believers, to talk to the apostles and elders about this question. 3 The church sent the delegates to Jerusalem, and they stopped along the way in Phoenicia and Samaria to visit the believers. They told them—much to everyone's joy—that the Gentiles, too, were being converted.

4 When they arrived in Jerusalem, Barnabas and Paul were welcomed by the whole church, including the apostles and elders. They reported everything God had done through them. 5 But then some of the believers who belonged to the sect of the Pharisees stood up and insisted, "The Gentile converts must be circumcised and required to follow the law of Moses."

6 So the apostles and elders met together to resolve this issue. 7 At the meeting, after a long discussion, Peter stood and addressed them as follows: "Brothers, you all know that God chose me from among you some time ago to preach to the Gentiles so that they could hear the Good News and believe. 8 God knows people's hearts, and he confirmed that he accepts Gentiles by giving them the Holy Spirit, just as he did to us. 9 He made no distinction between us and them, for he cleansed their hearts through faith. 10 So why are you now challenging God by burdening the Gentile believers* with a yoke that neither we nor our ancestors were able to bear? 11 We believe that we are all saved the same way, by the undeserved grace of the Lord Jesus."

12 Everyone listened quietly as Barnabas and Paul told about the miraculous signs and wonders God had done through them among the Gentiles.

13 When they had finished, James stood and said, "Brothers, listen to me. 14 Peter* has told you about the time God first visited the Gentiles to take from them a people for himself. 15 And this conversion of Gentiles is exactly what the prophets predicted. As it is written:

16 'Afterward I will return
    and restore the fallen house* of David.
  I will rebuild its ruins
    and restore it,
17 so that the rest of humanity might seek
    the LORD,
  including the Gentiles—
    all those I have called to be mine.
  The LORD has spoken—
18    he who made these things known so
    long ago.'*

19 "And so my judgment is that we should not make it difficult for the Gentiles who are turning to God. 20 Instead, we should write and tell them to abstain from eating food offered to idols, from sexual immorality, from eating the meat of strangled animals, and from consuming blood. 21 For these laws of Moses have been preached in Jewish synagogues in every city on every Sabbath for many generations."

## The Letter for Gentile Believers

22 Then the apostles and elders together with the whole church in Jerusalem chose delegates, and they sent them to Antioch of Syria with Paul and Barnabas to report on this decision. The men chosen were two of the church leaders*—Judas (also called Barsabbas) and Silas. 23 This is the letter they took with them:

"This letter is from the apostles and elders, your brothers in Jerusalem. It

15:1 Greek *brothers;* also in 15:3, 23, 32, 33, 36, 40.    15:10 Greek *disciples.*    15:14 Greek *Symeon.*    15:16 Or *kingdom;* Greek reads *tent.*    15:16-18 Amos 9:11-12 (Greek version); Isa 45:21.    15:22 Greek *were leaders among the brothers.*

is written to the Gentile believers in Antioch, Syria, and Cilicia. Greetings!

24"We understand that some men from here have troubled you and upset you with their teaching, but we did not send them! 25So we decided, having come to complete agreement, to send you official representatives, along with our beloved Barnabas and Paul, 26who have risked their lives for the name of our Lord Jesus Christ. 27We are sending Judas and Silas to confirm what we have decided concerning your question.

28"For it seemed good to the Holy Spirit and to us to lay no greater burden on you than these few requirements: 29You must abstain from eating food offered to idols, from consuming blood or the meat of strangled animals, and from sexual immorality. If you do this, you will do well. Farewell."

30The messengers went at once to Antioch, where they called a general meeting of the believers and delivered the letter. 31And there was great joy throughout the church that day as they read this encouraging message.

32Then Judas and Silas, both being prophets, spoke at length to the believers, encouraging and strengthening their faith. 33They stayed for a while, and then the believers sent them back to the church in Jerusalem with a blessing of peace.* 35Paul and Barnabas stayed in Antioch. They and many others taught and preached the word of the Lord there.

### Paul and Barnabas Separate

36After some time Paul said to Barnabas, "Let's go back and visit each city where we previously preached the word of the Lord, to see how the new believers are doing." 37Barnabas agreed and wanted to take along John Mark. 38But Paul disagreed strongly, since John Mark had deserted them in Pamphylia and had not continued with them in their work. 39Their disagreement was so sharp that they separated. Barnabas took John Mark with him and sailed for Cyprus. 40Paul chose Silas, and as he left, the believers entrusted him to the Lord's gracious care. 41Then he traveled throughout Syria and Cilicia, strengthening the churches there.

### Paul's Second Missionary Journey

**16** Paul went first to Derbe and then to Lystra, where there was a young disciple named Timothy. His mother was a Jewish believer, but his father was a Greek. 2Timothy was well thought of by the believers* in Lystra and Iconium, 3so Paul wanted him to join them on their journey. In deference to

15:33 Some manuscripts add verse 34, *But Silas decided to stay there.*   16:2 Greek *brothers;* also in 16:40.

## GET out of jail free
READ ACTS 16:22-28

It is a dangerous thing to look at the way God works in other people's lives and surmise He *has* to work exactly the same way in ours. God is sovereign and doesn't answer to us. Sometimes our prayers are answered exactly as we had hoped, but other times He doesn't do it *our* way.

Consider this story of Paul and Silas's miraculous release from jail. Had they compared themselves to others, they might not have thought an angelic jailbreak would happen. After all, John the Baptist, who prepared the way for Jesus, didn't get a miracle release; he was beheaded in prison. Don't forget what happened to the early church's deacon Stephen, who also was imprisoned. He never received a miracle "get-out-of-jail-free" card. Instead he was stoned to death. And even though Paul miraculously is freed here, later he is imprisoned and beheaded in Rome.

God cannot act contrary to His character, but He doesn't have to act in accordance with our plans or in the same way in each of our lives.

the Jews of the area, he arranged for Timothy to be circumcised before they left, for everyone knew that his father was a Greek. ⁴Then they went from town to town, instructing the believers to follow the decisions made by the apostles and elders in Jerusalem. ⁵So the churches were strengthened in their faith and grew larger every day.

## A Call from Macedonia

⁶Next Paul and Silas traveled through the area of Phrygia and Galatia, because the Holy Spirit had prevented them from preaching the word in the province of Asia at that time. ⁷Then coming to the borders of Mysia, they headed north for the province of Bithynia,* but again the Spirit of Jesus did not allow them to go there. ⁸So instead, they went on through Mysia to the seaport of Troas.

⁹That night Paul had a vision: A man from Macedonia in northern Greece was standing there, pleading with him, "Come over to Macedonia and help us!" ¹⁰So we* decided to leave for Macedonia at once, having concluded that God was calling us to preach the Good News there.

## Lydia of Philippi Believes in Jesus

¹¹We boarded a boat at Troas and sailed straight across to the island of Samothrace, and the next day we landed at Neapolis. ¹²From there we reached Philippi, a major city of that district of Macedonia and a Roman colony. And we stayed there several days.

¹³On the Sabbath we went a little way outside the city to a riverbank, where we thought people would be meeting for prayer, and we sat down to speak with some women who had gathered there. ¹⁴One of them was Lydia from Thyatira, a merchant of expensive purple cloth, who worshiped God. As she listened to us, the Lord opened her heart, and she accepted what Paul was saying. ¹⁵She was baptized along with other members of her household, and she asked us to be her guests. "If you agree that I am a true believer in the Lord," she said, "come and stay at my home." And she urged us until we agreed.

## Paul and Silas in Prison

¹⁶One day as we were going down to the place of prayer, we met a demon-possessed slave girl. She was a fortune-teller who earned a lot of money for her masters. ¹⁷She followed Paul and the rest of us, shouting, "These men are servants of the Most High God, and they have come to tell you how to be saved."

¹⁸This went on day after day until Paul got so exasperated that he turned and said to the demon within her, "I command you in the name of Jesus Christ to come out of her." And instantly it left her.

¹⁹Her masters' hopes of wealth were now shattered, so they grabbed Paul and Silas and dragged them before the authorities at the marketplace. ²⁰"The whole city is in an uproar because of these Jews!" they shouted to the city officials. ²¹"They are teaching customs that are illegal for us Romans to practice."

²²A mob quickly formed against Paul and Silas, and the city officials ordered them stripped and beaten with wooden rods. ²³They were severely beaten, and then they were thrown into prison. The jailer was ordered to make sure they didn't escape. ²⁴So the jailer put them into the inner dungeon and clamped their feet in the stocks.

²⁵Around midnight Paul and Silas were praying and singing hymns to God, and the other prisoners were listening. ²⁶Suddenly, there was a massive earthquake, and the prison was shaken to its foundations. All the doors immediately flew open, and the chains of every prisoner fell off! ²⁷The jailer woke up to see the prison doors wide open. He assumed the prisoners had escaped, so he drew his sword to kill himself. ²⁸But Paul shouted to him, "Stop! Don't kill yourself! We are all here!"

²⁹The jailer called for lights and ran to the dungeon and fell down trembling before Paul and Silas. ³⁰Then he brought them out and asked, "Sirs, what must I do to be saved?"

**31**They replied, "Believe in the Lord Jesus and you will be saved, along with everyone in your household." ³²And they shared the word of the Lord with him and with all who lived in his household. ³³Even at that hour of the night, the jailer cared for them and washed

16:6-7 *Phrygia, Galatia, Asia, Mysia,* and *Bithynia* were all districts in what is now Turkey.   16:10 Luke, the writer of this book, here joined Paul and accompanied him on his journey.

their wounds. Then he and everyone in his household were immediately baptized. [34] He brought them into his house and set a meal before them, and he and his entire household rejoiced because they all believed in God.

[35] The next morning the city officials sent the police to tell the jailer, "Let those men go!" [36] So the jailer told Paul, "The city officials have said you and Silas are free to leave. Go in peace."

[37] But Paul replied, "They have publicly beaten us without a trial and put us in prison—and we are Roman citizens. So now they want us to leave secretly? Certainly not! Let them come themselves to release us!"

[38] When the police reported this, the city officials were alarmed to learn that Paul and Silas were Roman citizens. [39] So they came to the jail and apologized to them. Then they brought them out and begged them to leave the city. [40] When Paul and Silas left the prison, they returned to the home of Lydia. There they met with the believers and encouraged them once more. Then they left town.

## Paul Preaches in Thessalonica

**17** Paul and Silas then traveled through the towns of Amphipolis and Apollonia and came to Thessalonica, where there was a Jewish synagogue. [2] As was Paul's custom, he went to the synagogue service, and for three Sabbaths in a row he used the Scriptures to reason with the people. [3] He explained the prophecies and proved that the Messiah must suffer and rise from the dead. He said, "This Jesus I'm telling you about is the Messiah." [4] Some of the Jews who listened were persuaded and joined Paul and Silas, along with many God-fearing Greek men and quite a few prominent women.*

[5] But some of the Jews were jealous, so they gathered some troublemakers from the marketplace to form a mob and start a riot. They attacked the home of Jason, searching for Paul and Silas so they could drag them out to the crowd.* [6] Not finding them there, they dragged out Jason and some of the other believers* instead and took them before the city council. "Paul and Silas have

caused trouble all over the world," they shouted, "and now they are here disturbing our city, too. [7] And Jason has welcomed them into his home. They are all guilty of treason against Caesar, for they profess allegiance to another king, named Jesus."

[8] The people of the city, as well as the city council, were thrown into turmoil by these reports. [9] So the officials forced Jason and the other believers to post bond, and then they released them.

## Paul and Silas in Berea

[10] That very night the believers sent Paul and Silas to Berea. When they arrived there, they went to the Jewish synagogue. [11] And the people of Berea were more open-minded than those in Thessalonica, and they listened eagerly to Paul's message. They searched the Scriptures day after day to see if Paul and Silas were teaching the truth. [12] As a result, many Jews believed, as did many of the prominent Greek women and men.

[13] But when some Jews in Thessalonica learned that Paul was preaching the word of God in Berea, they went there and stirred up trouble. [14] The believers acted at once, sending Paul on to the coast, while Silas and Timothy remained behind. [15] Those escorting Paul went with him all the way to Athens; then they returned to Berea with instructions for Silas and Timothy to hurry and join him.

## Paul Preaches in Athens

[16] While Paul was waiting for them in Athens, he was deeply troubled by all the idols he saw everywhere in the city. [17] He went to the synagogue to reason with the Jews and the God-fearing Gentiles, and he spoke daily in the public square to all who happened to be there.

[18] He also had a debate with some of the Epicurean and Stoic philosophers. When he told them about Jesus and his resurrection, they said, "What's this babbler trying to say with these strange ideas he's picked up?" Others said, "He seems to be preaching about some foreign gods."

[19] Then they took him to the high council of the city.* "Come and tell us about this new

---

17:4 Some manuscripts read *quite a few of the wives of the leading men.*   **17:5** Or *the city council.*   **17:6** Greek *brothers;* also in 17:10, 14.   **17:19** Or *the most learned society of philosophers in the city.* Greek reads *the Areopagus.*

teaching," they said. 20 "You are saying some rather strange things, and we want to know what it's all about." 21 (It should be explained that all the Athenians as well as the foreigners in Athens seemed to spend all their time discussing the latest ideas.)

22 So Paul, standing before the council,* addressed them as follows: "Men of Athens, I notice that you are very religious in every way, 23 for as I was walking along I saw your many shrines. And one of your altars had this inscription on it: 'To an Unknown God.' This God, whom you worship without knowing, is the one I'm telling you about.

24 "He is the God who made the world and everything in it. Since he is Lord of heaven and earth, he doesn't live in man-made temples, 25 and human hands can't serve his needs—for he has no needs. He himself gives life and breath to everything, and he satisfies every need. 26 From one man* he created all the nations throughout the whole earth. He decided beforehand when they should rise and fall, and he determined their boundaries.

27 "His purpose was for the nations to seek after God and perhaps feel their way toward him and find him—though he is not far from any one of us. 28 For in him we live and move and exist. As some of your* own poets have said, 'We are his offspring.' 29 And since this is true, we shouldn't think of God as an idol designed by craftsmen from gold or silver or stone.

30 "God overlooked people's ignorance about these things in earlier times, but now he commands everyone everywhere to repent of their sins and turn to him. 31 For he has set a day for judging the world with justice by the man he has appointed, and he proved to everyone who this is by raising him from the dead."

32 When they heard Paul speak about the resurrection of the dead, some laughed in contempt, but others said, "We want to hear more about this later." 33 That ended Paul's discussion with them, 34 but some joined him and became believers. Among them were Dionysius, a member of the council,* a woman named Damaris, and others with them.

## WHAT does God need?

READ ACTS 17:24-25

When we hear the term "the needy," we usually think of people who are poor and in need of charity and assistance from others. It's not a pleasant position in which to find ourselves. That's one of the reasons dealing with a health crisis is so upsetting—it shows us what we don't want to admit about ourselves: We are needy—in poor physical health, and maybe poor in spirit, too.

God, on the other hand, is *never* needy. Although He loves to hear our praises and is pleased by our obedience, there is nothing He actually needs from us. Tell Him today what you are lacking because He truly "satisfies every need."

### Paul Meets Priscilla and Aquila in Corinth

**18** Then Paul left Athens and went to Corinth.* 2 There he became acquainted with a Jew named Aquila, born in Pontus, who had recently arrived from Italy with his wife, Priscilla. They had left Italy when Claudius Caesar deported all Jews from Rome. 3 Paul lived and worked with them, for they were tentmakers* just as he was.

4 Each Sabbath found Paul at the synagogue, trying to convince the Jews and Greeks alike. 5 And after Silas and Timothy came down from Macedonia, Paul spent all his time preaching the word. He testified to the Jews that Jesus was the Messiah. 6 But when they opposed and insulted him, Paul shook the dust from his clothes and said, "Your blood is upon your own heads—I am innocent. From now on I will go preach to the Gentiles."

7 Then he left and went to the home of Titius Justus, a Gentile who worshiped God and lived next door to the synagogue. 8 Crispus, the leader of the synagogue, and everyone in his household believed in the Lord. Many others in Corinth also heard Paul, became believers, and were baptized.

9 One night the Lord spoke to Paul in a vision and told him, "Don't be afraid! Speak out! Don't be silent! 10 For I am with you, and no one will attack and harm you, for many

17:22 Traditionally rendered *standing in the middle of Mars Hill;* Greek reads *standing in the middle of the Areopagus.* 17:26 Greek *From one;* other manuscripts read *From one blood.* 17:28 Some manuscripts read *our.* 17:34 Greek *an Areopagite.* 18:1 *Athens* and *Corinth* were major cities in Achaia, the region in the southern portion of the Greek peninsula. 18:3 Or *leatherworkers.*

people in this city belong to me." ¹¹So Paul stayed there for the next year and a half, teaching the word of God.

¹²But when Gallio became governor of Achaia, some Jews rose up together against Paul and brought him before the governor for judgment. ¹³They accused Paul of "persuading people to worship God in ways that are contrary to our law."

¹⁴But just as Paul started to make his defense, Gallio turned to Paul's accusers and said, "Listen, you Jews, if this were a case involving some wrongdoing or a serious crime, I would have a reason to accept your case. ¹⁵But since it is merely a question of words and names and your Jewish law, take care of it yourselves. I refuse to judge such matters." ¹⁶And he threw them out of the courtroom.

¹⁷The crowd* then grabbed Sosthenes, the leader of the synagogue, and beat him right there in the courtroom. But Gallio paid no attention.

## Paul Returns to Antioch of Syria

¹⁸Paul stayed in Corinth for some time after that, then said good-bye to the brothers and sisters* and went to nearby Cenchrea. There he shaved his head according to Jewish custom, marking the end of a vow. Then he set sail for Syria, taking Priscilla and Aquila with him.

¹⁹They stopped first at the port of Ephesus, where Paul left the others behind. While he was there, he went to the synagogue to reason with the Jews. ²⁰They asked him to stay longer, but he declined. ²¹As he left, however, he said, "I will come back later,* God willing." Then he set sail from Ephesus. ²²The next stop was at the port of Caesarea. From there he went up and visited the church at Jerusalem* and then went back to Antioch.

²³After spending some time in Antioch, Paul went back through Galatia and Phrygia, visiting and strengthening all the believers.*

## Apollos Instructed at Ephesus

²⁴Meanwhile, a Jew named Apollos, an eloquent speaker who knew the Scriptures well, had arrived in Ephesus from Alexandria in Egypt. ²⁵He had been taught the way of the Lord, and he taught others about Jesus with an enthusiastic spirit* and with accuracy. However, he knew only about John's baptism. ²⁶When Priscilla and Aquila heard him preaching boldly in the synagogue, they took him aside and explained the way of God even more accurately.

²⁷Apollos had been thinking about going to Achaia, and the brothers and sisters in Ephesus encouraged him to go. They wrote to the believers in Achaia, asking them to welcome him. When he arrived there, he proved to be of great benefit to those who, by God's grace, had believed. ²⁸He refuted the Jews with powerful arguments in public debate. Using the Scriptures, he explained to them that Jesus was the Messiah.

## Paul's Third Missionary Journey

**19** While Apollos was in Corinth, Paul traveled through the interior regions until he reached Ephesus, on the coast, where he found several believers.* ²"Did you receive the Holy Spirit when you believed?" he asked them.

"No," they replied, "we haven't even heard that there is a Holy Spirit."

³"Then what baptism did you experience?" he asked.

And they replied, "The baptism of John."

⁴Paul said, "John's baptism called for repentance from sin. But John himself told the people to believe in the one who would come later, meaning Jesus."

⁵As soon as they heard this, they were baptized in the name of the Lord Jesus. ⁶Then when Paul laid his hands on them, the Holy Spirit came on them, and they spoke in other tongues and prophesied. ⁷There were about twelve men in all.

## Paul Ministers in Ephesus

⁸Then Paul went to the synagogue and preached boldly for the next three months, arguing persuasively about the Kingdom of God. ⁹But some became stubborn, rejecting his message and publicly speaking against the Way. So Paul left the synagogue and took

the believers with him. Then he held daily discussions at the lecture hall of Tyrannus. ¹⁰This went on for the next two years, so that people throughout the province of Asia—both Jews and Greeks—heard the word of the Lord.

¹¹God gave Paul the power to perform unusual miracles. ¹²When handkerchiefs or aprons that had merely touched his skin were placed on sick people, they were healed of their diseases, and evil spirits were expelled.

¹³A group of Jews was traveling from town to town casting out evil spirits. They tried to use the name of the Lord Jesus in their incantation, saying, "I command you in the name of Jesus, whom Paul preaches, to come out!" ¹⁴Seven sons of Sceva, a leading priest, were doing this. ¹⁵But one time when they tried it, the evil spirit replied, "I know Jesus, and I know Paul, but who are you?" ¹⁶Then the man with the evil spirit leaped on them, overpowered them, and attacked them with such violence that they fled from the house, naked and battered.

¹⁷The story of what happened spread quickly all through Ephesus, to Jews and Greeks alike. A solemn fear descended on the city, and the name of the Lord Jesus was greatly honored. ¹⁸Many who became believers confessed their sinful practices. ¹⁹A number of them who had been practicing sorcery brought their incantation books and burned them at a public bonfire. The value of the books was several million dollars.* ²⁰So the message about the Lord spread widely and had a powerful effect.

²¹Afterward Paul felt compelled by the Spirit* to go over to Macedonia and Achaia before going to Jerusalem. "And after that," he said, "I must go on to Rome!" ²²He sent his two assistants, Timothy and Erastus, ahead to Macedonia while he stayed awhile longer in the province of Asia.

## The Riot in Ephesus

²³About that time, serious trouble developed in Ephesus concerning the Way. ²⁴It began with Demetrius, a silversmith who had a large business manufacturing silver shrines of the Greek goddess Artemis.* He kept many craftsmen busy. ²⁵He called them together, along with others employed in similar trades, and addressed them as follows:

"Gentlemen, you know that our wealth comes from this business. ²⁶But as you have seen and heard, this man Paul has persuaded many people that handmade gods aren't really gods at all. And he's done this not only here in Ephesus but throughout the entire province! ²⁷Of course, I'm not just talking about the loss of public respect for our business. I'm also concerned that the temple of the great goddess Artemis will lose its influence and that Artemis—this magnificent goddess worshiped throughout the province of Asia and all around the world—will be robbed of her great prestige!"

²⁸At this their anger boiled, and they began shouting, "Great is Artemis of the Ephesians!" ²⁹Soon the whole city was filled with confusion. Everyone rushed to the amphitheater, dragging along Gaius and Aristarchus, who were Paul's traveling companions from Macedonia. ³⁰Paul wanted to go in, too, but the believers wouldn't let him. ³¹Some of the officials of the province, friends of Paul, also sent a message to him, begging him not to risk his life by entering the amphitheater.

³²Inside, the people were all shouting, some one thing and some another. Everything was in confusion. In fact, most of them didn't even know why they were there. ³³The Jews in the crowd pushed Alexander forward and told him to explain the situation. He motioned for silence and tried to speak. ³⁴But when the crowd realized he was a Jew, they started shouting again and kept it up for two hours: "Great is Artemis of the Ephesians! Great is Artemis of the Ephesians!"

³⁵At last the mayor was able to quiet them down enough to speak. "Citizens of Ephesus," he said. "Everyone knows that Ephesus is the official guardian of the temple of the great Artemis, whose image fell down to us from heaven. ³⁶Since this is an undeniable fact, you should stay calm and not do anything rash. ³⁷You have brought these men here, but they have stolen nothing from the temple and have not spoken against our goddess. ³⁸"If Demetrius and the craftsmen have a

---

**19:19** Greek *50,000 pieces of silver,* each of which was the equivalent of a day's wage.   **19:21** Or *decided in his spirit.*
**19:24** *Artemis* is otherwise known as Diana.

case against them, the courts are in session and the officials can hear the case at once. Let them make formal charges. 39And if there are complaints about other matters, they can be settled in a legal assembly. 40I am afraid we are in danger of being charged with rioting by the Roman government, since there is no cause for all this commotion. And if Rome demands an explanation, we won't know what to say." 41*Then he dismissed them, and they dispersed.

## Paul Goes to Macedonia and Greece

**20** When the uproar was over, Paul sent for the believers* and encouraged them. Then he said good-bye and left for Macedonia. 2While there, he encouraged the believers in all the towns he passed through. Then he traveled down to Greece, 3where he stayed for three months. He was preparing to sail back to Syria when he discovered a plot by some Jews against his life, so he decided to return through Macedonia.

4Several men were traveling with him. They were Sopater son of Pyrrhus from Berea; Aristarchus and Secundus from Thessalonica; Gaius from Derbe; Timothy; and Tychicus and Trophimus from the province of Asia. 5They went on ahead and waited for us at Troas. 6After the Passover* ended, we boarded a ship at Philippi in Macedonia and five days later joined them in Troas, where we stayed a week.

## GOOD-BYE blessings
READ ACTS 20:17-38

Once in a while some of us get the "blessing" of knowing our own death is imminent. The reason we say "blessing" is because such knowledge affords us the chance to say important things before we leave this earth. Here, Paul says good-bye to the leaders of the Ephesian church. He admonishes them, reminds them of eternal truths, and assures them of his love and care for them. Finally, he kneels and prays with them. Many tears were shed because they wouldn't see each other again, but there is no doubt these dear friends were blessed by those special last words Paul shared with them. Is there anyone you need to bless today?

## Paul's Final Visit to Troas
7On the first day of the week, we gathered with the local believers to share in the Lord's Supper.* Paul was preaching to them, and since he was leaving the next day, he kept talking until midnight. 8The upstairs room where we met was lighted with many flickering lamps. 9As Paul spoke on and on, a young man named Eutychus, sitting on the windowsill, became very drowsy. Finally, he fell sound asleep and dropped three stories to his death below. 10Paul went down, bent over him, and took him into his arms. "Don't worry," he said, "he's alive!" 11Then they all went back upstairs, shared in the Lord's Supper,* and ate together. Paul continued talking to them until dawn, and then he left. 12Meanwhile, the young man was taken home unhurt, and everyone was greatly relieved.

## Paul Meets the Ephesian Elders
13Paul went by land to Assos, where he had arranged for us to join him, while we traveled by ship. 14He joined us there, and we sailed together to Mitylene. 15The next day we sailed past the island of Kios. The following day we crossed to the island of Samos, and* a day later we arrived at Miletus. 16Paul had decided to sail on past Ephesus, for he didn't want to spend any more time in the province of Asia. He was hurrying to get to Jerusalem, if possible, in time for the Festival of Pentecost. 17But when we landed at Miletus, he sent a message to the elders of the church at Ephesus, asking them to come and meet him.

18When they arrived he declared, "You know that from the day I set foot in the province of Asia until now 19I have done the Lord's work humbly and with many tears. I have endured the trials that came to me from the plots of the Jews. 20I never shrank back from telling you what you needed to hear, either publicly or in your homes. 21I have had one message for Jews and Greeks alike—the necessity of repenting from sin and turning to God, and of having faith in our Lord Jesus. 22"And now I am bound by the Spirit* to go

19:41 Some translations include verse 41 as part of verse 40.
20:1 Greek *disciples.* 20:6 Greek *the days of unleavened bread.*
20:7 Greek *to break bread.* 20:11 Greek *broke the bread.*
20:15 Some manuscripts read *and having stayed at Trogyllium.*
20:22 Or *by my spirit,* or *by an inner compulsion;* Greek reads *by the spirit.*

to Jerusalem. I don't know what awaits me, [23]except that the Holy Spirit tells me in city after city that jail and suffering lie ahead. [24]But my life is worth nothing to me unless I use it for finishing the work assigned me by the Lord Jesus—the work of telling others the Good News about the wonderful grace of God.

[25]"And now I know that none of you to whom I have preached the Kingdom will ever see me again. [26]I declare today that I have been faithful. If anyone suffers eternal death, it's not my fault,* [27]for I didn't shrink from declaring all that God wants you to know.

[28]"So guard yourselves and God's people. Feed and shepherd God's flock—his church, purchased with his own blood*—over which the Holy Spirit has appointed you as elders.* [29]I know that false teachers, like vicious wolves, will come in among you after I leave, not sparing the flock. [30]Even some men from your own group will rise up and distort the truth in order to draw a following. [31]Watch out! Remember the three years I was with you—my constant watch and care over you night and day, and my many tears for you.

[32]"And now I entrust you to God and the message of his grace that is able to build you up and give you an inheritance with all those he has set apart for himself.

[33]"I have never coveted anyone's silver or gold or fine clothes. [34]You know that these hands of mine have worked to supply my own needs and even the needs of those who were with me. [35]And I have been a constant example of how you can help those in need by working hard. You should remember the words of the Lord Jesus: 'It is more blessed to give than to receive.'"

[36]When he had finished speaking, he knelt and prayed with them. [37]They all cried as they embraced and kissed him good-bye. [38]They were sad most of all because he had said that they would never see him again. Then they escorted him down to the ship.

## Paul's Journey to Jerusalem

**21** After saying farewell to the Ephesian elders, we sailed straight to the island of Cos. The next day we reached Rhodes and then went to Patara. [2]There we boarded a ship sailing for Phoenicia. [3]We sighted the island of Cyprus, passed it on our left, and landed at the harbor of Tyre, in Syria, where the ship was to unload its cargo.

[4]We went ashore, found the local believers,* and stayed with them a week. These believers prophesied through the Holy Spirit that Paul should not go on to Jerusalem. [5]When we returned to the ship at the end of the week, the entire congregation, including women* and children, left the city and came down to the shore with us. There we knelt, prayed, [6]and said our farewells. Then we went aboard, and they returned home.

[7]The next stop after leaving Tyre was Ptolemais, where we greeted the brothers and sisters* and stayed for one day. [8]The next day we went on to Caesarea and stayed at the home of Philip the Evangelist, one of the seven men who had been chosen to distribute food. [9]He had four unmarried daughters who had the gift of prophecy.

[10]Several days later a man named Agabus, who also had the gift of prophecy, arrived from Judea. [11]He came over, took Paul's belt, and bound his own feet and hands with it. Then he said, "The Holy Spirit declares, 'So shall the owner of this belt be bound by the Jewish leaders in Jerusalem and turned over to the Gentiles.'" [12]When we heard this, we and the local believers all begged Paul not to go on to Jerusalem.

[13]But he said, "Why all this weeping? You are breaking my heart! I am ready not only to be jailed at Jerusalem but even to die for the sake of the Lord Jesus." [14]When it was clear that we couldn't persuade him, we gave up and said, "The Lord's will be done."

## Paul Arrives at Jerusalem

[15]After this we packed our things and left for Jerusalem. [16]Some believers from Caesarea accompanied us, and they took us to the home of Mnason, a man originally from Cyprus and one of the early believers. [17]When we arrived, the brothers and sisters in Jerusalem welcomed us warmly.

[18]The next day Paul went with us to meet with James, and all the elders of the Jerusalem church were present. [19]After greeting

them, Paul gave a detailed account of the things God had accomplished among the Gentiles through his ministry.

20 After hearing this, they praised God. And then they said, "You know, dear brother, how many thousands of Jews have also believed, and they all follow the law of Moses very seriously. 21 But the Jewish believers here in Jerusalem have been told that you are teaching all the Jews who live among the Gentiles to turn their backs on the laws of Moses. They've heard that you teach them not to circumcise their children or follow other Jewish customs. 22 What should we do? They will certainly hear that you have come.

23 "Here's what we want you to do. We have four men here who have completed their vow. 24 Go with them to the Temple and join them in the purification ceremony, paying for them to have their heads ritually shaved. Then everyone will know that the rumors are all false and that you yourself observe the Jewish laws.

25 "As for the Gentile believers, they should do what we already told them in a letter: They should abstain from eating food offered to idols, from consuming blood or the meat of strangled animals, and from sexual immorality."

## Paul Is Arrested

26 So Paul went to the Temple the next day with the other men. They had already started the purification ritual, so he publicly announced the date when their vows would end and sacrifices would be offered for each of them.

27 The seven days were almost ended when some Jews from the province of Asia saw Paul in the Temple and roused a mob against him. They grabbed him, 28 yelling, "Men of Israel, help us! This is the man who preaches against our people everywhere and tells everybody to disobey the Jewish laws. He speaks against the Temple—and even defiles this holy place by bringing in Gentiles.*" 29 (For earlier that day they had seen him in the city with Trophimus, a Gentile from Ephesus,* and they assumed Paul had taken him into the Temple.)

30 The whole city was rocked by these accusations, and a great riot followed. Paul was grabbed and dragged out of the Temple, and immediately the gates were closed behind him. 31 As they were trying to kill him, word reached the commander of the Roman regiment that all Jerusalem was in an uproar. 32 He immediately called out his soldiers and officers* and ran down among the crowd. When the mob saw the commander and the troops coming, they stopped beating Paul.

33 Then the commander arrested him and ordered him bound with two chains. He asked the crowd who he was and what he had done. 34 Some shouted one thing and some another. Since he couldn't find out the truth in all the uproar and confusion, he ordered that Paul be taken to the fortress. 35 As Paul reached the stairs, the mob grew so violent the soldiers had to lift him to their shoulders to protect him. 36 And the crowd followed behind, shouting, "Kill him, kill him!"

## Paul Speaks to the Crowd

37 As Paul was about to be taken inside, he said to the commander, "May I have a word with you?"

"Do you know Greek?" the commander asked, surprised. 38 "Aren't you the Egyptian who led a rebellion some time ago and took 4,000 members of the Assassins out into the desert?"

39 "No," Paul replied, "I am a Jew and a citizen of Tarsus in Cilicia, which is an important city. Please, let me talk to these people." 40 The commander agreed, so Paul stood on the stairs and motioned to the people to be quiet. Soon a deep silence enveloped the crowd, and he addressed them in their own language, Aramaic.*

**22** "Brothers and esteemed fathers," Paul said, "listen to me as I offer my defense." 2 When they heard him speaking in their own language,* the silence was even greater.

3 Then Paul said, "I am a Jew, born in Tarsus, a city in Cilicia, and I was brought up and educated here in Jerusalem under Gamaliel. As his student, I was carefully trained in our Jewish laws and customs. I became very zeal-

21:28 Greek *Greeks.*   21:29 Greek *Trophimus, the Ephesian.*   21:32 Greek *centurions.*   21:40 Or *Hebrew.*   22:2 Greek *in Aramaic,* or *in Hebrew.*

ous to honor God in everything I did, just like all of you today. ⁴And I persecuted the followers of the Way, hounding some to death, arresting both men and women and throwing them in prison. ⁵The high priest and the whole council of elders can testify that this is so. For I received letters from them to our Jewish brothers in Damascus, authorizing me to bring the Christians from there to Jerusalem, in chains, to be punished.

⁶"As I was on the road, approaching Damascus about noon, a very bright light from heaven suddenly shone down around me. ⁷I fell to the ground and heard a voice saying to me, 'Saul, Saul, why are you persecuting me?'

⁸"'Who are you, lord?' I asked.

"And the voice replied, 'I am Jesus the Nazarene,* the one you are persecuting.' ⁹The people with me saw the light but didn't understand the voice speaking to me.

¹⁰"I asked, 'What should I do, Lord?'

"And the Lord told me, 'Get up and go into Damascus, and there you will be told everything you are to do.'

¹¹"I was blinded by the intense light and had to be led by the hand to Damascus by my companions. ¹²A man named Ananias lived there. He was a godly man, deeply devoted to the law, and well regarded by all the Jews of Damascus. ¹³He came and stood beside me and said, 'Brother Saul, regain your sight.' And that very moment I could see him!

¹⁴"Then he told me, 'The God of our ancestors has chosen you to know his will and to see the Righteous One and hear him speak. ¹⁵For you are to be his witness, telling everyone what you have seen and heard. ¹⁶What are you waiting for? Get up and be baptized. Have your sins washed away by calling on the name of the Lord.'

¹⁷"After I returned to Jerusalem, I was praying in the Temple and fell into a trance. ¹⁸I saw a vision of Jesus* saying to me, 'Hurry! Leave Jerusalem, for the people here won't accept your testimony about me.'

¹⁹"'But Lord,' I argued, 'they certainly know that in every synagogue I imprisoned and beat those who believed in you. ²⁰And I was in complete agreement when your witness Ste-

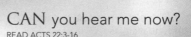

## CAN you hear me now?
READ ACTS 22:3-16

When did God first become real to you? It probably wasn't anything quite as spectacular as Paul's encounter. Maybe it did happen in an instant, but maybe it was a slow encounter over time. Perhaps it really hasn't happened at all. You still think God is "the man upstairs" or a cosmic cop writing down every bad thing you do. Maybe this health crisis is the time God finally will become very real to you. Author C. S. Lewis said that God "whispers to us in our pleasures, speaks in our conscience, but shouts in our pain: it is His megaphone to rouse a deaf world." God wants you to know Him up close and personal. Are you listening?

phen was killed. I stood by and kept the coats they took off when they stoned him.'

²¹"But the Lord said to me, 'Go, for I will send you far away to the Gentiles!'"

²²The crowd listened until Paul said that word. Then they all began to shout, "Away with such a fellow! He isn't fit to live!" ²³They yelled, threw off their coats, and tossed handfuls of dust into the air.

### Paul Reveals His Roman Citizenship
²⁴The commander brought Paul inside and ordered him lashed with whips to make him confess his crime. He wanted to find out why the crowd had become so furious. ²⁵When they tied Paul down to lash him, Paul said to the officer* standing there, "Is it legal for you to whip a Roman citizen who hasn't even been tried?"

²⁶When the officer heard this, he went to the commander and asked, "What are you doing? This man is a Roman citizen!"

²⁷So the commander went over and asked Paul, "Tell me, are you a Roman citizen?"

"Yes, I certainly am," Paul replied.

²⁸"I am, too," the commander muttered, "and it cost me plenty!"

Paul answered, "But I am a citizen by birth!"

²⁹The soldiers who were about to interrogate Paul quickly withdrew when they heard he was a Roman citizen, and the commander

22:8 Or *Jesus of Nazareth.*    22:18 Greek *him.*    22:25 Greek *the centurion;* also in 22:26.

was frightened because he had ordered him bound and whipped.

## Paul before the High Council

30 The next day the commander ordered the leading priests into session with the Jewish high council.* He wanted to find out what the trouble was all about, so he released Paul to have him stand before them.

**23** Gazing intently at the high council,* Paul began: "Brothers, I have always lived before God with a clear conscience!"

2 Instantly Ananias the high priest commanded those close to Paul to slap him on the mouth. 3 But Paul said to him, "God will slap you, you corrupt hypocrite!* What kind of judge are you to break the law yourself by ordering me struck like that?"

4 Those standing near Paul said to him, "Do you dare to insult God's high priest?"

5 "I'm sorry, brothers. I didn't realize he was the high priest," Paul replied, "for the Scriptures say, 'You must not speak evil of any of your rulers.'*"

6 Paul realized that some members of the high council were Sadducees and some were Pharisees, so he shouted, "Brothers, I am a Pharisee, as were my ancestors! And I am on trial because my hope is in the resurrection of the dead!"

7 This divided the council—the Pharisees against the Sadducees—8 for the Sadducees say there is no resurrection or angels or spirits, but the Pharisees believe in all of these. 9 So there was a great uproar. Some of the teachers of religious law who were Pharisees jumped up and began to argue forcefully. "We see nothing wrong with him," they shouted. "Perhaps a spirit or an angel spoke to him." 10 As the conflict grew more violent, the commander was afraid they would tear Paul apart. So he ordered his soldiers to go and rescue him by force and take him back to the fortress.

11 That night the Lord appeared to Paul and said, "Be encouraged, Paul. Just as you have been a witness to me here in Jerusalem, you must preach the Good News in Rome as well."

## The Plan to Kill Paul

12 The next morning a group of Jews* got together and bound themselves with an oath not to eat or drink until they had killed Paul. 13 There were more than forty of them in the conspiracy. 14 They went to the leading priests and elders and told them, "We have bound ourselves with an oath to eat nothing until we have killed Paul. 15 So you and the high council should ask the commander to bring Paul back to the council again. Pretend you want to examine his case more fully. We will kill him on the way."

16 But Paul's nephew—his sister's son— heard of their plan and went to the fortress and told Paul. 17 Paul called for one of the Roman officers* and said, "Take this young man to the commander. He has something important to tell him."

18 So the officer did, explaining, "Paul, the prisoner, called me over and asked me to bring this young man to you because he has something to tell you."

19 The commander took his hand, led him aside, and asked, "What is it you want to tell me?"

20 Paul's nephew told him, "Some Jews are going to ask you to bring Paul before the high council tomorrow, pretending they want to get some more information. 21 But don't do it! There are more than forty men hiding along the way ready to ambush him. They have vowed not to eat or drink anything until they have killed him. They are ready now, just waiting for your consent."

22 "Don't let anyone know you told me this," the commander warned the young man.

## Paul Is Sent to Caesarea

23 Then the commander called two of his officers and ordered, "Get 200 soldiers ready to leave for Caesarea at nine o'clock tonight. Also take 200 spearmen and 70 mounted troops. 24 Provide horses for Paul to ride, and get him safely to Governor Felix." 25 Then he wrote this letter to the governor:

26 "From Claudius Lysias, to his Excellency, Governor Felix: Greetings!

27 "This man was seized by some Jews, and they were about to kill him when I

---

22:30 Greek Sanhedrin. 23:1 Greek Sanhedrin; also in 23:6, 15, 20, 28. 23:3 Greek you whitewashed wall. 23:5 Exod 22:28. 23:12 Greek the Jews. 23:17 Greek centurions; also in 23:23.

arrived with the troops. When I learned that he was a Roman citizen, I removed him to safety. 28 Then I took him to their high council to try to learn the basis of the accusations against him. 29 I soon discovered the charge was something regarding their religious law—certainly nothing worthy of imprisonment or death. 30 But when I was informed of a plot to kill him, I immediately sent him on to you. I have told his accusers to bring their charges before you."

31 So that night, as ordered, the soldiers took Paul as far as Antipatris. 32 They returned to the fortress the next morning, while the mounted troops took him on to Caesarea. 33 When they arrived in Caesarea, they presented Paul and the letter to Governor Felix. 34 He read it and then asked Paul what province he was from. "Cilicia," Paul answered.

35 "I will hear your case myself when your accusers arrive," the governor told him. Then the governor ordered him kept in the prison at Herod's headquarters.*

## Paul Appears before Felix

**24** Five days later Ananias, the high priest, arrived with some of the Jewish elders and the lawyer* Tertullus, to present their case against Paul to the governor. 2 When Paul was called in, Tertullus presented the charges against Paul in the following address to the governor:

"Your Excellency, you have provided a long period of peace for us Jews and with foresight have enacted reforms for us. 3 For all of this we are very grateful to you. 4 But I don't want to bore you, so please give me your attention for only a moment. 5 We have found this man to be a troublemaker who is constantly stirring up riots among the Jews all over the world. He is a ringleader of the cult known as the Nazarenes. 6 Furthermore, he was trying to desecrate the Temple when we arrested him.* 8 You can find out the truth of our accusations by examining him yourself." 9 Then

the other Jews chimed in, declaring that everything Tertullus said was true.

10 The governor then motioned for Paul to speak. Paul said, "I know, sir, that you have been a judge of Jewish affairs for many years, so I gladly present my defense before you. 11 You can quickly discover that I arrived in Jerusalem no more than twelve days ago to worship at the Temple. 12 My accusers never found me arguing with anyone in the Temple, nor stirring up a riot in any synagogue or on the streets of the city. 13 These men cannot prove the things they accuse me of doing.

14 "But I admit that I follow the Way, which they call a cult. I worship the God of our ancestors, and I firmly believe the Jewish law and everything written in the prophets. 15 I have the same hope in God that these men have, that he will raise both the righteous and the unrighteous. 16 Because of this, I always try to maintain a clear conscience before God and all people.

17 "After several years away, I returned to Jerusalem with money to aid my people and to offer sacrifices to God. 18 My accusers saw me in the Temple as I was completing a purification ceremony. There was no crowd around me and no rioting. 19 But some Jews from the province of Asia were there—and they ought to be here to bring charges if they have anything against me! 20 Ask these men here what crime the Jewish high council* found me guilty of, 21 except for the one time I shouted

**23:35** Greek *Herod's Praetorium.*   **24:1** Greek *some elders and an orator.*   **24:6** Some manuscripts add an expanded conclusion to verse 6, all of verse 7, and an additional phrase in verse 8: *We would have judged him by our law,* ⁷*but Lysias, the commander of the garrison, came and violently took him away from us,* ⁸*commanding his accusers to come before you.*   **24:20** Greek *Sanhedrin.*

## YOU'RE in good hands
READ ACTS 26:22-23

How would you describe a life that had encountered the following events? Blinded for a short while, slandered by many, chased by an angry mob, stoned, beaten with wooden rods, placed in dungeon stocks, opposed and insulted by community leaders, plotted against, and finally arrested and placed in chains. Paul describes such a life—his life—as "protected" by God. We tend to think of protection as meaning "nothing bad will happen to me," but Paul obviously viewed it another way. He saw God's hand of protection in spite of all the difficulties and was able to trust that his life truly was safe in God's hands.

out, 'I am on trial before you today because I believe in the resurrection of the dead!'"

22At that point Felix, who was quite familiar with the Way, adjourned the hearing and said, "Wait until Lysias, the garrison commander, arrives. Then I will decide the case." 23He ordered an officer* to keep Paul in custody but to give him some freedom and allow his friends to visit him and take care of his needs.

24A few days later Felix came back with his wife, Drusilla, who was Jewish. Sending for Paul, they listened as he told them about faith in Christ Jesus. 25As he reasoned with them about righteousness and self-control and the coming day of judgment, Felix became frightened. "Go away for now," he replied. "When it is more convenient, I'll call for you again." 26He also hoped that Paul would bribe him, so he sent for him quite often and talked with him.

27After two years went by in this way, Felix was succeeded by Porcius Festus. And because Felix wanted to gain favor with the Jewish people, he left Paul in prison.

## Paul Appears before Festus

**25** Three days after Festus arrived in Caesarea to take over his new responsibilities, he left for Jerusalem, 2where the leading priests and other Jewish leaders met with him and made their accusations against Paul. 3They asked Festus as a favor to transfer Paul to Jerusalem (planning to ambush and kill him on the way). 4But Festus replied that Paul was at Caesarea and he himself would be returning there soon. 5So he said, "Those of you in authority can return with me. If Paul has done anything wrong, you can make your accusations."

6About eight or ten days later Festus returned to Caesarea, and on the following day he took his seat in court and ordered that Paul be brought in. 7When Paul arrived, the Jewish leaders from Jerusalem gathered around and made many serious accusations they couldn't prove.

8Paul denied the charges. "I am not guilty of any crime against the Jewish laws or the Temple or the Roman government," he said.

9Then Festus, wanting to please the Jews, asked him, "Are you willing to go to Jerusalem and stand trial before me there?"

10But Paul replied, "No! This is the official Roman court, so I ought to be tried right here. You know very well I am not guilty of harming the Jews. 11If I have done something worthy of death, I don't refuse to die. But if I am innocent, no one has a right to turn me over to these men to kill me. I appeal to Caesar!"

12Festus conferred with his advisers and then replied, "Very well! You have appealed to Caesar, and to Caesar you will go!"

13A few days later King Agrippa arrived with his sister, Bernice,* to pay their respects to Festus. 14During their stay of several days, Festus discussed Paul's case with the king. "There is a prisoner here," he told him, "whose case was left for me by Felix. 15When I was in Jerusalem, the leading priests and Jewish elders pressed charges against him and asked me to condemn him. 16I pointed out to them that Roman law does not convict people without a trial. They must be given an opportunity to confront their accusers and defend themselves.

17"When his accusers came here for the trial, I didn't delay. I called the case the very next day and ordered Paul brought in. 18But the accusations made against him weren't any of the crimes I expected. 19Instead, it was something about their religion and a dead man named Jesus, who Paul insists is alive. 20I was at a loss to know how to investigate these things, so I asked him whether he would be willing to stand trial on these charges in Jerusalem. 21But Paul appealed to have his case decided by the emperor. So I ordered that he be held in custody until I could arrange to send him to Caesar."

22"I'd like to hear the man myself," Agrippa said.

And Festus replied, "You will—tomorrow!"

## Paul Speaks to Agrippa

23So the next day Agrippa and Bernice arrived at the auditorium with great pomp, accompanied by military officers and prominent men of the city. Festus ordered that Paul be brought in. 24Then Festus said, "King Agrippa and all who are here, this is the man whose death is demanded by all the Jews,

24:23 Greek *a centurion.*   25:13 Greek *Agrippa the king and Bernice arrived.*

both here and in Jerusalem. 25 But in my opinion he has done nothing deserving death. However, since he appealed his case to the emperor, I have decided to send him to Rome.

26 "But what shall I write the emperor? For there is no clear charge against him. So I have brought him before all of you, and especially you, King Agrippa, so that after we examine him, I might have something to write. 27 For it makes no sense to send a prisoner to the emperor without specifying the charges against him!"

# 26

Then Agrippa said to Paul, "You may speak in your defense."

So Paul, gesturing with his hand, started his defense: 2 "I am fortunate, King Agrippa, that you are the one hearing my defense today against all these accusations made by the Jewish leaders, 3 for I know you are an expert on all Jewish customs and controversies. Now please listen to me patiently!

4 "As the Jewish leaders are well aware, I was given a thorough Jewish training from my earliest childhood among my own people and in Jerusalem. 5 If they would admit it, they know that I have been a member of the Pharisees, the strictest sect of our religion. 6 Now I am on trial because of my hope in the fulfillment of God's promise made to our ancestors. 7 In fact, that is why the twelve tribes of Israel zealously worship God night and day, and they share the same hope I have. Yet, Your Majesty, they accuse me for having this hope! 8 Why does it seem incredible to any of you that God can raise the dead?

9 "I used to believe that I ought to do everything I could to oppose the very name of Jesus the Nazarene.* 10 Indeed, I did just that in Jerusalem. Authorized by the leading priests, I caused many believers* there to be sent to prison. And I cast my vote against them when they were condemned to death. 11 Many times I had them punished in the synagogues to get them to curse Jesus.* I was so violently opposed to them that I even chased them down in foreign cities.

12 "One day I was on such a mission to Damascus, armed with the authority and commission of the leading priests. 13 About noon, Your Majesty, as I was on the road, a light from heaven brighter than the sun shone down on me and my companions. 14 We all fell down, and I heard a voice saying to me in Aramaic,* 'Saul, Saul, why are you persecuting me? It is useless for you to fight against my will.*'

15 "'Who are you, lord?' I asked.

"And the Lord replied, 'I am Jesus, the one you are persecuting. 16 Now get to your feet! For I have appeared to you to appoint you as my servant and witness. You are to tell the world what you have seen and what I will show you in the future. 17 And I will rescue you from both your own people and the Gentiles. Yes, I am sending you to the Gentiles 18 to open their eyes, so they may turn from darkness to light and from the power of Satan to God. Then they will receive forgiveness for their sins and be given a place among God's people, who are set apart by faith in me.'

19 "And so, King Agrippa, I obeyed that vision from heaven. 20 I preached first to those in Damascus, then in Jerusalem and throughout all Judea, and also to the Gentiles, that all must repent of their sins and turn to God—and prove they have changed by the good things they do. 21 Some Jews arrested me in the Temple for preaching this, and they tried to kill me. 22 But God has protected me right up to this present time so I can testify to everyone, from the least to the greatest. I teach nothing except what the prophets and Moses said would happen—23 that the Messiah would suffer and be the first to rise from the dead, and in this way announce God's light to Jews and Gentiles alike."

24 Suddenly, Festus shouted, "Paul, you are insane. Too much study has made you crazy!"

25 But Paul replied, "I am not insane, Most Excellent Festus. What I am saying is the sober truth. 26 And King Agrippa knows about these things. I speak boldly, for I am sure these events are all familiar to him, for they were not done in a corner! 27 King Agrippa, do you believe the prophets? I know you do—"

28 Agrippa interrupted him. "Do you think

---

26:9 Or Jesus of Nazareth.   26:10 Greek many of God's holy people.   26:11 Greek to blaspheme.   26:14a Or Hebrew.
26:14b Greek It is hard for you to kick against the oxgoads.

## WATCH this!

READ ACTS 26:31-32

"If only" . . . How many times have you uttered those words? If only I'd gone to the doctor sooner. If only there was a treatment that worked. If only I hadn't smoked. If only there had been a warning sign.

"If onlys" are painful. Here King Agrippa says Paul could have been set free if only he hadn't appealed to Caesar. It sounds like Paul made a mistake that cost him his freedom. But God loves to take "if onlys" and turn them into "watch this". He takes the things that "coulda-woulda-shoulda" happened and uses them for His glory. Is there an "if only" preying on your mind? Ask God to turn it into a "watch this!"

you can persuade me to become a Christian so quickly?"*

29 Paul replied, "Whether quickly or not, I pray to God that both you and everyone here in this audience might become the same as I am, except for these chains."

30 Then the king, the governor, Bernice, and all the others stood and left. 31 As they went out, they talked it over and agreed, "This man hasn't done anything to deserve death or imprisonment."

32 And Agrippa said to Festus, "He could have been set free if he hadn't appealed to Caesar."

### Paul Sails for Rome

**27** When the time came, we set sail for Italy. Paul and several other prisoners were placed in the custody of a Roman officer* named Julius, a captain of the Imperial Regiment. 2 Aristarchus, a Macedonian from Thessalonica, was also with us. We left on a ship whose home port was Adramyttium on the northwest coast of the province of Asia;* it was scheduled to make several stops at ports along the coast of the province.

3 The next day when we docked at Sidon, Julius was very kind to Paul and let him go ashore to visit with friends so they could provide for his needs. 4 Putting out to sea

from there, we encountered strong headwinds that made it difficult to keep the ship on course, so we sailed north of Cyprus between the island and the mainland. 5 Keeping to the open sea, we passed along the coast of Cilicia and Pamphylia, landing at Myra, in the province of Lycia. 6 There the commanding officer found an Egyptian ship from Alexandria that was bound for Italy, and he put us on board.

7 We had several days of slow sailing, and after great difficulty we finally neared Cnidus. But the wind was against us, so we sailed across to Crete and along the sheltered coast of the island, past the cape of Salmone. 8 We struggled along the coast with great difficulty and finally arrived at Fair Havens, near the town of Lasea. 9 We had lost a lot of time. The weather was becoming dangerous for sea travel because it was so late in the fall,* and Paul spoke to the ship's officers about it.

10 "Men," he said, "I believe there is trouble ahead if we go on—shipwreck, loss of cargo, and danger to our lives as well." 11 But the officer in charge of the prisoners listened more to the ship's captain and the owner than to Paul. 12 And since Fair Havens was an exposed harbor—a poor place to spend the winter—most of the crew wanted to go on to Phoenix, farther up the coast of Crete, and spend the winter there. Phoenix was a good harbor with only a southwest and northwest exposure.

### The Storm at Sea

13 When a light wind began blowing from the south, the sailors thought they could make it. So they pulled up anchor and sailed close to the shore of Crete. 14 But the weather changed abruptly, and a wind of typhoon strength (called a "northeaster") burst across the island and blew us out to sea. 15 The sailors couldn't turn the ship into the wind, so they gave up and let it run before the gale.

16 We sailed along the sheltered side of a small island named Cauda,* where with great difficulty we hoisted aboard the lifeboat being towed behind us. 17 Then the sailors bound ropes around the hull of the ship to strengthen it. They were afraid of being

driven across to the sandbars of Syrtis off the African coast, so they lowered the sea anchor to slow the ship and were driven before the wind.

18The next day, as gale-force winds continued to batter the ship, the crew began throwing the cargo overboard. 19The following day they even took some of the ship's gear and threw it overboard. 20The terrible storm raged for many days, blotting out the sun and the stars, until at last all hope was gone.

21No one had eaten for a long time. Finally, Paul called the crew together and said, "Men, you should have listened to me in the first place and not left Crete. You would have avoided all this damage and loss. 22But take courage! None of you will lose your lives, even though the ship will go down. 23For last night an angel of the God to whom I belong and whom I serve stood beside me, 24and he said, 'Don't be afraid, Paul, for you will surely stand trial before Caesar! What's more, God in his goodness has granted safety to everyone sailing with you.' 25So take courage! For I believe God. It will be just as he said. 26But we will be shipwrecked on an island."

### The Shipwreck

27About midnight on the fourteenth night of the storm, as we were being driven across the Sea of Adria,* the sailors sensed land was near. 28They dropped a weighted line and found that the water was 120 feet deep. But a little later they measured again and found it was only 90 feet deep.* 29At this rate they were afraid we would soon be driven against the rocks along the shore, so they threw out four anchors from the back of the ship and prayed for daylight.

30Then the sailors tried to abandon the ship; they lowered the lifeboat as though they were going to put out anchors from the front of the ship. 31But Paul said to the commanding officer and the soldiers, "You will all die unless the sailors stay aboard." 32So the soldiers cut the ropes to the lifeboat and let it drift away.

33Just as day was dawning, Paul urged everyone to eat. "You have been so worried that you haven't touched food for two weeks," he said. 34"Please eat something now for your own good. For not a hair of your heads will perish." 35Then he took some bread, gave thanks to God before them all, and broke off a piece and ate it. 36Then everyone was encouraged and began to eat—37all 276 of us who were on board. 38After eating, the crew lightened the ship further by throwing the cargo of wheat overboard.

39When morning dawned, they didn't recognize the coastline, but they saw a bay with a beach and wondered if they could get to shore by running the ship aground. 40So they cut off the anchors and left them in the sea. Then they lowered the rudders, raised the foresail, and headed toward shore. 41But they hit a shoal and ran the ship aground too soon. The bow of the ship stuck fast, while the stern was repeatedly smashed by the force of the waves and began to break apart.

42The soldiers wanted to kill the prisoners to make sure they didn't swim ashore and escape. 43But the commanding officer wanted to spare Paul, so he didn't let them carry out their plan. Then he ordered all who could swim to jump overboard first and make for land. 44The others held onto planks or debris from the broken ship.* So everyone escaped safely to shore.

### Paul on the Island of Malta

**28** Once we were safe on shore, we learned that we were on the island of Malta. 2The people of the island were very kind to us. It was cold and rainy, so they built a fire on the shore to welcome us.

3As Paul gathered an armful of sticks and was laying them on the fire, a poisonous snake, driven out by the heat, bit him on the hand. 4The people of the island saw it hanging from his hand and said to each other, "A murderer, no doubt! Though he escaped the sea, justice will not permit him to live." 5But Paul shook off the snake into the fire and was unharmed. 6The people waited for him to swell up or suddenly drop dead. But when they had waited a long time and saw that he wasn't harmed, they changed their minds and decided he was a god.

27:27 The *Sea of Adria* includes the central portion of the Mediterranean.    27:28 Greek *20 fathoms . . . 15 fathoms* [37 meters . . . 27 meters].    27:44 Or *or were helped by members of the ship's crew.*

7Near the shore where we landed was an estate belonging to Publius, the chief official of the island. He welcomed us and treated us kindly for three days. 8As it happened, Publius's father was ill with fever and dysentery. Paul went in and prayed for him, and laying his hands on him, he healed him. 9Then all the other sick people on the island came and were healed. 10As a result we were showered with honors, and when the time came to sail, people supplied us with everything we would need for the trip.

## Paul Arrives at Rome

11It was three months after the shipwreck that we set sail on another ship that had wintered at the island—an Alexandrian ship with the twin gods* as its figurehead. 12Our first stop was Syracuse,* where we stayed three days. 13From there we sailed across to Rhegium.* A day later a south wind began blowing, so the following day we sailed up the coast to Puteoli. 14There we found some believers,* who invited us to spend a week with them. And so we came to Rome. 15The brothers and sisters* in Rome had heard we were coming, and they came to meet us at the Forum* on the Appian Way. Others joined us at The Three Taverns.* When Paul saw them, he was encouraged and thanked God.

16When we arrived in Rome, Paul was permitted to have his own private lodging, though he was guarded by a soldier.

## Paul Preaches at Rome under Guard

17Three days after Paul's arrival, he called together the local Jewish leaders. He said to them, "Brothers, I was arrested in Jerusalem and handed over to the Roman government, even though I had done nothing against our people or the customs of our ancestors. 18The Romans tried me and wanted to release me, because they found no cause for the death sentence. 19But when the Jewish leaders protested the decision, I felt it necessary to appeal to Caesar, even though I had no desire to press charges against my own people. 20I asked you to come here today so we could get acquainted and so I could explain to you that I am bound with this chain because I believe that the hope of Israel—the Messiah—has already come."

21They replied, "We have had no letters from Judea or reports against you from anyone who has come here. 22But we want to hear what you believe, for the only thing we know about this movement is that it is denounced everywhere."

23So a time was set, and on that day a large number of people came to Paul's lodging. He explained and testified about the Kingdom of God and tried to persuade them about Jesus from the Scriptures. Using the law of Moses and the books of the prophets, he spoke to them from morning until evening. 24Some were persuaded by the things he said, but others did not believe. 25And after they had argued back and forth among themselves, they left with this final word from Paul: "The Holy Spirit was right when he said to your ancestors through Isaiah the prophet,

26'Go and say to this people:
 When you hear what I say,
  you will not understand.
 When you see what I do,
  you will not comprehend.
27For the hearts of these people are
  hardened,
 and their ears cannot hear,
 and they have closed their eyes—
so their eyes cannot see,
 and their ears cannot hear,
 and their hearts cannot understand,
and they cannot turn to me
 and let me heal them.'*

28So I want you to know that this salvation from God has also been offered to the Gentiles, and they will accept it."*

30For the next two years, Paul lived in Rome at his own expense.* He welcomed all who visited him, 31boldly proclaiming the Kingdom of God and teaching about the Lord Jesus Christ. And no one tried to stop him.

28:11 The *twin gods* were the Roman gods Castor and Pollux.   28:12 *Syracuse* was on the island of Sicily.   28:13 *Rhegium* was on the southern tip of Italy.   28:14 Greek *brothers*.   28:15a Greek *brothers*.   28:15b *The Forum* was about 43 miles (70 kilometers) from Rome.   28:15c *The Three Taverns* was about 35 miles (57 kilometers) from Rome.   28:26-27 Isa 6:9-10 (Greek version).
28:28 Some manuscripts add verse 29, *And when he had said these words, the Jews departed, greatly disagreeing with each other.*
28:30 Or *in his own rented quarters.*

# ROMANS

*And we know that God causes everything to work together for the good of those who love God and are called according to his purpose for them.*

ROMANS 8:28

Would it be easier for you to face your health crisis if you knew something good was going to come from it? Would it help to know that for believers there is no such thing as senseless suffering? Would it be too much for you to imagine that God actually wants to bring a blessing through your trial?

Paul's letter to the church at Rome contains the most complete explanation of Christian teachings in the New Testament, including God's promise that He can somehow miraculously take everything that happens to us—good or bad—and use it for good in His grand plan.

We can't tell you when or where God will bring a blessing through your trial of suffering, but we can tell you why—because Romans 8:28 promises it. God will bring blessing through your trial because you matter greatly to Him, and He longs to show you that. He may bless you with a physical healing, or He may bless you by healing you emotionally of some deep-seated hurts. He may bless you spiritually with the joy of knowing Him in ways you never have before. Or He may bless others through you in unimaginable ways.

But keep in mind the blessings we receive through trials often are *not* the ones we seek, but the ones God chooses for us. Because God knows you and loves you, He knows how to bless you. He can bless you through your trials . . . if you let Him decide the blessing.

## Greetings from Paul

**1** This letter is from Paul, a slave of Christ Jesus, chosen by God to be an apostle and sent out to preach his Good News. 2God promised this Good News long ago through his prophets in the holy Scriptures. 3The Good News is about his Son. In his earthly life he was born into King David's family line, 4and he was shown to be* the Son of God when he was raised from the dead by the power of the Holy Spirit.* He is Jesus Christ our Lord. 5Through Christ, God has given us the privilege* and authority as apostles to tell Gentiles everywhere what God has done for them, so that they will believe and obey him, bringing glory to his name.

6And you are included among those Gentiles who have been called to belong to Jesus Christ. 7I am writing to all of you in Rome who are loved by God and are called to be his own holy people.

May God our Father and the Lord Jesus Christ give you grace and peace.

## God's Good News

8Let me say first that I thank my God through Jesus Christ for all of you, because your faith in him is being talked about all over the world. 9God knows how often I pray for you. Day and night I bring you and your needs in prayer to God, whom I serve with all my heart* by spreading the Good News about his Son.

10One of the things I always pray for is the opportunity, God willing, to come at last to see you. 11For I long to visit you so I can bring you some spiritual gift that will help you grow strong in the Lord. 12When we get together, I want to encourage you in your faith, but I also want to be encouraged by yours.

13I want you to know, dear brothers and sisters,* that I planned many times to visit you, but I was prevented until now. I want to work among you and see spiritual fruit, just as I have seen among other Gentiles. 14For I have a great sense of obligation to people in both the civilized world and the rest of the world,* to the educated and uneducated alike. 15So I am eager to come to you in Rome, too, to preach the Good News.

16For I am not ashamed of this Good News about Christ. It is the power of God at work, saving everyone who believes—the Jew first and also the Gentile.* 17This Good News tells

1:4a Or *and was designated.* 1:4b Or *by the Spirit of holiness;* or *in the new realm of the Spirit.* 1:5 Or *the grace.* 1:9 Or *in my spirit.* 1:13 Greek *brothers.* 1:14 Greek *to Greeks and barbarians.* 1:16 Greek *also the Greek.*

## EVEN perfectionists aren't perfect

READ ROMANS 3:23-24

Have you ever worried whether you're "good enough" for God to put His healing touch on you? How about whether you're good enough to be loved by God in the first place?

Relax. You're not. You never have been and you never will be. Verse 23 makes it clear that nobody is "good enough" when compared to God's perfect, holy standard. No matter how hard we may have tried, we all have missed the mark. We've either done, said, or thought things we shouldn't have. We've also *not* done, said, or thought things we should have. We might stack up pretty well against our neighbor or our coworker or even our relatives, but compared to God's "glorious standard," we're not even close.

In today's politically correct terminology, we're all perfection-challenged. The Bible simply calls us sinful. But the good news is that once we acknowledge this, God's undeserved kindness wipes away our sins and makes us good enough. He has done for us what we could *never* do for ourselves.

us how God makes us right in his sight. This is accomplished from start to finish by faith. As the Scriptures say, "It is through faith that a righteous person has life."*

## God's Anger at Sin

18 But God shows his anger from heaven against all sinful, wicked people who suppress the truth by their wickedness.* 19 They know the truth about God because he has made it obvious to them. 20 For ever since the world was created, people have seen the earth and sky. Through everything God made, they can clearly see his invisible qualities—his eternal power and divine nature. So they have no excuse for not knowing God.

21 Yes, they knew God, but they wouldn't worship him as God or even give him thanks. And they began to think up foolish ideas of what God was like. As a result, their minds became dark and confused. 22 Claiming to be wise, they instead became utter fools. 23 And instead of worshiping the glorious, ever-living God, they worshiped idols made to look like mere people and birds and animals and reptiles.

24 So God abandoned them to do whatever shameful things their hearts desired. As a result, they did vile and degrading things with each other's bodies. 25 They traded the truth about God for a lie. So they worshiped and served the things God created instead of the Creator himself, who is worthy of eternal praise! Amen. 26 That is why God abandoned them to their shameful desires. Even the women turned against the natural way to have sex and instead indulged in sex with each other. 27 And the men, instead of having normal sexual relations with women, burned with lust for each other. Men did shameful things with other men, and as a result of this sin, they suffered within themselves the penalty they deserved.

28 Since they thought it foolish to acknowledge God, he abandoned them to their foolish thinking and let them do things that should never be done. 29 Their lives became full of every kind of wickedness, sin, greed, hate, envy, murder, quarreling, deception, malicious behavior, and gossip. 30 They

are backstabbers, haters of God, insolent, proud, and boastful. They invent new ways of sinning, and they disobey their parents. 31 They refuse to understand, break their promises, are heartless, and have no mercy. 32 They know God's justice requires that those who do these things deserve to die, yet they do them anyway. Worse yet, they encourage others to do them, too.

## God's Judgment of Sin

2 You may think you can condemn such people, but you are just as bad, and you have no excuse! When you say they are wicked and should be punished, you are condemning yourself, for you who judge others do these very same things. 2 And we know that God, in his justice, will punish anyone who does such things. 3 Since you judge others for doing these things, why do you think you can avoid God's judgment when you do the same things? 4 Don't you see how wonderfully kind, tolerant, and patient God is with you? Does this mean nothing to you? Can't you see that his kindness is intended to turn you from your sin?

5 But because you are stubborn and refuse to turn from your sin, you are storing up terrible punishment for yourself. For a day of anger is coming, when God's righteous judgment will be revealed. 6 He will judge everyone according to what they have done. 7 He will give eternal life to those who keep on doing good, seeking after the glory and honor and immortality that God offers. 8 But he will pour out his anger and wrath on those who live for themselves, who refuse to obey the truth and instead live lives of wickedness. 9 There will be trouble and calamity for everyone who keeps on doing what is evil—for the Jew first and also for the Gentile.* 10 But there will be glory and honor and peace from God for all who do good—for the Jew first and also for the Gentile. 11 For God does not show favoritism.

12 When the Gentiles sin, they will be destroyed, even though they never had God's written law. And the Jews, who do have God's law, will be judged by that law when they fail

1:17 Or "The righteous will live by faith." Hab 2:4.  1:18 Or who, by their wickedness, prevent the truth from being known.
2:9 Greek also for the Greek; also in 2:10.

to obey it. ¹³For merely listening to the law doesn't make us right with God. It is obeying the law that makes us right in his sight. ¹⁴Even Gentiles, who do not have God's written law, show that they know his law when they instinctively obey it, even without having heard it. ¹⁵They demonstrate that God's law is written in their hearts, for their own conscience and thoughts either accuse them or tell them they are doing right. ¹⁶And this is the message I proclaim—that the day is coming when God, through Christ Jesus, will judge everyone's secret life.

### The Jews and the Law

¹⁷You who call yourselves Jews are relying on God's law, and you boast about your special relationship with him. ¹⁸You know what he wants; you know what is right because you have been taught his law. ¹⁹You are convinced that you are a guide for the blind and a light for people who are lost in darkness. ²⁰You think you can instruct the ignorant and teach children the ways of God. For you are certain that God's law gives you complete knowledge and truth.

²¹Well then, if you teach others, why don't you teach yourself? You tell others not to steal, but do you steal? ²²You say it is wrong to commit adultery, but do you commit adultery? You condemn idolatry, but do you use items stolen from pagan temples?* ²³You are so proud of knowing the law, but you dishonor God by breaking it. ²⁴No wonder the Scriptures say, "The Gentiles blaspheme the name of God because of you."*

²⁵The Jewish ceremony of circumcision has value only if you obey God's law. But if you don't obey God's law, you are no better off than an uncircumcised Gentile. ²⁶And if the Gentiles obey God's law, won't God declare them to be his own people? ²⁷In fact, uncircumcised Gentiles who keep God's law will condemn you Jews who are circumcised and possess God's law but don't obey it.

²⁸For you are not a true Jew just because you were born of Jewish parents or because you have gone through the ceremony of circumcision. ²⁹No, a true Jew is one whose heart is right with God. And true circumci-

sion is not merely obeying the letter of the law; rather, it is a change of heart produced by God's Spirit. And a person with a changed heart seeks praise* from God, not from people.

### God Remains Faithful

**3** Then what's the advantage of being a Jew? Is there any value in the ceremony of circumcision? ²Yes, there are great benefits! First of all, the Jews were entrusted with the whole revelation of God.*

³True, some of them were unfaithful; but just because they were unfaithful, does that mean God will be unfaithful? ⁴Of course not! Even if everyone else is a liar, God is true. As the Scriptures say about him,

"You will be proved right in what you say,
and you will win your case in court."*

⁵"But," some might say, "our sinfulness serves a good purpose, for it helps people see how righteous God is. Isn't it unfair, then, for him to punish us?" (This is merely a human point of view.) ⁶Of course not! If God were not entirely fair, how would he be qualified to judge the world? ⁷"But," someone might still argue, "how can God condemn me as a sinner if my dishonesty highlights his truthfulness and brings him more glory?" ⁸And some people even slander us by claiming that we say, "The more we sin, the better it is!" Those who say such things deserve to be condemned.

### All People Are Sinners

⁹Well then, should we conclude that we Jews are better than others? No, not at all, for we have already shown that all people, whether Jews or Gentiles,* are under the power of sin. ¹⁰As the Scriptures say,

"No one is righteous—
	not even one.
¹¹ No one is truly wise;
	no one is seeking God.
¹² All have turned away;
	all have become useless.
No one does good,
	not a single one."*

---

2:22 Greek *do you steal from temples?*   2:24 Isa 52:5 (Greek version).   2:29 Or *receives praise.*   3:2 Greek *the oracles of God.*
3:4 Ps 51:4 (Greek version).   3:9 Greek *or Greeks.*   3:10-12 Pss 14:1-3; 53:1-3 (Greek version).

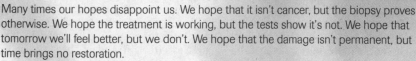

# HOPES dashed

READ ROMANS 5:3-5

Many times our hopes disappoint us. We hope that it isn't cancer, but the biopsy proves otherwise. We hope the treatment is working, but the tests show it's not. We hope that tomorrow we'll feel better, but we don't. We hope that the damage isn't permanent, but time brings no restoration.

All of us who have put our hope in something—or someone—in this world have at times been disappointed. But Paul says there is a hope that will never disappoint us. It's the "confident hope of salvation." And the amazing thing is our hope actually gets more confident *because* of the problems and trials we face. Struggles develop our endurance, which in turn strengthens our character, which in turns strengthens our hope of salvation. It is a *sure* hope—not one that changes with doctor reports or test results.

If you're tired of being disappointed, put all your hope in the One who will never disappoint you.

---

13 "Their talk is foul, like the stench from
  an open grave.
   Their tongues are filled with lies."
   "Snake venom drips from their lips."*
14   "Their mouths are full of cursing and
   bitterness."*
15 "They rush to commit murder.
16   Destruction and misery always follow
   them.
17 They don't know where to find peace."*
18   "They have no fear of God at all."*

19 Obviously, the law applies to those to whom it was given, for its purpose is to keep people from having excuses, and to show that the entire world is guilty before God. 20 For no one can ever be made right with God by doing what the law commands. The law simply shows us how sinful we are.

## Christ Took Our Punishment

21 But now God has shown us a way to be made right with him without keeping the requirements of the law, as was promised in the writings of Moses* and the prophets long ago. 22 We are made right with God by placing our faith in Jesus Christ. And this is true for everyone who believes, no matter who we are. 23 For everyone has sinned; we all fall short of God's glorious standard. 24 Yet God, with undeserved kindness, declares that we are righteous. He did this through Christ Jesus when he freed us from the penalty for our sins. 25 For God presented Jesus as the sacrifice for sin. People are made right with God when they believe that Jesus sacrificed his life, shedding his blood. This sacrifice shows that God was being fair when he held back and did not punish those who sinned in times past, 26 for he was looking ahead and including them in what he would do in this present time. God did this to demonstrate his righteousness, for he himself is fair and just, and he declares sinners to be right in his sight when they believe in Jesus.

27 Can we boast, then, that we have done anything to be accepted by God? No, because our acquittal is not based on obeying the law. It is based on faith. 28 So we are made right with God through faith and not by obeying the law.

29 After all, is God the God of the Jews only? Isn't he also the God of the Gentiles? Of course he is. 30 There is only one God, and he makes people right with himself only by faith, whether they are Jews or Gentiles.* 31 Well then, if we emphasize faith, does this mean that we can forget about the law? Of course not! In fact, only when we have faith do we truly fulfill the law.

3:13 Pss 5:9 (Greek version); 140:3.   3:14 Ps 10:7 (Greek version).   3:15-17 Isa 59:7-8.   3:18 Ps 36:1.   3:21 Greek *in the law.*
3:30 Greek *whether they are circumcised or uncircumcised.*

## The Faith of Abraham

**4** Abraham was, humanly speaking, the founder of our Jewish nation. What did he discover about being made right with God? [2] If his good deeds had made him acceptable to God, he would have had something to boast about. But that was not God's way. [3] For the Scriptures tell us, "Abraham believed God, and God counted him as righteous because of his faith."*

[4] When people work, their wages are not a gift, but something they have earned. [5] But people are counted as righteous, not because of their work, but because of their faith in God who forgives sinners. [6] David also spoke of this when he described the happiness of those who are declared righteous without working for it:

[7] "Oh, what joy for those
  whose disobedience is forgiven,
  whose sins are put out of sight.
[8] Yes, what joy for those
  whose record the LORD has cleared
  of sin."*

[9] Now, is this blessing only for the Jews, or is it also for uncircumcised Gentiles?* Well, we have been saying that Abraham was counted as righteous by God because of his faith. [10] But how did this happen? Was he counted as righteous only after he was circumcised, or was it before he was circumcised? Clearly, God accepted Abraham before he was circumcised!

[11] Circumcision was a sign that Abraham already had faith and that God had already accepted him and declared him to be righteous—even before he was circumcised. So Abraham is the spiritual father of those who have faith but have not been circumcised. They are counted as righteous because of their faith. [12] And Abraham is also the spiritual father of those who have been circumcised, but only if they have the same kind of faith Abraham had before he was circumcised.

[13] Clearly, God's promise to give the whole earth to Abraham and his descendants was based not on his obedience to God's law, but on a right relationship with God that comes

by faith. [14] If God's promise is only for those who obey the law, then faith is not necessary and the promise is pointless. [15] For the law always brings punishment on those who try to obey it. (The only way to avoid breaking the law is to have no law to break!)

[16] So the promise is received by faith. It is given as a free gift. And we are all certain to receive it, whether or not we live according to the law of Moses, if we have faith like Abraham's. For Abraham is the father of all who believe. [17] That is what the Scriptures mean when God told him, "I have made you the father of many nations."* This happened because Abraham believed in the God who brings the dead back to life and who creates new things out of nothing.

[18] Even when there was no reason for hope, Abraham kept hoping—believing that he would become the father of many nations. For God had said to him, "That's how many descendants you will have!"* [19] And Abraham's faith did not weaken, even though, at about 100 years of age, he figured his body was as good as dead—and so was Sarah's womb.

[20] Abraham never wavered in believing God's promise. In fact, his faith grew stronger, and in this he brought glory to God. [21] He was fully convinced that God is able to do whatever he promises. [22] And because of Abraham's faith, God counted him as righteous. [23] And when God counted him as righteous, it wasn't just for Abraham's benefit. It was recorded [24] for our benefit, too, assuring us that God will also count us as righteous if we believe in him, the one who raised Jesus our Lord from the dead. [25] He was handed over to die because of our sins, and he was raised to life to make us right with God.

## Faith Brings Joy

**5** Therefore, since we have been made right in God's sight by faith, we have peace with God because of what Jesus Christ our Lord has done for us. [2] Because of our faith, Christ has brought us into this place of undeserved privilege where we now stand, and we confidently and joyfully look forward to sharing God's glory.

[3] We can rejoice, too, when we run into

**4:3** Gen 15:6.  **4:7-8** Ps 32:1-2 (Greek version).  **4:9** Greek *is this blessing only for the circumcised, or is it also for the uncircumcised?*  **4:17** Gen 17:5.  **4:18** Gen 15:5.

problems and trials, for we know that they help us develop endurance. 4And endurance develops strength of character, and character strengthens our confident hope of salvation. 5And this hope will not lead to disappointment. For we know how dearly God loves us, because he has given us the Holy Spirit to fill our hearts with his love.

6When we were utterly helpless, Christ came at just the right time and died for us sinners. 7Now, most people would not be willing to die for an upright person, though someone might perhaps be willing to die for a person who is especially good. 8But God showed his great love for us by sending Christ to die for us while we were still sinners. 9And since we have been made right in God's sight by the blood of Christ, he will certainly save us from God's condemnation. 10For since our friendship with God was restored by the death of his Son while we were still his enemies, we will certainly be saved through the life of his Son. 11So now we can rejoice in our wonderful new relationship with God because our Lord Jesus Christ has made us friends of God.

## Adam and Christ Contrasted

12When Adam sinned, sin entered the world. Adam's sin brought death, so death spread to everyone, for everyone sinned. 13Yes, people sinned even before the law was given. But it was not counted as sin because there was not yet any law to break. 14Still, everyone died—from the time of Adam to the time of Moses—even those who did not disobey an explicit commandment of God, as Adam did. Now Adam is a symbol, a representation of Christ, who was yet to come. 15But there is a great difference between Adam's sin and God's gracious gift. For the sin of this one man, Adam, brought death to many. But even greater is God's wonderful grace and his gift of forgiveness to many through this other man, Jesus Christ. 16And the result of God's gracious gift is very different from the result of that one man's sin. For Adam's sin led to condemnation, but God's free gift leads to our being made right with God, even though we are guilty of many sins. 17For the sin of this one man, Adam, caused death to rule over many. But even greater is God's wonderful grace and his gift of righteousness, for all who receive it will live in triumph over sin and death through this one man, Jesus Christ.

18Yes, Adam's one sin brings condemnation for everyone, but Christ's one act of righteousness brings a right relationship with God and new life for everyone. 19Because one person disobeyed God, many became sinners. But because one other person obeyed God, many will be made righteous.

20God's law was given so that all people could see how sinful they were. But as people sinned more and more, God's wonderful grace became more abundant. 21So just as sin ruled over all people and brought them to death, now God's wonderful grace rules instead, giving us right standing with God and resulting in eternal life through Jesus Christ our Lord.

## Sin's Power Is Broken

6 Well then, should we keep on sinning so that God can show us more and more of his wonderful grace? 2Of course not! Since we have died to sin, how can we continue to live in it? 3Or have you forgotten that when we were joined with Christ Jesus in baptism, we joined him in his death? 4For we died and were buried with Christ by baptism. And just as Christ was raised from the dead by the glorious power of the Father, now we also may live new lives.

5Since we have been united with him in his death, we will also be raised to life as he was. 6We know that our old sinful selves were crucified with Christ so that sin might lose its power in our lives. We are no longer slaves to sin. 7For when we died with Christ we were set free from the power of sin. 8And since we died with Christ, we know we will also live with him. 9We are sure of this because Christ was raised from the dead, and he will never die again. Death no longer has any power over him. 10When he died, he died once to break the power of sin. But now that he lives, he lives for the glory of God. 11So you also should consider yourselves to be dead to the power of sin and alive to God through Christ Jesus.

¹²Do not let sin control the way you live;* do not give in to sinful desires. ¹³Do not let any part of your body become an instrument of evil to serve sin. Instead, give yourselves completely to God, for you were dead, but now you have new life. So use your whole body as an instrument to do what is right for the glory of God. ¹⁴Sin is no longer your master, for you no longer live under the requirements of the law. Instead, you live under the freedom of God's grace.

¹⁵Well then, since God's grace has set us free from the law, does that mean we can go on sinning? Of course not! ¹⁶Don't you realize that you become the slave of whatever you choose to obey? You can be a slave to sin, which leads to death, or you can choose to obey God, which leads to righteous living. ¹⁷Thank God! Once you were slaves of sin, but now you wholeheartedly obey this teaching we have given you. ¹⁸Now you are free from your slavery to sin, and you have become slaves to righteous living.

¹⁹Because of the weakness of your human nature, I am using the illustration of slavery to help you understand all this. Previously, you let yourselves be slaves to impurity and lawlessness, which led ever deeper into sin. Now you must give yourselves to be slaves to righteous living so that you will become holy.

²⁰When you were slaves to sin, you were free from the obligation to do right. ²¹And what was the result? You are now ashamed of the things you used to do, things that end in eternal doom. ²²But now you are free from the power of sin and have become slaves of God. Now you do those things that lead to holiness and result in eternal life. ²³For the wages of sin is death, but the free gift of God is eternal life through Christ Jesus our Lord.

### No Longer Bound to the Law

**7** Now, dear brothers and sisters*—you who are familiar with the law—don't you know that the law applies only while a person is living? ²For example, when a woman marries, the law binds her to her husband as long as he is alive. But if he dies, the laws of marriage no longer apply to her. ³So while her husband is alive, she would be committing adultery if she married another man. But if her husband dies, she is free from that law and does not commit adultery when she remarries.

⁴So, my dear brothers and sisters, this is the point: You died to the power of the law when you died with Christ. And now you are united with the one who was raised from the dead. As a result, we can produce a harvest of good deeds for God. ⁵When we were con-

6:12 Or *Do not let sin reign in your body, which is subject to death.*     7:1 Greek *brothers;* also in 7:4.

## PRAYING when you can't

READ ROMANS 8:26-27

Sometimes in the midst of a health crisis, we may feel as if we can't pray or we don't know what to pray. In such times, we need to apply these two wonderful verses about how to pray even when we can't pray. Paul assures us that it's okay at times not to be able to pray, because the Holy Spirit will pray for us. He will take our groans too deep for words right to God Himself. And even better than that, the Spirit knows what to pray for us and will pray according to God's will.

How awesome—God understands that at the times we need Him most, we may not be able to express ourselves, so He has His own Spirit do it for us! Go ahead and let the Spirit pray for you today. He can take your innermost thoughts, your deepest fears, and your heartfelt longings to the very throne of God. You don't even have to say a word.

trolled by our old nature,* sinful desires were at work within us, and the law aroused these evil desires that produced a harvest of sinful deeds, resulting in death. 6 But now we have been released from the law, for we died to it and are no longer captive to its power. Now we can serve God, not in the old way of obeying the letter of the law, but in the new way of living in the Spirit.

## God's Law Reveals Our Sin

7 Well then, am I suggesting that the law of God is sinful? Of course not! In fact, it was the law that showed me my sin. I would never have known that coveting is wrong if the law had not said, "You must not covet."* 8 But sin used this command to arouse all kinds of covetous desires within me! If there were no law, sin would not have that power. 9 At one time I lived without understanding the law. But when I learned the command not to covet, for instance, the power of sin came to life, 10 and I died. So I discovered that the law's commands, which were supposed to bring life, brought spiritual death instead. 11 Sin took advantage of those commands and deceived me; it used the commands to kill me. 12 But still, the law itself is holy, and its commands are holy and right and good.

13 But how can that be? Did the law, which is good, cause my death? Of course not! Sin used what was good to bring about my condemnation to death. So we can see how terrible sin really is. It uses God's good commands for its own evil purposes.

## Struggling with Sin

14 So the trouble is not with the law, for it is spiritual and good. The trouble is with me, for I am all too human, a slave to sin. 15 I don't really understand myself, for I want to do what is right, but I don't do it. Instead, I do what I hate. 16 But if I know that what I am doing is wrong, this shows that I agree that the law is good. 17 So I am not the one doing wrong; it is sin living in me that does it.

18 And I know that nothing good lives in me, that is, in my sinful nature.* I want to do what is right, but I can't. 19 I want to do what is good, but I don't. I don't want to do what is wrong, but I do it anyway. 20 But if I do what I don't want to do, I am not really the one doing wrong; it is sin living in me that does it.

21 I have discovered this principle of life— that when I want to do what is right, I inevitably do what is wrong. 22 I love God's law with all my heart. 23 But there is another power* within me that is at war with my mind. This power makes me a slave to the sin that is still within me. 24 Oh, what a miserable person I am! Who will free me from this life that is dominated by sin and death? 25 Thank God! The answer is in Jesus Christ our Lord. So you see how it is: In my mind I really want to obey God's law, but because of my sinful nature I am a slave to sin.

## Life in the Spirit

8 ¹ So now there is no condemnation for those who belong to Christ Jesus. 2 And because you belong to him, the power* of the life-giving Spirit has freed you* from the power of sin that leads to death. 3 The law of Moses was unable to save us because of the weakness of our sinful nature.* So God did what the law could not do. He sent his own Son in a body like the bodies we sinners have. And in that body God declared an end to sin's control over us by giving his Son as a sacrifice for our sins. 4 He did this so that the just requirement of the law would be fully satisfied for us, who no longer follow our sinful nature but instead follow the Spirit.

5 Those who are dominated by the sinful nature think about sinful things, but those who are controlled by the Holy Spirit think about things that please the Spirit. 6 So letting your sinful nature control your mind leads to death. But letting the Spirit control your mind leads to life and peace. 7 For the sinful nature is always hostile to God. It never did obey God's laws, and it never will. 8 That's why those who are still under the control of their sinful nature can never please God.

9 But you are not controlled by your sinful nature. You are controlled by the Spirit if you have the Spirit of God living in you. (And remember that those who do not have the

---

7:5 Greek When we were in the flesh.   7:7 Exod 20:17; Deut 5:21.   7:18 Greek my flesh; also in 7:25.   7:23 Greek law; also in 7:23b.   8:2a Greek the law; also in 8:2b.   8:2b Some manuscripts read me.   8:3 Greek our flesh; similarly in 8:4, 5, 6, 7, 8, 9, 12.

Spirit of Christ living in them do not belong to him at all.) [10]And Christ lives within you, so even though your body will die because of sin, the Spirit gives you life* because you have been made right with God. [11]The Spirit of God, who raised Jesus from the dead, lives in you. And just as God raised Christ Jesus from the dead, he will give life to your mortal bodies by this same Spirit living within you.

[12]Therefore, dear brothers and sisters,* you have no obligation to do what your sinful nature urges you to do. [13]For if you live by its dictates, you will die. But if through the power of the Spirit you put to death the deeds of your sinful nature,* you will live. [14]For all who are led by the Spirit of God are children* of God.

[15]So you have not received a spirit that makes you fearful slaves. Instead, you received God's Spirit when he adopted you as his own children.* Now we call him, "Abba, Father."* [16]For his Spirit joins with our spirit to affirm that we are God's children. [17]And since we are his children, we are his heirs. In fact, together with Christ we are heirs of God's glory. But if we are to share his glory, we must also share his suffering.

### The Future Glory

[18]Yet what we suffer now is nothing compared to the glory he will reveal to us later. [19]For all creation is waiting eagerly for that future day when God will reveal who his children really are. [20]Against its will, all creation was subjected to God's curse. But with eager hope, [21]the creation looks forward to the day when it will join God's children in glorious freedom from death and decay. [22]For we know that all creation has been groaning as in the pains of childbirth right up to the present time. [23]And we believers also groan, even though we have the Holy Spirit within us as a foretaste of future glory, for we long for our bodies to be released from sin and suffering. We, too, wait with eager hope for the day when God will give us our full rights as his adopted children,* including the new bodies he has promised us. [24]We were given this hope when we were

saved. (If we already have something, we don't need to hope* for it. [25]But if we look forward to something we don't yet have, we must wait patiently and confidently.)

[26]And the Holy Spirit helps us in our weakness. For example, we don't know what God wants us to pray for. But the Holy Spirit prays for us with groanings that cannot be expressed in words. [27]And the Father who knows all hearts knows what the Spirit is saying, for the Spirit pleads for us believers* in harmony with God's own will. [28]And we know that God causes everything to work together* for the good of those who love God and are called according to his purpose for them. [29]For God knew his people in advance, and he chose them to become like his Son, so that his Son would be the firstborn among many brothers and sisters. [30]And having chosen them, he called them to come to him. And having called them, he gave them right standing with himself. And having given them right standing, he gave them his glory.

### Nothing Can Separate Us from God's Love

[31]What shall we say about such wonderful things as these? If God is for us, who can ever be against us? [32]Since he did not spare even his own Son but gave him up for us all, won't he also give us everything else? [33]Who dares accuse us whom God has chosen for his own? No one—for God himself has given us right standing with himself. [34]Who will condemn us? No one—for Christ Jesus died for us and was raised to life for us, and he is sitting in the place of honor at God's right hand, pleading for us.

[35]Can anything ever separate us from Christ's love? Does it mean he no longer loves us if we have trouble or calamity, or are persecuted, or hungry, or destitute, or in danger, or threatened with death? [36](As the Scriptures say, "For your sake we are killed every day; we are being slaughtered like sheep."*) [37]No, despite all these things, overwhelming victory is ours through Christ, who loved us.

---

8:10 Or *your spirit is alive.*   8:12 Greek *brothers;* also in 8:29.   8:13 Greek *deeds of the body.*   8:14 Greek *sons;* also in 8:19.
8:15a Greek *you received a spirit of sonship.*   8:15b *Abba* is an Aramaic term for "father."   8:23 Greek *wait anxiously for sonship.*
8:24 Some manuscripts read *wait.*   8:27 Greek *for God's holy people.*   8:28 Some manuscripts read *And we know that everything works together.*   8:36 Ps 44:22.

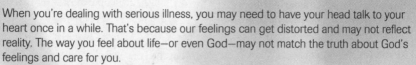

# FEELINGS vs. reality

READ ROMANS 8:35-39

When you're dealing with serious illness, you may need to have your head talk to your heart once in a while. That's because our feelings can get distorted and may not reflect reality. The way you feel about life—or even God—may not match the truth about God's feelings and care for you.

Are you *convinced* that neither chemo nor radiation, neither scans nor surgery, neither disappointments nor bad news, neither predictions nor seemingly unanswered prayers, nor anything else in the world of illness will be able to separate you from the love of God that is yours in Christ Jesus?

Don't let your "fears for today" or your "worries about tomorrow" rob you of the absolute certainty that the God of the universe loves you and that nothing, absolutely nothing, can diminish that love for you. Whether your heart feels it or not, your head has a message for you: No matter what happens or doesn't happen in your life today, *nothing* can keep your heavenly Father from loving you.

**38**And I am convinced that nothing can ever separate us from God's love. Neither death nor life, neither angels nor demons,* neither our fears for today nor our worries about tomorrow—not even the powers of hell can separate us from God's love. 39No power in the sky above or in the earth below—indeed, nothing in all creation will ever be able to separate us from the love of God that is revealed in Christ Jesus our Lord.

## God's Selection of Israel

**9** With Christ as my witness, I speak with utter truthfulness. My conscience and the Holy Spirit confirm it. 2My heart is filled with bitter sorrow and unending grief 3for my people, my Jewish brothers and sisters.* I would be willing to be forever cursed—cut off from Christ!—if that would save them. 4They are the people of Israel, chosen to be God's adopted children.* God revealed his glory to them. He made covenants with them and gave them his law. He gave them the privilege of worshiping him and receiving his wonderful promises. 5Abraham, Isaac, and Jacob are their ancestors, and Christ himself was an Israelite as far as his human nature is concerned. And he is God,

the one who rules over everything and is worthy of eternal praise! Amen.*

6Well then, has God failed to fulfill his promise to Israel? No, for not all who are born into the nation of Israel are truly members of God's people! 7Being descendants of Abraham doesn't make them truly Abraham's children. For the Scriptures say, "Isaac is the son through whom your descendants will be counted,"* though Abraham had other children, too. 8This means that Abraham's physical descendants are not necessarily children of God. Only the children of the promise are considered to be Abraham's children. 9For God had promised, "I will return about this time next year, and Sarah will have a son."*

10This son was our ancestor Isaac. When he married Rebekah, she gave birth to twins.* 11But before they were born, before they had done anything good or bad, she received a message from God. (This message shows that God chooses people according to his own purposes; 12he calls people, but not according to their good or bad works.) She was told, "Your older son will serve your younger son."* 13In the words of the Scriptures, "I loved Jacob, but I rejected Esau."*

**8:38** Greek *nor rulers.* **9:3** Greek *my brothers.* **9:4** Greek *chosen for sonship.* **9:5** Or *May God, the one who rules over everything, be praised forever. Amen.* **9:7** Gen 21:12. **9:9** Gen 18:10, 14. **9:10** Greek *she conceived children through this one man.* **9:12** Gen 25:23. **9:13** Mal 1:2-3.

¹⁴Are we saying, then, that God was unfair? Of course not! ¹⁵For God said to Moses,

"I will show mercy to anyone I choose,
    and I will show compassion to anyone
    I choose."*

¹⁶So it is God who decides to show mercy. We can neither choose it nor work for it.

¹⁷For the Scriptures say that God told Pharaoh, "I have appointed you for the very purpose of displaying my power in you and to spread my fame throughout the earth."* ¹⁸So you see, God chooses to show mercy to some, and he chooses to harden the hearts of others so they refuse to listen.

¹⁹Well then, you might say, "Why does God blame people for not responding? Haven't they simply done what he makes them do?"

²⁰No, don't say that. Who are you, a mere human being, to argue with God? Should the thing that was created say to the one who created it, "Why have you made me like this?" ²¹When a potter makes jars out of clay, doesn't he have a right to use the same lump of clay to make one jar for decoration and another to throw garbage into? ²²In the same way, even though God has the right to show his anger and his power, he is very patient with those on whom his anger falls, who are destined for destruction. ²³He does this to make the riches of his glory shine even brighter on those to whom he shows mercy, who were prepared in advance for glory. ²⁴And we are among those whom he selected, both from the Jews and from the Gentiles.

²⁵Concerning the Gentiles, God says in the prophecy of Hosea,

"Those who were not my people,
    I will now call my people.
And I will love those
    whom I did not love before."*

²⁶And,

"Then, at the place where they were told,
    'You are not my people,'
there they will be called
    'children of the living God.'"*

²⁷And concerning Israel, Isaiah the prophet cried out,

"Though the people of Israel are as
        numerous as the sand of the
        seashore,
    only a remnant will be saved.
²⁸For the LORD will carry out his sentence
        upon the earth
    quickly and with finality."*

²⁹And Isaiah said the same thing in another place:

"If the LORD of Heaven's Armies
    had not spared a few of our children,
we would have been wiped out like
        Sodom,
    destroyed like Gomorrah."*

## Israel's Unbelief

³⁰What does all this mean? Even though the Gentiles were not trying to follow God's standards, they were made right with God. And it was by faith that this took place. ³¹But the people of Israel, who tried so hard to get right with God by keeping the law, never succeeded. ³²Why not? Because they were trying to get right with God by keeping the law* instead of by trusting in him. They stumbled over the great rock in their path. ³³God warned them of this in the Scriptures when he said,

"I am placing a stone in Jerusalem* that
        makes people stumble,
    a rock that makes them fall.
But anyone who trusts in him
    will never be disgraced."*

**10** Dear brothers and sisters,* the longing of my heart and my prayer to God is for the people of Israel to be saved. ²I know what enthusiasm they have for God, but it is misdirected zeal. ³For they don't understand God's way of making people right with himself. Refusing to accept God's way, they cling to their own way of getting right with God by trying to keep the law. ⁴For Christ has already accomplished the purpose for which the law was given.* As a re-

9:15 Exod 33:19.   9:17 Exod 9:16 (Greek version).   9:25 Hos 2:23.   9:26 Greek *sons of the living God.* Hos 1:10.   9:27-28 Isa 10:22-23 (Greek version).   9:29 Isa 1:9.   9:32 Greek *by works.*   9:33a Greek *in Zion.*   9:33b Isa 8:14; 28:16 (Greek version).   10:1 Greek *Brothers.*   10:4 Or *For Christ is the end of the law.*

sult, all who believe in him are made right with God.

### Salvation Is for Everyone

⁵For Moses writes that the law's way of making a person right with God requires obedience to all of its commands.* ⁶But faith's way of getting right with God says, "Don't say in your heart, 'Who will go up to heaven' (to bring Christ down to earth). ⁷And don't say, 'Who will go down to the place of the dead' (to bring Christ back to life again)." ⁸In fact, it says,

> "The message is very close
>     at hand;
>   it is on your lips and in your heart."*

And that message is the very message about faith that we preach: ⁹If you confess with your mouth that Jesus is Lord and believe in your heart that God raised him from the dead, you will be saved. ¹⁰For it is by believing in your heart that you are made right with God, and it is by confessing with your mouth that you are saved. ¹¹As the Scriptures tell us, "Anyone who trusts in him will never be disgraced."* ¹²Jew and Gentile* are the same in this respect. They have the same Lord, who gives generously to all who call on him. ¹³For "Everyone who calls on the name of the Lord will be saved."*

¹⁴But how can they call on him to save them unless they believe in him? And how can they believe in him if they have never heard about him? And how can they hear about him unless someone tells them? ¹⁵And how will anyone go and tell them without being sent? That is why the Scriptures say, "How beautiful are the feet of messengers who bring good news!"*

¹⁶But not everyone welcomes the Good News, for Isaiah the prophet said, "Lord, who has believed our message?"* ¹⁷So faith comes from hearing, that is, hearing the Good News about Christ. ¹⁸But I ask, have the people of Israel actually heard the message? Yes, they have:

> "The message has gone throughout
>     the earth,
>   and the words to all the world."*

¹⁹But I ask, did the people of Israel really understand? Yes, they did, for even in the time of Moses, God said,

> "I will rouse your jealousy through
>     people who are not even a nation.
>   I will provoke your anger through the
>     foolish Gentiles."*

²⁰And later Isaiah spoke boldly for God, saying,

> "I was found by people who were not
>     looking for me.
>   I showed myself to those who were not
>     asking for me."*

²¹But regarding Israel, God said,

> "All day long I opened my arms to them,
>   but they were disobedient and
>     rebellious."*

### God's Mercy on Israel

**11** I ask, then, has God rejected his own people, the nation of Israel? Of course not! I myself am an Israelite, a descendant of Abraham and a member of the tribe of Benjamin.

²No, God has not rejected his own people, whom he chose from the very beginning. Do you realize what the Scriptures say about

---

10:5 See Lev 18:5.   10:6-8 Deut 30:12-14.   10:11 Isa 28:16 (Greek version).   10:12 Greek *and Greek*.   10:13 Joel 2:32.   10:15 Isa 52:7.   10:16 Isa 53:1.   10:18 Ps 19:4.   10:19 Deut 32:21.   10:20 Isa 65:1 (Greek version).   10:21 Isa 65:2 (Greek version).

---

## ANOTHER ashtray?

READ ROMANS 9:20-21

Ever wonder about the differences in our physical bodies? Why are some people drop-dead gorgeous and others have a face only a mother could love? Why do some have genetic mutations for disease while others sail through with great health?

It's hard to accept our physical imperfections, and sometimes we may even question why God made us this way. But that's like a lump of clay asking the Potter why it has to be an ashtray, not a vase. The answer is the same for both questions: The creation can't argue with the Creator. He knows what He's doing and uses every lump of clay for His purpose.

this? Elijah the prophet complained to God about the people of Israel and said, ³"LORD, they have killed your prophets and torn down your altars. I am the only one left, and now they are trying to kill me, too."*

⁴And do you remember God's reply? He said, "No, I have 7,000 others who have never bowed down to Baal!"*

⁵It is the same today, for a few of the people of Israel* have remained faithful because of God's grace—his undeserved kindness in choosing them. ⁶And since it is through God's kindness, then it is not by their good works. For in that case, <u>God's grace would not be what it really is—free and undeserved.</u>

⁷So this is the situation: Most of the people of Israel have not found the favor of God they are looking for so earnestly. A few have—the ones God has chosen—but the hearts of the rest were hardened. ⁸As the Scriptures say,

"God has put them into a deep sleep.
To this day he has shut their eyes so they
    do not see,
    and closed their ears so they do
    not hear."*

⁹Likewise, David said,

"Let their bountiful table become a snare,
    a trap that makes them think all is well.
Let their blessings cause them to
    stumble,
    and let them get what they deserve.
¹⁰Let their eyes go blind so they cannot see,
    and let their backs be bent forever."*

¹¹Did God's people stumble and fall beyond recovery? Of course not! They were disobedient, so God made salvation available to the Gentiles. But he wanted his own people to become jealous and claim it for themselves. ¹²Now if the Gentiles were enriched because the people of Israel turned down God's offer of salvation, think how much greater a blessing the world will share when they finally accept it.

¹³I am saying all this especially for you Gentiles. God has appointed me as the apostle to the Gentiles. I stress this, ¹⁴for I want somehow to make the people of Israel jealous of what you Gentiles have, so I might save some of them. ¹⁵For since their rejection meant that God offered salvation to the rest of the world, their acceptance will be even more wonderful. It will be life for those who were dead! ¹⁶And since Abraham and the other patriarchs were holy, their descendants will also be holy—just as the entire batch of dough is holy because the portion given as an offering is holy. For if the roots of the tree are holy, the branches will be, too.

¹⁷But some of these branches from Abraham's tree—some of the people of Israel—have been broken off. And you Gentiles, who were branches from a wild olive tree, have been grafted in. So now you also receive the blessing God has promised Abraham and his children, sharing in the rich nourishment from the root of God's special olive tree. ¹⁸But you must not brag about being grafted in to replace the branches that were broken off. You are just a branch, not the root.

¹⁹"Well," you may say, "those branches were broken off to make room for me." ²⁰Yes, but remember—those branches were broken off because they didn't believe in Christ, and you are there because you do believe. So don't think highly of yourself, but fear what could happen. ²¹For if God did not spare the original branches, he won't* spare you either.

²²Notice how God is both kind and severe. He is severe toward those who disobeyed, but kind to you if you continue to trust in his kindness. But if you stop trusting, you also will be cut off. ²³And if the people of Israel turn from their unbelief, they will be grafted in again, for God has the power to graft them back into the tree. ²⁴You, by nature, were a branch cut from a wild olive tree. So if God was willing to do something contrary to nature by grafting you into his cultivated tree, he will be far more eager to graft the original branches back into the tree where they belong.

## God's Mercy Is for Everyone

²⁵I want you to understand this mystery, dear brothers and sisters,* so that you will

**11:3** 1 Kgs 19:10, 14.   **11:4** 1 Kgs 19:18.   **11:5** Greek *for a remnant.*   **11:8** Isa 29:10; Deut 29:4.   **11:9-10** Ps 69:22-23 (Greek version).   **11:21** Some manuscripts read *perhaps he won't.*   **11:25** Greek *brothers.*

not feel proud about yourselves. Some of the people of Israel have hard hearts, but this will last only until the full number of Gentiles comes to Christ. 26And so all Israel will be saved. As the Scriptures say,

> "The one who rescues will come from
>     Jerusalem,*
> and he will turn Israel* away from
>     ungodliness.
> 27 And this is my covenant with them,
>     that I will take away their sins."*

28Many of the people of Israel are now enemies of the Good News, and this benefits you Gentiles. Yet they are still the people he loves because he chose their ancestors Abraham, Isaac, and Jacob. 29For God's gifts and his call can never be withdrawn. 30Once, you Gentiles were rebels against God, but when the people of Israel rebelled against him, God was merciful to you instead. 31Now they are the rebels, and God's mercy has come to you so that they, too, will share* in God's mercy. 32For God has imprisoned everyone in disobedience so he could have mercy on everyone.

33Oh, how great are God's riches and wisdom and knowledge! How impossible it is for us to understand his decisions and his ways!

> 34 For who can know the LORD's thoughts?
>     Who knows enough to give him
>     advice?*
> 35 And who has given him so much
>     that he needs to pay it back?*

36For everything comes from him and exists by his power and is intended for his glory. All glory to him forever! Amen.

## A Living Sacrifice to God

**12** And so, dear brothers and sisters,* I plead with you to give your bodies to God because of all he has done for you. Let them be a living and holy sacrifice—the kind he will find acceptable. This is truly the way to worship him.* 2Don't copy the behavior and customs of this world, but let God transform you into a new person by changing the way you think. Then you will learn to know God's will for you, which is good and pleasing and perfect.

3Because of the privilege and authority* God has given me, I give each of you this warning: Don't think you are better than you really are. Be honest in your evaluation of yourselves, measuring yourselves by the faith God has given us.* 4Just as our bodies have many parts and each part has a special function, 5so it is with Christ's body. We are many parts of one body, and we all belong to each other.

6In his grace, God has given us different gifts for doing certain things well. So if God has given you the ability to prophesy, speak out with as much faith as God has given you. 7If your gift is serving others, serve them well. If you are a teacher, teach well. 8If your gift is to encourage others, be encouraging. If it is giving, give generously. If God has given you leadership ability, take the responsibility seriously. And if you have a gift for showing kindness to others, do it gladly.

9Don't just pretend to love others. Really love them. Hate what is wrong. Hold tightly to what is good. 10Love each other with genuine affection,* and take delight in honoring each other. 11Never be lazy, but work hard and serve the Lord enthusiastically.* 12Rejoice in our confident hope. Be patient in trouble, and keep on praying. 13When God's people are in need, be ready to help them. Always be eager to practice hospitality.

14Bless those who persecute you. Don't curse them; pray that God will bless them. 15Be happy with those who are happy, and weep with those who weep. 16Live in harmony with each other. Don't be too proud to enjoy the company of ordinary people. And don't think you know it all!

17Never pay back evil with more evil. Do things in such a way that everyone can see you are honorable. 18Do all that you can to live in peace with everyone.

19Dear friends, never take revenge. Leave

---

11:26a Greek *from Zion.*   11:26b Greek *Jacob.*   11:26-27 Isa 59:20-21; 27:9 (Greek version).   11:31 Other manuscripts read *will now share;* still others read *will someday share.*   11:34 Isa 40:13 (Greek version).   11:35 See Job 41:11.   12:1a Greek *brothers.*   12:1b Or *This is your spiritual worship;* or *This is your reasonable service.*   12:3a Or *Because of the grace;* compare 1:5.   12:3b Or *by the faith God has given you;* or *by the standard of our God-given faith.*   12:10 Greek *with brotherly love.*   12:11 Or *but serve the Lord with a zealous spirit;* or *but let the Spirit excite you as you serve the Lord.*

that to the righteous anger of God. For the Scriptures say,

"I will take revenge;
   I will pay them back,"*
   says the LORD.

20 Instead,

"If your enemies are hungry,
   feed them.
If they are thirsty, give them something
   to drink.
In doing this, you will heap
   burning coals of shame on their
   heads."*

21 Don't let evil conquer you, but conquer evil by doing good.

### Respect for Authority

**13** Everyone must submit to governing authorities. For all authority comes from God, and those in positions of authority have been placed there by God. 2 So anyone who rebels against authority is rebelling against what God has instituted, and they will be punished. 3 For the authorities do not strike fear in people who are doing right, but in those who are doing wrong. Would you like to live without fear of the authorities? Do what is right, and they will honor you. 4 The authorities are God's servants, sent for your good. But if you are doing wrong, of course you should be afraid, for they have the power to punish you. They are God's servants, sent for the very purpose of punishing those who do what is wrong. 5 So you must submit to them, not only to avoid punishment, but also to keep a clear conscience.

6 Pay your taxes, too, for these same reasons. For government workers need to be paid. They are serving God in what they do. 7 Give to everyone what you owe them: Pay your taxes and government fees to those who collect them, and give respect and honor to those who are in authority.

### Love Fulfills God's Requirements

8 Owe nothing to anyone—except for your obligation to love one another. If you love your neighbor, you will fulfill the requirements of God's law. 9 For the commandments say, "You must not commit adultery. You must not murder. You must not steal. You must not covet."* These—and other such commandments—are summed up in this one commandment: "Love your neighbor as yourself."* 10 Love does no wrong to others, so love fulfills the requirements of God's law.

11 This is all the more urgent, for you know how late it is; time is running out. Wake up, for our salvation is nearer now than when we first believed. 12 The night is

**12:19** Deut 32:35.  **12:20** Prov 25:21-22.  **13:9a** Exod 20:13-15, 17.  **13:9b** Lev 19:18.

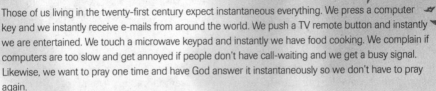

## MICROWAVE prayers

READ ROMANS 12:12

Those of us living in the twenty-first century expect instantaneous everything. We press a computer key and we instantly receive e-mails from around the world. We push a TV remote button and instantly we are entertained. We touch a microwave keypad and instantly we have food cooking. We complain if computers are too slow and get annoyed if people don't have call-waiting and we get a busy signal. Likewise, we want to pray one time and have God answer it instantaneously so we don't have to pray again.

But even though we pray and God *instantly hears* us, He may or may not *instantly answer* us. Prayer can be hard work as we bring our requests to God time and time again. This verse reminds us to be patient in trouble and not to give up praying even when the answer seems "slow" in coming. God will answer in His own time and in His own way.

After all, the best things in life are worth waiting for.

almost gone; the day of salvation will soon be here. So remove your dark deeds like dirty clothes, and put on the shining armor of right living. 13Because we belong to the day, we must live decent lives for all to see. Don't participate in the darkness of wild parties and drunkenness, or in sexual promiscuity and immoral living, or in quarreling and jealousy. 14Instead, clothe yourself with the presence of the Lord Jesus Christ. And don't let yourself think about ways to indulge your evil desires.

## The Danger of Criticism

**14** Accept other believers who are weak in faith, and don't argue with them about what they think is right or wrong. 2For instance, one person believes it's all right to eat anything. But another believer with a sensitive conscience will eat only vegetables. 3Those who feel free to eat anything must not look down on those who don't. And those who don't eat certain foods must not condemn those who do, for God has accepted them. 4Who are you to condemn someone else's servants? They are responsible to the Lord, so let him judge whether they are right or wrong. And with the Lord's help, they will do what is right and will receive his approval.

5In the same way, some think one day is more holy than another day, while others think every day is alike. You should each be fully convinced that whichever day you choose is acceptable. 6Those who worship the Lord on a special day do it to honor him. Those who eat any kind of food do so to honor the Lord, since they give thanks to God before eating. And those who refuse to eat certain foods also want to please the Lord and give thanks to God. 7For we don't live for ourselves or die for ourselves. 8If we live, it's to honor the Lord. And if we die, it's to honor the Lord. So whether we live or die, we belong to the Lord. 9Christ died and rose again for this very purpose—to be Lord both of the living and of the dead.

10So why do you condemn another believer*? Why do you look down on another believer? Remember, we will all stand before the judgment seat of God. 11For the Scriptures say,

"'As surely as I live,' says the LORD,
'every knee will bend to me,
    and every tongue will confess and give
        praise to God.*'"

12Yes, each of us will give a personal account to God. 13So let's stop condemning each other. Decide instead to live in such a way that you will not cause another believer to stumble and fall.

14I know and am convinced on the authority of the Lord Jesus that no food, in and of itself, is wrong to eat. But if someone believes it is wrong, then for that person it is wrong. 15And if another believer is distressed by what you eat, you are not acting in love if you eat it. Don't let your eating ruin someone for whom Christ died. 16Then you will not be criticized for doing something you believe is good. 17For the Kingdom of God is not a matter of what we eat or drink, but of living a life of goodness and peace and joy in the Holy Spirit. 18If you serve Christ with this attitude, you will please God, and others will approve of you, too. 19So then, let us aim for harmony in the church and try to build each other up.

20Don't tear apart the work of God over what you eat. Remember, all foods are acceptable, but it is wrong to eat something if it makes another person stumble. 21It is better not to eat meat or drink wine or do anything else if it might cause another believer to stumble. 22You may believe there's nothing wrong with what you are doing, but keep it between yourself and God. Blessed are those who don't feel guilty for doing something they have decided is right. 23But if you have doubts about whether or not you should eat something, you are sinning if you go ahead and do it. For you are not following your convictions. If you do anything you believe is not right, you are sinning.

## Living to Please Others

**15** We who are strong must be considerate of those who are sensitive about things like this. We must not just please ourselves. 2We should help others do what is right and build them up in the Lord. 3For even Christ didn't live to please himself. As

---

**14:10** Greek *your brother;* also in 14:10b, 13, 15, 21.   **14:11** Or *confess allegiance to God.* Isa 49:18; 45:23 (Greek version).

the Scriptures say, "The insults of those who insult you, O God, have fallen on me."* [4]Such things were written in the Scriptures long ago to teach us. And the Scriptures give us hope and encouragement as we wait patiently for God's promises to be fulfilled.

[5]May God, who gives this patience and encouragement, help you live in complete harmony with each other, as is fitting for followers of Christ Jesus. [6]Then all of you can join together with one voice, giving praise and glory to God, the Father of our Lord Jesus Christ.

[7]Therefore, accept each other just as Christ has accepted you so that God will be given glory. [8]Remember that Christ came as a servant to the Jews* to show that God is true to the promises he made to their ancestors. [9]He also came so that the Gentiles might give glory to God for his mercies to them. That is what the psalmist meant when he wrote:

"For this, I will praise you among the
    Gentiles;
  I will sing praises to your name."*

[10]And in another place it is written,

"Rejoice with his people,
  you Gentiles."*

[11]And yet again,

"Praise the Lord, all you Gentiles.
  Praise him, all you people of the earth."*

[12]And in another place Isaiah said,

"The heir to David's throne* will come,
  and he will rule over the Gentiles.
They will place their hope on him."*

[13]I pray that God, the source of hope, will fill you completely with joy and peace because you trust in him. Then you will overflow with confident hope through the power of the Holy Spirit.

## Paul's Reason for Writing

[14]I am fully convinced, my dear brothers and sisters,* that you are full of goodness. You know these things so well you can teach each other all about them. [15]Even so, I have been bold enough to write about some of these points, knowing that all you need is this reminder. For by God's grace, [16]I am a special messenger from Christ Jesus to you Gentiles. I bring you the Good News so that I might present you as an acceptable offering to God, made holy by the Holy Spirit. [17]So I have reason to be enthusiastic about all Christ Jesus has done through me in my service to God. [18]Yet I dare not boast about anything except what Christ has done through me, bringing the Gentiles to God by my message and by the way I worked among them. [19]They were convinced by the power of miraculous signs and wonders and by the power of God's Spirit.* In this way, I have fully presented the Good News of Christ from Jerusalem all the way to Illyricum.*

[20]My ambition has always been to preach the Good News where the name of Christ has never been heard, rather than where a church has already been started by someone else. [21]I have been following the plan spoken of in the Scriptures, where it says,

"Those who have never been told about
    him will see,
  and those who have never heard of
    him will understand."*

[22]In fact, my visit to you has been delayed so long because I have been preaching in these places.

## Paul's Travel Plans

[23]But now I have finished my work in these regions, and after all these long years of waiting, I am eager to visit you. [24]I am planning to go to Spain, and when I do, I will stop off in Rome. And after I have enjoyed your fellowship for a little while, you can provide for my journey.

[25]But before I come, I must go to Jerusalem to take a gift to the believers* there. [26]For you see, the believers in Macedonia and Achaia* have eagerly taken up an offering for the poor among the believers in Jerusalem. [27]They were glad to do this because they feel they

15:3 Greek *who insult you have fallen on me.* Ps 69:9.   15:8 Greek *servant of circumcision.*   15:9 Ps 18:49.   15:10 Deut 32:43.
15:11 Ps 117:1.   15:12a Greek *The root of Jesse.* David was the son of Jesse.   15:12b Isa 11:10 (Greek version).   15:14 Greek
*brothers;* also in 15:30.   15:19a Other manuscripts read *the Spirit;* still others read *the Holy Spirit.*   15:19b *Illyricum* was a region
northeast of Italy.   15:21 Isa 52:15 (Greek version).   15:25 Greek *God's holy people;* also in 15:26, 31.   15:26 *Macedonia* and
*Achaia* were the northern and southern regions of Greece.

owe a real debt to them. Since the Gentiles received the spiritual blessings of the Good News from the believers in Jerusalem, they feel the least they can do in return is to help them financially. 28As soon as I have delivered this money and completed this good deed of theirs, I will come to see you on my way to Spain. 29And I am sure that when I come, Christ will richly bless our time together.

30Dear brothers and sisters, I urge you in the name of our Lord Jesus Christ to join in my struggle by praying to God for me. Do this because of your love for me, given to you by the Holy Spirit. 31Pray that I will be rescued from those in Judea who refuse to obey God. Pray also that the believers there will be willing to accept the donation* I am taking to Jerusalem. 32Then, by the will of God, I will be able to come to you with a joyful heart, and we will be an encouragement to each other.

33And now may God, who gives us his peace, be with you all. Amen.*

## Paul Greets His Friends

**16** I commend to you our sister Phoebe, who is a deacon in the church in Cenchrea. 2Welcome her in the Lord as one who is worthy of honor among God's people. Help her in whatever she needs, for she has been helpful to many, and especially to me.

3Give my greetings to Priscilla and Aquila, my co-workers in the ministry of Christ Jesus. 4In fact, they once risked their lives for me. I am thankful to them, and so are all the Gentile churches. 5Also give my greetings to the church that meets in their home.

Greet my dear friend Epenetus. He was the first person from the province of Asia to become a follower of Christ. 6Give my greetings to Mary, who has worked so hard for your benefit. 7Greet Andronicus and Junia,* my fellow Jews,* who were in prison with me. They are highly respected among the apostles and became followers of Christ before I did. 8Greet Ampliatus, my dear friend in the Lord. 9Greet Urbanus, our co-worker in Christ, and my dear friend Stachys.

10Greet Apelles, a good man whom Christ

I pray that God, the source of hope,

will fill you completely with

joy and peace

because you trust in him.

Then you will overflow with

confident hope

through the power of the Holy Spirit.

ROMANS 15:13

approves. And give my greetings to the believers from the household of Aristobulus. 11Greet Herodion, my fellow Jew.* Greet the Lord's people from the household of Narcissus. 12Give my greetings to Tryphena and Tryphosa, the Lord's workers, and to dear Persis, who has worked so hard for the Lord. 13Greet Rufus, whom the Lord picked out to be his very own; and also his dear mother, who has been a mother to me.

14Give my greetings to Asyncritus, Phlegon, Hermes, Patrobas, Hermas, and the brothers and sisters* who meet with them. 15Give my greetings to Philologus, Julia, Nereus and his sister, and to Olympas and all the believers* who meet with them. 16Greet each other in Christian love.* All the churches of Christ send you their greetings.

## Paul's Final Instructions

17And now I make one more appeal, my dear brothers and sisters. Watch out for people who cause divisions and upset people's faith by teaching things contrary to what you have been taught. Stay away from them. 18Such people are not serving Christ our Lord; they are serving their own personal interests. By smooth talk and glowing words they deceive innocent people. 19But everyone knows that you are obedient to the Lord. This makes me

**15:31** Greek *the ministry;* other manuscripts read *the gift.*   **15:33** Some manuscripts omit *Amen.* One very early manuscript places 16:25-27 here.   **16:7a** *Junia* is a feminine name. Some late manuscripts accent the word so it reads *Junias,* a masculine name; still others read *Julia* (feminine).   **16:7b** Or *compatriots;* also in 16:21.   **16:11** Or *compatriot.*   **16:14** Greek *brothers;* also in 16:17. **16:15** Greek *all of God's holy people.*   **16:16** Greek *with a sacred kiss.*

very happy. I want you to be wise in doing right and to stay innocent of any wrong. ²⁰The God of peace will soon crush Satan under your feet. May the grace of our Lord Jesus* be with you.

²¹Timothy, my fellow worker, sends you his greetings, as do Lucius, Jason, and Sosipater, my fellow Jews.

²²I, Tertius, the one writing this letter for Paul, send my greetings, too, as one of the Lord's followers.

²³Gaius says hello to you. He is my host and also serves as host to the whole church.

Erastus, the city treasurer, sends you his greetings, and so does our brother Quartus.*

²⁵Now all glory to God, who is able to make you strong, just as my Good News says. This message about Jesus Christ has revealed his plan for you Gentiles, a plan kept secret from the beginning of time. ²⁶But now as the prophets* foretold and as the eternal God has commanded, this message is made known to all Gentiles everywhere, so that they too might believe and obey him. ²⁷All glory to the only wise God, through Jesus Christ, forever. Amen.

**16:20** Some manuscripts read *Lord Jesus Christ.*   **16:23** Some manuscripts add verse 24, *May the grace of our Lord Jesus Christ be with you all. Amen.* Still others add this sentence after verse 27.   **16:26** Greek *the prophetic writings.*

# 1 CORINTHIANS

*If one part suffers, all the parts suffer with it, and if one part is honored, all the parts are glad.*

1 CORINTHIANS 12:26

We need each other. That's a lesson serious illness drives home very quickly. Hopefully, your family is standing strong with you right now. Regardless, how is your spiritual family doing? Are you even a part of the "family of God"? We're not talking just about whether you're a believer going to heaven, but are you a part of His family right now here on earth? Do you have a worship home where people pray regularly with you, teach you God's Word, and help with practical needs in your life? If not, you are missing out on one of God's greatest gifts.

Sure, there are hypocrites in churches and swindling preachers and everything else rotten you can imagine, but don't let people's failures keep you from the truth that we were *created for community*. And if you aren't a part of a congregation because you've been hurt in the past—or for any other reason—we pray you won't let anything keep you from finding a worship home.

There are no perfect churches, as this letter from Paul to the church at Corinth confirms. These new believers were struggling with things like marriage, immorality, dietary laws, and lawsuits, so Paul paints for them a picture of what the family of God needs to look like.

He makes it clear that we were not meant to be lone rangers. God wants to touch you through His family. He wants *you* to touch others in His family, too. Find a spiritual family where together your joys can be doubled and your sorrows halved.

## Greetings from Paul

**1** This letter is from Paul, chosen by the will of God to be an apostle of Christ Jesus, and from our brother Sosthenes.

2 I am writing to God's church in Corinth,* to you who have been called by God to be his own holy people. He made you holy by means of Christ Jesus,* just as he did for all people everywhere who call on the name of our Lord Jesus Christ, their Lord and ours.

3 May God our Father and the Lord Jesus Christ give you grace and peace.

## Paul Gives Thanks to God

4 I always thank my God for you and for the gracious gifts he has given you, now that you belong to Christ Jesus. 5 Through him, God has enriched your church in every way—with all of your eloquent words and all of your knowledge. 6 This confirms that what I told you about Christ is true. 7 Now you have every spiritual gift you need as you eagerly wait for the return of our Lord Jesus Christ. 8 He will keep you strong to the end so that you will be free from all blame on the day when our Lord Jesus Christ returns. 9 God will do this, for he is faithful to do what he says, and he has invited you into partnership with his Son, Jesus Christ our Lord.

## Divisions in the Church

10 I appeal to you, dear brothers and sisters,* by the authority of our Lord Jesus Christ, to live in harmony with each other. Let there be no divisions in the church. Rather, be of one mind, united in thought and purpose. 11 For some members of Chloe's household have told me about your quarrels, my dear brothers and sisters. 12 Some of you are saying, "I am a follower of Paul." Others are saying, "I follow Apollos," or "I follow Peter,*" or "I follow only Christ."

13 Has Christ been divided into factions? Was I, Paul, crucified for you? Were any of you baptized in the name of Paul? Of course not! 14 I thank God that I did not baptize any of you except Crispus and Gaius, 15 for now no one can say they were baptized in my name. 16 (Oh yes, I also baptized the household of Stephanas, but I don't remember baptizing anyone else.) 17 For Christ didn't send me to baptize, but to preach the Good News—and not with clever speech, for fear that the cross of Christ would lose its power.

## The Wisdom of God

18 The message of the cross is foolish to those who are headed for destruction! But we who are being saved know it is the very power of God. 19 As the Scriptures say,

"I will destroy the wisdom of the wise
    and discard the intelligence of the
        intelligent."*

20 So where does this leave the philosophers, the scholars, and the world's brilliant debaters? God has made the wisdom of this world look foolish. 21 Since God in his wisdom saw to it that the world would never know him through human wisdom, he has used our foolish preaching to save those who believe. 22 It is foolish to the Jews, who ask for signs from heaven. And it is foolish to the Greeks, who seek human wisdom. 23 So when we preach that Christ was crucified, the Jews are offended and the Gentiles say it's all nonsense.

24 But to those called by God to salvation, both Jews and Gentiles,* Christ is the power of God and the wisdom of God. 25 This foolish plan of God is wiser than the wisest of human plans, and God's weakness is stronger than the greatest of human strength.

26 Remember, dear brothers and sisters, that few of you were wise in the world's eyes or powerful or wealthy* when God called you. 27 Instead, God chose things the world considers foolish in order to shame those who think they are wise. And he chose things that are powerless to shame those who are

1:2a *Corinth* was the capital city of Achaia, the southern region of the Greek peninsula.   1:2b Or *because you belong to Christ Jesus.*   1:10 Greek *brothers;* also in 1:11, 26.   1:12 Greek *Cephas.*   1:19 Isa 29:14.   1:24 Greek *and Greeks.*   1:26 Or *high born.*

powerful. 28 God chose things despised by the world,* things counted as nothing at all, and used them to bring to nothing what the world considers important. 29 As a result, no one can ever boast in the presence of God.

30 God has united you with Christ Jesus. For our benefit God made him to be wisdom itself. Christ made us right with God; he made us pure and holy, and he freed us from sin. 31 Therefore, as the Scriptures say, "If you want to boast, boast only about the LORD."*

### Paul's Message of Wisdom

**2** When I first came to you, dear brothers and sisters,* I didn't use lofty words and impressive wisdom to tell you God's secret plan.* 2 For I decided that while I was with you I would forget everything except Jesus Christ, the one who was crucified. 3 I came to you in weakness—timid and trembling. 4 And my message and my preaching were very plain. Rather than using clever and persuasive speeches, I relied only on the power of the Holy Spirit. 5 I did this so you would trust not in human wisdom but in the power of God.

6 Yet when I am among mature believers, I do speak with words of wisdom, but not the kind of wisdom that belongs to this world or to the rulers of this world, who are soon forgotten. 7 No, the wisdom we speak of is the mystery of God*—his plan that was previously hidden, even though he made it for our ultimate glory before the world began. 8 But the rulers of this world have not understood it; if they had, they would not have crucified our glorious Lord. 9 That is what the Scriptures mean when they say,

"No eye has seen, no ear has heard,
  and no mind has imagined
what God has prepared
  for those who love him."*

10 But* it was to us that God revealed these things by his Spirit. For his Spirit searches out everything and shows us God's deep secrets. 11 No one can know a person's thoughts except that person's own spirit, and no one

## WEAK disease vs. strong God
READ 1 CORINTHIANS 1:25

Researchers always are looking for ways to fool growing tumors or outsmart errant cells. Unfortunately, many diseases and conditions continue to flourish despite the best minds and muscle. But never forget that the serious illness you face is not smarter or stronger than the Lord. In fact, the "smartest," most powerful illness is foolish and weak in comparison to Him. Pray for those people who are looking for cures that they might look to God for answers and strength to defeat these attacks on our bodies. And pray for your physicians that God might supernaturally give them wisdom as they make decisions about your care.

can know God's thoughts except God's own Spirit. 12 And we have received God's Spirit (not the world's spirit), so we can know the wonderful things God has freely given us.

13 When we tell you these things, we do not use words that come from human wisdom. Instead, we speak words given to us by the Spirit, using the Spirit's words to explain spiritual truths.* 14 But people who aren't spiritual* can't receive these truths from God's Spirit. It all sounds foolish to them and they can't understand it, for only those who are spiritual can understand what the Spirit means. 15 Those who are spiritual can evaluate all things, but they themselves cannot be evaluated by others. 16 For,

"Who can know the LORD's thoughts?
  Who knows enough to teach him?"*

But we understand these things, for we have the mind of Christ.

### Paul and Apollos, Servants of Christ

**3** Dear brothers and sisters,* when I was with you I couldn't talk to you as I would to spiritual people.* I had to talk as though you belonged to this world or as though you were infants in the Christian life.* 2 I had to feed you with milk, not with solid food,

1:28 Or God chose those who are low born.   1:31 Jer 9:24.   2:1a Greek brothers.   2:1b Greek God's mystery; other manuscripts read God's testimony.   2:7 Greek But we speak God's wisdom in a mystery.   2:9 Isa 64:4.   2:10 Some manuscripts read For.   2:13 Or explaining spiritual truths in spiritual language, or explaining spiritual truths to spiritual people.   2:14 Or who don't have the Spirit; or who have only physical life.   2:16 Isa 40:13 (Greek version).   3:1a Greek Brothers.   3:1b Or to people who have the Spirit.   3:1c Greek in Christ.

because you weren't ready for anything stronger. And you still aren't ready, ³for you are still controlled by your sinful nature. You are jealous of one another and quarrel with each other. Doesn't that prove you are controlled by your sinful nature? Aren't you living like people of the world? ⁴When one of you says, "I am a follower of Paul," and another says, "I follow Apollos," aren't you acting just like people of the world?

⁵After all, who is Apollos? Who is Paul? We are only God's servants through whom you believed the Good News. Each of us did the work the Lord gave us. ⁶I planted the seed in your hearts, and Apollos watered it, but it was God who made it grow. ⁷It's not important who does the planting, or who does the watering. What's important is that God makes the seed grow. ⁸The one who plants and the one who waters work together with the same purpose. And both will be rewarded for their own hard work. ⁹For we are both God's workers. And you are God's field. You are God's building.

¹⁰Because of God's grace to me, I have laid the foundation like an expert builder. Now others are building on it. But whoever is building on this foundation must be very careful. ¹¹For no one can lay any foundation other than the one we already have—Jesus Christ.

¹²Anyone who builds on that foundation may use a variety of materials—gold, silver, jewels, wood, hay, or straw. ¹³But on the judgment day, fire will reveal what kind of work each builder has done. The fire will show if a person's work has any value. ¹⁴If the work survives, that builder will receive a reward. ¹⁵But if the work is burned up, the builder will suffer great loss. The builder will be saved, but like someone barely escaping through a wall of flames.

¹⁶Don't you realize that all of you together are the temple of God and that the Spirit of God lives in* you? ¹⁷God will destroy anyone who destroys this temple. For God's temple is holy, and you are that temple.

¹⁸Stop deceiving yourselves. If you think you are wise by this world's standards, you need to become a fool to be truly wise. ¹⁹For the wisdom of this world is foolishness to God. As the Scriptures say,

"He traps the wise
in the snare of their own cleverness."*

²⁰And again,

"The LORD knows the thoughts
of the wise;
he knows they are worthless."*

²¹So don't boast about following a particular human leader. For everything belongs to you—²²whether Paul or Apollos or Peter,* or the world, or life and death, or the present and the future. Everything belongs to you, ²³and you belong to Christ, and Christ belongs to God.

### Paul's Relationship with the Corinthians

**4** So look at Apollos and me as mere servants of Christ who have been put in charge of explaining God's mysteries. ²Now, a person who is put in charge as a manager must be faithful. ³As for me, it matters very little how I might be evaluated by you or by any human authority. I don't even trust my own judgment on this point. ⁴My conscience is clear, but that doesn't prove I'm right. It is the Lord himself who will examine me and decide.

⁵So don't make judgments about anyone ahead of time—before the Lord returns. For he will bring our darkest secrets to light and

3:16 Or *among.*   3:19 Job 5:13.   3:20 Ps 94:11.   3:22 Greek *Cephas.*

will reveal our private motives. Then God will give to each one whatever praise is due.

⁶Dear brothers and sisters,* I have used Apollos and myself to illustrate what I've been saying. If you pay attention to what I have quoted from the Scriptures,* you won't be proud of one of your leaders at the expense of another. ⁷For what gives you the right to make such a judgment? What do you have that God hasn't given you? And if everything you have is from God, why boast as though it were not a gift?

⁸You think you already have everything you need. You think you are already rich. You have begun to reign in God's kingdom without us! I wish you really were reigning already, for then we would be reigning with you. ⁹Instead, I sometimes think God has put us apostles on display, like prisoners of war at the end of a victor's parade, condemned to die. We have become a spectacle to the entire world—to people and angels alike.

¹⁰Our dedication to Christ makes us look like fools, but you claim to be so wise in Christ! We are weak, but you are so powerful! You are honored, but we are ridiculed. ¹¹Even now we go hungry and thirsty, and we don't have enough clothes to keep warm. We are often beaten and have no home. ¹²We work wearily with our own hands to earn our living. We bless those who curse us. We are patient with those who abuse us. ¹³We appeal gently when evil things are said about us. Yet we are treated like the world's garbage, like everybody's trash—right up to the present moment.

¹⁴I am not writing these things to shame you, but to warn you as my beloved children. ¹⁵For even if you had ten thousand others to teach you about Christ, you have only one spiritual father. For I became your father in Christ Jesus when I preached the Good News to you. ¹⁶So I urge you to imitate me.

¹⁷That's why I have sent Timothy, my beloved and faithful child in the Lord. He will remind you of how I follow Christ Jesus, just as I teach in all the churches wherever I go.

¹⁸Some of you have become arrogant, thinking I will not visit you again. ¹⁹But I will come—and soon—if the Lord lets me, and then I'll find out whether these arrogant people just give pretentious speeches or whether they really have God's power. ²⁰For the Kingdom of God is not just a lot of talk; it is living by God's power. ²¹Which do you choose? Should I come with a rod to punish you, or should I come with love and a gentle spirit?

## Paul Condemns Spiritual Pride

**5** I can hardly believe the report about the sexual immorality going on among you—something that even pagans don't do. I am told that a man in your church is living in sin with his stepmother.* ²You are so proud of yourselves, but you should be mourning in sorrow and shame. And you should remove this man from your fellowship.

³Even though I am not with you in person, I am with you in the Spirit.* And as though I were there, I have already passed judgment on this man ⁴in the name of the Lord Jesus. You must call a meeting of the church.* I will be present with you in spirit, and so will the power of our Lord Jesus. ⁵Then you must throw this man out and hand him over to Satan so that his sinful nature will be destroyed* and he himself* will be saved on the day the Lord* returns.

⁶Your boasting about this is terrible. Don't you realize that this sin is like a little yeast that spreads through the whole batch of dough? ⁷Get rid of the old "yeast" by removing this wicked person from among you. Then you will be like a fresh batch of dough made without yeast, which is what you really are. Christ, our Passover Lamb, has been sacrificed for us.* ⁸So let us celebrate the festival, not with the old bread* of wickedness and evil, but with the new bread* of sincerity and truth.

⁹When I wrote to you before, I told you not to associate with people who indulge in sexual sin. ¹⁰But I wasn't talking about unbelievers who indulge in sexual sin, or are greedy, or cheat people, or worship idols.

---

4:6a Greek *Brothers.*    4:6b Or *If you learn not to go beyond "what is written."*    5:1 Greek *his father's wife.*    5:3 Or *in spirit.*
5:4 Or *In the name of the Lord Jesus, you must call a meeting of the church.*    5:5a Or *so that his body will be destroyed;* Greek reads
*for the destruction of the flesh.*    5:5b Greek *and the spirit.*    5:5c Other manuscripts read *the Lord Jesus;* still others read *our Lord
Jesus Christ.*    5:7 Greek *has been sacrificed.*    5:8a Greek *not with old leaven.*    5:8b Greek *but with unleavened (bread).*

You would have to leave this world to avoid people like that. 11I meant that you are not to associate with anyone who claims to be a believer* yet indulges in sexual sin, or is greedy, or worships idols, or is abusive, or is a drunkard, or cheats people. Don't even eat with such people.

12It isn't my responsibility to judge outsiders, but it certainly is your responsibility to judge those inside the church who are sinning. 13God will judge those on the outside; but as the Scriptures say, "You must remove the evil person from among you."*

### Avoiding Lawsuits with Christians

**6** When one of you has a dispute with another believer, how dare you file a lawsuit and ask a secular court to decide the matter instead of taking it to other believers*! 2Don't you realize that someday we believers will judge the world? And since you are going to judge the world, can't you decide even these little things among yourselves? 3Don't you realize that we will judge angels? So you should surely be able to resolve ordinary disputes in this life. 4If you have legal disputes about such matters, why go to outside judges who are not respected by the church? 5I am saying this to shame you. Isn't there anyone in all the church who is wise enough to decide these issues? 6But instead, one believer* sues another—right in front of unbelievers!

7Even to have such lawsuits with one another is a defeat for you. Why not just accept the injustice and leave it at that? Why not let yourselves be cheated? 8Instead, you yourselves are the ones who do wrong and cheat even your fellow believers.*

9Don't you realize that those who do wrong will not inherit the Kingdom of God? Don't fool yourselves. Those who indulge in sexual sin, or who worship idols, or commit adultery, or are male prostitutes, or practice homosexuality, 10or are thieves, or greedy people, or drunkards, or are abusive, or cheat people—none of these will inherit the Kingdom of God. 11Some of you were once like that. But you were cleansed; you were made holy; you were made right with God

by calling on the name of the Lord Jesus Christ and by the Spirit of our God.

### Avoiding Sexual Sin

12You say, "I am allowed to do anything"—but not everything is good for you. And even though "I am allowed to do anything," I must not become a slave to anything. 13You say, "Food was made for the stomach, and the stomach for food." (This is true, though someday God will do away with both of them.) But you can't say that our bodies were made for sexual immorality. They were made for the Lord, and the Lord cares about our bodies. 14And God will raise us from the dead by his power, just as he raised our Lord from the dead.

15Don't you realize that your bodies are actually parts of Christ? Should a man take his body, which is part of Christ, and join it to a prostitute? Never! 16And don't you realize that if a man joins himself to a prostitute, he becomes one body with her? For the Scriptures say, "The two are united into one."* 17But the person who is joined to the Lord is one spirit with him.

18Run from sexual sin! No other sin so clearly affects the body as this one does. For sexual immorality is a sin against your own body. 19Don't you realize that your body is the temple of the Holy Spirit, who lives in you and was given to you by God? You do not belong to yourself, 20for God bought you with a high price. So you must honor God with your body.

### Instruction on Marriage •

**7** Now regarding the questions you asked in your letter. Yes, it is good to abstain from sexual relations.* 2But because there is so much sexual immorality, each man should have his own wife, and each woman should have her own husband.

3The husband should fulfill his wife's sexual needs, and the wife should fulfill her husband's needs. 4The wife gives authority over her body to her husband, and the husband gives authority over his body to his wife.

5Do not deprive each other of sexual relations, unless you both agree to refrain from sexual intimacy for a limited time so you can

5:11 Greek a brother.    5:13 Deut 17:7.    6:1 Greek God's holy people; also in 6:2.    6:6 Greek one brother.    6:8 Greek even the brothers.    6:16 Gen 2:24.    7:1 Or to live a celibate life; Greek reads It is good for a man not to touch a woman.

give yourselves more completely to prayer. Afterward, you should come together again so that Satan won't be able to tempt you because of your lack of self-control. 6I say this as a concession, not as a command. 7But I wish everyone were single, just as I am. Yet each person has a special gift from God, of one kind or another.

8So I say to those who aren't married and to widows—it's better to stay unmarried, just as I am. 9But if they can't control themselves, they should go ahead and marry. It's better to marry than to burn with lust.

10But for those who are married, I have a command that comes not from me, but from the Lord.* A wife must not leave her husband. 11But if she does leave him, let her remain single or else be reconciled to him. And the husband must not leave his wife.

12Now, I will speak to the rest of you, though I do not have a direct command from the Lord. If a Christian man* has a wife who is not a believer and she is willing to continue living with him, he must not leave her. 13And if a Christian woman has a husband who is not a believer and he is willing to continue living with her, she must not leave him. 14For the Christian wife brings holiness to her marriage, and the Christian husband* brings holiness to his marriage. Otherwise, your children would not be holy, but now they are holy. 15(But if the husband or wife who isn't a believer insists on leaving, let them go. In such cases the Christian husband or wife* is no longer bound to the other, for God has called you* to live in peace.) 16Don't you wives realize that your husbands might be saved because of you? And don't you husbands realize that your wives might be saved because of you?

17Each of you should continue to live in whatever situation the Lord has placed you, and remain as you were when God first called you. This is my rule for all the churches. 18For instance, a man who was circumcised before he became a believer should not try to reverse it. And the man who was uncircumcised when he became a believer should not be circumcised now. 19For it makes no difference

## GOD'S expensive purchase
READ 1 CORINTHIANS 6:19-20

Sometimes illness is a result of things we put into our bodies or ways we neglect them. Other times we do everything "right," but our bodies still break down. Nobody would disagree that a desire for good health should spur us to care for ourselves. But the Bible gives us an even bigger motivation—we need to honor God with our bodies because they belong to Him. He bought us at the highest price when He paid for us with His only Son's life. Whether you're sick or well, honor God with your body.

whether or not a man has been circumcised. The important thing is to keep God's commandments.

20Yes, each of you should remain as you were when God called you. 21Are you a slave? Don't let that worry you—but if you get a chance to be free, take it. 22And remember, if you were a slave when the Lord called you, you are now free in the Lord. And if you were free when the Lord called you, you are now a slave of Christ. 23God paid a high price for you, so don't be enslaved by the world.* 24Each of you, dear brothers and sisters,* should remain as you were when God first called you.

25Now regarding your question about the young women who are not yet married. I do not have a command from the Lord for them. But the Lord in his mercy has given me wisdom that can be trusted, and I will share it with you. 26Because of the present crisis,* I think it is best to remain as you are. 27If you have a wife, do not seek to end the marriage. If you do not have a wife, do not seek to get married. 28But if you do get married, it is not a sin. And if a young woman gets married, it is not a sin. However, those who get married at this time will have troubles, and I am trying to spare you those problems.

29But let me say this, dear brothers and

7:10 See Matt 5:32; 19:9; Mark 10:11-12; Luke 16:18.   7:12 Greek a brother.   7:14 Greek the brother.   7:15a Greek the brother or sister.   7:15b Some manuscripts read us.   7:23 Greek don't become slaves of people.   7:24 Greek brothers; also in 7:29.   7:26 Or the pressures of life.

sisters: The time that remains is very short. So from now on, those with wives should not focus only on their marriage. <sup>30</sup>Those who weep or who rejoice or who buy things should not be absorbed by their weeping or their joy or their possessions. <sup>31</sup>Those who use the things of the world should not become attached to them. For this world as we know it will soon pass away.

<sup>32</sup>I want you to be free from the concerns of this life. An unmarried man can spend his time doing the Lord's work and thinking how to please him. <sup>33</sup>But a married man has to think about his earthly responsibilities and how to please his wife. <sup>34</sup>His interests are divided. In the same way, a woman who is no longer married or has never been married can be devoted to the Lord and holy in body and in spirit. But a married woman has to think about her earthly responsibilities and how to please her husband. <sup>35</sup>I am saying this for your benefit, not to place restrictions on you. I want you to do whatever will help you serve the Lord best, with as few distractions as possible.

<sup>36</sup>But if a man thinks that he's treating his fiancée improperly and will inevitably give in to his passion, let him marry her as he wishes. It is not a sin. <sup>37</sup>But if he has decided firmly not to marry and there is no urgency and he can control his passion, he does well not to marry. <sup>38</sup>So the person who marries his fiancée does well, and the person who doesn't marry does even better.

<sup>39</sup>A wife is bound to her husband as long as he lives. If her husband dies, she is free to marry anyone she wishes, but only if he loves the Lord.* <sup>40</sup>But in my opinion it would be better for her to stay single, and I think I am giving you counsel from God's Spirit when I say this.

## Food Sacrificed to Idols

**8** Now regarding your question about food that has been offered to idols. Yes, we know that "we all have knowledge" about this issue. But while knowledge makes us feel important, it is love that strengthens the church. <sup>2</sup>Anyone who claims to know all the answers doesn't really know very much.

<sup>3</sup>But the person who loves God is the one whom God recognizes.*

<sup>4</sup>So, what about eating meat that has been offered to idols? Well, we all know that an idol is not really a god and that there is only one God. <sup>5</sup>There may be so-called gods both in heaven and on earth, and some people actually worship many gods and many lords. <sup>6</sup>But we know that there is only one God, the Father, who created everything, and we live for him. And there is only one Lord, Jesus Christ, through whom God made everything and through whom we have been given life.

<sup>7</sup>However, not all believers know this. Some are accustomed to thinking of idols as being real, so when they eat food that has been offered to idols, they think of it as the worship of real gods, and their weak consciences are violated. <sup>8</sup>It's true that we can't win God's approval by what we eat. We don't lose anything if we don't eat it, and we don't gain anything if we do.

<sup>9</sup>But you must be careful so that your freedom does not cause others with a weaker conscience to stumble. <sup>10</sup>For if others see you—with your "superior knowledge"—eating in the temple of an idol, won't they be encouraged to violate their conscience by eating food that has been offered to an idol? <sup>11</sup>So because of your superior knowledge, a weak believer* for whom Christ died will be destroyed. <sup>12</sup>And when you sin against other believers* by encouraging them to do something they believe is wrong, you are sinning against Christ. <sup>13</sup>So if what I eat causes another believer to sin, I will never eat meat again as long as I live—for I don't want to cause another believer to stumble.

## Paul Gives Up His Rights

**9** Am I not as free as anyone else? Am I not an apostle? Haven't I seen Jesus our Lord with my own eyes? Isn't it because of my work that you belong to the Lord? <sup>2</sup>Even if others think I am not an apostle, I certainly am to you. You yourselves are proof that I am the Lord's apostle.

<sup>3</sup>This is my answer to those who question my authority.* <sup>4</sup>Don't we have the right to live in your homes and share your meals?

**7:39** Greek *but only in the Lord*.   **8:3** Some manuscripts read *the person who loves has full knowledge*.   **8:11** Greek *brother*; also in 8:13.   **8:12** Greek *brothers*.   **9:3** Greek *those who examine me*.

5Don't we have the right to bring a Christian wife with us as the other apostles and the Lord's brothers do, and as Peter* does? 6Or is it only Barnabas and I who have to work to support ourselves?

7What soldier has to pay his own expenses? What farmer plants a vineyard and doesn't have the right to eat some of its fruit? What shepherd cares for a flock of sheep and isn't allowed to drink some of the milk? 8Am I expressing merely a human opinion, or does the law say the same thing? 9For the law of Moses says, "You must not muzzle an ox to keep it from eating as it treads out the grain."* Was God thinking only about oxen when he said this? 10Wasn't he actually speaking to us? Yes, it was written for us, so that the one who plows and the one who threshes the grain might both expect a share of the harvest.

11Since we have planted spiritual seed among you, aren't we entitled to a harvest of physical food and drink? 12If you support others who preach to you, shouldn't we have an even greater right to be supported? But we have never used this right. We would rather put up with anything than be an obstacle to the Good News about Christ.

13Don't you realize that those who work in the temple get their meals from the offerings brought to the temple? And those who serve at the altar get a share of the sacrificial offerings. 14In the same way, the Lord ordered that those who preach the Good News should be supported by those who benefit from it. 15Yet I have never used any of these rights. And I am not writing this to suggest that I want to start now. In fact, I would rather die than lose my right to boast about preaching without charge. 16Yet preaching the Good News is not something I can boast about. I am compelled by God to do it. How terrible for me if I didn't preach the Good News!

17If I were doing this on my own initiative, I would deserve payment. But I have no choice, for God has given me this sacred trust. 18What then is my pay? It is the opportunity to preach the Good News without charging anyone. That's why I never demand my rights when I preach the Good News.

19Even though I am a free man with no master, I have become a slave to all people to bring many to Christ. 20When I was with the Jews, I lived like a Jew to bring the Jews to Christ. When I was with those who follow the Jewish law, I too lived under that law. Even though I am not subject to the law, I did this so I could bring to Christ those who are under the law. 21When I am with the Gentiles who do not follow the Jewish law,* I too live apart from that law so I can bring them to Christ. But I do not ignore the law of God; I obey the law of Christ.

22When I am with those who are weak, I share their weakness, for I want to bring the weak to Christ. Yes, I try to find common ground with everyone, doing everything I can to save some. 23I do everything to spread the Good News and share in its blessings.

24Don't you realize that in a race everyone runs, but only one person gets the prize? So run to win! 25All athletes are disciplined in their training. They do it to win a prize that will fade away, but we do it for an eternal prize. 26So I run with purpose in every step. I am not just shadowboxing. 27I discipline my body like an athlete, training it to do what it should. Otherwise, I fear that after preaching to others I myself might be disqualified.

## Lessons from Israel's Idolatry

**10** I don't want you to forget, dear brothers and sisters,* about our ancestors in the wilderness long ago. All of them were guided by a cloud that moved ahead of them, and all of them walked through the sea on dry ground. 2In the cloud and in the sea, all of them were baptized as followers of Moses. 3All of them ate the same spiritual food, 4and all of them drank the same spiritual water. For they drank from the spiritual rock that traveled with them, and that rock was Christ. 5Yet God was not pleased with most of them, and their bodies were scattered in the wilderness.

6These things happened as a warning to us, so that we would not crave evil things as they did, 7or worship idols as some of them did. As the Scriptures say, "The people celebrated with feasting and drinking, and they indulged in pagan revelry."* 8And we must

9:5 Greek *Cephas.*   9:9 Deut 25:4.   9:21 Greek *those without the law.*   10:1 Greek *brothers.*   10:7 Exod 32:6.

not engage in sexual immorality as some of them did, causing 23,000 of them to die in one day.

⁹Nor should we put Christ* to the test, as some of them did and then died from snakebites. ¹⁰And don't grumble as some of them did, and then were destroyed by the angel of death. ¹¹These things happened to them as examples for us. They were written down to warn us who live at the end of the age.

¹²If you think you are standing strong, be careful not to fall. ¹³The temptations in your life are no different from what others experience. And God is faithful. He will not allow the temptation to be more than you can stand. When you are tempted, he will show you a way out so that you can endure.

¹⁴So, my dear friends, flee from the worship of idols. ¹⁵You are reasonable people. Decide for yourselves if what I am saying is true. ¹⁶When we bless the cup at the Lord's Table, aren't we sharing in the blood of Christ? And when we break the bread, aren't we sharing in the body of Christ? ¹⁷And though we are many, we all eat from one loaf of bread, showing that we are one body. ¹⁸Think about the people of Israel. Weren't they united by eating the sacrifices at the altar?

¹⁹What am I trying to say? Am I saying that food offered to idols has some signifi-cance, or that idols are real gods? ²⁰No, not at all. I am saying that these sacrifices are of-fered to demons, not to God. And I don't want you to participate with demons. ²¹You cannot drink from the cup of the Lord and from the cup of demons, too. You cannot eat at the Lord's Table and at the table of de-mons, too. ²²What? Do we dare to rouse the Lord's jealousy? Do you think we are stron-ger than he is?

²³You say, "I am allowed to do anything"*—but not everything is good for you. You say, "I am allowed to do anything"—but not every-thing is beneficial. ²⁴Don't be concerned for your own good but for the good of others.

²⁵So you may eat any meat that is sold in the marketplace without raising questions of conscience. ²⁶For "the earth is the Lord's, and everything in it."*

²⁷If someone who isn't a believer asks you home for dinner, accept the invitation if you want to. Eat whatever is offered to you with-out raising questions of conscience. ²⁸(But suppose someone tells you, "This meat was offered to an idol." Don't eat it, out of con-sideration for the conscience of the one who told you. ²⁹It might not be a matter of con-science for you, but it is for the other per-son.) For why should my freedom be limited by what someone else thinks? ³⁰If I can thank God for the food and enjoy it, why should I be condemned for eating it?

**10:9** Some manuscripts read *the Lord.*    **10:23** Greek *All things are lawful;* also in 10:23b.    **10:26** Ps 24:1.

## MORE than you can handle?
READ 1 CORINTHIANS 10:13

God doesn't give you more than you can handle. Does that phrase sound familiar? A lot of people console themselves with this thought even as the trials are piling up. Many people even quote this verse as "proof" this won't happen. We firmly believe there is never a time we are *tempted* to sin and simply have no choice but to give in. God always does provide a way of escape so we can withstand the temptation. However, we also believe that sometimes trials come into our lives that *are* more than we can bear on our own. Perhaps that already is true in your life.

Take heart. While your troubles may be more than you can handle, they are *not* more than God can handle. Even if your own resources are exhausted, God's resources never will be. Your strength might be sapped, but He still can move mountains. Everything may be chang-ing around you, but He always will be your Rock.

³¹So whether you eat or drink, or whatever you do, do it all for the glory of God. ³²Don't give offense to Jews or Gentiles* or the church of God. ³³I, too, try to please everyone in everything I do. I don't just do what is best for me; I do what is best for others so that many may be saved. ¹¹:¹And you should imitate me, just as I imitate Christ.

## Instructions for Public Worship

**11** ²I am so glad that you always keep me in your thoughts, and that you are following the teachings I passed on to you. ³But there is one thing I want you to know: The head of every man is Christ, the head of woman is man, and the head of Christ is God.* ⁴A man dishonors his head* if he covers his head while praying or prophesying. ⁵But a woman dishonors her head* if she prays or prophesies without a covering on her head, for this is the same as shaving her head. ⁶Yes, if she refuses to wear a head covering, she should cut off all her hair! But since it is shameful for a woman to have her hair cut or her head shaved, she should wear a covering.*

⁷A man should not wear anything on his head when worshiping, for man is made in God's image and reflects God's glory. And woman reflects man's glory. ⁸For the first man didn't come from woman, but the first woman came from man. ⁹And man was not made for woman, but woman was made for man. ¹⁰For this reason, and because the angels are watching, a woman should wear a covering on her head to show she is under authority.*

¹¹But among the Lord's people, women are not independent of men, and men are not independent of women. ¹²For although the first woman came from man, every other man was born from a woman, and everything comes from God.

¹³Judge for yourselves. Is it right for a woman to pray to God in public without covering her head? ¹⁴Isn't it obvious that it's disgraceful for a man to have long hair? ¹⁵And isn't long hair a woman's pride and

joy? For it has been given to her as a covering. ¹⁶But if anyone wants to argue about this, I simply say that we have no other custom than this, and neither do God's other churches.

## Order at the Lord's Supper

¹⁷But in the following instructions, I cannot praise you. For it sounds as if more harm than good is done when you meet together. ¹⁸First, I hear that there are divisions among you when you meet as a church, and to some extent I believe it. ¹⁹But, of course, there must be divisions among you so that you who have God's approval will be recognized!

²⁰When you meet together, you are not really interested in the Lord's Supper. ²¹For some of you hurry to eat your own meal without sharing with others. As a result, some go hungry while others get drunk. ²²What? Don't you have your own homes for eating and drinking? Or do you really want to disgrace God's church and shame the poor? What am I supposed to say? Do you want me to praise you? Well, I certainly will not praise you for this!

²³For I pass on to you what I received from the Lord himself. On the night when he was betrayed, the Lord Jesus took some bread ²⁴and gave thanks to God for it. Then he broke it in pieces and said, " This is my body, which is given for you.* Do this to remember me." ²⁵In the same way, he took the cup of wine after supper, saying, " This cup is the new covenant between God and his people—an agreement confirmed with my blood. Do this to remember me as often as you drink it." ²⁶For every time you eat this bread and drink this cup, you are announcing the Lord's death until he comes again.

²⁷So anyone who eats this bread or drinks this cup of the Lord unworthily is guilty of sinning against* the body and blood of the Lord. ²⁸That is why you should examine yourself before eating the bread and drinking the cup. ²⁹For if you eat the bread or drink the cup without honoring the body of

---

**10:32** Greek *or Greeks.*    **11:3** Or *to know: The source of every man is Christ, the source of woman is man, and the source of Christ is God.* Or *to know: Every man is responsible to Christ, a woman is responsible to her husband, and Christ is responsible to God.*    **11:4** Or *dishonors Christ.*    **11:5** Or *dishonors her husband.*    **11:6** Or *should have long hair.*    **11:10** Greek *should have an authority on her head.*    **11:24** Greek *which is for you;* other manuscripts read *which is broken for you.*    **11:27** Or *is responsible for.*

Christ,* you are eating and drinking God's judgment upon yourself. 30That is why many of you are weak and sick and some have even died.

31But if we would examine ourselves, we would not be judged by God in this way. 32Yet when we are judged by the Lord, we are being disciplined so that we will not be condemned along with the world.

33So, my dear brothers and sisters,* when you gather for the Lord's Supper, wait for each other. 34If you are really hungry, eat at home so you won't bring judgment upon yourselves when you meet together. I'll give you instructions about the other matters after I arrive.

## Spiritual Gifts

**12** Now, dear brothers and sisters,* regarding your question about the special abilities the Spirit gives us. I don't want you to misunderstand this. 2You know that when you were still pagans, you were led astray and swept along in worshiping speechless idols. 3So I want you to know that no one speaking by the Spirit of God will curse Jesus, and no one can say Jesus is Lord, except by the Holy Spirit.

4There are different kinds of spiritual gifts, but the same Spirit is the source of them all. 5There are different kinds of service, but we serve the same Lord. 6God works in different ways, but it is the same God who does the work in all of us.

7A spiritual gift is given to each of us so we can help each other. 8To one person the Spirit gives the ability to give wise advice*; to another the same Spirit gives a message of special knowledge.* 9The same Spirit gives great faith to another, and to someone else the one Spirit gives the gift of healing. 10He gives one person the power to perform miracles, and another the ability to prophesy. He gives someone else the ability to discern whether a message is from the Spirit of God or from another spirit. Still another person is given the ability to speak in unknown languages,* while another is given the ability to interpret what is being said. 11It is the one and only Spirit who distributes all these gifts. He alone decides which gift each person should have.

## One Body with Many Parts

12The human body has many parts, but the many parts make up one whole body. So it is with the body of Christ. 13Some of us are Jews, some are Gentiles,* some are slaves, and some are free. But we have all been baptized into one body by one Spirit, and we all share the same Spirit.*

14Yes, the body has many different parts, not just one part. 15If the foot says, "I am not a part of the body because I am not a hand," that does not make it any less a part of the body. 16And if the ear says, "I am not part of the body because I am not an eye," would that make it any less a part of the body? 17If the whole body were an eye, how would you hear? Or if your whole body were an ear, how would you smell anything?

18But our bodies have many parts, and God has put each part just where he wants it. 19How strange a body would be if it had only one part! 20Yes, there are many parts, but only one body. 21The eye can never say to the hand, "I don't need you." The head can't say to the feet, "I don't need you."

22In fact, some parts of the body that seem weakest and least important are actually the most necessary. 23And the parts we regard as less honorable are those we clothe with the greatest care. So we carefully protect those parts that should not be seen, 24while the more honorable parts do not require this special care. So God has put the body together such that extra honor and care are given to those parts that have less dignity. 25This makes for harmony among the members, so that all the members care for each other. 26If one part suffers, all the parts suffer with it, and if one part is honored, all the parts are glad.

27All of you together are Christ's body, and each of you is a part of it. 28Here are some of the parts God has appointed for the church:

first are apostles,
second are prophets,

**11:29** Greek *the body;* other manuscripts read *the Lord's body.* **11:33** Greek *brothers.* **12:1** Greek *brothers.* **12:8a** Or *gives a word of wisdom.* **12:8b** Or *gives a word of knowledge.* **12:10** Or *in various tongues;* also in 12:28, 30. **12:13a** Greek *some are Greeks.* **12:13b** Greek *we were all given one Spirit to drink.*

Love is patient and kind. Love is not jealous or boastful or proud or rude. It does not demand its own way. It is not irritable, and it keeps no record of being wronged. It does not rejoice about injustice but rejoices whenever the truth wins out. Love never gives up, never loses faith, is always hopeful, and endures through every circumstance.

1 CORINTHIANS 13:4-7

---

third are teachers,
then those who do miracles,
those who have the gift of healing,
those who can help others,
those who have the gift of leadership,
those who speak in unknown languages.

29 Are we all apostles? Are we all prophets? Are we all teachers? Do we all have the power to do miracles? 30 Do we all have the gift of healing? Do we all have the ability to speak in unknown languages? Do we all have the ability to interpret unknown languages? Of course not! 31 So you should earnestly desire the most helpful gifts.

But now let me show you a way of life that is best of all.

## Love Is the Greatest

**13** If I could speak all the languages of earth and of angels, but didn't love others, I would only be a noisy gong or a clanging cymbal. 2 If I had the gift of prophecy, and if I understood all of God's secret plans and possessed all knowledge, and if I had such faith that I could move mountains, but didn't love others, I would be nothing. 3 If I gave everything I have to the poor and even sacrificed my body, I could boast about it;* but if I didn't love others, I would have gained nothing.

4 Love is patient and kind. Love is not jeal-ous or boastful or proud 5 or rude. It does not demand its own way. It is not irritable, and it keeps no record of being wronged. 6 It does not rejoice about injustice but rejoices whenever the truth wins out. 7 Love never gives up, never loses faith, is always hopeful, and endures through every circumstance.

8 Prophecy and speaking in unknown lan-guages* and special knowledge will become useless. But love will last forever! 9 Now our knowledge is partial and incomplete, and even the gift of prophecy reveals only part of the whole picture! 10 But when the time of perfection comes, these partial things will become useless.

11 When I was a child, I spoke and thought and reasoned as a child. But when I grew up, I put away childish things. 12 Now we see things imperfectly, like puzzling reflections in a mirror, but then we will see everything with perfect clarity.* All that I know now is partial and incomplete, but then I will know everything completely, just as God now knows me completely.

13 Three things will last forever—faith, hope, and love—and the greatest of these is love.

## Tongues and Prophecy

**14** Let love be your highest goal! But you should also desire the special abilities the Spirit gives—especially the ability to

13:3 Some manuscripts read *sacrificed my body to be burned.*   13:8 Or *in tongues.*   13:12 Greek *see face to face.*

prophecy. [2]For if you have the ability to speak in tongues,* you will be talking only to God, since people won't be able to understand you. You will be speaking by the power of the Spirit,* but it will all be mysterious. [3]But one who prophesies strengthens others, encourages them, and comforts them. [4]A person who speaks in tongues is strengthened personally, but one who speaks a word of prophecy strengthens the entire church.

[5]I wish you could all speak in tongues, but even more I wish you could all prophesy. For prophecy is greater than speaking in tongues, unless someone interprets what you are saying so that the whole church will be strengthened.

[6]Dear brothers and sisters,* if I should come to you speaking in an unknown language,* how would that help you? But if I bring you a revelation or some special knowledge or prophecy or teaching, that will be helpful. [7]Even lifeless instruments like the flute or the harp must play the notes clearly, or no one will recognize the melody. [8]And if the bugler doesn't sound a clear call, how will the soldiers know they are being called to battle?

[9]It's the same for you. If you speak to people in words they don't understand, how will they know what you are saying? You might as well be talking into empty space.

[10]There are many different languages in the world, and every language has meaning. [11]But if I don't understand a language, I will be a foreigner to someone who speaks it, and the one who speaks it will be a foreigner to me. [12]And the same is true for you. Since you are so eager to have the special abilities the Spirit gives, seek those that will strengthen the whole church.

[13]So anyone who speaks in tongues should pray also for the ability to interpret what has been said. [14]For if I pray in tongues, my spirit is praying, but I don't understand what I am saying.

[15]Well then, what shall I do? I will pray in the spirit,* and I will also pray in words I understand. I will sing in the spirit, and I will also sing in words I understand. [16]For if you

praise God only in the spirit, how can those who don't understand you praise God along with you? How can they join you in giving thanks when they don't understand what you are saying? [17]You will be giving thanks very well, but it won't strengthen the people who hear you.

[18]I thank God that I speak in tongues more than any of you. [19]But in a church meeting I would rather speak five understandable words to help others than ten thousand words in an unknown language.

[20]Dear brothers and sisters, don't be childish in your understanding of these things. Be innocent as babies when it comes to evil, but be mature in understanding matters of this kind. [21]It is written in the Scriptures*:

"I will speak to my own people
    through strange languages
    and through the lips of foreigners.
But even then, they will not listen
        to me,"*
    says the LORD.

[22]So you see that speaking in tongues is a sign, not for believers, but for unbelievers. Prophecy, however, is for the benefit of believers, not unbelievers. [23]Even so, if unbelievers or people who don't understand these things come into your church meeting and hear everyone speaking in an unknown language, they will think you are crazy. [24]But if all of you are prophesying, and unbelievers or people who don't understand these things come into your meeting, they will be convicted of sin and judged by what you say. [25]As they listen, their secret thoughts will be exposed, and they will fall to their knees and worship God, declaring, "God is truly here among you."

### A Call to Orderly Worship

[26]Well, my brothers and sisters, let's summarize. When you meet together, one will sing, another will teach, another will tell some special revelation God has given, one will speak in tongues, and another will interpret what is said. But everything that is done must strengthen all of you.

**14:2a** Or *in unknown languages;* also in 14:4, 5, 13, 14, 18, 22, 26, 27, 28, 39.   **14:2b** Or *speaking in your spirit.*   **14:6a** Greek *brothers;* also in 14:20, 26, 39.   **14:6b** Or *in tongues;* also in 14:19, 23.   **14:15** Or *in the Spirit;* also in 14:15b, 16.   **14:21a** Greek *in the law.*   **14:21b** Isa 28:11-12.

27No more than two or three should speak in tongues. They must speak one at a time, and someone must interpret what they say. 28But if no one is present who can interpret, they must be silent in your church meeting and speak in tongues to God privately.

29Let two or three people prophesy, and let the others evaluate what is said. 30But if someone is prophesying and another person receives a revelation from the Lord, the one who is speaking must stop. 31In this way, all who prophesy will have a turn to speak, one after the other, so that everyone will learn and be encouraged. 32Remember that people who prophesy are in control of their spirit and can take turns. 33For God is not a God of disorder but of peace, as in all the meetings of God's holy people.*

34Women should be silent during the church meetings. It is not proper for them to speak. They should be submissive, just as the law says. 35If they have any questions, they should ask their husbands at home, for it is improper for women to speak in church meetings.*

36Or do you think God's word originated with you Corinthians? Are you the only ones to whom it was given? 37If you claim to be a prophet or think you are spiritual, you should recognize that what I am saying is a command from the Lord himself. 38But if you do not recognize this, you yourself will not be recognized.*

39So, my dear brothers and sisters, be eager to prophesy, and don't forbid speaking in tongues. 40But be sure that everything is done properly and in order.

## The Resurrection of Christ

**15** Let me now remind you, dear brothers and sisters,* of the Good News I preached to you before. You welcomed it then, and you still stand firm in it. 2It is this Good News that saves you if you continue to believe the message I told you—unless, of course, you believed something that was never true in the first place.*

3I passed on to you what was most impor-

tant and what had also been passed on to me. Christ died for our sins, just as the Scriptures said. 4He was buried, and he was raised from the dead on the third day, just as the Scriptures said. 5He was seen by Peter* and then by the Twelve. 6After that, he was seen by more than 500 of his followers* at one time, most of whom are still alive, though some have died. 7Then he was seen by James and later by all the apostles. 8Last of all, as though I had been born at the wrong time, I also saw him. 9For I am the least of all the apostles. In fact, I'm not even worthy to be called an apostle after the way I persecuted God's church.

10But whatever I am now, it is all because God poured out his special favor on me—and not without results. For I have worked harder than any of the other apostles; yet it was not I but God who was working through me by his grace. 11So it makes no difference whether I preach or they preach, for we all preach the same message you have already believed.

## The Resurrection of the Dead

12But tell me this—since we preach that Christ rose from the dead, why are some of you saying there will be no resurrection of the dead? 13For if there is no resurrection of the dead, then Christ has not been raised either. 14And if Christ has not been raised, then all our preaching is useless, and your faith is useless. 15And we apostles would all be lying about God—for we have said that God raised Christ from the grave. But that can't be true if there is no resurrection of the dead. 16And if there is no resurrection of the dead, then Christ has not been raised. 17And if Christ has not been raised, then your faith is useless and you are still guilty of your sins. 18In that case, all who have died believing in Christ are lost! 19And if our hope in Christ is only for this life, we are more to be pitied than anyone in the world.

20But in fact, Christ has been raised from the dead. He is the first of a great harvest of all who have died.

21So you see, just as death came into the

---

14:33 The phrase *as in all the meetings of God's holy people* could instead be joined to the beginning of 14:34.    14:35 Some manuscripts place verses 34-35 after 14:40.    14:38 Some manuscripts read *If you are ignorant of this, stay in your ignorance.* 15:1 Greek *brothers;* also in 15:31, 50, 58.    15:2 Or *unless you never believed it in the first place.*    15:5 Greek *Cephas.*    15:6 Greek *the brothers.*

world through a man, now the resurrection from the dead has begun through another man. 22Just as everyone dies because we all belong to Adam, everyone who belongs to Christ will be given new life. 23But there is an order to this resurrection: Christ was raised as the first of the harvest; then all who belong to Christ will be raised when he comes back.

24After that the end will come, when he will turn the Kingdom over to God the Father, having destroyed every ruler and authority and power. 25For Christ must reign until he humbles all his enemies beneath his feet. 26And the last enemy to be destroyed is death. 27For the Scriptures say, "God has put all things under his authority."* (Of course, when it says "all things are under his authority," that does not include God himself, who gave Christ his authority.) 28Then, when all things are under his authority, the Son will put himself under God's authority, so that God, who gave his Son authority over all things, will be utterly supreme over everything everywhere.

29If the dead will not be raised, what point is there in people being baptized for those who are dead? Why do it unless the dead will someday rise again?

30And why should we ourselves risk our lives hour by hour? 31For I swear, dear brothers and sisters, that I face death daily. This is as certain as my pride in what Christ Jesus our Lord has done in you. 32And what value was there in fighting wild beasts—those people of Ephesus*—if there will be no resurrection from the dead? And if there is no resurrection, "Let's feast and drink, for tomorrow we die!"* 33Don't be fooled by those who say such things, for "bad company corrupts good character." 34Think carefully about what is right, and stop sinning. For to your shame I say that some of you don't know God at all.

## The Resurrection Body

35But someone may ask, "How will the dead be raised? What kind of bodies will they have?" 36What a foolish question! When you put a seed into the ground, it doesn't grow into a plant unless it dies first. 37And what you put in the ground is not the plant that will grow, but only a bare seed of wheat or whatever you are planting. 38Then God gives it the new body he wants it to have. A different plant grows from each kind of seed. 39Similarly there are different kinds of flesh—one kind for humans, another for animals, another for birds, and another for fish.

40There are also bodies in the heavens and bodies on the earth. The glory of the heavenly bodies is different from the glory of the earthly bodies. 41The sun has one

15:27 Ps 8:6.   15:32a Greek *fighting wild beasts in Ephesus.*   15:32b Isa 22:13.

# WANT a new body?
READ 1 CORINTHIANS 15:35-44, 50-55

When you think about the complexity of the human body, it's actually pretty amazing that it doesn't fall apart more often! Think about it: 656 muscles, 206 bones, about 5 feet of colon, and estimates of 100,000 billion cells—that's a lot of stuff to go wrong!

But it can be very frustrating to have a body that is not working properly. Maybe you've even wished you could trade in your worn-out model. Perhaps get something a little newer, less rusty, and with a lot fewer trips to the mechanic! One day you will get to make such a trade. But it won't be for something just a little better; it will be the swap of a lifetime.

You'll get to trade this used-up body for a new one that will never grow weary or get diseased. And it won't be backed by a 100,000-mile guarantee—or even a 100,000-year warranty. This new one will be guaranteed for all eternity. Now that's a good trade.

kind of glory, while the moon and stars each have another kind. And even the stars differ from each other in their glory.

42 It is the same way with the resurrection of the dead. Our earthly bodies are planted in the ground when we die, but they will be raised to live forever. 43 Our bodies are buried in brokenness, but they will be raised in glory. They are buried in weakness, but they will be raised in strength. 44 They are buried as natural human bodies, but they will be raised as spiritual bodies. For just as there are natural bodies, there are also spiritual bodies.

45 The Scriptures tell us, "The first man, Adam, became a living person."* But the last Adam—that is, Christ—is a life-giving Spirit. 46 What comes first is the natural body, then the spiritual body comes later. 47 Adam, the first man, was made from the dust of the earth, while Christ, the second man, came from heaven. 48 Earthly people are like the earthly man, and heavenly people are like the heavenly man. 49 Just as we are now like the earthly man, we will someday be like* the heavenly man.

50 What I am saying, dear brothers and sisters, is that our physical bodies cannot inherit the Kingdom of God. These dying bodies cannot inherit what will last forever.

51 But let me reveal to you a wonderful secret. We will not all die, but we will all be transformed! 52 It will happen in a moment, in the blink of an eye, when the last trumpet is blown. For when the trumpet sounds, those who have died will be raised to live forever. And we who are living will also be transformed. 53 For our dying bodies must be transformed into bodies that will never die; our mortal bodies must be transformed into immortal bodies.

54 Then, when our dying bodies have been transformed into bodies that will never die,* this Scripture will be fulfilled:

"Death is swallowed up in
victory.*
55 O death, where is your victory?
O death, where is your sting?*"

56 For sin is the sting that results in death, and the law gives sin its power. 57 But thank God! He gives us victory over sin and death through our Lord Jesus Christ.

58 So, my dear brothers and sisters, be strong and immovable. Always work enthusiastically for the Lord, for you know that nothing you do for the Lord is ever useless.

## The Collection for Jerusalem

**16** Now regarding your question about the money being collected for God's people in Jerusalem. You should follow the same procedure I gave to the churches in Galatia. 2 On the first day of each week, you should each put aside a portion of the money you have earned. Don't wait until I get there and then try to collect it all at once. 3 When I come, I will write letters of recommendation for the messengers you choose to deliver your gift to Jerusalem. 4 And if it seems appropriate for me to go along, they can travel with me.

## Paul's Final Instructions

5 I am coming to visit you after I have been to Macedonia,* for I am planning to travel through Macedonia. 6 Perhaps I will stay awhile with you, possibly all winter, and then you can send me on my way to my next destination. 7 This time I don't want to make just a short visit and then go right on. I want to come and stay awhile, if the Lord will let me. 8 In the meantime, I will be staying here at Ephesus until the Festival of Pentecost. 9 There is a wide-open door for a great work here, although many oppose me.

10 When Timothy comes, don't intimidate him. He is doing the Lord's work, just as I am. 11 Don't let anyone treat him with contempt. Send him on his way with your blessing when he returns to me. I expect him to come with the other believers.*

12 Now about our brother Apollos—I urged him to visit you with the other believers, but he was not willing to go right now.

15:45 Gen 2:7.   15:49 Some manuscripts read *let us be like.*   15:54a Some manuscripts add *and our mortal bodies have been transformed into immortal bodies.*   15:54b Isa 25:8.   15:55 Hos 13:14 (Greek version).   16:5 *Macedonia* was in the northern region of Greece.   16:11 Greek *with the brothers;* also in 16:12.

He will see you later when he has the opportunity.

13Be on guard. Stand firm in the faith. Be courageous.* Be strong. 14And do everything with love.

15 You know that Stephanas and his household were the first of the harvest of believers in Greece,* and they are spending their lives in service to God's people. I urge you, dear brothers and sisters,* 16to submit to them and others like them who serve with such devotion. 17I am very glad that Stephanas, Fortunatus, and Achaicus have come here. They have been providing the help you weren't here to give me. 18They have been a wonderful encouragement to me, as they have been to you. You must show your appreciation to all who serve so well.

## Paul's Final Greetings

19The churches here in the province of Asia* send greetings in the Lord, as do Aquila and Priscilla* and all the others who gather in their home for church meetings. 20All the brothers and sisters here send greetings to you. Greet each other with Christian love.*

21 HERE IS MY GREETING IN MY OWN HANDWRITING—PAUL.

22If anyone does not love the Lord, that person is cursed. Our Lord, come!*

23 May the grace of the Lord Jesus be with you.

24My love to all of you in Christ Jesus.*

16:13 Greek *Be men.*    16:15a Greek *in Achaia,* the southern region of the Greek peninsula.    16:15b Greek *brothers;* also in 16:20.
16:19a *Asia* was a Roman province in what is now western Turkey.    16:19b Greek *Prisca.*    16:20 Greek *with a sacred kiss.*
16:22 From Aramaic, *Marana tha.* Some manuscripts read *Maran atha,* "Our Lord has come."    16:24 Some manuscripts add *Amen.*

# 2 CORINTHIANS

*He comforts us in all our troubles so that we can comfort others.*

2 CORINTHIANS 1:4

"I know exactly how you feel."

Ever have someone try to encourage you with those words? While it's doubtful anyone knows *exactly* what you're feeling, it *is* great when those who have walked in our shoes come alongside us during hard times. These special people seem to know when to speak and when to be silent; when to drop by and when to drop a note. Their prayers seem to have more strength as they put into words what we're having trouble expressing. While they may not have the power to change our circumstances, they are empowered with a comfort that touches us in the middle of our trials. These are the ones who have been comforted by God during their own "dark night of the soul" and now share that same comfort with others.

Paul's second letter to the church at Corinth speaks a great deal about triumphing over adversity. (Paul was speaking from firsthand experience as the church had wronged him personally, even questioning his authority as an apostle of God.) One of the good things Paul says can come out of our troubles is a newfound ability to empathize with others and comfort them during their difficult times.

Why don't you begin to triumph over your adversity today and ask God, the source of all comfort, to bring His comfort to you so that you can share it with others in similar circumstances? It's a prayer He loves to answer.

## Greetings from Paul

**1** This letter is from Paul, chosen by the will of God to be an apostle of Christ Jesus, and from our brother Timothy.

I am writing to God's church in Corinth and to all of his holy people throughout Greece.*

2May God our Father and the Lord Jesus Christ give you grace and peace.

## God Offers Comfort to All

3All praise to God, the Father of our Lord Jesus Christ. God is our merciful Father and the source of all comfort. 4He comforts us in all our troubles so that we can comfort others. When they are troubled, we will be able to give them the same comfort God has given us. 5For the more we suffer for Christ, the more God will shower us with his comfort through Christ. 6Even when we are weighed down with troubles, it is for your comfort and salvation! For when we ourselves are comforted, we will certainly comfort you. Then you can patiently endure the same things we suffer. 7We are confident that as you share in our sufferings, you will also share in the comfort God gives us.

8We think you ought to know, dear brothers and sisters,* about the trouble we went through in the province of Asia. We were crushed and overwhelmed beyond our ability to endure, and we thought we would never live through it. 9In fact, we expected to die. But as a result, we stopped relying on ourselves and learned to rely only on God, who raises the dead. 10And he did rescue us from mortal danger, and he will rescue us again. We have placed our confidence in him, and he will continue to rescue us. 11And you are helping us by praying for us. Then many people will give thanks because God has graciously answered so many prayers for our safety.

## Paul's Change of Plans

12We can say with confidence and a clear conscience that we have lived with a God-given holiness* and sincerity in all our dealings. We have depended on God's grace, not on our own human wisdom. That is how we have conducted ourselves before the world, and especially toward you. 13Our letters have been straightforward, and there is nothing written between the lines and nothing you can't understand. I hope someday you will fully understand us, 14even if you don't understand us now. Then on the day when the Lord Jesus* returns, you will be proud of us in the same way we are proud of you.

15Since I was so sure of your understanding and trust, I wanted to give you a double blessing by visiting you twice— 16first on my way to Macedonia and again when I returned from Macedonia.* Then you could send me on my way to Judea.

17You may be asking why I changed my plan. Do you think I make my plans carelessly? Do you think I am like people of the world who say "Yes" when they really mean "No"? 18As surely as God is faithful, my word to you does not waver between "Yes" and "No." 19For Jesus Christ, the Son of God, does not waver between "Yes" and "No." He is the one whom Silas,* Timothy, and I preached to you, and as God's ultimate "Yes," he always does what he says. 20For all of God's promises have been fulfilled in Christ with a resounding "Yes!" And through Christ, our "Amen" (which means "Yes") ascends to God for his glory.

21It is God who enables us, along with you, to stand firm for Christ. He has commissioned us, 22and he has identified us as his own by placing the Holy Spirit in our hearts as the first installment that guarantees everything he has promised us.

23Now I call upon God as my witness that I am telling the truth. The reason I didn't return to Corinth was to spare you from a severe rebuke. 24But that does not mean we want to dominate you by telling you how to

**1:1** Greek *Achaia,* the southern region of the Greek peninsula.   **1:8** Greek *brothers.*   **1:12** Some manuscripts read *honesty.*
**1:14** Some manuscripts read *our Lord Jesus.*   **1:16** *Macedonia* was in the northern region of Greece.   **1:19** Greek *Silvanus.*

put your faith into practice. We want to work together with you so you will be full of joy, for it is by your own faith that you stand firm.

**2** So I decided that I would not bring you grief with another painful visit. [2] For if I cause you grief, who will make me glad? Certainly not someone I have grieved. [3] That is why I wrote to you as I did, so that when I do come, I won't be grieved by the very ones who ought to give me the greatest joy. Surely you all know that my joy comes from your being joyful. [4] I wrote that letter in great anguish, with a troubled heart and many tears. I didn't want to grieve you, but I wanted to let you know how much love I have for you.

### Forgiveness for the Sinner

[5] I am not overstating it when I say that the man who caused all the trouble hurt all of you more than he hurt me. [6] Most of you opposed him, and that was punishment enough. [7] Now, however, it is time to forgive and comfort him. Otherwise he may be overcome by discouragement. [8] So I urge you now to reaffirm your love for him.

[9] I wrote to you as I did to test you and see if you would fully comply with my instructions. [10] When you forgive this man, I forgive him, too. And when I forgive whatever needs to be forgiven, I do so with Christ's authority for your benefit, [11] so that Satan will not outsmart us. For we are familiar with his evil schemes.

[12] When I came to the city of Troas to preach the Good News of Christ, the Lord opened a door of opportunity for me. [13] But I had no peace of mind because my dear brother Titus hadn't yet arrived with a report from you. So I said good-bye and went on to Macedonia to find him.

### Ministers of the New Covenant

[14] But thank God! He has made us his captives and continues to lead us along in Christ's triumphal procession. Now he uses us to spread the knowledge of Christ everywhere, like a sweet perfume. [15] Our lives are a Christ-like fragrance rising up to God. But this fragrance is perceived differently by

## BEEN there, done that
READ 2 CORINTHIANS 1:8-10

Are you at the end of your rope? Out of medical options? On borrowed time? The apostle Paul has been there and done that. He and his fellow travelers ran into some serious trouble on one of their journeys and even expected to die. With their backs up against the wall, they came to the end of themselves. And that's when everything changed. Why? Because they stopped relying on themselves and learned to rely on God.

You'll never know how much you have in Him until He's all you have.

those who are being saved and by those who are perishing. [16] To those who are perishing, we are a dreadful smell of death and doom. But to those who are being saved, we are a life-giving perfume. And who is adequate for such a task as this?

[17] You see, we are not like the many hucksters* who preach for personal profit. We preach the word of God with sincerity and with Christ's authority, knowing that God is watching us.

**3** Are we beginning to praise ourselves again? Are we like others, who need to bring you letters of recommendation, or who ask you to write such letters on their behalf? Surely not! [2] The only letter of recommendation we need is you yourselves. Your lives are a letter written in our* hearts; everyone can read it and recognize our good work among you. [3] Clearly, you are a letter from Christ showing the result of our ministry among you. This "letter" is written not with pen and ink, but with the Spirit of the living God. It is carved not on tablets of stone, but on human hearts.

[4] We are confident of all this because of our great trust in God through Christ. [5] It is not that we think we are qualified to do anything on our own. Our qualification comes from God. [6] He has enabled us to be ministers of

2:17 Some manuscripts read *the rest of the hucksters.*     3:2 Some manuscripts read *your.*

his new covenant. This is a covenant not of written laws, but of the Spirit. The old written covenant ends in death; but under the new covenant, the Spirit gives life.

### The Glory of the New Covenant

[7] The old way,* with laws etched in stone, led to death, though it began with such glory that the people of Israel could not bear to look at Moses' face. For his face shone with the glory of God, even though the brightness was already fading away. [8] Shouldn't we expect far greater glory under the new way, now that the Holy Spirit is giving life? [9] If the old way, which brings condemnation, was glorious, how much more glorious is the new way, which makes us right with God! [10] In fact, that first glory was not glorious at all compared with the overwhelming glory of the new way. [11] So if the old way, which has been replaced, was glorious, how much more glorious is the new, which remains forever!

[12] Since this new way gives us such confidence, we can be very bold. [13] We are not like Moses, who put a veil over his face so the people of Israel would not see the glory, even though it was destined to fade away. [14] But the people's minds were hardened, and to this day whenever the old covenant is being read, the same veil covers their minds so they cannot understand the truth. And this veil can be removed only by believing in Christ. [15] Yes, even today when they read Moses' writings, their hearts are covered with that veil, and they do not understand.

[16] But whenever someone turns to the Lord, the veil is taken away. [17] For the Lord is the Spirit, and wherever the Spirit of the Lord is, there is freedom. [18] So all of us who have had that veil removed can see and reflect the glory of the Lord. And the Lord—who is the Spirit—makes us more and more like him as we are changed into his glorious image.

### Treasure in Fragile Clay Jars

**4** Therefore, since God in his mercy has given us this new way,* we never give up. [2] We reject all shameful deeds and underhanded methods. We don't try to trick anyone or distort the word of God. We tell the truth before God, and all who are honest know this.

[3] If the Good News we preach is hidden behind a veil, it is hidden only from people who are perishing. [4] Satan, who is the god of this world, has blinded the minds of those who don't believe. They are unable to see the glorious light of the Good News. They don't understand this message about the glory of Christ, who is the exact likeness of God.

[5] You see, we don't go around preaching about ourselves. We preach that Jesus Christ is Lord, and we ourselves are your servants for Jesus' sake. [6] For God, who said, "Let there be light in the darkness," has made this light shine in our hearts so we could know the glory of God that is seen in the face of Jesus Christ.

[7] We now have this light shining in our hearts, but we ourselves are like fragile clay jars containing this great treasure.* This makes it clear that our great power is from God, not from ourselves.

[8] We are pressed on every side by troubles, but we are not crushed. We are perplexed, but not driven to despair. [9] We are hunted down, but never abandoned by God. We get knocked down, but we are not destroyed. [10] Through suffering, our bodies continue to share in the death of Jesus so that the life of Jesus may also be seen in our bodies.

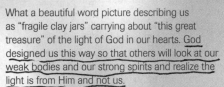

## PERPLEXED
### but not despairing
READ 2 CORINTHIANS 4:7-10

What a beautiful word picture describing us as "fragile clay jars" carrying about "this great treasure" of the light of God in our hearts. <u>God designed us this way so that others will look at our weak bodies and our strong spirits and realize the light is from Him and not us.</u>

The Bible never promises us a rose garden, but it does promise a light at the end of the tunnel (and *no*, it's not a train!). We will be pressed on every side but not crushed; perplexed but not despairing; hunted down but not abandoned; knocked down but not destroyed. Keep your eyes on the treasure inside; not on the cracked jar outside.

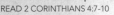

**3:7** Or *ministry;* also in 3:8, 9, 10, 11, 12. **4:1** Or *ministry.*
**4:7** Greek *We now have this treasure in clay jars.*

225

CORINTHIANS 5

**11**Yes, we live under constant danger of death because we serve Jesus, so that the life of Jesus will be evident in our dying bodies. **12**So we live in the face of death, but this has resulted in eternal life for you.

**13**But we continue to preach because we have the same kind of faith the psalmist had when he said, "I believed in God, so I spoke."* **14**We know that God, who raised the Lord Jesus,* will also raise us with Jesus and present us to himself together with you. **15**All of this is for your benefit. And as God's grace reaches more and more people, there will be great thanksgiving, and God will receive more and more glory.

**16**That is why we never give up. Though our bodies are dying, our spirits are* being renewed every day. **17**For our present troubles are small and won't last very long. Yet they produce for us a glory that vastly outweighs them and will last forever! **18**So we don't look at the troubles we can see now; rather, we fix our gaze on things that cannot be seen. For the things we see now will soon be gone, but the things we cannot see will last forever.

## New Bodies

**5** **1**For we know that when this earthly tent we live in is taken down (that is, when we die and leave this earthly body), we will have a house in heaven, an eternal body made for us by God himself and not by human hands. **2**We grow weary in our present bodies, and we long to put on our heavenly bodies like new clothing. **3**For we will put on heavenly bodies; we will not be spirits without bodies.* **4**While we live in these earthly bodies, we groan and sigh, but it's not that we want to die and get rid of these bodies that clothe us. Rather, we want to put on our new bodies so that these dying bodies will be swallowed up by life. **5**God himself has prepared us for this, and as a guarantee he has given us his Holy Spirit.

**6**So we are always confident, even though we know that as long as we live in these bodies we are not at home with the Lord. **7**For we live by believing and not by seeing. **8**Yes, we are fully confident, and we would rather be away from these earthly bodies, for then we will be at home with the Lord. **9**So whether we are here in this body or away from this body, our goal is to please him. **10**For we must all stand before Christ to be judged. We will each receive whatever we deserve for the good or evil we have done in this earthly body.

## We Are God's Ambassadors

**11**Because we understand our fearful responsibility to the Lord, we work hard to persuade others. God knows we are sincere, and I hope you know this, too. **12**Are we commending ourselves to you again? No, we are giving you a reason to be proud of us,* so you can answer those who brag about having a spectacular ministry rather than having a sincere heart. **13**If it seems we are crazy, it is to bring glory to God. And if we are in our right minds, it is for your benefit. **14**Either way, Christ's love controls us.* Since we believe that Christ died for all, we also believe that we have all died to our old life.* **15**He died for everyone so that those who receive his new life will no longer live for themselves. Instead, they will live for Christ, who died and was raised for them.

**16**So we have stopped evaluating others from a human point of view. At one time we thought of Christ merely from a human point of view. How differently we know him now! **17**This means that anyone who belongs to Christ has become a new person. The old life is gone; a new life has begun!

**18**And all of this is a gift from God, who brought us back to himself through Christ. And God has given us this task of reconciling people to him. **19**For God was in Christ, reconciling the world to himself, no longer counting people's sins against them. And he gave us this wonderful message of reconciliation. **20**So we are Christ's ambassadors; God is making his appeal through us. We speak for Christ when we plead, "Come back to God!" **21**For God made Christ, who never sinned, to be the offering for our sin,* so that we could be made right with God through Christ.

**4:13** Ps 116:10. **4:14** Some manuscripts read *who raised Jesus.* **4:16** Greek *our inner being is.* **5:3** Greek *we will not be naked.* **5:12** Some manuscripts read *proud of yourselves.* **5:14a** Or *urges us on.* **5:14b** Greek *Since one died for all, then all died.* **5:21** Or *to become sin itself.*

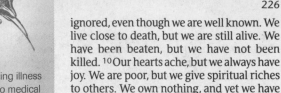

# WHY we never give up

READ 2 CORINTHIANS 4:16, 18

Maybe you're dealing with a life-threatening illness today or already have been told there's no medical cure for your problem. Paul has really good news for you—no matter what is happening to your body, your spirit can be renewed every single day.

In fact, whatever you are going through is really quite small and short compared to the really big, eternal glory God has waiting for all His children. Right now your troubles certainly may not seem small or short, but Paul says that's because you're looking *at* them rather than *beyond* them. His advice is to "fix our gaze" on eternal things; that will give us a true perspective so we will not give up.

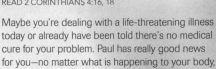

**6** As God's partners,* we beg you not to accept this marvelous gift of God's kindness and then ignore it. **2** For God says,

"At just the right time, I heard you.
On the day of salvation, I helped you."*

Indeed, the "right time" is now. Today is the day of salvation.

### Paul's Hardships

**3** We live in such a way that no one will stumble because of us, and no one will find fault with our ministry. **4** In everything we do, we show that we are true ministers of God. We patiently endure troubles and hardships and calamities of every kind. **5** We have been beaten, been put in prison, faced angry mobs, worked to exhaustion, endured sleepless nights, and gone without food. **6** We prove ourselves by our purity, our understanding, our patience, our kindness, by the Holy Spirit within us,* and by our sincere love. **7** We faithfully preach the truth. God's power is working in us. We use the weapons of righteousness in the right hand for attack and the left hand for defense. **8** We serve God whether people honor us or despise us, whether they slander us or praise us. We are honest, but they call us impostors. **9** We are

ignored, even though we are well known. We live close to death, but we are still alive. We have been beaten, but we have not been killed. **10** Our hearts ache, but we always have joy. We are poor, but we give spiritual riches to others. We own nothing, and yet we have everything.

**11** Oh, dear Corinthian friends! We have spoken honestly with you, and our hearts are open to you. **12** There is no lack of love on our part, but you have withheld your love from us. **13** I am asking you to respond as if you were my own children. Open your hearts to us!

### The Temple of the Living God

**14** Don't team up with those who are unbelievers. How can righteousness be a partner with wickedness? How can light live with darkness? **15** What harmony can there be between Christ and the devil*? How can a believer be a partner with an unbeliever? **16** And what union can there be between God's temple and idols? For we are the temple of the living God. As God said:

"I will live in them
and walk among them.
I will be their God,
and they will be my people.*
**17** Therefore, come out from among
unbelievers,
and separate yourselves from them,
says the LORD.
Don't touch their filthy things,
and I will welcome you.*
**18** And I will be your Father,
and you will be my sons and daughters,
says the LORD Almighty.*"

**7** Because we have these promises, dear friends, let us cleanse ourselves from everything that can defile our body or spirit. And let us work toward complete holiness because we fear God.

**2** Please open your hearts to us. We have not done wrong to anyone, nor led anyone astray, nor taken advantage of anyone. **3** I'm not saying this to condemn you. I said before that you are in our hearts, and we live or die

**6:1** Or *As we work together.* **6:2** Isa 49:8 (Greek version). **6:6** Or *by our holiness of spirit.* **6:15** Greek *Beliar;* various other manuscripts render this proper name of the devil as *Belian, Beliab,* or *Belial.* **6:16** Lev 26:12; Ezek 37:27. **6:17** Isa 52:11; Ezek 20:34 (Greek version). **6:18** 2 Sam 7:14.

together with you. ⁴I have the highest confidence in you, and I take great pride in you. You have greatly encouraged me and made me happy despite all our troubles.

### Paul's Joy at the Church's Repentance

⁵When we arrived in Macedonia, there was no rest for us. We faced conflict from every direction, with battles on the outside and fear on the inside. ⁶But God, who encourages those who are discouraged, encouraged us by the arrival of Titus. ⁷His presence was a joy, but so was the news he brought of the encouragement he received from you. When he told us how much you long to see me, and how sorry you are for what happened, and how loyal you are to me, I was filled with joy!

⁸I am not sorry that I sent that severe letter to you, though I was sorry at first, for I know it was painful to you for a little while. ⁹Now I am glad I sent it, not because it hurt you, but because the pain caused you to repent and change your ways. It was the kind of sorrow God wants his people to have, so you were not harmed by us in any way. ¹⁰For the kind of sorrow God wants us to experience leads us away from sin and results in salvation. There's no regret for that kind of sorrow. But worldly sorrow, which lacks repentance, results in spiritual death.

¹¹Just see what this godly sorrow produced in you! Such earnestness, such concern to clear yourselves, such indignation, such alarm, such longing to see me, such zeal, and such a readiness to punish wrong. You showed that you have done everything necessary to make things right. ¹²My purpose, then, was not to write about who did the wrong or who was wronged. I wrote to you so that in the sight of God you could see for yourselves how loyal you are to us. ¹³We have been greatly encouraged by this.

In addition to our own encouragement, we were especially delighted to see how happy Titus was about the way all of you welcomed him and set his mind* at ease. ¹⁴I had told him how proud I was of you—and you didn't disappoint me. I have always told you the truth, and now my boasting to Titus

has also proved true! ¹⁵Now he cares for you more than ever when he remembers the way all of you obeyed him and welcomed him with such fear and deep respect. ¹⁶I am very happy now because I have complete confidence in you.

### A Call to Generous Giving

**8** Now I want you to know, dear brothers and sisters,* what God in his kindness has done through the churches in Macedonia. ²They are being tested by many troubles, and they are very poor. But they are also filled with abundant joy, which has overflowed in rich generosity.

³For I can testify that they gave not only what they could afford, but far more. And they did it of their own free will. ⁴They begged us again and again for the privilege of sharing in the gift for the believers* in Jerusalem. ⁵They even did more than we had hoped, for their first action was to give themselves to the Lord and to us, just as God wanted them to do.

⁶So we have urged Titus, who encouraged your giving in the first place, to return to you and encourage you to finish this ministry of giving. ⁷Since you excel in so many ways—in your faith, your gifted speakers, your knowledge, your enthusiasm, and your love from us*—I want you to excel also in this gracious act of giving.

⁸I am not commanding you to do this. But I am testing how genuine your love is by

---

## ENCOURAGING the discouraged
READ 2 CORINTHIANS 7:5-6

When we are facing a health crisis, we, like Paul, can face "battles on the outside and fear on the inside." Sometimes our spirits need refreshing as much as our bodies. Never forget that we serve a God who "encourages those who are discouraged." When Paul "faced conflict from every direction," God sent his friend Titus at just the right time to fill the apostle with joy. God knows exactly what you need to deal with today's pressures. Ask Him to send a "Titus" to encourage you and then wait to see Him answer.

---

**7:13** Greek *his spirit.*   **8:1** Greek *brothers.*   **8:4** Greek *for God's holy people.*   **8:7** Some manuscripts read *your love for us.*

comparing it with the eagerness of the other churches.

⁹You know the generous grace of our Lord Jesus Christ. Though he was rich, yet for your sakes he became poor, so that by his poverty he could make you rich.

¹⁰Here is my advice: It would be good for you to finish what you started a year ago. Last year you were the first who wanted to give, and you were the first to begin doing it. ¹¹Now you should finish what you started. Let the eagerness you showed in the beginning be matched now by your giving. <u>Give in proportion to what you have</u>. ¹²Whatever you give is acceptable if you give it eagerly. And give according to what you have, not what you don't have. ¹³Of course, I don't mean your giving should make life easy for others and hard for yourselves. I only mean that there should be some equality. ¹⁴Right now you have plenty and can help those who are in need. Later, they will have plenty and can share with you when you need it. In this way, things will be equal. ¹⁵As the Scriptures say,

"Those who gathered a lot had nothing
    left over,
and those who gathered only a little
    had enough."*

### Titus and His Companions

¹⁶But thank God! He has given Titus the same enthusiasm for you that I have. ¹⁷Titus welcomed our request that he visit you again. In fact, he himself was very eager to go and see you. ¹⁸We are also sending another brother with Titus. All the churches praise him as a preacher of the Good News. ¹⁹He was appointed by the churches to accompany us as we take the offering to Jerusalem*—a service that glorifies the Lord and shows our eagerness to help.

²⁰We are traveling together to guard against any criticism for the way we are handling this generous gift. ²¹We are careful to be honorable before the Lord, but we also want everyone else to see that we are honorable.

²²We are also sending with them another of our brothers who has proven himself many times and has shown on many occasions how eager he is. He is now even more enthusiastic because of his great confidence in you. ²³If anyone asks about Titus, say that he is my partner who works with me to help you. And the brothers with him have been sent by the churches,* and they bring honor to Christ. ²⁴So show them your love, and prove to all the churches that our boasting about you is justified.

### The Collection for Christians in Jerusalem

**9** I really don't need to write to you about this ministry of giving for the believers in Jerusalem.* ²For I know how eager you are to help, and I have been boasting to the churches in Macedonia that you in Greece* were ready to send an offering a year ago. In fact, it was your enthusiasm that stirred up many of the Macedonian believers to begin giving.

³But I am sending these brothers to be sure you really are ready, as I have been telling them, and that your money is all collected. I don't want to be wrong in my boasting about you. ⁴We would be embarrassed—not to mention your own embarrassment—if some Macedonian believers came with me and found that you weren't ready after all I had told them! ⁵So I thought I should send these brothers ahead of me to make sure the gift you promised is ready. But I want it to be a willing gift, not one given grudgingly.

⁶Remember this—a farmer who plants only a few seeds will get a small crop. But the one who plants generously will get a generous crop. ⁷You must each decide in your heart how much to give. And don't give reluctantly or in response to pressure. "For God loves a person who gives cheerfully."* ⁸And God will generously provide all you need. Then you will always have everything you need and plenty left over to share with others. ⁹As the Scriptures say,

"They share freely and give generously
    to the poor.
Their good deeds will be remembered
    forever."*

---

**8:15** Exod 16:18.   **8:19** See 1 Cor 16:3-4.   **8:23** Greek *are apostles of the churches.*   **9:1** Greek *about the offering for God's holy people.*   **9:2** Greek *in Achaia,* the southern region of the Greek peninsula. *Macedonia* was in the northern region of Greece.   **9:7** See footnote on Prov 22:8.   **9:9** Ps 112:9.

¹⁰For God is the one who provides seed for the farmer and then bread to eat. In the same way, he will provide and increase your resources and then produce a great harvest of generosity* in you.

¹¹Yes, you will be enriched in every way so that you can always be generous. And when we take your gifts to those who need them, they will thank God. ¹²So two good things will result from this ministry of giving—the needs of the believers in Jerusalem* will be met, and they will joyfully express their thanks to God.

¹³As a result of your ministry, they will give glory to God. For your generosity to them and to all believers will prove that you are obedient to the Good News of Christ. ¹⁴And they will pray for you with deep affection because of the overflowing grace God has given to you. ¹⁵Thank God for this gift* too wonderful for words!

## Paul Defends His Authority

**10** Now I, Paul, appeal to you with the gentleness and kindness of Christ—though I realize you think I am timid in person and bold only when I write from far away. ²Well, I am begging you now so that when I come I won't have to be bold with those who think we act from human motives.

³We are human, but we don't wage war as humans do. ⁴*We use God's mighty weapons, not worldly weapons, to knock down the strongholds of human reasoning and to destroy false arguments. ⁵We destroy every proud obstacle that keeps people from knowing God. We capture their rebellious thoughts and teach them to obey Christ. ⁶And after you have become fully obedient, we will punish everyone who remains disobedient.

⁷Look at the obvious facts.* Those who say they belong to Christ must recognize that we belong to Christ as much as they do. ⁸I may seem to be boasting too much about the authority given to us by the Lord. But our authority builds you up; it doesn't tear you down. So I will not be ashamed of using my authority.

### THE weakest link
READ 2 CORINTHIANS 11:30

Have you "boasted" in your weaknesses lately?

"You think you have no energy; I have less than that!"

"So you were a nervous wreck waiting for your test results; I was a bigger mess!"

Okay, maybe you don't have to take Paul quite so literally, but hopefully you get the idea that when bad things happen to God's people, it's all right to feel weak. In fact, when we come up against huge obstacles, they become good reminders of how much we all need the Lord—even though we're sometimes tempted to forget that truth when we're feeling fine. This is one time it's okay to be the weakest link.

⁹I'm not trying to frighten you by my letters. ¹⁰For some say, "Paul's letters are demanding and forceful, but in person he is weak, and his speeches are worthless!" ¹¹Those people should realize that our actions when we arrive in person will be as forceful as what we say in our letters from far away.

¹²Oh, don't worry; we wouldn't dare say that we are as wonderful as these other men who tell you how important they are! But they are only comparing themselves with each other, using themselves as the standard of measurement. How ignorant!

¹³We will not boast about things done outside our area of authority. We will boast only about what has happened within the boundaries of the work God has given us, which includes our working with you. ¹⁴We are not reaching beyond these boundaries when we claim authority over you, as if we had never visited you. For we were the first to travel all the way to Corinth with the Good News of Christ.

¹⁵Nor do we boast and claim credit for the work someone else has done. Instead, we hope that your faith will grow so that the boundaries of our work among you will be extended. ¹⁶Then we will be able to go and preach the Good News in other places far beyond you, where no one else is working.

**9:10** Greek *righteousness.* **9:12** Greek *of God's holy people.* **9:15** Greek *his gift.* **10:4** English translations divide verses 4 and 5 in various ways. **10:7** Or *You look at things only on the basis of appearance.*

Then there will be no question of our boasting about work done in someone else's territory. [17]As the Scriptures say, "If you want to boast, boast only about the LORD."*

[18]When people commend themselves, it doesn't count for much. The important thing is for the Lord to commend them.

### Paul and the False Apostles

**11** I hope you will put up with a little more of my foolishness. Please bear with me. [2]For I am jealous for you with the jealousy of God himself. I promised you as a pure bride* to one husband—Christ. [3]But I fear that somehow your pure and undivided devotion to Christ will be corrupted, just as Eve was deceived by the cunning ways of the serpent. [4]You happily put up with whatever anyone tells you, even if they preach a different Jesus than the one we preach, or a different kind of Spirit than the one you received, or a different kind of gospel than the one you believed.

[5]But I don't consider myself inferior in any way to these "super apostles" who teach such things. [6]I may be unskilled as a speaker, but I'm not lacking in knowledge. We have made this clear to you in every possible way.

[7]Was I wrong when I humbled myself and honored you by preaching God's Good News to you without expecting anything in return? [8]I "robbed" other churches by accepting their contributions so I could serve you at no cost. [9]And when I was with you and didn't have enough to live on, I did not become a financial burden to anyone. For the brothers who came from Macedonia brought me all that I needed. I have never been a burden to you, and I never will be. [10]As surely as the truth of Christ is in me, no one in all of Greece* will ever stop me from boasting about this. [11]Why? Because I don't love you? God knows that I do.

[12]But I will continue doing what I have always done. This will undercut those who are looking for an opportunity to boast that their work is just like ours. [13]These people are false apostles. They are deceitful workers who disguise themselves as apostles of Christ. [14]But I am not surprised! Even Satan disguises himself as an angel of light. [15]So it is no wonder that his servants also disguise themselves as servants of righteousness. In the end they will get the punishment their wicked deeds deserve.

### Paul's Many Trials

[16]Again I say, don't think that I am a fool to talk like this. But even if you do, listen to me, as you would to a foolish person, while I also boast a little. [17]Such boasting is not from the Lord, but I am acting like a fool. [18]And since others boast about their human achievements, I will, too. [19]After all, you think you are so wise, but you enjoy putting up with fools! [20]You put up with it when someone enslaves you, takes everything you have, takes advantage of you, takes control of everything, and slaps you in the face. [21]I'm ashamed to say that we've been too "weak" to do that!

But whatever they dare to boast about—I'm talking like a fool again—I dare to boast about it, too. [22]Are they Hebrews? So am I. Are they Israelites? So am I. Are they descendants of Abraham? So am I. [23]Are they servants of Christ? I know I sound like a madman, but I have served him far more! I have worked harder, been put in prison more often, been whipped times without number, and faced death again and again. [24]Five different times the Jewish leaders gave me thirty-nine lashes. [25]Three times I was beaten with rods. Once I was stoned. Three times I was shipwrecked. Once I spent a whole night and a day adrift at sea. [26]I have traveled on many long journeys. I have faced danger from rivers and from robbers. I have faced danger from my own people, the Jews, as well as from the Gentiles. I have faced danger in the cities, in the deserts, and on the seas. And I have faced danger from men who claim to be believers but are not.* [27]I have worked hard and long, enduring many sleepless nights. I have been hungry and thirsty and have often gone without food. I have shivered in the cold, without enough clothing to keep me warm.

**10:17** Jer 9:24.  **11:2** Greek *a virgin*.  **11:10** Greek *Achaia*, the southern region of the Greek peninsula.  **11:26** Greek *from false brothers*.

[28] Then, besides all this, I have the daily burden of my concern for all the churches. [29] Who is weak without my feeling that weakness? Who is led astray, and I do not burn with anger?

[30] If I must boast, I would rather boast about the things that show how weak I am. [31] God, the Father of our Lord Jesus, who is worthy of eternal praise, knows I am not lying. [32] When I was in Damascus, the governor under King Aretas kept guards at the city gates to catch me. [33] I had to be lowered in a basket through a window in the city wall to escape from him.

## Paul's Vision and His Thorn in the Flesh

**12** This boasting will do no good, but I must go on. I will reluctantly tell about visions and revelations from the Lord. [2]* I was caught up to the third heaven fourteen years ago. Whether I was in my body or out of my body, I don't know—only God knows. [3] Yes, only God knows whether I was in my body or outside my body. But I do know [4] that I was caught up* to paradise and heard things so astounding that they cannot be expressed in words, things no human is allowed to tell.

[5] That experience is worth boasting about, but I'm not going to do it. I will boast only about my weaknesses. [6] If I wanted to boast, I would be no fool in doing so, because I would be telling the truth. But I won't do it, because I don't want anyone to give me credit beyond what they can see in my life or hear in my message, [7] even though I have received such wonderful revelations from God. So to keep me from becoming proud, I was given a thorn in my flesh, a messenger from Satan to torment me and keep me from becoming proud.

[8] Three different times I begged the Lord to take it away. [9] Each time he said, "My grace is all you need. My power works best in weakness." So now I am glad to boast about my weaknesses, so that the power of Christ can work through me. [10] That's why I take pleasure in my weaknesses, and in the insults, hardships, persecutions, and troubles

12:2 Greek *I know a man in Christ who.* 12:3-4 Greek *But I know such a man, 'that he was caught up.* 12:11 Some manuscripts omit *boasting like this.*

that I suffer for Christ. For when I am weak, then I am strong.

## Paul's Concern for the Corinthians

[11] You have made me act like a fool—boasting like this.* You ought to be writing commendations for me, for I am not at all inferior to these "super apostles," even though I am nothing at all. [12] When I was with you, I certainly gave you proof that I am an apostle. For I patiently did many signs and wonders and miracles among you. [13] The only thing I failed to do, which I do in the other churches, was to become a financial burden to you. Please forgive me for this wrong!

[14] Now I am coming to you for the third time, and I will not be a burden to you. I don't want what you have—I want you. After all, children don't provide for their parents. Rather, parents provide for their children. [15] I will gladly spend myself and all I have for you, even though it seems that the more I love you, the less you love me.

[16] Some of you admit I was not a burden to you. But others still think I was sneaky and took advantage of you by trickery. [17] But how? Did any of the men I sent to you take advantage of you? [18] When I urged Titus to visit you and sent our other brother with him, did Titus take advantage of you? No! For we have the same spirit and walk in each other's steps, doing things the same way.

# WHEN God says no

READ 2 CORINTHIANS 12:7-10

The next time someone promises you that God absolutely will heal you in answer to your prayers, ask them to read these verses. The greatest apostle of the early church asked God three times to take away his thorn in the flesh. Three times he got the same answer: "My grace is all you need. My power works best in weakness."

We absolutely believe God may heal you completely, but we also know that sometimes we see His power in our lives in even greater ways when we don't get healed the way we had hoped. Whatever His answer for you may be, trust that His grace always will be enough.

¹⁹Perhaps you think we're saying these things just to defend ourselves. No, we tell you this as Christ's servants, and with God as our witness. Everything we do, dear friends, is to strengthen you. ²⁰For I am afraid that when I come I won't like what I find, and you won't like my response. I am afraid that I will find quarreling, jealousy, anger, self-ishness, slander, gossip, arrogance, and dis-orderly behavior. ²¹Yes, I am afraid that when I come again, God will humble me in your presence. And I will be grieved be-cause many of you have not given up your old sins. You have not repented of your im-purity, sexual immorality, and eagerness for lustful pleasure.

## Paul's Final Advice

**13** This is the third time I am coming to visit you (and as the Scriptures say, "The facts of every case must be established by the testimony of two or three witnesses"*). ²I have already warned those who had been sinning when I was there on my second visit. Now I again warn them and all others, just as I did before, that next time I will not spare them.

³I will give you all the proof you want that Christ speaks through me. Christ is not weak when he deals with you; he is powerful among you. ⁴Although he was crucified in weakness, he now lives by the power of God. We, too, are weak, just as Christ was, but when we deal with you we will be alive with him and will have God's power.

⁵Examine yourselves to see if your faith is genuine. Test yourselves. Surely you know that Jesus Christ is among you*; if not, you have failed the test of genuine faith. ⁶As you test yourselves, I hope you will recognize that we have not failed the test of apostolic au-thority.

⁷We pray to God that you will not do what is wrong by refusing our correction. I hope we won't need to demonstrate our authority when we arrive. Do the right thing before we come—even if that makes it look like we have failed to demonstrate our authority. ⁸For we cannot oppose the truth, but must always stand for the truth. ⁹We are glad to seem weak if it helps show that you are actually strong. We pray that you will become mature.

¹⁰I am writing this to you before I come, hoping that I won't need to deal severely with you when I do come. For I want to use the authority the Lord has given me to strengthen you, not to tear you down.

## Paul's Final Greetings

¹¹Dear brothers and sisters,* I close my let-ter with these last words: Be joyful. Grow to maturity. Encourage each other. Live in har-mony and peace. Then the God of love and peace will be with you.

¹²Greet each other with Christian love.* ¹³All of God's people here send you their greetings.

¹⁴*May the grace of the Lord Jesus Christ, the love of God, and the fellowship of the Holy Spirit be with you all.

**13:1** Deut 19:15. **13:5** Or *in you*. **13:11** Greek *Brothers*. **13:12** Greek *with a sacred kiss*. **13:14** Some English translations include verse 13 as part of verse 12, and then verse 14 becomes verse 13.

# GALATIANS

*I ask you again, does God give you the Holy Spirit and work miracles among you because you obey the law? Of course not! It is because you believe the message you heard about Christ.*

GALATIANS 3:5

Isn't it amazing all the advice you get when you're dealing with a serious illness? Everybody seems to know somebody who tried this herb or brewed that tea. Each has the formula they think will make things right with your body.

You may even hear formulas for faith—certain things to do so that your prayers for a cure will be answered. Be very careful here. It is so easy for all of us to slip into rituals and tasks to try and earn favor with God. In this letter to the believers at Galatia, Paul warns them that the outward symbols of their Jewish faith (things like circumcision and dietary rules) are not nearly as crucial as faith in the Messiah.

We, like the Galatians, need to live by God's grace. God's healing touch is not something we wrench from His closed fist by our concerted efforts. There's nothing you can do to make God love you any more or any less than He already does. He proved that a long time ago when He carried a cross to a hill called Calvary. Instead, let this be your only "formula" for life: "It is no longer I who live, but Christ lives in me. So I live in this earthly body by trusting in the Son of God, who loved me and gave himself for me" (2:20).

## Greetings from Paul

**1** This letter is from Paul, an apostle. I was not appointed by any group of people or any human authority, but by Jesus Christ himself and by God the Father, who raised Jesus from the dead.

2 All the brothers and sisters* here join me in sending this letter to the churches of Galatia.

3 May God our Father and the Lord Jesus Christ* give you grace and peace. 4 Jesus gave his life for our sins, just as God our Father planned, in order to rescue us from this evil world in which we live. 5 All glory to God forever and ever! Amen.

## There Is Only One Good News

6 I am shocked that you are turning away so soon from God, who called you to himself through the loving mercy of Christ.* You are following a different way that pretends to be the Good News 7 but is not the Good News at all. You are being fooled by those who deliberately twist the truth concerning Christ.

8 Let God's curse fall on anyone, including us or even an angel from heaven, who preaches a different kind of Good News than the one we preached to you. 9 I say again what we have said before: If anyone preaches any other Good News than the one you welcomed, let that person be cursed.

10 Obviously, I'm not trying to win the approval of people, but of God. If pleasing people were my goal, I would not be Christ's servant.

## Paul's Message Comes from Christ

11 Dear brothers and sisters, I want you to understand that the gospel message I preach is not based on mere human reasoning. 12 I received my message from no human source, and no one taught me. Instead, I received it by direct revelation from Jesus Christ.*

13 You know what I was like when I followed the Jewish religion—how I violently persecuted God's church. I did my best to destroy it. 14 I was far ahead of my fellow Jews in my zeal for the traditions of my ancestors.

15 But even before I was born, God chose me and called me by his marvelous grace. Then it pleased him 16 to reveal his Son to me* so that I would proclaim the Good News about Jesus to the Gentiles.

When this happened, I did not rush out to consult with any human being.* 17 Nor did I go up to Jerusalem to consult with those who were apostles before I was. Instead, I went away into Arabia, and later I returned to the city of Damascus.

18 Then three years later I went to Jerusalem to get to know Peter,* and I stayed with him for fifteen days. 19 The only other apostle I met at that time was James, the Lord's brother. 20 I declare before God that what I am writing to you is not a lie.

21 After that visit I went north into the provinces of Syria and Cilicia. 22 And still the Christians in the churches in Judea didn't know me personally. 23 All they knew was that people were saying, "The one who used to persecute us is now preaching the very faith he tried to destroy!" 24 And they praised God because of me.

## The Apostles Accept Paul

**2** Then fourteen years later I went back to Jerusalem again, this time with Barnabas; and Titus came along, too. 2 I went there because God revealed to me that I should go. While I was there I met privately with those considered to be leaders of the church and shared with them the message I had been preaching to the Gentiles. I wanted to make sure that we were in agreement, for fear that all my efforts had been wasted and I was running the race for nothing. 3 And they sup-

---

**1:2** Greek *brothers;* also in 1:11.    **1:3** Some manuscripts read *God the Father and our Lord Jesus Christ.*    **1:6** Some manuscripts read *through loving mercy.*    **1:12** Or *by the revelation of Jesus Christ.*    **1:16a** Or *in me.*    **1:16b** Greek *with flesh and blood.*    **1:18** Greek *Cephas.*

ported me and did not even demand that my companion Titus be circumcised, though he was a Gentile.*

⁴Even that question came up only because of some so-called Christians there—false ones, really*—who were secretly brought in. They sneaked in to spy on us and take away the freedom we have in Christ Jesus. They wanted to enslave us and force us to follow their Jewish regulations. ⁵But we refused to give in to them for a single moment. We wanted to preserve the truth of the gospel message for you.

⁶And the leaders of the church had nothing to add to what I was preaching. (By the way, their reputation as great leaders made no difference to me, for God has no favorites.) ⁷Instead, they saw that <u>God had given me the responsibility of preaching the gospel to the Gentiles, just as he had given Peter the responsibility of preaching to the Jews.</u> ⁸For the same God who worked through Peter as the apostle to the Jews also worked through me as the apostle to the Gentiles.

⁹In fact, James, Peter,* and John, who were known as pillars of the church, recognized the gift God had given me, and they accepted Barnabas and me as their co-workers. They encouraged us to keep preaching to the Gentiles, while they continued their work with the Jews. ¹⁰Their only suggestion was that we keep on helping the poor, which I have always been eager to do.

### Paul Confronts Peter

¹¹But when Peter came to Antioch, I had to oppose him to his face, for what he did was very wrong. ¹²When he first arrived, he ate with the Gentile Christians, who were not circumcised. But afterward, when some friends of James came, Peter wouldn't eat with the Gentiles anymore. He was afraid of criticism from these people who insisted on the necessity of circumcision. ¹³As a result, other Jewish Christians followed Peter's hypocrisy, and even Barnabas was led astray by their hypocrisy.

¹⁴When I saw that they were not following the truth of the gospel message, I said to Peter in front of all the others, "Since you, a Jew by birth, have discarded the Jewish laws and are living like a Gentile, why are you now trying to make these Gentiles follow the Jewish traditions?

¹⁵"You and I are Jews by birth, not 'sinners' like the Gentiles. ¹⁶Yet we know that a person is made right with God by faith in Jesus Christ, not by obeying the law. And we have believed in Christ Jesus, so that we might be made right with God because of our faith in Christ, not because we have obeyed the law. For no one will ever be made right with God by obeying the law."*

¹⁷But suppose we seek to be made right with God through faith in Christ and then we are found guilty because we have abandoned the law. Would that mean Christ has led us into sin? Absolutely not! ¹⁸Rather, I am a sinner if I rebuild the old system of law I already tore down. ¹⁹For when I tried to keep the law, it condemned me. So I died to the law—I stopped trying to meet all its requirements—so that I might live for God. ²⁰My old self has been crucified with Christ.* It is no longer I who live, but Christ lives in me. So I live in this earthly body by trusting in the Son of God, who loved me and gave himself for me. ²¹I do not treat the grace of God as meaningless. For if keeping the law could make us right with God, then there was no need for Christ to die.

### The Law and Faith in Christ

**3** Oh, foolish Galatians! Who has cast an evil spell on you? For the meaning of Jesus Christ's death was made as clear to you as if you had seen a picture of his death on the cross. ²Let me ask you this one question: Did you receive the Holy Spirit by obeying the law of Moses? Of course not! You received the Spirit because you believed the message you heard about Christ. ³How foolish can you be? After starting your Christian lives in the Spirit, why are you now trying to become perfect by your own human effort? ⁴Have you experienced* so much for nothing? Surely it was not in vain, was it?

⁵I ask you again, does God give you the

2:3 Greek *a Greek.*    2:4 Greek *some false brothers.*    2:9 Greek *Cephas;* also in 2:11, 14.    2:16 Some translators hold that the quotation extends through verse 14; others through verse 16; and still others through verse 21.    2:20 Some English translations put this sentence in verse 19.    3:4 Or *Have you suffered.*

Holy Spirit and work miracles among you because you obey the law? Of course not! It is because you believe the message you heard about Christ.

6In the same way, "Abraham believed God, and God counted him as righteous because of his faith."* 7The real children of Abraham, then, are those who put their faith in God.

8What's more, the Scriptures looked forward to this time when God would declare the Gentiles to be righteous because of their faith. God proclaimed this good news to Abraham long ago when he said, "All nations will be blessed through you."* 9So all who put their faith in Christ share the same blessing Abraham received because of his faith.

10But those who depend on the law to make them right with God are under his curse, for the Scriptures say, "Cursed is everyone who does not observe and obey all the commands that are written in God's Book of the Law."* 11So it is clear that no one can be made right with God by trying to keep the law. For the Scriptures say, "It is through faith that a righteous person has life."* 12This way of faith is very different from the way of law, which says, "It is through obeying the law that a person has life."*

13But Christ has rescued us from the curse pronounced by the law. When he was hung on the cross, he took upon himself the curse for our wrongdoing. For it is written in the Scriptures, "Cursed is everyone who is hung on a tree."* 14Through Christ Jesus, God has blessed the Gentiles with the same blessing he promised to Abraham, so that we who are believers might receive the promised* Holy Spirit through faith.

### The Law and God's Promise

15Dear brothers and sisters,* here's an example from everyday life. Just as no one can set aside or amend an irrevocable agreement, so it is in this case. 16God gave the promises to Abraham and his child.* And notice that the Scripture doesn't say "to his children,*" as if it meant many descendants. Rather, it says "to his child"—and that, of course, means Christ. 17This is what I am trying to say: The agreement God made with Abraham could not be canceled 430 years later when God gave the law to Moses. God would be breaking his promise. 18For if the inheritance could be received by keeping the law, then it would not be the result of accepting God's promise. But God graciously gave it to Abraham as a promise.

19Why, then, was the law given? It was given alongside the promise to show people their sins. But the law was designed to last only until the coming of the child who was promised. God gave his law through angels to Moses, who was the mediator between God and the people. 20Now a mediator is helpful if more than one party must reach an agreement. But God, who is one, did not use a mediator when he gave his promise to Abraham.

21Is there a conflict, then, between God's law and God's promises?* Absolutely not! If the law could give us new life, we could be made right with God by obeying it. 22But the Scriptures declare that we are all prisoners of sin, so we receive God's promise of freedom only by believing in Jesus Christ.

### God's Children through Faith

23Before the way of faith in Christ was available to us, we were placed under guard by the law. We were kept in protective custody, so to speak, until the way of faith was revealed.

24Let me put it another way. The law was our guardian until Christ came; it protected us until we could be made right with God through faith. 25And now that the way of faith has come, we no longer need the law as our guardian.

26For you are all children* of God through faith in Christ Jesus. 27And all who have been united with Christ in baptism have put on Christ, like putting on new clothes.* 28There is no longer Jew or Gentile,* slave or free, male and female. For you are all one in Christ Jesus. 29And now that you belong to Christ, you are the true children* of Abraham. You are his heirs, and God's promise to Abraham belongs to you.

3:6 Gen 15:6.   3:8 Gen 12:3; 18:18; 22:18.   3:10 Deut 27:26.   3:11 Hab 2:4.   3:12 Lev 18:5.   3:13 Deut 21:23 (Greek version). 3:14 Some manuscripts read *the blessing of the.*   3:15 Greek *Brothers.*   3:16a Greek *seed;* also in 3:16c, 19. See notes on Gen 12:7 and 13:15.   3:16b Greek *seeds.*   3:21 Some manuscripts read *and the promises?*   3:26 Greek *sons.*   3:27 Greek *have put on Christ.*   3:28 Greek *Jew or Greek.*   3:29 Greek *seed.*

**4** Think of it this way. If a father dies and leaves an inheritance for his young children, those children are not much better off than slaves until they grow up, even though they actually own everything their father had. ²They have to obey their guardians until they reach whatever age their father set. ³And that's the way it was with us before Christ came. We were like children; we were slaves to the basic spiritual principles* of this world.

⁴But when the right time came, God sent his Son, born of a woman, subject to the law. ⁵God sent him to buy freedom for us who were slaves to the law, so that he could adopt us as his very own children.* ⁶And because we* are his children, God has sent the Spirit of his Son into our hearts, prompting us to call out, "Abba, Father."* ⁷Now you are no longer a slave but God's own child.* And since you are his child, God has made you his heir.

### Paul's Concern for the Galatians

⁸Before you Gentiles knew God, you were slaves to so-called gods that do not even exist. ⁹So now that you know God (or should I say, now that God knows you), why do you want to go back again and become slaves once more to the weak and useless spiritual principles of this world? ¹⁰You are trying to earn favor with God by observing certain days or months or seasons or years. ¹¹I fear for you. Perhaps all my hard work with you was for nothing. ¹²Dear brothers and sisters,* I plead with you to live as I do in freedom from these things, for I have become like you Gentiles—free from those laws.

You did not mistreat me when I first preached to you. ¹³Surely you remember that I was sick when I first brought you the Good News. ¹⁴But even though my condition tempted you to reject me, you did not despise me or turn me away. No, you took me in and cared for me as though I were an angel from God or even Christ Jesus himself. ¹⁵Where is that joyful and grateful spirit you felt then? I am sure you would have taken out your own eyes and given them to me if it had been possible. ¹⁶Have I now become your enemy because I am telling you the truth?

## IN the same boat together
READ GALATIANS 3:28

Disease often puts us together with people whom we otherwise never might have met. Those waiting for transplants form a bond regardless of race or color. Those receiving chemo side-by-side enjoy a friendship irrespective of social status. Those sharing in a disease-related support group develop intimacy despite their uncommon backgrounds. There's a sense they're together in the same boat.

It's like that for true believers, too. We become children of God through our faith in Jesus, and we gain a whole new family of people in the same boat—maybe not like us on the outside, but exactly the same on the inside because of what Christ has done for us all.

¹⁷Those false teachers are so eager to win your favor, but their intentions are not good. They are trying to shut you off from me so that you will pay attention only to them. ¹⁸If someone is eager to do good things for you, that's all right; but let them do it all the time, not just when I'm with you.

¹⁹Oh, my dear children! I feel as if I'm going through labor pains for you again, and they will continue until Christ is fully developed in your lives. ²⁰I wish I were with you right now so I could change my tone. But at this distance I don't know how else to help you.

### Abraham's Two Children

²¹Tell me, you who want to live under the law, do you know what the law actually says? ²²The Scriptures say that Abraham had two sons, one from his slave wife and one from his freeborn wife.* ²³The son of the slave wife was born in a human attempt to bring about the fulfillment of God's promise. But the son of the freeborn wife was born as God's own fulfillment of his promise.

²⁴These two women serve as an illustration of God's two covenants. The first woman, Hagar, represents Mount Sinai where people received the law that enslaved them. ²⁵And now Jerusalem is just like Mount Sinai in Arabia,* because she and her children live in

**4:3** Or *powers;* also in 4:9.   **4:5** Greek *sons;* also in 4:6.   **4:6a** Greek *you.*   **4:6b** *Abba* is an Aramaic term for "father."   **4:7** Greek *son;* also in 4:7b.   **4:12** Greek *brothers;* also in 4:28, 31.   **4:22** See Gen 16:15; 21:2-3.   **4:25** Greek *And Hagar, which is Mount Sinai in Arabia, is now like Jerusalem;* other manuscripts read *And Mount Sinai in Arabia is now like Jerusalem.*

# THE EXHAUSTED caregiver

Being a caregiver is one of the most exhausting jobs on the face of the planet. Some of our loved ones need help with all the daily tasks of living, and we barely have enough strength left to care for ourselves. And some of our loved ones are reeling from the side effects of treatments while we sit helplessly wishing there was something more we could do. We even might feel it would be easier to be the patient than to stand by feeling power-less to change the situation. Sometimes we may even get tired of doing the good we know we need to do.

Paul encourages us not to give up. You will never regret the sacrifices you make for your loved one, so take every chance to do good for them today. They may not notice or appreci-ate each good deed, but God does and promises a "harvest of blessing" to you for your faithfulness.

---

slavery to the law. 26But the other woman, Sarah, represents the heavenly Jerusalem. She is the free woman, and she is our mother. 27As Isaiah said,

"Rejoice, O childless woman,
  you who have never given birth!
Break into a joyful shout,
  you who have never been in labor!
For the desolate woman now has more
    children
  than the woman who lives with her
    husband!"*

28And you, dear brothers and sisters, are children of the promise, just like Isaac. 29But you are now being persecuted by those who want you to keep the law, just as Ishmael, the child born by human effort, persecuted Isaac, the child born by the power of the Spirit.

30But what do the Scriptures say about that? "Get rid of the slave and her son, for the son of the slave woman will not share the in-heritance with the free woman's son."* 31So, dear brothers and sisters, we are not chil-dren of the slave woman; we are children of the free woman.

## Freedom in Christ

**5** So Christ has truly set us free. Now make sure that you stay free, and don't get tied up again in slavery to the law.

2Listen! I, Paul, tell you this: If you are counting on circumcision to make you right with God, then Christ will be of no benefit to you. 3I'll say it again. If you are trying to find favor with God by being circumcised, you must obey every regulation in the whole law of Moses. 4For if you are trying to make yourselves right with God by keeping the law, you have been cut off from Christ! You have fallen away from God's grace.

5But we who live by the Spirit eagerly wait to receive by faith the righteousness God has promised to us. 6For when we place our faith in Christ Jesus, there is no benefit in being circumcised or being uncircumcised. What is important is faith expressing itself in love.

7You were running the race so well. Who has held you back from following the truth? 8It certainly isn't God, for he is the one who called you to freedom. 9This false teaching is like a little yeast that spreads through the whole batch of dough! 10I am trusting the Lord to keep you from believing false teach-ings. God will judge that person, whoever he is, who has been confusing you.

11Dear brothers and sisters,* if I were still preaching that you must be circum-cised—as some say I do—why am I still be-ing persecuted? If I were no longer preaching salvation through the cross of Christ, no one would be offended. 12I just

4:27 Isa 54:1.   4:30 Gen 21:10.   5:11 Greek *Brothers;* similarly in 5:13.

wish that those troublemakers who want to
mutilate you by circumcision would mutilate themselves.*
13For you have been called to live in freedom, my brothers and sisters. But don't use
your freedom to satisfy your sinful nature. Instead, use your freedom to serve one another
in love. 14For the whole law can be summed
up in this one command: "Love your neighbor as yourself."* 15But if you are always bit-
ing and devouring one another, watch out!
Beware of destroying one another.

*Living by the Spirit's Power*

16So I say, let the Holy Spirit guide your
lives. Then you won't be doing what your
sinful nature craves. 17The sinful nature
wants to do evil, which is just the opposite
of what the Spirit wants. And the Spirit
gives us desires that are the opposite of
what the sinful nature desires. These two
forces are constantly fighting each other, so
you are not free to carry out your good intentions. 18But when you are directed by
the Spirit, you are not under obligation to
the law of Moses.
19When you follow the desires of your sinful nature, the results are very clear: sexual
immorality, impurity, lustful pleasures,
20idolatry, sorcery, hostility, quarreling, jealousy, outbursts of anger, selfish ambition,
dissension, division, 21envy, drunkenness,
wild parties, and other sins like these. Let me
tell you again, as I have before, that anyone
living that sort of life will not inherit the
Kingdom of God.
22But the Holy Spirit produces this kind
of fruit in our lives: love, joy, peace, patience,
kindness, goodness, faithfulness, 23gentle-
ness, and self-control. There is no law
against these things!
24Those who belong to Christ Jesus have
nailed the passions and desires of their sinful
nature to his cross and crucified them there.
25Since we are living by the Spirit, let us follow the Spirit's leading in every part of our
lives. 26Let us not become conceited, or provoke one another, or be jealous of one another.

*We Harvest What We Plant*

6 Dear brothers and sisters, if another
believer* is overcome by some sin, you
who are godly* should gently and humbly
help that person back onto the right path.
And be careful not to fall into the same
temptation yourself. 2Share each other's
burdens, and in this way obey the law of
Christ. 3If you think you are too important
to help someone, you are only fooling yourself. You are not that important.
4Pay careful attention to your own work,
for then you will get the satisfaction of a job
well done, and you won't need to compare
yourself to anyone else. 5For we are each responsible for our own conduct.
6Those who are taught the word of God
should provide for their teachers, sharing all
good things with them.
7Don't be misled—you cannot mock the
justice of God. You will always harvest what
you plant. 8Those who live only to satisfy
their own sinful nature will harvest decay
and death from that sinful nature. But those
who live to please the Spirit will harvest
everlasting life from the Spirit. 9So let's not
get tired of doing what is good. At just the
right time we will reap a harvest of blessing
if we don't give up. 10Therefore, whenever
we have the opportunity, we should do good
to everyone—especially to those in the
family of faith.

Caregiver

Fruit of the Spirit

## RIPE for the picking

READ GALATIANS 5:22-23

Illness has a way of sending our emotions on a roller coaster. We're ecstatic when the CT scan has good news and then our joy plummets when the PET scan reveals bad news. We feel peaceful heading into surgery, but that calm disappears when we hear what has been found.

Author-pastor Rick Warren explains in *The Purpose-Driven Life* that godly characteristics (fruits of the Spirit) are developed in our lives when we're put in situations where we are tempted to respond exactly the *opposite* way.

So next time the doctor is running late, take a deep breath and smile because God is ready to produce some great fruit in your life!

**5:12** Or *castrate themselves,* or *cut themselves off from you;* Greek reads *cut themselves off.* **5:14** Lev 19:18. **6:1a** Greek *Brothers, if a man.* **6:1b** Greek *spiritual.*

*Paul's Final Advice*

11 NOTICE WHAT LARGE LETTERS I USE AS I WRITE THESE CLOSING WORDS IN MY OWN HANDWRITING.

12Those who are trying to force you to be circumcised want to look good to others. They don't want to be persecuted for teaching that the cross of Christ alone can save. 13And even those who advocate circumcision don't keep the whole law themselves. They only want you to be circumcised so they can boast about it and claim you as their disciples.

14As for me, may I never boast about anything except the cross of our Lord Jesus Christ. Because of that cross,* my interest in this world has been crucified, and the world's interest in me has also died. 15It doesn't matter whether we have been circumcised or not. What counts is whether we have been transformed into a new creation. 16May God's peace and mercy be upon all who live by this principle; they are the new people of God.*

17From now on, don't let anyone trouble me with these things. For I bear on my body the scars that show I belong to Jesus.

18Dear brothers and sisters,* may the grace of our Lord Jesus Christ be with your spirit. Amen.

6:14 Or *Because of him.*   6:16 Greek *this principle, and upon the Israel of God.*   6:18 Greek *Brothers.*

# PHILIPPIANS

*Always be full of
joy in the Lord.
I say it again—
rejoice!*

PHILIPPIANS 4:4

Illness has a nasty habit of taking things away from
people. Sometimes it takes them away for a short while,
and sometimes it takes them away permanently. Sickness
might affect how happy we feel or whether we laugh a lot.
But it needn't take away our joy.

That's because happiness and laughter are based on
what is happening (to) us, while joy is based on what God
has done (in) us. It's an attitude that we can choose each
day regardless of whether we're lying in a hospital bed,
sitting in a chemo room, riding in a wheelchair, or even
chained in a Roman prison as the apostle Paul was when
he penned this letter to the church in Philippi. Paul was
not a masochist: His joy was *not* in being chained. He
wasn't a Pollyanna: His joy was *not* in a belief that being
in prison wasn't really that bad. No, he was full of joy
(he uses the word fifteen times in these 104 verses!)
because his joy was in his personal relationship with
Jesus the Messiah.

No matter what the status of our health or our loved
one's health is, we can have joy. It is our choice to make
each day.

In a changing, uncertain world, joy is one thing that
doesn't have to change, because true joy is found in the
Lord and not in ourselves. Choose JOY today.

## Greetings from Paul

**1** This letter is from Paul and Timothy, slaves of Christ Jesus.

I am writing to all of God's holy people in Philippi who belong to Christ Jesus, including the elders* and deacons.

2 May God our Father and the Lord Jesus Christ give you grace and peace.

## Paul's Thanksgiving and Prayer

3 Every time I think of you, I give thanks to my God. 4 Whenever I pray, I make my requests for all of you with joy, 5 for you have been my partners in spreading the Good News about Christ from the time you first heard it until now. 6 And I am certain that God, who began the good work within you, will continue his work until it is finally finished on the day when Christ Jesus returns.

7 So it is right that I should feel as I do about all of you, for you have a special place in my heart. You share with me the special favor of God, both in my imprisonment and in defending and confirming the truth of the Good News. 8 God knows how much I love you and long for you with the tender compassion of Christ Jesus.

9 I pray that your love will overflow more and more, and that you will keep on growing in knowledge and understanding. 10 For I want you to understand what really matters, so that you may live pure and blameless lives until the day of Christ's return. 11 May you always be filled with the fruit of your salvation—the righteous character produced in your life by Jesus Christ*—for this will bring much glory and praise to God.

## Paul's Joy That Christ Is Preached

12 And I want you to know, my dear brothers and sisters,* that everything that has happened to me here has helped to spread the Good News. 13 For everyone here, including the whole palace guard,* knows that I am in chains because of Christ. 14 And because of my imprisonment, most of the believers* here have gained confidence and boldly speak God's message* without fear.

15 It's true that some are preaching out of jealousy and rivalry. But others preach about Christ with pure motives. 16 They preach because they love me, for they know I have been appointed to defend the Good News. 17 Those others do not have pure motives as they preach about Christ. They preach with selfish ambition, not sincerely, intending to make my chains more painful to me. 18 But that doesn't matter. Whether their motives are false or genuine, the message about Christ is being preached either way, so I rejoice. And I will continue to rejoice. 19 For I know that as you pray for me and the Spirit of Jesus Christ helps me, this will lead to my deliverance.

## Paul's Life for Christ

20 For I fully expect and hope that I will never be ashamed, but that I will continue to be bold for Christ, as I have been in the past. And I trust that my life will bring honor to Christ, whether I live or die. 21 For to me, living means living for Christ, and dying is even better. 22 But if I live, I can do more fruitful work for Christ. So I really don't know which is better. 23 I'm torn between two desires: I long to go and be with Christ, which would be far better for me. 24 But for your sakes, it is better that I continue to live.

25 Knowing this, I am convinced that I will remain alive so I can continue to help all of you grow and experience the joy of your faith. 26 And when I come to you again, you will have even more reason to take pride in Christ Jesus because of what he is doing through me.

## Live as Citizens of Heaven

27 Above all, you must live as citizens of heaven, conducting yourselves in a manner worthy of the Good News about Christ. Then,

1:1 Or *overseers;* or *bishops.*   1:11 Greek *with the fruit of righteousness through Jesus Christ.*   1:12 Greek *brothers.*   1:13 Greek *including all the Praetorium.*   1:14a Greek *brothers in the Lord.*   1:14b Some manuscripts read *speak the message.*

whether I come and see you again or only hear about you, I will know that you are standing together with one spirit and one purpose, fighting together for the faith, which is the Good News. ²⁸Don't be intimidated in any way by your enemies. This will be a sign to them that they are going to be destroyed, but that you are going to be saved, even by God himself. ²⁹For you have been given not only the privilege of trusting in Christ but also the privilege of suffering for him. ³⁰We are in this struggle together. You have seen my struggle in the past, and you know that I am still in the midst of it.

### Have the Attitude of Christ

**2** Is there any encouragement from belonging to Christ? Any comfort from his love? Any fellowship together in the Spirit? Are your hearts tender and compassionate? ²Then make me truly happy by agreeing wholeheartedly with each other, loving one another, and working together with one mind and purpose.

³Don't be selfish; don't try to impress others. Be humble, thinking of others as better than yourselves. ⁴Don't look out only for your own interests, but take an interest in others, too.

⁵You must have the same attitude that Christ Jesus had.

⁶Though he was God,*
    he did not think of equality with God
        as something to cling to.
⁷Instead, he gave up his divine privileges*;
    he took the humble position
        of a slave*
    and was born as a human being.
  When he appeared in human form,*
⁸    he humbled himself in obedience
        to God
    and died a criminal's death on
        a cross.

⁹Therefore, God elevated him to the place
        of highest honor
    and gave him the name above all
        other names,
¹⁰that at the name of Jesus every knee
        should bow,
    in heaven and on earth and under
        the earth,
¹¹and every tongue confess that Jesus
        Christ is Lord,
    to the glory of God the Father.

### Shine Brightly for Christ

¹²Dear friends, you always followed my instructions when I was with you. And now that I am away, it is even more important. Work hard to show the results of your salvation, obeying God with deep reverence and

**2:6** Or *Being in the form of God.*    **2:7a** Greek *he emptied himself.*    **2:7b** Or *the form of a slave.*    **2:7c** Some English translations put this phrase in verse 8.

## AFRAID of heaven?
READ PHILIPPIANS 1:20-24

It's kind of funny how so many of us talk about how awesome heaven will be, and yet we will do just about anything to stay here on earth another day! Dave Dravecky's Outreach of Hope has even published a booklet entitled *If Heaven Is So Great, Why Am I Afraid to Go There?*

Paul has no such fear. He describes how he loves his earthly life but is actually looking forward to dying. He adds that he is really "torn between two desires": longing to be with Jesus and knowing that many people on earth need him.

Perhaps you feel those conflicting tugs on your heart today: longing to be with Jesus and yet knowing people here still need you. Take heart that you as a believer are in a win-win situation. "And I trust that my life will bring honor to Christ, whether I live or die."

fear. <sup>13</sup>For God is working in you, giving you the desire and the power to do what pleases him.

<sup>14</sup>Do everything without complaining and arguing, <sup>15</sup>so that no one can criticize you. Live clean, innocent lives as children of God, shining like bright lights in a world full of crooked and perverse people. <sup>16</sup>Hold firmly to the word of life; then, on the day of Christ's return, I will be proud that I did not run the race in vain and that my work was not useless. <sup>17</sup>But I will rejoice even if I lose my life, pouring it out like a liquid offering to God,* just like your faithful service is an offering to God. And I want all of you to share that joy. <sup>18</sup>Yes, you should rejoice, and I will share your joy.

### Paul Commends Timothy

<sup>19</sup>If the Lord Jesus is willing, I hope to send Timothy to you soon for a visit. Then he can cheer me up by telling me how you are getting along. <sup>20</sup>I have no one else like Timothy, who genuinely cares about your welfare. <sup>21</sup>All the others care only for themselves and not for what matters to Jesus Christ. <sup>22</sup>But you know how Timothy has proved himself. Like a son with his father, he has served with me in preaching the Good News. <sup>23</sup>I hope to send him to you just as soon as I find out what is going to happen to me here. <sup>24</sup>And I have confidence from the Lord that I myself will come to see you soon.

### Paul Commends Epaphroditus

<sup>25</sup>Meanwhile, I thought I should send Epaphroditus back to you. He is a true brother, co-worker, and fellow soldier. And he was your messenger to help me in my need. <sup>26</sup>I am sending him because he has been longing to see you, and he was very distressed that you heard he was ill. <sup>27</sup>And he certainly was ill; in fact, he almost died. But God had mercy on him—and also on me, so that I would not have one sorrow after another.

<sup>28</sup>So I am all the more anxious to send him back to you, for I know you will be glad to see him, and then I will not be so worried about you. <sup>29</sup>Welcome him with Christian love* and with great joy, and give him the honor that people like him deserve. <sup>30</sup>For he risked his life for the work of Christ, and he was at the point of death while doing for me what you couldn't do from far away.

### The Priceless Value of Knowing Christ

**3** Whatever happens, my dear brothers and sisters,* rejoice in the Lord. I never get tired of telling you these things, and I do it to safeguard your faith.

<sup>2</sup>Watch out for those dogs, those people who do evil, those mutilators who say you must be circumcised to be saved. <sup>3</sup>For we who worship by the Spirit of God* are the ones who are truly circumcised. We rely on what Christ Jesus has done for us. We put no confidence in human effort, <sup>4</sup>though I could have confidence in my own effort if anyone could. Indeed, if others have reason for confidence in their own efforts, I have even more!

<sup>5</sup>I was circumcised when I was eight days old. I am a pure-blooded citizen of Israel and a member of the tribe of Benjamin—a real Hebrew if there ever was one! I was a member of the Pharisees, who demand the strictest obedience to the Jewish law. <sup>6</sup>I was so zealous that I harshly persecuted the church. And as for righteousness, I obeyed the law without fault.

<sup>7</sup>I once thought these things were valuable, but now I consider them worthless because of what Christ has done. <sup>8</sup>Yes, everything else is worthless when compared with the infinite value of knowing Christ Jesus my Lord. For his sake I have discarded everything else, counting it all as garbage, so that I could gain Christ <sup>9</sup>and become one with him. I no longer count on my own righteousness through obeying the law; rather, I become righteous through faith in Christ.* For God's way of making us right with himself depends on faith. <sup>10</sup>I want to know Christ and experience the mighty power that raised him from the dead. I want to suffer with him, sharing in his death, <sup>11</sup>so that one way or another I will experience the resurrection from the dead!

---

**2:17** Greek *I will rejoice even if I am to be poured out as a liquid offering.*   **2:29** Greek *in the Lord.*   **3:1** Greek *brothers;* also in 3:13, 17.   **3:3** Some manuscripts read *worship God in spirit;* one early manuscript reads *worship in spirit.*   **3:9** Or *through the faithfulness of Christ.*

253

### Pressing toward the Goal

¹²I don't mean to say that I have already achieved these things or that I have already reached perfection. But I press on to possess that perfection for which Christ Jesus first possessed me. ¹³No, dear brothers and sisters, I have not achieved it,* but I focus on this one thing: Forgetting the past and looking forward to what lies ahead, ¹⁴I press on to reach the end of the race and receive the heavenly prize for which God, through Christ Jesus, is calling us.

¹⁵Let all who are spiritually mature agree on these things. If you disagree on some point, I believe God will make it plain to you. ¹⁶But we must hold on to the progress we have already made.

¹⁷Dear brothers and sisters, pattern your lives after mine, and learn from those who follow our example. ¹⁸For I have told you often before, and I say it again with tears in my eyes, that there are many whose conduct shows they are really enemies of the cross of Christ. ¹⁹They are headed for destruction. Their god is their appetite, they brag about shameful things, and they think only about this life here on earth. ²⁰But we are citizens of heaven, where the Lord Jesus Christ lives. And we are eagerly waiting for him to return as our Savior. ²¹He will take our weak mortal bodies and change them into glorious bodies like his own, using the same power with which he will bring everything under his control.

**4** Therefore, my dear brothers and sisters,* stay true to the Lord. I love you and long to see you, dear friends, for you are my joy and the crown I receive for my work.

### Words of Encouragement

²Now I appeal to Euodia and Syntyche. Please, because you belong to the Lord, settle your disagreement. ³And I ask you, my true partner,* to help these two women, for they worked hard with me in telling others the Good News. They worked along with Clement and the rest of my co-workers, whose names are written in the Book of Life.

⁴Always be full of joy in the Lord. I say it again—rejoice! ⁵Let everyone see that you

> Don't worry about anything; instead, pray about everything. Tell God what you need, and thank him for all he has done. Then you will experience God's peace, which exceeds anything we can understand. His peace will guard your hearts and minds as you live in Christ Jesus.
>
> PHILIPPIANS 4:6-7

are considerate in all you do. Remember, the Lord is coming soon.

⁶Don't worry about anything; instead, pray about everything. Tell God what you need, and thank him for all he has done. ⁷Then you will experience God's peace, which exceeds anything we can understand. His peace will guard your hearts and minds as you live in Christ Jesus.

⁸And now, dear brothers and sisters, one final thing. Fix your thoughts on what is true, and honorable, and right, and pure, and lovely, and admirable. Think about things that are excellent and worthy of praise. ⁹Keep putting into practice all you learned and received from me—everything you heard from me and saw me doing. Then the God of peace will be with you.

### Paul's Thanks for Their Gifts

¹⁰How I praise the Lord that you are concerned about me again. I know you have always been concerned for me, but you didn't have the chance to help me. ¹¹Not that I was ever in need, for I have learned how to be content with whatever I have. ¹²I know how to live on almost nothing or with everything. I have learned the secret of living in every situation, whether it is with a full stomach or empty, with plenty or little. ¹³For I can do everything through Christ,*

---

**3:13** Some manuscripts read *not yet achieved it.*    **4:1** Greek *brothers;* also in 4:8.    **4:3** Or *loyal Syzygus.*    **4:13** Greek *through the one.*

who gives me strength. [14]Even so, you have done well to share with me in my present difficulty.

[15]As you know, you Philippians were the only ones who gave me financial help when I first brought you the Good News and then traveled on from Macedonia. No other church did this. [16]Even when I was in Thessalonica you sent help more than once. [17]I don't say this because I want a gift from you. Rather, I want you to receive a reward for your kindness.

[18]At the moment I have all I need—and more! I am generously supplied with the gifts you sent me with Epaphroditus. They are a sweet-smelling sacrifice that is acceptable and pleasing to God. [19]And this same God who takes care of me will supply all your needs from his glorious riches, which have been given to us in Christ Jesus.

[20]Now all glory to God our Father forever and ever! Amen.

## Paul's Final Greetings

[21]Give my greetings to each of God's holy people—all who belong to Christ Jesus. The brothers who are with me send you their greetings. [22]And all the rest of God's people send you greetings, too, especially those in Caesar's household.

[23]May the grace of the Lord Jesus Christ be with your spirit.

# COLOSSIANS

*That's why I work and struggle so hard, depending on Christ's mighty power that works within me.*

COLOSSIANS 1:29

We all start out in life completely dependent on another person to sustain us. Then as a toddler we begin to insist, "I can do it myself!" We continue that loud cry as we become an "I don't need you" teenager and finally emerge as an independent adult who always "can take care of myself."

Then illness hits.

We may have to depend on others for rides to the doctor. We may need help taking care of our children. We may even need assistance with personal routines like getting dressed and using the bathroom. Usually, the more independent we are, the worse patients we will make.

Self-reliance is built into our human natures. And while it's good to have a strong work ethic and a fighting spirit, we need to realize that there's a dependency we *want* to foster each day. We need to depend on the Lord's mighty power that works within us. If we are weak, He offers a mighty power to strengthen us. Even if we still feel pretty strong, He offers a supernatural power that is not available naturally within us.

Colossians is another one of the apostle Paul's letters written from a Roman prison. Paul was an incredibly independent, capable man, who had discovered that the strongest people are the ones who are most dependent . . . on the mighty power of Christ.

## Greetings from Paul

**1** This letter is from Paul, chosen by the will of God to be an apostle of Christ Jesus, and from our brother Timothy.

² We are writing to God's holy people in the city of Colosse, who are faithful brothers and sisters* in Christ.

May God our Father give you grace and peace.

## Paul's Thanksgiving and Prayer

³ We always pray for you, and we give thanks to God, the Father of our Lord Jesus Christ. ⁴ For we have heard of your faith in Christ Jesus and your love for all of God's people, ⁵ which come from your confident hope of what God has reserved for you in heaven. You have had this expectation ever since you first heard the truth of the Good News.

⁶ This same Good News that came to you is going out all over the world. It is bearing fruit everywhere by changing lives, just as it changed your lives from the day you first heard and understood the truth about God's wonderful grace.

⁷ You learned about the Good News from Epaphras, our beloved co-worker. He is Christ's faithful servant, and he is helping us on your behalf.* ⁸ He has told us about the love for others that the Holy Spirit has given you.

⁹ So we have not stopped praying for you since we first heard about you. We ask God to give you complete knowledge of his will and to give you spiritual wisdom and understanding. ¹⁰ Then the way you live will always honor and please the Lord, and your lives will produce every kind of good fruit. All the while, you will grow as you learn to know God better and better.

¹¹ We also pray that you will be strengthened with all his glorious power so you will have all the endurance and patience you need. May you be filled with joy,* ¹² always thanking the Father. He has enabled you to share in the inheritance that belongs to his people, who live in the light. ¹³ For he has rescued us from the kingdom of darkness and transferred us into the Kingdom of his dear Son, ¹⁴ who purchased our freedom* and forgave our sins.

## Christ Is Supreme

¹⁵ Christ is the visible image of the invisible God.
   He existed before anything was created
      and is supreme over all creation,*
¹⁶ for through him God created everything
      in the heavenly realms and on earth.
   He made the things we can see
      and the things we can't see—
   such as thrones, kingdoms, rulers, and
      authorities in the unseen world.
   Everything was created through him
      and for him.
¹⁷ He existed before anything else,
      and he holds all creation together.
¹⁸ Christ is also the head of the church,
      which is his body.
   He is the beginning,
      supreme over all who rise from the dead.*
   So he is first in everything.
¹⁹ For God in all his fullness
      was pleased to live in Christ,
²⁰ and through him God reconciled
      everything to himself.
   He made peace with everything in
      heaven and on earth
   by means of Christ's blood on the cross.

²¹ This includes you who were once far away from God. You were his enemies, separated from him by your evil thoughts and actions. ²² Yet now he has reconciled you to himself through the death of Christ in his physical body. As a result, he has brought you into his own presence, and you are holy and blameless as you stand before him without a single fault.

²³ But you must continue to believe this truth and stand firmly in it. Don't drift away

---

**1:2** Greek *faithful brothers.* **1:7** Or *he is ministering on your behalf;* some manuscripts read *he is ministering on our behalf.* **1:11** Or *all the patience and endurance you need with joy.* **1:14** Some manuscripts add *with his blood.* **1:15** Or *He is the firstborn of all creation.* **1:18** Or *the firstborn from the dead.*

from the assurance you received when you heard the Good News. The Good News has been preached all over the world, and I, Paul, have been appointed as God's servant to proclaim it.

### Paul's Work for the Church

24 I am glad when I suffer for you in my body, for I am participating in the sufferings of Christ that continue for his body, the church. 25 God has given me the responsibility of serving his church by proclaiming his entire message to you. 26 This message was kept secret for centuries and generations past, but now it has been revealed to God's people. 27 For God wanted them to know that the riches and glory of Christ are for you Gentiles, too. And this is the secret: Christ lives in you. This gives you assurance of sharing his glory.

28 So we tell others about Christ, warning everyone and teaching everyone with all the wisdom God has given us. We want to present them to God, perfect* in their relationship to Christ. 29 That's why I work and struggle so hard, depending on Christ's mighty power that works within me.

**2** I want you to know how much I have agonized for you and for the church at Laodicea, and for many other believers who have never met me personally. 2 I want them to be encouraged and knit together by strong ties of love. I want them to have complete confidence that they understand God's mysterious plan, which is Christ himself. 3 In him lie hidden all the treasures of wisdom and knowledge.

4 I am telling you this so no one will deceive you with well-crafted arguments. 5 For though I am far away from you, my heart is with you. And I rejoice that you are living as you should and that your faith in Christ is strong.

### Freedom from Rules and New Life in Christ

6 And now, just as you accepted Christ Jesus as your Lord, you must continue to follow him. 7 Let your roots grow down into him, and let your lives be built on him. Then your faith will grow strong in the truth you were taught, and you will overflow with thankfulness.

8 Don't let anyone capture you with empty philosophies and high-sounding nonsense that come from human thinking and from the spiritual powers* of this world, rather than from Christ. 9 For in Christ lives all the fullness of God in a human body.* 10 So you also are complete through your union with Christ, who is the head over every ruler and authority.

11 When you came to Christ, you were "circumcised," but not by a physical procedure.

1:28 Or *mature.*    2:8 Or *the spiritual principles;* also in 2:20.    2:9 Or *in him dwells all the completeness of the Godhead bodily.*

Christ is the visible image of the invisible God. He existed before anything was created and is supreme over all creation, for through him God created everything in the heavenly realms and on earth. He made the things we can see and the things we can't see— such as thrones, kingdoms, rulers, and authorities in the unseen world. Everything was created through him and for him.

COLOSSIANS 1:15-16

Christ performed a spiritual circumcision—
the cutting away of your sinful nature.* ¹²For
you were buried with Christ when you were
baptized. And with him you were raised to
new life because you trusted the mighty
power of God, who raised Christ from the
dead.

¹³You were dead because of your sins and
because your sinful nature was not yet cut
away. Then God made you alive with Christ,
for he forgave all our sins. ¹⁴He canceled the
record of the charges against us and took it
away by nailing it to the cross. ¹⁵In this way,
he disarmed* the spiritual rulers and authorities. He shamed them publicly by his
victory over them on the cross.

¹⁶So don't let anyone condemn you for
what you eat or drink, or for not celebrating
certain holy days or new moon ceremonies
or Sabbaths. ¹⁷For these rules are only shadows of the reality yet to come. And Christ
himself is that reality. ¹⁸Don't let anyone
condemn you by insisting on pious self-
denial or the worship of angels,* saying they
have had visions about these things. Their
sinful minds have made them proud, ¹⁹and
they are not connected to Christ, the head of
the body. For he holds the whole body together with its joints and ligaments, and it
grows as God nourishes it.

²⁰You have died with Christ, and he has set
you free from the spiritual powers of this
world. So why do you keep on following the
rules of the world, such as, ²¹"Don't handle!
Don't taste! Don't touch!"? ²²Such rules are
mere human teachings about things that de-
teriorate as we use them. ²³These rules may
seem wise because they require strong devotion, pious self-denial, and severe bodily
discipline. But they provide no help in con-
quering a person's evil desires.

## Living the New Life

**3** Since you have been raised to new life
with Christ, set your sights on the realities of heaven, where Christ sits in the place
of honor at God's right hand. ²Think about
the things of heaven, not the things of earth.
³For you died to this life, and your real life is

hidden with Christ in God. ⁴And when Christ,
who is your* life, is revealed to the whole
world, you will share in all his glory.

⁵So put to death the sinful, earthly things
lurking within you. Have nothing to do with
sexual immorality, impurity, lust, and evil
desires. Don't be greedy, for a greedy person
is an idolater, worshiping the things of this
world. ⁶Because of these sins, the anger of
God is coming.* ⁷You used to do these
things when your life was still part of this
world. ⁸But now is the time to get rid of anger, rage, malicious behavior, slander, and
dirty language. ⁹Don't lie to each other, for
you have stripped off your old sinful nature
and all its wicked deeds. ¹⁰Put on your new
nature, and be renewed as you learn to know
your Creator and become like him. ¹¹In this
new life, it doesn't matter if you are a Jew or
a Gentile,* circumcised or uncircumcised,
barbaric, uncivilized,* slave, or free. Christ
is all that matters, and he lives in all of us.

¹²Since God chose you to be the holy people he loves, you must clothe yourselves with
tenderhearted mercy, kindness, humility,
gentleness, and patience. ¹³<u>Make allowance
for each other's faults, and forgive anyone
who offends you</u>. Remember, the Lord forgave you, so you must forgive others. ¹⁴Above
all, clothe yourselves with love, which binds
us all together in perfect harmony. ¹⁵And let
the peace that comes from Christ rule in
your hearts. For as members of one body you
are called to live in peace. And always be
thankful.

¹⁶Let the message about Christ, in all its
richness, fill your lives. Teach and counsel
each other with all the wisdom he gives.
Sing psalms and hymns and spiritual songs
to God with thankful hearts. ¹⁷And whatever
you do or say, do it as a representative of the
Lord Jesus, giving thanks through him to
God the Father.

## Instructions for Christian Households

¹⁸Wives, submit to your husbands, as is fitting for those who belong to the Lord.

¹⁹Husbands, love your wives and never
treat them harshly.

[20]Children, always obey your parents, for this pleases the Lord. [21]Fathers, do not aggravate your children, or they will become discouraged.

[22]Slaves, obey your earthly masters in everything you do. Try to please them all the time, not just when they are watching you. Serve them sincerely because of your reverent fear of the Lord. [23]Work willingly at whatever you do, as though you were working for the Lord rather than for people. [24]Remember that the Lord will give you an inheritance as your reward, and that the Master you are serving is Christ.* [25]But if you do what is wrong, you will be paid back for the wrong you have done. For God has no favorites.

**4** Masters, be just and fair to your slaves. Remember that you also have a Master—in heaven.

### An Encouragement for Prayer

[2]Devote yourselves to prayer with an alert mind and a thankful heart. [3]Pray for us, too, that God will give us many opportunities to speak about his mysterious plan concerning Christ. That is why I am here in chains. [4]Pray that I will proclaim this message as clearly as I should.

[5]Live wisely among those who are not believers, and make the most of every opportunity. [6]Let your conversation be gracious and attractive* so that you will have the right response for everyone.

### Paul's Final Instructions and Greetings

[7]Tychicus will give you a full report about how I am getting along. He is a beloved brother and faithful helper who serves with me in the Lord's work. [8]I have sent him to you for this very purpose—to let you know how we are doing and to encourage you. [9]I am also sending Onesimus, a faithful and beloved brother, one of your own people. He and Tychicus will tell you everything that's happening here.

[10]Aristarchus, who is in prison with me, sends you his greetings, and so does Mark, Barnabas's cousin. As you were instructed

---

## SETTING goals

READ COLOSSIANS 3:2

Setting goals for ourselves while dealing with a health crisis is a great motivator. Some days our goal may be to be dressed by noon, knowing that even a morning shower will exhaust us. Other days we may determine to take a short walk around the yard.

Some goals are long-term: to be healthy enough to walk a daughter down the aisle, to be strong enough to work full-time again, or to be alive to hold a first grandchild. Setting our sights on the future can help spur us to wellness. And if you really want to be blessed, set your sights even further—set them on heaven where our goal of becoming just like Jesus finally will come true.

---

before, make Mark welcome if he comes your way. [11]Jesus (the one we call Justus) also sends his greetings. These are the only Jewish believers among my co-workers; they are working with me here for the Kingdom of God. And what a comfort they have been!

[12]Epaphras, a member of your own fellowship and a servant of Christ Jesus, sends you his greetings. He always prays earnestly for you, asking God to make you strong and perfect, fully confident that you are following the whole will of God. [13]I can assure you that he prays hard for you and also for the believers in Laodicea and Hierapolis.

[14]Luke, the beloved doctor, sends his greetings, and so does Demas. [15]Please give my greetings to our brothers and sisters* at Laodicea, and to Nympha and the church that meets in her house.

[16]After you have read this letter, pass it on to the church at Laodicea so they can read it, too. And you should read the letter I wrote to them.

[17]And say to Archippus, "Be sure to carry out the ministry the Lord gave you."

[18]HERE IS MY GREETING IN MY OWN HANDWRITING—PAUL.

Remember my chains.

May God's grace be with you.

---

**3:24** Or *and serve Christ as your Master.*    **4:6** Greek *and seasoned with salt.*    **4:15** Greek *brothers.*

# DAVID vs. Goliath

If you or your loved one is up against a particularly scary diagnosis, we encourage you to think of the shepherd boy David as he went into battle armed only with a slingshot and five stones to fight against the giant Goliath. Do you know what his battle cry was? He wasn't like the Little Engine That Could, chugging along and repeating, "I think I can, I think I can."

No, his thinking was more like, "I know I can't. I know I can't." David was the youngest and smallest boy in his family—too small to wear a protective suit of armor—and Goliath was more than nine feet tall. But David's battle cry was "I know God can. I know God can." If you read 1 Samuel 17:47 in the Old Testament, you'll see his exact words: "The battle is the LORD's" (NIV).

That phrase appears many times throughout the Old Testament as mighty warriors went up against even mightier opponents. It's a phrase you may want to pray when you wake up each morning. (Just fill in the blank with your illness.)

*Lord, I feel like a little shepherd boy with a slingshot facing a giant named _____, and it is more than I can handle. But I choose to believe it is not more than You can handle. The battle belongs to You, Lord. Fight for me and through me. Do what I cannot do on my own.*

We believe that sometimes we do face more than we can handle in our own strength, but we also believe in the promise of Philippians 4:13, which says: "For I can do everything through Christ, who gives me strength."

**You don't have to reach down inside yourself and muster up some super strength.** Even if you feel you can't "live strong," you can live *by His strength* because "the battle is the LORD's."

The Old Testament prophet Isaiah described that strength: "He gives power to the weak and strength to the powerless. Even youths will become weak and tired, and young men will fall in exhaustion. But those who trust in the LORD will find new strength. They will soar high on wings like eagles. They will run and not grow weary. They will walk and not faint" (Isaiah 40:29-31).

Live strong BY HIS STRENGTH.

# 1 THESSALONIANS

*We want you to know what will happen to the believers who have died so you will not grieve like people who have no hope.*

1 THESSALONIANS 4:13

What are the worst words we can hear coming out of a physician's mouth?

You have AIDS. . . . I'm afraid the heart is severely damaged. . . . Yes, Alzheimer's has started. . . . I'm sorry, but it will be a chronic condition.

How about this one?

There's no hope.

It's the one pronouncement that blows away all the other difficult diagnoses, because it steals the one thing we all must have to live . . . hope. We face another day of blood sticks and needles because we have hope that we will feel better tomorrow. We undergo another round of nauseating chemo because we have hope that the tumor will shrink. We endure another day of swollen, aching joints because we have hope that one day we may have a short respite from our pain.

Do you realize that for a believer in Jesus, the phrase "there's no hope" is *never* true? Oh, there may come a time when medical science runs out of options and our prayers for an earthly cure are not answered. But that's when our best hope comes true.

Paul explains this blessed hope in 4:16-17: "For the Lord himself will come down from heaven with a commanding shout, with the voice of the archangel, and with the trumpet call of God. First, the Christians who have died will rise from their graves. Then, together with them, we who are still alive and remain on the earth will be caught up in the clouds to meet the Lord in the air. Then we will be with the Lord forever. So encourage each other with these words."

### Greetings from Paul

**1** This letter is from Paul, Silas,* and Timothy.

We are writing to the church in Thessalonica, to you who belong to God the Father and the Lord Jesus Christ.

May God give you grace and peace.

### The Faith of the Thessalonian Believers

² We always thank God for all of you and pray for you constantly. ³ As we pray to our God and Father about you, we think of your faithful work, your loving deeds, and the enduring hope you have because of our Lord Jesus Christ.

⁴ We know, dear brothers and sisters,* that God loves you and has chosen you to be his own people. ⁵ For when we brought you the Good News, it was not only with words but also with power, for the Holy Spirit gave you full assurance* that what we said was true. And you know of our concern for you from the way we lived when we were with you. ⁶ So you received the message with joy from the Holy Spirit in spite of the severe suffering it brought you. In this way, you imitated both us and the Lord. ⁷ As a result, you have become an example to all the believers in Greece—throughout both Macedonia and Achaia.*

⁸ And now the word of the Lord is ringing out from you to people everywhere, even beyond Macedonia and Achaia, for wherever we go we find people telling us about your faith in God. We don't need to tell them about it, ⁹ for they keep talking about the wonderful welcome you gave us and how you turned away from idols to serve the living and true God. ¹⁰ And they speak of how you are looking forward to the coming of God's Son from heaven—Jesus, whom God raised from the dead. He is the one who has rescued us from the terrors of the coming judgment.

### Paul Remembers His Visit

**2** You yourselves know, dear brothers and sisters,* that our visit to you was not a failure. ² You know how badly we had been treated at Philippi just before we came to you and how much we suffered there. Yet our God gave us the courage to declare his Good News to you boldly, in spite of great opposition. ³ So you can see we were not preaching with any deceit or impure motives or trickery.

⁴ For we speak as messengers approved by God to be entrusted with the Good News. <u>Our purpose is to please God, not people.</u> He alone examines the motives of our hearts. ⁵ Never once did we try to win you with flattery, as you well know. And God is our witness that we were not pretending to be your friends just to get your money! ⁶ As for human praise, we have never sought it from you or anyone else.

⁷ As apostles of Christ we certainly had a right to make some demands of you, but instead we were like children* among you. Or

---

## YOU should try this!

READ 1 THESSALONIANS 2:4

People facing a health crisis usually get a lot of advice—most of it *not* from those with a medical degree! Well-meaning friends and family offer suggestions on what diet to follow, which vitamins to swallow, and which Web sites to study. Such an outpouring of unsolicited opinions can overwhelm the patient and family who must make health-related decisions. Many of us don't like to hurt another's feelings and may feel we *should* try every eating hint offered or even visit every acclaimed medical center. But our purpose is not to please others—not when we are sick and not when we are well. We need to consider options, <u>ask God for guidance</u>, and seek only to please Him.

---

1:1 Greek *Silvanus*, the Greek form of the name.   1:4 Greek *brothers*.   1:5 Or *with the power of the Holy Spirit, so you can have full assurance.*   1:7 *Macedonia* and *Achaia* were the northern and southern regions of Greece.   2:1 Greek *brothers*; also in 2:9, 14, 17.   2:7 Some manuscripts read *we were gentle.*

we were like a mother feeding and caring for her own children. [8] We loved you so much that we shared with you not only God's Good News but our own lives, too.

[9] Don't you remember, dear brothers and sisters, how hard we worked among you? Night and day we toiled to earn a living so that we would not be a burden to any of you as we preached God's Good News to you. [10] You yourselves are our witnesses—and so is God—that we were devout and honest and faultless toward all of you believers. [11] And you know that we treated each of you as a father treats his own children. [12] We pleaded with you, encouraged you, and urged you to live your lives in a way that God would consider worthy. For he called you to share in his Kingdom and glory.

[13] Therefore, we never stop thanking God that when you received his message from us, you didn't think of our words as mere human ideas. You accepted what we said as the very word of God—which, of course, it is. And this word continues to work in you who believe.

[14] And then, dear brothers and sisters, you suffered persecution from your own countrymen. In this way, you imitated the believers in God's churches in Judea who, because of their belief in Christ Jesus, suffered from their own people, the Jews. [15] For some of the Jews killed the prophets, and some even killed the Lord Jesus. Now they have persecuted us, too. They fail to please God and work against all humanity [16] as they try to keep us from preaching the Good News of salvation to the Gentiles. By doing this, they continue to pile up their sins. But the anger of God has caught up with them at last.

*Timothy's Good Report about the Church*
[17] Dear brothers and sisters, after we were separated from you for a little while (though our hearts never left you), we tried very hard to come back because of our intense longing to see you again. [18] We wanted very much to come to you, and I, Paul, tried again and again, but Satan prevented us. [19] After all, what gives us hope and joy, and what will be

## BOUND to come some trouble
READ 1 THESSALONIANS 3:1-4

If you ever imagined that faith in God would keep troubles away, then these verses will give you a truer picture. Certainly, many problems can be avoided in life when we choose to live God's way, but a life of faith *doesn't* guarantee a trouble-free life. Everyone in this world has troubles, but those of us with faith also have the answer to life's problems. In the words of songwriter Rich Mullins: "There's bound to come some trouble in your life, but it ain't nothing to be afraid of. . . . That ain't no reason to fear. . ,. . Reach out to Jesus, hold on tight. He's been there before and He knows what it's like. You'll find He's there."

our proud reward and crown as we stand before our Lord Jesus when he returns? It is you! [20] Yes, you are our pride and joy.

**3** Finally, when we could stand it no longer, we decided to stay alone in Athens, [2] and we sent Timothy to visit you. He is our brother and God's co-worker* in proclaiming the Good News of Christ. We sent him to strengthen you, to encourage you in your faith, [3] and to keep you from being shaken by the troubles you were going through. But you know that we are destined for such troubles. [4] Even while we were with you, we warned you that troubles would soon come—and they did, as you well know. [5] That is why, when I could bear it no longer, I sent Timothy to find out whether your faith was still strong. I was afraid that the tempter had gotten the best of you and that our work had been useless.

[6] But now Timothy has just returned, bringing us good news about your faith and love. He reports that you always remember our visit with joy and that you want to see us as much as we want to see you. [7] So we have been greatly encouraged in the midst of our troubles and suffering, dear brothers and sisters,* because you have remained strong in your faith. [8] It gives us new life to know that you are standing firm in the Lord.

[9] How we thank God for you! Because of

3:2 Other manuscripts read *and God's servant;* still others read *and a co-worker,* or *and a servant and co-worker for God,* or *and God's servant and our co-worker.* 3:7 Greek *brothers.*

you we have great joy as we enter God's presence. [10]Night and day we pray earnestly for you, asking God to let us see you again to fill the gaps in your faith.

[11]May God our Father and our Lord Jesus bring us to you very soon. [12]And may the Lord make your love for one another and for all people grow and overflow, just as our love for you overflows. [13]May he, as a result, make your hearts strong, blameless, and holy as you stand before God our Father when our Lord Jesus comes again with all his holy people. Amen.

## Live to Please God

**4** Finally, dear brothers and sisters,* we urge you in the name of the Lord Jesus to live in a way that pleases God, as we have taught you. You live this way already, and we encourage you to do so even more. [2]For you remember what we taught you by the authority of the Lord Jesus.

[3]God's will is for you to be holy, so stay away from all sexual sin. [4]Then each of you will control his own body* and live in holiness and honor—[5]not in lustful passion like the pagans who do not know God and his ways. [6]Never harm or cheat a Christian brother in this matter by violating his wife,* for the Lord avenges all such sins, as we have solemnly warned you before. [7]God has called us to live holy lives, not impure lives. [8]Therefore, anyone who refuses to live by these rules is not disobeying human teach-

ing but is rejecting God, who gives his Holy Spirit to you.

[9]But we don't need to write to you about the importance of loving each other,* for God himself has taught you to love one another. [10]Indeed, you already show your love for all the believers* throughout Macedonia. Even so, dear brothers and sisters, we urge you to love them even more.

[11]Make it your goal to live a quiet life, minding your own business and working with your hands, just as we instructed you before. [12]Then people who are not Christians will respect the way you live, and you will not need to depend on others.

## The Hope of the Resurrection

[13]And now, dear brothers and sisters, we want you to know what will happen to the believers who have died* so you will not grieve like people who have no hope. [14]For since we believe that Jesus died and was raised to life again, we also believe that when Jesus returns, God will bring back with him the believers who have died.

[15]We tell you this directly from the Lord: We who are still living when the Lord returns will not meet him ahead of those who have died.* [16]For the Lord himself will come down from heaven with a commanding shout, with the voice of the archangel, and with the trumpet call of God. First, the Christians who have died* will rise from their graves. [17]Then, together with them, we who are still alive and remain on the earth will be caught up in the clouds to meet the Lord in the air. Then we will be with the Lord forever. [18]So encourage each other with these words.

**5** Now concerning how and when all this will happen, dear brothers and sisters,* we don't really need to write you. [2]For you know quite well that the day of the Lord's return will come unexpectedly, like a thief in the night. [3]When people are saying, "Everything is peaceful and secure," then disaster

---

# WHAT'S God's will for me?

READ 1 THESSALONIANS 5:16-18

People often remark that they wish they knew what God's will was for their life. Well, here it is in black-and-white: "Always be joyful. Never stop praying. Be thankful in all circumstances, for this is God's will for you who belong to Christ Jesus." So if this is God's will for us, we must be able to do it whether we are feeling fine, not feeling fine, or caring for someone who's not feeling fine. We talked about being joyful in Philippians (page 249) and we'll talk about praying in 1 Timothy (page 271). But how do we be thankful for infirmities and illness? We don't. We do choose to be grateful to God *in* all our circumstances, not *for* them.

---

**4:1** Greek *brothers;* also in 4:10, 13. **4:4** Or *will know how to take a wife for himself;* or *will learn to live with his own wife;* Greek reads *will know how to possess his own vessel.* **4:6** Greek *Never harm or cheat a brother in this matter.* **4:9** Greek *about brotherly love.* **4:10** Greek *the brothers.* **4:13** Greek *those who have fallen asleep;* also in 4:14. **4:15** Greek *those who have fallen asleep.* **4:16** Greek *the dead in Christ.* **5:1** Greek *brothers;* also in 5:4, 12, 14, 25, 26, 27.

will fall on them as suddenly as a pregnant woman's labor pains begin. And there will be no escape.

⁴But you aren't in the dark about these things, dear brothers and sisters, and you won't be surprised when the day of the Lord comes like a thief.* ⁵For you are all children of the light and of the day; we don't belong to darkness and night. ⁶So be on your guard, not asleep like the others. Stay alert and be clearheaded. ⁷Night is the time when people sleep and drinkers get drunk. ⁸But let us who live in the light be clearheaded, protected by the armor of faith and love, and wearing as our helmet the confidence of our salvation.

⁹For God chose to save us through our Lord Jesus Christ, not to pour out his anger on us. ¹⁰Christ died for us so that, whether we are dead or alive when he returns, we can live with him forever. ¹¹So encourage each other and build each other up, just as you are already doing.

## Paul's Final Advice

¹²Dear brothers and sisters, honor those who are your leaders in the Lord's work. They work hard among you and give you spiritual guidance. ¹³Show them great respect and wholehearted love because of their work. And live peacefully with each other.

¹⁴Brothers and sisters, we urge you to warn those who are lazy. Encourage those who are timid. Take tender care of those who are weak. Be patient with everyone.

¹⁵See that no one pays back evil for evil, but always try to do good to each other and to all people.

¹⁶Always be joyful. ¹⁷Never stop praying. ¹⁸Be thankful in all circumstances, for this is God's will for you who belong to Christ Jesus.

¹⁹Do not stifle the Holy Spirit. ²⁰Do not scoff at prophecies, ²¹but test everything that is said. Hold on to what is good. ²²Stay away from every kind of evil.

## Paul's Final Greetings

²³Now may the God of peace make you holy in every way, and may your whole spirit and soul and body be kept blameless until our Lord Jesus Christ comes again. ²⁴God will make this happen, for he who calls you is faithful.

²⁵Dear brothers and sisters, pray for us.

²⁶Greet all the brothers and sisters with Christian love.*

²⁷I command you in the name of the Lord to read this letter to all the brothers and sisters.

²⁸May the grace of our Lord Jesus Christ be with you.

5:4 Some manuscripts read *comes upon you as if you were thieves.*    5:26 Greek *with a holy kiss.*

# ENTRUSTING our families
## to God's care

When serious illness hits someone in a family, it's as if the whole family "has" the disease because it disrupts their lifestyle and affects everyone in the home. When we face such a situation, we wish we could prevent its impact, but that's not possible.

Those of us who have been diagnosed with a life-threatening illness may even soberly imagine what life would be like for our families without us.

And when we do, the bottom-line question we must face is: *Which do I love more—my relationships on earth or my relationship with God?* It's fairly easy to say we love God most of all, but when push comes to shove (or illness comes our way), will we be longing for our heavenly home or only hanging on to our earthly one? Don't get us wrong; we don't think God wants us to turn our backs on our family or our home with some sort of misdirected heavenly gaze.

> He wants us to love our family with an unending, unconditional love.
> ### *But He still wants us to love Him more.*
> He wants us to love life with a passion and a purpose.
> ### *But He still wants us to love Him more.*
> He wants us to love this world with care and concern.
> ### *But He still wants us to love Him more.*

Have you been able to entrust your family to God's care no matter what happens to you?

> But they want me. They love me and I love them so very much.
> ### *I love them even more than you do.*
> I know You love them, but I want to take care of them.
> ### *I love them even more than you do.*
> I know You love them, but they need me.
> ### *I love them even more than you do.*
> I don't want to entrust them to You, Lord. I want them to be entrusted to me. I . . . I . . . I . . .
> ### *I love them even more than you do.*

It's time to walk by faith and not by sight. God loves your loved ones even more than you do.

# 2 THESSALONIANS

*Now may the
Lord of peace
himself give you
his peace at all
times and in
every situation.*

2 THESSALONIANS 3:16

People don't usually talk about being "peacefully sick" or "peacefully caring" for an ill relative. Somehow peace just doesn't seem to fit those situations.

In this letter to the church in Thessalonica, Paul prays that the believers there would experience God's peace "at all times and in every situation." Peace doesn't seem to fit the Thessalonians' situation either: They were being persecuted for their faith. People were being beaten with rods, thrown into prison, and made to suffer great hardships. Not exactly a situation that breeds peace.

You, too, may be in a situation that doesn't exactly seem conducive to peace: newly diagnosed and in shock, praying there's been some mistake; facing surgery, hoping the doctor can get it all; trudging through treatments, praying they work; undergoing tests, longing for good news; at the end of medical hope, praying for a little more time; holding the hand of a loved one, trying to be strong.

But true peace doesn't come out of a situation. It comes from Jesus Himself. He is the very Lord of peace, and whenever He is invited into a situation, He brings His own personal *shalom*.

He brings a peace that makes no sense. It's a peace that cannot be explained. It's a peace that goes beyond our human minds. It's a peace that only He can give. It's a peace we pray you'll feel today and at all times and in every situation.

## Greetings from Paul

**1** This letter is from Paul, Silas,* and Timothy.

We are writing to the church in Thessalonica, to you who belong to God our Father and the Lord Jesus Christ.

2May God our Father* and the Lord Jesus Christ give you grace and peace.

## Encouragement during Persecution

3Dear brothers and sisters,* we can't help but thank God for you, because your faith is flourishing and your love for one another is growing. 4We proudly tell God's other churches about your endurance and faithfulness in all the persecutions and hardships you are suffering. 5And God will use this persecution to show his justice and to make you worthy of his Kingdom, for which you are suffering. 6In his justice he will pay back those who persecute you.

7And God will provide rest for you who are being persecuted and also for us when the Lord Jesus appears from heaven. He will come with his mighty angels, 8in flaming fire, bringing judgment on those who don't know God and on those who refuse to obey the Good News of our Lord Jesus. 9They will be punished with eternal destruction, forever separated from the Lord and from his glorious power. 10When he comes on that day, he will receive glory from his holy people—praise from all who believe. And this includes you, for you believed what we told you about him.

11So we keep on praying for you, asking our God to enable you to live a life worthy of his call. May he give you the power to accomplish all the good things your faith prompts you to do. 12Then the name of our Lord Jesus will be honored because of the way you live, and you will be honored along with him. This is all made possible because of the grace of our God and Lord, Jesus Christ.*

## Events prior to the Lord's Second Coming

**2** Now, dear brothers and sisters,* let us clarify some things about the coming of our Lord Jesus Christ and how we will be gathered to meet him. 2Don't be so easily shaken or alarmed by those who say that the day of the Lord has already begun. Don't believe them, even if they claim to have had a spiritual vision, a revelation, or a letter supposedly from us. 3Don't be fooled by what they say. For that day will not come until there is a great rebellion against God and the man of lawlessness* is revealed—the one who brings destruction.* 4He will exalt himself and defy everything that people call god and every object of worship. He will even sit in the temple of God, claiming that he himself is God.

5Don't you remember that I told you about all this when I was with you? 6And you know what is holding him back, for he can be revealed only when his time comes. 7For this lawlessness is already at work secretly, and it will remain secret until the one who is holding it back steps out of the way. 8Then the man of lawlessness will be revealed, but the Lord Jesus will kill him with the breath of his mouth and destroy him by the splendor of his coming.

9This man will come to do the work of Satan with counterfeit power and signs and miracles. 10He will use every kind of evil deception to fool those on their way to destruction, because they refuse to love and accept the truth that would save them. 11So God will cause them to be greatly deceived, and they will believe these lies. 12Then they will be condemned for enjoying evil rather than believing the truth.

## Believers Should Stand Firm

13As for us, we can't help but thank God for you, dear brothers and sisters loved by the Lord. We are always thankful that God chose

1:1 Greek *Silvanus,* the Greek form of the name.   1:2 Some manuscripts read *God the Father.*   1:3 Greek *Brothers.*   1:12 Or *of our God and our Lord Jesus Christ.*   2:1 Greek *brothers;* also in 2:13, 15.   2:3a Some manuscripts read *the man of sin.*   2:3b Greek *the son of destruction.*

you to be among the first* to experience salvation—a salvation that came through the Spirit who makes you holy and through your belief in the truth. ¹⁴He called you to salvation when we told you the Good News; now you can share in the glory of our Lord Jesus Christ.

¹⁵With all these things in mind, dear brothers and sisters, stand firm and keep a strong grip on the teaching we passed on to you both in person and by letter.

¹⁶Now may our Lord Jesus Christ himself and God our Father, who loved us and by his grace gave us eternal comfort and a wonderful hope, ¹⁷comfort you and strengthen you in every good thing you do and say.

### Paul's Request for Prayer

**3** Finally, dear brothers and sisters,* we ask you to pray for us. Pray that the Lord's message will spread rapidly and be honored wherever it goes, just as when it came to you. ²Pray, too, that we will be rescued from wicked and evil people, for not everyone is a believer. ³But the Lord is faithful; he will strengthen you and guard you from the evil one.* ⁴And we are confident in the Lord that you are doing and will continue to do the things we commanded you. ⁵May the Lord lead your hearts into a full understanding and expression of the love of God and the patient endurance that comes from Christ.

### An Exhortation to Proper Living

⁶And now, dear brothers and sisters, we give you this command in the name of our Lord Jesus Christ: Stay away from all believers* who live idle lives and don't follow the tradition they received* from us. ⁷For you know that you ought to imitate us. We were not idle when we were with you. ⁸We never accepted food from anyone without paying for it. We worked hard day and night so we would not be a burden to any of you. ⁹We certainly had the right to ask you to feed us,

## TODAY'S to-do list
READ 2 THESSALONIANS 1:11

Wouldn't it be great to have the strength to accomplish everything you wanted to get done in a day? How wonderful to have enough stamina to do household chores or put in a full workday or at least not collapse after doing such things.

Sick people and those caring for them probably pray for strength as much as anything. The Bible never promises we will have the strength to get everything done on our to-do list, but it does assure us that God will give us the power to do whatever He calls us to do.

but we wanted to give you an example to follow. ¹⁰Even while we were with you, we gave you this command: "Those unwilling to work will not get to eat."

¹¹Yet we hear that some of you are living idle lives, refusing to work and meddling in other people's business. ¹²We command such people and urge them in the name of the Lord Jesus Christ to settle down and work to earn their own living. ¹³As for the rest of you, dear brothers and sisters, never get tired of doing good.

¹⁴Take note of those who refuse to obey what we say in this letter. Stay away from them so they will be ashamed. ¹⁵Don't think of them as enemies, but warn them as you would a brother or sister.*

### Paul's Final Greetings

¹⁶Now may the Lord of peace himself give you his peace at all times and in every situation. The Lord be with you all.

¹⁷HERE IS MY GREETING IN MY OWN HANDWRITING—PAUL. I DO THIS IN ALL MY LETTERS TO PROVE THEY ARE FROM ME.

¹⁸May the grace of our Lord Jesus Christ be with you all.

**2:13** Some manuscripts read *chose you from the very beginning. from every brother.* **3:6b** Some manuscripts read *you received.* **3:1** Greek *brothers;* also in 3:6, 13. **3:3** Or *from evil.* **3:6a** Greek **3:15** Greek *as a brother.*

# LOSING your faith?

Have the trials of life caused you to lose your faith in God? Or are the doubts starting to pile up and you're wondering if you're on the verge of turning your back on Him?

Oh, you still believe God exists, but you don't feel like you can or want to trust Him anymore. The difficulties of life and especially serious health concerns can lead to a spiritual crisis in many lives.

"Doubt rises up to obscure His presence and disillusionment settles into despair," writes Dr. James Dobson in *When God Doesn't Make Sense*. "The greatest frustration is knowing that He created the entire universe by simply speaking it into existence, and He has all the power and all understanding. He could rescue. He could heal. He could save. But why won't He do it?"[1]

Feeling abandoned by God is especially terrible to experience after you earlier felt closeness with Him.

"Satan then drops by for a little visit and whispers, 'He is not there! You are alone!'" Dobson adds.[2]

We can't begin to explain to you why yet another family member is sick or why your child has a life-threatening illness or why you've received such a dismal diagnosis. We agree with you that **it doesn't make sense, it doesn't seem right, and it certainly doesn't *feel* like God cares.**

But we also believe that despite life's tough situations, we all are *deeply* loved by our heavenly Father. We believe He proved that once and for all 2,000 years ago when He sent His one and only, perfectly sinless Son to die on the cross for your sins and for ours. We believe that even if God never answered another single prayer on our behalf, He already has done enough because when He raised Jesus to life, He defeated our greatest enemy: Death.

So go ahead and ask Him all your questions. As the praise chorus says, "Give Him all your tears and sorrow. Give Him all your years of pain."

But remember, God is not going to defend His actions (or seeming in-actions) to you, and you may never know the reasons for the suffering that has touched your life.

He asks only one thing of you—to trust Him even when it doesn't make sense.

[1] James Dobson, *When God Doesn't Make Sense* (Carol Stream, IL: Tyndale House Publishers, 1993), 18.    [2] Ibid.

# 1 TIMOTHY

> *I urge you, first of all, to pray for all people. Ask God to help them; intercede on their behalf, and give thanks for them.*
>
> 1 TIMOTHY 2:1

Have you prayed less or more since you or your loved one was diagnosed with a serious illness? Are fewer or more people praying for you since that diagnosis? Pretty obvious answers here.

Can you even imagine turning down any prayers? ("No, thanks, please don't pray, we have too many prayers already.") Not likely to happen.

When people tell us they're praying for us, we don't take those words glibly. We actually might be tempted to ask, "Are you really?" because we know we are hanging on by the thin threads of those prayers. We not only don't turn down prayer; we are counting on it to see us through.

Go ahead and get your name on every church telephone prayer chain in the country. Gather up as many friends as you can and let them pray over you. Don't be shy about asking that others lift your needs to God. But don't forget your part: You can "pray for all people," too. An hour in an MRI tube is a great chance for you to ask God "to help them." A thirty-minute echocardiogram gives you plenty of time to "intercede on their behalf." Fifteen minutes waiting in an exam room for a running-late doctor is the perfect opportunity to "give thanks for them."

It is an incredible joy to be prayed for . . . and an awesome joy to pray for others.

## Greetings from Paul

**1** This letter is from Paul, an apostle of Christ Jesus, appointed by the command of God our Savior and Christ Jesus, who gives us hope.

²I am writing to Timothy, my true son in the faith.

May God the Father and Christ Jesus our Lord give you grace, mercy, and peace.

## Warnings against False Teachings

³When I left for Macedonia, I urged you to stay there in Ephesus and stop those whose teaching is contrary to the truth. ⁴Don't let them waste their time in endless discussion of myths and spiritual pedigrees. These things only lead to meaningless speculations,* which don't help people live a life of faith in God.*

⁵The purpose of my instruction is that all believers would be filled with love that comes from a pure heart, a clear conscience, and genuine faith. ⁶But some people have missed this whole point. They have turned away from these things and spend their time in meaningless discussions. ⁷They want to be known as teachers of the law of Moses, but they don't know what they are talking about, even though they speak so confidently.

⁸We know that the law is good when used correctly. ⁹For the law was not intended for people who do what is right. It is for people who are lawless and rebellious, who are ungodly and sinful, who consider nothing sacred and defile what is holy, who kill their father or mother or commit other murders. ¹⁰The law is for people who are sexually immoral, or who practice homosexuality, or are slave traders,* liars, promise breakers, or who do anything else that contradicts the wholesome teaching ¹¹that comes from the glorious Good News entrusted to me by our blessed God.

## Paul's Gratitude for God's Mercy

¹²I thank Christ Jesus our Lord, who has given me strength to do his work. He considered me trustworthy and appointed me to serve him, ¹³even though I used to blaspheme the name of Christ. In my insolence, I persecuted his people. But God had mercy on me because I did it in ignorance and unbelief. ¹⁴Oh, how generous and gracious our Lord was! He filled me with the faith and love that come from Christ Jesus.

¹⁵This is a trustworthy saying, and everyone should accept it: "Christ Jesus came into the world to save sinners"—and I am the worst of them all. ¹⁶But God had mercy on me so that Christ Jesus could use me as a prime example of his great patience with even the worst sinners. Then others will realize that they, too, can believe in him and receive eternal life. ¹⁷All honor and glory to God forever and ever! He is the eternal King, the unseen one who never dies; he alone is God. Amen.

## Timothy's Responsibility

¹⁸Timothy, my son, here are my instructions for you, based on the prophetic words spoken about you earlier. May they help you fight well in the Lord's battles. ¹⁹Cling to your faith in Christ, and keep your conscience clear. For some people have deliberately violated their consciences; as a result, their faith has been shipwrecked. ²⁰Hymenaeus and Alexander are two examples. I threw them out and handed them over to Satan so they might learn not to blaspheme God.

## Instructions about Worship

**2** I urge you, first of all, to pray for all people. Ask God to help them; intercede on their behalf, and give thanks for them. ²Pray this way for kings and all who are in authority so that we can live peaceful and quiet lives marked by godliness and dignity. ³This is good and pleases God our Savior, ⁴who wants everyone to be saved and to under-

---

1:4a Greek *in myths and endless genealogies, which cause speculation.* 1:4b Greek *a stewardship of God in faith.* 1:10 Or *kidnappers.*

stand the truth. **5**For there is only one God and one Mediator who can reconcile God and humanity—the man Christ Jesus. **6**He gave his life to purchase freedom for everyone. This is the message God gave to the world at just the right time. **7**And I have been chosen as a preacher and apostle to teach the Gentiles this message about faith and truth. I'm not exaggerating—just telling the truth.

**8**In every place of worship, I want men to pray with holy hands lifted up to God, free from anger and controversy.

**9**And I want women to be modest in their appearance.* They should wear decent and appropriate clothing and not draw attention to themselves by the way they fix their hair or by wearing gold or pearls or expensive clothes. **10**For women who claim to be devoted to God should make themselves attractive by the good things they do.

**11**Women should learn quietly and submissively. **12**I do not let women teach men or have authority over them.* Let them listen quietly. **13**For God made Adam first, and afterward he made Eve. **14**And it was not Adam who was deceived by Satan. The woman was deceived, and sin was the result. **15**But women will be saved through childbearing,* assuming they continue to live in faith, love, holiness, and modesty.

## Leaders in the Church  Elder

**3** This is a trustworthy saying: "If someone aspires to be an elder,* he desires an honorable position." **2**So an elder must be a man whose life is above reproach. He must be faithful to his wife.* He must exercise self-control, live wisely, and have a good reputation. He must enjoy having guests in his home, and he must be able to teach. **3**He must not be a heavy drinker* or be violent. He must be gentle, not quarrelsome, and not love money. **4**He must manage his own family well, having children who respect and obey him. **5**For if a man cannot manage his own household, how can he take care of God's church?

### PATHWAYS to healing
READ 1 TIMOTHY 2:5

If you've been dealing with a health crisis very long, you've probably noticed medicine isn't always an exact science, and decisions aren't always crystal clear. Sometimes a physician offers various choices, or a second opinion yields additional ways to approach a problem. Most of us like having options rather than just a single choice.

But while there may be many pathways to physical health, there is only one pathway to true spiritual health. We may be told there are many ways to reach God and we can choose our own path. But this verse and others in Scripture make it clear there is only one way to get right with God—through His Son, Jesus. One God, one Savior, one path.

**6**An elder must not be a new believer, because he might become proud, and the devil would cause him to fall.* **7**Also, people outside the church must speak well of him so that he will not be disgraced and fall into the devil's trap.

**8**In the same way, deacons must be well respected and have integrity. They must not be heavy drinkers or dishonest with money. **9**They must be committed to the mystery of the faith now revealed and must live with a clear conscience. **10**Before they are appointed as deacons, let them be closely examined. If they pass the test, then let them serve as deacons.

**11**In the same way, their wives* must be respected and must not slander others. They must exercise self-control and be faithful in everything they do.

**12**A deacon must be faithful to his wife, and he must manage his children and household well. **13**Those who do well as deacons will be rewarded with respect from others and will have increased confidence in their faith in Christ Jesus.

### The Truths of Our Faith
**14**I am writing these things to you now, even though I hope to be with you soon, **15**so that

2:9 Or to pray in modest apparel.   2:12 Or teach men or usurp their authority.   2:15 Or will be saved by accepting their role as mothers, or will be saved by the birth of the Child.   3:1 Or an overseer, or a bishop; also in 3:2, 6.   3:2 Or must have only one wife, or must be married only once; Greek reads must be the husband of one wife; also in 3:12.   3:3 Greek must not drink too much wine; similarly in 3:8.   3:6 Or he might fall into the same judgment as the devil.   3:11 Or the women deacons. The Greek word can be translated women or wives.

Remember when you were a kid and indignantly informed your parents: "That's not fair!"

They probably responded with some important information for you: "Life's not fair." Their response only made you madder!

Nobody who's being treated unfairly wants to hear it. It's a logical response to a heartfelt emotion. But the longer we live, the more we all realize how true that statement is. Perhaps life has been unfair to you or your loved one recently—or perhaps for a very long time. Either way, life has disappointed you. **Maybe if you're really honest, you'll admit you even feel disappointed with God.**

We have another truth we'd like to share: Don't confuse life with God.

In Philip Yancey's book *Disappointment with God*, he writes about a man named Douglas whom he interviewed because he thought Douglas might feel a great disappointment with God. Life, as Yancey describes it, had been very unfair to Douglas. While his wife was battling advanced breast cancer, Douglas was in a car accident with a drunk driver and suffered a terrible head injury that left him permanently disabled, often in pain, and unable to work full-time.

But when Yancey asked this victim of unfairness to describe his disappointment with God, Douglas said he didn't feel any and instead told Yancey the following:

> "I have learned to see beyond the physical reality in this world to the spiritual reality. We tend to think, 'Life should be fair because God is fair.' But God is not life. And if I confuse God with the physical reality of life—by expecting constant good health, for example—then I set myself up for crashing disappointment.
>
> "If we develop a relationship with God *apart* from our life circumstances," said Douglas, "then we may be able to hang in there when the physical reality breaks down. We can learn to trust God in spite of the unfairness of life."[1]

Disease is very unfair. Even if you "did" something to "get" it or didn't do something *not* to get it, it's still unfair. Maybe you are a smoker diagnosed with some smoking-related illness. It's still unfair because many smokers never develop a disease from their habit (only about 20 percent get lung cancer). Maybe you quit smoking ten or twenty years ago and you still have been afflicted. Hardly fair.

Perhaps you didn't get regular mammograms, Pap smears, or PSA tests and now you have cancer. Guess what—it's still not fair, because lots of people don't get those screening tests and they don't get cancer. Besides, some people get them faithfully and the cancer isn't even detected! That seems even more unfair.

Maybe you are overweight or out of shape or didn't get regular physicals and now you have a serious illness. It's still not very fair because you know many others in your same circumstances with great health. Or perhaps you received the ultimate insult by being diagnosed with a serious disease in spite of taking the *best* care possible of yourself and doing everything right not to get sick.

**Go ahead and say it.**

**It's not fair that I have this.**

**It's not fair that my loved one has this.**

**It's not fair that this has happened to us right now.**

Say it, but don't be confused that life should be fair because God is. Life is not fair, but God is not life.

Yancey says, "Every time a believer struggles with sorrow or loneliness or ill health or pain and chooses to trust and serve God anyhow, a bell rings out across heaven and the angels give a great shout. Why? Because one more pilgrim has shown again that he or she understands that Jesus is worth it all. God is faithful."[2]

There's a law firm that advertises on the radio by spotlighting people who have had awful, unfair things happen to them and then hired a lawyer to try and rectify the situation. The commercial concludes that you, too, should call this law firm "when life hands you moments you just don't deserve."

We think we have even better advice: When life hands you moments you just don't deserve, put your trust in the Lord; because even when life is unfair, God is faithful.

[1]Philip Yancey, *Disappointment with God* (Grand Rapids, MI: Zondervan, 1988), 182–184.   [2]Ibid., 170.

if I am delayed, you will know how people must conduct themselves in the household of God. This is the church of the living God, which is the pillar and foundation of the truth.

16Without question, this is the great mystery of our faith*:

Christ* was revealed in a human body
and vindicated by the Spirit.*
He was seen by angels
and announced to the nations.
He was believed in throughout
the world
and taken to heaven in glory.

## Warnings against False Teachers

**4** Now the Holy Spirit tells us clearly that in the last times some will turn away from the true faith; they will follow deceptive spirits and teachings that come from demons. 2These people are hypocrites and liars, and their consciences are dead.* 3They will say it is wrong to be married and wrong to eat certain foods. But God created those foods to be eaten with thanks by faithful people who know the truth. 4Since everything God created is good, we should not reject any of it but receive it with thanks. 5For we know it is made acceptable* by the word of God and prayer.

## A Good Servant of Christ Jesus

6If you explain these things to the brothers and sisters,* Timothy, you will be a worthy servant of Christ Jesus, one who is nourished by the message of faith and the good teaching you have followed. 7Do not waste time arguing over godless ideas and old wives' tales. Instead, train yourself to be godly. 8"Physical training is good, but training for godliness is much better, promising benefits in this life and in the life to come." 9This is a trustworthy saying, and everyone should accept it. 10This is why we work hard and continue to struggle,* for our hope is in the living God, who is the Savior of all people and particularly of all believers.

11Teach these things and insist that everyone learn them. 12Don't let anyone think less of you because you are young. Be an example to all believers in what you say, in the way you live, in your love, your faith, and your purity. 13Until I get there, focus on reading the Scriptures to the church, encouraging the believers, and teaching them.

14Do not neglect the spiritual gift you received through the prophecy spoken over you when the elders of the church laid their hands on you. 15Give your complete attention to these matters. Throw yourself into your tasks so that everyone will see your progress. 16Keep a close watch on how you live and on your teaching. Stay true to what is right for the sake of your own salvation and the salvation of those who hear you.

## Advice about Widows, Elders, and Slaves

**5** Never speak harshly to an older man,* but appeal to him respectfully as you would to your own father. Talk to younger men as you would to your own brothers. 2Treat older women as you would your mother, and treat younger women with all purity as you would your own sisters.

3Take care of* any widow who has no one else to care for her. 4But if she has children or grandchildren, their first responsibility is to show godliness at home and repay their parents by taking care of them. This is something that pleases God.

5Now a true widow, a woman who is truly alone in this world, has placed her hope in God. She prays night and day, asking God for his help. 6But the widow who lives only for pleasure is spiritually dead even while she lives. 7Give these instructions to the church so that no one will be open to criticism.

8But those who won't care for their relatives, especially those in their own household, have denied the true faith. Such people are worse than unbelievers.

9A widow who is put on the list for support must be a woman who is at least sixty years old and was faithful to her husband.* 10She must be well respected by everyone because of the good she has done. Has she brought up her children well? Has she been kind to strangers and served other believers

3:16a Or of godliness. 3:16b Greek He who; other manuscripts read God. 3:16c Or in his spirit. 4:2 Greek are seared. 4:5 Or made holy. 4:6 Greek brothers. 4:10 Some manuscripts read continue to suffer. 5:1 Or an elder. 5:3 Or Honor. 5:9 Greek was the wife of one husband.

humbly?* Has she helped those who are in trouble? Has she always been ready to do good?

¹¹The younger widows should not be on the list, because their physical desires will overpower their devotion to Christ and they will want to remarry. ¹²Then they would be guilty of breaking their previous pledge. ¹³And if they are on the list, they will learn to be lazy and will spend their time gossiping from house to house, meddling in other people's business and talking about things they shouldn't. ¹⁴So I advise these younger widows to marry again, have children, and take care of their own homes. Then the enemy will not be able to say anything against them. ¹⁵For I am afraid that some of them have already gone astray and now follow Satan.

¹⁶If a woman who is a believer has relatives who are widows, she must take care of them and not put the responsibility on the church. Then the church can care for the widows who are truly alone.

¹⁷Elders who do their work well should be respected and paid well,* especially those who work hard at both preaching and teaching. ¹⁸For the Scripture says, "You must not muzzle an ox to keep it from eating as it treads out the grain." And in another place, " Those who work deserve their pay!"*

¹⁹Do not listen to an accusation against an elder unless it is confirmed by two or three witnesses. ²⁰Those who sin should be reprimanded in front of the whole church; this will serve as a strong warning to others.

²¹I solemnly command you in the presence of God and Christ Jesus and the holy angels to obey these instructions without taking sides or showing favoritism to anyone.

²²Never be in a hurry about appointing a church leader.* Do not share in the sins of others. Keep yourself pure.

²³Don't drink only water. You ought to drink a little wine for the sake of your stomach because you are sick so often.

²⁴Remember, the sins of some people are obvious, leading them to certain judgment. But there are others whose sins will not be revealed until later. ²⁵In the same way, the

good deeds of some people are obvious. And the good deeds done in secret will someday come to light.

**6** All slaves should show full respect for their masters so they will not bring shame on the name of God and his teaching. ²If the masters are believers, that is no excuse for being disrespectful. Those slaves should work all the harder because their efforts are helping other believers* who are well loved.

### False Teaching and True Riches

Teach these things, Timothy, and encourage everyone to obey them. ³Some people may contradict our teaching, but these are the wholesome teachings of the Lord Jesus Christ. These teachings promote a godly life. ⁴Anyone who teaches something different is arrogant and lacks understanding. Such a person has an unhealthy desire to quibble over the meaning of words. This stirs up arguments ending in jealousy, division, slander, and evil suspicions. ⁵These people always cause trouble. Their minds are corrupt, and they have turned their backs on the truth. To them, a show of godliness is just a way to become wealthy.

⁶Yet true godliness with contentment is itself great wealth. ⁷After all, we brought nothing with us when we came into the world, and we can't take anything with us when we leave

## IN God we trust

READ 1 TIMOTHY 6:10, 17

Illness has a funny way of putting us all on the same level. Both the rich and the poor can be devastated by a disease, sidelined by sickness, or crippled with a condition. Just read the newspapers and you'll see that even those famous headline-makers with money to burn do fall victim to illness and even death. Surely, if money could buy health, these rich folks would have found a way. The Bible doesn't say money is the root of all kinds of evil—it says "the love of money" is. Whether you have a little or a lot of money, never put your trust in anything but the inscription engraved upon it.

5:10 Greek *and washed the feet of God's holy people?*
5:17 Greek *should be worthy of double honor.*   5:18 Deut 25:4; Luke 10:7.   5:22 Greek *about the laying on of hands.*
6:2 Greek *brothers.*

it. ⁸So if we have enough food and clothing, let us be content.

⁹But people who long to be rich fall into temptation and are trapped by many foolish and harmful desires that plunge them into ruin and destruction. ¹⁰For the love of money is the root of all kinds of evil. And some people, craving money, have wandered from the true faith and pierced themselves with many sorrows.

### Paul's Final Instructions

¹¹But you, Timothy, are a man of God; so run from all these evil things. Pursue righteousness and a godly life, along with faith, love, perseverance, and gentleness. **12**Fight the good fight for the true faith. Hold tightly to the eternal life to which God has called you, which you have confessed so well before many witnesses. ¹³And I charge you before God, who gives life to all, and before Christ Jesus, who gave a good testimony before Pontius Pilate, ¹⁴that you obey this command without wavering. Then no one can find fault with you from now until our Lord Jesus Christ comes again. ¹⁵For at just the right time Christ will be revealed from heaven by the blessed and only almighty God, the King of all kings and Lord of all lords. ¹⁶He alone can never die, and he lives in light so brilliant that no human can approach him. No human eye has ever seen him, nor ever will. All honor and power to him forever! Amen.

¹⁷Teach those who are rich in this world not to be proud and not to trust in their money, which is so unreliable. Their trust should be in God, who richly gives us all we need for our enjoyment. ¹⁸Tell them to use their money to do good. They should be rich in good works and generous to those in need, always being ready to share with others. ¹⁹By doing this they will be storing up their treasure as a good foundation for the future so that they may experience true life.

²⁰Timothy, guard what God has entrusted to you. Avoid godless, foolish discussions with those who oppose you with their so-called knowledge. ²¹Some people have wandered from the faith by following such foolishness.

May God's grace be with you all.

# 2 TIMOTHY

> *For I know the one in whom I trust, and I am sure that he is able to guard what I have entrusted to him until the day of his return.*
>
> 2 TIMOTHY 1:12

It's crucial to have trust in our medical teams and in our treatments. That doesn't mean we don't ask questions or seek out information on our own, but we need to have a level of trust that our life or our loved one's life is in good, trustworthy hands. And if we find that our trust is wavering because a health professional does not listen to our concerns or is unavailable for our medical needs, it may be time to put together a new team. Some of us have had *too* much trust in a less-than-competent physician and we ended up not getting the right tests done in a timely fashion, delaying our diagnosis or treatment.

In yet another letter from prison, the apostle Paul talks about how he has entrusted his life to someone and knows it's safe in His hands. That person is the Lord Jesus, and Paul is very confident in that trust. That's because it is *not* a blind trust, as Paul asserts, "I know the one in whom I trust."

We can't really trust the Lord with our lives or our loved one's life unless we *know* Him well enough to trust Him. So go ahead and ask Him questions and seek out reliable information about Him. You won't be disappointed. He always listens to our concerns and is available for our needs. The more you see Him work in your life today, the more you'll trust Him with all of your tomorrows.

# 1

This letter is from Paul, chosen by the will of God to be an apostle of Christ Jesus. I have been sent out to tell others about the life he has promised through faith in Christ Jesus.

²I am writing to Timothy, my dear son.

May God the Father and Christ Jesus our Lord give you grace, mercy, and peace.

## Encouragement to Be Faithful

³Timothy, I thank God for you—the God I serve with a clear conscience, just as my ancestors did. Night and day I constantly remember you in my prayers. ⁴I long to see you again, for I remember your tears as we parted. And I will be filled with joy when we are together again.

⁵I remember your genuine faith, for you share the faith that first filled your grandmother Lois and your mother, Eunice. And I know that same faith continues strong in you. ⁶This is why I remind you to fan into flames the spiritual gift God gave you when I laid my hands on you. ⁷For God has not given us a spirit of fear and timidity, but of power, love, and self-discipline.

⁸So never be ashamed to tell others about our Lord. And don't be ashamed of me, either, even though I'm in prison for him. With the strength God gives you, be ready to suffer with me for the sake of the Good News. ⁹For God saved us and called us to live a holy life. He did this, not because we deserved it, but because that was his plan from before the beginning of time—to show us his grace through Christ Jesus. ¹⁰And now he has made all of this plain to us by the appearing of Christ Jesus, our Savior. He broke the power of death and illuminated the way to life and immortality through the Good News. ¹¹And God chose me to be a preacher, an apostle, and a teacher of this Good News.

¹²That is why I am suffering here in prison. But I am not ashamed of it, for I know the one in whom I trust, and I am sure that he

1:12 Or *what has been entrusted to me.*

is able to guard what I have entrusted to him* until the day of his return.

¹³Hold on to the pattern of wholesome teaching you learned from me—a pattern shaped by the faith and love that you have in Christ Jesus. ¹⁴Through the power of the Holy Spirit who lives within us, carefully guard the precious truth that has been entrusted to you.

¹⁵As you know, everyone from the province of Asia has deserted me—even Phygelus and Hermogenes.

¹⁶May the Lord show special kindness to Onesiphorus and all his family because he often visited and encouraged me. He was never ashamed of me because I was in chains. ¹⁷When he came to Rome, he searched everywhere until he found me. ¹⁸May the Lord show him special kindness on the day of Christ's return. And you know very well how helpful he was in Ephesus.

## A Good Soldier of Christ Jesus

# 2

Timothy, my dear son, be strong through the grace that God gives you in Christ Jesus. ²You have heard me teach things that have been confirmed by many reliable witnesses. Now teach these truths to other trustworthy people who will be able to pass them on to others.

³Endure suffering along with me, as a good soldier of Christ Jesus. ⁴Soldiers don't get tied up in the affairs of civilian life, for then they cannot please the officer who enlisted them. ⁵And athletes cannot win the prize unless they follow the rules. ⁶And hardworking farmers should be the first to enjoy the fruit of their labor. ⁷Think about what I am saying. The Lord will help you understand all these things.

⁸Always remember that Jesus Christ, a descendant of King David, was raised from the dead. This is the Good News I preach. ⁹And because I preach this Good News, I am suffering and have been chained like a criminal. But the word of God cannot be chained.

¹⁰So I am willing to endure anything if it will bring salvation and eternal glory in Christ Jesus to those God has chosen. ¹¹This is a trustworthy saying:

If we die with him,
we will also live with him.
¹² If we endure hardship,
we will reign with him.
If we deny him,
he will deny us.
¹³ If we are unfaithful,
he remains faithful,
for he cannot deny who he is.

¹⁴Remind everyone about these things, and command them in God's presence to stop fighting over words. Such arguments are useless, and they can ruin those who hear them.

### An Approved Worker

¹⁵Work hard so you can present yourself to God and receive his approval. Be a good worker, one who does not need to be ashamed and who correctly explains the word of truth. ¹⁶Avoid worthless, foolish talk that only leads to more godless behavior. ¹⁷This kind of talk spreads like cancer, as in the case of Hymenaeus and Philetus. ¹⁸They have left the path of truth, claiming that the resurrection of the dead has already occurred; in this way, they have turned some people away from the faith.

¹⁹But God's truth stands firm like a foundation stone with this inscription: "The LORD knows those who are his,"* and "All who belong to the LORD must turn away from evil."*

²⁰In a wealthy home some utensils are made of gold and silver, and some are made of wood and clay. The expensive utensils are used for special occasions, and the cheap ones are for everyday use. ²¹If you keep yourself pure, you will be a special utensil for honorable use. Your life will be clean, and you will be ready for the Master to use you for every good work.

²²Run from anything that stimulates youthful lusts. Instead, pursue righteous living, faithfulness, love, and peace. Enjoy the companionship of those who call on the Lord with pure hearts.

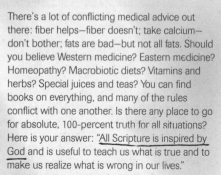

## CONFLICTING
### medical advice
READ 2 TIMOTHY 3:16-17

There's a lot of conflicting medical advice out there: fiber helps—fiber doesn't; take calcium—don't bother; fats are bad—but not all fats. Should you believe Western medicine? Eastern medicine? Homeopathy? Macrobiotic diets? Vitamins and herbs? Special juices and teas? You can find books on everything, and many of the rules conflict with one another. Is there any place to go for absolute, 100-percent truth for all situations? Here is your answer: "All Scripture is inspired by God and is useful to teach us what is true and to make us realize what is wrong in our lives."

²³Again I say, don't get involved in foolish, ignorant arguments that only start fights. ²⁴A servant of the Lord must not quarrel but must be kind to everyone, be able to teach, and be patient with difficult people. ²⁵Gently instruct those who oppose the truth. Perhaps God will change those people's hearts, and they will learn the truth. ²⁶Then they will come to their senses and escape from the devil's trap. For they have been held captive by him to do whatever he wants.

### The Dangers of the Last Days

**3** You should know this, Timothy, that in the last days there will be very difficult times. ²For people will love only themselves and their money. They will be boastful and proud, scoffing at God, disobedient to their parents, and ungrateful. They will consider nothing sacred. ³They will be unloving and unforgiving; they will slander others and have no self-control. They will be cruel and hate what is good. ⁴They will betray their friends, be reckless, be puffed up with pride, and love pleasure rather than God. ⁵They will act religious, but they will reject the power that could make them godly. Stay away from people like that!

⁶They are the kind who work their way into people's homes and win the confidence of* vulnerable women who are burdened with the guilt of sin and controlled by various

2:19a Num 16:5.   2:19b See Isa 52:11.   3:6 Greek *and take captive.*

desires. 7(Such women are forever following new teachings, but they are never able to understand the truth.) 8These teachers oppose the truth just as Jannes and Jambres opposed Moses. They have depraved minds and a counterfeit faith. 9But they won't get away with this for long. Someday everyone will recognize what fools they are, just as with Jannes and Jambres.

### Paul's Charge to Timothy

10But you, Timothy, certainly know what I teach, and how I live, and what my purpose in life is. You know my faith, my patience, my love, and my endurance. 11You know how much persecution and suffering I have endured. You know all about how I was persecuted in Antioch, Iconium, and Lystra—but the Lord rescued me from all of it. 12Yes, and everyone who wants to live a godly life in Christ Jesus will suffer persecution. 13But evil people and impostors will flourish. They will deceive others and will themselves be deceived.

14But you must remain faithful to the things you have been taught. You know they are true, for you know you can trust those who taught you. 15You have been taught the holy Scriptures from childhood, and they have given you the wisdom to receive the salvation that comes by trusting in Christ Jesus. 16All Scripture is inspired by God and is useful to teach us what is true and to make us realize what is wrong in our lives. It corrects us when we are wrong and teaches us to do what is right. 17God uses it to prepare and equip his people to do every good work.

4 I solemnly urge you in the presence of God and Christ Jesus, who will someday judge the living and the dead when he appears to set up his Kingdom: 2Preach the word of God. Be prepared, whether the time is favorable or not. Patiently correct, rebuke, and encourage your people with good teaching.

3For a time is coming when people will no longer listen to sound and wholesome teaching. They will follow their own desires and will look for teachers who will tell them whatever their itching ears want to hear. 4They will reject the truth and chase after myths.

5But you should keep a clear mind in every situation. Don't be afraid of suffering for the Lord. Work at telling others the Good News, and fully carry out the ministry God has given you.

6As for me, my life has already been poured out as an offering to God. The time of my death is near. 7I have fought the good fight, I have finished the race, and I have remained faithful. 8And now the prize awaits me—the crown of righteousness, which the Lord, the righteous Judge, will give me on the day of his return. And the prize is not just for me but for all who eagerly look forward to his appearing.

### Paul's Final Words

9Timothy, please come as soon as you can. 10Demas has deserted me because he loves the things of this life and has gone to Thessalonica. Crescens has gone to Galatia, and Titus has gone to Dalmatia. 11Only Luke is with me. Bring Mark with you when you come, for he will be helpful to me in my ministry. 12I sent Tychicus to Ephesus. 13When you come, be sure to bring the coat I left with Carpus at Troas. Also bring my books, and especially my papers.*

14Alexander the coppersmith did me much harm, but the Lord will judge him for what he has done. 15Be careful of him, for he fought against everything we said.

4:13 Greek *especially the parchments.*

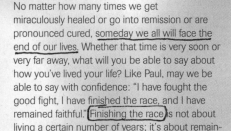

# FINISHING
## the race
READ 2 TIMOTHY 4:7-8

No matter how many times we get miraculously healed or go into remission or are pronounced cured, someday we all will face the end of our lives. Whether that time is very soon or very far away, what will you be able to say about how you've lived your life? Like Paul, may we be able to say with confidence: "I have fought the good fight, I have finished the race, and I have remained faithful." Finishing the race is not about living a certain number of years; it's about remaining faithful in the years God gives us.

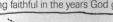

¹⁶The first time I was brought before the judge, no one came with me. Everyone abandoned me. May it not be counted against them. ¹⁷But the Lord stood with me and gave me strength so that I might preach the Good News in its entirety for all the Gentiles to hear. And he rescued me from certain death.* ¹⁸Yes, and the Lord will deliver me from every evil attack and will bring me safely into his heavenly Kingdom. All glory to God forever and ever! Amen.

**4:17** Greek *from the mouth of a lion.*   **4:21** Greek *brothers.*

### Paul's Final Greetings

¹⁹Give my greetings to Priscilla and Aquila and those living in the household of Onesiphorus. ²⁰Erastus stayed at Corinth, and I left Trophimus sick at Miletus.

²¹Do your best to get here before winter. Eubulus sends you greetings, and so do Pudens, Linus, Claudia, and all the brothers and sisters.*

²²May the Lord be with your spirit. And may his grace be with all of you.

# HOW could God let this happen?

When you believe in God, it can be hard to come to terms with the fact that He has allowed adversity to come into your life or your loved one's. David Biebel talks about this fact in his book *If God Is So Good, Why Do I Hurt So Bad?* He says there are two truths suffering people have to reconcile: sometimes life is agony, and our loving God is in control.

Think about it.

If God knows everything, this diagnosis did not surprise Him.

If God sees everything, He saw the bad news coming.

If God has power over everything, He could have stopped it.

But He didn't.

He didn't stop you or your loved one from getting cancer or AIDS or lupus or Alzheimer's or kidney disease or whatever else has afflicted you. He didn't stop it from happening to you or your loved one or many other people or their loved ones.

But the reality is that God's Word never promises that He will stop all bad things from happening to us. On the contrary, it promises us that He is prepared for each battle and will equip us, too.

*The MESSAGE* Bible paraphrases 2 Corinthians 4:8-9 this way: "We've been surrounded and battered by troubles, but we're not demoralized; **we're not sure what to do, but we know that God knows what to do;** we've been spiritually terrorized; but God hasn't left our side; we've been thrown down, but we haven't broken."

God is in control.

Errant cells aren't.

Toxic medicine isn't.

White-coated doctors aren't.

Herbs and vitamins aren't.

We aren't.

The sooner we learn this truth, the easier our fight against illness will be. It's actually quite freeing once you get it right. **You can relax knowing Someone else is in charge**—Someone much more intelligent, powerful, and vigilant than we are or could ever hope to be.

Be encouraged that this health crisis has not taken God by surprise. He is in control and knows how to equip you for the fight.

# TITUS

*This truth gives them confidence that they have eternal life, which God—who does not lie—promised them before the world began.*

TITUS 1:2

How much confidence do you have in your medical team? How about in the drugs you're taking? How confident are you about your chances for recovery?

Confidence is great, but it's not an ironclad guarantee of a desired outcome. Most of us know someone who has been let down by a doctor in whom they had confidence. Some of us confidently have taken drugs only to be disappointed in the results. And some who have been absolutely confident of a miracle haven't gotten it.

But there is one matter about which we can have absolute, certain confidence—yes, an ironclad guarantee. We can know where we are going to spend eternity—whether we will have eternal life with God or eternal separation from God. It is possible to know for certain that if we died tonight we would wake up in heaven.

We don't have to keep our fingers crossed and "hope" we're going to heaven. We don't have to wonder if we will make it there. We can have *confidence* that we have eternal life. That's because our confidence is not in ourselves, but in God who does not lie.

If you don't have confidence about where you will spend eternity and want to learn more, please turn to page 486 to find out how this promise can be yours, because having this certain confidence gives us the confidence to face life's uncertainties.

### Greetings from Paul

**1** This letter is from Paul, a slave of God and an apostle of Jesus Christ. I have been sent to proclaim faith to* those God has chosen and to teach them to know the truth that shows them how to live godly lives. 2 This truth gives them confidence that they have eternal life, which God—who does not lie—promised them before the world began. 3And now at just the right time he has revealed this message, which we announce to everyone. It is by the command of God our Savior that I have been entrusted with this work for him.

4 I am writing to Titus, my true son in the faith that we share.

May God the Father and Christ Jesus our Savior give you grace and peace.

### Titus's Work in Crete

5 I left you on the island of Crete so you could complete our work there and appoint elders in each town as I instructed you. 6An elder must live a blameless life. He must be faithful to his wife,* and his children must be believers who don't have a reputation for being wild or rebellious. 7For an elder* must live a blameless life. He must not be arrogant or quick-tempered; he must not be a heavy drinker,* violent, or dishonest with money.

8Rather, he must enjoy having guests in his home, and he must love what is good. He must live wisely and be just. He must live a devout and disciplined life. 9He must have a strong belief in the trustworthy message he was taught; then he will be able to encourage others with wholesome teaching and show those who oppose it where they are wrong.

10For there are many rebellious people who engage in useless talk and deceive others. This is especially true of those who insist on circumcision for salvation. 11They must be silenced, because they are turning whole families away from the truth by their false teaching. And they do it only for money. 12Even one of their own men, a prophet from Crete, has said about them, "The people of Crete are all liars, cruel animals, and lazy gluttons."* 13This is true. So reprimand them sternly to make them strong in the faith. 14They must stop listening to Jewish myths and the commands of people who have turned away from the truth.

15Everything is pure to those whose hearts are pure. But nothing is pure to those who are corrupt and unbelieving, because their minds and consciences are corrupted. 16Such people claim they know God, but they deny him by the way they live. They are detestable and disobedient, worthless for doing anything good.

### Promote Right Teaching

**2** As for you, Titus, promote the kind of living that reflects wholesome teaching. 2Teach the older men to exercise self-control, to be worthy of respect, and to live wisely. They must have sound faith and be filled with love and patience.

3 Similarly, teach the older women to live in a way that honors God. They must not slander others or be heavy drinkers.* Instead, they should teach others what is good. 4These older women must train the younger women to love their husbands and their children, 5to live wisely and be pure, to work in their homes,* to do good, and to be submissive to their husbands. Then they will not bring shame on the word of God.

6In the same way, encourage the young men to live wisely. 7And you yourself must be an example to them by doing good works of every kind. Let everything you do reflect the integrity and seriousness of your teaching. 8Teach the truth so that your teaching can't be criticized. Then those who oppose us will be ashamed and have nothing bad to say about us.

---

1:1 Or *to strengthen the faith of.*   1:6 Or *must have only one wife,* or *must be married only once;* Greek reads *must be the husband of one wife.*   1:7a Or *an overseer,* or *a bishop.*   1:7b Greek *must not drink too much wine.*   1:12 This quotation is from Epimenides of Knossos.   2:3 Greek *be enslaved to much wine.*   2:5 Some manuscripts read *to care for their homes.*

⁹Slaves must always obey their masters and do their best to please them. They must not talk back ¹⁰or steal, but must show themselves to be entirely trustworthy and good. Then they will make the teaching about God our Savior attractive in every way.

¹¹For the grace of God has been revealed, bringing salvation to all people. ¹²And we are instructed to turn from godless living and sinful pleasures. We should live in this evil world with wisdom, righteousness, and devotion to God, ¹³while we look forward with hope to that wonderful day when the glory of our great God and Savior, Jesus Christ, will be revealed. ¹⁴He gave his life to free us from every kind of sin, to cleanse us, and to make us his very own people, totally committed to doing good deeds.

¹⁵You must teach these things and encourage the believers to do them. You have the authority to correct them when necessary, so don't let anyone disregard what you say.

### Do What Is Good

**3** Remind the believers to submit to the government and its officers. They should be obedient, always ready to do what is good. ²They must not slander anyone and must avoid quarreling. Instead, they should be gentle and show true humility to everyone.

³Once we, too, were foolish and disobedient. We were misled and became slaves to many lusts and pleasures. Our lives were full of evil and envy, and we hated each other. ⁴But—"When God our Savior revealed his kindness and love, ⁵he saved us, not because of the righteous things we had done, but because of his mercy. He washed away our sins, giving us a new birth and new life through the Holy Spirit.* ⁶He generously poured out the Spirit upon us through Jesus Christ our Savior. ⁷Because of his grace he declared us righteous and gave us confidence that we will inherit eternal life." ⁸This is a trustworthy saying, and I want you to insist on these teachings so that all who trust in God will devote

themselves to doing good. These teachings are good and beneficial for everyone.

⁹Do not get involved in foolish discussions about spiritual pedigrees* or in quarrels and fights about obedience to Jewish laws. These things are useless and a waste of time. ¹⁰If people are causing divisions among you, give a first and second warning. After that, have nothing more to do with them. ¹¹For people like that have turned away from the truth, and their own sins condemn them.

### Paul's Final Remarks and Greetings

¹²I am planning to send either Artemas or Tychicus to you. As soon as one of them arrives, do your best to meet me at Nicopolis, for I have decided to stay there for the winter. ¹³Do everything you can to help Zenas the lawyer and Apollos with their trip. See that they are given everything they need. ¹⁴Our people must learn to do good by meeting the urgent needs of others; then they will not be unproductive.

¹⁵Everybody here sends greetings. Please give my greetings to the believers—all who love us.

May God's grace be with you all.

3:5 Greek *He saved us through the washing of regeneration and renewing of the Holy Spirit.*   3:9 Or *spiritual genealogies.*

# FAMILIES facing uncertain futures together

As adults we instinctively want to protect our children or grandchildren from harm or from bad news. But we'd like to suggest that a serious diagnosis can bring a wonderful real-life lesson of God's faithfulness . . . if we allow our youngsters to walk with us along this unwanted journey.

*ALS*
*Alzheimers*
*Cancer*
*Heart Attack*

The journey starts with <u>naming the "Enemy."</u> Go ahead and use the word: cancer or multiple sclerosis or heart disease or whatever has struck your family. If you don't use it, chances are someone else will, and the kids will hear it from them. Next, try to give them age-appropriate information and a little idea of what they might expect to happen in the coming days. Give them an opportunity to ask questions, but be careful not to give them so much specific information that it overwhelms them. **(If you don't tell children anything, what they imagine in their young minds may be even *worse* than what the situation really is.)**

We've also found that it's important not to make promises we can't keep. <u>Each person's diagnosis has a different prognosis</u>, but it's best not to *promise* that "Mommy is going to be fine" or "Grandpa won't die." Instead, assure your children that "the doctors will do everything possible to make Mommy better" or "the doctors will do their best to help Grandpa."

And after you've had this emotionally painful conversation, **have your children or grandchildren place their hands in yours and together place all of your hands in the Lord's.** It's the best decision you can make, because time and again they will be able to see what it means to trust God in hard times. It is a much more powerful lesson for children to walk with you firsthand as you deal with a serious disease in your life or a loved one's life rather than to hear about the journey later after the fact.

They need to see that sometimes you are afraid . . . and yet you find courage.

They need to hear that you have worries . . . and yet you find hope.

They need to know that you don't have all the answers . . . and yet you talk to the One who does.

They need to experience how God supernaturally gives our families courage to face things we never thought we could.

# PHILEMON

*Your love has given me much joy and comfort, my brother, for your kindness has often refreshed the hearts of God's people.*

PHILEMON 1:7

It's amazing how little acts of kindness don't seem little at all when we're facing a health crisis. Cards with scribbled personal notes become treasures to read daily. A lasagna dinner dropped off by a friend allows energies to be focused on other tasks. A well-timed phone call gives the strength to face yet another exhausting day.

This letter from the apostle Paul was written to a friend named Philemon, because Paul needed a favor for another friend named Onesimus. Normally that might have been an easy thing for Philemon to do, but there was a catch this time: Onesimus was Philemon's slave who had run away, and now Paul wanted him welcomed back as a friend and brother. We don't know Philemon's response, but Paul is clear that he expects kindness to be shown no matter how difficult. Who knows, it might even have been hard for Onesimus to accept that kindness.

We need to be willing to allow others to do kind things for us even though most of us would rather be on the giving end instead of the receiving end. It's humbling to let a friend scrub your toilets or mow your yard or drive you to a doctor's appointment; but when we turn down acts of kindness, we're robbing others of the joy of doing good things for us.

Hopefully, eventually we will have the strength, time, and energy to demonstrate acts of kindness to others. But in the meantime, let's allow others to refresh our hearts by their kindnesses to us.

## Greetings from Paul

This letter is from Paul, a prisoner for preaching the Good News about Christ Jesus, and from our brother Timothy.

I am writing to Philemon, our beloved co-worker, [2] and to our sister Apphia, and to our fellow soldier Archippus, and to the church that meets in your* house.

[3] May God our Father and the Lord Jesus Christ give you grace and peace.

## Paul's Thanksgiving and Prayer

[4] I always thank my God when I pray for you, Philemon, [5] because I keep hearing about your faith in the Lord Jesus and your love for all of God's people. [6] And I am praying that you will put into action the generosity that comes from your faith as you understand and experience all the good things we have in Christ. [7] Your love has given me much joy and comfort, my brother, for your kindness has often refreshed the hearts of God's people.

## Paul's Appeal for Onesimus

[8] That is why I am boldly asking a favor of you. I could demand it in the name of Christ because it is the right thing for you to do. [9] But because of our love, I prefer simply to ask you. Consider this as a request from me—Paul, an old man and now also a prisoner for the sake of Christ Jesus.*

[10] I appeal to you to show kindness to my child, Onesimus. I became his father in the faith while here in prison. [11] Onesimus* hasn't been of much use to you in the past, but now he is very useful to both of us. [12] I am sending him back to you, and with him comes my own heart.

[13] I wanted to keep him here with me while I am in these chains for preaching the Good News, and he would have helped me on your behalf. [14] But I didn't want to do anything without your consent. I wanted you to help because you were willing, not because you were forced. [15] It seems you lost Onesimus for a little while so that you could have him back forever. [16] He is no longer like a slave to you. He is more than a slave, for he is a beloved brother, especially to me. Now he will mean much more to you, both as a man and as a brother in the Lord.

[17] So if you consider me your partner, welcome him as you would welcome me. [18] If he has wronged you in any way or owes you anything, charge it to me. [19] I, PAUL, WRITE THIS WITH MY OWN HAND: I WILL REPAY IT. AND I WON'T MENTION THAT YOU OWE ME YOUR VERY SOUL!

[20] Yes, my brother, please do me this favor* for the Lord's sake. Give me this encouragement in Christ.

[21] I am confident as I write this letter that you will do what I ask and even more! [22] One more thing—please prepare a guest room for me, for I am hoping that God will answer your prayers and let me return to you soon.

## Paul's Final Greetings

[23] Epaphras, my fellow prisoner in Christ Jesus, sends you his greetings. [24] So do Mark, Aristarchus, Demas, and Luke, my co-workers.

[25] May the grace of the Lord Jesus Christ be with your spirit.

**2** Throughout this letter, *you* and *your* are singular except in verses 3, 22, and 25. **9** Or *a prisoner of Christ Jesus*. **11** *Onesimus* means "useful." **20** Greek *onaimen*, a play on the name Onesimus.

# HEBREWS

*Faith is the
confidence that
what we hope for
will actually
happen; it gives
us assurance
about things we
cannot see.*

HEBREWS 11:1

Some people seem to find it easy to have great faith. Others are more skeptical and not quite so eager to take those giant leaps of confidence. The Scriptures tell us that it's not so much the size of our faith that matters but rather the *object* of our faith that makes all the difference.

The anonymous author of this letter to Jewish (Hebrew) believers assures them that faith in the Messiah is enough—they don't need any of the old ways of trying to get right with God, like blood sacrifices or priests interceding for them. Jesus has become the perfect sacrifice and the perfect, holy High Priest. And their faith should be in Him alone.

We hope you have "faith" in competent doctors, confidence in excellent medical facilities, and even firm beliefs in the healing power of treatments. But we hope your ultimate faith is in Jesus. If it is, you won't need good luck or to keep your fingers crossed, because your trust will be in the One who can meet your deepest needs and give you assurance about the things you cannot see. God is so awesome and so much bigger than whatever you or your loved one are facing. He's even bigger than your faith! God doesn't *need* anything to show His power, including just the right amount of faith. Isn't that incredibly freeing? Doesn't that take the pressure off? Your faith doesn't have to be bigger than your disease or condition or disorder, because God already is. Just have faith in Him.

## Jesus Christ Is God's Son

**1** Long ago God spoke many times and in many ways to our ancestors through the prophets. **2** And now in these final days, he has spoken to us through his Son. God promised everything to the Son as an inheritance, and through the Son he created the universe. **3** The Son radiates God's own glory and expresses the very character of God, and he sustains everything by the mighty power of his command. When he had cleansed us from our sins, he sat down in the place of honor at the right hand of the majestic God in heaven. **4** This shows that the Son is far greater than the angels, just as the name God gave him is greater than their names.

### The Son Is Greater Than the Angels

**5** For God never said to any angel what he said to Jesus:

"You are my Son.
  Today I have become your Father.*"

God also said,

"I will be his Father,
  and he will be my Son."*

**6** And when he brought his firstborn Son into the world, God said,*

"Let all of God's angels worship him."*

**7** Regarding the angels, he says,

"He sends his angels like the winds,
  his servants like flames of fire."*

**8** But to the Son he says,

"Your throne, O God, endures forever
  and ever.
You rule with a scepter of justice.
**9** You love justice and hate evil.
  Therefore, O God, your God has
    anointed you,
  pouring out the oil of joy on you more
    than on anyone else."*

**10** He also says to the Son,

"In the beginning, Lord, you laid the
    foundation of the earth
  and made the heavens with your hands.
**11** They will perish, but you remain forever.
  They will wear out like old clothing.
**12** You will fold them up like a cloak
  and discard them like old clothing.
But you are always the same;
  you will live forever."*

**13** And God never said to any of the angels,

"Sit in the place of honor at my right hand
  until I humble your enemies,
  making them a footstool under your
    feet."*

**14** Therefore, angels are only servants—spirits sent to care for people who will inherit salvation.

### A Warning against Drifting Away

**2** So we must listen very carefully to the truth we have heard, or we may drift away from it. **2** For the message God delivered through angels has always stood firm, and every violation of the law and every act of disobedience was punished. **3** So what makes us think we can escape if we ignore this great salvation that was first announced by the Lord Jesus himself and then delivered to us by those who heard him speak? **4** And God confirmed the message by giving signs and wonders and various miracles and gifts of the Holy Spirit whenever he chose.

### Jesus, the Man

**5** And furthermore, it is not angels who will control the future world we are talking about. **6** For in one place the Scriptures say,

"What are mere mortals that you should
    think about them,
  or a son of man* that you should care
    for him?

---

**1:5a** Or *Today I reveal you as my Son.* Ps 2:7. **1:5b** 2 Sam 7:14. **1:6a** Or *when he again brings his firstborn son into the world, God will say.* **1:6b** Deut 32:43. **1:7** Ps 104:4 (Greek version). **1:8-9** Ps 45:6-7. **1:10-12** Ps 102:25-27. **1:13** Ps 110:1. **2:6** Or *the Son of Man.*

7 Yet you made them only a little lower
than the angels
and crowned them with glory and honor.*
8 You gave them authority over all
things."*

Now when it says "all things," it means nothing is left out. But we have not yet seen all things put under their authority. 9 What we do see is Jesus, who was given a position "a little lower than the angels"; and because he suffered death for us, he is now "crowned with glory and honor." Yes, by God's grace, Jesus tasted death for everyone. 10 God, for whom and through whom everything was made, chose to bring many children into glory. And it was only right that he should make Jesus, through his suffering, a perfect leader, fit to bring them into their salvation.

11 So now Jesus and the ones he makes holy have the same Father. That is why Jesus is not ashamed to call them his brothers and sisters.* 12 For he said to God,

"I will proclaim your name to my
brothers and sisters.
I will praise you among your
assembled people."*

13 He also said,

"I will put my trust in him,"
that is, "I and the children God has
given me."*

14 Because God's children are human beings—made of flesh and blood—the Son also became flesh and blood. For only as a human being could he die, and only by dying could he break the power of the devil, who had* the power of death. 15 Only in this way could he set free all who have lived their lives as slaves to the fear of dying.

16 We also know that the Son did not come to help angels; he came to help the descendants of Abraham. 17 Therefore, it was necessary for him to be made in every respect like us, his brothers and sisters,* so that he could be our merciful and faithful High Priest before God. Then he could offer a sacrifice that would take away the sins of the people. 18 Since he himself has gone through suffer-

## TOUCHED by an angel
READ HEBREWS 1:4, 13-14

Angels never seem to lose popularity. We see them heralded in songs, books, TV shows, movies, and as lapel pins. The Bible contains more than 300 verses about angels including these here, which explain they are servants of God sent to care for us believers. How wonderful it is when God sends an angel to rescue or protect us! Unfortunately, many people today view affection for angels as a kind of spirituality that doesn't involve commitment to God or His laws—help that doesn't require us to go directly to God. But heavenly angels carry out only God's will, not ours or theirs. Don't get lost in the angel craze; it's God's touch you really want.

ing and testing, he is able to help us when we are being tested.

### Jesus Is Greater Than Moses

3 And so, dear brothers and sisters who belong to God and* are partners with those called to heaven, think carefully about this Jesus whom we declare to be God's messenger* and High Priest. 2 For he was faithful to God, who appointed him, just as Moses served faithfully when he was entrusted with God's entire* house.

3 But Jesus deserves far more glory than Moses, just as a person who builds a house deserves more praise than the house itself. 4 For every house has a builder, but the one who built everything is God. 5 Moses was certainly faithful in God's house as a servant. His work was an illustration of the truths God would reveal later. 6 But Christ, as the Son, is in charge of God's entire house. And we are God's house, if we keep our courage and remain confident in our hope in Christ.*

7 That is why the Holy Spirit says,

"Today when you hear his voice,
8    don't harden your hearts
as Israel did when they rebelled,
when they tested me in the wilderness.
9 There your ancestors tested and tried
my patience,

2:7 Some manuscripts add *You gave them charge of everything you made.* 2:6-8 Ps 8:4-6 (Greek version). 2:11 Greek *brothers;* also in 2:12. 2:12 Ps 22:22. 2:13 Isa 8:17-18. 2:14 Or *has.* 2:17 Greek *like the brothers.* 3:1a Greek *And so, holy brothers who.* 3:1b Greek *God's apostle.* 3:2 Some manuscripts omit *entire.* 3:6 Some manuscripts add *faithful to the end.*

even though they saw my miracles for forty years.
¹⁰ So I was angry with them, and I said,
'Their hearts always turn away from me.
They refuse to do what I tell them.'
¹¹ So in my anger I took an oath:
'They will never enter my place of rest.' "*

¹²Be careful then, dear brothers and sisters.* Make sure that your own hearts are not evil and unbelieving, turning you away from the living God. ¹³You must warn each other every day, while it is still "today," so that none of you will be deceived by sin and hardened against God. ¹⁴For if we are faithful to the end, trusting God just as firmly as when we first believed, we will share in all that belongs to Christ. ¹⁵Remember what it says:

"Today when you hear his voice,
don't harden your hearts
as Israel did when they rebelled."*

¹⁶And who was it who rebelled against God, even though they heard his voice? Wasn't it the people Moses led out of Egypt? ¹⁷And who made God angry for forty years? Wasn't it the people who sinned, whose corpses lay in the wilderness? ¹⁸And to whom was God speaking when he took an oath that they would never enter his rest? Wasn't it the people who disobeyed him? ¹⁹So we see that because of their unbelief they were not able to enter his rest.

*Promised Rest for God's People*

**4** God's promise of entering his rest still stands, so we ought to tremble with fear that some of you might fail to experience it. ²For this good news—that God has prepared this rest—has been announced to us just as it was to them. But it did them no good because they didn't share the faith of those who listened to God.* ³For only we who believe can enter his rest. As for the others, God said,

"In my anger I took an oath:
'They will never enter my place of rest,'"*

even though this rest has been ready since he made the world. ⁴We know it is ready because of the place in the Scriptures where it mentions the seventh day: "On the seventh day God rested from all his work."* ⁵But in the other passage God said, "They will never enter my place of rest."*

⁶So God's rest is there for people to enter, but those who first heard this good news failed to enter because they disobeyed God. ⁷So God set another time for entering his rest, and that time is today. God announced this through David much later in the words already quoted:

"Today when you hear his voice,
don't harden your hearts."*

⁸Now if Joshua had succeeded in giving them this rest, God would not have spoken about another day of rest still to come. ⁹So there is a special rest* still waiting for the people of God. ¹⁰For all who have entered into God's rest have rested from their labors, just as God did after creating the world. ¹¹So let us do our best to enter that rest. But if we disobey God, as the people of Israel did, we will fall.

¹²For the word of God is alive and powerful. It is sharper than the sharpest two-edged sword, cutting between soul and spirit, between joint and marrow. It exposes our innermost thoughts and desires. ¹³Nothing in all creation is hidden from God. Everything is naked and exposed before his eyes, and he is the one to whom we are accountable.

*Christ Is Our High Priest*

¹⁴So then, since we have a great High Priest who has entered heaven, Jesus the Son of God, let us hold firmly to what we believe. ¹⁵This High Priest of ours understands our weaknesses, for he faced all of the same testings we do, yet he did not sin. ¹⁶So let us come boldly to the throne of our gracious God. There we will receive his mercy, and we will find grace to help us when we need it most.

**5** Every high priest is a man chosen to represent other people in their dealings with God. He presents their gifts to God and offers sacrifices for their sins. ²And he is able

---

**3:7-11** Ps 95:7-11. **3:12** Greek *brothers*. **3:15** Ps 95:7-8. **4:2** Some manuscripts read *they didn't combine what they heard with faith*. **4:3** Ps 95:11. **4:4** Gen 2:2. **4:5** Ps 95:11. **4:7** Ps 95:7-8. **4:9** Or *a Sabbath rest*.

to deal gently with ignorant and wayward people because he himself is subject to the same weaknesses. ³That is why he must offer sacrifices for his own sins as well as theirs.

⁴And no one can become a high priest simply because he wants such an honor. He must be called by God for this work, just as Aaron was. ⁵That is why Christ did not honor himself by assuming he could become High Priest. No, he was chosen by God, who said to him,

"You are my Son.
Today I have become your Father.*"

⁶And in another passage God said to him,

"You are a priest forever in the order
of Melchizedek."*

⁷While Jesus was here on earth, he offered prayers and pleadings, with a loud cry and tears, to the one who could rescue him from death. And God heard his prayers because of his deep reverence for God. ⁸Even though Jesus was God's Son, he learned obedience from the things he suffered. ⁹In this way, God qualified him as a perfect High Priest, and he became the source of eternal salvation for all those who obey him. ¹⁰And God designated him to be a High Priest in the order of Melchizedek.

### A Call to Spiritual Growth

¹¹There is much more we would like to say about this, but it is difficult to explain, especially since you are spiritually dull and don't seem to listen. ¹²You have been believers so long now that you ought to be teaching others. Instead, you need someone to teach you again the basic things about God's word.* You are like babies who need milk and cannot eat solid food. ¹³For someone who lives on milk is still an infant and doesn't know how to do what is right. ¹⁴Solid food is for those who are mature, who through training have the skill to recognize the difference between right and wrong.

**6** So let us stop going over the basic teachings about Christ again and again. Let us go on instead and become mature in our understanding. Surely we don't need to start

again with the fundamental importance of repenting from evil deeds and placing our faith in God. ²You don't need further instruction about baptisms, the laying on of hands, the resurrection of the dead, and eternal judgment. ³And so, God willing, we will move forward to further understanding.

⁴For it is impossible to bring back to repentance those who were once enlightened—those who have experienced the good things of heaven and shared in the Holy Spirit, ⁵who have tasted the goodness of the word of God and the power of the age to come—⁶and who then turn away from God. It is impossible to bring such people back to repentance; by rejecting the Son of God, they themselves are nailing him to the cross once again and holding him up to public shame.

⁷When the ground soaks up the falling rain and bears a good crop for the farmer, it has God's blessing. ⁸But if a field bears thorns and thistles, it is useless. The farmer will soon condemn that field and burn it.

⁹Dear friends, even though we are talking this way, we really don't believe it applies to you. We are confident that you are meant for better things, things that come with salvation. **10**For God is not unjust. He will not forget how hard you have worked for him and how you have shown your love to him by caring for other believers,* as you still do. ¹¹Our great desire is that you will keep on loving others as long as life lasts, in order to make certain that what you hope for will come true. ¹²Then you will not become spiritually dull and indifferent. Instead, you will follow the example of those who are going to inherit God's promises because of their faith and endurance.

### God's Promises Bring Hope

¹³For example, there was God's promise to Abraham. Since there was no one greater to swear by, God took an oath in his own name, saying:

¹⁴ "I will certainly bless you,
and I will multiply your descendants
beyond number."*

¹⁵Then Abraham waited patiently, and he received what God had promised.

5:5 Or *Today I reveal you as my Son*. Ps 2:7.   5:6 Ps 110:4.   5:12 Or *about the oracles of God*.   6:10 Greek *for God's holy people*.
6:14 Gen 22:17.

¹⁶Now when people take an oath, they call on someone greater than themselves to hold them to it. And without any question that oath is binding. ¹⁷God also bound himself with an oath, so that those who received the promise could be perfectly sure that he would never change his mind. ¹⁸So God has given both his promise and his oath. These two things are unchangeable because it is impossible for God to lie. Therefore, we who have fled to him for refuge can have great confidence as we hold to the hope that lies before us. ¹⁹This hope is a strong and trustworthy anchor for our souls. It leads us through the curtain into God's inner sanctuary. ²⁰Jesus has already gone in there for us. He has become our eternal High Priest in the order of Melchizedek.

### Melchizedek Is Greater Than Abraham

**7** This Melchizedek was king of the city of Salem and also a priest of God Most High. When Abraham was returning home after winning a great battle against the kings, Melchizedek met him and blessed him. ²Then Abraham took a tenth of all he had captured in battle and gave it to Melchizedek. The name Melchizedek means "king of justice," and king of Salem means "king of peace." ³There is no record of his father or mother or any of his ancestors—no beginning or end to his life. He remains a priest forever, resembling the Son of God.

⁴Consider then how great this Melchizedek was. Even Abraham, the great patriarch of Israel, recognized this by giving him a tenth of what he had taken in battle. ⁵Now the law of Moses required that the priests, who are descendants of Levi, must collect a tithe from the rest of the people of Israel,* who are also descendants of Abraham. ⁶But Melchizedek, who was not a descendant of Levi, collected a tenth from Abraham. And Melchizedek placed a blessing upon Abraham, the one who had already received the promises of God. ⁷And without question, the person who has the power to give a blessing is greater than the one who is blessed.

⁸The priests who collect tithes are men who die, so Melchizedek is greater than they are, because we are told that he lives on. ⁹In addition, we might even say that these Levites—the ones who collect the tithe—paid a tithe to Melchizedek when their ancestor Abraham paid a tithe to him. ¹⁰For although Levi wasn't born yet, the seed from which he came was in Abraham's body when Melchizedek collected the tithe from him.

¹¹So if the priesthood of Levi, on which the law was based, could have achieved the perfection God intended, why did God need to establish a different priesthood, with a priest in the order of Melchizedek instead of the order of Levi and Aaron?* ¹²And if the priesthood is changed, the law must also be changed to permit it. ¹³For the priest we are talking about belongs to a different tribe, whose members have never served at the altar as priests. ¹⁴What I mean is, our Lord came from the tribe of Judah, and Moses never mentioned priests coming from that tribe.

### Jesus Is like Melchizedek

¹⁵This change has been made very clear since a different priest, who is like Melchizedek, has appeared. ¹⁶Jesus became a priest, not by meeting the physical requirement of belonging to the tribe of Levi, but by the power of a life that cannot be destroyed. ¹⁷And the psalmist pointed this out when he prophesied,

"You are a priest forever in the order
of Melchizedek."*

**7:5** Greek *from their brothers.*   **7:11** Greek *the order of Aaron?*
**7:17** Ps 110:4.

---

## SURGERY with a purpose

READ HEBREWS 4:12-13

Be careful as you hold this book; you have a weapon in your hands. The words of Scripture are not like any other words written anywhere. They're alive and powerful, like a sword that is able to cut away all the junk in our lives. When we read the Bible, it exposes our innermost thoughts and desires. We also find out two important truths about ourselves: God loves us just the way we are, but He doesn't want us to stay that way. Let God do His "surgery" on you today and begin cutting away the things that are keeping you from becoming all you were meant to be.

18 Yes, the old requirement about the priesthood was set aside because it was weak and useless. 19 For the law never made anything perfect. But now we have confidence in a better hope, through which we draw near to God.

20 This new system was established with a solemn oath. Aaron's descendants became priests without such an oath, 21 but there was an oath regarding Jesus. For God said to him,

"The LORD has taken an oath and will not break his vow:
'You are a priest forever.'"*

22 Because of this oath, Jesus is the one who guarantees this better covenant with God.

23 There were many priests under the old system, for death prevented them from remaining in office. 24 But because Jesus lives forever, his priesthood lasts forever. 25 Therefore he is able, once and forever, to save* those who come to God through him. He lives forever to intercede with God on their behalf.

26 He is the kind of high priest we need because he is holy and blameless, unstained by sin. He has been set apart from sinners and has been given the highest place of honor in heaven.* 27 Unlike those other high priests, he does not need to offer sacrifices every day. They did this for their own sins first and then for the sins of the people. But Jesus did this once for all when he offered himself as the sacrifice for the people's sins. 28 The law appointed high priests who were limited by human weakness. But after the law was given, God appointed his Son with an oath, and his Son has been made the perfect High Priest forever.

## Christ Is Our High Priest

**8** Here is the main point: We have a High Priest who sat down in the place of honor beside the throne of the majestic God in heaven. 2 There he ministers in the heavenly Tabernacle,* the true place of worship that was built by the Lord and not by human hands. 3 And since every high priest is required to offer gifts and sacrifices, our High Priest must make an offering, too. 4 If he were here on earth, he would not even be a priest, since there already are priests who offer the gifts required by the law. 5 They serve in a system of worship that is only a copy, a shadow of the real one in heaven. For when Moses was getting ready to build the Tabernacle, God gave him this warning: "Be sure that you make everything according to the pattern I have shown you here on the mountain."*

6 But now Jesus, our High Priest, has been given a ministry that is far superior to the old priesthood, for he is the one who mediates for us a far better covenant with God, based on better promises.

7 If the first covenant had been faultless, there would have been no need for a second covenant to replace it. 8 But when God found fault with the people, he said:

"The day is coming, says the LORD,
    when I will make a new covenant
    with the people of Israel and Judah.
9 This covenant will not be like the one
    I made with their ancestors
when I took them by the hand
    and led them out of the land
        of Egypt.
They did not remain faithful to my
        covenant,
    so I turned my back on them, says the
        LORD.
10 But this is the new covenant I will
        make
    with the people of Israel on that
        day,* says the LORD:
I will put my laws in their minds,
    and I will write them on their hearts.
I will be their God,
    and they will be my people.
11 And they will not need to teach their
        neighbors,
    nor will they need to teach their
        relatives,*
    saying, 'You should know the
        LORD.'
For everyone, from the least to the
        greatest,
    will know me already.
12 And I will forgive their wickedness,
    and I will never again remember their
        sins."*

---

7:21 Ps 110:4.   7:25 Or *is able to save completely.*   7:26 Or *has been exalted higher than the heavens.*   8:2 Or *tent;* also in 8:5.
8:5 Exod 25:40; 26:30.   8:10 Greek *after those days.*   8:11 Greek *their brother.*   8:8-12 Jer 31:31-34.

13When God speaks of a "new" covenant, it means he has made the first one obsolete. It is now out of date and will soon disappear.

## Old Rules about Worship

**9** That first covenant between God and Israel had regulations for worship and a place of worship here on earth. 2There were two rooms in that Tabernacle.* In the first room were a lampstand, a table, and sacred loaves of bread on the table. This room was called the Holy Place. 3Then there was a curtain, and behind the curtain was the second room* called the Most Holy Place. 4In that room were a gold incense altar and a wooden chest called the Ark of the Covenant, which was covered with gold on all sides. Inside the Ark were a gold jar containing manna, Aaron's staff that sprouted leaves, and the stone tablets of the covenant. 5Above the Ark were the cherubim of divine glory, whose wings stretched out over the Ark's cover, the place of atonement. But we cannot explain these things in detail now.

6When these things were all in place, the priests regularly entered the first room* as they performed their religious duties. 7But only the high priest ever entered the Most Holy Place, and only once a year. And he always offered blood for his own sins and for the sins the people had committed in ignorance. 8By these regulations the Holy Spirit revealed that the entrance to the Most Holy Place was not freely open as long as the Tabernacle* and the system it represented were still in use.

9This is an illustration pointing to the present time. For the gifts and sacrifices that the priests offer are not able to cleanse the consciences of the people who bring them. 10For that old system deals only with food and drink and various cleansing ceremonies—physical regulations that were in effect only until a better system could be established.

## Christ Is the Perfect Sacrifice

11So Christ has now become the High Priest over all the good things that have come.* He has entered that greater, more perfect Tabernacle in heaven, which was not made by human hands and is not part of this created world. 12With his own blood—not the blood of goats and calves—he entered the Most Holy Place once for all time and secured our redemption forever.

13Under the old system, the blood of goats and bulls and the ashes of a young cow could cleanse people's bodies from ceremonial impurity. 14Just think how much more the blood of Christ will purify our consciences from sinful deeds* so that we can worship the living God. For by the power of the eternal Spirit, Christ offered himself to God as a perfect sacrifice for our sins. 15That is why he is the one who mediates a new covenant between God and people, so that all who are called can receive the eternal inheritance God has promised them. For Christ died to set them free from the penalty of the sins they had committed under that first covenant.

16Now when someone leaves a will,* it is necessary to prove that the person who made it is dead.* 17The will goes into effect only after the person's death. While the person who made it is still alive, the will cannot be put into effect.

18That is why even the first covenant was put into effect with the blood of an animal. 19For after Moses had read each of God's commandments to all the people, he took the blood of calves and goats,* along with water, and sprinkled both the book of God's law and all the people, using hyssop branches and scarlet wool. 20Then he said, "This blood confirms the covenant God has made with you."* 21And in the same way, he sprinkled blood on the Tabernacle and on everything used for worship. 22In fact, according to the law of Moses, nearly everything was purified with blood. For without the shedding of blood, there is no forgiveness.

23That is why the Tabernacle and everything in it, which were copies of things in heaven, had to be purified by the blood of animals. But the real things in heaven had to be purified with far better sacrifices than the blood of animals.

24For Christ did not enter into a holy place

9:2 Or *tent;* also in 9:11, 21.    9:3 Greek *second tent.*    9:6 Greek *first tent.*    9:8 Or *the first room;* Greek reads *the first tent.*    9:11 Some manuscripts read *that are about to come.*    9:14 Greek *from dead works.*    9:16a Or *covenant;* also in 9:17    9:16b Or *Now when someone makes a covenant, it is necessary to ratify it with the death of a sacrifice.*    9:19 Some manuscripts omit *and goats.*    9:20 Exod 24:8.

made with human hands, which was only a copy of the true one in heaven. He entered into heaven itself to appear now before God on our behalf. 25And he did not enter heaven to offer himself again and again, like the high priest here on earth who enters the Most Holy Place year after year with the blood of an animal. 26If that had been necessary, Christ would have had to die again and again, ever since the world began. But now, once for all time, he has appeared at the end of the age* to remove sin by his own death as a sacrifice.

27And just as each person is destined to die once and after that comes judgment, 28so also Christ died once for all time as a sacrifice to take away the sins of many people. He will come again, not to deal with our sins, but to bring salvation to all who are eagerly waiting for him.

*Christ's Sacrifice Once for All*

**10** The old system under the law of Moses was only a shadow, a dim preview of the good things to come, not the good things themselves. The sacrifices under that system were repeated again and again, year after year, but they were never able to provide perfect cleansing for those who came to worship. 2If they could have provided perfect cleansing, the sacrifices would have stopped, for the worshipers would have been purified once for all time, and their feelings of guilt would have disappeared.

3But instead, those sacrifices actually reminded them of their sins year after year. 4For it is not possible for the blood of bulls and goats to take away sins. 5That is why, when Christ* came into the world, he said to God,

"You did not want animal sacrifices or
   sin offerings.
 But you have given me a body to offer.
6 You were not pleased with burnt offerings
   or other offerings for sin.
7 Then I said, 'Look, I have come to do your
   will, O God—
 as is written about me in the
   Scriptures.'"*

8First, Christ said, "You did not want animal sacrifices or sin offerings or burnt offerings

or other offerings for sin, nor were you pleased with them" (though they are required by the law of Moses). 9Then he said, "Look, I have come to do your will." He cancels the first covenant in order to put the second into effect. 10For God's will was for us to be made holy by the sacrifice of the body of Jesus Christ, once for all time.

11Under the old covenant, the priest stands and ministers before the altar day after day, offering the same sacrifices again and again, which can never take away sins. 12But our High Priest offered himself to God as a single sacrifice for sins, good for all time. Then he sat down in the place of honor at God's right hand. 13There he waits until his enemies are humbled and made a footstool under his feet. 14For by that one offering he forever made perfect those who are being made holy.

15And the Holy Spirit also testifies that this is so. For he says,

16 "This is the new covenant I will make
   with my people on that day,* says the
   LORD:
 I will put my laws in their hearts,
   and I will write them on their
     minds."*

17Then he says,

"I will never again remember
   their sins and lawless deeds."*

---

## I KNOW how you feel
READ HEBREWS 4:14-16

Ever wish somebody *really* understood how you feel? Really knew all you've been through and cared about all that still lies ahead? There is One who does. Jesus "understands our weaknesses, for he faced all of the same testings we do." Oh, sure, He never had the exact same diagnosis as you or your loved one, but He lived with a death sentence hanging over Him. He experienced the unfairness of life and the temptation to ask, "Why me?" He endured the breakdown of His physical body and the temptation to go to someone besides His heavenly Father to satisfy His needs. That's why we need to go to Jesus to find compassion when we need it most—because He truly understands.

---

9:26 Greek *the ages.* 10:5 Greek *he;* also in 10:8. 10:5-7 Ps 40:6-8 (Greek version). 10:16a Greek *after those days.* 10:16b Jer 31:33a. 10:17 Jer 31:34b.

18And when sins have been forgiven, there is no need to offer any more sacrifices.

## A Call to Persevere

19And so, dear brothers and sisters,* we can boldly enter heaven's Most Holy Place because of the blood of Jesus. 20By his death,* Jesus opened a new and life-giving way through the curtain into the Most Holy Place. 21And since we have a great High Priest who rules over God's house, 22let us go right into the presence of God with sincere hearts fully trusting him. For our guilty consciences have been sprinkled with Christ's blood to make us clean, and our bodies have been washed with pure water.

23Let us hold tightly without wavering to the hope we affirm, for God can be trusted to keep his promise. 24Let us think of ways to motivate one another to acts of love and good works. 25And let us not neglect our meeting together, as some people do, but encourage one another, especially now that the day of his return is drawing near.

26Dear friends, if we deliberately continue sinning after we have received knowledge of the truth, there is no longer any sacrifice that will cover these sins. 27There is only the terrible expectation of God's judgment and the raging fire that will consume his enemies. 28For anyone who refused to obey the law of Moses was put to death without mercy on the testimony of two or three witnesses. 29Just think how much worse the punishment will be for those who have trampled on the Son of God, and have treated the blood of the covenant, which made us holy, as if it were common and unholy, and have insulted and disdained the Holy Spirit who brings God's mercy to us. 30For we know the one who said,

"I will take revenge.
I will pay them back."*

He also said,

"The LORD will judge his own people."*

31It is a terrible thing to fall into the hands of the living God.

32Think back on those early days when you first learned about Christ.* Remember how you remained faithful even though it meant terrible suffering. 33Sometimes you were exposed to public ridicule and were beaten, and sometimes you helped others who were suffering the same things. 34You suffered along with those who were thrown into jail, and when all you owned was taken from you, you accepted it with joy. You knew there were better things waiting for you that will last forever.

35So do not throw away this confident trust in the Lord. Remember the great reward it brings you! 36Patient endurance is what you need now, so that you will continue to do God's will. Then you will receive all that he has promised.

37"For in just a little while,
  the Coming One will come and not delay.
38 And my righteous ones will live by faith.*
  But I will take no pleasure in anyone
    who turns away."*

39But we are not like those who turn away from God to their own destruction. We are the faithful ones, whose souls will be saved.

## Great Examples of Faith

**11** Faith is the confidence that what we hope for will actually happen; it gives us assurance about things we cannot see. 2Through their faith, the people in days of old earned a good reputation.

3By faith we understand that the entire universe was formed at God's command, that what we now see did not come from anything that can be seen.

4It was by faith that Abel brought a more acceptable offering to God than Cain did. Abel's offering gave evidence that he was a righteous man, and God showed his approval of his gifts. Although Abel is long dead, he still speaks to us by his example of faith.

5It was by faith that Enoch was taken up to heaven without dying—"he disappeared, because God took him."* For before he was taken up, he was known as a person who pleased God. 6And it is impossible to please

10:19 Greek brothers.   10:20 Greek Through his flesh.   10:30a Deut 32:35.   10:30b Deut 32:36.   10:32 Greek when you were first enlightened.   10:38 Or my righteous ones will live by their faithfulness; Greek reads my righteous one will live by faith.   10:37-38 Hab 2:3-4.   11:5 Gen 5:24.

God without faith. Anyone who wants to come to him must believe that God exists and that he rewards those who sincerely seek him.

7 It was by faith that Noah built a large boat to save his family from the flood. He obeyed God, who warned him about things that had never happened before. By his faith Noah condemned the rest of the world, and he received the righteousness that comes by faith.

8 It was by faith that Abraham obeyed when God called him to leave home and go to another land that God would give him as his inheritance. He went without knowing where he was going. 9 And even when he reached the land God promised him, he lived there by faith—for he was like a foreigner, living in tents. And so did Isaac and Jacob, who inherited the same promise. 10 Abraham was confidently looking forward to a city with eternal foundations, a city designed and built by God.

11 It was by faith that even Sarah was able to have a child, though she was barren and was too old. She believed* that God would keep his promise. 12 And so a whole nation came from this one man who was as good as dead—a nation with so many people that, like the stars in the sky and the sand on the seashore, there is no way to count them.

13 All these people died still believing what God had promised them. They did not receive what was promised, but they saw it all from a distance and welcomed it. They agreed that they were foreigners and nomads here on earth. 14 Obviously people who say such things are looking forward to a country they can call their own. 15 If they had longed for the country they came from, they could have gone back. 16 But they were looking for a better place, a heavenly homeland. That is why God is not ashamed to be called their God, for he has prepared a city for them.

17 It was by faith that Abraham offered Isaac as a sacrifice when God was testing him. Abraham, who had received God's promises, was ready to sacrifice his only son, Isaac, 18 even though God had told him, "Isaac is the son through whom your descendants will be counted."* 19 Abraham reasoned that if Isaac died, God was able to bring him back to life again. And in a sense, Abraham did receive his son back from the dead.

20 It was by faith that Isaac promised blessings for the future to his sons, Jacob and Esau.

21 It was by faith that Jacob, when he was old and dying, blessed each of Joseph's sons and bowed in worship as he leaned on his staff.

22 It was by faith that Joseph, when he was about to die, said confidently that the people of Israel would leave Egypt. He even commanded them to take his bones with them when they left.

23 It was by faith that Moses' parents hid him for three months when he was born. They saw that God had given them an unusual child, and they were not afraid to disobey the king's command.

24 It was by faith that Moses, when he grew up, refused to be called the son of Pharaoh's daughter. 25 He chose to share the oppression of God's people instead of enjoying the fleeting pleasures of sin. 26 He thought it was better to suffer for the sake of Christ than to own the treasures of Egypt, for he was looking ahead to his great reward. 27 It was by faith that Moses left the land of Egypt, not fearing the king's anger. He kept right on going because he kept his eyes on the one who is invisible. 28 It was by faith

11:11 Or *It was by faith that he [Abraham] was able to have a child, even though Sarah was barren and he was too old. He believed.*    11:18 Gen 21:12.

---

## EXCUSES, excuses

READ HEBREWS 10:23-25

So what's your excuse for not worshipping regularly with a group of believers? Sometimes people facing a health crisis can get so busy and burned-out that weekends become a time for catching up on rest or housecleaning or yard work. Whatever else you are choosing to do on the Sabbath is not nearly as important as worshipping together with others of like faith. As long as you have enough strength to get to worship, get there! Sit in the back in case you have to leave quickly. Don't shake hands if you're worried about germs. But do whatever it takes to be with God's people, because that is where you will find the encouragement you need.

that Moses commanded the people of Israel to keep the Passover and to sprinkle blood on the doorposts so that the angel of death would not kill their firstborn sons.

29 It was by faith that the people of Israel went right through the Red Sea as though they were on dry ground. But when the Egyptians tried to follow, they were all drowned.

30 It was by faith that the people of Israel marched around Jericho for seven days, and the walls came crashing down.

31 It was by faith that Rahab the prostitute was not destroyed with the people in her city who refused to obey God. For she had given a friendly welcome to the spies.

32 How much more do I need to say? It would take too long to recount the stories of the faith of Gideon, Barak, Samson, Jephthah, David, Samuel, and all the prophets. 33 By faith these people overthrew kingdoms, ruled with justice, and received what God had promised them. They shut the mouths of lions, 34 quenched the flames of fire, and escaped death by the edge of the sword. Their weakness was turned to strength. They became strong in battle and put whole armies to flight. 35 Women received their loved ones back again from death.

But others were tortured, refusing to turn from God in order to be set free. They placed their hope in a better life after the resurrection. 36 Some were jeered at, and their backs were cut open with whips. Others were chained in prisons. 37 Some died by stoning, some were sawed in half,* and others were killed with the sword. Some went about wearing skins of sheep and goats, destitute and oppressed and mistreated. 38 They were too good for this world, wandering over deserts and mountains, hiding in caves and holes in the ground.

39 All these people earned a good reputation because of their faith, yet none of them received all that God had promised. 40 For God had something better in mind for us, so that they would not reach perfection without us.

## God's Discipline Proves His Love

**12** Therefore, since we are surrounded by such a huge crowd of witnesses to the life of faith, let us strip off every weight that slows us down, especially the sin that so easily trips us up. And let us run with endurance the race God has set before us. 2 We do this by keeping our eyes on Jesus, the champion who initiates and perfects our faith.* Because of the joy* awaiting him, he endured the cross, disregarding its shame. Now he is seated in the place of honor beside God's throne. 3 Think of all the hostility he endured from sinful people;* then you won't become weary and give up. 4 After all, you have not yet given your lives in your struggle against sin.

5 And have you forgotten the encouraging words God spoke to you as his children?* He said,

"My child,* don't make light of the LORD's discipline,
    and don't give up when he corrects you.
6 For the LORD disciplines those he loves,
    and he punishes each one he accepts
        as his child."*

7 As you endure this divine discipline, remember that God is treating you as his own children. Who ever heard of a child who is never disciplined by its father? 8 If God doesn't discipline you as he does all of his children, it means that you are illegitimate and are not really his children at all. 9 Since we respected our earthly fathers who disciplined us, shouldn't we submit even more to the discipline of the Father of our spirits, and live forever?* 10 For our earthly fathers disciplined us for a few years, doing the best they knew how. But God's discipline is always good for us, so that we might share in his holiness. 11 No discipline is enjoyable while it is happening—it's painful! But afterward there will be a peaceful harvest of right living for those who are trained in this way.

12 So take a new grip with your tired hands and strengthen your weak knees. 13 Mark out a straight path for your feet so that those

---

11:37 Some manuscripts add *some were tested.*   12:2a Or *Jesus, the originator and perfecter of our faith.*   12:2b Or *Instead of the joy.*   12:3 Some manuscripts read *Think of how people hurt themselves by opposing him.*   12:5a Greek *sons;* also in 12:7, 8.   12:5b Greek *son;* also in 12:6, 7.   12:5-6 Prov 3:11-12 (Greek version).   12:9 Or *and really live?*

who are weak and lame will not fall but become strong.

### A Call to Listen to God

14 Work at living in peace with everyone, and work at living a holy life, for those who are not holy will not see the Lord. 15 Look after each other so that none of you fails to receive the grace of God. Watch out that no poisonous root of bitterness grows up to trouble you, corrupting many. 16 Make sure that no one is immoral or godless like Esau, who traded his birthright as the firstborn son for a single meal. 17 You know that afterward, when he wanted his father's blessing, he was rejected. It was too late for repentance, even though he begged with bitter tears.

18 You have not come to a physical mountain,* to a place of flaming fire, darkness, gloom, and whirlwind, as the Israelites did at Mount Sinai. 19 For they heard an awesome trumpet blast and a voice so terrible that they begged God to stop speaking. 20 They staggered back under God's command: "If even an animal touches the mountain, it must be stoned to death."* 21 Moses himself was so frightened at the sight that he said, "I am terrified and trembling."*

22 No, you have come to Mount Zion, to the city of the living God, the heavenly Jerusalem, and to countless thousands of angels in a joyful gathering. 23 You have come to the assembly of God's firstborn children, whose names are written in heaven. You have come to God himself, who is the judge over all things. You have come to the spirits of the righteous ones in heaven who have now been made perfect. 24 You have come to Jesus, the one who mediates the new covenant between God and people, and to the sprinkled blood, which speaks of forgiveness instead of crying out for vengeance like the blood of Abel.

25 Be careful that you do not refuse to listen to the One who is speaking. For if the people of Israel did not escape when they refused to listen to Moses, the earthly messenger, we will certainly not escape if we reject the One who speaks to us from heaven! 26 When God spoke from Mount Sinai his voice shook the earth, but now he makes another promise:

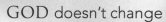

## GOD doesn't change
READ HEBREWS 13:8 AND 11:32-40

People often say that God doesn't change, that He's "the same yesterday, today, and forever." We wholeheartedly agree that His *character* doesn't change, but His ways sometimes do. He cannot act contrary to His character, but He doesn't have to act the same way in each of our lives. Look at the stories of faith in chapter 11: Some people were miraculously rescued and even revived from the dead; others were mistreated and even murdered.

God is the same for us as He was for them. The same God of love. The same God of mercy. The same God of justice. The same God of holiness. The same God who can do things as differently in our lives as He chooses.

"Once again I will shake not only the earth but the heavens also."* 27 This means that all of creation will be shaken and removed, so that only unshakable things will remain.

28 Since we are receiving a Kingdom that is unshakable, let us be thankful and please God by worshiping him with holy fear and awe. 29 For our God is a devouring fire.

### Concluding Words

**13** Keep on loving each other as brothers and sisters.* 2 Don't forget to show hospitality to strangers, for some who have done this have entertained angels without realizing it! 3 Remember those in prison, as if you were there yourself. Remember also those being mistreated, as if you felt their pain in your own bodies.

4 Give honor to marriage, and remain faithful to one another in marriage. God will surely judge people who are immoral and those who commit adultery.

5 Don't love money; be satisfied with what you have. For God has said,

"I will never fail you.
I will never abandon you."*

6 So we can say with confidence,

"The Lord is my helper,
so I will have no fear.
What can mere people do to me?"*

7 Remember your leaders who taught you the word of God. Think of all the good that has come from their lives, and follow the example of their faith.

8 Jesus Christ is the same yesterday, today, and forever. 9 So do not be attracted by strange, new ideas. Your strength comes from God's grace, not from rules about food, which don't help those who follow them.

10 We have an altar from which the priests in the Tabernacle* have no right to eat. 11 Under the old system, the high priest brought the blood of animals into the Holy Place as a sacrifice for sin, and the bodies of the animals were burned outside the camp. 12 So also Jesus suffered and died outside the city gates to make his people holy by means of his own blood. 13 So let us go out to him, outside the camp, and bear the disgrace he bore. 14 For this world is not our permanent home; we are looking forward to a home yet to come.

15 Therefore, let us offer through Jesus a continual sacrifice of praise to God, proclaiming our allegiance to his name. 16 And don't forget to do good and to share with those in need. These are the sacrifices that please God.

17 Obey your spiritual leaders, and do what they say. Their work is to watch over your souls, and they are accountable to God. Give them reason to do this with joy and not with sorrow. That would certainly not be for your benefit.

18 Pray for us, for our conscience is clear and we want to live honorably in everything we do. 19 And especially pray that I will be able to come back to you soon.

20 Now may the God of peace—
who brought up from the dead our
Lord Jesus,
the great Shepherd of the sheep,
and ratified an eternal covenant with
his blood—
21 may he equip you with all you need
for doing his will.
May he produce in you,*
through the power of Jesus Christ,
every good thing that is pleasing
to him.
All glory to him forever and ever!
Amen.

22 I urge you, dear brothers and sisters,* to pay attention to what I have written in this brief exhortation.

23 I want you to know that our brother Timothy has been released from jail. If he comes here soon, I will bring him with me to see you.

24 Greet all your leaders and all the believers there.* The believers from Italy send you their greetings.

25 May God's grace be with you all.

13:10 Or *tent*.   13:21 Some manuscripts read *in us*.   13:22 Greek *brothers*.   13:24 Greek *all of God's holy people*.

# JAMES

*Dear brothers and sisters, when troubles come your way, consider it an opportunity for great joy.*

JAMES 1:2

What was your reaction when you heard the dreaded words?

"You have cancer."

"It's a heart attack."

"This is very serious."

Shock, disbelief, concern, worry, fear, and even anger are emotions that come to mind. Joy is hardly on the short or long list of our reactions to serious illness. If given a choice about whether to face a trial, which of us would wildly wave our hands gleefully exclaiming, "Pick me! Pick me!"?

And yet James, the half-brother of Jesus and a leader in the early church, makes an amazing statement: "When troubles come your way, consider it an opportunity for great joy." The words "troubles" and "great joy" don't seem to belong together in the same sentence, let alone fit together in the same life.

How can James make such an assertion?

He's *not* joyful because something bad has happened. But he is joyful about what good thing *can* happen *in* us because something bad has happened *to* us. He knows that troubles, including illness, are the perfect opportunity for us to grow and see God's character developed in us. "For you know that when your faith is tested, your endurance has a chance to grow. So let it grow, for when your endurance is fully developed, you will be perfect and complete, needing nothing" (James 1:3-4).

Any opportunities for great joy in your life today?

305

### Greetings from James

**1** This letter is from James, a slave of God and of the Lord Jesus Christ.

I am writing to the "twelve tribes"—Jewish believers scattered abroad.

Greetings!

### Faith and Endurance

2 Dear brothers and sisters,* when troubles come your way, consider it an opportunity for great joy. 3 For you know that when your faith is tested, your endurance has a chance to grow. 4 So let it grow, for when your endurance is fully developed, you will be perfect and complete, needing nothing.

5 If you need wisdom, ask our generous God, and he will give it to you. He will not rebuke you for asking. 6 But when you ask him, be sure that your faith is in God alone. Do not waver, for a person with divided loyalty is as unsettled as a wave of the sea that is blown and tossed by the wind. 7 Such people should not expect to receive anything from the Lord. 8 Their loyalty is divided between God and the world, and they are unstable in everything they do.

9 Believers who are* poor have something to boast about, for God has honored them. 10 And those who are rich should boast that God has humbled them. They will fade away like a little flower in the field. 11 The hot sun rises and the grass withers; the little flower droops and falls, and its beauty fades away. In the same way, the rich will fade away with all of their achievements.

12 God blesses those who patiently endure testing and temptation. Afterward they will receive the crown of life that God has promised to those who love him. 13 And remember, when you are being tempted, do not say, "God is tempting me." God is never tempted to do wrong,* and he never tempts anyone else. 14 Temptation comes from our own desires, which entice us and drag us away.

15 These desires give birth to sinful actions. And when sin is allowed to grow, it gives birth to death.

16 So don't be misled, my dear brothers and sisters. 17 Whatever is good and perfect comes down to us from God our Father, who created all the lights in the heavens.* He never changes or casts a shifting shadow.* 18 He chose to give birth to us by giving us his true word. And we, out of all creation, became his prized possession.*

### Listening and Doing

19 Understand this, my dear brothers and sisters: You must all be quick to listen, slow to speak, and slow to get angry. 20 Human anger* does not produce the righteousness* God desires. 21 So get rid of all the filth and evil in your lives, and humbly accept the word God has planted in your hearts, for it has the power to save your souls.

22 But don't just listen to God's word. You must do what it says. Otherwise, you are only fooling yourselves. 23 For if you listen to the word and don't obey, it is like glancing at your face in a mirror. 24 You see yourself, walk away, and forget what you look like. 25 But if you look carefully into the perfect law that sets you free, and if you do what it says and don't forget what you heard, then God will bless you for doing it.

26 If you claim to be religious but don't control your tongue, you are fooling yourself, and your religion is worthless. 27 Pure and genuine religion in the sight of God the Father means caring for orphans and widows in their distress and refusing to let the world corrupt you.

### A Warning against Prejudice

**2** My dear brothers and sisters,* how can you claim to have faith in our glorious Lord Jesus Christ if you favor some people over others?

1:2 Greek brothers; also in 1:16, 19.  1:9 Greek The brother who is.  1:13 Or God should not be put to a test by evil people.  1:17a Greek from above, from the Father of lights.  1:17b Some manuscripts read He never changes, as a shifting shadow does.  1:18 Greek we became a kind of firstfruit of his creatures.  1:20a Greek A man's anger.  1:20b Or the justice.  2:1 Greek brothers; also in 2:5, 14.

2For example, suppose someone comes into your meeting* dressed in fancy clothes and expensive jewelry, and another comes in who is poor and dressed in dirty clothes. 3If you give special attention and a good seat to the rich person, but you say to the poor one, "You can stand over there, or else sit on the floor"—well, 4doesn't this discrimination show that your judgments are guided by evil motives?

5Listen to me, dear brothers and sisters. Hasn't God chosen the poor in this world to be rich in faith? Aren't they the ones who will inherit the Kingdom he promised to those who love him? 6But you dishonor the poor! Isn't it the rich who oppress you and drag you into court? 7Aren't they the ones who slander Jesus Christ, whose noble name* you bear?

8Yes indeed, it is good when you obey the royal law as found in the Scriptures: "Love your neighbor as yourself."* 9But if you favor some people over others, you are committing a sin. You are guilty of breaking the law.

10For the person who keeps all of the laws except one is as guilty as a person who has broken all of God's laws. 11For the same God who said, "You must not commit adultery," also said, "You must not murder."* So if you murder someone but do not commit adultery, you have still broken the law.

12So whatever you say or whatever you do, remember that you will be judged by the law that sets you free. 13There will be no mercy for those who have not shown mercy to others. But if you have been merciful, God will be merciful when he judges you.

### Faith without Good Deeds Is Dead

14What good is it, dear brothers and sisters, if you say you have faith but don't show it by your actions? Can that kind of faith save anyone? 15Suppose you see a brother or sister who has no food or clothing, 16and you say, "Good-bye and have a good day; stay warm and eat well"—but then you don't give that person any food or clothing. What good does that do?

17So you see, <u>faith by itself isn't enough.</u>

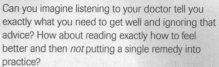

## GETTING God's blessing
READ JAMES 1:22-25

Can you imagine listening to your doctor tell you exactly what you need to get well and ignoring that advice? How about reading exactly how to feel better and then *not* putting a single remedy into practice?

Nobody in his or her right mind would ignore such valuable information and still hope to become well physically.

We can make that same mistake with God's Word. If we just hear it or read it but fail to take its advice, obey its commands, and believe its promises, we are only fooling ourselves. We will never be well spiritually and emotionally.

If you want God's blessing, live His Word.

---

<u>Unless it produces good deeds, it is dead and useless.</u>
18Now someome people have faith; others have good deeds." But I say, "How can you show me your faith if you don't have good deeds? I will show you my faith by my good deeds."

19You say you have faith, for you believe that there is one God.* Good for you! Even the demons believe this, and they tremble in terror. 20How foolish! Can't you see that faith without good deeds is useless?

21Don't you remember that our ancestor Abraham was shown to be right with God by his actions when he offered his son Isaac on the altar? 22You see, his faith and his actions worked together. His actions made his faith complete. 23And so it happened just as the Scriptures say: "Abraham believed God, and God counted him as righteous because of his faith."* He was even called the friend of God.* 24So you see, we are shown to be right with God by what we do, not by faith alone.

25Rahab the prostitute is another example. She was shown to be right with God by her actions when she hid those messengers and sent them safely away by a different road. 26Just as the body is dead without breath,* so also faith is dead without good works.

---

2:2 Greek *your synagogue.*   2:7 Greek *slander the noble name.*   2:8 Lev 19:18.   2:11 Exod 20:13-14; Deut 5:17-18.   2:19 Some manuscripts read *that God is one;* see Deut 6:4.   2:23a Gen 15:6.   2:23b See Isa 41:8.   2:26 Or *without spirit.*

## Controlling the Tongue

**3** Dear brothers and sisters,* not many of you should become teachers in the church, for we who teach will be judged more strictly. ²Indeed, we all make many mistakes. For if we could control our tongues, we would be perfect and could also control ourselves in every other way.

³We can make a large horse go wherever we want by means of a small bit in its mouth. ⁴And a small rudder makes a huge ship turn wherever the pilot chooses to go, even though the winds are strong. ⁵In the same way, the tongue is a small thing that makes grand speeches.

But a tiny spark can set a great forest on fire. ⁶And the tongue is a flame of fire. It is a whole world of wickedness, corrupting your entire body. It can set your whole life on fire, for it is set on fire by hell itself.*

⁷People can tame all kinds of animals, birds, reptiles, and fish, ⁸but no one can tame the tongue. It is restless and evil, full of deadly poison. ⁹Sometimes it praises our Lord and Father, and sometimes it curses those who have been made in the image of God. ¹⁰And so blessing and cursing come pouring out of the same mouth. Surely, my brothers and sisters, this is not right! ¹¹Does a spring of water bubble out with both fresh water and bitter water? ¹²Does a fig tree produce olives, or a grapevine produce figs? No, and you can't draw fresh water from a salty spring.*

## True Wisdom Comes from God

¹³If you are wise and understand God's ways, prove it by living an honorable life, doing good works with the humility that comes from wisdom. ¹⁴But if you are bitterly jealous and there is selfish ambition in your heart, don't cover up the truth with boasting and lying. ¹⁵For jealousy and selfishness are not God's kind of wisdom. Such things are earthly, unspiritual, and demonic. ¹⁶For wherever there is jealousy and selfish ambition, there you will find dis-order and evil of every kind.

¹⁷But the wisdom from above is first of all pure. It is also peace loving, gentle at all times, and willing to yield to others. It is full of mercy and good deeds. It shows no favoritism and is always sincere. ¹⁸And those who are peacemakers will plant seeds of peace and reap a harvest of righteousness.*

## Drawing Close to God

**4** What is causing the quarrels and fights among you? Don't they come from the evil desires at war within you? ²You want what you don't have, so you scheme and kill to get it. You are jealous of what others have, but you can't get it, so you fight and wage war to take it away from them. Yet you don't have what you want because you don't ask God for it. ³And even when you ask, you don't get it because your motives are all wrong—you want only what will give you pleasure.

⁴You adulterers!* Don't you realize that friendship with the world makes you an enemy of God? I say it again: If you want to be a friend of the world, you make yourself an enemy of God. ⁵What do you think the Scriptures mean when they say that the spirit God has placed within us is filled with envy?* ⁶But he gives us even more grace to stand against such evil desires. As the Scriptures say,

"God opposes the proud
   but favors the humble."*

⁷So humble yourselves before God. Resist the devil, and he will flee from you. ⁸Come close to God, and God will come close to you. Wash your hands, you sinners; purify your hearts, for your loyalty is divided between God and the world. ⁹Let there be tears for what you have done. Let there be sorrow and deep grief. Let there be sadness instead of laughter, and gloom instead of joy. ¹⁰Humble yourselves before the Lord, and he will lift you up in honor.

## Warning against Judging Others

¹¹Don't speak evil against each other, dear brothers and sisters.* If you criticize and judge each other, then you are criticizing

**3:1** Greek *brothers;* also in 3:10.   **3:6** Or *for it will burn in hell* (Greek *Gehenna*).   **3:12** Greek *from salt.*   **3:18** Or *of good things,* or *of justice.*   **4:4** Greek *You adulteresses!*   **4:5** Or *that God longs jealously for the human spirit he has placed within us?* or *that the Holy Spirit, whom God has placed within us, opposes our envy?*   **4:6** Prov 3:34 (Greek version).   **4:11** Greek *brothers.*

and judging God's law. But your job is to obey the law, not to judge whether it applies to you. ¹²God alone, who gave the law, is the Judge. He alone has the power to save or to destroy. So what right do you have to judge your neighbor?

## Warning about Self-Confidence

¹³Look here, you who say, "Today or tomorrow we are going to a certain town and will stay there a year. We will do business there and make a profit." ¹⁴How do you know what your life will be like tomorrow? Your life is like the morning fog—it's here a little while, then it's gone. ¹⁵What you ought to say is, "If the Lord wants us to, we will live and do this or that." ¹⁶Otherwise you are boasting about your own plans, and all such boasting is evil.

¹⁷Remember, it is sin to know what you ought to do and then not do it.

## Warning to the Rich

**5** Look here, you rich people: Weep and groan with anguish because of all the terrible troubles ahead of you. ²Your wealth is rotting away, and your fine clothes are moth-eaten rags. ³Your gold and silver have become worthless. The very wealth you were counting on will eat away your flesh like fire. This treasure you have accumulated will stand as evidence against you on the day of judgment. ⁴For listen! Hear the cries of the field workers whom you have cheated of their pay. The wages you held back cry out against you. The cries of those who harvest your fields have reached the ears of the LORD of Heaven's Armies.

⁵You have spent your years on earth in luxury, satisfying your every desire. You have fattened yourselves for the day of slaughter. ⁶You have condemned and killed innocent people,* who do not resist you.*

## Patience and Endurance

⁷Dear brothers and sisters,* be patient as you wait for the Lord's return. Consider the farmers who patiently wait for the rains in the fall and in the spring. They eagerly look for the valuable harvest to ripen. ⁸You, too, must be patient. Take courage, for the coming of the Lord is near.

⁹Don't grumble about each other, brothers and sisters, or you will be judged. For look—the Judge is standing at the door!

¹⁰For examples of patience in suffering, dear brothers and sisters, look at the prophets who spoke in the name of the Lord. ¹¹We give great honor to those who endure under suffering. For instance, you know about Job, a man of great endurance. You can see how the Lord was kind to him at the end, for the Lord is full of tenderness and mercy.

¹²But most of all, my brothers and sisters, never take an oath, by heaven or earth or anything else. Just say a simple yes or no, so that you will not sin and be condemned.

## The Power of Prayer

¹³Are any of you suffering hardships? You should pray. Are any of you happy? You should sing praises. ¹⁴Are any of you sick? You should call for the elders of the church to come and pray over you, anointing you with oil in the name of the Lord. ¹⁵Such a prayer offered in faith will heal the sick, and the Lord will make you well. And if you have committed any sins, you will be forgiven.

¹⁶Confess your sins to each other and pray for each other so that you may be healed. The earnest prayer of a righteous

> Are any of you suffering hardships? You should pray.
>
> Are any of you happy? You should sing praises.
>
> Are any of you sick? You should call for the elders of the church to come and pray over you, anointing you with oil in the name of the Lord.
>
> JAMES 5:13-14

**5:6a** Or *killed the Righteous One.*　**5:6b** Or *Don't they resist you?* or *Doesn't God oppose you?* or *Aren't they now accusing you before God?*　**5:7** Greek *brothers;* also in 5:9, 10, 12, 19.

person has great power and produces wonderful results. [17]Elijah was as human as we are, and yet when he prayed earnestly that no rain would fall, none fell for three and a half years! [18]Then, when he prayed again, the sky sent down rain and the earth began to yield its crops.

## Restore Wandering Believers

[19]My dear brothers and sisters, if someone among you wanders away from the truth and is brought back, [20]you can be sure that whoever brings the sinner back will save that person from death and bring about the forgiveness of many sins.

# 1 PETER

> *Dear friends,*
> *don't be*
> *surprised at the*
> *fiery trials you*
> *are going*
> *through, as if*
> *something*
> *strange were*
> *happening to*
> *you.*
>
> 1 PETER 4:12

Illness often catches us by surprise. Cancer is an especially sneaky disease. By the time the headache occurs, the brain tumor is probably the size of a golf ball. By the time the cough appears, the lung tumor likely is inoperable. By the time the pain is felt, the ovarian tumor usually has spread. Heart attacks can be silent. Diabetes can surface without warning. It is possible to look fine and even *feel* fine and yet surprisingly be seriously ill.

Sometimes it's hard to believe that anything is really wrong after we've been so healthy all our lives. Illness seems a strange foreigner to us and we may even protest, "This shouldn't be happening."

In this letter to several of the early churches, the apostle Peter tries to warn believers that they should not be surprised that suffering, persecution, and trials are coming their way—not exactly the kind of news that makes your day! (His words were very timely as the Emperor Nero soon would set Rome on fire so he could rebuild it his way. He blamed the fire on the Christians and began a systematic persecution of them, including using them as lighted torches in his gardens.)

And while Peter's words are directed especially at those being persecuted for their faith, they apply also to those of us having our faith tested through other kinds of "fiery trials." We really should not be surprised that our bodies betray us and break down. Neither should we be surprised that God can and will see us through.

## Greetings from Peter

**1** This letter is from Peter, an apostle of Jesus Christ.

I am writing to God's chosen people who are living as foreigners in the provinces of Pontus, Galatia, Cappadocia, Asia, and Bithynia.* ²God the Father knew you and chose you long ago, and his Spirit has made you holy. As a result, you have obeyed him and have been cleansed by the blood of Jesus Christ.

May God give you more and more grace and peace.

## The Hope of Eternal Life

³All praise to God, the Father of our Lord Jesus Christ. It is by his great mercy that we have been born again, because God raised Jesus Christ from the dead. Now we live with great expectation, ⁴and we have a priceless inheritance—an inheritance that is kept in heaven for you, pure and undefiled, beyond the reach of change and decay. ⁵And through your faith, God is protecting you by his power until you receive this salvation, which is ready to be revealed on the last day for all to see.

⁶So be truly glad.* There is wonderful joy ahead, even though you have to endure many trials for a little while. ⁷These trials will show that your faith is genuine. It is being tested as fire tests and purifies gold—though your faith is far more precious than mere gold. So when your faith remains strong through many trials, it will bring you much praise and glory and honor on the day when Jesus Christ is revealed to the whole world.

⁸You love him even though you have never seen him. Though you do not see him now, you trust him; and you rejoice with a glorious, inexpressible joy. ⁹The reward for trusting him will be the salvation of your souls.

¹⁰This salvation was something even the prophets wanted to know more about when they prophesied about this gracious salvation prepared for you. ¹¹They wondered what time or situation the Spirit of Christ within them was talking about when he told them in advance about Christ's suffering and his great glory afterward.

¹²They were told that their messages were not for themselves, but for you. And now this Good News has been announced to you by those who preached in the power of the Holy Spirit sent from heaven. It is all so wonderful that even the angels are eagerly watching these things happen.

## A Call to Holy Living

¹³So think clearly and exercise self-control. Look forward to the gracious salvation that will come to you when Jesus Christ is revealed to the world. ¹⁴So you must live as God's obedient children. Don't slip back into your old ways of living to satisfy your own desires. You didn't know any better then. ¹⁵But now you must be holy in everything you do, just as God who chose you is holy. ¹⁶For the Scriptures say, "You must be holy because I am holy."*

¹⁷And remember that the heavenly Father to whom you pray has no favorites. He will judge or reward you according to what you do. So you must live in reverent fear of him during your time as "foreigners in the land." ¹⁸For you know that God paid a ransom to save you from the empty life you inherited from your ancestors. And the ransom he paid was not mere gold or silver. ¹⁹It was the precious blood of Christ, the sinless, spotless Lamb of God. ²⁰God chose him as your ransom long before the world began, but he has now revealed him to you in these last days.

²¹Through Christ you have come to trust in God. And you have placed your faith and hope in God because he raised Christ from the dead and gave him great glory.

²²You were cleansed from your sins when you obeyed the truth, so now you must show

---

**1:1** *Pontus, Galatia, Cappadocia, Asia,* and *Bithynia* were Roman provinces in what is now Turkey.  **1:6** Or *So you are truly glad.*
**1:16** Lev 11:44-45; 19:2; 20:7.

sincere love to each other as brothers and sisters.* Love each other deeply with all your heart.*

**23** For you have been born again, but not to a life that will quickly end. Your new life will last forever because it comes from the eternal, living word of God. <sup>24</sup>As the Scriptures say,

> "People are like grass;
>     their beauty is like a flower in
>         the field.
> The grass withers and the flower fades.
> <sup>25</sup>    But the word of the Lord remains
>         forever."*

And that word is the Good News that was preached to you.

**2** So get rid of all evil behavior. Be done with all deceit, hypocrisy, jealousy, and all unkind speech. <sup>2</sup>Like newborn babies, you must crave pure spiritual milk so that you will grow into a full experience of salvation. Cry out for this nourishment, <sup>3</sup>now that you have had a taste of the Lord's kindness.

### Living Stones for God's House

<sup>4</sup>You are coming to Christ, who is the living cornerstone of God's temple. He was rejected by people, but he was chosen by God for great honor.

<sup>5</sup>And you are living stones that God is building into his spiritual temple. What's more, you are his holy priests.* Through the mediation of Jesus Christ, you offer spiritual sacrifices that please God. <sup>6</sup>As the Scriptures say,

> "I am placing a cornerstone in
>     Jerusalem,*
> chosen for great honor,
> and anyone who trusts in him
>     will never be disgraced."*

<sup>7</sup>Yes, you who trust him recognize the honor God has given him. But for those who reject him,

> "The stone that the builders rejected
>     has now become the cornerstone."*

## FEELING the heat?
READ 1 PETER 1:7

Heating up a pot of gold will turn the normally hard precious metal into liquid and cause impurities to rise to the surface. The refiner then scoops them out. Turning the heat up even more causes more impurities to rise and be discarded, leaving a purer, more valuable gold.

Has the heat been turned up on you as you sit like gold in a pot? The heavenly Refiner's goal is *not* to destroy you, but to "bring you much praise and glory and honor on the day when Jesus Christ is revealed to the whole world."

<sup>8</sup>And,

> "He is the stone that makes people
>     stumble,
>     the rock that makes them fall."*

They stumble because they do not obey God's word, and so they meet the fate that was planned for them.

<sup>9</sup>But you are not like that, for you are a chosen people. You are royal priests,* a holy nation, God's very own possession. As a result, you can show others the goodness of God, for he called you out of the darkness into his wonderful light.

<sup>10</sup>"Once you had no identity as
>     a people;
> now you are God's people.
> Once you received no mercy;
>     now you have received God's
>         mercy."*

<sup>11</sup>Dear friends, I warn you as "temporary residents and foreigners" to keep away from worldly desires that wage war against your very souls. <sup>12</sup>Be careful to live properly among your unbelieving neighbors. Then even if they accuse you of doing wrong, they will see your honorable behavior, and they will give honor to God when he judges the world.*

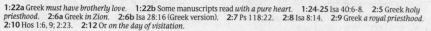

**1:22a** Greek *must have brotherly love.*    **1:22b** Some manuscripts read *with a pure heart.*    **1:24-25** Isa 40:6-8.    **2:5** Greek *holy priesthood.*    **2:6a** Greek *in Zion.*    **2:6b** Isa 28:16 (Greek version).    **2:7** Ps 118:22.    **2:8** Isa 8:14.    **2:9** Greek *a royal priesthood.*    **2:10** Hos 1:6, 9; 2:23.    **2:12** Or *on the day of visitation.*

## Respecting People in Authority

¹³For the Lord's sake, respect all human authority—whether the king as head of state, ¹⁴or the officials he has appointed. For the king has sent them to punish those who do wrong and to honor those who do right.

¹⁵It is God's will that your honorable lives should silence those ignorant people who make foolish accusations against you. ¹⁶For you are free, yet you are God's slaves, so don't use your freedom as an excuse to do evil. ¹⁷Respect everyone, and love your Christian brothers and sisters.* Fear God, and respect the king.

## Slaves

¹⁸You who are slaves must accept the authority of your masters with all respect.* Do what they tell you—not only if they are kind and reasonable, but even if they are cruel. ¹⁹For God is pleased with you when you do what you know is right and patiently endure unfair treatment. ²⁰Of course, you get no credit for being patient if you are beaten for doing wrong. But if you suffer for doing good and endure it patiently, God is pleased with you.

²¹For God called you to do good, even if it means suffering, just as Christ suffered* for you. He is your example, and you must follow in his steps.

²²He never sinned,
    nor ever deceived anyone.*
²³He did not retaliate when he was
        insulted,
    nor threaten revenge when he
        suffered.
    He left his case in the hands of God,
        who always judges fairly.
²⁴He personally carried our sins
        in his body on the cross
    so that we can be dead to sin
        and live for what is right.
    By his wounds
        you are healed.
²⁵Once you were like sheep
        who wandered away.
    But now you have turned to your
        Shepherd,
    the Guardian of your souls.

## Wives

**3** In the same way, you wives must accept the authority of your husbands. Then, even if some refuse to obey the Good News, your godly lives will speak to them without any words. They will be won over ²by observing your pure and reverent lives.

³Don't be concerned about the outward beauty of fancy hairstyles, expensive jewelry, or beautiful clothes. ⁴You should clothe yourselves instead with the beauty that comes from within, the unfading beauty of a gentle and quiet spirit, which is so precious to God. ⁵This is how the holy women of old made themselves beautiful. They trusted God and accepted the authority of their husbands. ⁶For instance, Sarah obeyed her husband, Abraham, and called him her master. You are her daughters when you do what is right without fear of what your husbands might do.

## Husbands

⁷In the same way, you husbands must give honor to your wives. Treat your wife with understanding as you live together. She may be weaker than you are, but she is your equal partner in God's gift of new life. Treat her as you should so your prayers will not be hindered.

## All Christians

⁸Finally, all of you should be of one mind. Sympathize with each other. Love each other as brothers and sisters.* Be tenderhearted, and keep a humble attitude. ⁹Don't repay evil for evil. Don't retaliate with insults when people insult you. Instead, pay them back with a blessing. That is what God has called you to do, and he will bless you for it. ¹⁰For the Scriptures say,

"If you want to enjoy life
    and see many happy days,
keep your tongue from speaking evil
    and your lips from telling lies.
¹¹Turn away from evil and do good.
    Search for peace, and work to
        maintain it.

**2:17** Greek *love the brotherhood.* **2:18** Or *because you fear God.* **2:21** Some manuscripts read *died.* **2:22** Isa 53:9. **3:8** Greek *Show brotherly love.*

<sup>12</sup> The eyes of the Lord watch over those
        who do right,
    and his ears are open to their prayers.
    But the Lord turns his face
        against those who do evil."*

## Suffering for Doing Good

<sup>13</sup> Now, who will want to harm you if you are eager to do good? <sup>14</sup> But even if you suffer for doing what is right, God will reward you for it. So don't worry or be afraid of their threats. <sup>15</sup> Instead, you must worship Christ as Lord of your life. And if someone asks about your Christian hope, always be ready to explain it. <sup>16</sup> But do this in a gentle and respectful way.* Keep your conscience clear. Then if people speak against you, they will be ashamed when they see what a good life you live because you belong to Christ. <sup>17</sup> Remember, it is better to suffer for doing good, if that is what God wants, than to suffer for doing wrong!

<sup>18</sup> Christ suffered* for our sins once for all time. He never sinned, but he died for sinners to bring you safely home to God. He suffered physical death, but he was raised to life in the Spirit.*

<sup>19</sup> So he went and preached to the spirits in prison—<sup>20</sup> those who disobeyed God long ago when God waited patiently while Noah was building his boat. Only eight people were saved from drowning in that terrible flood.* <sup>21</sup> And that water is a picture of baptism, which now saves you, not by removing dirt from your body, but as a response to God from* a clean conscience. It is effective because of the resurrection of Jesus Christ.

<sup>22</sup> Now Christ has gone to heaven. He is seated in the place of honor next to God, and all the angels and authorities and powers accept his authority.

## Living for God

**4** So then, since Christ suffered physical pain, you must arm yourselves with the same attitude he had, and be ready to suffer, too. For if you have suffered physically for Christ, you have finished with sin.* <sup>2</sup> You won't spend the rest of your lives chasing your own desires, but you will be anxious to do the will of God. <sup>3</sup> You have had enough in the past of the evil things that godless people enjoy—their immorality and lust, their feasting and drunkenness and wild parties, and their terrible worship of idols.

<sup>4</sup> Of course, your former friends are surprised when you no longer plunge into the flood of wild and destructive things they do. So they slander you. <sup>5</sup> But remember that they will have to face God, who will judge everyone, both the living and the dead. <sup>6</sup> That is why the Good News was preached to those who are now dead*—so although they were destined to die like all people,* they now live forever with God in the Spirit.*

<sup>7</sup> The end of the world is coming soon. Therefore, be earnest and disciplined in your prayers. <sup>8</sup> Most important of all, continue to show deep love for each other, for love covers a multitude of sins. <sup>9</sup> Cheerfully share your home with those who need a meal or a place to stay.

<sup>10</sup> God has given each of you a gift from his great variety of spiritual gifts. Use them well to serve one another. <sup>11</sup> Do you have the gift of speaking? Then speak as though God himself were speaking through you. Do you have the gift of helping others? Do it with all the strength and energy that God supplies. Then everything you do will bring glory to

**3:10-12** Ps 34:12-16.   **3:16** Some English translations put this sentence in verse 15.   **3:18a** Some manuscripts read *died.* **3:18b** Or *in spirit.*   **3:20** Greek *saved through water.*   **3:21** Or *as an appeal to God for.*   **4:1** Or *For the one* [or One] *who has suffered physically has finished with sin.*   **4:6a** Greek *preached even to the dead.*   **4:6b** Or *so although people had judged them worthy of death.*   **4:6c** Or *in spirit.*

## IMPORTANT vs. unimportant
READ 1 PETER 4:2

You and your loved ones have faced a tremendous challenge. You have come face-to-face with your own mortality. You have endured difficulties you probably never thought you could. You have learned to distinguish between important and unimportant stuff. You know better than most that life is a tremendous gift not to be wasted.

Do you need to set any new priorities? Hopefully, "you won't spend the rest of your lives chasing your own desires, but you will be anxious to do the will of God."

God through Jesus Christ. All glory and power to him forever and ever! Amen.

### Suffering for Being a Christian

¹²Dear friends, don't be surprised at the fiery trials you are going through, as if something strange were happening to you. ¹³Instead, be very glad—for these trials make you partners with Christ in his suffering, so that you will have the wonderful joy of seeing his glory when it is revealed to all the world.

¹⁴So be happy when you are insulted for being a Christian,* for then the glorious Spirit of God* rests upon you.* ¹⁵If you suffer, however, it must not be for murder, stealing, making trouble, or prying into other people's affairs. ¹⁶But it is no shame to suffer for being a Christian. Praise God for the privilege of being called by his name! ¹⁷For the time has come for judgment, and it must begin with God's household. And if judgment begins with us, what terrible fate awaits those who have never obeyed God's Good News? ¹⁸And also,

"If the righteous are barely saved,
    what will happen to godless sinners?"*

¹⁹So if you are suffering in a manner that pleases God, keep on doing what is right, and trust your lives to the God who created you, for he will never fail you.

### Advice for Elders and Young Men

**5** And now, a word to you who are elders in the churches. I, too, am an elder and a witness to the sufferings of Christ. And I, too, will share in his glory when he is revealed to the whole world. As a fellow elder, I appeal to you: ²Care for the flock that God has entrusted to you. Watch over it willingly, not grudgingly—not for what you will get out of it, but because you are eager to serve

God. ³Don't lord it over the people assigned to your care, but lead them by your own good example. ⁴And when the Great Shepherd appears, you will receive a crown of never-ending glory and honor.

⁵In the same way, you younger men must accept the authority of the elders. And all of you, serve each other in humility, for

"God opposes the proud
    but favors the humble."*

⁶So humble yourselves under the mighty power of God, and at the right time he will lift you up in honor. ⁷Give all your worries and cares to God, for he cares about you.

⁸Stay alert! Watch out for your great enemy, the devil. He prowls around like a roaring lion, looking for someone to devour. ⁹Stand firm against him, and be strong in your faith. Remember that your Christian brothers and sisters* all over the world are going through the same kind of suffering you are.

¹⁰In his kindness God called you to share in his eternal glory by means of Christ Jesus. So after you have suffered a little while, he will restore, support, and strengthen you, and he will place you on a firm foundation. ¹¹All power to him forever! Amen.

### Peter's Final Greetings

¹²I have written and sent this short letter to you with the help of Silas,* whom I commend to you as a faithful brother. My purpose in writing is to encourage you and assure you that what you are experiencing is truly part of God's grace for you. Stand firm in this grace.

¹³Your sister church here in Babylon* sends you greetings, and so does my son Mark. ¹⁴Greet each other with Christian love.*

Peace be with all of you who are in Christ.

---

**4:14a** Greek *for the name of Christ.*    **4:14b** Or *for the glory of God, which is his Spirit.*    **4:14c** Some manuscripts add *On their part he is blasphemed, but on your part he is glorified.*    **4:18** Prov 11:31 (Greek version).    **5:5** Prov 3:34 (Greek version).    **5:9** Greek *your brothers.*    **5:12** Greek *Silvanus.*    **5:13** Greek *The elect one in Babylon.* Babylon was probably symbolic for Rome.    **5:14** Greek *with a kiss of love.*

# 2 PETER

*A day is like a thousand years to the Lord, and a thousand years is like a day.*

2 PETER 3:8

Waiting is one of the worst aspects of serious illness. We wait to hear the biopsy report. We wait to get the test results. We wait for the doctor's call. Those waiting days each can seem like a thousand years.

So why do we hate waiting so much? When we wait for others, it puts us at their mercy. They are controlling our schedules, our pace of life, and our agendas. Things are out of our hands.

Let's be honest: Most of us do not like to be at the mercy of someone or something else. Waiting goes against our very nature as any parent knows who has taken a long car ride with a small, are-we-there-yet child. But waiting can draw us closer to the Lord better than just about anything else.

When you're waiting, don't give up. Give in . . . to God. Go ahead and put yourself at His mercy. That's where we already are anyway. We might as well admit it, because when we do, we can start to experience the transforming power waiting can have on our character. It's not the waiting that changes us; it's how we respond to it. Try these "waiting" responses:

I'm not waiting on test results. I'm learning to depend more on God.

I'm not waiting for a doctor's call. I'm learning to be patient as God is with me.

I'm not waiting to be cured. I'm becoming more like Jesus.

317

## Greetings from Peter

**1** This letter is from Simon* Peter, a slave and apostle of Jesus Christ.

I am writing to you who share the same precious faith we have. This faith was given to you because of the justice and fairness* of Jesus Christ, our God and Savior.

<sup></sup>2May God give you more and more grace and peace as you grow in your knowledge of God and Jesus our Lord.

## Growing in Faith

3By his divine power, God has given us everything we need for living a godly life. We have received all of this by coming to know him, the one who called us to himself by means of his marvelous glory and excellence. 4And because of his glory and excellence, he has given us great and precious promises. These are the promises that enable you to share his divine nature and escape the world's corruption caused by human desires.

5In view of all this, make every effort to respond to God's promises. Supplement your faith with a generous provision of moral excellence, and moral excellence with knowledge, 6and knowledge with self-control, and self-control with patient endurance, and patient endurance with godliness, 7and godliness with brotherly affection, and brotherly affection with love for everyone.

8The more you grow like this, the more productive and useful you will be in your knowledge of our Lord Jesus Christ. 9But those who fail to develop in this way are shortsighted or blind, forgetting that they have been cleansed from their old sins.

10So, dear brothers and sisters,* work hard to prove that you really are among those God has called and chosen. Do these things, and you will never fall away. 11Then God will give you a grand entrance into the eternal Kingdom of our Lord and Savior Jesus Christ.

## Paying Attention to Scripture

12Therefore, I will always remind you about these things—even though you already know them and are standing firm in the truth you have been taught. 13And it is only right that I should keep on reminding you as long as I live.* 14For our Lord Jesus Christ has shown me that I must soon leave this earthly life,* 15so I will work hard to make sure you always remember these things after I am gone.

16For we were not making up clever stories when we told you about the powerful coming of our Lord Jesus Christ. We saw his majestic splendor with our own eyes 17when he received honor and glory from God the Father. The voice from the majestic glory of God said to him, "This is my dearly loved Son, who brings me great joy."* 18We ourselves heard that voice from heaven when we were with him on the holy mountain.

19Because of that experience, we have even greater confidence in the message proclaimed by the prophets. You must pay close attention to what they wrote, for their words are like a lamp shining in a dark place—until the Day dawns, and Christ the Morning Star shines* in your hearts. 20Above all, you must realize that no prophecy in Scripture ever came from the prophet's own understanding,* 21or from human initiative. No, those prophets were moved by the Holy Spirit, and they spoke from God.

## The Danger of False Teachers

**2** But there were also false prophets in Israel, just as there will be false teachers among you. They will cleverly teach destructive heresies and even deny the Master who bought them. In this way, they will bring sudden destruction on themselves. 2Many will follow their evil teaching and shameful immorality. And because of these teachers, the way of truth will be slandered. 3In their

---

**1:1a** Greek *Symeon.*   **1:1b** Or *to you in the righteousness*   **1:10** Greek *brothers.*   **1:13** Greek *as long as I am in this tent* [or *tabernacle*].   **1:14** Greek *I must soon put off my tent* [or *tabernacle*].   **1:17** Matt 17:5; Mark 9:7; Luke 9:35.   **1:19** Or *rises.*
**1:20** Or *is a matter of one's own interpretation.*

greed they will make up clever lies to get hold of your money. But God condemned them long ago, and their destruction will not be delayed.

⁴For God did not spare even the angels who sinned. He threw them into hell,* in gloomy pits of darkness,* where they are being held until the day of judgment. ⁵And God did not spare the ancient world—except for Noah and the seven others in his family. Noah warned the world of God's righteous judgment. So God protected Noah when he destroyed the world of ungodly people with a vast flood. ⁶Later, God condemned the cities of Sodom and Gomorrah and turned them into heaps of ashes. He made them an example of what will happen to ungodly people. ⁷But God also rescued Lot out of Sodom because he was a righteous man who was sick of the shameful immorality of the wicked people around him. ⁸Yes, Lot was a righteous man who was tormented in his soul by the wickedness he saw and heard day after day. ⁹So you see, the Lord knows how to rescue godly people from their trials, even while keeping the wicked under punishment until the day of final judgment. ¹⁰He is especially hard on those who follow their own twisted sexual desire, and who despise authority.

These people are proud and arrogant, daring even to scoff at supernatural beings* without so much as trembling. ¹¹But the angels, who are far greater in power and strength, do not dare to bring from the Lord* a charge of blasphemy against those supernatural beings.

¹²These false teachers are like unthinking animals, creatures of instinct, born to be caught and destroyed. They scoff at things they do not understand, and like animals, they will be destroyed. ¹³Their destruction is their reward for the harm they have done. They love to indulge in evil pleasures in broad daylight. They are a disgrace and a stain among you. They delight in deception* even as they eat with you in your fellowship meals. ¹⁴They commit adultery with their eyes, and their desire for sin is

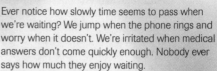

## WAITING is the worst
READ 2 PETER 3:14

Ever notice how slowly time seems to pass when we're waiting? We jump when the phone rings and worry when it doesn't. We're irritated when medical answers don't come quickly enough. Nobody ever says how much they enjoy waiting.

But some things are worth the wait: eight hours on a plane for a dream vacation; nine months to hold a new baby; ten years to welcome home a wayward child; a lifetime for a new heaven and earth.

Waiting is not optional. How we wait is our choice. "And so, dear friends, while you are waiting for these things to happen, make every effort to be found living peaceful lives that are pure and blameless in his sight."

never satisfied. They lure unstable people into sin, and they are well trained in greed. They live under God's curse. ¹⁵They have wandered off the right road and followed the footsteps of Balaam son of Beor,* who loved to earn money by doing wrong. ¹⁶But Balaam was stopped from his mad course when his donkey rebuked him with a human voice.

¹⁷These people are as useless as dried-up springs or as mist blown away by the wind. They are doomed to blackest darkness. ¹⁸They brag about themselves with empty, foolish boasting. With an appeal to twisted sexual desires, they lure back into sin those who have barely escaped from a lifestyle of deception. ¹⁹They promise freedom, but they themselves are slaves of sin and corruption. For you are a slave to whatever controls you. ²⁰And when people escape from the wickedness of the world by knowing our Lord and Savior Jesus Christ and then get tangled up and enslaved by sin again, they are worse off than before. ²¹It would be better if they had never known the way to righteousness than to know it and then reject the command they were given to live a holy life. ²²They prove the truth of this proverb: "A dog returns to its vomit."* And another says, "A washed pig returns to the mud."

2:4a Greek *Tartarus*.　2:4b Some manuscripts read *in chains of gloom*.　2:10 Greek *at glorious ones*, which are probably evil angels.　2:11 Other manuscripts read *to the Lord;* still others omit this phrase.　2:13 Some manuscripts read *in fellowship meals*.　2:15 Some manuscripts read *Bosor*.　2:22 Prov 26:11.

*The Day of the Lord Is Coming*

**3** This is my second letter to you, dear friends, and in both of them I have tried to stimulate your wholesome thinking and refresh your memory. [2] I want you to remember what the holy prophets said long ago and what our Lord and Savior commanded through your apostles.

[3] Most importantly, I want to remind you that in the last days scoffers will come, mocking the truth and following their own desires. [4] They will say, "What happened to the promise that Jesus is coming again? From before the times of our ancestors, everything has remained the same since the world was first created."

[5] They deliberately forget that God made the heavens by the word of his command, and he brought the earth out from the water and surrounded it with water. [6] Then he used the water to destroy the ancient world with a mighty flood. [7] And by the same word, the present heavens and earth have been stored up for fire. They are being kept for the day of judgment, when ungodly people will be destroyed.

[8] But you must not forget this one thing, dear friends: A day is like a thousand years to the Lord, and a thousand years is like a day. [9] The Lord isn't really being slow about his promise, as some people think. No, he is being patient for your sake. He does not want anyone to be destroyed, but wants everyone to repent. [10] But the day of the Lord will come as unexpectedly as a thief. Then the heavens will pass away with a terrible noise, and the very elements themselves will disappear in fire, and the earth and everything on it will be found to deserve judgment.*

[11] Since everything around us is going to be destroyed like this, what holy and godly lives you should live, [12] looking forward to the day of God and hurrying it along. On that day, he will set the heavens on fire, and the elements will melt away in the flames. [13] But we are looking forward to the new heavens and new earth he has promised, a world filled with God's righteousness.

[14] And so, dear friends, while you are waiting for these things to happen, make every effort to be found living peaceful lives that are pure and blameless in his sight.

[15] And remember, the Lord's patience gives people time to be saved. This is what our beloved brother Paul also wrote to you with the wisdom God gave him—[16] speaking of these things in all of his letters. Some of his comments are hard to understand, and those who are ignorant and unstable have twisted his letters to mean something quite different, just as they do with other parts of Scripture. And this will result in their destruction.

*Peter's Final Words*

[17] I am warning you ahead of time, dear friends. Be on guard so that you will not be carried away by the errors of these wicked people and lose your own secure footing. [18] Rather, you must grow in the grace and knowledge of our Lord and Savior Jesus Christ.

All glory to him, both now and forever! Amen.

3:10 Other manuscripts read *will be burned up;* still others read *will be found destroyed.*

# 1 JOHN

*Such love has no fear, because perfect love expels all fear.*

1 JOHN 4:18

Fear is a funny thing. Not "ha-ha" funny, but peculiar funny. You need a certain amount of it in order to live safely; but if you have too much of it, it paralyzes you from really living.

The late psychiatrist M. Scott Peck had some great thoughts on the subject. He said, "The absence of fear is not courage; the absence of fear is some kind of brain damage. Courage is the capacity to go on in spite of the fear, or in spite of the pain."[1]

So how do we do that? Tell ourselves we're not really afraid? Pretend that we have no fear? No, the apostle John (the same one who wrote the Gospel of John) shows us a much better way. He writes that when we truly experience the love of God, His perfect love gets rid of all the fear. If you believe with your mind and your heart that God truly loves you, you will not fear today or tomorrow because everything that touches you first will be sifted through His loving hands. "We know how much God loves us, and we have put our trust in His love" (1 John 4:16).

Is your back up against the wall? GOD loves you.

Are you sick and tired of being sick and tired? God LOVES you.

Are your days numbered? God loves YOU.

Trust in that love.

---

[1] M. Scott Peck, *Further Along the Road Less Traveled* (New York: Touchstone, 1993), 23.

## Introduction

**1** We proclaim to you the one who existed from the beginning,* whom we have heard and seen. We saw him with our own eyes and touched him with our own hands. He is the Word of life. ²This one who is life itself was revealed to us, and we have seen him. And now we testify and proclaim to you that he is the one who is eternal life. He was with the Father, and then he was revealed to us. ³We proclaim to you what we ourselves have actually seen and heard so that you may have fellowship with us. And our fellowship is with the Father and with his Son, Jesus Christ. ⁴We are writing these things so that you may fully share our joy.*

## Living in the Light

⁵This is the message we heard from Jesus* and now declare to you: God is light, and there is no darkness in him at all. ⁶So we are lying if we say we have fellowship with God but go on living in spiritual darkness; we are not practicing the truth. ⁷But if we are living in the light, as God is in the light, then we have fellowship with each other, and the blood of Jesus, his Son, cleanses us from all sin.

⁸If we claim we have no sin, we are only fooling ourselves and not living in the truth. ⁹But if we confess our sins to him, he is faithful and just to forgive us our sins and to cleanse us from all wickedness. ¹⁰If we claim we have not sinned, we are calling God a liar and showing that his word has no place in our hearts.

**2** ¹My dear children, I am writing this to you so that you will not sin. But if anyone does sin, we have an advocate who pleads our case before the Father. He is Jesus Christ, the one who is truly righteous. ²He himself is the sacrifice that atones for our sins—and not only our sins but the sins of all the world.

³And we can be sure that we know him if we obey his commandments. ⁴If someone claims, "I know God," but doesn't obey God's commandments, that person is a liar and is not living in the truth. ⁵But those who obey God's word truly show how completely they love him. That is how we know we are living in him. ⁶Those who say they live in God should live their lives as Jesus did.

## A New Commandment

⁷Dear friends, I am not writing a new commandment for you; rather it is an old one you have had from the very beginning. This old commandment—to love one another—is the same message you heard before. ⁸Yet it is also new. Jesus lived the truth of this commandment, and you also are living it. For the darkness is disappearing, and the true light is already shining.

⁹If anyone claims, "I am living in the light," but hates a Christian brother or sister,* that person is still living in darkness. ¹⁰Anyone who loves another brother or sister* is living in the light and does not cause others to stumble. ¹¹But anyone who hates another brother or sister is still living and walking in darkness. Such a person does not know the way to go, having been blinded by the darkness.

¹² I am writing to you who are God's children
   because your sins have been forgiven through Jesus.*
¹³ I am writing to you who are mature in the faith*
   because you know Christ, who existed from the beginning.
   I am writing to you who are young in the faith
   because you have won your battle with the evil one.
¹⁴ I have written to you who are God's children

because you know the Father.
I have written to you who are mature in
the faith
because you know Christ, who existed
from the beginning.
I have written to you who are young in
the faith
because you are strong.
God's word lives in your hearts,
and you have won your battle with the
evil one.

## Do Not Love This World

15 Do not love this world nor the things it of-fers you, for when you love the world, you do not have the love of the Father in you. 16 For the world offers only a craving for physical pleasure, a craving for everything we see, and pride in our achievements and posses-sions. These are not from the Father, but are from this world. 17 And this world is fading away, along with everything that people crave. But anyone who does what pleases God will live forever.

## Warning about Antichrists

18 Dear children, the last hour is here. You have heard that the Antichrist is coming, and already many such antichrists have ap-peared. From this we know that the last hour has come. 19 These people left our churches, but they never really belonged with us; otherwise they would have stayed with us. When they left, it proved that they did not belong with us.

20 But you are not like that, for the Holy One has given you his Spirit,* and all of you know the truth. 21 So I am writing to you not be-cause you don't know the truth but because you know the difference between truth and lies. 22 And who is a liar? Anyone who says that Jesus is not the Christ.* Anyone who de-nies the Father and the Son is an antichrist.* 23 Anyone who denies the Son doesn't have the Father, either. But anyone who acknowl-edges the Son has the Father also.

24 So you must remain faithful to what you have been taught from the beginning. If you do, you will remain in fellowship with the Son and with the Father. 25 And in this

SAME old message
READ 1 JOHN 2:7

When we're facing a health crisis, we realize more than ever that life is not about how much we have or how much we've accomplished. It's about how much we're loved and how much we love. John readily acknowledges that his message is "an old one you have had from the very beginning." His simple, yet profound message is for us to "love one another."

There are admittedly many things that cannot be done while we're ill. But the good news is we always can be loved . . . and we can love others.

fellowship we enjoy the eternal life he prom-ised us.

26 I am writing these things to warn you about those who want to lead you astray. 27 But you have received the Holy Spirit,* and he lives within you, so you don't need anyone to teach you what is true. For the Spirit* teaches you everything you need to know, and what he teaches is true—it is not a lie. So just as he has taught you, remain in fellowship with Christ.

## Living as Children of God

28 And now, dear children, remain in fellow-ship with Christ so that when he returns, you will be full of courage and not shrink back from him in shame.

29 Since we know that Christ is righteous, we also know that all who do what is right are God's children.

**3** See how very much our Father loves us, for he calls us his children, and that is what we are! But the people who belong to this world don't recognize that we are God's children because they don't know him. 2 Dear friends, we are already God's children, but he has not yet shown us what we will be like when Christ appears. But we do know that we will be like him, for we will see him as he really is. 3 And all who have this eager expectation will keep themselves pure, just as he is pure.

⁴Everyone who sins is breaking God's law, for all sin is contrary to the law of God. ⁵And you know that Jesus came to take away our sins, and there is no sin in him. ⁶Anyone who continues to live in him will not sin. But anyone who keeps on sinning does not know him or understand who he is.

⁷Dear children, don't let anyone deceive you about this: When people do what is right, it shows that they are righteous, even as Christ is righteous. ⁸But when people keep on sinning, it shows that they belong to the devil, who has been sinning since the beginning. But the Son of God came to destroy the works of the devil. ⁹Those who have been born into God's family do not make a practice of sinning, because God's life* is in them. So they can't keep on sinning, because they are children of God. ¹⁰So now we can tell who are children of God and who are children of the devil. Anyone who does not live righteously and does not love other believers* does not belong to God.

## Love One Another

¹¹This is the message you have heard from the beginning: We should love one another. ¹²We must not be like Cain, who belonged to the evil one and killed his brother. And why did he kill him? Because Cain had been doing what was evil, and his brother had been doing what was righteous. ¹³So don't be surprised, dear brothers and sisters,* if the world hates you.

¹⁴If we love our Christian brothers and sisters,* it proves that we have passed from death to life. But a person who has no love is still dead. ¹⁵Anyone who hates another brother or sister* is really a murderer at heart. And you know that murderers don't have eternal life within them.

¹⁶We know what real love is because Jesus gave up his life for us. So we also ought to give up our lives for our brothers and sisters. ¹⁷If someone has enough money to live well and sees a brother or sister* in need but shows no compassion—how can God's love be in that person?

¹⁸Dear children, let's not merely say that we love each other; let us show the truth by our actions. ¹⁹Our actions will show that we belong to the truth, so we will be confident when we stand before God. ²⁰Even if we feel guilty, God is greater than our feelings, and he knows everything.

²¹Dear friends, if we don't feel guilty, we can come to God with bold confidence. ²²And we will receive from him whatever we ask because we obey him and do the things that please him.

²³And this is his commandment: We must believe in the name of his Son, Jesus Christ, and love one another, just as he commanded us. ²⁴Those who obey God's commandments remain in fellowship with him, and he with them. And we know he lives in us because the Spirit he gave us lives in us.

## Discerning False Prophets

**4** Dear friends, do not believe everyone who claims to speak by the Spirit. You must test them to see if the spirit they have comes from God. For there are many false prophets in the world. ²This is how we know if they have the Spirit of God: If a person claiming to be a prophet* acknowledges that Jesus Christ came in a real body, that person has the Spirit of God. ³But if someone claims to be a prophet and does not acknowledge the truth about Jesus, that person is not from God. Such a person has the spirit of the Antichrist, which you heard is coming into the world and indeed is already here.

⁴But you belong to God, my dear children. You have already won a victory over those people, because the Spirit who lives in you is greater than the spirit who lives in the world. ⁵Those people belong to this world, so they speak from the world's viewpoint, and the world listens to them. ⁶But we belong to God, and those who know God listen to us. If they do not belong to God, they do not listen to us. That is how we know if someone has the Spirit of truth or the spirit of deception.

## Loving One Another

⁷Dear friends, let us continue to love one another, for love comes from God. Anyone

3:9 Greek *because his seed.*    3:10 Greek *does not love his brother.*    3:13 Greek *brothers.*    3:14 Greek *the brothers;* similarly in 3:16.
3:15 Greek *hates his brother.*    3:17 Greek *sees his brother.*    4:2 Greek *If a spirit;* similarly in 4:3.

who loves is a child of God and knows God. [8] But anyone who does not love does not know God, for God is love.

[9] God showed how much he loved us by sending his one and only Son into the world so that we might have eternal life through him. [10] This is real love—not that we loved God, but that he loved us and sent his Son as a sacrifice to take away our sins.

[11] Dear friends, since God loved us that much, we surely ought to love each other. [12] No one has ever seen God. But if we love each other, God lives in us, and his love is brought to full expression in us.

[13] And God has given us his Spirit as proof that we live in him and he in us. [14] Furthermore, we have seen with our own eyes and now testify that the Father sent his Son to be the Savior of the world. [15] All who confess that Jesus is the Son of God have God living in them, and they live in God. [16] We know how much God loves us, and we have put our trust in his love.

God is love, and all who live in love live in God, and God lives in them. [17] And as we live in God, our love grows more perfect. So we will not be afraid on the day of judgment, but we can face him with confidence because we live like Jesus here in this world. [18] Such love has no fear, because perfect love expels all fear. If we are afraid, it is for fear of punishment, and this shows that we have not fully experienced his perfect love. [19] We love each other* because he loved us first.

[20] If someone says, "I love God," but hates a Christian brother or sister,* that person is a liar; for if we don't love people we can see, how can we love God, whom we cannot see? [21] And he has given us this command: Those who love God must also love their Christian brothers and sisters.*

### Faith in the Son of God

**5** Everyone who believes that Jesus is the Christ* has become a child of God. And everyone who loves the Father loves his children, too. [2] We know we love God's children if we love God and obey his commandments. [3] Loving God means keeping his commandments, and his commandments are not burdensome. [4] For every child of God defeats this evil world, and we achieve this victory through our faith. [5] And who can win this battle against the world? Only those who believe that Jesus is the Son of God.

[6] And Jesus Christ was revealed as God's Son by his baptism in water and by shedding his blood on the cross*—not by water only, but by water and blood. And the Spirit, who is truth, confirms it with his testimony.

4:19 Greek *We love*. Other manuscripts read *We love God;* still others read *We love him.*    **4:20** Greek *hates his brother.*    **4:21** Greek *The one who loves God must also love his brother.*    **5:1** Or *the Messiah.*    **5:6** Greek *This is he who came by water and blood.*

## MAKE my day

READ 1 JOHN 4:12

Are you looking for God today? Where are you looking for Him? Is it just in prayers related to your health or your loved one's health, or are you watching for Him in other places? Do you wish God would just show up in person and make your day?

Go ahead and ask Him to do just that, but don't be waiting for an old, white-haired guy with a long beard to arrive. You'll need to watch for Him in unexpected places.

He might be in the friend who stops by and takes you to lunch.

He might be in the note that comes in the mail with a special word of blessing.

He might be in the phone call that ends with a prayer for you.

And He might even be in the knock on the door that leads to someone *you* can encourage.

However it happens, don't miss these "God moments." He may not always show up exactly the way you imagined, but He'll be there.

*Joy Bombs!*

7So we have these three witnesses*—8the Spirit, the water, and the blood—and all three agree. 9Since we believe human testimony, surely we can believe the greater testimony that comes from God. And God has testified about his Son. 10All who believe in the Son of God know in their hearts that this testimony is true. Those who don't believe this are actually calling God a liar because they don't believe what God has testified about his Son.

11And this is what God has testified: He has given us eternal life, and this life is in his Son. 12Whoever has the Son has life; whoever does not have God's Son does not have life.

## Conclusion

13I have written this to you who believe in the name of the Son of God, so that you may know you have eternal life. 14And we are confident that he hears us whenever we ask for anything that pleases him. 15And since we know he hears us when we make our requests, we also know that he will give us what we ask for.

16If you see a Christian brother or sister* sinning in a way that does not lead to death, you should pray, and God will give that person life. But there is a sin that leads to death, and I am not saying you should pray for those who commit it. 17All wicked actions are sin, but not every sin leads to death.

18We know that God's children do not make a practice of sinning, for God's Son holds them securely, and the evil one cannot touch them. 19We know that we are children of God and that the world around us is under the control of the evil one.

20And we know that the Son of God has come, and he has given us understanding so that we can know the true God.* And now we live in fellowship with the true God because we live in fellowship with his Son, Jesus Christ. He is the only true God, and he is eternal life.

21Dear children, keep away from anything that might take God's place in your hearts.*

5:7 A few very late manuscripts add *in heaven—the Father, the Word, and the Holy Spirit, and these three are one. And we have three witnesses on earth.* 5:16 Greek *a brother.* 5:20 Greek *the one who is true.* 5:21 Greek *keep yourselves from idols.*

# 2 JOHN

Many people say they don't want to know the truth about their illness, somehow assuming that what they don't know can't hurt them. But while we don't have to surf every disease-related Web site or memorize every discouraging statistic, we need to know the truth about what we face. Ignorance is not bliss.

Correct diagnoses are true, but prognoses may or may not be. Just because a doctor tells you or your loved one that you have "only six months to live" does not mean that statement will come true in your life. We've all known people who were *supposed* to be dead years and even decades ago. Don't accept as gospel truth a prediction that may or may not come true for you. (When you get right down to it, everyone has the same two survival statistics—we're all 100 percent alive now and we all eventually will be 0 percent alive on planet Earth!)

So let's not live in statistics or any other what-ifs. Let's live as the apostle John suggests: "in truth." Let's compare what we're thinking, believing, and feeling about our situation to the absolute, unchanging truth. That kind of unchanging truth won't be found in any medical book (revised editions keep coming out). And that kind of absolute truth won't be found in any randomized trial (there always are objections to the accuracy of study results).

The only place to find that kind of you-can-bet-your-life-on-it truth is within the Word of God. Keep reading it and living in its truth.

## Greetings

This letter is from John, the elder.*

I am writing to the chosen lady and to her children,* whom I love in the truth—as does everyone else who knows the truth—²because the truth lives in us and will be with us forever.

³Grace, mercy, and peace, which come from God the Father and from Jesus Christ—the Son of the Father—will continue to be with us who live in truth and love.

## Live in the Truth

⁴How happy I was to meet some of your children and find them living according to the truth, just as the Father commanded.

⁵I am writing to remind you, dear friends,* that we should love one another. This is not a new commandment, but one we have had from the beginning. ⁶Love means doing what God has commanded us, and he has commanded us to love one another, just as you heard from the beginning.

⁷I say this because many deceivers have gone out into the world. They deny that Jesus Christ came* in a real body. Such a person is a deceiver and an antichrist. ⁸Watch out that you do not lose what we* have worked so hard to achieve. Be diligent so that you receive your full reward. ⁹Anyone who wanders away from this teaching has no relationship with God. But anyone who remains in the teaching of Christ has a relationship with both the Father and the Son.

¹⁰If anyone comes to your meeting and does not teach the truth about Christ, don't invite that person into your home or give any kind of encouragement. ¹¹Anyone who encourages such people becomes a partner in their evil work.

## Conclusion

¹²I have much more to say to you, but I don't want to do it with paper and ink. For I hope to visit you soon and talk with you face to face. Then our joy will be complete.

¹³Greetings from the children of your sister,* chosen by God.

1a Greek *From the elder.*   1b Or *the church God has chosen and its members.*   5 Greek *I urge you, lady.*   7 Or *will come.*   8 Some manuscripts read *you.*   13 Or *from the members of your sister church.*

# 3 JOHN

> *Dear friend,*
> *I hope all is well*
> *with you and*
> *that you are as*
> *healthy in body*
> *as you are strong*
> *in spirit.*
>
> 3 JOHN 1:2

A holistic approach to health has become very popular in recent years, and many physicians are realizing that treating the whole person—body, mind, and spirit—is crucial for wellness. However, that concept is not a new one at all.

The Scriptures are full of stories of Jesus treating the whole person—laying hands on them and restoring their physical bodies (the original therapeutic touch!), and speaking a word to them and healing their souls (no crystal pendant needed!).

But it can be hard to be strong in spirit when we don't feel well in body or mind. Mental or physical fatigue and pain can discourage and depress the best of us. That's why it is so crucial to care for and "feed" all our parts. It's pretty obvious that our bodies need the right food (no, Ben & Jerry's Cherry Garcia does not count as a fruit serving), rest (listen when your body wants a nap), and exercise (even if it's just a walk to the mailbox).

We know we can "feed" our minds by filling them with such things as soothing music, positive thoughts, and mental stimulation. But how do we feed our spirits?

Actually, you're doing it right now. As you read the Word of God and truths about His Word, you are supplying the spiritual nourishment you need. Even if you can't strengthen your body some days, don't ever let your spirit go hungry—feed it every day with God's Word and you will be strong in spirit.

### Greetings

This letter is from John, the elder.*

I am writing to Gaius, my dear friend, whom I love in the truth.

2 Dear friend, I hope all is well with you and that you are as healthy in body as you are strong in spirit. 3 Some of the traveling teachers* recently returned and made me very happy by telling me about your faithfulness and that you are living according to the truth. 4 I could have no greater joy than to hear that my children are following the truth.

### Caring for the Lord's Workers

5 Dear friend, you are being faithful to God when you care for the traveling teachers who pass through, even though they are strangers to you. 6 They have told the church here of your loving friendship. Please continue providing for such teachers in a manner that pleases God. 7 For they are traveling for the Lord,* and they accept nothing from people who are not believers.* 8 So we ourselves should support them so that we can be their partners as they teach the truth.

9 I wrote to the church about this, but Diotrephes, who loves to be the leader, refuses to have anything to do with us. 10 When I come, I will report some of the things he is doing and the evil accusations he is making against us. Not only does he refuse to welcome the traveling teachers, he also tells others not to help them. And when they do help, he puts them out of the church.

11 Dear friend, don't let this bad example influence you. Follow only what is good. Remember that those who do good prove that they are God's children, and those who do evil prove that they do not know God.*

12 Everyone speaks highly of Demetrius, as does the truth itself. We ourselves can say the same for him, and you know we speak the truth.

### Conclusion

13 I have much more to say to you, but I don't want to write it with pen and ink. 14 For I hope to see you soon, and then we will talk face to face.

15 *Peace be with you.

Your friends here send you their greetings. Please give my personal greetings to each of our friends there.

---

1 Greek *From the elder.*  3 Greek *the brothers;* also in verses 5 and 10.  7a Greek *They went out on behalf of the Name.*  7b Greek *from Gentiles.*  11 Greek *they have not seen God.*  15 Some English translations combine verses 14 and 15 into verse 14.

# JUDE

*May God give
you more and
more mercy,
peace, and love.*

JUDE 1:2

It's wonderful when merciful healthcare professionals care for us. These are the doctors who don't get irritated when we interrupt their sleep with our frightened phone calls. These are the nurses who smile while cleaning up the lunch that didn't stay down. These are the ones who show compassion when we forget appointments, get prescriptions confused, and beg to be squeezed in to see the doctor on a busy day.

People facing a health crisis need a lot of mercy.

But even when we're well, we need a lot of mercy. We need God's mercy.

Jude, the half-brother of Jesus and writer of this short letter, probably understood mercy very well. We know from other Scriptures that Jesus' blood relatives at first did not believe He was the Messiah, and some even thought He was crazy. At some point Jude obviously realized the truth about his sibling and no doubt felt anguish over his former words and actions. It was then that he must have experienced God's mercy.

God's mercy is Him *not* giving us what we deserve. (Grace, on the other hand, is God giving us what we *don't* deserve!) In God's mercy, He doesn't turn a deaf ear to our prayers (who are we that the Creator would listen to us?). In God's mercy, He doesn't punish our forgiven sins (even though He knows we will mess up again). And in God's mercy, He sees the doubts and darkness of our hearts, but loves us just the same.

331

### Greetings from Jude

This letter is from Jude, a slave of Jesus Christ and a brother of James.

I am writing to all who have been called by God the Father, who loves you and keeps you safe in the care of Jesus Christ.*

2 May God give you more and more mercy, peace, and love.

### The Danger of False Teachers

3 Dear friends, I had been eagerly planning to write to you about the salvation we all share. But now I find that I must write about something else, urging you to defend the faith that God has entrusted once for all time to his holy people. 4 I say this because some ungodly people have wormed their way into your churches, saying that God's marvelous grace allows us to live immoral lives. The condemnation of such people was recorded long ago, for they have denied our only Master and Lord, Jesus Christ.

5 So I want to remind you, though you already know these things, that Jesus* first rescued the nation of Israel from Egypt, but later he destroyed those who did not remain faithful. 6 And I remind you of the angels who did not stay within the limits of authority God gave them but left the place where they be-longed. God has kept them securely chained in prisons of darkness, waiting for the great day of judgment. 7 And don't forget Sodom and Gomorrah and their neighboring towns, which were filled with immorality and every kind of sexual perversion. Those cities were destroyed by fire and serve as a warning of the eternal fire of God's judgment.

8 In the same way, these people—who claim authority from their dreams—live immoral lives, defy authority, and scoff at supernatural beings.* 9 But even Michael, one of the mightiest of the angels,* did not dare accuse the devil of blasphemy, but simply said, "The Lord rebuke you!" (This took place when Michael was arguing with the devil about Moses' body.) 10 But these people scoff at things they do not understand. Like unthinking animals, they do whatever their instincts tell them, and so they bring about their own destruction. 11 What sorrow awaits them! For they follow in the footsteps of Cain, who killed his brother. Like Balaam, they deceive people for money. And like Korah, they perish in their rebellion.

12 When these people eat with you in your fellowship meals commemorating the Lord's love, they are like dangerous reefs that can shipwreck you.* They are like shameless shepherds who care only for themselves. They are like clouds blowing over the land without giving any rain. They are like trees in autumn that are doubly dead, for they bear no fruit and have been pulled up by the roots. 13 They are like wild waves of the sea, churning up the foam of their shameful deeds. They are like wandering stars, doomed forever to blackest darkness.

14 Enoch, who lived in the seventh generation after Adam, prophesied about these people. He said, "Listen! The Lord is coming with countless thousands of his holy ones 15 to execute judgment on the people of the

---

Now all glory to God, who is able to keep you from falling away and will bring you with great joy into his glorious presence without a single fault. All glory to him who alone is God, our Savior through Jesus Christ our Lord. All glory, majesty, power, and authority are his before all time, and in the present, and beyond all time!

JUDE 1:24-25

---

1 Or *keeps you for Jesus Christ.*   5 As in the best manuscripts; various other manuscripts read *[the] Lord,* or *God,* or *Christ;* one reads *God Christ.*   8 Greek *at glorious ones,* which are probably evil angels.   9 Greek *Michael, the archangel.*   12 Or *they are contaminants among you;* or *they are stains.*

world. He will convict every person of all the ungodly things they have done and for all the insults that ungodly sinners have spoken against him."*

<sup>16</sup>These people are grumblers and complainers, living only to satisfy their desires. They brag loudly about themselves, and they flatter others to get what they want.

### A Call to Remain Faithful

<sup>17</sup>But you, my dear friends, must remember what the apostles of our Lord Jesus Christ said. <sup>18</sup>They told you that in the last times there would be scoffers whose purpose in life is to satisfy their ungodly desires. <sup>19</sup>These people are the ones who are creating divisions among you. They follow their natural instincts because they do not have God's Spirit in them.

<sup>20</sup>But you, dear friends, must build each other up in your most holy faith, pray in the power of the Holy Spirit,* <sup>21</sup>and await the mercy of our Lord Jesus Christ, who will bring you eternal life. In this way, you will keep yourselves safe in God's love.

<sup>22</sup>And you must show mercy to* those whose faith is wavering. <sup>23</sup>Rescue others by snatching them from the flames of judgment. Show mercy to still others,* but do so with great caution, hating the sins that contaminate their lives.*

### A Prayer of Praise

<sup>24</sup>Now all glory to God, who is able to keep you from falling away and will bring you with great joy into his glorious presence without a single fault. <sup>25</sup>All glory to him who alone is God, our Savior through Jesus Christ our Lord. All glory, majesty, power, and authority are his before all time, and in the present, and beyond all time! Amen.

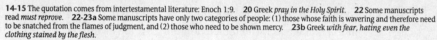

**14-15** The quotation comes from intertestamental literature: Enoch 1:9.   **20** Greek *pray in the Holy Spirit.*   **22** Some manuscripts read *must reprove.*   **22-23a** Some manuscripts have only two categories of people: (1) those whose faith is wavering and therefore need to be snatched from the flames of judgment, and (2) those who need to be shown mercy.   **23b** Greek *with fear, hating even the clothing stained by the flesh.*

# GOING to the party

Imagine someone takes you to a party. You see a few friends there, enjoy a couple of good conversations, a little laughter, and some decent appetizers. The party's all right, but you keep hoping it will get better. Give it another hour, and maybe it will. Suddenly, your friend says, "I need to take you home."

*Now?*

You're disappointed—nobody wants to leave a party early—but you leave, and your friend drops you off at your house. As you approach the door, **you're feeling all alone and sorry for yourself.** As you open the door and reach for the light switch, you sense someone's there. Your heart's in your throat. You flip on the light.

"Surprise!" Your house is full of smiling people, familiar faces.

It's a party—for *you*. You smell your favorites—barbecued ribs and pecan pie right out of the oven. The tables are full. It's a feast. You recognize the guests, people you haven't seen for a long time. Then, one by one, the people you most enjoyed at the other party show up at your house, grinning. This turns out to be the *real* party. You realize that if you'd stayed longer at the other party, as you'd wanted, you wouldn't be *at* the real party—you'd be *away* from it.

Christians faced with terminal illness or imminent death often feel they're leaving the party before it's over. They have to go home early. They're disappointed, thinking of all they'll miss when they leave. But the truth is, the real party is underway at home—precisely where they're going. They're not the ones missing the party; those of us left behind are. (Fortunately, if we know Jesus, we'll get there eventually.)

One by one, occasionally a few of us at a time, we'll disappear from this world. Those we leave behind will grieve that their loved ones have left home. In reality, however, their believing loved ones aren't *leaving* home, they're *going* home. They'll be home before us. We'll be arriving at the party a little later.[1]

[1] Randy Alcorn, *Heaven* (Carol Stream, IL: Tyndale House Publishers, 2004), 441–442.

# REVELATION

*He will wipe every tear from their eyes, and there will be no more death or sorrow or crying or pain. All these things are gone forever.*

REVELATION 21:4

Knowing the end of a book or movie ahead of time can ruin the story for us. But knowing how this earth ends and how a new earth and heaven begin only enhances our life story.

Don't be afraid of reading Revelation because it's about the end times. And don't get hung up trying to figure out all the dates and symbolism. The book is a revelation—or unveiling of the future—from Jesus to His disciple John when the latter was an old man exiled for his faith to the isle of Patmos. It basically tells us three things: that Jesus will save the church (all true believers), judge the nations, and reign over His Kingdom. Look for what it teaches about the Trinity (God the Father, God the Son, and God the Holy Spirit) and what it explains about our *real* home. When things are going well here on earth, we get lulled into thinking this is our happy home and we want to keep on living here. But when serious illness comes along, it's a good reminder that we're only passing through.

That longing inside of you for things to be better here—for there to be no sadness, no crying, no sickness, no death—that's a longing for heaven. In the Old Testament, Ecclesiastes 3:11 explains that God has "planted eternity in the human heart." Whether we long for pure happiness or a cure for a disease, it's a longing that earth can never satisfy, because it's a longing for our real home—heaven.

## Prologue

**1** This is a revelation from* Jesus Christ, which God gave him to show his servants the events that must soon* take place. He sent an angel to present this revelation to his servant John, ²who faithfully reported everything he saw. This is his report of the word of God and the testimony of Jesus Christ.

³God blesses the one who reads the words of this prophecy to the church, and he blesses all who listen to its message and obey what it says, for the time is near.

## John's Greeting to the Seven Churches

⁴This letter is from John to the seven churches in the province of Asia.*

Grace and peace to you from the one who is, who always was, and who is still to come; from the sevenfold Spirit* before his throne; ⁵and from Jesus Christ. He is the faithful witness to these things, the first to rise from the dead, and the ruler of all the kings of the world.

All glory to him who loves us and has freed us from our sins by shedding his blood for us. ⁶He has made us a Kingdom of priests for God his Father. All glory and power to him forever and ever! Amen.

⁷Look! He comes with the clouds
　　of heaven.
And everyone will see him—
　　even those who pierced him.
And all the nations of the world
　　will mourn for him.
Yes! Amen!

⁸"I am the Alpha and the Omega—the beginning and the end,"* says the Lord God. "I am the one who is, who always was, and who is still to come—the Almighty One."

## Vision of the Son of Man

⁹I, John, am your brother and your partner in suffering and in God's Kingdom and in the patient endurance to which Jesus calls us. I was exiled to the island of Patmos for preaching the word of God and for my testimony about Jesus. ¹⁰It was the Lord's Day, and I was worshiping in the Spirit.* Suddenly, I heard behind me a loud voice like a trumpet blast. ¹¹It said, " Write in a book* everything you see, and send it to the seven churches in the cities of Ephesus, Smyrna, Pergamum, Thyatira, Sardis, Philadelphia, and Laodicea."

¹²When I turned to see who was speaking to me, I saw seven gold lampstands. ¹³And standing in the middle of the lampstands was someone like the Son of Man.* He was wearing a long robe with a gold sash across his chest. ¹⁴His head and his hair were white like wool, as white as snow. And his eyes were like flames of fire. ¹⁵His feet were like polished bronze refined in a furnace, and his voice thundered like mighty ocean waves. ¹⁶He held seven stars in his right hand, and a sharp two-edged sword came from his mouth. And his face was like the sun in all its brilliance.

¹⁷When I saw him, I fell at his feet as if I were dead. But he laid his right hand on me and said, "Don't be afraid! I am the First and the Last. ¹⁸I am the living one. I died, but look—I am alive forever and ever! And I hold the keys of death and the grave.*

¹⁹"Write down what you have seen—both the things that are now happening and the things that will happen.* ²⁰This is the meaning of the mystery of the seven stars you saw in my right hand and the seven gold lampstands: The seven stars are the angels* of the seven churches, and the seven lampstands are the seven churches.

## The Message to the Church in Ephesus

**2** "Write this letter to the angel* of the church in Ephesus. This is the message from the one who holds the seven stars in

---

**1:1a** Or *of.*　**1:1b** Or *suddenly,* or *quickly.*　**1:4a** *Asia* was a Roman province in what is now western Turkey.　**1:4b** Greek *the seven spirits.*　**1:8** Greek *I am the Alpha and the Omega,* referring to the first and last letters of the Greek alphabet.　**1:10** Or *in spirit.*　**1:11** Or *on a scroll.*　**1:13** Or *like a son of man.* See Dan 7:13. "Son of Man" is a title Jesus used for himself.　**1:18** Greek *and Hades.*　**1:19** Or *what you have seen and what they mean—the things that have already begun to happen.*　**1:20** Or *the messengers.*　**2:1** Or *the messenger;* also in 2:8, 12, 18.

his right hand, the one who walks among the seven gold lampstands:

2"I know all the things you do. I have seen your hard work and your patient endurance. I know you don't tolerate evil people. You have examined the claims of those who say they are apostles but are not. You have discovered they are liars. 3 You have patiently suffered for me without quitting.

4"But I have this complaint against you. You don't love me or each other as you did at first!* 5 Look how far you have fallen! Turn back to me and do the works you did at first. If you don't repent, I will come and remove your lampstand from its place among the churches. 6 But this is in your favor: You hate the evil deeds of the Nicolaitans, just as I do.

7"Anyone with ears to hear must listen to the Spirit and understand what he is saying to the churches. To everyone who is victorious I will give fruit from the tree of life in the paradise of God.

## The Message to the Church in Smyrna

8 " Write this letter to the angel of the church in Smyrna. This is the message from the one who is the First and the Last, who was dead but is now alive:

9"I know about your suffering and your poverty—but you are rich! I know the blasphemy of those opposing you. They say they are Jews, but they are not, because their synagogue belongs to Satan. 10 Don't be afraid of what you are about to suffer. The devil will throw some of you into prison to test you. You will suffer for ten days. But if you remain faithful even when facing death, I will give you the crown of life.

11"Anyone with ears to hear must listen to the Spirit and understand what he is saying to the churches. Whoever is victorious will not be harmed by the second death.

## The Message to the Church in Pergamum

12"Write this letter to the angel of the church in Pergamum. This is the message

from the one with the sharp two-edged sword:

13"I know that you live in the city where Satan has his throne, yet you have remained loyal to me. You refused to deny me even when Antipas, my faithful witness, was martyred among you there in Satan's city.

14"But I have a few complaints against you. You tolerate some among you whose teaching is like that of Balaam, who showed Balak how to trip up the people of Israel. He taught them to sin by eating food offered to idols and by committing sexual sin. 15 In a similar way, you have some Nicolaitans among you who follow the same teaching. 16 Repent of your sin, or I will come to you suddenly and fight against them with the sword of my mouth.

17"Anyone with ears to hear must listen to the Spirit and understand what he is saying to the churches. To everyone who is victorious I will give some of the manna that has been hidden away in heaven. And I will give to each one a white stone, and on the stone will be engraved a new name that no one understands except the one who receives it.

## The Message to the Church in Thyatira

18"Write this letter to the angel of the church in Thyatira. This is the message from the Son of God, whose eyes are like flames of fire, whose feet are like polished bronze:

19"I know all the things you do. I have seen your love, your faith, your service, and your patient endurance. And I can see your constant improvement in all these things.

20"But I have this complaint against you. You are permitting that woman— that Jezebel who calls herself a prophet— to lead my servants astray. She teaches them to commit sexual sin and to eat food offered to idols. 21 I gave her time to repent, but she does not want to turn away from her immorality.

2:4 Greek You have lost your first love.

22"Therefore, I will throw her on a bed of suffering,* and those who commit adultery with her will suffer greatly unless they repent and turn away from her evil deeds. 23 I will strike her children dead. Then all the churches will know that I am the one who searches out the thoughts and intentions of every person. And I will give to each of you whatever you deserve. 24"But I also have a message for the rest of you in Thyatira who have not followed this false teaching ('deeper truths,' as they call them—depths of Satan, actually). I will ask nothing more of you 25 except that you hold tightly to what you have until I come. 26 To all who are victorious, who obey me to the very end,

To them I will give authority over all the nations.
27 They will rule the nations with an iron rod
and smash them like clay pots.*

28 They will have the same authority I received from my Father, and I will also give them the morning star! 29"Anyone with ears to hear must listen to the Spirit and understand what he is saying to the churches.

## The Message to the Church in Sardis

**3** " Write this letter to the angel* of the church in Sardis. This is the message from the one who has the sevenfold Spirit* of God and the seven stars:

"I know all the things you do, and that you have a reputation for being alive— but you are dead. 2 Wake up! Strengthen what little remains, for even what is left is almost dead. I find that your actions do not meet the requirements of my God. 3 Go back to what you heard and believed at first; hold to it firmly. Repent and turn to me again.
If you don't wake up, I will come to you suddenly, as unexpected as a thief.
4" Yet there are some in the church in Sardis who have not soiled their clothes with evil. They will walk with me in white,

for they are worthy. 5 All who are victorious will be clothed in white. I will never erase their names from the Book of Life, but I will announce before my Father and his angels that they are mine.
6"Anyone with ears to hear must listen to the Spirit and understand what he is saying to the churches.

## The Message to the Church in Philadelphia

7"Write this letter to the angel of the church in Philadelphia.

This is the message from the one who is holy and true,
the one who has the key of David.
What he opens, no one can close;
and what he closes, no one can open:*

8"I know all the things you do, and I have opened a door for you that no one can close. You have little strength, yet you obeyed my word and did not deny me. 9 Look, I will force those who belong to Satan's synagogue—those liars who say they are Jews but are not—to come and bow down at your feet. They will acknowledge that you are the ones I love. 10"Because you have obeyed my command to persevere, I will protect you from the great time of testing that will come upon the whole world to test those who belong to this world. 11 I am coming soon.* Hold on to what you have, so that no one will take away your crown. 12 All who are victorious will become pillars in the Temple of my God, and they will never have to leave it. And I will write on them the name of my God, and they will be citizens in the city of my God—the new Jerusalem that comes down from heaven from my God. And I will also write on them my new name. 13"Anyone with ears to hear must listen to the Spirit and understand what he is saying to the churches.

## The Message to the Church in Laodicea

14"Write this letter to the angel of the church in Laodicea. This is the message

2:22 Greek *a bed.*  2:26-27 Ps 2:8-9 (Greek Version).  3:1a Or *the messenger;* also in 3:7, 14.  3:1b Greek *the seven spirits.*  3:7 Isa 22:22.  3:11 Or *suddenly,* or *quickly.*

from the one who is the Amen—the faithful and true witness, the beginning* of God's new creation:

15"I know all the things you do, that you are neither hot nor cold. I wish that you were one or the other! 16But since you are like lukewarm water, neither hot nor cold, I will spit you out of my mouth! 17You say, 'I am rich. I have everything I want. I don't need a thing!' And you don't realize that you are wretched and miserable and poor and blind and naked. 18So I advise you to buy gold from me—gold that has been purified by fire. Then you will be rich. Also buy white garments from me so you will not be shamed by your nakedness, and ointment for your eyes so you will be able to see. 19I correct and discipline everyone I love. So be diligent and turn from your indifference.

20"Look! I stand at the door and knock. If you hear my voice and open the door, I will come in, and we will share a meal together as friends. 21Those who are victorious will sit with me on my throne, just as I was victorious and sat with my Father on his throne.

22"Anyone with ears to hear must listen to the Spirit and understand what he is saying to the churches."

## Worship in Heaven

4 Then as I looked, I saw a door standing open in heaven, and the same voice I had heard before spoke to me like a trumpet blast. The voice said, "Come up here, and I will show you what must happen after this." 2And instantly I was in the Spirit,* and I saw a throne in heaven and someone sitting on it. 3The one sitting on the throne was as brilliant as gemstones—like jasper and carnelian. And the glow of an emerald circled his throne like a rainbow. 4Twenty-four thrones surrounded him, and twenty-four elders sat on them. They were all clothed in white and had gold crowns on their heads. 5From the throne came flashes of lightning and the rumble of thunder. And in front of the throne were seven torches with burning flames. This is the

## SOMEONE'S at the door
READ REVELATION 3:20

If you heard a knocking at your door, chances are you'd first check that you knew who it was, and then you'd open the door and let the person in. But what if someone was knocking on the door of your heart? Not pounding, just politely knocking. Would you even hear? Would you open the door?

For many of you reading this today, Jesus is knocking at the door of your heart. Some of you only started hearing the knocking after illness hit. Others opened the door to Him when you were young, but then your home got busy and crowded and He got pushed out. Will you let Jesus in—or back in—today? The only doorknob is on your side.

sevenfold Spirit* of God. 6In front of the throne was a shiny sea of glass, sparkling like crystal.

In the center and around the throne were four living beings, each covered with eyes, front and back. 7The first of these living beings was like a lion; the second was like an ox; the third had a human face; and the fourth was like an eagle in flight. 8Each of these living beings had six wings, and their wings were covered all over with eyes, inside and out. Day after day and night after night they keep on saying,

"Holy, holy, holy is the Lord God, the Almighty—
    the one who always was, who is, and
    who is still to come."

9Whenever the living beings give glory and honor and thanks to the one sitting on the throne (the one who lives forever and ever), 10the twenty-four elders fall down and worship the one sitting on the throne (the one who lives forever and ever). And they lay their crowns before the throne and say,

11"You are worthy, O Lord our God,
    to receive glory and honor and
    power.
For you created all things,
    and they exist because you created
    what you pleased."

3:14 Or the ruler, or the source.   4:2 Or in spirit.   4:5 Greek They are the seven spirits.

### The Lamb Opens the Scroll

**5** Then I saw a scroll* in the right hand of the one who was sitting on the throne. There was writing on the inside and the outside of the scroll, and it was sealed with seven seals. ²And I saw a strong angel, who shouted with a loud voice: "Who is worthy to break the seals on this scroll and open it?" ³But no one in heaven or on earth or under the earth was able to open the scroll and read it.

⁴Then I began to weep bitterly because no one was found worthy to open the scroll and read it. ⁵But one of the twenty-four elders said to me, "Stop weeping! Look, the Lion of the tribe of Judah, the heir to David's throne,* has won the victory. He is worthy to open the scroll and its seven seals."

⁶Then I saw a Lamb that looked as if it had been slaughtered, but it was now standing between the throne and the four living beings and among the twenty-four elders. He had seven horns and seven eyes, which represent the sevenfold Spirit* of God that is sent out into every part of the earth. ⁷He stepped forward and took the scroll from the right hand of the one sitting on the throne. ⁸And when he took the scroll, the four living beings and the twenty-four elders fell down before the Lamb. Each one had a harp, and they held gold bowls filled with incense, which are the prayers of God's people. ⁹And they sang a new song with these words:

"You are worthy to take the scroll
    and break its seals and open it.
For you were slaughtered, and your blood
        has ransomed people for God
    from every tribe and language and
        people and nation.
¹⁰ And you have caused them to become
    a Kingdom of priests for our God.
    And they will reign* on the earth."

¹¹Then I looked again, and I heard the voices of thousands and millions of angels around the throne and of the living beings and the elders. ¹²And they sang in a mighty chorus:

"Worthy is the Lamb who was
    slaughtered—
    to receive power and riches
and wisdom and strength
    and honor and glory and blessing."

¹³And then I heard every creature in heaven and on earth and under the earth and in the sea. They sang:

"Blessing and honor and glory and power
    belong to the one sitting on the throne
    and to the Lamb forever and ever."

¹⁴And the four living beings said, "Amen!" And the twenty-four elders fell down and worshiped the Lamb.

### The Lamb Breaks the First Six Seals

**6** As I watched, the Lamb broke the first of the seven seals on the scroll.* Then I heard one of the four living beings say with a voice like thunder, "Come!" ²I looked up and saw a white horse standing there. Its rider carried a bow, and a crown was placed on his head. He rode out to win many battles and gain the victory.

³When the Lamb broke the second seal, I heard the second living being say, "Come!" ⁴Then another horse appeared, a red one. Its rider was given a mighty sword and the authority to take peace from the earth. And there was war and slaughter everywhere.

⁵When the Lamb broke the third seal, I heard the third living being say, "Come!" I looked up and saw a black horse, and its rider was holding a pair of scales in his hand. ⁶And I heard a voice from among the four living beings say, "A loaf of wheat bread or three loaves of barley will cost a day's pay.* And don't waste* the olive oil and wine."

⁷When the Lamb broke the fourth seal, I heard the fourth living being say, "Come!" ⁸I looked up and saw a horse whose color was pale green. Its rider was named Death, and his companion was the Grave.* These two were given authority over one-fourth of the earth, to kill with the sword and famine and disease* and wild animals.

⁹When the Lamb broke the fifth seal,

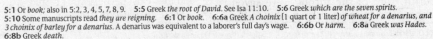

**5:1** Or *book;* also in 5:2, 3, 4, 5, 7, 8, 9. **5:5** Greek *the root of David.* See Isa 11:10. **5:6** Greek *which are the seven spirits.* **5:10** Some manuscripts read *they are reigning.* **6:1** Or *book.* **6:6a** Greek *A choinix* [1 quart or 1 liter] *of wheat for a denarius, and 3 choinix of barley for a denarius.* A denarius was equivalent to a laborer's full day's wage. **6:6b** Or *harm.* **6:8a** Greek *was Hades.* **6:8b** Greek *death.*

I saw under the altar the souls of all who had been martyred for the word of God and for being faithful in their testimony. 10 They shouted to the Lord and said, "O Sovereign Lord, holy and true, how long before you judge the people who belong to this world and avenge our blood for what they have done to us?" 11 Then a white robe was given to each of them. And they were told to rest a little longer until the full number of their brothers and sisters*—their fellow servants of Jesus who were to be martyred—had joined them.

12 I watched as the Lamb broke the sixth seal, and there was a great earthquake. The sun became as dark as black cloth, and the moon became as red as blood. 13 Then the stars of the sky fell to the earth like green figs falling from a tree shaken by a strong wind. 14 The sky was rolled up like a scroll, and all of the mountains and islands were moved from their places.

15 Then everyone—the kings of the earth, the rulers, the generals, the wealthy, the powerful, and every slave and free person—all hid themselves in the caves and among the rocks of the mountains. 16 And they cried to the mountains and the rocks, "Fall on us and hide us from the face of the one who sits on the throne and from the wrath of the Lamb. 17 For the great day of their wrath has come, and who is able to survive?"

## God's People Will Be Preserved

**7** Then I saw four angels standing at the four corners of the earth, holding back the four winds so they did not blow on the earth or the sea, or even on any tree. 2 And I saw another angel coming up from the east, carrying the seal of the living God. And he shouted to those four angels, who had been given power to harm land and sea, 3 "Wait! Don't harm the land or the sea or the trees until we have placed the seal of God on the foreheads of his servants."

4 And I heard how many were marked with the seal of God—144,000 were sealed from all the tribes of Israel:

| | |
|---|---|
| 5 from Judah | 12,000 |
| from Reuben | 12,000 |

6:11 Greek *their brothers*.

| | |
|---|---|
| from Gad | 12,000 |
| 6 from Asher | 12,000 |
| from Naphtali | 12,000 |
| from Manasseh | 12,000 |
| 7 from Simeon | 12,000 |
| from Levi | 12,000 |
| from Issachar | 12,000 |
| 8 from Zebulun | 12,000 |
| from Joseph | 12,000 |
| from Benjamin | 12,000 |

## Praise from the Great Crowd

9 After this I saw a vast crowd, too great to count, from every nation and tribe and people and language, standing in front of the throne and before the Lamb. They were clothed in white robes and held palm branches in their hands. 10 And they were shouting with a mighty shout,

"Salvation comes from our God who sits
    on the throne
    and from the Lamb!"

11 And all the angels were standing around the throne and around the elders and the four living beings. And they fell before the throne with their faces to the ground and worshiped God. 12 They sang,

"Amen! Blessing and glory and wisdom
    and thanksgiving and honor
and power and strength belong to our
    God
    forever and ever! Amen."

## SWEET smell of prayers

READ REVELATION 5:8 AND 8:3-4

If you lived during the "flower-child" sixties, you probably remember the distinctive smell of incense burning. Maybe it brings back good memories, or maybe it conjures up things you'd rather forget.

You're still burning incense, you know. Every time you lift your voice in prayer to God, that prayer becomes sweet incense to your heavenly Father as John describes in these verses.

The next time you're not sure your prayers are making it through the ceiling above you, picture each prayer traveling to the very throne of God and becoming a sweet fragrance to Him. He loves to hear you pray. Go ahead and fill up another bowl.

*incense*

13Then one of the twenty-four elders asked me, "Who are these who are clothed in white? Where did they come from?"

14And I said to him, "Sir, you are the one who knows."

Then he said to me, "These are the ones who died in* the great tribulation.* They have washed their robes in the blood of the Lamb and made them white.

15 "That is why they stand in front of God's throne
and serve him day and night in his Temple.
And he who sits on the throne
will give them shelter.
16They will never again be hungry or thirsty;
they will never be scorched by the heat of the sun.
17 For the Lamb on the throne*
will be their Shepherd.
He will lead them to springs of life-giving water.
And God will wipe every tear from their eyes."

## The Lamb Breaks the Seventh Seal

**8** When the Lamb broke the seventh seal on the scroll,* there was silence throughout heaven for about half an hour. 2I saw the seven angels who stand before God, and they were given seven trumpets.

3Then another angel with a gold incense burner came and stood at the altar. And a great amount of incense was given to him to mix with the prayers of God's people as an offering on the gold altar before the throne. 4The smoke of the incense, mixed with the prayers of God's holy people, ascended up to God from the altar where the angel had poured them out. 5Then the angel filled the incense burner with fire from the altar and threw it down upon the earth; and thunder crashed, lightning flashed, and there was a terrible earthquake.

### The First Four Trumpets

6Then the seven angels with the seven trumpets prepared to blow their mighty blasts.

7The first angel blew his trumpet, and hail and fire mixed with blood were thrown down on the earth. One-third of the earth was set on fire, one-third of the trees were burned, and all the green grass was burned.

8Then the second angel blew his trumpet, and a great mountain of fire was thrown into the sea. One-third of the water in the sea became blood, 9one-third of all things living in the sea died, and one-third of all the ships on the sea were destroyed.

10Then the third angel blew his trumpet, and a great star fell from the sky, burning like a torch. It fell on one-third of the rivers and on the springs of water. 11The name of the star was Bitterness.* It made one-third of the water bitter, and many people died from drinking the bitter water.

12Then the fourth angel blew his trumpet, and one-third of the sun was struck, and one-third of the moon, and one-third of the stars, and they became dark. And one-third of the day was dark, and also one-third of the night.

13Then I looked, and I heard a single eagle crying loudly as it flew through the air, "Terror, terror, terror to all who belong to this world because of what will happen when the last three angels blow their trumpets."

### The Fifth Trumpet Brings the First Terror

**9** Then the fifth angel blew his trumpet, and I saw a star that had fallen to earth from the sky, and he was given the key to the shaft of the bottomless pit.* 2When he opened it, smoke poured out as though from a huge furnace, and the sunlight and air turned dark from the smoke.

3Then locusts came from the smoke and descended on the earth, and they were given power to sting like scorpions. 4They were told not to harm the grass or plants or trees, but only the people who did not have the seal of God on their foreheads. 5They were told not to kill them but to torture them for five months with pain like the pain of a scorpion sting. 6In those days people will seek death but will not find it.

7:14a Greek *who came out of.* 7:14b Or *the great suffering.* 7:17 Greek *on the center of the throne.* 8:1 Or *book.* 8:11 Greek *Wormwood.* 9:1 Or *the abyss,* or *the underworld;* also in 9:11.

They will long to die, but death will flee from them!

7 The locusts looked like horses prepared for battle. They had what looked like gold crowns on their heads, and their faces looked like human faces. 8 They had hair like women's hair and teeth like the teeth of a lion. 9 They wore armor made of iron, and their wings roared like an army of chariots rushing into battle. 10 They had tails that stung like scorpions, and for five months they had the power to torment people. 11 Their king is the angel from the bottomless pit; his name in Hebrew is *Abaddon,* and in Greek, *Apollyon*—the Destroyer.

12 The first terror is past, but look, two more terrors are coming!

## The Sixth Trumpet Brings the Second Terror

13 Then the sixth angel blew his trumpet, and I heard a voice speaking from the four horns of the gold altar that stands in the presence of God. 14 And the voice said to the sixth angel who held the trumpet, "Release the four angels who are bound at the great Euphrates River." 15 Then the four angels who had been prepared for this hour and day and month and year were turned loose to kill one-third of all the people on earth. 16 I heard the size of their army, which was 200 million mounted troops.

17 And in my vision, I saw the horses and the riders sitting on them. The riders wore armor that was fiery red and dark blue and yellow. The horses had heads like lions, and fire and smoke and burning sulfur billowed from their mouths. 18 One-third of all the people on earth were killed by these three plagues—by the fire and smoke and burning sulfur that came from the mouths of the horses. 19 Their power was in their mouths and in their tails. For their tails had heads like snakes, with the power to injure people.

20 But the people who did not die in these plagues still refused to repent of their evil deeds and turn to God. They continued to worship demons and idols made of gold, silver, bronze, stone, and wood—idols that can neither see nor hear nor walk! 21 And they did not repent of their murders or their witchcraft or their sexual immorality or their thefts.

## The Angel and the Small Scroll

**10** Then I saw another mighty angel coming down from heaven, surrounded by a cloud, with a rainbow over his head. His face shone like the sun, and his feet were like pillars of fire. 2 And in his hand was a small scroll* that had been opened. He stood with his right foot on the sea and his left foot on the land. 3 And he gave a great shout like the roar of a lion. And when he shouted, the seven thunders answered.

4 When the seven thunders spoke, I was about to write. But I heard a voice from heaven saying, "Keep secret* what the seven thunders said, and do not write it down."

5 Then the angel I saw standing on the sea and on the land raised his right hand toward heaven. 6 He swore an oath in the name of the one who lives forever and ever, who created the heavens and everything in them, the earth and everything in it, and the sea and everything in it. He said, "There will be no more delay. 7 When the seventh angel blows his trumpet, God's mysterious plan will be fulfilled. It will happen just as he announced it to his servants the prophets."

8 Then the voice from heaven spoke to me again: "Go and take the open scroll from the hand of the angel who is standing on the sea and on the land."

9 So I went to the angel and told him to give me the small scroll. "Yes, take it and eat it," he said. "It will be sweet as honey in your mouth, but it will turn sour in your stomach!" 10 So I took the small scroll from the hand of the angel, and I ate it! It was sweet in my mouth, but when I swallowed it, it turned sour in my stomach.

11 Then I was told, "You must prophesy again about many peoples, nations, languages, and kings."

**10:2** Or *book;* also in 10:8, 9, 10. **10:4** Greek *Seal up.*

# NO more tears

READ REVELATION 7:15-17

Tears are an amazingly complex combination of proteins, enzymes, lipids, metabolites, and electrolytes (and you thought they were just salty water!). Every tear has three layers, and scientists even can distinguish between "normal" lubricating tears and emotional tears. Some researchers theorize that emotional tears carry hormones from our brains, flush toxins from our bloodstreams, and return our bodies to a reduced-stress state. Isn't it amazing how much intricacy the Creator put into tiny tears!

Whether your eyes are brimming with tears or whether you manage to choke them back, the day is coming when you will do neither. Instead, God will wipe every tear from our eyes.

## The Two Witnesses

**11** Then I was given a measuring stick, and I was told, "Go and measure the Temple of God and the altar, and count the number of worshipers. 2But do not measure the outer courtyard, for it has been turned over to the nations. They will trample the holy city for 42 months. 3And I will give power to my two witnesses, and they will be clothed in burlap and will prophesy during those 1,260 days."

4These two prophets are the two olive trees and the two lampstands that stand before the Lord of all the earth. 5If anyone tries to harm them, fire flashes from their mouths and consumes their enemies. This is how anyone who tries to harm them must die. 6They have power to shut the sky so that no rain will fall for as long as they prophesy. And they have the power to turn the rivers and oceans into blood, and to strike the earth with every kind of plague as often as they wish.

7When they complete their testimony, the beast that comes up out of the bottomless pit* will declare war against them, and he will conquer them and kill them. 8And their bodies will lie in the main street of Jerusalem,* the city that is figuratively called "Sodom" and "Egypt," the city where their Lord was crucified. 9And for three and a half days, all peoples, tribes, languages, and na-

tions will stare at their bodies. No one will be allowed to bury them. 10All the people who belong to this world will gloat over them and give presents to each other to celebrate the death of the two prophets who had tormented them.

11But after three and a half days, God breathed life into them, and they stood up! Terror struck all who were staring at them. 12Then a loud voice from heaven called to the two prophets, "Come up here!" And they rose to heaven in a cloud as their enemies watched.

13At the same time there was a terrible earthquake that destroyed a tenth of the city. Seven thousand people died in that earthquake, and everyone else was terrified and gave glory to the God of heaven.

14The second terror is past, but look, the third terror is coming quickly.

## The Seventh Trumpet Brings the Third Terror

15Then the seventh angel blew his trumpet, and there were loud voices shouting in heaven:

> "The world has now become the
>     Kingdom of our Lord and of his
>     Christ,*
>     and he will reign forever and ever."

16The twenty-four elders sitting on their thrones before God fell with their faces to the ground and worshiped him. 17And they said,

> "We give thanks to you, Lord God, the
>     Almighty,
> the one who is and who always was,
> for now you have assumed your great
>     power
> and have begun to reign.
18 The nations were filled with wrath,
> but now the time of your wrath has
>     come.
> It is time to judge the dead
> and reward your servants the
>     prophets,
>     as well as your holy people,
> and all who fear your name,
>     from the least to the greatest.

**11:7** Or *the abyss,* or *the underworld.*   **11:8** Greek *the great city.*   **11:15** Or *his Messiah.*

It is time to destroy
　all who have caused destruction on the
　　earth."

¹⁹Then, in heaven, the Temple of God was opened and the Ark of his covenant could be seen inside the Temple. Lightning flashed, thunder crashed and roared, and there was an earthquake and a terrible hailstorm.

## The Woman and the Dragon (Satan)

**12** Then I witnessed in heaven an event of great significance. I saw a woman clothed with the sun, with the moon beneath her feet, and a crown of twelve stars on her head. ²She was pregnant, and she cried out because of her labor pains and the agony of giving birth.

³Then I witnessed in heaven another significant event. I saw a large red dragon with seven heads and ten horns, with seven crowns on his heads. ⁴His tail swept away one-third of the stars in the sky, and he threw them to the earth. He stood in front of the woman as she was about to give birth, ready to devour her baby as soon as it was born.

⁵She gave birth to a son who was to rule all nations with an iron rod. And her child was snatched away from the dragon and was caught up to God and to his throne. ⁶And the woman fled into the wilderness, where God had prepared a place to care for her for 1,260 days.

⁷Then there was war in heaven. Michael and his angels fought against the dragon and his angels. ⁸And the dragon lost the battle, and he and his angels were forced out of heaven. ⁹This great dragon—the ancient serpent called the devil, or Satan, the one deceiving the whole world—was thrown down to the earth with all his angels.

¹⁰Then I heard a loud voice shouting across the heavens,

"It has come at last—
　salvation and power
and the Kingdom of our God,
　and the authority of his Christ.*
For the accuser of our brothers and
　　sisters*
has been thrown down to earth—

the one who accuses them
　before our God day and night.
¹¹ And they have defeated him by the blood
　of the Lamb
　and by their testimony.
And they did not love their lives so much
　that they were afraid to die.
¹² Therefore, rejoice, O heavens!
　And you who live in the heavens,
　　rejoice!
But terror will come on the earth and
　the sea,
　for the devil has come down to you
　　in great anger,
　knowing that he has little time."

¹³When the dragon realized that he had been thrown down to the earth, he pursued the woman who had given birth to the male child. ¹⁴But she was given two wings like those of a great eagle so she could fly to the place prepared for her in the wilderness. There she would be cared for and protected from the dragon* for a time, times, and half a time.

¹⁵Then the dragon tried to drown the woman with a flood of water that flowed from his mouth. ¹⁶But the earth helped her by opening its mouth and swallowing the river that gushed out from the mouth of the dragon. ¹⁷And the dragon was angry at the woman and declared war against the rest of her children—all who keep God's commandments and maintain their testimony for Jesus.

¹⁸Then the dragon took his stand* on the shore beside the sea.

## The Beast out of the Sea

**13** Then I saw a beast rising up out of the sea. It had seven heads and ten horns, with ten crowns on its horns. And written on each head were names that blasphemed God. ²This beast looked like a leopard, but it had the feet of a bear and the mouth of a lion! And the dragon gave the beast his own power and throne and great authority.

³I saw that one of the heads of the beast seemed wounded beyond recovery—but the

**12:10a** Or *his Messiah.*　**12:10b** Greek *brothers.*　**12:14** Greek *the serpent;* also in 12:15. See 12:9.　**12:18** Greek *Then he took his stand;* some manuscripts read *Then I took my stand.* Some translations put this entire sentence into 13:1.

fatal wound was healed! The whole world marveled at this miracle and gave allegiance to the beast. 4 They worshiped the dragon for giving the beast such power, and they also worshiped the beast. "Who is as great as the beast?" they exclaimed. "Who is able to fight against him?"

5 Then the beast was allowed to speak great blasphemies against God. And he was given authority to do whatever he wanted for forty-two months. 6 And he spoke terrible words of blasphemy against God, slandering his name and his dwelling—that is, those who dwell in heaven.* 7 And the beast was allowed to wage war against God's holy people and to conquer them. And he was given authority to rule over every tribe and people and language and nation. 8 And all the people who belong to this world worshiped the beast. They are the ones whose names were not written in the Book of Life before the world was made—the Book that belongs to the Lamb who was slaughtered.*

9 Anyone with ears to hear
should listen and understand.
10 Anyone who is destined for prison
will be taken to prison.
Anyone destined to die by the sword
will die by the sword.

This means that God's holy people must endure persecution patiently and remain faithful.

### The Beast out of the Earth

11 Then I saw another beast come up out of the earth. He had two horns like those of a lamb, but he spoke with the voice of a dragon. 12 He exercised all the authority of the first beast. And he required all the earth and its people to worship the first beast, whose fatal wound had been healed. 13 He did astounding miracles, even making fire flash down to earth from the sky while everyone was watching. 14 And with all the miracles he was allowed to perform on behalf of the first beast, he deceived all the people who belong to this world. He ordered the people to make a great statue of the first beast, who was fatally wounded and then came back to life. 15 He was then permitted to give life to this statue so that it could speak. Then the statue of the beast commanded that anyone refusing to worship it must die.

16 He required everyone—small and great, rich and poor, free and slave—to be given a mark on the right hand or on the forehead. 17 And no one could buy or sell anything without that mark, which was either the name of the beast or the number representing his name. 18 Wisdom is needed here. Let the one with understanding solve the meaning of the number of the beast, for it is the number of a man.* His number is 666.*

### The Lamb and the 144,000

**14** Then I saw the Lamb standing on Mount Zion, and with him were 144,000 who had his name and his Father's name written on their foreheads. 2 And I heard a sound from heaven like the roar of mighty ocean waves or the rolling of loud thunder. It was like the sound of many harpists playing together.

3 This great choir sang a wonderful new song in front of the throne of God and before the four living beings and the twenty-four elders. No one could learn this song except the 144,000 who had been redeemed from the earth. 4 They have kept themselves as pure as virgins,* following the Lamb wherever he goes. They have been purchased from among the people on the earth as a special offering* to God and to the Lamb. 5 They have told no lies; they are without blame.

### The Three Angels

6 And I saw another angel flying through the sky, carrying the eternal Good News to proclaim to the people who belong to this world—to every nation, tribe, language, and people. 7 "Fear God," he shouted. "Give glory to him. For the time has come when he will sit as judge. Worship him who made the heavens, the earth, the sea, and all the springs of water."

8 Then another angel followed him

---

**13:6** Some manuscripts read *and his dwelling and all who dwell in heaven.* **13:8** Or *not written in the Book of Life that belongs to the Lamb who was slaughtered before the world was made.* **13:18a** Or *of humanity.* **13:18b** Some manuscripts read *616.* **14:4a** Greek *They are virgins who have not defiled themselves with women.* **14:4b** Greek *as firstfruits.*

through the sky, shouting, "Babylon is fallen—that great city is fallen—because she made all the nations of the world drink the wine of her passionate immorality."

⁹Then a third angel followed them, shouting, "Anyone who worships the beast and his statue or who accepts his mark on the forehead or on the hand ¹⁰must drink the wine of God's anger. It has been poured full strength into God's cup of wrath. And they will be tormented with fire and burning sulfur in the presence of the holy angels and the Lamb. ¹¹The smoke of their torment will rise forever and ever, and they will have no relief day or night, for they have worshiped the beast and his statue and have accepted the mark of his name."

¹²This means that God's holy people must endure persecution patiently, obeying his commands and maintaining their faith in Jesus.

¹³And I heard a voice from heaven saying, "Write this down: Blessed are those who die in the Lord from now on. Yes, says the Spirit, they are blessed indeed, for they will rest from their hard work; for their good deeds follow them!"

### The Harvest of the Earth

¹⁴Then I saw a white cloud, and seated on the cloud was someone like the Son of Man.* He had a gold crown on his head and a sharp sickle in his hand.

¹⁵Then another angel came from the Temple and shouted to the one sitting on the cloud, "Swing the sickle, for the time of harvest has come; the crop on earth is ripe." ¹⁶So the one sitting on the cloud swung his sickle over the earth, and the whole earth was harvested.

¹⁷After that, another angel came from the Temple in heaven, and he also had a sharp sickle. ¹⁸Then another angel, who had power to destroy with fire, came from the altar. He shouted to the angel with the sharp sickle, "Swing your sickle now to gather the clusters of grapes from the vines of the earth, for they are ripe for judgment." ¹⁹So the angel swung his sickle over the earth and loaded the grapes into the great winepress of God's wrath. ²⁰The grapes were trampled in the winepress outside the city, and blood flowed from the winepress in a stream about 180 miles* long and as high as a horse's bridle.

### The Song of Moses and of the Lamb

**15** Then I saw in heaven another marvelous event of great significance. Seven angels were holding the seven last plagues, which would bring God's wrath to completion. ²I saw before me what seemed to be a glass sea mixed with fire. And on it stood all the people who had been victorious over the beast and his statue and the number representing his name. They were all holding harps that God had given them. ³And they were singing the song of Moses, the servant of God, and the song of the Lamb:

"Great and marvelous are your
    works,
  O Lord God, the Almighty.
Just and true are your ways,
  O King of the nations.*
⁴Who will not fear you, Lord,
  and glorify your name?
  For you alone are holy.
All nations will come and worship
    before you,
  for your righteous deeds have been
    revealed."

## THE TRUTH about angels

READ REVELATION 19:9-10 AND 22:8-9

If we saw an angel as John did, we, too, might be tempted to bow down in worship. But twice John tells us that the angels would not allow him to worship them. Twice he is reminded to "worship only God."

There is a real fascination with angels today, and much of it has nothing to do with their status as true servants of God. People dealing with serious illness often seem to be especially enamored with these messengers.

Don't make the mistake John did by giving angels more attention and significance than they are due. Let every representation of an angel you see remind you to praise God and Him alone.

---

**14:14** Or *like a son of man.* See Dan 7:13. "Son of Man" is a title Jesus used for himself.    **14:20** Greek *1,600 stadia* [296 kilometers].    **15:3** Some manuscripts read *King of the ages.*

*The Seven Bowls of the Seven Plagues*

5 Then I looked and saw that the Temple in heaven, God's Tabernacle, was thrown wide open. 6 The seven angels who were holding the seven plagues came out of the Temple. They were clothed in spotless white linen* with gold sashes across their chests. 7 Then one of the four living beings handed each of the seven angels a gold bowl filled with the wrath of God, who lives forever and ever. 8 The Temple was filled with smoke from God's glory and power. No one could enter the Temple until the seven angels had completed pouring out the seven plagues.

# 16

Then I heard a mighty voice from the Temple say to the seven angels, "Go your ways and pour out on the earth the seven bowls containing God's wrath."

2 So the first angel left the Temple and poured out his bowl on the earth, and horrible, malignant sores broke out on everyone who had the mark of the beast and who worshiped his statue.

3 Then the second angel poured out his bowl on the sea, and it became like the blood of a corpse. And everything in the sea died.

4 Then the third angel poured out his bowl on the rivers and springs, and they became blood. 5 And I heard the angel who had authority over all water saying,

"You are just, O Holy One, who is and who always was,
   because you have sent these judgments.
6 Since they shed the blood
   of your holy people and your prophets,
you have given them blood to drink.
   It is their just reward."

7 And I heard a voice from the altar,* saying,

"Yes, O Lord God, the Almighty,
   your judgments are true and just."

8 Then the fourth angel poured out his bowl on the sun, causing it to scorch everyone with its fire. 9 Everyone was burned by this blast of heat, and they cursed the name of God, who had control over all these plagues. They did not repent of their sins and turn to God and give him glory.

10 Then the fifth angel poured out his bowl on the throne of the beast, and his kingdom was plunged into darkness. His subjects ground their teeth in anguish, 11 and they cursed the God of heaven for their pains and sores. But they did not repent of their evil deeds and turn to God.

12 Then the sixth angel poured out his bowl on the great Euphrates River, and it dried up so that the kings from the east could march their armies toward the west without hindrance. 13 And I saw three evil* spirits that looked like frogs leap from the mouths of the dragon, the beast, and the false prophet. 14 They are demonic spirits who work miracles and go out to all the rulers of the world to gather them for battle against the Lord on that great judgment day of God the Almighty.

15 "Look, I will come as unexpectedly as a thief! Blessed are all who are watching for me, who keep their clothing ready so they will not have to walk around naked and ashamed."

16 And the demonic spirits gathered all the rulers and their armies to a place with the Hebrew name *Armageddon*.*

17 Then the seventh angel poured out his bowl into the air. And a mighty shout came from the throne in the Temple, saying, "It is finished!" 18 Then the thunder crashed and rolled, and lightning flashed. And a great earthquake struck—the worst since people were placed on the earth. 19 The great city of Babylon split into three sections, and the cities of many nations fell into heaps of rubble. So God remembered all of Babylon's sins, and he made her drink the cup that was filled with the wine of his fierce wrath. 20 And every island disappeared, and all the mountains were leveled. 21 There was a terrible hailstorm, and hailstones weighing seventy-five pounds* fell from the sky onto the people below. They cursed God because of the terrible plague of the hailstorm.

15:6 Other manuscripts read *white stone;* still others read *white [garments] made of linen.*    16:7 Greek *I heard the altar.*
16:13 Greek *unclean.*    16:16 Or *Harmagedon.*    16:21 Greek *1 talent* [34 kilograms].

## The Great Prostitute

**17** One of the seven angels who had poured out the seven bowls came over and spoke to me. "Come with me," he said, "and I will show you the judgment that is going to come on the great prostitute, who rules over many waters. ²The kings of the world have committed adultery with her, and the people who belong to this world have been made drunk by the wine of her immorality."

³So the angel took me in the Spirit* into the wilderness. There I saw a woman sitting on a scarlet beast that had seven heads and ten horns, and blasphemies against God were written all over it. ⁴The woman wore purple and scarlet clothing and beautiful jewelry made of gold and precious gems and pearls. In her hand she held a gold goblet full of obscenities and the impurities of her immorality. ⁵A mysterious name was written on her forehead: "Babylon the Great, Mother of All Prostitutes and Obscenities in the World." ⁶I could see that she was drunk—drunk with the blood of God's holy people who were witnesses for Jesus. I stared at her in complete amazement.

⁷"Why are you so amazed?" the angel asked. "I will tell you the mystery of this woman and of the beast with seven heads and ten horns on which she sits. ⁸The beast you saw was once alive but isn't now. And yet he will soon come up out of the bottomless pit* and go to eternal destruction. And the people who belong to this world, whose names were not written in the Book of Life before the world was made, will be amazed at the reappearance of this beast who had died.

⁹"This calls for a mind with understanding: The seven heads of the beast represent the seven hills where the woman rules. They also represent seven kings. ¹⁰Five kings have already fallen, the sixth now reigns, and the seventh is yet to come, but his reign will be brief. ¹¹"The scarlet beast that was, but is no longer, is the eighth king. He is like the other seven, and he, too, is headed for destruction. ¹²The ten horns of the beast are ten kings who have not yet risen to power. They will be appointed to their kingdoms for one brief moment to reign with the beast. ¹³They will all agree to give him their power and author-

ity. ¹⁴Together they will go to war against the Lamb, but the Lamb will defeat them because he is Lord of all lords and King of all kings. And his called and chosen and faithful ones will be with him."

¹⁵Then the angel said to me, "The waters where the prostitute is ruling represent masses of people of every nation and language. ¹⁶The scarlet beast and his ten horns all hate the prostitute. They will strip her naked, eat her flesh, and burn her remains with fire. ¹⁷For God has put a plan into their minds, a plan that will carry out his purposes. They will agree to give their authority to the scarlet beast, and so the words of God will be fulfilled. ¹⁸And this woman you saw in your vision represents the great city that rules over the kings of the world."

## The Fall of Babylon

**18** After all this I saw another angel come down from heaven with great authority, and the earth grew bright with his splendor. ²He gave a mighty shout:

> "Babylon is fallen—that great city is fallen!
> She has become a home for demons.
> She is a hideout for every foul* spirit,
> a hideout for every foul vulture

**17:3** Or *in spirit*.   **17:8** Or *the abyss,* or *the underworld*.   **18:2a** Greek *unclean;* also in each of the two following phrases.

---

## OTHER side of truth
READ REVELATION 19:11-16

Doctors and patients don't always see things from the same perspective. The physician may focus more on the fact that a drug can treat symptoms, while a patient may concentrate more on the drug's side effects. Both sides are true, and together they form the complete picture of the situation.

The Gospels gave us a great picture of Jesus' life on earth. And now John gives us a different perspective, as we get a glimpse of Jesus when He returns to earth. The first time He came as a suffering servant, but He will come back as a battling king. We may not be as fond of this "side," but together they form the complete picture of our Lord.

and every foul and dreadful animal.*
³ For all the nations have fallen*
  because of the wine of her passionate
  immorality.
The kings of the world
  have committed adultery with her.
Because of her desires for extravagant
  luxury,
  the merchants of the world have grown
  rich."

⁴ Then I heard another voice calling from
heaven,

"Come away from her, my people.
  Do not take part in her sins,
  or you will be punished with her.
⁵ For her sins are piled as high as heaven,
  and God remembers her evil deeds.
⁶ Do to her as she has done to others.
  Double her penalty* for all her evil
  deeds.
She brewed a cup of terror for others,
  so brew twice as much* for her.
⁷ She glorified herself and lived in luxury,
  so match it now with torment and
  sorrow.
She boasted in her heart,
  'I am queen on my throne.
I am no helpless widow,
  and I have no reason to mourn.'
⁸ Therefore, these plagues will overtake
  her in a single day—
  death and mourning and famine.
She will be completely consumed
  by fire,
  for the Lord God who judges her is
  mighty."

⁹ And the kings of the world who committed adultery with her and enjoyed her great
luxury will mourn for her as they see the
smoke rising from her charred remains.
¹⁰ They will stand at a distance, terrified by
her great torment. They will cry out,

"How terrible, how terrible for you,
  O Babylon, you great city!
In a single moment
  God's judgment came on you."

¹¹ The merchants of the world will weep
and mourn for her, for there is no one left to
buy their goods. ¹² She bought great quanti-
ties of gold, silver, jewels, and pearls; fine
linen, purple, silk, and scarlet cloth; things
made of fragrant thyine wood, ivory goods,
and objects made of expensive wood; and
bronze, iron, and marble. ¹³ She also bought
cinnamon, spice, incense, myrrh, frankincense, wine, olive oil, fine flour, wheat, cattle,
sheep, horses, chariots, and bodies—that is,
human slaves.

¹⁴ "The fancy things you loved so much
  are gone," they cry.
"All your luxuries and splendor
  are gone forever,
  never to be yours again."

¹⁵ The merchants who became wealthy by
selling her these things will stand at a distance, terrified by her great torment. They
will weep and cry out,

¹⁶ "How terrible, how terrible for that
  great city!
She was clothed in finest purple and
  scarlet linens,
  decked out with gold and precious
  stones and pearls!
¹⁷ In a single moment
  all the wealth of the city is gone!"

And all the captains of the merchant ships
and their passengers and sailors and crews
will stand at a distance. ¹⁸ They will cry out as
they watch the smoke ascend, and they will
say, "Where is there another city as great as
this?" ¹⁹ And they will weep and throw dust
on their heads to show their grief. And they
will cry out,

"How terrible, how terrible for that
  great city!
The shipowners became wealthy
  by transporting her great wealth
  on the seas.
In a single moment it is all gone."

²⁰ Rejoice over her fate, O heaven
  and people of God and apostles
  and prophets!
For at last God has judged her
  for your sakes.

---

18:2b Some manuscripts condense the last two lines to read *a hideout for every foul [unclean] and dreadful vulture.*   **18:3** Some
manuscripts read *have drunk.*   **18:6a** Or *Give her an equal penalty.*   **18:6b** Or *brew just as much.*

²¹ Then a mighty angel picked up a boulder the size of a huge millstone. He threw it into the ocean and shouted,

"Just like this, the great city Babylon
   will be thrown down with violence
   and will never be found again.
²² The sound of harps, singers, flutes,
     and trumpets
   will never be heard in you again.
No craftsmen and no trades
   will ever be found in you again.
The sound of the mill
   will never be heard in you again.
²³ The light of a lamp
   will never shine in you again.
The happy voices of brides and
    grooms
   will never be heard in you again.
For your merchants were the greatest in
    the world,
   and you deceived the nations with your
    sorceries.
²⁴ In your* streets flowed the blood
   of the prophets and of God's holy
    people
   and the blood of people slaughtered
    all over the world."

### Songs of Victory in Heaven

**19** After this, I heard what sounded like a vast crowd in heaven shouting,

"Praise the Lord!*
   Salvation and glory and power belong
    to our God.
² His judgments are true and just.
   He has punished the great prostitute
who corrupted the earth with her
    immorality.
   He has avenged the murder of his
    servants."

³ And again their voices rang out:

"Praise the Lord!
   The smoke from that city ascends
    forever and ever!"

⁴ Then the twenty-four elders and the four living beings fell down and worshiped God,

who was sitting on the throne. They cried out, "Amen! Praise the Lord!"

⁵ And from the throne came a voice that said,

"Praise our God,
   all his servants,
all who fear him,
   from the least to the greatest."

⁶ Then I heard again what sounded like the shout of a vast crowd or the roar of mighty ocean waves or the crash of loud thunder:

"Praise the Lord!
   For the Lord our God,* the Almighty,
    reigns.
⁷ Let us be glad and rejoice,
   and let us give honor to him.
For the time has come for the wedding
    feast of the Lamb,
   and his bride has prepared herself.
⁸ She has been given the finest of pure
    white linen to wear."
For the fine linen represents the good
   deeds of God's holy people.

⁹ And the angel said to me, "Write this: Blessed are those who are invited to the wedding feast of the Lamb." And he added, "These are true words that come from God."

¹⁰ Then I fell down at his feet to worship him, but he said, "No, don't worship me. I am a servant of God, just like you and your brothers and sisters* who testify about their

---

**18:24** Greek *her.*   **19:1** Greek *Hallelujah;* also in 19:3, 4, 6. *Hallelujah* is the transliteration of a Hebrew term that means "Praise the Lord."   **19:6** Some manuscripts read *the Lord God.* **19:10a** Greek *brothers.*

---

## EVERYTHING made new
READ REVELATION 21:3-4

Don't you wish these verses were a description of life on earth now? Wouldn't it be awesome if God's home were right here among us? How incredible it would be if He would wipe away all our tears, take away all our pain, and protect us from any more deaths! We want these verses to come true *now* for all the sick people we know.

But these are not promises for now. They won't happen until the first heaven and the first earth pass away and God makes everything new. In the meantime, we hope for what we do not have . . . knowing that one day it *will* come.

faith in Jesus. <u>Worship only God.</u> For the essence of prophecy is to <u>give a clear witness for Jesus.*"</u>

## The Rider on the White Horse

11 Then I saw heaven opened, and <u>a white horse</u> was standing there. <u>Its rider was named Faithful and True,</u> for he judges fairly and wages a righteous war. 12 His eyes were like flames of fire, and on his head were many crowns. A name was written on him that no one understood except himself. 13 He wore a robe dipped in blood, and his title was the Word of God. 14 The armies of heaven, dressed in the finest of pure white linen, followed him on white horses. 15 From his mouth came a sharp sword to strike down the nations. He will rule them with an iron rod. He will release the fierce wrath of God, the Almighty, like juice flowing from a winepress. 16 On his robe at his thigh* was written this title: King of all kings and Lord of all lords.

17 Then I saw an angel standing in the sun, shouting to the vultures flying high in the sky: "Come! Gather together for the great banquet God has prepared. 18 Come and eat the flesh of kings, generals, and strong warriors; of horses and their riders; and of all humanity, both free and slave, small and great."

19 Then I saw the beast and the kings of the world and their armies gathered together to fight against the one sitting on the horse and his army. 20 And the beast was captured, and with him the false prophet who did mighty miracles on behalf of the beast—miracles that deceived all who had accepted the mark of the beast and who worshiped his statue. Both the beast and his false prophet were thrown alive into the fiery lake of burning sulfur. 21 Their entire army was killed by the sharp sword that came from the mouth of the one riding the white horse. And the vultures all gorged themselves on the dead bodies.

## The Thousand Years

**20** Then I saw an angel coming down from heaven with the key to the bottomless pit* and a heavy chain in his hand. 2 He seized the dragon—that old serpent, who is the devil, Satan—and bound

him in chains for a thousand years. 3 The angel threw him into the bottomless pit, which he then shut and locked so Satan could not deceive the nations anymore until the thousand years were finished. Afterward he must be released for a little while.

4 Then I saw thrones, and the people sitting on them had been given the authority to judge. And I saw the souls of those who had been beheaded for their testimony about Jesus and for proclaiming the word of God. They had not worshiped the beast or his statue, nor accepted his mark on their forehead or their hands. They all came to life again, and they reigned with Christ for a thousand years.

5 <u>This is the first resurrection.</u> (The rest of the dead did not come back to life until the thousand years had ended.) 6 Blessed and holy are those who share in the first resurrection. For them the second death holds no power, but they will be priests of God and of Christ and will reign with him a thousand years.

## The Defeat of Satan

7 When the thousand years come to an end, Satan will be let out of his prison. 8 He will go out to deceive the nations—called Gog and Magog—in every corner of the earth. He will gather them together for battle—a mighty army, as numberless as sand along the seashore. 9 And I saw them as they went up on the broad plain of the earth and surrounded God's people and the beloved city. But fire from heaven came down on the attacking armies and consumed them.

10 Then the devil, who had deceived them, was thrown into the fiery lake of burning sulfur, joining the beast and the false prophet. There they will be tormented day and night forever and ever.

## The Final Judgment

11 And I saw a great white throne and the one sitting on it. The earth and sky fled from his presence, but they found no place to hide. 12 I saw the dead, both great and small, standing before God's throne. And the books were opened, including the Book of

**19:10b** Or *is the message confirmed by Jesus.*     **19:16** Or *On his robe and thigh.*     **20:1** Or *the abyss,* or *the underworld;* also in 20:3.

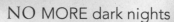

Life. And the dead were judged according to what they had done, as recorded in the books. ¹³The sea gave up its dead, and death and the grave* gave up their dead. And all were judged according to their deeds. ¹⁴Then death and the grave were thrown into the lake of fire. This lake of fire is the second death. ¹⁵And anyone whose name was not found recorded in the Book of Life was thrown into the lake of fire.

### The New Jerusalem

**21** Then I saw a new heaven and a new earth, for the old heaven and the old earth had disappeared. And the sea was also gone. ²And I saw the holy city, the new Jerusalem, coming down from God out of heaven like a bride beautifully dressed for her husband.

³I heard a loud shout from the throne, saying, "Look, God's home is now among his people! He will live with them, and they will be his people. God himself will be with them.* ⁴He will wipe every tear from their eyes, and there will be no more death or sorrow or crying or pain. All these things are gone forever."

⁵And the one sitting on the throne said, "Look, I am making everything new!" And then he said to me, "Write this down, for what I tell you is trustworthy and true." ⁶And he also said, "It is finished! I am the Alpha and the Omega—the Beginning and the End. To all who are thirsty I will give freely from the springs of the water of life. ⁷All who are victorious will inherit all these blessings, and I will be their God, and they will be my children.

⁸"But cowards, unbelievers, the corrupt, murderers, the immoral, those who practice witchcraft, idol worshipers, and all liars—their fate is in the fiery lake of burning sulfur. This is the second death."

⁹Then one of the seven angels who held the seven bowls containing the seven last plagues came and said to me, "Come with me! I will show you the bride, the wife of the Lamb."

¹⁰So he took me in the Spirit* to a great, high mountain, and he showed me the holy city, Jerusalem, descending out of heaven

## NO MORE dark nights

READ REVELATION 21:23 AND 22:5

Our lives often are filled with darkness. Sometimes it's the darkness of a disease attacking our bodies or the darkness of a disorder robbing our minds. Sometimes it's the darkness of despair because there's no medical hope or the darkness of depression as we are crushed beneath our trials.

At times we can't catch our breath. Other times we're afraid to fall asleep. If only there was an end to the darkness.

There is.

In heaven there will be no darkness or night—and no need for sun or moon—because the glory of God will illuminate everything and Jesus, the Light of the World, will shine on us. Now that's worth waiting for.

from God. ¹¹It shone with the glory of God and sparkled like a precious stone—like jasper as clear as crystal. ¹²The city wall was broad and high, with twelve gates guarded by twelve angels. And the names of the twelve tribes of Israel were written on the gates. ¹³There were three gates on each side—east, north, south, and west. ¹⁴The wall of the city had twelve foundation stones, and on them were written the names of the twelve apostles of the Lamb.

¹⁵The angel who talked to me held in his hand a gold measuring stick to measure the city, its gates, and its wall. ¹⁶When he measured it, he found it was a square, as wide as it was long. In fact, its length and width and height were each 1,400 miles.* ¹⁷Then he measured the walls and found them to be 216 feet thick* (according to the human standard used by the angel).

¹⁸The wall was made of jasper, and the city was pure gold, as clear as glass. ¹⁹The wall of the city was built on foundation stones inlaid with twelve precious stones:* the first was jasper, the second sapphire, the third agate, the fourth emerald, ²⁰the fifth onyx, the sixth carnelian, the seventh chrysolite, the eighth beryl, the ninth topaz, the tenth chrysoprase, the eleventh jacinth, the twelfth amethyst.

20:13 Greek and Hades; also in 20:14. 21:3 Some manuscripts read God himself will be with them, their God. 21:10 Or in spirit. 21:16 Greek 12,000 stadia [2,220 kilometers]. 21:17 Greek 144 cubits [65 meters]. 21:19 The identification of some of these gemstones is uncertain.

Our world could use some good news, couldn't it? In many ways it's a frightening time in which to be living—wars, rumors of wars, the constant threat of terrorism, the ups and downs of the stock market, violence in the classrooms, so many friends and relatives with cancer, and families torn apart by abuse and divorce. **Life is not only hard; it's often downright unfair, as some people seem to have more than their share of troubles.** You might even be one of those people.

A gentleman was overheard saying: "Every time I think I have my life together, something happens and it's falling apart again."

Wouldn't it be wonderful if we lived in a world where everything was fair and people didn't get sick and sad things didn't happen and nobody had to die? Who wouldn't want to call such a place their "home"?

Did you ever wonder why there's such a longing in each of us for just such a place? It's a longing for home, you know. A longing for our real home. You see, we weren't created to live in California or New York or Florida or anywhere else on the face of this planet. We were created for our real home—heaven.

**The Bible describes heaven in Revelation 21:4 as a place where God "will wipe every tear from their eyes, and there will be no more death or sorrow or crying or pain."**

And why won't there be any more tears or death or sorrow or pain? Not because we'll have all the money we ever wanted or all the fame or all the knowledge or any other earthly pursuit.

It's because we'll have God Himself.

In Revelation 21:3, the verse right before the one about no more tears, pain, or death, it says: "Look, God's home is now among his people! He will live with them, and they will be his people."

That's why there won't be any more tears or pain or death. We'll have what we always really needed to be whole—the constant presence of God Himself.

# call home

The great seventeenth-century philosopher and mathematician Blaise Pascal wrote that each of us has a "God-shaped vacuum" in us. There's a hole, so to speak, in our hearts that leaves us longing for something more than this world has to offer. It's a hole and a longing that God *put in us* when He created us. He knows only He can fill that hole even though we try to fill it ourselves with all sorts of other things. Some of us try to fill it with "stuff" we purchase or with relationships or with work or with sports or with learning or with religious rituals. Some even try things like food or sex or drugs or alcohol. But none of these can fill the God-shaped vacuum in us . . . instead, they only make it bigger.

The only thing that fills that hole and makes us *whole* is when God fills it with Himself by putting His very Spirit inside us, one life at a time. And when God's Spirit lives inside us, we discover our purpose for living.

A health crisis often makes us realize how precious life is, and it can send us scurrying to discover the meaning of life.

**So, why are we here?**

It's really quite simple. Do you know what it is?

**We were created to praise God.**

That's right. We find true joy, true fulfillment when we realize there's Someone bigger than us. Someone greater than us. Someone worthy of every bit of praise we can give.

We were created to praise God with our lips . . . and our lives.

And when we do, a feeling of peace and power comes over us that hardly can be described. It's a feeling that reminds us this world is not our real home.

If you've never really had praise for God well up in your heart, we pray that you will as you read *He Cares* today. The book of Revelation gives us just a teeny glimpse of what it's going to be like in heaven, standing and praising God before His throne with Jesus at His right hand.

And if you're still trying to fill that God-shaped vacuum with other things, we pray you'll allow God to fill you with Himself and satisfy that longing for your real home, heaven.

21 The twelve gates were made of pearls—each gate from a single pearl! And the main street was pure gold, as clear as glass.

22 I saw no temple in the city, for the Lord God Almighty and the Lamb are its temple. 23 And the city has no need of sun or moon, for the glory of God illuminates the city, and the Lamb is its light. 24 The nations will walk in its light, and the kings of the world will enter the city in all their glory. 25 Its gates will never be closed at the end of day because there is no night there. 26 And all the nations will bring their glory and honor into the city. 27 Nothing evil* will be allowed to enter, nor anyone who practices shameful idolatry and dishonesty—but only those whose names are written in the Lamb's Book of Life.

# 22

Then the angel showed me a river with the water of life, clear as crystal, flowing from the throne of God and of the Lamb. 2 It flowed down the center of the main street. On each side of the river grew a tree of life, bearing twelve crops of fruit,* with a fresh crop each month. The leaves were used for medicine to heal the nations.

3 No longer will there be a curse upon anything. For the throne of God and of the Lamb will be there, and his servants will worship him. 4 And they will see his face, and his name will be written on their foreheads. 5 And there will be no night there—no need for lamps or sun—for the Lord God will shine on them. And they will reign forever and ever.

6 Then the angel said to me, "Everything you have heard and seen is trustworthy and true. The Lord God, who inspires his prophets,* has sent his angel to tell his servants what will happen soon.*"

## Jesus Is Coming

7 "Look, I am coming soon! Blessed are those who obey the words of prophecy written in this book.*"

8 I, John, am the one who heard and saw all these things. And when I heard and saw

them, I fell down to worship at the feet of the angel who showed them to me. 9 But he said, "No, don't worship me. I am a servant of God, just like you and your brothers the prophets, as well as all who obey what is written in this book. Worship only God!"

10 Then he instructed me, "Do not seal up the prophetic words in this book, for the time is near. 11 Let the one who is doing harm continue to do harm; let the one who is vile continue to be vile; let the one who is righteous continue to live righteously; let the one who is holy continue to be holy."

12 "Look, I am coming soon, bringing my reward with me to repay all people according to their deeds. 13 I am the Alpha and the Omega, the First and the Last, the Beginning and the End."

14 Blessed are those who wash their robes. They will be permitted to enter through the gates of the city and eat the fruit from the tree of life. 15 Outside the city are the dogs—the sorcerers, the sexually immoral, the murderers, the idol worshipers, and all who love to live a lie.

16 "I, Jesus, have sent my angel to give you this message for the churches. I am both the source of David and the heir to his throne.* I am the bright morning star."

17 The Spirit and the bride say, "Come." Let anyone who hears this say, "Come." Let anyone who is thirsty come. Let anyone who desires drink freely from the water of life. 18 And I solemnly declare to everyone who hears the words of prophecy written in this book: If anyone adds anything to what is written here, God will add to that person the plagues described in this book. 19 And if anyone removes any of the words from this book of prophecy, God will remove that person's share in the tree of life and in the holy city that are described in this book.

20 He who is the faithful witness to all these things says, " Yes, I am coming soon!" Amen! Come, Lord Jesus!

21 May the grace of the Lord Jesus be with God's holy people.*

21:27 Or ceremonially unclean.    22:2 Or twelve kinds of fruit.    22:6a Or The Lord, the God of the spirits of the prophets.
22:6b Or suddenly, or quickly; also in 22:7, 12, 20.    22:7 Or scroll; also in 22:9, 10, 18, 19.    22:16 Greek I am the root and offspring
of David.    22:21 Other manuscripts read be with all; still others read be with all of God's holy people. Some manuscripts add Amen.

# PSALMS

Pity parties are great once in a while. Hopefully you have a friend with whom you can trade poor-me complaints—just keep the party short and make sure you find something to laugh about when you finish all your moaning!

The Psalms are ancient Hebrew poetry, but they also are perfect "food" for a pity party. Most of these poems were written by David, the shepherd boy who became king, and he had plenty of hardships to complain about. He lived under a "death sentence" much of his life as his royal predecessor and enemy, King Saul, pursued him for years trying to kill him. Today, you're facing a different kind of enemy, but an enemy nonetheless. What's the name of your enemy? Maybe it's cancer or AIDS, or maybe it's depression or despair. Name your "enemy" and when you see that word in the Psalms, substitute your own personal foe there.

Reading the Psalms, which were sung to instrumental music, will make you feel better about any complaining or whining you've been doing. And they'll also help you find new ways to praise and thank God even in the midst of adversity. Many of us who have faced serious illness have found that Psalms, more than any book in the Bible, mirrored our changing temperaments and allowed us to verbalize those deep emotions to God. Use the psalms as your own prayers. You can start with Psalm 17:6: "I am praying to you because I know you will answer, O God. Bend down and listen as I pray."

## BOOK ONE (Psalms 1–41)

## PSALM 1

1 Oh, the joys of those who do not
    follow the advice of the wicked,
    or stand around with sinners,
    or join in with mockers.
2 But they delight in the law of the LORD,
    meditating on it day and night.
3 They are like trees planted along the
        riverbank,
    bearing fruit each season.
Their leaves never wither,
    and they prosper in all they do.

4 But not the wicked!
    They are like worthless chaff, scattered
        by the wind.
5 They will be condemned at the time of
        judgment.
    Sinners will have no place among the
        godly.
6 For the LORD watches over the path of
        the godly,
    but the path of the wicked leads to
        destruction.

## PSALM 2

1 Why are the nations so angry?
    Why do they waste their time with
        futile plans?
2 The kings of the earth prepare for battle;
    the rulers plot together
against the LORD
    and against his anointed one.
3 "Let us break their chains," they cry,
    "and free ourselves from slavery
        to God."

4 But the one who rules in heaven laughs.
    The Lord scoffs at them.
5 Then in anger he rebukes them,
    terrifying them with his fierce fury.
6 For the Lord declares, "I have placed my
        chosen king on the throne
    in Jerusalem,* on my holy mountain."

7 The king proclaims the LORD's decree:
    "The LORD said to me, 'You are my son.*
    Today I have become your Father.*
8 Only ask, and I will give you the nations
        as your inheritance,
    the whole earth as your possession.
9 You will break* them with an iron rod
    and smash them like clay pots.'"

10 Now then, you kings, act wisely!
    Be warned, you rulers of the earth!
11 Serve the LORD with reverent fear,
    and rejoice with trembling.
12 Submit to God's royal son,* or he will
        become angry,
    and you will be destroyed in the midst
        of all your activities—
for his anger flares up in an instant.
    But what joy for all who take refuge
        in him!

## PSALM 3

*A psalm of David, regarding the time David
fled from his son Absalom.*

1 O LORD, I have so many enemies;
    so many are against me.
2 So many are saying,
    "God will never rescue him!"
                                        *Interlude**

3 But you, O LORD, are a shield around me;
    you are my glory, the one who holds my
        head high.
4 I cried out to the LORD,
    and he answered me from his holy
        mountain.                    *Interlude*

5 I lay down and slept,
    yet I woke up in safety,
    for the LORD was watching over me.
6 I am not afraid of ten thousand enemies
    who surround me on every side.

7 Arise, O LORD!
    Rescue me, my God!
    Slap all my enemies in the face!

2:6 Hebrew *on Zion.*  2:7a Or *Son;* also in 2:12.  2:7b Or *Today I reveal you as my son.*  2:9 Greek version reads *rule.* Compare Rev 2:27.  2:12 The meaning of the Hebrew is uncertain.  3:2 Hebrew *Selah.* The meaning of this word is uncertain, though it is probably a musical or literary term. It is rendered *Interlude* throughout the Psalms.

Shatter the teeth of the wicked!
8 Victory comes from you, O LORD.
  May you bless your people.     *Interlude*

## PSALM 4

*For the choir director: A psalm of David, to be
accompanied by stringed instruments.*

1 Answer me when I call to you,
    O God who declares me innocent.
  Free me from my troubles.
    Have mercy on me and hear my
      prayer.

2 How long will you people ruin my
      reputation?
    How long will you make groundless
      accusations?
    How long will you continue your lies?
                              *Interlude*

3 You can be sure of this:
    The LORD set apart the godly for
      himself.
    The LORD will answer when I call
      to him.

4 Don't sin by letting anger control you.
    Think about it overnight and remain
      silent.                    *Interlude*
5 Offer sacrifices in the right spirit,
    and trust the LORD.

6 Many people say, "Who will show us
      better times?"
    Let your face smile on us, LORD.

7 You have given me greater joy
    than those who have abundant
      harvests of grain and new wine.
8 In peace I will lie down and sleep,
    for you alone, O LORD, will keep
      me safe.

## PSALM 5

*For the choir director: A psalm of David, to be
accompanied by the flute.*

1 O LORD, hear me as I pray;
    pay attention to my groaning.
2 Listen to my cry for help, my King and my
      God,
    for I pray to no one but you.
3 Listen to my voice in the morning, LORD.
    Each morning I bring my requests to
      you and wait expectantly.

4 O God, you take no pleasure in
      wickedness;
    you cannot tolerate the sins of the
      wicked.
5 Therefore, the proud may not stand in
      your presence,
    for you hate all who do evil.
6 You will destroy those who tell lies.
    The LORD detests murderers and
      deceivers.

7 Because of your unfailing love, I can
      enter your house;
    I will worship at your Temple with
      deepest awe.

# SMILE of God

READ PSALM 4:6-8

If you're waiting for things to get better so you can feel some joy, you needn't wait anymore.
The psalmist David apparently had some friends who were wishing somebody would cut them a break
and make life a little easier. But David didn't feel the same way. Instead, he found such joy in his relationship with the Lord that it didn't really matter that life wasn't going so well. He found his joy in the
smile of God.

And just how do we experience that "smile" from our heavenly Father? In his book *The Purpose-
Driven Life*, Rick Warren writes that our first purpose in life is to please God. Or as Warren puts it,
"The smile of God is the goal of your life."

Dealing with health problems or caring for those with problems can rob us of many things, but it
needn't take away our goal in life—to please God and make Him smile. And it's His smile that will give
us our greatest joy.

8 Lead me in the right path, O LORD,
  or my enemies will conquer me.
Make your way plain for me to follow.

9 My enemies cannot speak a truthful word.
  Their deepest desire is to destroy
    others.
  Their talk is foul, like the stench from an
    open grave.
  Their tongues are filled with flattery.*
10 O God, declare them guilty.
  Let them be caught in their own traps.
  Drive them away because of their many
    sins,
  for they have rebelled against you.

11 But let all who take refuge in you rejoice;
  let them sing joyful praises forever.
  Spread your protection over them,
  that all who love your name may be
    filled with joy.
12 For you bless the godly, O LORD;
  you surround them with your shield
    of love.

## PSALM 6

*For the choir director: A psalm of David, to be
accompanied by an eight-stringed instrument.**

1 O LORD, don't rebuke me in your anger
  or discipline me in your rage.
2 Have compassion on me, LORD, for I am
    weak.
  Heal me, LORD, for my bones are in
    agony.
3 I am sick at heart.
  How long, O LORD, until you restore me?

4 Return, O LORD, and rescue me.
  Save me because of your unfailing love.
5 For the dead do not remember you.
  Who can praise you from the grave?*

6 I am worn out from sobbing.
  All night I flood my bed with weeping,
  drenching it with my tears.
7 My vision is blurred by grief;
  my eyes are worn out because of all my
    enemies.

8 Go away, all you who do evil,
  for the LORD has heard my weeping.

9 The LORD has heard my plea;
  the LORD will answer my prayer.
10 May all my enemies be disgraced and
    terrified.
  May they suddenly turn back in shame.

## PSALM 7

*A psalm of David, which he sang to the LORD
concerning Cush of the tribe of Benjamin.*

1 I come to you for protection, O LORD
    my God.
  Save me from my persecutors—
    rescue me!
2 If you don't, they will maul me like a lion,
  tearing me to pieces with no one to
    rescue me.
3 O LORD my God, if I have done wrong
  or am guilty of injustice,
4 if I have betrayed a friend
  or plundered my enemy without cause,
5 then let my enemies capture me.
  Let them trample me into the ground
  and drag my honor in the dust.
                                    *Interlude*

6 Arise, O LORD, in anger!
  Stand up against the fury of my
    enemies!
  Wake up, my God, and bring justice!
7 Gather the nations before you.
  Rule over them from on high.
8   The LORD judges the nations.
  Declare me righteous, O LORD,
  for I am innocent, O Most High!
9 End the evil of those who are wicked,
  and defend the righteous.
  For you look deep within the mind
    and heart,
  O righteous God.

10 God is my shield,
  saving those whose hearts are true
    and right.
11 God is an honest judge.
  He is angry with the wicked every day.

12 If a person does not repent,
  God* will sharpen his sword;
  he will bend and string his bow.
13 He will prepare his deadly weapons
  and shoot his flaming arrows.

5:9 Greek version reads *with lies.* Compare Rom 3:12.   6:TITLE Hebrew *with stringed instruments; according to the sheminith.*
6:5 Hebrew *from Sheol?*   7:12 Hebrew *he.*

¹⁴ The wicked conceive evil;
    they are pregnant with trouble
    and give birth to lies.
¹⁵ They dig a deep pit to trap others,
    then fall into it themselves.
¹⁶ The trouble they make for others
    backfires on them.
    The violence they plan falls on their
    own heads.

¹⁷ I will thank the LORD because he is just;
    I will sing praise to the name of the
    LORD Most High.

## PSALM 8

*For the choir director: A psalm of David, to be
accompanied by a stringed instrument.* *

¹ O LORD, our Lord, your majestic name
    fills the earth!
    Your glory is higher than the heavens.
² You have taught children and infants
    to tell of your strength,*
    silencing your enemies
    and all who oppose you.

³ When I look at the night sky and see the
    work of your fingers—
    the moon and the stars you set in
    place—
⁴ what are mere mortals that you should
    think about them,
    human beings that you should care
    for them?*
⁵ Yet you made them only a little lower
    than God*
    and crowned them* with glory and
    honor.
⁶ You gave them charge of everything you
    made,
    putting all things under their
    authority—
⁷ the flocks and the herds
    and all the wild animals,
⁸ the birds in the sky, the fish in the
    sea,
    and everything that swims the ocean
    currents.

⁹ O LORD, our Lord, your majestic name
    fills the earth!

## PRESCRIPTION
### for the blues
READ PSALM 8

Feeling a little down today? Are you discouraged about all that has happened? Maybe you're even despairing over all you still have to face. Medications can be helpful and even necessary at times when we can't lift the fog of depression. But there's something else you might want to try when you're down—worshipping God. Seriously. Even if you don't feel like giving honor and reverence to anybody or anything, use this psalm to do it anyway. You see, we're "wired for worship." It's built into our brains by our Creator and if we don't do it, there's a part of us that's just not going to feel right. Worship is not only pleasing to God; it's healing for us.

## PSALM 9

*For the choir director: A psalm of David, to be
sung to the tune "Death of the Son."*

¹ I will praise you, LORD, with all my
    heart;
    I will tell of all the marvelous things
    you have done.
² I will be filled with joy because of you.
    I will sing praises to your name,
    O Most High.

³ My enemies retreated;
    they staggered and died when you
    appeared.
⁴ For you have judged in my favor;
    from your throne you have judged
    with fairness.
⁵ You have rebuked the nations and
    destroyed the wicked;
    you have erased their names forever.
⁶ The enemy is finished, in endless ruins;
    the cities you uprooted are now
    forgotten.

⁷ But the LORD reigns forever,
    executing judgment from his throne.
⁸ He will judge the world with justice
    and rule the nations with fairness.
⁹ The LORD is a shelter for the oppressed,
    a refuge in times of trouble.

**8:TITLE** Hebrew *according to the gittith.* **8:2** Greek version reads *to give you praise.* Compare Matt 21:16. **8:4** Hebrew *what is man that you should think of him, / the son of man that you should care for him?* **8:5a** Or *Yet you made them only a little lower than the angels;* Hebrew reads *Yet you made him* [i.e., man] *a little lower than Elohim.* **8:5b** Hebrew *him* [i.e., man]; similarly in 8:6.

10 Those who know your name trust in you,
for you, O Lord, do not abandon those
who search for you.

11 Sing praises to the Lord who reigns
in Jerusalem.*
Tell the world about his unforgettable
deeds.
12 For he who avenges murder cares for
the helpless.
He does not ignore the cries of those
who suffer.

13 Lord, have mercy on me.
See how my enemies torment me.
Snatch me back from the jaws
of death.
14 Save me so I can praise you publicly at
Jerusalem's gates,
so I can rejoice that you have rescued me.

15 The nations have fallen into the pit they
dug for others.
Their own feet have been caught in the
trap they set.
16 The Lord is known for his justice.
The wicked are trapped by their own
deeds.            *Quiet Interlude**

17 The wicked will go down to the grave.*
This is the fate of all the nations who
ignore God.
18 But the needy will not be ignored forever;
the hopes of the poor will not always
be crushed.

19 Arise, O Lord!
Do not let mere mortals defy you!
Judge the nations!
20 Make them tremble in fear, O Lord.
Let the nations know they are merely
human.            *Interlude*

## PSALM 10

1 O Lord, why do you stand so far away?
Why do you hide when I am in
trouble?
2 The wicked arrogantly hunt down the
poor.
Let them be caught in the evil they
plan for others.
3 For they brag about their evil desires;

they praise the greedy and curse
the Lord.

4 The wicked are too proud to seek God.
They seem to think that God is dead.
5 Yet they succeed in everything they do.
They do not see your punishment
awaiting them.
They sneer at all their enemies.
6 They think, "Nothing bad will ever
happen to us!
We will be free of trouble forever!"

7 Their mouths are full of cursing, lies, and
threats.*
Trouble and evil are on the tips of their
tongues.
8 They lurk in ambush in the villages,
waiting to murder innocent people.
They are always searching for helpless
victims.
9 Like lions crouched in hiding,
they wait to pounce on the helpless.
Like hunters they capture the helpless
and drag them away in nets.
10 Their helpless victims are crushed;
they fall beneath the strength
of the wicked.
11 The wicked think, "God isn't watching us!
He has closed his eyes and won't
even see what we do!"

12 Arise, O Lord!
Punish the wicked, O God!
Do not ignore the helpless!
13 Why do the wicked get away with
despising God?
They think, "God will never call us
to account."
14 But you see the trouble and grief they
cause.
You take note of it and punish them.
The helpless put their trust in you.
You defend the orphans.

15 Break the arms of these wicked, evil
people!
Go after them until the last one is
destroyed.
16 The Lord is king forever and ever!
The godless nations will vanish from
the land.

**9:11** Hebrew *Zion;* also in 9:14.    **9:16** Hebrew *Higgaion Selah.* The meaning of this phrase is uncertain.    **9:17** Hebrew *to Sheol.*
**10:7** Greek version reads *cursing and bitterness.* Compare Rom 3:14.

¹⁷ LORD, you know the hopes of the helpless.
  Surely you will hear their cries and
     comfort them.
¹⁸ You will bring justice to the orphans and
     the oppressed,
  so mere people can no longer terrify
     them.

## PSALM 11
*For the choir director: A psalm of David.*

¹ I trust in the LORD for protection.
  So why do you say to me,
     "Fly like a bird to the mountains for
        safety!
² The wicked are stringing their bows
     and fitting their arrows on the
        bowstrings.
  They shoot from the shadows
     at those whose hearts are right.
³ The foundations of law and order have
     collapsed.
  What can the righteous do?"

⁴ But the LORD is in his holy Temple;
     the LORD still rules from heaven.
  He watches everyone closely,
     examining every person on earth.
⁵ The LORD examines both the righteous
     and the wicked.
  He hates those who love violence.
⁶ He will rain down blazing coals and
     burning sulfur on the wicked,
  punishing them with scorching winds.
⁷ For the righteous LORD loves justice.
  The virtuous will see his face.

## PSALM 12
*For the choir director: A psalm of David, to be
accompanied by an eight-stringed instrument.* *

¹ Help, O LORD, for the godly are fast
     disappearing!
  The faithful have vanished from the
     earth!
² Neighbors lie to each other,
     speaking with flattering lips and
        deceitful hearts.
³ May the LORD cut off their flattering lips
     and silence their boastful tongues.
⁴ They say, "We will lie to our hearts'
     content.
  Our lips are our own—who can stop us?"

12:TITLE Hebrew *according to the sheminith.*

⁵ The LORD replies, "I have seen violence
     done to the helpless,
  and I have heard the groans of the poor.
  Now I will rise up to rescue them,
     as they have longed for me to do."
⁶ The LORD's promises are pure,
     like silver refined in a furnace,
  purified seven times over.
⁷ Therefore, LORD, we know you will
     protect the oppressed,
  preserving them forever from this lying
     generation,
⁸ even though the wicked strut about,
     and evil is praised throughout the land.

## PSALM 13
*For the choir director: A psalm of David.*

¹ O LORD, how long will you forget me?
     Forever?
  How long will you look the other way?
² How long must I struggle with anguish
     in my soul,
  with sorrow in my heart every day?
  How long will my enemy have the
     upper hand?

³ Turn and answer me, O LORD my God!
  Restore the sparkle to my eyes, or
     I will die.
⁴ Don't let my enemies gloat, saying, "We
     have defeated him!"
  Don't let them rejoice at my downfall.

⁵ But I trust in your unfailing love.
  I will rejoice because you have
     rescued me.
⁶ I will sing to the LORD
  because he is good to me.

## PSALM 14
*For the choir director: A psalm of David.*

¹ Only fools say in their hearts,
     "There is no God."
  They are corrupt, and their actions are
     evil;
  not one of them does good!

² The LORD looks down from heaven
     on the entire human race;
  he looks to see if anyone is truly wise,
     if anyone seeks God.

³ But no, all have turned away;
    all have become corrupt.*
No one does good,
    not a single one!

⁴ Will those who do evil never learn?
    They eat up my people like bread
    and wouldn't think of praying to the
        LORD.
⁵ Terror will grip them,
    for God is with those who obey him.
⁶ The wicked frustrate the plans of the
       oppressed,
    but the LORD will protect his people.

⁷ Who will come from Mount Zion to
       rescue Israel?
When the LORD restores his people,
    Jacob will shout with joy, and Israel
    will rejoice.

## PSALM 15
*A psalm of David.*

¹ Who may worship in your sanctuary,
    LORD?
Who may enter your presence on your
    holy hill?
² Those who lead blameless lives and do
    what is right,
    speaking the truth from sincere
       hearts.
³ Those who refuse to gossip
    or harm their neighbors
    or speak evil of their friends.

⁴ Those who despise flagrant sinners,
    and honor the faithful followers
       of the LORD,
    and keep their promises even when
       it hurts.
⁵ Those who lend money without charging
       interest,
    and who cannot be bribed to lie about
       the innocent.
Such people will stand firm forever.

## PSALM 16
*A psalm of David.*

¹ Keep me safe, O God,
    for I have come to you for refuge.

² I said to the LORD, "You are my
    Master!
    Every good thing I have comes from
    you."
³ The godly people in the land
    are my true heroes!
    I take pleasure in them!
⁴ Troubles multiply for those who chase
    after other gods.
    I will not take part in their sacrifices
    of blood
    or even speak the names of their
    gods.

⁵ LORD, you alone are my inheritance, my
    cup of blessing.
    You guard all that is mine.
⁶ The land you have given me is a pleasant
    land.
    What a wonderful inheritance!

⁷ I will bless the LORD who guides me;
    even at night my heart instructs me.
⁸ I know the LORD is always with me.
    I will not be shaken, for he is right
    beside me.

⁹ No wonder my heart is glad, and
    I rejoice.*
    My body rests in safety.
¹⁰ For you will not leave my soul among
    the dead*
    or allow your holy one* to rot in the
    grave.

**14:3** Greek version reads *have become useless.* Compare Rom 3:12. **16:9** Greek version reads *and my tongue shouts his praises.* Compare Acts 2:26. **16:10a** Hebrew *in Sheol.* **16:10b** Or *your Holy One.*

## WHAT'S in a name?
READ PSALM 9:9-10

How would you like to be stuck with one of these real, but comical names: Wayne Dwopp, Chanda Lear, Warren Pease, and identical twins Kate and Duplicate.

    This psalm says that those who know God's name will trust Him. Do you know God's name? He uses more than 600+ terms in the Bible to describe Himself. Here are a few of His Hebrew names to consider today: Yahweh-Yireh (the Lord our Provider); Yahweh-Rapha (the Lord our Healer); and Yahweh-Shalom (the Lord our Peace). And perhaps the one you most need to hear: El-Shaddai (the God who is sufficient for the needs of His people.)

11 You will show me the way of life,
    granting me the joy of your presence
    and the pleasures of living with you
        forever.*

## PSALM 17
*A prayer of David.*

1 O LORD, hear my plea for justice.
    Listen to my cry for help.
  Pay attention to my prayer,
    for it comes from honest lips.
2 Declare me innocent,
    for you see those who do right.

3 You have tested my thoughts and
        examined my heart in the night.
    You have scrutinized me and found
        nothing wrong.
    I am determined not to sin in what
        I say.
4 I have followed your commands,
    which keep me from following cruel
        and evil people.
5 My steps have stayed on your path;
    I have not wavered from following
        you.

6 I am praying to you because I know you
        will answer, O God.
    Bend down and listen as I pray.
7 Show me your unfailing love in
        wonderful ways.
    By your mighty power you rescue
        those who seek refuge from their
        enemies.
8 Guard me as you would guard your
        own eyes.*
    Hide me in the shadow of your
        wings.
9 Protect me from wicked people who
        attack me,
    from murderous enemies who
        surround me.
10 They are without pity.
    Listen to their boasting!
11 They track me down and surround me,
    watching for the chance to throw me
        to the ground.
12 They are like hungry lions, eager to tear
        me apart—
    like young lions hiding in ambush.

13 Arise, O LORD!
    Stand against them, and bring them
        to their knees!
    Rescue me from the wicked with your
        sword!
14 By the power of your hand, O LORD,
    destroy those who look to this world
        for their reward.
    But satisfy the hunger of your treasured
        ones.
    May their children have plenty,
    leaving an inheritance for their
        descendants.
15 Because I am righteous, I will see you.
    When I awake, I will see you face to
        face and be satisfied.

## PSALM 18
*For the choir director: A psalm of David, the
servant of the LORD. He sang this song to the
LORD on the day the LORD rescued him from
all his enemies and from Saul. He sang:*

1 I love you, LORD;
    you are my strength.
2 The LORD is my rock, my fortress, and my
        savior;
    my God is my rock, in whom I find
        protection.
  He is my shield, the power that saves me,
    and my place of safety.
3 I called on the LORD, who is worthy
        of praise,
    and he saved me from my enemies.

4 The ropes of death entangled me;
    floods of destruction swept over me.
5 The grave* wrapped its ropes around me;
    death laid a trap in my path.
6 But in my distress I cried out to the LORD;
    yes, I prayed to my God for help.
  He heard me from his sanctuary;
    my cry to him reached his ears.

7 Then the earth quaked and trembled.
    The foundations of the mountains
        shook;
    they quaked because of his anger.
8 Smoke poured from his nostrils;
    fierce flames leaped from his mouth.
    Glowing coals blazed forth from him.

16:11 Greek version reads *You have shown me the way of life, / and you will fill me with the joy of your presence.* Compare Acts 2:28.
17:8 Hebrew *as the pupil of your eye.*    18:5 Hebrew *Sheol.*

⁹ He opened the heavens and came down;
   dark storm clouds were beneath his
   feet.
¹⁰ Mounted on a mighty angelic being,*
   he flew,
   soaring on the wings of the wind.
¹¹ He shrouded himself in darkness,
   veiling his approach with dark rain
   clouds.
¹² Thick clouds shielded the brightness
   around him
   and rained down hail and burning
   coals.*
¹³ The LORD thundered from heaven;
   the voice of the Most High resounded
   amid the hail and burning coals.
¹⁴ He shot his arrows and scattered his
   enemies;
   his lightning flashed, and they were
   greatly confused.
¹⁵ Then at your command, O LORD,
   at the blast of your breath,
   the bottom of the sea could be seen,
   and the foundations of the earth were
   laid bare.

¹⁶ He reached down from heaven and
   rescued me;
   he drew me out of deep waters.
¹⁷ He rescued me from my powerful
   enemies,
   from those who hated me and were
   too strong for me.
¹⁸ They attacked me at a moment when
   I was in distress,
   but the LORD supported me.
¹⁹ He led me to a place of safety;
   he rescued me because he delights
   in me.
²⁰ The LORD rewarded me for doing right;
   he restored me because of my
   innocence.
²¹ For I have kept the ways of the LORD;
   I have not turned from my God
   to follow evil.
²² I have followed all his regulations;
   I have never abandoned his decrees.
²³ I am blameless before God;
   I have kept myself from sin.
²⁴ The LORD rewarded me for doing right.
   He has seen my innocence.

²⁵ To the faithful you show yourself faithful;
   to those with integrity you show
   integrity.
²⁶ To the pure you show yourself pure,
   but to the wicked you show yourself
   hostile.
²⁷ You rescue the humble,
   but you humiliate the proud.
²⁸ You light a lamp for me.
   The LORD, my God, lights up my
   darkness.
²⁹ In your strength I can crush an army;
   with my God I can scale any wall.

³⁰ God's way is perfect.
   All the LORD's promises prove true.
   He is a shield for all who look to him
   for protection.
³¹ For who is God except the LORD?
   Who but our God is a solid rock?
³² God arms me with strength,
   and he makes my way perfect.
³³ He makes me as surefooted as a deer,
   enabling me to stand on mountain
   heights.
³⁴ He trains my hands for battle;
   he strengthens my arm to draw
   a bronze bow.
³⁵ You have given me your shield of victory.
   Your right hand supports me;
   your help has made me great.
³⁶ You have made a wide path for my feet
   to keep them from slipping.

³⁷ I chased my enemies and caught them;
   I did not stop until they were
   conquered.
³⁸ I struck them down so they could not
   get up;
   they fell beneath my feet.
³⁹ You have armed me with strength for the
   battle;
   you have subdued my enemies under
   my feet.
⁴⁰ You placed my foot on their necks.
   I have destroyed all who hated me.
⁴¹ They called for help, but no one came
   to their rescue.
   They even cried to the LORD, but he
   refused to answer.
⁴² I ground them as fine as dust in the wind.
   I swept them into the gutter like dirt.

18:10 Hebrew *a cherub.*    18:12 Or *and lightning bolts;* also in 18:13.

43 You gave me victory over my accusers.
   You appointed me ruler over nations;
   people I don't even know now serve me.
44 As soon as they hear of me, they submit;
   foreign nations cringe before me.
45 They all lose their courage
   and come trembling from their
      strongholds.

46 The LORD lives! Praise to my Rock!
   May the God of my salvation be exalted!
47 He is the God who pays back those who
      harm me;
   he subdues the nations under me
48    and rescues me from my enemies.
   You hold me safe beyond the reach
      of my enemies;
   you save me from violent opponents.
49 For this, O LORD, I will praise you among
      the nations;
   I will sing praises to your name.
50 You give great victories to your king;
   you show unfailing love to your anointed,
   to David and all his descendants
      forever.

## PSALM 19
*For the choir director: A psalm of David.*

1. The heavens proclaim the glory of God.
   The skies display his craftsmanship.
2 Day after day they continue to speak;
   night after night they make him known.

19:3 Or *There is no speech or language where their voice is not heard.*

3 They speak without a sound or word;
   their voice is never heard.*
4 Yet their message has gone throughout
      the earth,
   and their words to all the world.

God has made a home in the heavens for
      the sun.
5 It bursts forth like a radiant bridegroom
      after his wedding.
   It rejoices like a great athlete eager
      to run the race.
6 The sun rises at one end of the heavens
   and follows its course to the other end.
   Nothing can hide from its heat.

7 The instructions of the LORD are perfect,
   reviving the soul.
   The decrees of the LORD are trustworthy,
   making wise the simple.
8 The commandments of the LORD are
      right,
   bringing joy to the heart.
   The commands of the LORD are clear,
   giving insight for living.
9 Reverence for the LORD is pure,
   lasting forever.
   The laws of the LORD are true;
   each one is fair.
10 They are more desirable than gold,
   even the finest gold.
   They are sweeter than honey,
   even honey dripping from the comb.

# WORDS that hurt
READ PSALM 19:14

Dealing with a health crisis can lead to short tempers, harsh words, and hurtful thoughts about others. We often take out our frustrations on those closest to us—the ones we care about the most—because deep inside we know they'll still love us. (Who knows what the doctor would do if we gave him or her a piece of our mind!) It's hard to control our tongues and sometimes even harder not to harbor hurts in our heart. But while our unkind words injure our listeners and our bad-tempered thoughts eat away at our own peace of mind, both responses do even more damage . . . they displease God.

   This psalm is a great prayer to memorize and pray whenever we are tempted to be rude, unfeeling, brusque, discourteous, or uncivil to another person—especially those under our own roof. It's also a great question to ask ourselves before we speak or when we're brooding over something. Are these words I'm about to utter pleasing to God? Are these thoughts I'm having pleasing to God?

*Have compassion on me, LORD, for I am weak. Heal me, LORD, for my bones are in agony.* PSALM 6:2

**O LORD my God, I cried to you for help, and you restored my health.** PSALM 30:2

*"O LORD," I prayed, "have mercy on me. Heal me, for I have sinned against you."* PSALM 41:4

**Let all that I am praise the LORD; may I never forget the good things he does for me. He forgives all my sins and heals all my diseases.** PSALM 103:2-3

*"LORD, help!" they cried in their trouble, and he saved them from their distress. He sent out his word and healed them, snatching them from the door of death.* PSALM 107:19-20

**Don't be impressed with your own wisdom. Instead, fear the LORD and turn away from evil. Then you will have healing for your body and strength for your bones.** PROVERBS 3:7-8

*My child, pay attention to what I say. Listen carefully to my words. Don't lose sight of them. Let them penetrate deep into your heart, for they bring life to those who find them, and healing to their whole body.* PROVERBS 4:20-22

**A cheerful look brings joy to the heart; good news makes for good health.** PROVERBS 15:30

*News about him spread as far as Syria, and people soon began bringing to him all who were sick. And whatever their sickness or disease, or if they were demon possessed or epileptic or paralyzed—he healed them all.* MATTHEW 4:24

*That evening many demon-possessed people were brought to Jesus. He cast out the evil spirits with a simple command, and he healed all the sick. This fulfilled the word of the Lord through the prophet Isaiah, who said,* **"He took our sicknesses and removed our diseases."** MATTHEW 8:16-17

*Jesus traveled through all the towns and villages of that area, teaching in the synagogues and announcing the Good News about the Kingdom. And he healed every kind of disease and illness.* MATTHEW 9:35

# Scripture verses

*Jesus called his twelve disciples together and gave them author-ity to cast out evil spirits and to heal every kind of disease and illness.* MATTHEW 10:1

*"Go and announce to them that the Kingdom of Heaven is near. Heal the sick, raise the dead, cure those with leprosy, and cast out demons. Give as freely as you have received!"* MATTHEW 10:7-8

*Jesus saw the huge crowd as he stepped from the boat, and **he had compassion on them and healed their sick.*** MATTHEW 14:14

*A vast crowd brought to him people who were lame, blind, crippled, those who couldn't speak, and many others. They laid them before Jesus, and he healed them all. The crowd was amazed! Those who hadn't been able to speak were talking, the crippled were made well, the lame were walk-ing, and the blind could see again! And they praised the God of Israel.* MATTHEW 15:30-31

*Large crowds followed him there, and he healed their sick.* MATTHEW 19:2

*And Jesus said to him, "Go, for your faith has healed you." Instantly the man could see, and he followed Jesus down the road.* MARK 10:52

*One day Jesus called together his twelve disciples and gave them power and authority to cast out all demons and to heal all diseases. Then he sent them out to tell everyone about the Kingdom of God and to heal the sick. . . . So they began their circuit of the villages, preaching the Good News and healing the sick.* LUKE 9:1-2, 6

*"And you know that **God anointed Jesus of Nazareth with the Holy Spirit and with power**. Then Jesus went around doing good and healing all who were oppressed by the devil, for God was with him."* ACTS 10:38

*Are any of you sick? You should call for the elders of the church to come and pray over you, anointing you with oil in the name of the Lord. Such a prayer offered in faith will heal the sick, and the Lord will make you well. And if you have committed any sins, you will be forgiven. Confess your sins to each other and pray for each other so that you may be healed. The earnest prayer of a righteous person has great power and produces won-derful results.* JAMES 5:14-16

**He personally carried our sins in his body on the cross so that we can be dead to sin and live for what is right. By his wounds you are healed.** 1 PETER 2:24

11 They are a warning to your servant,
    a great reward for those who obey
      them.
**12**How can I know all the sins lurking
      in my heart?
    Cleanse me from these hidden faults.
13 Keep your servant from deliberate sins!
    Don't let them control me.
    Then I will be free of guilt
    and innocent of great sin.

14 May the words of my mouth
    and the meditation of my heart
  be pleasing to you,
    O LORD, my rock and my redeemer.

## PSALM 20
*For the choir director: A psalm of David.*

1 In times of trouble, may the LORD answer
      your cry.
    May the name of the God of Jacob keep
      you safe from all harm.
2 May he send you help from his
      sanctuary
    and strengthen you from Jerusalem.*
3 May he remember all your gifts
    and look favorably on your burnt
      offerings.                    *Interlude*

4 May he grant your heart's desires
    and make all your plans succeed.
5 May we shout for joy when we hear
      of your victory
    and raise a victory banner in the name
      of our God.
    May the LORD answer all your prayers.

6 Now I know that the LORD rescues his
      anointed king.
    He will answer him from his holy
      heaven
    and rescue him by his great power.
7 Some nations boast of their chariots and
      horses,
    but we boast in the name of the LORD
      our God.
8 Those nations will fall down and
      collapse,
    but we will rise up and stand firm.

9 Give victory to our king, O LORD!
    Answer our cry for help.

20:2 Hebrew *Zion*.

## PSALM 21
*For the choir director: A psalm of David.*

1 How the king rejoices in your strength,
      O LORD!
    He shouts with joy because you give
      him victory.
2 For you have given him his heart's
      desire;
    you have withheld nothing he
      requested.                   *Interlude*

3 You welcomed him back with success
      and prosperity.
    You placed a crown of finest gold
      on his head.
4 He asked you to preserve his life,
    and you granted his request.
    The days of his life stretch
      on forever.
5 Your victory brings him great honor,
    and you have clothed him with
      splendor and majesty.
6 You have endowed him with eternal
      blessings
    and given him the joy of your
      presence.
7 For the king trusts in the LORD.
    The unfailing love of the Most High
      will keep him from stumbling.

8 You will capture all your enemies.
    Your strong right hand will seize all
      who hate you.
9 You will throw them in a flaming
      furnace
    when you appear.
    The LORD will consume them in his
      anger;
    fire will devour them.
10 You will wipe their children from the
      face of the earth;
    they will never have descendants.
11 Although they plot against you,
    their evil schemes will never
      succeed.
12 For they will turn and run
    when they see your arrows aimed
      at them.
13 Rise up, O LORD, in all your power.
    With music and singing we
      celebrate your mighty acts.

## PSALM 22

*For the choir director: A psalm of David, to be
sung to the tune "Doe of the Dawn."*

¹ My God, my God, why have you
    abandoned me?
  Why are you so far away when I groan
    for help?
² Every day I call to you, my God, but you
    do not answer.
  Every night you hear my voice, but
    I find no relief.

³ Yet you are holy,
    enthroned on the praises of Israel.
⁴ Our ancestors trusted in you,
    and you rescued them.
⁵ They cried out to you and were saved.
    They trusted in you and were never
    disgraced.

⁶ But I am a worm and not a man.
    I am scorned and despised by all!
⁷ Everyone who sees me mocks me.
    They sneer and shake their heads,
    saying,
⁸ "Is this the one who relies on the Lord?
    Then let the Lord save him!
  If the Lord loves him so much,
    let the Lord rescue him!"

⁹ Yet you brought me safely from my
    mother's womb
  and led me to trust you at my mother's
    breast.
¹⁰ I was thrust into your arms at my birth.
    You have been my God from the
    moment I was born.

¹¹ Do not stay so far from me,
    for trouble is near,
    and no one else can help me.
¹² My enemies surround me like a herd
    of bulls;
  fierce bulls of Bashan have hemmed
    me in!
¹³ Like lions they open their jaws
    against me,
    roaring and tearing into their prey.
¹⁴ My life is poured out like water,
    and all my bones are out of joint.
  My heart is like wax,
    melting within me.

¹⁵ My strength has dried up like sunbaked
    clay.
  My tongue sticks to the roof of my
    mouth.
  You have laid me in the dust and left
    me for dead.
¹⁶ My enemies surround me like a pack
    of dogs;
  an evil gang closes in on me.
  They have pierced my hands and feet.
¹⁷ I can count all my bones.
    My enemies stare at me and gloat.
¹⁸ They divide my garments among
    themselves
  and throw dice* for my clothing.

¹⁹ O Lord, do not stay far away!
  You are my strength; come quickly
    to my aid!
²⁰ Save me from the sword;
  spare my precious life from these
    dogs.
²¹ Snatch me from the lion's jaws
  and from the horns of these wild oxen.

²² I will proclaim your name to my brothers
    and sisters.*
  I will praise you among your
    assembled people.
²³ Praise the Lord, all you who fear him!
  Honor him, all you descendants
    of Jacob!
  Show him reverence, all you
    descendants of Israel!
²⁴ For he has not ignored or belittled the
    suffering of the needy.
  He has not turned his back on them,
    but has listened to their cries for help.

²⁵ I will praise you in the great assembly.
  I will fulfill my vows in the presence
    of those who worship you.
²⁶ The poor will eat and be satisfied.
  All who seek the Lord will praise him.
  Their hearts will rejoice with
    everlasting joy.
²⁷ The whole earth will acknowledge the
    Lord and return to him.
  All the families of the nations will bow
    down before him.
²⁸ For royal power belongs to the Lord.
  He rules all the nations.

22:18 Hebrew *cast lots.*    22:22 Hebrew *my brothers.*

29 Let the rich of the earth feast and worship.
   Bow before him, all who are mortal,
   all whose lives will end as dust.
30 Our children will also serve him.
   Future generations will hear about the
      wonders of the Lord.
31 His righteous acts will be told to those
      not yet born.
   They will hear about everything he
      has done.

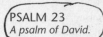

## PSALM 23
*A psalm of David.*

1 The LORD is my shepherd;
   I have all that I need.
2 He lets me rest in green meadows;
   he leads me beside peaceful streams.
3   He renews my strength.
 He guides me along right paths,
   bringing honor to his name.
4 Even when I walk
   through the darkest valley,*
 I will not be afraid,
   for you are close beside me.
 Your rod and your staff
   protect and comfort me.
5 You prepare a feast for me
   in the presence of my enemies.
 You honor me by anointing my head
   with oil.
 My cup overflows with blessings.

23:4 Or *the dark valley of death.*

6 Surely your goodness and unfailing love
   will pursue me
 all the days of my life,
 and I will live in the house of the LORD
   forever.

## PSALM 24
*A psalm of David.*

1 The earth is the LORD's, and everything
   in it.
 The world and all its people belong
   to him.
2 For he laid the earth's foundation
   on the seas
 and built it on the ocean depths.

3 Who may climb the mountain of the
   LORD?
 Who may stand in his holy place?
4 Only those whose hands and hearts
   are pure,
 who do not worship idols
 and never tell lies.
5 They will receive the LORD's blessing
 and have a right relationship with God
   their savior.
6 Such people may seek you
 and worship in your presence,
   O God of Jacob.      *Interlude*

7 Open up, ancient gates!
 Open up, ancient doors,

# LET DOWN by God
READ PSALM 22:1-21

Have you been able to be honest—really honest—with God? It sure beats putting on a happy face and pretending you're okay when you're not. It sure beats stuffing all those emotions deep down inside where they'll only find some other (unhealthy) way to come out. And it sure beats not talking to Him at all.

Go ahead and tell Him that you're mad at Him or that you feel let down and even ignored by Him.
   *But nice people don't say not-nice things to God!* Oh, really? God called David "a man after my own heart" (Acts 13:22), and here in this psalm David sounds very disappointed with God. He also sounds painfully honest with his Father.

   Honesty with God is a real step toward emotional and spiritual healing. As we take all our difficult questions to God, it moves us closer to the only One who truly has all the answers.

and let the King of glory enter.
⁸ Who is the King of glory?
The Lᴏʀᴅ, strong and mighty;
the Lᴏʀᴅ, invincible in battle.
⁹ Open up, ancient gates!
Open up, ancient doors,
and let the King of glory enter.
¹⁰ Who is the King of glory?
The Lᴏʀᴅ of Heaven's Armies—
he is the King of glory.          *Interlude*

## PSALM 25*
*A psalm of David.*

¹ O Lᴏʀᴅ, I give my life to you.
² I trust in you, my God!
Do not let me be disgraced,
or let my enemies rejoice in my
defeat.
³ No one who trusts in you will ever be
disgraced,
but disgrace comes to those who try
to deceive others.

⁴ Show me the right path, O Lᴏʀᴅ;
point out the road for me to follow.
⁵ Lead me by your truth and teach me,
for you are the God who saves me.
All day long I put my hope in you.
⁶ Remember, O Lᴏʀᴅ, your compassion
and unfailing love,
which you have shown from long ages
past.
⁷ Do not remember the rebellious sins
of my youth.
Remember me in the light of your
unfailing love,
for you are merciful, O Lᴏʀᴅ.

⁸ The Lᴏʀᴅ is good and does what is right;
he shows the proper path to those who
go astray.
⁹ He leads the humble in doing right,
teaching them his way.
¹⁰ The Lᴏʀᴅ leads with unfailing love and
faithfulness
all who keep his covenant and obey
his demands.

¹¹ For the honor of your name, O Lᴏʀᴅ,
forgive my many, many sins.
¹² Who are those who fear the Lᴏʀᴅ?

The Lᴏʀᴅ is my shepherd; I have all that
I need.
He lets me rest in green meadows; he leads
me beside peaceful streams.
He renews my strength.
He guides me along right paths, bringing
honor to his name.
Even when I walk through the darkest valley,
I will not be afraid, for you are close beside
me.
Your rod and your staff protect and comfort
me.

PSALM 23:1-4

He will show them the path they
should choose.
¹³ They will live in prosperity,
and their children will inherit the land.
¹⁴ The Lᴏʀᴅ is a friend to those who fear
him.
He teaches them his covenant.
¹⁵ My eyes are always on the Lᴏʀᴅ,
for he rescues me from the traps
of my enemies.

¹⁶ Turn to me and have mercy,
for I am alone and in deep distress.
¹⁷ My problems go from bad to worse.
Oh, save me from them all!
¹⁸ Feel my pain and see my trouble.
Forgive all my sins.
¹⁹ See how many enemies I have
and how viciously they hate me!
²⁰ Protect me! Rescue my life from them!
Do not let me be disgraced, for in you
I take refuge.
²¹ May integrity and honesty protect me,
for I put my hope in you.

²² O God, ransom Israel
from all its troubles.

## PSALM 26
*A psalm of David.*

¹ Declare me innocent, O Lᴏʀᴅ,
for I have acted with integrity;

**25** This psalm is a Hebrew acrostic poem; each verse begins with a successive letter of the Hebrew alphabet.

I have trusted in the LORD without
    wavering.
2 Put me on trial, LORD, and cross-
    examine me.
Test my motives and my heart.
3 For I am always aware of your unfailing
    love,
    and I have lived according to your
    truth.
4 I do not spend time with liars
    or go along with hypocrites.
5 I hate the gatherings of those who do
    evil,
    and I refuse to join in with the wicked.
6 I wash my hands to declare my
    innocence.
I come to your altar, O LORD,
7 singing a song of thanksgiving
    and telling of all your wonders.
8 I love your sanctuary, LORD,
    the place where your glorious presence
    dwells.

9 Don't let me suffer the fate of sinners.
    Don't condemn me along with
    murderers.
10 Their hands are dirty with evil schemes,
    and they constantly take bribes.
11 But I am not like that; I live with integrity.
    So redeem me and show me mercy.
12 Now I stand on solid ground,
    and I will publicly praise the LORD.

## PSALM 27
*A psalm of David.*

1 The LORD is my light and my salvation—
    so why should I be afraid?
The LORD is my fortress, protecting me
    from danger,
    so why should I tremble?
2 When evil people come to devour me,
    when my enemies and foes attack me,
    they will stumble and fall.
3 Though a mighty army surrounds me,
    my heart will not be afraid.
Even if I am attacked,
    I will remain confident.

4 The one thing I ask of the LORD—
    the thing I seek most—
    is to live in the house of the LORD all the
    days of my life,

delighting in the LORD's perfections
    and meditating in his Temple.
5 For he will conceal me there when
    troubles come;
    he will hide me in his sanctuary.
    He will place me out of reach on a high
    rock.
6 Then I will hold my head high
    above my enemies who surround me.
At his sanctuary I will offer sacrifices
    with shouts of joy,
    singing and praising the LORD with
    music.

7 Hear me as I pray, O LORD.
    Be merciful and answer me!
8 My heart has heard you say, "Come and
    talk with me."
    And my heart responds, "LORD, I am
    coming."
9 Do not turn your back on me.
    Do not reject your servant in anger.
    You have always been my helper.
Don't leave me now; don't abandon me,
    O God of my salvation!
10 Even if my father and mother
    abandon me,
    the LORD will hold me close.

11 Teach me how to live, O LORD.
    Lead me along the right path,
    for my enemies are waiting for me.
12 Do not let me fall into their hands.
    For they accuse me of things I've never
    done;
    with every breath they threaten me
    with violence.
13 Yet I am confident I will see the LORD's
    goodness
    while I am here in the land of the
    living.

14 Wait patiently for the LORD.
    Be brave and courageous.
    Yes, wait patiently for the LORD.

## PSALM 28
*A psalm of David.*

1 I pray to you, O LORD, my rock.
    Do not turn a deaf ear to me.
For if you are silent,
    I might as well give up and die.
2 Listen to my prayer for mercy

as I cry out to you for help,
as I lift my hands toward your holy
sanctuary.

³ Do not drag me away with the wicked—
with those who do evil—
those who speak friendly words to their
neighbors
while planning evil in their hearts.
⁴ Give them the punishment they so richly
deserve!
Measure it out in proportion to their
wickedness.
Pay them back for all their evil deeds!
Give them a taste of what they have
done to others.
⁵ They care nothing for what the LORD has
done
or for what his hands have made.
So he will tear them down,
and they will never be rebuilt!

⁶Praise the LORD!
For he has heard my cry for mercy.
⁷ The LORD is my strength and shield.
I trust him with all my heart.
He helps me, and my heart is filled with
joy.
I burst out in songs of thanksgiving.

⁸ The LORD gives his people strength.
He is a safe fortress for his anointed
king.
⁹ Save your people!
Bless Israel, your special possession.*
Lead them like a shepherd,
and carry them in your arms forever.

PSALM 29
*A psalm of David.*

¹ Honor the LORD, you heavenly beings*;
honor the LORD for his glory and
strength.
² Honor the LORD for the glory of his
name.
Worship the LORD in the splendor of
his holiness.

³ The voice of the LORD echoes above
the sea.
The God of glory thunders.

The LORD thunders over the mighty sea.
⁴ The voice of the LORD is powerful;
the voice of the LORD is majestic.
⁵ The voice of the LORD splits the mighty
cedars;
the LORD shatters the cedars of
Lebanon.
⁶ He makes Lebanon's mountains skip like
a calf;
he makes Mount Hermon* leap like a
young wild ox.
⁷ The voice of the LORD strikes
with bolts of lightning.
⁸ The voice of the LORD makes the barren
wilderness quake;
the LORD shakes the wilderness of
Kadesh.
⁹ The voice of the LORD twists mighty oaks*
and strips the forests bare.
In his Temple everyone shouts, "Glory!"

¹⁰ The LORD rules over the floodwaters.
The LORD reigns as king forever.
¹¹ The LORD gives his people strength.
The LORD blesses them with peace.

PSALM 30
*A psalm of David. A song for the dedication
of the Temple.*

¹ I will exalt you, LORD, for you rescued me.
You refused to let my enemies triumph
over me.
² O LORD my God, I cried to you for help,
and you restored my health.

## WISHIN' and hopin'
READ PSALM 25:4-5

Sometimes we say things like "I hope the
test results are good" or "I hope I feel better" or
"I hope I can get through these treatments."
    But a better choice would be to use the word
"wish" instead of "hope." There's only one place to
put true hope and that is in God Almighty. That's
why the Bible says "hope" never disappoints us. It's
not talking about all our wishes; of course, many of
those won't happen and we'll be disappointed. But
when our absolute hope is in our loving, heavenly
Father, we won't be let down.
    Wish for anything you want, but hope in one
thing only: God Himself.

³ You brought me up from the grave,*
 O Lord.
 You kept me from falling into the pit
 of death.

⁴ Sing to the Lord, all you godly ones!
 Praise his holy name.
⁵ For his anger lasts only a moment,
 but his favor lasts a lifetime!
 Weeping may last through the night,
 but joy comes with the morning.

⁶ When I was prosperous, I said,
 "Nothing can stop me now!"
⁷ Your favor, O Lord, made me as secure
 as a mountain.
 Then you turned away from me, and
 I was shattered.

⁸ I cried out to you, O Lord.
 I begged the Lord for mercy, saying,
⁹ "What will you gain if I die,
 if I sink into the grave?
 Can my dust praise you?
 Can it tell of your faithfulness?
¹⁰ Hear me, Lord, and have mercy on me.
 Help me, O Lord."

¹¹ You have turned my mourning into joyful
 dancing.
 You have taken away my clothes of
 mourning and clothed me with joy,
¹² that I might sing praises to you and not
 be silent.
 O Lord my God, I will give you thanks
 forever!

## PSALM 31
*For the choir director: A psalm of David.*

¹ O Lord, I have come to you for
 protection;
 don't let me be disgraced.
 Save me, for you do what is right.
² Turn your ear to listen to me;
 rescue me quickly.
 Be my rock of protection,
 a fortress where I will be safe.
³ You are my rock and my fortress.
 For the honor of your name, lead me
 out of this danger.
⁴ Pull me from the trap my enemies set
 for me,

for I find protection in you alone.
⁵ I entrust my spirit into your hand.
 Rescue me, Lord, for you are a faithful
 God.

⁶ I hate those who worship worthless idols.
 I trust in the Lord.
⁷ I will be glad and rejoice in your unfailing
 love,
 for you have seen my troubles,
 and you care about the anguish
 of my soul.
⁸ You have not handed me over to my
 enemies
 but have set me in a safe place.

⁹ Have mercy on me, Lord, for I am
 in distress.
 Tears blur my eyes.
 My body and soul are withering away.
¹⁰ I am dying from grief;
 my years are shortened by sadness.
 Sin has drained my strength;
 I am wasting away from within.
¹¹ I am scorned by all my enemies
 and despised by my neighbors—
 even my friends are afraid to come
 near me.
 When they see me on the street,
 they run the other way.
¹² I am ignored as if I were dead,
 as if I were a broken pot.
¹³ I have heard the many rumors
 about me,
 and I am surrounded by terror.
 My enemies conspire against me,
 plotting to take my life.

¹⁴ But I am trusting you, O Lord,
 saying, "You are my God!"
¹⁵ My future is in your hands.
 Rescue me from those who hunt me
 down relentlessly.
¹⁶ Let your favor shine on your servant.
 In your unfailing love, rescue me.
¹⁷ Don't let me be disgraced, O Lord,
 for I call out to you for help.
 Let the wicked be disgraced;
 let them lie silent in the grave.*
¹⁸ Silence their lying lips—
 those proud and arrogant lips that
 accuse the godly.

**30:3** Hebrew *from Sheol.*    **31:17** Hebrew *in Sheol.*

¹⁹ How great is the goodness
    you have stored up for those who
        fear you.
You lavish it on those who come to you
    for protection,
        blessing them before the watching
        world.
²⁰ You hide them in the shelter of your
        presence,
    safe from those who conspire against
        them.
You shelter them in your presence,
    far from accusing tongues.

²¹ Praise the LORD,
    for he has shown me the wonders of
        his unfailing love.
He kept me safe when my city was
    under attack.
²² In panic I cried out,
    "I am cut off from the LORD!"
But you heard my cry for mercy
    and answered my call for help.

²³ Love the LORD, all you godly ones!
    For the LORD protects those who are
        loyal to him,
    but he harshly punishes the arrogant.
²⁴ So be strong and courageous,
    all you who put your hope in the LORD!

## PSALM 32
*A psalm\* of David.*

¹ Oh, what joy for those
    whose disobedience is forgiven,
    whose sin is put out of sight!
² Yes, what joy for those
    whose record the LORD has cleared
        of guilt,\*
    whose lives are lived in complete
        honesty!
³ When I refused to confess my sin,
    my body wasted away,
    and I groaned all day long.
⁴ Day and night your hand of discipline
    was heavy on me.
My strength evaporated like water in
    the summer heat.        *Interlude*

⁵ Finally, I confessed all my sins to you
    and stopped trying to hide my guilt.

## COME a little bit closer
READ PSALM 27:8

Have you heard the voice of God lately? Don't expect it to sound like the deep bass voice Charlton Heston heard as he portrayed Moses in *The Ten Commandments* movie. It's more likely it won't be an audible sound at all, but more of a whispering in your mind or a tugging at your heart.

Whoever you are, wherever you are—whatever you've done or *not* done—the Lord is calling you. He's calling you closer to Himself. More than anything, He wants to have a more intimate relationship with you. Will you respond as David did? "LORD, I am coming."

It's your move.

I said to myself, "I will confess my
    rebellion to the LORD."
And you forgave me! All my guilt
    is gone.        *Interlude*

⁶ Therefore, let all the godly pray to you
    while there is still time,
    that they may not drown in the
        floodwaters of judgment.
⁷ For you are my hiding place;
    you protect me from trouble.
    You surround me with songs of victory.
        *Interlude*

⁸ The LORD says, "I will guide you along the
    best pathway for your life.
    I will advise you and watch over you.
⁹ Do not be like a senseless horse or mule
    that needs a bit and bridle to keep it
        under control."

¹⁰ Many sorrows come to the wicked,
    but unfailing love surrounds those
        who trust the LORD.
¹¹ So rejoice in the LORD and be glad, all you
    who obey him!
Shout for joy, all you whose hearts
    are pure!

## PSALM 33
¹ Let the godly sing for joy to the LORD;
    it is fitting for the pure to praise him.

---

**32:TITLE** Hebrew *maskil*. This may be a literary or musical term.    **32:2** Greek version reads *of sin.* Compare Rom 4:7.

2 Praise the Lord with melodies on the
    lyre;
    make music for him on the ten-
        stringed harp.
3 Sing a new song of praise to him;
    play skillfully on the harp, and sing
        with joy.
4 For the word of the Lord holds true,
    and we can trust everything he does.
5 He loves whatever is just and good;
    the unfailing love of the Lord fills
        the earth.

6 The Lord merely spoke,
    and the heavens were created.
  He breathed the word,
    and all the stars were born.
7 He assigned the sea its boundaries
    and locked the oceans in vast
        reservoirs.
8 Let the whole world fear the Lord,
    and let everyone stand in awe of him.
9 For when he spoke, the world began!
    It appeared at his command.

10 The Lord frustrates the plans of the
        nations
    and thwarts all their schemes.
11 But the Lord's plans stand firm forever;
    his intentions can never be shaken.

12 What joy for the nation whose God is
        the Lord,
    whose people he has chosen as his
        inheritance.

13 The Lord looks down from heaven
    and sees the whole human race.
14 From his throne he observes
    all who live on the earth.
15 He made their hearts,
    so he understands everything they do.
16 The best-equipped army cannot save
        a king,
    nor is great strength enough to save
        a warrior.
17 Don't count on your warhorse to give you
        victory—
    for all its strength, it cannot save you.

18 But the Lord watches over those who
        fear him,
    those who rely on his unfailing love.

19 He rescues them from death
    and keeps them alive in times of
        famine.

20 We put our hope in the Lord.
    He is our help and our shield.
21 In him our hearts rejoice,
    for we trust in his holy name.
22 Let your unfailing love surround us, Lord,
    for our hope is in you alone.

## PSALM 34*

*A psalm of David, regarding the time he
pretended to be insane in front of Abimelech,
who sent him away.*

1 I will praise the Lord at all times.
    I will constantly speak his praises.
2 I will boast only in the Lord;
    let all who are helpless take heart.
3 Come, let us tell of the Lord's greatness;
    let us exalt his name together.

4 I prayed to the Lord, and he answered me.
    He freed me from all my fears.
5 Those who look to him for help will be
        radiant with joy;
    no shadow of shame will darken their
        faces.
6 In my desperation I prayed, and the Lord
        listened;
    he saved me from all my troubles.
7 For the angel of the Lord is a guard;
    he surrounds and defends all who fear
        him.

8 Taste and see that the Lord is good.
    Oh, the joys of those who take refuge
        in him!
9 Fear the Lord, you his godly people,
    for those who fear him will have all
        they need.
10 Even strong young lions sometimes go
        hungry,
    but those who trust in the Lord will
        lack no good thing.

11 Come, my children, and listen to me,
    and I will teach you to fear the Lord.
12 Does anyone want to live a life
    that is long and prosperous?
13 Then keep your tongue from speaking
        evil
    and your lips from telling lies!

**34** This psalm is a Hebrew acrostic poem; each verse begins with a successive letter of the Hebrew alphabet.

¹⁴ Turn away from evil and do good.
Search for peace, and work to
maintain it.

**15** The eyes of the LORD watch over those
who do right;
his ears are open to their cries for help.
¹⁶ But the LORD turns his face against those
who do evil;
he will erase their memory from the
earth.
¹⁷ The LORD hears his people when they call
to him for help.
He rescues them from all their
troubles.
¹⁸ The LORD is close to the brokenhearted;
he rescues those whose spirits are
crushed.

¹⁹ The righteous person faces many
troubles,
but the LORD comes to the rescue each
time.
²⁰ For the LORD protects the bones of the
righteous;
not one of them is broken!

²¹ Calamity will surely overtake the wicked,
and those who hate the righteous will
be punished.
²² But the LORD will redeem those who
serve him.
No one who takes refuge in him will be
condemned.

## PSALM 35
*A psalm of David.*

¹ O LORD, oppose those who oppose me.
Fight those who fight against me.
² Put on your armor, and take up your
shield.
Prepare for battle, and come to my aid.
³ Lift up your spear and javelin
against those who pursue me.
Let me hear you say,
"I will give you victory!"
⁴ Bring shame and disgrace on those trying
to kill me;
turn them back and humiliate those
who want to harm me.
⁵ Blow them away like chaff in the wind—
a wind sent by the angel of the LORD.
⁶ Make their path dark and slippery,

with the angel of the LORD pursuing
them.
⁷ I did them no wrong, but they laid a trap
for me.
I did them no wrong, but they dug a pit
to catch me.
⁸ So let sudden ruin come upon them!
Let them be caught in the trap they set
for me!
Let them be destroyed in the pit they
dug for me.

⁹ Then I will rejoice in the LORD.
I will be glad because he rescues me.
¹⁰ With every bone in my body I will praise
him:
"LORD, who can compare with you?
Who else rescues the helpless from the
strong?
Who else protects the helpless and
poor from those who rob them?"

¹¹ Malicious witnesses testify against me.
They accuse me of crimes I know
nothing about.
¹² They repay me evil for good.
I am sick with despair.
¹³ Yet when they were ill, I grieved for them.
I denied myself by fasting for them,
but my prayers returned unanswered.
¹⁴ I was sad, as though they were my friends
or family,
as if I were grieving for my own
mother.
¹⁵ But they are glad now that I am in
trouble;
they gleefully join together
against me.
I am attacked by people I don't even
know;
they slander me constantly.
¹⁶ They mock me and call me names;
they snarl at me.

¹⁷ How long, O Lord, will you look on and
do nothing?
Rescue me from their fierce attacks.
Protect my life from these lions!
¹⁸ Then I will thank you in front of the great
assembly.
I will praise you before all the people.
¹⁹ Don't let my treacherous enemies rejoice
over my defeat.

Don't let those who hate me without
cause gloat over my sorrow.
20 They don't talk of peace;
they plot against innocent people who
mind their own business.
21 They shout, "Aha! Aha!
With our own eyes we saw him do it!"

22 O Lord, you know all about this.
Do not stay silent.
Do not abandon me now, O Lord.
23 Wake up! Rise to my defense!
Take up my case, my God and my Lord.
24 Declare me not guilty, O Lord my God,
for you give justice.
Don't let my enemies laugh about me
in my troubles.
25 Don't let them say, "Look, we got what we
wanted!
Now we will eat him alive!"

26 May those who rejoice at my troubles
be humiliated and disgraced.
May those who triumph over me
be covered with shame and dishonor.
27 But give great joy to those who came to
my defense.
Let them continually say, "Great is the
Lord,
who delights in blessing his servant
with peace!"
28 Then I will proclaim your justice,
and I will praise you all day long.

## PSALM 36
*For the choir director: A psalm of David, the
servant of the LORD.*

1 Sin whispers to the wicked, deep within
their hearts.
They have no fear of God at all.
2 In their blind conceit,
they cannot see how wicked they
really are.
3 Everything they say is crooked and
deceitful.
They refuse to act wisely or do good.
4 They lie awake at night, hatching
sinful plots.
Their actions are never good.
They make no attempt to turn
from evil.

5 Your unfailing love, O Lord, is as vast
as the heavens;
your faithfulness reaches beyond
the clouds.
6 Your righteousness is like the mighty
mountains,
your justice like the ocean depths.
You care for people and animals alike,
O Lord.
7 How precious is your unfailing love,
O God!
All humanity finds shelter
in the shadow of your wings.
8 You feed them from the abundance
of your own house,
letting them drink from your river
of delights.
9 For you are the fountain of life,
the light by which we see.

10 Pour out your unfailing love on those
who love you;
give justice to those with honest
hearts.
11 Don't let the proud trample me
or the wicked push me around.
12 Look! Those who do evil have fallen!
They are thrown down, never to rise
again.

## PSALM 37*
*A psalm of David.*

1 Don't worry about the wicked
or envy those who do wrong.
2 For like grass, they soon fade away.
Like spring flowers, they soon
wither.

3 Trust in the Lord and do good.
Then you will live safely in the land
and prosper.
4 Take delight in the Lord,
and he will give you your heart's
desires.

5 Commit everything you do to the Lord.
Trust him, and he will help you.
6 He will make your innocence radiate like
the dawn,
and the justice of your cause will shine
like the noonday sun.

---

**37** This psalm is a Hebrew acrostic poem; each stanza begins with a successive letter of the Hebrew alphabet.

7 Be still in the presence of the LORD,
   and wait patiently for him to act.
Don't worry about evil people who
      prosper
   or fret about their wicked schemes.

8 Stop being angry!
   Turn from your rage!
Do not lose your temper—
   it only leads to harm.
9 For the wicked will be destroyed,
   but those who trust in the LORD will
      possess the land.

10 Soon the wicked will disappear.
   Though you look for them, they will be
      gone.
11 The lowly will possess the land
   and will live in peace and prosperity.

12 The wicked plot against the godly;
   they snarl at them in defiance.
13 But the Lord just laughs,
   for he sees their day of judgment
      coming.

14 The wicked draw their swords
   and string their bows
to kill the poor and the oppressed,
   to slaughter those who do right.
15 But their swords will stab their own
      hearts,
   and their bows will be broken.

16 It is better to be godly and have little
   than to be evil and rich.
17 For the strength of the wicked will be
      shattered,
   but the LORD takes care of the godly.

18 Day by day the LORD takes care of the
      innocent,
   and they will receive an inheritance
      that lasts forever.
19 They will not be disgraced in hard times;
   even in famine they will have more
      than enough.

20 But the wicked will die.
   The LORD's enemies are like flowers
      in a field—
   they will disappear like smoke.

21 The wicked borrow and never repay,
   but the godly are generous givers.

22 Those the LORD blesses will possess
      the land,
   but those he curses will die.

23 The LORD directs the steps of the godly.
   He delights in every detail of their
      lives.
24 Though they stumble, they will never fall,
   for the LORD holds them by the hand.

25 Once I was young, and now I am old.
   Yet I have never seen the godly
      abandoned
   or their children begging for bread.
26 The godly always give generous loans
      to others,
   and their children are a blessing.

27 Turn from evil and do good,
   and you will live in the land forever.
28 For the LORD loves justice,
   and he will never abandon the godly.

   He will keep them safe forever,
   but the children of the wicked will die.
29 The godly will possess the land
   and will live there forever.

30 The godly offer good counsel;
   they teach right from wrong.
31 They have made God's law their own,
   so they will never slip from his path.

32 The wicked wait in ambush for the godly,
   looking for an excuse to kill them.

## PEACE of heart
READ PSALMS 29:11 AND 85:8

How long has it been since you felt at peace?
Maybe you can't get your mind to turn off when
you try to sleep. Perhaps you can't stop feeling
apprehensive about the future. Being at peace
seems unimaginable in your circumstances.

But it is possible to experience a peace that
doesn't even make sense in the midst of difficult
situations. God's peace is that kind of a supernatural peace. It goes beyond our human understanding. But it happens. And it can be yours today.

The psalmist says that God blesses His people
with both strength and peace. Tell your Father you
need Him to speak His peace to your heart today.

<sup>33</sup> But the Lord will not let the wicked
succeed
   or let the godly be condemned when
they are put on trial.

<sup>34</sup> Put your hope in the Lord.
   Travel steadily along his path.
He will honor you by giving you the land.
You will see the wicked destroyed.

<sup>35</sup> I have seen wicked and ruthless people
flourishing like a tree in its native soil.
<sup>36</sup> But when I looked again, they were
gone!
   Though I searched for them, I could
not find them!

<sup>37</sup> Look at those who are honest and good,
for a wonderful future awaits those
who love peace.
<sup>38</sup> But the rebellious will be destroyed;
they have no future.

<sup>39</sup> The Lord rescues the godly;
   he is their fortress in times of trouble.
<sup>40</sup> The Lord helps them,
rescuing them from the wicked.
He saves them,
   and they find shelter in him.

## PSALM 38
*A psalm of David, asking God to remember
him.*

<sup>1</sup> O Lord, don't rebuke me in your anger
or discipline me in your rage!
<sup>2</sup> Your arrows have struck deep,
and your blows are crushing me.
<sup>3</sup> Because of your anger, my whole body
is sick;
   my health is broken because of my
sins.
<sup>4</sup> My guilt overwhelms me—
it is a burden too heavy to bear.
<sup>5</sup> My wounds fester and stink
because of my foolish sins.
<sup>6</sup> I am bent over and racked with pain.
All day long I walk around filled with
grief.
<sup>7</sup> A raging fever burns within me,
and my health is broken.
<sup>8</sup> I am exhausted and completely crushed.
My groans come from an anguished
heart.

<sup>9</sup> You know what I long for, Lord;
you hear my every sigh.
<sup>10</sup> My heart beats wildly, my strength fails,
and I am going blind.
<sup>11</sup> My loved ones and friends stay away,
fearing my disease.
   Even my own family stands at
a distance.
<sup>12</sup> Meanwhile, my enemies lay traps
to kill me.
   Those who wish me harm make plans
to ruin me.
   All day long they plan their treachery.

<sup>13</sup> But I am deaf to all their threats.
I am silent before them as one who
cannot speak.
<sup>14</sup> I choose to hear nothing,
and I make no reply.
<sup>15</sup> For I am waiting for you, O Lord.
You must answer for me, O Lord
my God.
<sup>16</sup> I prayed, "Don't let my enemies gloat
over me
   or rejoice at my downfall."

<sup>17</sup> I am on the verge of collapse,
facing constant pain.
<sup>18</sup> But I confess my sins;
I am deeply sorry for what I have done.
<sup>19</sup> I have many aggressive enemies;
they hate me without reason.
<sup>20</sup> They repay me evil for good
and oppose me for pursuing good.
<sup>21</sup> Do not abandon me, O Lord.
Do not stand at a distance, my God.
<sup>22</sup> Come quickly to help me,
O Lord my savior.

## PSALM 39
*For Jeduthun, the choir director: A psalm
of David.*

<sup>1</sup> I said to myself, "I will watch what I do
and not sin in what I say.
I will hold my tongue
when the ungodly are around me."
<sup>2</sup> But as I stood there in silence—
not even speaking of good things—
the turmoil within me grew worse.
<sup>3</sup> The more I thought about it,
the hotter I got,
igniting a fire of words:

⁴ "LORD, remind me how brief my time on
    earth will be.
  Remind me that my days are
    numbered—
  how fleeting my life is.
⁵ You have made my life no longer than the
    width of my hand.
  My entire lifetime is just a moment
    to you;
  at best, each of us is but a breath."
                                        *Interlude*

⁶ We are merely moving shadows,
  and all our busy rushing ends in
    nothing.
  We heap up wealth,
    not knowing who will spend it.
⁷ And so, Lord, where do I put my hope?
  My only hope is in you.
⁸ Rescue me from my rebellion.
  Do not let fools mock me.
⁹ I am silent before you; I won't say a word,
  for my punishment is from you.
¹⁰ But please stop striking me!
  I am exhausted by the blows from
    your hand.
¹¹ When you discipline us for our sins,
  you consume like a moth what is
    precious to us.
  Each of us is but a breath.     *Interlude*

¹² Hear my prayer, O LORD!
  Listen to my cries for help!
  Don't ignore my tears.
  For I am your guest—
    a traveler passing through,
  as my ancestors were before me.
¹³ Leave me alone so I can smile again
  before I am gone and exist no more.

♦ PSALM 40
*For the choir director: A psalm of David.*

  ¹ I waited patiently for the LORD to
      help me,
    and he turned to me and heard my cry.
  ² He lifted me out of the pit of despair,
    out of the mud and the mire.
  He set my feet on solid ground
    and steadied me as I walked along.
  ³ He has given me a new song to sing,
    a hymn of praise to our God.

Many will see what he has done and be
    amazed.
  They will put their trust in the LORD.

⁴ Oh, the joys of those who trust the LORD,
  who have no confidence in the proud
  or in those who worship idols.
⁵ O LORD my God, you have performed
    many wonders for us.
  Your plans for us are too numerous
    to list.
  You have no equal.
  If I tried to recite all your wonderful
    deeds,
  I would never come to the end
    of them.

⁶ You take no delight in sacrifices or
    offerings.
  Now that you have made me listen,
    I finally understand*—
  you don't require burnt offerings or
    sin offerings.
⁷ Then I said, "Look, I have come.
  As is written about me in the
    Scriptures:
⁸ I take joy in doing your will,
    my God,
  for your instructions are written
    on my heart."

⁹ I have told all your people about your
    justice.
  I have not been afraid to speak out,
    as you, O LORD, well know.
¹⁰ I have not kept the good news of your
    justice hidden in my heart;
  I have talked about your faithfulness
    and saving power.
  I have told everyone in the great
    assembly
  of your unfailing love and
    faithfulness.

¹¹ LORD, don't hold back your tender
    mercies from me.
  Let your unfailing love and
    faithfulness always protect me.
¹² For troubles surround me—
    too many to count!
  My sins pile up so high
    I can't see my way out.

**40:6** Greek text reads *You have given me a body.* Compare Heb 10:5.

They outnumber the hairs on my head.
I have lost all courage.

13 Please, LORD, rescue me!
Come quickly, LORD, and help me.
14 May those who try to destroy me
be humiliated and put to shame.
May those who take delight in my
trouble
be turned back in disgrace.
15 Let them be horrified by their shame,
for they said, "Aha! We've got him
now!"

16 But may all who search for you
be filled with joy and gladness in you.
May those who love your salvation
repeatedly shout, "The LORD is
great!"
17 As for me, since I am poor and needy,
let the Lord keep me in his thoughts.
You are my helper and my savior.
O my God, do not delay.

## PSALM 41
*For the choir director: A psalm of David.*

1 Oh, the joys of those who are kind to the
poor!
The LORD rescues them when they are
in trouble.
2 The LORD protects them
and keeps them alive.
He gives them prosperity in the land
and rescues them from their enemies.
3 The LORD nurses them when they are
sick
and restores them to health.

4 "O LORD," I prayed, "have mercy on me.
Heal me, for I have sinned against you."
5 But my enemies say nothing but evil
about me.
"How soon will he die and be
forgotten?" they ask.
6 They visit me as if they were my
friends,
but all the while they gather gossip,
and when they leave, they spread it
everywhere.
7 All who hate me whisper about me,
imagining the worst.

8 "He has some fatal disease," they say.
"He will never get out of that bed!"
9 Even my best friend, the one I trusted
completely,
the one who shared my food, has
turned against me.

10 LORD, have mercy on me.
Make me well again, so I can pay them
back!
11 I know you are pleased with me,
for you have not let my enemies
triumph over me.
12 You have preserved my life because
I am innocent;
you have brought me into your
presence forever.

13 Praise the LORD, the God of Israel,
who lives from everlasting to
everlasting.
Amen and amen!

BOOK TWO (Psalms 42–72)

## PSALM 42
*For the choir director: A psalm\* of the
descendants of Korah.*

1 As the deer longs for streams of water,
so I long for you, O God.
2 I thirst for God, the living God.
When can I go and stand before
him?
3 Day and night I have only tears for food,
while my enemies continually taunt
me, saying,
"Where is this God of yours?"

4 My heart is breaking
as I remember how it used to be:
I walked among the crowds of
worshipers,
leading a great procession to the house
of God,
singing for joy and giving thanks
amid the sound of a great celebration!

5 Why am I discouraged?
Why is my heart so sad?
I will put my hope in God!
I will praise him again—
my Savior and 6my God!

**42:TITLE** Hebrew *maskil.* This may be a literary or musical term.

385

Now I am deeply discouraged,
but I will remember you—
even from distant Mount Hermon, the
source of the Jordan,
from the land of Mount Mizar.
7 I hear the tumult of the raging seas
as your waves and surging tides sweep
over me.
8 But each day the LORD pours his unfailing
love upon me,
and through each night I sing his songs,
praying to God who gives me life.

9 "O God my rock," I cry,
"Why have you forgotten me?
Why must I wander around in grief,
oppressed by my enemies?"
10 Their taunts break my bones.
They scoff, "Where is this God
of yours?"

11 Why am I discouraged?
Why is my heart so sad?
I will put my hope in God!
I will praise him again—
my Savior and my God!

## PSALM 43
1 Declare me innocent, O God!
Defend me against these ungodly
people.
Rescue me from these unjust liars.
2 For you are God, my only safe haven.
Why have you tossed me aside?
Why must I wander around in grief,
oppressed by my enemies?
3 Send out your light and your truth;
let them guide me.
Let them lead me to your holy
mountain,
to the place where you live.
4 There I will go to the altar of God,
to God—the source of all my joy.
I will praise you with my harp,
O God, my God!

5 Why am I discouraged?
Why is my heart so sad?
I will put my hope in God!
I will praise him again—
my Savior and my God!

# CONTROL freaks
READ PSALM 31:1-5, 14-15

Many of us would have to admit that we are
"control freaks." We like to make plans, carry
them out, and then smile at how well they went.
We like to call the shots. We'd rather tell God what
we think we need than have Him tell us. If we're
truly honest, we even may admit that it's hard to
pray for God's will because we know it may not
be the same as ours.

Illness can be a real wake-up call for us. We are
forced to realize we are *not* in control of everything.
But no matter how many (or how few) tomorrows
doctors may have told you to expect, those tomorrows are safely in God's control.

## PSALM 44
*For the choir director: A psalm\* of the
descendants of Korah.*

1 O God, we have heard it with our own
ears—
our ancestors have told us
of all you did in their day,
in days long ago:
2 You drove out the pagan nations by your
power
and gave all the land to our ancestors.
You crushed their enemies
and set our ancestors free.
3 They did not conquer the land with their
swords;
it was not their own strong arm that
gave them victory.
It was your right hand and strong arm
and the blinding light from your face
that helped them,
for you loved them.

4 You are my King and my God.
You command victories for Israel.\*
5 Only by your power can we push back
our enemies;
only in your name can we trample
our foes.
6 I do not trust in my bow;
I do not count on my sword
to save me.

44:TITLE Hebrew *maskil*. This may be a literary or musical term.   44:4 Hebrew *for Jacob*. The names "Jacob" and "Israel" are often
interchanged throughout the Old Testament, referring sometimes to the individual patriarch and sometimes to the nation.

7 You are the one who gives us victory over
  our enemies;
  you disgrace those who hate us.
8 O God, we give glory to you all day long
  and constantly praise your name.

*Interlude*

9 But now you have tossed us aside in
  dishonor.
  You no longer lead our armies to
  battle.
10 You make us retreat from our enemies
  and allow those who hate us to plunder
  our land.
11 You have butchered us like sheep
  and scattered us among the nations.
12 You sold your precious people for a
  pittance,
  making nothing on the sale.
13 You let our neighbors mock us.
  We are an object of scorn and derision
  to those around us.
14 You have made us the butt of their jokes;
  they shake their heads at us in scorn.
15 We can't escape the constant
  humiliation;
  shame is written across our faces.
16 All we hear are the taunts of our mockers.
  All we see are our vengeful enemies.

17 All this has happened though we have
  not forgotten you.
  We have not violated your covenant.
18 Our hearts have not deserted you.
  We have not strayed from your path.
19 Yet you have crushed us in the jackal's
  desert home.
  You have covered us with darkness and
  death.
20 If we had forgotten the name of our God
  or spread our hands in prayer to
  foreign gods,
21 God would surely have known it,
  for he knows the secrets of every heart.
22 But for your sake we are killed every day;
  we are being slaughtered like sheep.

23 Wake up, O Lord! Why do you sleep?
  Get up! Do not reject us forever.
24 Why do you look the other way?
  Why do you ignore our suffering and
  oppression?

25 We collapse in the dust,
  lying face down in the dirt.
26 Rise up! Help us!
  Ransom us because of your unfailing
  love.

## PSALM 45

*For the choir director: A love song to be sung
to the tune "Lilies." A psalm\* of the descendants of Korah.*

1 Beautiful words stir my heart.
  I will recite a lovely poem about
  the king,
  for my tongue is like the pen of a
  skillful poet.

2 You are the most handsome of all.
  Gracious words stream from
  your lips.
  God himself has blessed you forever.
3 Put on your sword, O mighty warrior!
  You are so glorious, so majestic!
4 In your majesty, ride out to victory,
  defending truth, humility, and justice.
  Go forth to perform awe-inspiring
  deeds!
5 Your arrows are sharp, piercing your
  enemies' hearts.
  The nations fall beneath your feet.

6 Your throne, O God,\* endures forever and
  ever.
  You rule with a scepter of justice.
7 You love justice and hate evil.
  Therefore God, your God, has anointed
  you,
  pouring out the oil of joy on you more
  than on anyone else.
8 Myrrh, aloes, and cassia perfume your
  robes.
  In ivory palaces the music of strings
  entertains you.
9 Kings' daughters are among your noble
  women.
  At your right side stands the queen,
  wearing jewelry of finest gold from
  Ophir!

10 Listen to me, O royal daughter; take to
  heart what I say.
  Forget your people and your family far
  away.

45:TITLE Hebrew *maskil*. This may be a literary or musical term.    45:6 Or *Your divine throne.*

11 For your royal husband delights in your
  beauty;
    honor him, for he is your lord.
12 The princess of Tyre* will shower you
  with gifts.
    The wealthy will beg your favor.
13 The bride, a princess, looks glorious
  in her golden gown.
14 In her beautiful robes, she is led
  to the king,
    accompanied by her bridesmaids.
15 What a joyful and enthusiastic
  procession
    as they enter the king's palace!

16 Your sons will become kings like their
  father.
    You will make them rulers over many
    lands.
17 I will bring honor to your name in every
  generation.
    Therefore, the nations will praise you
    forever and ever.

## PSALM 46
*For the choir director: A song of the
descendants of Korah, to be sung by soprano
voices.*

1 God is our refuge and strength,
  always ready to help in times
  of trouble.
2 So we will not fear when earthquakes
  come
  and the mountains crumble into the
  sea.
3 Let the oceans roar and foam.
  Let the mountains tremble as the
  waters surge!               *Interlude*

4 A river brings joy to the city of our God,
  the sacred home of the Most High.
5 God dwells in that city; it cannot be
  destroyed.
  From the very break of day, God will
  protect it.
6 The nations are in chaos,
  and their kingdoms crumble!
  God's voice thunders,
  and the earth melts!

45:12 Hebrew *The daughter of Tyre.*   46:TITLE Hebrew
*according to alamoth.*   46:7 Hebrew *of Jacob;* also in 46:11.
See note on 44:4.

7 The LORD of Heaven's Armies is here
  among us;
    the God of Israel* is our fortress.
                              *Interlude*

8 Come, see the glorious works of the
  LORD:
    See how he brings destruction upon
    the world.
9 He causes wars to end throughout the
  earth.
    He breaks the bow and snaps the
    spear;
    he burns the shields with fire.

10 "Be still, and know that I am God!
    I will be honored by every nation.
    I will be honored throughout the
    world."

11 The LORD of Heaven's Armies is here
  among us;
    the God of Israel is our fortress.
                              *Interlude*

## PSALM 47
*For the choir director: A psalm of the
descendants of Korah.*

1 Come, everyone! Clap your hands!
  Shout to God with joyful praise!
2 For the LORD Most High is awesome.
  He is the great King of all the earth.
3 He subdues the nations before us,
  putting our enemies beneath our feet.

## CAUGHT off-guard
READ PSALM 33:6-11

Your or your loved one's diagnosis may have
taken you by surprise, but we guarantee it has not
taken God by surprise.
  He is all-knowing. He is all-seeing. He is all-
powerful. He is in control of everything. He merely
spoke words to create the heavens and the stars.
He's in charge of the oceans and the seas, and He
can thwart the schemes of the nations' greatest
leaders. Nothing and no one can deter His intentions for this world.
  He's not wondering what to do next for you. He's
not scrambling to get a plan together. He saw it all
coming and He's ready, willing, and able to supply
what you need.

4 He chose the Promised Land as our
    inheritance,
   the proud possession of Jacob's
      descendants, whom he loves.
                                    *Interlude*

5 God has ascended with a mighty shout.
   The LORD has ascended with trumpets
      blaring.
6 Sing praises to God, sing praises;
   sing praises to our King, sing praises!
7 For God is the King over all the earth.
   Praise him with a psalm!
8 God reigns above the nations,
   sitting on his holy throne.
9 The rulers of the world have gathered
      together
   with the people of the God of Abraham.
   For all the kings of the earth belong
      to God.
   He is highly honored everywhere.

## PSALM 48

*A song. A psalm of the descendants of Korah.*

1 How great is the LORD,
   how deserving of praise,
 in the city of our God,
   which sits on his holy mountain!
2 It is high and magnificent;
   the whole earth rejoices to see it!
 Mount Zion, the holy mountain,*
   is the city of the great King!
3 God himself is in Jerusalem's towers,
   revealing himself as its defender.

4 The kings of the earth joined forces
   and advanced against the city.
5 But when they saw it, they were stunned;
   they were terrified and ran away.
6 They were gripped with terror
   and writhed in pain like a woman in
      labor.
7 You destroyed them like the mighty ships
      of Tarshish
   shattered by a powerful east wind.

8 We had heard of the city's glory,
   but now we have seen it ourselves—
   the city of the LORD of Heaven's Armies.
 It is the city of our God;
   he will make it safe forever.     *Interlude*

9 O God, we meditate on your unfailing
      love
   as we worship in your Temple.
10 As your name deserves, O God,
   you will be praised to the ends of the
      earth.
   Your strong right hand is filled with
      victory.
11 Let the people on Mount Zion rejoice.
   Let all the towns of Judah be glad
   because of your justice.

12 Go, inspect the city of Jerusalem.*
   Walk around and count the many
      towers.
13 Take note of the fortified walls,
   and tour all the citadels,
 that you may describe them
   to future generations.
14 For that is what God is like.
   He is our God forever and ever,
   and he will guide us until we die.

## PSALM 49

*For the choir director: A psalm of the
descendants of Korah.*

1 Listen to this, all you people!
   Pay attention, everyone in the world!
2 High and low,
   rich and poor—listen!
3 For my words are wise,
   and my thoughts are filled with
      insight.
4 I listen carefully to many proverbs
   and solve riddles with inspiration from
      a harp.

5 Why should I fear when trouble comes,
   when enemies surround me?
6 They trust in their wealth
   and boast of great riches.
7 Yet they cannot redeem themselves from
      death*
   by paying a ransom to God.
8 Redemption does not come so easily,
   for no one can ever pay enough
9 to live forever
   and never see the grave.

10 Those who are wise must finally die,
   just like the foolish and senseless,

48:2 Or *Mount Zion, in the far north;* Hebrew reads *Mount Zion, the heights of Zaphon.*     48:12 Hebrew *Zion.*     49:7 Or *no one can redeem the life of another.*

leaving all their wealth behind.
<sup>11</sup> The grave is their eternal home,
   where they will stay forever.
They may name their estates after
      themselves,
<sup>12</sup>   but their fame will not last.
   They will die, just like animals.
<sup>13</sup> This is the fate of fools,
   though they are remembered as
      being wise.*                    *Interlude*

<sup>14</sup> Like sheep, they are led to the grave,*
   where death will be their shepherd.
In the morning the godly will rule over
      them.
   Their bodies will rot in the grave,
   far from their grand estates.
<sup>15</sup> But as for me, God will redeem
      my life.
He will snatch me from the power
   of the grave.                      *Interlude*

<sup>16</sup> So don't be dismayed when the wicked
      grow rich
and their homes become ever more
      splendid.
<sup>17</sup> For when they die, they take nothing
      with them.
Their wealth will not follow them into
      the grave.
<sup>18</sup> In this life they consider themselves
      fortunate
and are applauded for their success.
<sup>19</sup> But they will die like all before them
   and never again see the light of day.
<sup>20</sup> People who boast of their wealth don't
      understand;
   they will die, just like animals.

## PSALM 50
*A psalm of Asaph.*

<sup>1</sup> The LORD, the Mighty One, is God,
   and he has spoken;
he has summoned all humanity
   from where the sun rises to where
      it sets.
<sup>2</sup> From Mount Zion, the perfection of
      beauty,
   God shines in glorious radiance.
<sup>3</sup> Our God approaches,
   and he is not silent.

Fire devours everything in his way,
   and a great storm rages around him.
<sup>4</sup> He calls on the heavens above and earth
      below
   to witness the judgment of his people.
<sup>5</sup> "Bring my faithful people to me—
   those who made a covenant with me
      by giving sacrifices."
<sup>6</sup> Then let the heavens proclaim his justice,
   for God himself will be the judge.
                                    *Interlude*

<sup>7</sup> "O my people, listen as I speak.
   Here are my charges against you,
      O Israel:
   I am God, your God!
<sup>8</sup> I have no complaint about your sacrifices
   or the burnt offerings you constantly
      offer.
<sup>9</sup> But I do not need the bulls from your
      barns
   or the goats from your pens.
<sup>10</sup> For all the animals of the forest are mine,
   and I own the cattle on a thousand
      hills.
<sup>11</sup> I know every bird on the mountains,
   and all the animals of the field are
      mine.
<sup>12</sup> If I were hungry, I would not tell you,
   for all the world is mine and everything
      in it.
<sup>13</sup> Do I eat the meat of bulls?
   Do I drink the blood of goats?
<sup>14</sup> Make thankfulness your sacrifice to God,
   and keep the vows you made to the
      Most High.
<sup>15</sup> Then call on me when you are in trouble,
   and I will rescue you,
      and you will give me glory."

<sup>16</sup> But God says to the wicked:
   "Why bother reciting my decrees
   and pretending to obey my covenant?
<sup>17</sup> For you refuse my discipline
   and treat my words like trash.
<sup>18</sup> When you see thieves, you approve of
      them,
   and you spend your time with
      adulterers.
<sup>19</sup> Your mouth is filled with wickedness,
   and your tongue is full of lies.

**49:13** The meaning of the Hebrew is uncertain.   **49:14** Hebrew *Sheol;* also in 49:14b, 15.

20 You sit around and slander your brother—
      your own mother's son.
21 While you did all this, I remained silent,
      and you thought I didn't care.
   But now I will rebuke you,
      listing all my charges against you.
22 Repent, all of you who forget me,
      or I will tear you apart,
      and no one will help you.
23 But giving thanks is a sacrifice that truly
      honors me.
   If you keep to my path,
      I will reveal to you the salvation of God."

## PSALM 51

*For the choir director: A psalm of David,*
*regarding the time Nathan the prophet came*
*to him after David had committed adultery*
*with Bathsheba.*

**1** Have mercy on me, O God,
      because of your unfailing love.
   Because of your great compassion,
      blot out the stain of my sins.
2 Wash me clean from my guilt.
      Purify me from my sin.
3 For I recognize my rebellion;
      it haunts me day and night.
4 Against you, and you alone, have I sinned;
      I have done what is evil in your sight.
   You will be proved right in what you say,
      and your judgment against me is just.*

5 For I was born a sinner—
      yes, from the moment my mother
         conceived me.
6 But you desire honesty from the
         womb,*
      teaching me wisdom even there.

**7** Purify me from my sins,* and I will be
         clean;
      wash me, and I will be whiter than
         snow.
8 Oh, give me back my joy again;
      you have broken me—
      now let me rejoice.
9 Don't keep looking at my sins.
      Remove the stain of my guilt.
10 Create in me a clean heart, O God.
      Renew a loyal spirit within me.
11 Do not banish me from your presence,
      and don't take your Holy Spirit*
         from me.

12 Restore to me the joy of your salvation,
      and make me willing to obey you.
13 Then I will teach your ways to rebels,
      and they will return to you.
14 Forgive me for shedding blood, O God
         who saves;
      then I will joyfully sing of your
         forgiveness.
15 Unseal my lips, O Lord,
      that my mouth may praise you.

51:4 Greek version reads *and you will win your case in court.* Compare Rom 3:4.    51:6 Or *from the heart;* Hebrew reads *in the*
*inward parts.*    51:7 Hebrew *Purify me with the hyssop branch.*    51:11 Or *your spirit of holiness.*

# THE PAIN of waiting

READ PSALMS 38:15; 5:3; AND 27:14

"Why does it take so long to get back my blood work?"
   "I have to wait the whole weekend for the test results!"
   "What do you mean the doctor can't see me until next week?"
   "This waiting is killing me!"
   Most of us are not very good "wait-ers." Waiting goes against our very nature, but we can be thankful
for times we have to wait.
   *Thankful for waiting? You've got to be kidding!*
   Yes, thankful, because waiting reminds us that we are not God. We, of course, would never declare,
"I am God." But every time we get impatient, annoyed, and frustrated with waiting, we demonstrate our
need to be in charge.
   When we wait on God for answers to our prayers, it reminds us that He is in charge. Waiting forces
us to slow down and trust that He eventually will answer. It won't kill you to wait, but it may bless you.

¹⁶ You do not desire a sacrifice, or I would
offer one.
You do not want a burnt offering.
¹⁷ The sacrifice you desire is a broken spirit.
You will not reject a broken and
repentant heart, O God.
¹⁸ Look with favor on Zion and help her;
rebuild the walls of Jerusalem.
¹⁹ Then you will be pleased with sacrifices
offered in the right spirit—
with burnt offerings and whole burnt
offerings.
Then bulls will again be sacrificed
on your altar.

## PSALM 52

*For the choir director: A psalm\* of David,
regarding the time Doeg the Edomite said to
Saul, "David has gone to see Ahimelech."*

¹ Why do you boast about your crimes,
great warrior?
Don't you realize God's justice
continues forever?
² All day long you plot destruction.
Your tongue cuts like a sharp razor;
you're an expert at telling lies.
³ You love evil more than good
and lies more than truth.          *Interlude*

⁴ You love to destroy others with your words,
you liar!
⁵ But God will strike you down once and
for all.
He will pull you from your home
and uproot you from the land of the
living.                            *Interlude*

⁶ The righteous will see it and be amazed.
They will laugh and say,
⁷ "Look what happens to mighty warriors
who do not trust in God.
They trust their wealth instead
and grow more and more bold in their
wickedness."

⁸ But I am like an olive tree, thriving in the
house of God.
I will always trust in God's unfailing
love.
⁹ I will praise you forever, O God,
for what you have done.

I will trust in your good name
in the presence of your faithful people.

## PSALM 53

*For the choir director: A meditation; a psalm\*
of David.*

¹ Only fools say in their hearts,
"There is no God."
They are corrupt, and their actions
are evil;
not one of them does good!

² God looks down from heaven
on the entire human race;
he looks to see if anyone is truly wise,
if anyone seeks God.
³ But no, all have turned away;
all have become corrupt.\*
No one does good,
not a single one!

⁴ Will those who do evil never learn?
They eat up my people like bread
and wouldn't think of praying to God.
⁵ Terror will grip them,
terror like they have never known
before.
God will scatter the bones of your
enemies.
You will put them to shame, for God
has rejected them.

⁶ Who will come from Mount Zion to
rescue Israel?
When God restores his people,
Jacob will shout with joy, and Israel
will rejoice.

## PSALM 54

*For the choir director: A psalm\* of David,
regarding the time the Ziphites came and said
to Saul, "We know where David is hiding." To
be accompanied by stringed instruments.*

¹ Come with great power, O God, and
rescue me!
Defend me with your might.
² Listen to my prayer, O God.
Pay attention to my plea.
³ For strangers are attacking me;
violent people are trying to kill me.
They care nothing for God.     *Interlude*

**52:TITLE** Hebrew *maskil*. This may be a literary or musical term.    **53:TITLE** Hebrew *maskil*. This may be a literary or musical term.
**53:3** Greek version reads *have become useless*. Compare Rom 3:12.    **54:TITLE** Hebrew *maskil*. This may be a literary or musical term.

4 But God is my helper.
   The Lord keeps me alive!
5 May the evil plans of my enemies be
      turned against them.
   Do as you promised and put an end
      to them.

6 I will sacrifice a voluntary offering to you;
   I will praise your name, O Lord,
      for it is good.
7 For you have rescued me from my
      troubles
   and helped me to triumph over my
      enemies.

## PSALM 55
*For the choir director: A psalm\* of David, to
be accompanied by stringed instruments.*

1 Listen to my prayer, O God.
   Do not ignore my cry for help!
2 Please listen and answer me,
   for I am overwhelmed by my troubles.
3 My enemies shout at me,
      making loud and wicked threats.
   They bring trouble on me
   and angrily hunt me down.

4 My heart pounds in my chest.
   The terror of death assaults me.
5 Fear and trembling overwhelm me,
   and I can't stop shaking.
6 Oh, that I had wings like a dove;
   then I would fly away and rest!
7 I would fly far away
   to the quiet of the wilderness.
                                          *Interlude*
8 How quickly I would escape—
   far from this wild storm of hatred.

9 Confuse them, Lord, and frustrate their
      plans,
   for I see violence and conflict in the
      city.
10 Its walls are patrolled day and night
      against invaders,
   but the real danger is wickedness
      within the city.
11 Everything is falling apart;
   threats and cheating are rampant
      in the streets.

12 It is not an enemy who taunts me—
   I could bear that.

It is not my foes who so arrogantly insult
      me—
   I could have hidden from them.
13 Instead, it is you—my equal,
   my companion and close friend.
14 What good fellowship we once enjoyed
   as we walked together to the house
      of God.

15 Let death stalk my enemies;
   let the grave\* swallow them alive,
   for evil makes its home within them.

16 But I will call on God,
   and the Lord will rescue me.
17 Morning, noon, and night
   I cry out in my distress,
   and the Lord hears my voice.
18 He ransoms me and keeps me safe
   from the battle waged against me,
   though many still oppose me.
19 God, who has ruled forever,
   will hear me and humble them.
                                          *Interlude*
   For my enemies refuse to change their
      ways;
   they do not fear God.

20 As for my companion, he betrayed his
      friends;
   he broke his promises.
21 His words are as smooth as butter,
   but in his heart is war.
   His words are as soothing as lotion,
   but underneath are daggers!

22 Give your burdens to the Lord,
   and he will take care of you.
   He will not permit the godly to slip and
      fall.

23 But you, O God, will send the wicked
   down to the pit of destruction.
   Murderers and liars will die young,
   but I am trusting you to save me.

## PSALM 56
*For the choir director: A psalm of David,
regarding the time the Philistines seized him
in Gath. To be sung to the tune "Dove on
Distant Oaks."*

1 O God, have mercy on me,
   for people are hounding me.

---

55:TITLE Hebrew *maskil*. This may be a literary or musical term.   55:15 Hebrew *let Sheol*.

My foes attack me all day long.
2 I am constantly hounded by those who
slander me,
and many are boldly attacking me.
3 But when I am afraid,
I will put my trust in you.
4 I praise God for what he has promised.
I trust in God, so why should I be
afraid?
What can mere mortals do to me?

5 They are always twisting what I say;
they spend their days plotting to
harm me.
6 They come together to spy on me—
watching my every step, eager to
kill me.
7 Don't let them get away with their
wickedness;
in your anger, O God, bring them down.

8 You keep track of all my sorrows.*
You have collected all my tears in your
bottle.
You have recorded each one in your
book.

9 My enemies will retreat when I call to you
for help.
This I know: God is on my side!
10 I praise God for what he has promised;
Yes, I praise the LORD for what he has
promised.
11 I trust in God, so why should I be afraid?
What can mere mortals do to me?

12 I will fulfill my vows to you, O God,
and will offer a sacrifice of thanks for
your help.
13 For you have rescued me from death;
you have kept my feet from slipping.
So now I can walk in your presence,
O God,
in your life-giving light.

- PSALM 57
*For the choir director: A psalm of David,
regarding the time he fled from Saul and went
into the cave. To be sung to the tune "Do Not
Destroy!"*

1 Have mercy on me, O God, have mercy!
I look to you for protection.

56:8 Or *my wanderings.*  57:2 Hebrew *El-Elyon.*

## A CRISIS opportunity
READ PSALM 40:1-3

Even though it's only a popular myth that the
Chinese character for "crisis" is a combination of
the symbols "danger" and "opportunity," this psalm
shows how your health crisis *can* be an opportunity
for others to see God at work in your life and be
inspired to trust Him, too.
   Most of us would rather not be an "inspiration"
if it requires any pain on our part! But when painful
times come, they're the perfect crisis-opportunity
for others to be amazed at God's work in us. It's
not just physically healed people who inspire others
to trust in God, but it's also those who sing a new
song of praise to God *in spite of* their circumstances. Your crisis is His opportunity.

I will hide beneath the shadow of your
wings
until the danger passes by.
2 I cry out to God Most High,*
to God who will fulfill his purpose
for me.
3 He will send help from heaven to
rescue me,
disgracing those who hound me.
                                    *Interlude*
My God will send forth his unfailing love
and faithfulness.

4 I am surrounded by fierce lions
who greedily devour human prey—
whose teeth pierce like spears and arrows,
and whose tongues cut like swords.

5 Be exalted, O God, above the highest
heavens!
May your glory shine over all the earth.

6 My enemies have set a trap for me.
I am weary from distress.
They have dug a deep pit in my path,
but they themselves have fallen into it.
                                    *Interlude*

7 My heart is confident in you, O God;
my heart is confident.
No wonder I can sing your praises!
8 Wake up, my heart!
Wake up, O lyre and harp!

I will wake the dawn with my song.
⁹ I will thank you, Lord, among all the
people.
I will sing your praises among the
nations.
¹⁰ For your unfailing love is as high as the
heavens.
Your faithfulness reaches to the clouds.

¹¹ Be exalted, O God, above the highest
heavens.
May your glory shine over all the earth.

## PSALM 58

*For the choir director: A psalm of David, to be
sung to the tune "Do Not Destroy!"*

¹ Justice—do you rulers* know the
meaning of the word?
Do you judge the people fairly?
² No! You plot injustice in your hearts.
You spread violence throughout the
land.
³ These wicked people are born sinners;
even from birth they have lied and
gone their own way.
⁴ They spit venom like deadly snakes;
they are like cobras that refuse to listen,
⁵ ignoring the tunes of the snake charmers,
no matter how skillfully they play.

⁶ Break off their fangs, O God!
Smash the jaws of these lions, O LORD!
⁷ May they disappear like water into thirsty
ground.
Make their weapons useless in their
hands.*
⁸ May they be like snails that dissolve into
slime,
like a stillborn child who will never see
the sun.
⁹ God will sweep them away, both young
and old,
faster than a pot heats over burning
thorns.

¹⁰ The godly will rejoice when they see
injustice avenged.
They will wash their feet in the blood
of the wicked.
¹¹ Then at last everyone will say,
"There truly is a reward for those who
live for God;

surely there is a God who judges justly
here on earth."

## PSALM 59

*For the choir director: A psalm of David,
regarding the time Saul sent soldiers to
watch David's house in order to kill him.
To be sung to the tune "Do Not Destroy!"*

¹ Rescue me from my enemies, O God.
Protect me from those who have come
to destroy me.
² Rescue me from these criminals;
save me from these murderers.
³ They have set an ambush for me.
Fierce enemies are out there waiting,
LORD,
though I have not sinned or offended
them.
⁴ I have done nothing wrong,
yet they prepare to attack me.
Wake up! See what is happening and
help me!
⁵ O LORD God of Heaven's Armies, the God
of Israel,
wake up and punish those hostile
nations.
Show no mercy to wicked traitors.
*Interlude*

⁶ They come out at night,
snarling like vicious dogs
as they prowl the streets.
⁷ Listen to the filth that comes from
their mouths;
their words cut like swords.
"After all, who can hear us?" they sneer.
⁸ But LORD, you laugh at them.
You scoff at all the hostile nations.
⁹ You are my strength; I wait for you to
rescue me,
for you, O God, are my fortress.
¹⁰ In his unfailing love, my God will stand
with me.
He will let me look down in triumph
on all my enemies.

¹¹ Don't kill them, for my people soon
forget such lessons;
stagger them with your power, and
bring them to their knees,
O Lord our shield.
¹² Because of the sinful things they say,

---

**58:1** Or *you gods.*   **58:7** Or *Let them be trodden down and wither like grass.* The meaning of the Hebrew is uncertain.

because of the evil that is on their lips,
let them be captured by their pride,
their curses, and their lies.
13 Destroy them in your anger!
Wipe them out completely!
Then the whole world will know
that God reigns in Israel.*     *Interlude*

14 My enemies come out at night,
snarling like vicious dogs
as they prowl the streets.
15 They scavenge for food
but go to sleep unsatisfied.*

16 But as for me, I will sing about your power.
Each morning I will sing with joy about
your unfailing love.
For you have been my refuge,
a place of safety when I am in distress.
17 O my Strength, to you I sing praises,
for you, O God, are my refuge,
the God who shows me unfailing love.

## PSALM 60
*For the choir director: A psalm of David*
*useful for teaching, regarding the time David*
*fought Aram-naharaim and Aram-zobah, and*
*Joab returned and killed 12,000 Edomites in*
*the Valley of Salt. To be sung to the tune "Lily*
*of the Testimony."*

1 You have rejected us, O God, and broken
our defenses.
You have been angry with us; now
restore us to your favor.
2 You have shaken our land and split it
open.
Seal the cracks, for the land trembles.
3 You have been very hard on us,
making us drink wine that sent us
reeling.
4 But you have raised a banner for those
who fear you—
a rallying point in the face of attack.
*Interlude*

5 Now rescue your beloved people.
Answer and save us by your power.
6 God has promised this by his holiness*:
"I will divide up Shechem with joy.
I will measure out the valley of Succoth.
7 Gilead is mine,
and Manasseh, too.

Ephraim, my helmet, will produce my
warriors,
and Judah, my scepter, will produce
my kings.
8 But Moab, my washbasin, will become
my servant,
and I will wipe my feet on Edom
and shout in triumph over Philistia."

9 Who will bring me into the fortified
city?
Who will bring me victory over Edom?
10 Have you rejected us, O God?
Will you no longer march with our
armies?
11 Oh, please help us against our
enemies,
for all human help is useless.
12 With God's help we will do mighty
things,
for he will trample down our foes.

## PSALM 61
*For the choir director: A psalm of David, to be*
*accompanied by stringed instruments.*

1 O God, listen to my cry!
Hear my prayer!
2 From the ends of the earth,
I cry to you for help
when my heart is overwhelmed.
Lead me to the towering rock of safety,
3     for you are my safe refuge,
a fortress where my enemies cannot
reach me.
4 Let me live forever in your sanctuary,
safe beneath the shelter of your wings!
*Interlude*

5 For you have heard my vows, O God.
You have given me an inheritance
reserved for those who fear your
name.
6 Add many years to the life of the king!
May his years span the generations!
7 May he reign under God's protection
forever.
May your unfailing love and
faithfulness watch over him.
8 Then I will sing praises to your name
forever
as I fulfill my vows each day.

59:13 Hebrew *in Jacob.* See note on 44:4.    59:15 Or *and growl if they don't get enough.*    60:6 Or *in his sanctuary.*

## PSALM 62

*For Jeduthun, the choir director: A psalm
of David.*

¹ I wait quietly before God,
for my victory comes from him.
² He alone is my rock and my salvation,
my fortress where I will never be shaken.

³ So many enemies against one man—
all of them trying to kill me.
To them I'm just a broken-down wall
or a tottering fence.
⁴ They plan to topple me from my high
position.
They delight in telling lies about me.
They praise me to my face
but curse me in their hearts.  *Interlude*

⁵ Let all that I am wait quietly before God,
for my hope is in him.
⁶ He alone is my rock and my salvation,
my fortress where I will not be shaken.
⁷ My victory and honor come from God
alone.
He is my refuge, a rock where no
enemy can reach me.
⁸ O my people, trust in him at all times.
Pour out your heart to him,
for God is our refuge.          *Interlude*

⁹ Common people are as worthless as a
puff of wind,
and the powerful are not what they
appear to be.
If you weigh them on the scales,
together they are lighter than a breath
of air.

¹⁰ Don't make your living by extortion
or put your hope in stealing.
And if your wealth increases,
don't make it the center of your life.

¹¹ God has spoken plainly,
and I have heard it many times:
Power, O God, belongs to you;
¹² unfailing love, O Lord, is yours.
Surely you repay all people
according to what they have done.

## PSALM 63

*A psalm of David, regarding a time when
David was in the wilderness of Judah.*

¹ O God, you are my God;
I earnestly search for you.
My soul thirsts for you;
my whole body longs for you
in this parched and weary land
where there is no water.
² I have seen you in your sanctuary
and gazed upon your power and glory.
³ Your unfailing love is better than life
itself;
how I praise you!
⁴ I will praise you as long as I live,
lifting up my hands to you in prayer.
⁵ You satisfy me more than the richest
feast.
I will praise you with songs of joy.

⁶ I lie awake thinking of you,
meditating on you through the night.
⁷ Because you are my helper,
I sing for joy in the shadow of your
wings.
⁸ I cling to you;
your strong right hand holds me
securely.

⁹ But those plotting to destroy me will
come to ruin.
They will go down into the depths of
the earth.
¹⁰ They will die by the sword
and become the food of jackals.
¹¹ But the king will rejoice in God.
All who trust in him will praise him,
while liars will be silenced.

## PSALM 64

*For the choir director: A psalm of David.*

¹ O God, listen to my complaint.
Protect my life from my enemies'
threats.
² Hide me from the plots of this evil mob,
from this gang of wrongdoers.
³ They sharpen their tongues like
swords
and aim their bitter words like
arrows.
⁴ They shoot from ambush at the
innocent,
attacking suddenly and fearlessly.
⁵ They encourage each other to do evil
and plan how to set their traps in
secret.
"Who will ever notice?" they ask.

⁶ As they plot their crimes, they say,
   "We have devised the perfect plan!"
   Yes, the human heart and mind are
      cunning.

⁷ But God himself will shoot them with
      his arrows,
   suddenly striking them down.
⁸ Their own tongues will ruin them,
   and all who see them will shake their
      heads in scorn.
⁹ Then everyone will be afraid;
   they will proclaim the mighty acts
      of God
   and realize all the amazing things he
      does.
¹⁰ The godly will rejoice in the LORD
   and find shelter in him.
   And those who do what is right
      will praise him.

## PSALM 65
*For the choir director: A song. A psalm
of David.*

¹ What mighty praise, O God,
   belongs to you in Zion.
   We will fulfill our vows to you,
²    for you answer our prayers.
   All of us must come to you.
³ Though we are overwhelmed by our sins,
   you forgive them all.
⁴ What joy for those you choose to bring
      near,
   those who live in your holy courts.
   What festivities await us
   inside your holy Temple.

⁵ You faithfully answer our prayers with
      awesome deeds,
   O God our savior.
   You are the hope of everyone on earth,
   even those who sail on distant seas.
⁶ You formed the mountains by your
      power
   and armed yourself with mighty
      strength.
⁷ You quieted the raging oceans
   with their pounding waves
   and silenced the shouting of the
      nations.
⁸ Those who live at the ends of the earth
   stand in awe of your wonders.

From where the sun rises to where
      it sets,
   you inspire shouts of joy.

⁹ You take care of the earth and water it,
   making it rich and fertile.
   The river of God has plenty of water;
   it provides a bountiful harvest
      of grain,
   for you have ordered it so.
¹⁰ You drench the plowed ground with rain,
   melting the clods and leveling the
      ridges.
   You soften the earth with showers
   and bless its abundant crops.
¹¹ You crown the year with a bountiful
      harvest;
   even the hard pathways overflow with
      abundance.
¹² The grasslands of the wilderness become
   a lush pasture,
   and the hillsides blossom with joy.
¹³ The meadows are clothed with flocks
      of sheep,
   and the valleys are carpeted with
      grain.
   They all shout and sing for joy!

## • PSALM 66
*For the choir director: A song. A psalm.*

¹ Shout joyful praises to God, all the earth!
²    Sing about the glory of his name!
   Tell the world how glorious he is.

## NEED a superhero?
READ PSALM 46:1-3, 10

Comic book superheroes always are ready to
help those in distress, but each has a limitation.
Superman can't handle kryptonite. Daredevil can't
see. And even though the Incredible Hulk can really
jump, gravity always pulls him back to earth!

Not only is God always ready to help in times of
trouble, He also has no weakness or limitation.
Instead He is our refuge and our strength as He
either hides us from the calamity or gives us what
we need to face it head-on.

When the rug gets pulled out from underneath
your world, be still and know that your Rescuer
already is on the scene.

3 Say to God, "How awesome are your
     deeds!
   Your enemies cringe before your
     mighty power.
4 Everything on earth will worship you;
   they will sing your praises,
   shouting your name in glorious songs."
                                              *Interlude*

5 Come and see what our God has done,
   what awesome miracles he performs
     for people!
6 He made a dry path through the Red
     Sea,*
   and his people went across on foot.
   There we rejoiced in him.
7 For by his great power he rules forever.
   He watches every movement of the
     nations;
   let no rebel rise in defiance.   *Interlude*

8 Let the whole world bless our God
   and loudly sing his praises.
9 Our lives are in his hands,
   and he keeps our feet from stumbling.
10 You have tested us, O God;
   you have purified us like silver.
11 You captured us in your net
   and laid the burden of slavery on our
     backs.
12 Then you put a leader over us.*
   We went through fire and flood,
   but you brought us to a place of great
     abundance.

13 Now I come to your Temple with burnt
     offerings
   to fulfill the vows I made to you—
14 yes, the sacred vows that I made
   when I was in deep trouble.
15 That is why I am sacrificing burnt
     offerings to you—
   the best of my rams as a pleasing
     aroma,
   and a sacrifice of bulls and male goats.
                                              *Interlude*

16 Come and listen, all you who fear God,
   and I will tell you what he did for me.
17 For I cried out to him for help,
   praising him as I spoke.
18 If I had not confessed the sin in my heart,
   the Lord would not have listened.

19 But God did listen!
   He paid attention to my prayer.
20 Praise God, who did not ignore my prayer
   or withdraw his unfailing love
     from me.

## PSALM 67
*For the choir director: A song. A psalm, to be
accompanied by stringed instruments.*

1 May God be merciful and bless us.
   May his face smile with favor on us.
                                              *Interlude*

2 May your ways be known throughout the
     earth,
   your saving power among people
     everywhere.
3 May the nations praise you, O God.
   Yes, may all the nations praise you.
4 Let the whole world sing for joy,
   because you govern the nations with
     justice
   and guide the people of the whole
     world.                          *Interlude*

5 May the nations praise you, O God.
   Yes, may all the nations praise you.
6 Then the earth will yield its harvests,
   and God, our God, will richly
     bless us.
7 Yes, God will bless us,
   and people all over the world will fear
     him.

## PSALM 68
*For the choir director: A song. A psalm
of David.*

1 Rise up, O God, and scatter your enemies.
   Let those who hate God run for their
     lives.
2 Blow them away like smoke.
   Melt them like wax in a fire.
   Let the wicked perish in the presence
     of God.
3 But let the godly rejoice.
   Let them be glad in God's
     presence.
   Let them be filled with joy.
4 Sing praises to God and to his name!
   Sing loud praises to him who rides the
     clouds.

**66:6** Hebrew *the sea.*   **66:12** Or *You made people ride over our heads.*

His name is the Lord—
rejoice in his presence!

5 Father to the fatherless, defender of
widows—
this is God, whose dwelling is holy.
6 God places the lonely in families;
he sets the prisoners free and gives
them joy.
But he makes the rebellious live in
a sun-scorched land.

7 O God, when you led your people out
from Egypt,
when you marched through the dry
wasteland,                   *Interlude*
8 the earth trembled, and the heavens
poured down rain
before you, the God of Sinai,
before God, the God of Israel.
9 You sent abundant rain, O God,
to refresh the weary land.
10 There your people finally settled,
and with a bountiful harvest, O God,
you provided for your needy people.

11 The Lord gives the word,
and a great army* brings the good
news.
12 Enemy kings and their armies flee,
while the women of Israel divide the
plunder.
13 Even those who lived among the
sheepfolds found treasures—
doves with wings of silver
and feathers of gold.
14 The Almighty scattered the enemy kings
like a blowing snowstorm on Mount
Zalmon.

15 The mountains of Bashan are majestic,
with many peaks stretching high into
the sky.
16 Why do you look with envy, O rugged
mountains,
at Mount Zion, where God has chosen
to live,
where the Lord himself will live
forever?

17 Surrounded by unnumbered thousands
of chariots,

**68:11** Or *a host of women.*

## HOW many teardrops?
READ PSALM 56:8

Can you imagine all the tears you've shed in your
life? Remember the ones when your pet died, and
when your first love broke your heart? Remember
the ones when you were given the bad health
news? Don't forget those tears you let slip in the
shower so no one could see.

But someone did see. The same One who created
tears saw—and remembers—every one of yours.

Why does God collect and record all those tear-
drops? Author Joni Eareckson Tada, a quadriplegic
since 1967, says that in heaven every tear of suffering will be rewarded. "Every tear you've cried
will be redeemed," she says. "God will give you
indescribable glory for your grief."

the Lord came from Mount Sinai into
his sanctuary.
18 When you ascended to the heights,
you led a crowd of captives.
You received gifts from the people,
even from those who rebelled against
you.
Now the Lord God will live among
us there.

19 Praise the Lord; praise God our savior!
For each day he carries us in his arms.
                   *Interlude*
20 Our God is a God who saves!
The Sovereign Lord rescues us from
death.

21 But God will smash the heads of his
enemies,
crushing the skulls of those who love
their guilty ways.
22 The Lord says, "I will bring my enemies
down from Bashan;
I will bring them up from the depths
of the sea.
23 You, my people, will wash your feet in
their blood,
and even your dogs will get their share!"

24 Your procession has come into view,
O God—
the procession of my God and King as
he goes into the sanctuary.

<sup>25</sup> Singers are in front, musicians behind;
  between them are young women
    playing tambourines.
<sup>26</sup> Praise God, all you people of Israel;
  praise the LORD, the source of Israel's
    life.
<sup>27</sup> Look, the little tribe of Benjamin leads
    the way.
  Then comes a great throng of rulers
    from Judah
  and all the rulers of Zebulun and
    Naphtali.

<sup>28</sup> Summon your might, O God.
  Display your power, O God, as you have
    in the past.
<sup>29</sup> The kings of the earth are bringing
    tribute
  to your Temple in Jerusalem.
<sup>30</sup> Rebuke these enemy nations—
  these wild animals lurking in the reeds,
  this herd of bulls among the weaker
    calves.
  Make them bring bars of silver in humble
    tribute.
  Scatter the nations that delight in war.
<sup>31</sup> Let Egypt come with gifts of precious
    metals*;
  let Ethiopia* bow in submission to God.
<sup>32</sup> Sing to God, you kingdoms of the earth.
  Sing praises to the Lord.          *Interlude*
<sup>33</sup> Sing to the one who rides across the
    ancient heavens,
  his mighty voice thundering from the
    sky.
<sup>34</sup> Tell everyone about God's power.
  His majesty shines down on Israel;
  his strength is mighty in the heavens.
<sup>35</sup> God is awesome in his sanctuary.
  The God of Israel gives power and
    strength to his people.

  Praise be to God!


## PSALM 69

*For the choir director: A psalm of David, to be
sung to the tune "Lilies."*

<sup>1</sup> Save me, O God,
  for the floodwaters are up to my neck.
<sup>2</sup> Deeper and deeper I sink into the mire;
  I can't find a foothold.

I am in deep water,
  and the floods overwhelm me.
<sup>3</sup> I am exhausted from crying for help;
  my throat is parched.
My eyes are swollen with weeping,
  waiting for my God to help me.
<sup>4</sup> Those who hate me without cause
  outnumber the hairs on my head.
Many enemies try to destroy me with lies,
  demanding that I give back what
    I didn't steal.

<sup>5</sup> O God, you know how foolish I am;
  my sins cannot be hidden from you.
<sup>6</sup> Don't let those who trust in you be
    ashamed because of me,
  O Sovereign LORD of Heaven's Armies.
Don't let me cause them to be
    humiliated,
  O God of Israel.
<sup>7</sup> For I endure insults for your sake;
  humiliation is written all over my face.
<sup>8</sup> Even my own brothers pretend they don't
    know me;
  they treat me like a stranger.

<sup>9</sup> Passion for your house has
    consumed me,
  and the insults of those who insult you
    have fallen on me.
<sup>10</sup> When I weep and fast,
  they scoff at me.
<sup>11</sup> When I dress in burlap to show sorrow,
  they make fun of me.
<sup>12</sup> I am the favorite topic of town gossip,
  and all the drunks sing about me.

<sup>13</sup> But I keep praying to you, LORD,
  hoping this time you will show me
    favor.
In your unfailing love, O God,
  answer my prayer with your sure
    salvation.
<sup>14</sup> Rescue me from the mud;
  don't let me sink any deeper!
Save me from those who hate me,
  and pull me from these deep waters.
<sup>15</sup> Don't let the floods overwhelm me,
  or the deep waters swallow me,
  or the pit of death devour me.

<sup>16</sup> Answer my prayers, O LORD,
  for your unfailing love is wonderful.

**68:31a** Or *of rich cloth.*    **68:31b** Hebrew *Cush.*

Take care of me,
for your mercy is so plentiful.
17 Don't hide from your servant;
answer me quickly, for I am in deep
trouble!
18 Come and redeem me;
free me from my enemies.

19 You know of my shame, scorn, and
disgrace.
You see all that my enemies are doing.
20 Their insults have broken my heart,
and I am in despair.
If only one person would show some
pity;
if only one would turn and
comfort me.
21 But instead, they give me poison* for
food;
they offer me sour wine for my thirst.

22 Let the bountiful table set before them
become a snare
and their prosperity become a trap.*
23 Let their eyes go blind so they cannot see,
and make their bodies shake
continually.*
24 Pour out your fury on them;
consume them with your burning
anger.
25 Let their homes become desolate
and their tents be deserted.
26 To the one you have punished, they add
insult to injury;
they add to the pain of those you have
hurt.
27 Pile their sins up high,
and don't let them go free.
28 Erase their names from the Book of Life;
don't let them be counted among the
righteous.

29 I am suffering and in pain.
Rescue me, O God, by your saving
power.

30 Then I will praise God's name with
singing,
and I will honor him with thanksgiving.
31 For this will please the LORD more than
sacrificing cattle,

more than presenting a bull with its
horns and hooves.
32 The humble will see their God at work
and be glad.
Let all who seek God's help be
encouraged.
33 For the LORD hears the cries of the needy;
he does not despise his imprisoned
people.

34 Praise him, O heaven and earth,
the seas and all that move in them.
35 For God will save Jerusalem*
and rebuild the towns of Judah.
His people will live there
and settle in their own land.
36 The descendants of those who obey him
will inherit the land,
and those who love him will live there
in safety.

## PSALM 70
*For the choir director: A psalm of David,
asking God to remember him.*

1 Please, God, rescue me!
Come quickly, LORD, and help me.
2 May those who try to kill me
be humiliated and put to shame.
May those who take delight in my
trouble
be turned back in disgrace.
3 Let them be horrified by their shame,
for they said, "Aha! We've got him
now!"
4 But may all who search for you
be filled with joy and gladness
in you.
May those who love your salvation
repeatedly shout, "God is great!"
5 But as for me, I am poor and needy;
please hurry to my aid, O God.
You are my helper and my savior;
O LORD, do not delay.

## PSALM 71
1 O LORD, I have come to you for protection;
don't let me be disgraced.
2 Save me and rescue me,
for you do what is right.

---

69:21 Or *gall.*    69:22 Greek version reads *Let their bountiful table set before them become a snare, / a trap that makes them think all
is well. / Let their blessings cause them to stumble, / and let them get what they deserve.* Compare Rom 11:9.    69:23 Greek version
reads *and let their backs be bent forever.* Compare Rom 11:10.    69:35 Hebrew *Zion.*

Turn your ear to listen to me,
and set me free.
[3] Be my rock of safety
where I can always hide.
Give the order to save me,
for you are my rock and my fortress.
[4] My God, rescue me from the power
of the wicked,
from the clutches of cruel
oppressors.
[5] O Lord, you alone are my hope.
I've trusted you, O Lord, from
childhood.
[6] Yes, you have been with me from birth;
from my mother's womb you have
cared for me.
No wonder I am always praising you!

[7] My life is an example to many,
because you have been my strength
and protection.
[8] That is why I can never stop praising
you;
I declare your glory all day long.
[9] And now, in my old age, don't set me
aside.
Don't abandon me when my strength
is failing.
[10] For my enemies are whispering
against me.
They are plotting together to kill me.
[11] They say, "God has abandoned him.
Let's go and get him,
for no one will help him now."

[12] O God, don't stay away.
My God, please hurry to help me.
[13] Bring disgrace and destruction on my
accusers.
Humiliate and shame those who want
to harm me.
[14] But I will keep on hoping for your help;
I will praise you more and more.
[15] I will tell everyone about your
righteousness.
All day long I will proclaim your saving
power,
though I am not skilled with words.*
[16] I will praise your mighty deeds,
O Sovereign Lord.
I will tell everyone that you alone
are just.

[17] O God, you have taught me from my
earliest childhood,
and I constantly tell others about the
wonderful things you do.
[18] Now that I am old and gray,
do not abandon me, O God.
Let me proclaim your power to this new
generation,
your mighty miracles to all who come
after me.

[19] Your righteousness, O God, reaches to the
highest heavens.
You have done such wonderful things.
Who can compare with you,
O God?
[20] You have allowed me to suffer much
hardship,
but you will restore me to life again
and lift me up from the depths
of the earth.
[21] You will restore me to even greater honor
and comfort me once again.

*"In the Pits"
PS 71:17*

[22] Then I will praise you with music on the
harp,
because you are faithful to your
promises, O my God.
I will sing praises to you with a lyre,
O Holy One of Israel.
[23] I will shout for joy and sing your praises,
for you have ransomed me.
[24] I will tell about your righteous deeds
all day long,
for everyone who tried to hurt me
has been shamed and humiliated.

## PSALM 72
*A psalm of Solomon.*

[1] Give your love of justice to the king,
O God,
and righteousness to the king's son.
[2] Help him judge your people in the
right way;
let the poor always be treated fairly.
[3] May the mountains yield prosperity
for all,
and may the hills be fruitful.
[4] Help him to defend the poor,
to rescue the children of the needy,
and to crush their oppressors.

71:15 Or *though I cannot count it.*

5 May they fear you as long as the sun shines,
    as long as the moon remains in the sky.
    Yes, forever!

6 May the king's rule be refreshing like
        spring rain on freshly cut grass,
    like the showers that water the earth.
7 May all the godly flourish during his
        reign.
    May there be abundant prosperity
        until the moon is no more.
8 May he reign from sea to sea,
    and from the Euphrates River* to the
        ends of the earth.
9 Desert nomads will bow before him;
    his enemies will fall before him in the
        dust.
10 The western kings of Tarshish and other
        distant lands
    will bring him tribute.
    The eastern kings of Sheba and Seba
    will bring him gifts.
11 All kings will bow before him,
    and all nations will serve him.

12 He will rescue the poor when they cry
        to him;
    he will help the oppressed, who have
        no one to defend them.
13 He feels pity for the weak and the needy,
    and he will rescue them.
14 He will redeem them from oppression
        and violence,
    for their lives are precious to him.

15 Long live the king!
    May the gold of Sheba be given
        to him.
    May the people always pray for him
    and bless him all day long.
16 May there be abundant grain throughout
        the land,
    flourishing even on the hilltops.
    May the fruit trees flourish like the trees
        of Lebanon,
    and may the people thrive like grass
        in a field.
17 May the king's name endure forever;
    may it continue as long as the sun
        shines.
    May all nations be blessed through him
    and bring him praise.

72:8 Hebrew *the river.*

18 Praise the LORD God, the God of Israel,
    who alone does such wonderful things.
19 Praise his glorious name forever!
    Let the whole earth be filled with his
        glory.
    Amen and amen!

20 (This ends the prayers of David son
        of Jesse.)

• BOOK THREE (Psalms 73–89)

## PSALM 73
*A psalm of Asaph.*

1 Truly God is good to Israel,
    to those whose hearts are pure.
2 But as for me, I almost lost my footing.
    My feet were slipping, and I was
        almost gone.
3 For I envied the proud
    when I saw them prosper despite their
        wickedness.
4 They seem to live such painless lives;
    their bodies are so healthy and strong.
5 They don't have troubles like other
        people;
    they're not plagued with problems like
        everyone else.
6 They wear pride like a jeweled necklace
    and clothe themselves with cruelty.
7 These fat cats have everything
    their hearts could ever wish for!
8 They scoff and speak only evil;
    in their pride they seek to crush others.
9 They boast against the very heavens,
    and their words strut throughout the
        earth.
10 And so the people are dismayed and
        confused,
    drinking in all their words.
11 "What does God know?" they ask.
    "Does the Most High even know what's
        happening?"
12 Look at these wicked people—
    enjoying a life of ease while their
        riches multiply.

13 Did I keep my heart pure for nothing?
    Did I keep myself innocent for no
        reason?
14 I get nothing but trouble all day long;
    every morning brings me pain.

15 If I had really spoken this way to others,
  I would have been a traitor to your
    people.
16 So I tried to understand why the wicked
    prosper.
  But what a difficult task it is!
17 Then I went into your sanctuary,
    O God,
  and I finally understood the destiny of
    the wicked.
18 Truly, you put them on a slippery path
  and send them sliding over the cliff
    to destruction.
19 In an instant they are destroyed,
  completely swept away by terrors.
20 When you arise, O Lord,
  you will laugh at their silly ideas
  as a person laughs at dreams in the
    morning.

21 Then I realized that my heart was bitter,
  and I was all torn up inside.
22 I was so foolish and ignorant—
  I must have seemed like a senseless
    animal to you.
23 Yet I still belong to you;
  you hold my right hand.
24 You guide me with your counsel,
  leading me to a glorious destiny.
25 Whom have I in heaven but you?
  I desire you more than anything on
    earth.
26 My health may fail, and my spirit may
  grow weak,

but God remains the strength of my
  heart;
he is mine forever.

27 Those who desert him will perish,
  for you destroy those who abandon
    you.
28 But as for me, how good it is to be near
    God!
  I have made the Sovereign LORD my
    shelter,
  and I will tell everyone about the
    wonderful things you do.

# PSALM 74
*A psalm\* of Asaph.*

1 O God, why have you rejected us so long?
  Why is your anger so intense against
    the sheep of your own pasture?
2 Remember that we are the people you
    chose long ago,
  the tribe you redeemed as your own
    special possession!
  And remember Jerusalem,* your home
    here on earth.
3 Walk through the awful ruins of the city;
  see how the enemy has destroyed your
    sanctuary.

4 There your enemies shouted their
    victorious battle cries;
  there they set up their battle
    standards.
5 They swung their axes
  like woodcutters in a forest.
6 With axes and picks,
  they smashed the carved paneling.
7 They burned your sanctuary to the
    ground.
  They defiled the place that bears your
    name.
8 Then they thought, "Let's destroy
    everything!"
  So they burned down all the places
    where God was worshiped.

9 We no longer see your miraculous signs.
  All the prophets are gone,
  and no one can tell us when it will end.
10 How long, O God, will you allow our
    enemies to insult you?

74:TITLE Hebrew *maskil*. This may be a literary or musical term.
74:2 Hebrew *Mount Zion*.

## IN the wilderness
READ PSALM 63:1-8

Whether or not we like camping or
hiking in the wilderness, we can all
identify with the desire to be prepared before
we head into the unknown.

When a serious disease strikes, it can feel like
being dropped right into the middle of the wilderness. So much is unfamiliar, and the paths to take
are often uncharted. It's a world of terms and treatments we never even knew existed before—and
wish we didn't have to know now!

David wrote this psalm when he was in the
wilderness—literally. We pray you can identify not
just with his problems but with his solutions for
finding joy again, too.

Will you let them dishonor your name
  forever?
11 Why do you hold back your strong right
  hand?
  Unleash your powerful fist and destroy
  them.
12 You, O God, are my king from ages past,
  bringing salvation to the earth.
13 You split the sea by your strength
  and smashed the heads of the sea
  monsters.
14 You crushed the heads of Leviathan*
  and let the desert animals eat him.
15 You caused the springs and streams to
  gush forth,
  and you dried up rivers that never
  run dry.
16 Both day and night belong to you;
  you made the starlight* and the sun.
17 You set the boundaries of the earth,
  and you made both summer and
  winter.

18 See how these enemies insult you, LORD.
  A foolish nation has dishonored your
  name.
19 Don't let these wild beasts destroy your
  turtledoves.
  Don't forget your suffering people
  forever.

20 Remember your covenant promises,
  for the land is full of darkness and
  violence!
21 Don't let the downtrodden be humiliated
  again.
  Instead, let the poor and needy praise
  your name.

22 Arise, O God, and defend your cause.
  Remember how these fools insult you
  all day long.
23 Don't overlook what your enemies have
  said
  or their growing uproar.

## PSALM 75

*For the choir director: A psalm of Asaph. A song
to be sung to the tune "Do Not Destroy!"*

1 We thank you, O God!
  We give thanks because you are near.

People everywhere tell of your
  wonderful deeds.

2 God says, "At the time I have planned,
  I will bring justice against the
  wicked.
3 When the earth quakes and its people
  live in turmoil,
  I am the one who keeps its foundations
  firm.                                *Interlude*

4 "I warned the proud, 'Stop your
  boasting!'
  I told the wicked, 'Don't raise your
  fists!
5 Don't raise your fists in defiance at the
  heavens
  or speak with such arrogance.'"

6 For no one on earth—from east or west,
  or even from the wilderness—
  should raise a defiant fist.*
7 It is God alone who judges;
  he decides who will rise and who
  will fall.
8 For the LORD holds a cup in his hand
  that is full of foaming wine mixed
  with spices.
  He pours out the wine in judgment,
  and all the wicked must drink it,
  draining it to the dregs.

9 But as for me, I will always proclaim what
  God has done;
  I will sing praises to the God of Jacob.
10 For God says, "I will break the strength
  of the wicked,
  but I will increase the power of the
  godly."

## PSALM 76

*For the choir director: A psalm of Asaph.
A song to be accompanied by stringed
instruments.*

1 God is honored in Judah;
  his name is great in Israel.
2 Jerusalem* is where he lives;
  Mount Zion is his home.
3 There he has broken the fiery arrows
  of the enemy,
  the shields and swords and weapons
  of war.                              *Interlude*

---

74:14 The identification of Leviathan is disputed, ranging from an earthly creature to a mythical sea monster in ancient literature.
74:16 Or *moon;* Hebrew reads *light.*   75:6 Hebrew *should lift.*   76:2 Hebrew *Salem,* another name for Jerusalem.

4 You are glorious and more majestic
  than the everlasting mountains.*
5 Our boldest enemies have been plundered.
  They lie before us in the sleep of death.
  No warrior could lift a hand against us.
6 At the blast of your breath, O God of
  Jacob,
  their horses and chariots lay still.

7 No wonder you are greatly feared!
  Who can stand before you when your
  anger explodes?
8 From heaven you sentenced your
  enemies;
  the earth trembled and stood silent
  before you.
9 You stand up to judge those who do evil,
  O God,
  and to rescue the oppressed
  of the earth.                    *Interlude*
10 Human defiance only enhances your glory,
  for you use it as a weapon.*

11 Make vows to the LORD your God, and
  keep them.
  Let everyone bring tribute to the
  Awesome One.
12 For he breaks the pride of princes,
  and the kings of the earth fear him.

## PSALM 77
*For Jeduthun, the choir director: A psalm
of Asaph.*

1 I cry out to God; yes, I shout.
  Oh, that God would listen to me!
2 When I was in deep trouble,
  I searched for the Lord.
  All night long I prayed, with hands lifted
  toward heaven,
  but my soul was not comforted.
3 I think of God, and I moan,
  overwhelmed with longing
  for his help.                    *Interlude*

4 You don't let me sleep.
  I am too distressed even to pray!
5 I think of the good old days,
  long since ended,
6 when my nights were filled with joyful
  songs.
  I search my soul and ponder the
  difference now.

7 Has the Lord rejected me forever?
  Will he never again be kind to me?
8 Is his unfailing love gone forever?
  Have his promises permanently failed?
9 Has God forgotten to be gracious?
  Has he slammed the door on his
  compassion?                      *Interlude*

10 And I said, "This is my fate;
  the Most High has turned his hand
  against me."
11 But then I recall all you have done,
  O LORD;
  I remember your wonderful deeds
  of long ago.
12 They are constantly in my thoughts.
  I cannot stop thinking about your
  mighty works.

13 O God, your ways are holy.
  Is there any god as mighty as you?
14 You are the God of great wonders!
  You demonstrate your awesome power
  among the nations.
15 By your strong arm, you redeemed your
  people,
  the descendants of Jacob and Joseph.
                                   *Interlude*

16 When the Red Sea* saw you, O God,
  its waters looked and trembled!
  The sea quaked to its very depths.
17 The clouds poured down rain;
  the thunder rumbled in the sky.
  Your arrows of lightning flashed.
18 Your thunder roared from the whirlwind;
  the lightning lit up the world!
  The earth trembled and shook.
19 Your road led through the sea,
  your pathway through the mighty
  waters—
  a pathway no one knew was there!
20 You led your people along that road like a
  flock of sheep,
  with Moses and Aaron as their
  shepherds.

## PSALM 78
*A psalm* of Asaph.*

1 O my people, listen to my instructions.
  Open your ears to what I am saying,

---

**76:4** As in Greek version; Hebrew reads *than mountains filled with beasts of prey.*   **76:10** The meaning of the Hebrew is uncertain.
**77:16** Hebrew *the waters.*   **78:TITLE** Hebrew *maskil.* This may be a literary or musical term.

2   for I will speak to you in a parable.
    I will teach you hidden lessons from
        our past—
3     stories we have heard and known,
      stories our ancestors handed down
          to us.
4  We will not hide these truths from our
        children;
    we will tell the next generation
  about the glorious deeds of the LORD,
    about his power and his mighty
        wonders.
5  For he issued his laws to Jacob;
    he gave his instructions to Israel.
  He commanded our ancestors
    to teach them to their children,
6  so the next generation might know
        them—
    even the children not yet born—
    and they in turn will teach their own
        children.
7  So each generation should set its hope
        anew on God,
    not forgetting his glorious miracles
    and obeying his commands.
8  Then they will not be like their
        ancestors—
    stubborn, rebellious, and unfaithful,
    refusing to give their hearts to God.

9  The warriors of Ephraim, though armed
        with bows,
    turned their backs and fled on the day
        of battle.
10  They did not keep God's covenant
    and refused to live by his instructions.
11  They forgot what he had done—
    the great wonders he had shown them,
12  the miracles he did for their ancestors
    on the plain of Zoan in the land of
        Egypt.
13  For he divided the sea and led them
        through,
    making the water stand up like walls!
14  In the daytime he led them by a cloud,
    and all night by a pillar of fire.
15  He split open the rocks in the wilderness
    to give them water, as from a gushing
        spring.
16  He made streams pour from the rock,
    making the waters flow down like
        a river!

17  Yet they kept on sinning against him,
    rebelling against the Most High in the
        desert.
18  They stubbornly tested God in their
        hearts,
    demanding the foods they craved.
19  They even spoke against God himself,
        saying,
    "God can't give us food in the
        wilderness.
20  Yes, he can strike a rock so water gushes
        out,
    but he can't give his people bread
        and meat."
21  When the LORD heard them, he was
        furious.
    The fire of his wrath burned against
        Jacob.
    Yes, his anger rose against Israel,
22  for they did not believe God
    or trust him to care for them.
23  But he commanded the skies to open;
    he opened the doors of heaven.
24  He rained down manna for them to eat;
    he gave them bread from heaven.
25  They ate the food of angels!
    God gave them all they could hold.
26  He released the east wind in the heavens
    and guided the south wind by his
        mighty power.
27  He rained down meat as thick as dust—
    birds as plentiful as the sand on the
        seashore!
28  He caused the birds to fall within their
        camp
    and all around their tents.
29  The people ate their fill.
    He gave them what they craved.
30  But before they satisfied their craving,
    while the meat was yet in their
        mouths,
31  the anger of God rose against them,
    and he killed their strongest men.
    He struck down the finest of Israel's
        young men.
32  But in spite of this, the people kept
        sinning.
    Despite his wonders, they refused to
        trust him.
33  So he ended their lives in failure,
    their years in terror.

34 When God began killing them,
  they finally sought him.
  They repented and took God seriously.
35 Then they remembered that God was
    their rock,
  that God Most High* was their
    redeemer.
36 But all they gave him was lip service;
  they lied to him with their tongues.
37 Their hearts were not loyal to him.
  They did not keep his covenant.
38 Yet he was merciful and forgave their
    sins
  and did not destroy them all.
  Many times he held back his anger
  and did not unleash his fury!
39 For he remembered that they were
    merely mortal,
  gone like a breath of wind that never
    returns.

40 Oh, how often they rebelled against him
    in the wilderness
  and grieved his heart in that dry
    wasteland.
41 Again and again they tested God's
    patience
  and provoked the Holy One of Israel.
42 They did not remember his power
  and how he rescued them from their
    enemies.
43 They did not remember his miraculous
    signs in Egypt,
  his wonders on the plain of Zoan.
44 For he turned their rivers into blood,
  so no one could drink from the
    streams.
45 He sent vast swarms of flies to consume
    them
  and hordes of frogs to ruin them.
46 He gave their crops to caterpillars;
  their harvest was consumed by locusts.
47 He destroyed their grapevines with hail
  and shattered their sycamore-figs
    with sleet.
48 He abandoned their cattle to the hail,
  their livestock to bolts of lightning.
49 He loosed on them his fierce anger—
  all his fury, rage, and hostility.
  He dispatched against them
  a band of destroying angels.

50 He turned his anger against them;
  he did not spare the Egyptians' lives
  but ravaged them with the plague.
51 He killed the oldest son in each Egyptian
    family,
  the flower of youth throughout the
    land of Egypt.*
52 But he led his own people like a flock
    of sheep,
  guiding them safely through the
    wilderness.
53 He kept them safe so they were not afraid;
  but the sea covered their enemies.
54 He brought them to the border of his
    holy land,
  to this land of hills he had won for
    them.
55 He drove out the nations before them;
  he gave them their inheritance by lot.
  He settled the tribes of Israel into their
    homes.

56 But they kept testing and rebelling
    against God Most High.
  They did not obey his laws.
57 They turned back and were as faithless as
    their parents.
  They were as undependable as
    a crooked bow.
58 They angered God by building shrines to
    other gods;
  they made him jealous with their idols.
59 When God heard them, he was very
    angry,
  and he completely rejected Israel.
60 Then he abandoned his dwelling
    at Shiloh,
  the Tabernacle where he had lived
    among the people.
61 He allowed the Ark of his might to be
    captured;
  he surrendered his glory into enemy
    hands.
62 He gave his people over to be butchered
    by the sword,
  because he was so angry with his
    own people—his special
    possession.
63 Their young men were killed by fire;
  their young women died before
    singing their wedding songs.

78:35 Hebrew *El-Elyon*.    78:51 Hebrew *in the tents of Ham*.

⁶⁴ Their priests were slaughtered,
  and their widows could not mourn
    their deaths.

⁶⁵ Then the Lord rose up as though waking
    from sleep,
  like a warrior aroused from a drunken
    stupor.
⁶⁶ He routed his enemies
  and sent them to eternal shame.
⁶⁷ But he rejected Joseph's descendants;
  he did not choose the tribe of Ephraim.
⁶⁸ He chose instead the tribe of Judah,
  and Mount Zion, which he loved.
⁶⁹ There he built his sanctuary as high as
    the heavens,
  as solid and enduring as the earth.
⁷⁰ He chose his servant David,
  calling him from the sheep pens.
⁷¹ He took David from tending the ewes
    and lambs
  and made him the shepherd of Jacob's
    descendants—
  God's own people, Israel.
⁷² He cared for them with a true heart
  and led them with skillful hands.

## PSALM 79
*A psalm of Asaph.*

¹ O God, pagan nations have conquered
    your land,
  your special possession.
  They have defiled your holy Temple
  and made Jerusalem a heap of ruins.
² They have left the bodies of your servants
    as food for the birds of heaven.
  The flesh of your godly ones
    has become food for the wild animals.
³ Blood has flowed like water all around
    Jerusalem;
  no one is left to bury the dead.
⁴ We are mocked by our neighbors,
  an object of scorn and derision to
    those around us.

⁵ O LORD, how long will you be angry with
    us? Forever?
  How long will your jealousy burn like
    fire?
⁶ Pour out your wrath on the nations that
  refuse to acknowledge you—

on kingdoms that do not call upon
    your name.
⁷ For they have devoured your people Israel,*
  making the land a desolate wilderness.
⁸ Do not hold us guilty for the sins of our
    ancestors!
  Let your compassion quickly meet our
    needs,
  for we are on the brink of despair.

⁹ Help us, O God of our salvation!
  Help us for the glory of your name.
  Save us and forgive our sins
    for the honor of your name.
¹⁰ Why should pagan nations be allowed
    to scoff,
  asking, "Where is their God?"
  Show us your vengeance against the
    nations,
  for they have spilled the blood of your
    servants.
¹¹ Listen to the moaning of the prisoners.
  Demonstrate your great power by
    saving those condemned to die.

¹² O Lord, pay back our neighbors seven
    times
  for the scorn they have hurled at you.
¹³ Then we your people, the sheep of your
    pasture,
  will thank you forever and ever,
  praising your greatness from
    generation to generation.

## ◄ PSALM 80
*For the choir director: A psalm of Asaph, to be*
*sung to the tune "Lilies of the Covenant."*

¹ Please listen, O Shepherd of Israel,
  you who lead Joseph's descendants like
    a flock.
  O God, enthroned above the cherubim,
    display your radiant glory
²   to Ephraim, Benjamin, and Manasseh.
  Show us your mighty power.
  Come to rescue us!

³ Turn us again to yourself, O God.
  Make your face shine down upon us.
  Only then will we be saved.
⁴ O LORD God of Heaven's Armies,
  how long will you be angry with our
    prayers?

**79:7** Hebrew *devoured Jacob.* See note on 44:4.

5 You have fed us with sorrow
and made us drink tears by the
bucketful.
6 You have made us the scorn* of
neighboring nations.
Our enemies treat us as a joke.

7 Turn us again to yourself, O God of
Heaven's Armies.
Make your face shine down upon us.
Only then will we be saved.
8 You brought us from Egypt like a
grapevine;
you drove away the pagan nations and
transplanted us into your land.
9 You cleared the ground for us,
and we took root and filled the land.
10 Our shade covered the mountains;
our branches covered the mighty cedars.
11 We spread our branches west to the
Mediterranean Sea;
our shoots spread east to the
Euphrates River.*
12 But now, why have you broken down our
walls
so that all who pass by may steal our
fruit?
13 The wild boar from the forest devours it,
and the wild animals feed on it.

14 Come back, we beg you, O God of
Heaven's Armies.
Look down from heaven and see our
plight.
Take care of this grapevine
15 that you yourself have planted,
this son you have raised for yourself.
16 For we are chopped up and burned
by our enemies.
May they perish at the sight of your
frown.
17 Strengthen the man you love,
the son of your choice.
18 Then we will never abandon you again.
Revive us so we can call on your name
once more.

19 Turn us again to yourself, O LORD God
of Heaven's Armies.
Make your face shine down upon us.
Only then will we be saved.

## PSALM 81

*For the choir director: A psalm of Asaph, to be
accompanied by a stringed instrument.* *

1 Sing praises to God, our strength.
Sing to the God of Jacob.
2 Sing! Beat the tambourine.
Play the sweet lyre and the harp.
3 Blow the ram's horn at new moon,
and again at full moon to call a
festival!
4 For this is required by the decrees of
Israel;
it is a regulation of the God of Jacob.
5 He made it a law for Israel*
when he attacked Egypt to set
us free.

I heard an unknown voice say,
6 "Now I will take the load from your
shoulders;
I will free your hands from their heavy
tasks.
7 You cried to me in trouble, and I saved
you;
I answered out of the thundercloud
and tested your faith when there was
no water at Meribah.          *Interlude*

8 "Listen to me, O my people, while I give
you stern warnings.
O Israel, if you would only listen
to me!
9 You must never have a foreign god;
you must not bow down before a false
god.
10 For it was I, the LORD your God,
who rescued you from the land
of Egypt.
Open your mouth wide, and I will fill it
with good things.

11 "But no, my people wouldn't listen.
Israel did not want me around.
12 So I let them follow their own stubborn
desires,
living according to their own ideas.
13 Oh, that my people would listen to me!
Oh, that Israel would follow me,
walking in my paths!
14 How quickly I would then subdue their
enemies!

---

**80:6** As in Syriac version; Hebrew reads *the strife.*    **80:11** Hebrew *west to the sea, . . . east to the river.*    **81:TITLE** Hebrew *according to the gittith.*    **81:5** Hebrew *for Joseph.*

How soon my hands would be upon
their foes!
¹⁵ Those who hate the Lord would cringe
before him;
they would be doomed forever.
¹⁶ But I would feed you with the finest
wheat.
I would satisfy you with wild honey
from the rock."

## PSALM 82
*A psalm of Asaph.*

¹ God presides over heaven's court;
he pronounces judgment on the
heavenly beings:
² "How long will you hand down unjust
decisions
by favoring the wicked?          *Interlude*

³ "Give justice to the poor and the orphan;
uphold the rights of the oppressed and
the destitute.
⁴ Rescue the poor and helpless;
deliver them from the grasp of evil
people.
⁵ But these oppressors know nothing;
they are so ignorant!
They wander about in darkness,
while the whole world is shaken
to the core.
⁶ I say, 'You are gods;
you are all children of the Most High.
⁷ But you will die like mere mortals
and fall like every other ruler.'"

⁸ Rise up, O God, and judge the earth,
for all the nations belong to you.

## PSALM 83
*A song. A psalm of Asaph.*

¹ O God, do not be silent!
Do not be deaf.
Do not be quiet, O God.
² Don't you hear the uproar of your
enemies?
Don't you see that your arrogant
enemies are rising up?
³ They devise crafty schemes against your
people;
they conspire against your precious
ones.

⁴ "Come," they say, "let us wipe out Israel
as a nation.
We will destroy the very memory
of its existence."
⁵ Yes, this was their unanimous decision.
They signed a treaty as allies against
you—
⁶ these Edomites and Ishmaelites;
Moabites and Hagrites;
⁷ Gebalites, Ammonites, and Amalekites;
and people from Philistia and Tyre.
⁸ Assyria has joined them, too,
and is allied with the descendants
of Lot.                              *Interlude*

⁹ Do to them as you did to the Midianites
and as you did to Sisera and Jabin at
the Kishon River.
¹⁰ They were destroyed at Endor,
and their decaying corpses fertilized
the soil.
¹¹ Let their mighty nobles die as Oreb and
Zeeb did.
Let all their princes die like Zebah and
Zalmunna,
¹² for they said, "Let us seize for our
own use
these pasturelands of God!"
¹³ O my God, scatter them like tumbleweed,
like chaff before the wind!
¹⁴ As a fire burns a forest
and as a flame sets mountains
ablaze,
¹⁵ chase them with your fierce storm;
terrify them with your tempest.
¹⁶ Utterly disgrace them
until they submit to your name, O Lord.
¹⁷ Let them be ashamed and terrified
forever.
Let them die in disgrace.
¹⁸ Then they will learn that you alone are
called the Lord,
that you alone are the Most High,
supreme over all the earth.

## PSALM 84
*For the choir director: A psalm of the
descendants of Korah, to be accompanied
by a stringed instrument.* *

¹ How lovely is your dwelling place,
O Lord of Heaven's Armies.

84:TITLE Hebrew *according to the gittith.*

2 I long, yes, I faint with longing
 to enter the courts of the LORD.
With my whole being, body and soul,
 I will shout joyfully to the living God.
3 Even the sparrow finds a home,
 and the swallow builds her nest and
  raises her young
at a place near your altar,
 O LORD of Heaven's Armies, my King
  and my God!
4 What joy for those who can live in your
  house,
 always singing your praises.   *Interlude*

5 What joy for those whose strength comes
  from the LORD,
 who have set their minds on a
  pilgrimage to Jerusalem.
6 When they walk through the Valley
  of Weeping,*
 it will become a place of refreshing
  springs.
 The autumn rains will clothe it with
  blessings.
7 They will continue to grow stronger,
 and each of them will appear before
  God in Jerusalem.*

8 O LORD God of Heaven's Armies, hear my
  prayer.
 Listen, O God of Jacob.   *Interlude*

9 O God, look with favor upon the king,
  our shield!
 Show favor to the one you have
  anointed.

10 A single day in your courts
 is better than a thousand anywhere
  else!
 I would rather be a gatekeeper in the
  house of my God
 than live the good life in the homes of
  the wicked.
11 For the LORD God is our sun and
  our shield.
 He gives us grace and glory.
 The LORD will withhold no good thing
  from those who do what is right.
12 O LORD of Heaven's Armies,
 what joy for those who trust
  in you.

## PSALM 85
*For the choir director: A psalm of the descendants of Korah.*

1 LORD, you poured out blessings
  on your land!
 You restored the fortunes
  of Israel.*
2 You forgave the guilt of your people—
 yes, you covered all their sins.
                                    *Interlude*

3 You held back your fury.
 You kept back your blazing anger.

4 Now restore us again, O God of our
  salvation.
 Put aside your anger against us once
  more.
5 Will you be angry with us always?
 Will you prolong your wrath to all
  generations?
6 Won't you revive us again,
 so your people can rejoice in you?
7 Show us your unfailing love,
  O LORD,
 and grant us your salvation.

8 I listen carefully to what God the LORD is
  saying,
 for he speaks peace to his faithful
  people.
 But let them not return to their foolish
  ways.
9 Surely his salvation is near to those
  who fear him,
 so our land will be filled with his
  glory.

10 Unfailing love and truth have met
  together.
 Righteousness and peace have
  kissed!
11 Truth springs up from the earth,
 and righteousness smiles down
  from heaven.
12 Yes, the LORD pours down his
  blessings.
 Our land will yield its bountiful
  harvest.
13 Righteousness goes as a herald
  before him,
 preparing the way for his steps.

**84:6** Or *Valley of Poplars;* Hebrew reads *valley of Baca.*   **84:7** Hebrew *Zion.*   **85:1** Hebrew *of Jacob.* See note on 44:4.

## PSALM 86
*A prayer of David.*

¹ Bend down, O Lᴏʀᴅ, and hear my prayer;
  answer me, for I need your help.
² Protect me, for I am devoted to you.
  Save me, for I serve you and trust you.
  You are my God.
³ Be merciful to me, O Lord,
  for I am calling on you constantly.
⁴ Give me happiness, O Lord,
  for I give myself to you.
⁵ O Lord, you are so good, so ready to
  forgive,
  so full of unfailing love for all who ask
  for your help.
⁶ Listen closely to my prayer, O Lᴏʀᴅ;
  hear my urgent cry.
⁷ I will call to you whenever I'm in trouble,
  and you will answer me.

⁸ No pagan god is like you, O Lord.
  None can do what you do!
⁹ All the nations you made
  will come and bow before you, Lord;
  they will praise your holy name.
¹⁰ For you are great and perform wonderful
  deeds.
  You alone are God.

¹¹ Teach me your ways, O Lᴏʀᴅ,
  that I may live according to your truth!
  Grant me purity of heart,
  so that I may honor you.
¹² With all my heart I will praise you,
  O Lord my God.
  I will give glory to your name forever,
¹³ for your love for me is very great.
  You have rescued me from the depths
  of death.*

¹⁴ O God, insolent people rise up against me;
  a violent gang is trying to kill me.
  You mean nothing to them.
¹⁵ But you, O Lord,
  are a God of compassion and mercy,
  slow to get angry
  and filled with unfailing love and
  faithfulness.
¹⁶ Look down and have mercy on me.
  Give your strength to your servant;
  save me, the son of your servant.

## IN deep waters
READ PSALM 69:1-3, 29

Illness can take us through deep waters not only physically but emotionally and spiritually as well. We don't know how deep your waters are. Maybe they're waist deep and rising fast. Or maybe you're like David bobbing up and down, searching for something to help you stay afloat.

No matter what your "water level" or "swimming ability," God can and will rescue you with His supernatural presence. Be encouraged by His words from Isaiah 43:2: "When you go through deep waters, I will be with you. When you go through rivers of difficulty, you will not drown."

¹⁷ Send me a sign of your favor.
  Then those who hate me will be
  put to shame,
  for you, O Lᴏʀᴅ, help and comfort me.

## PSALM 87
*A song. A psalm of the descendants
of Korah.*

¹ On the holy mountain
  stands the city founded by the Lᴏʀᴅ.
² He loves the city of Jerusalem
  more than any other city in Israel.*
³ O city of God,
  what glorious things are said of you!
                                    *Interlude*

⁴ I will count Egypt* and Babylon among
  those who know me—
  also Philistia and Tyre, and even distant
  Ethiopia.*
  They have all become citizens of
  Jerusalem!
⁵ Regarding Jerusalem* it will be said,
  "Everyone enjoys the rights of
  citizenship there."
  And the Most High will personally
  bless this city.
⁶ When the Lᴏʀᴅ registers the nations, he
  will say,
  "They have all become citizens of
  Jerusalem." *Interlude*

**86:13** Hebrew *of Sheol.*   **87:2** Hebrew *He loves the gates of Zion more than all the dwellings of Jacob.* See note on 44:4.
**87:4a** Hebrew *Rahab,* the name of a mythical sea monster that represents chaos in ancient literature. The name is used here as a poetic name for Egypt.   **87:4b** Hebrew *Cush.*   **87:5** Hebrew *Zion.*

7 The people will play flutes* and sing,
  "The source of my life springs from
    Jerusalem!"

## PSALM 88

*For the choir director: A psalm of the
descendants of Korah. A song to be sung
to the tune "The Suffering of Affliction."
A psalm\* of Heman the Ezrahite.*

1 O Lord, God of my salvation,
    I cry out to you by day.
    I come to you at night.
2 Now hear my prayer;
    listen to my cry.
3 For my life is full of troubles,
    and death* draws near.
4 I am as good as dead,
    like a strong man with no strength left.
5 They have left me among the dead,
    and I lie like a corpse in a grave.
  I am forgotten,
    cut off from your care.
6 You have thrown me into the lowest pit,
    into the darkest depths.
7 Your anger weighs me down;
    with wave after wave you have
      engulfed me.          *Interlude*

8 You have driven my friends away
    by making me repulsive to them.
  I am in a trap with no way of escape.
9   My eyes are blinded by my tears.
  Each day I beg for your help, O Lord;
    I lift my hands to you for mercy.
10 Are your wonderful deeds of any use
      to the dead?
    Do the dead rise up and praise you?
                            *Interlude*

11 Can those in the grave declare your
      unfailing love?
    Can they proclaim your faithfulness in
      the place of destruction?*
12 Can the darkness speak of your
      wonderful deeds?
    Can anyone in the land of forgetfulness
      talk about your righteousness?
13 O Lord, I cry out to you.
    I will keep on pleading day by day.
14 O Lord, why do you reject me?
    Why do you turn your face from me?

15 I have been sick and close to death since
    my youth.
  I stand helpless and desperate before
    your terrors.
16 Your fierce anger has overwhelmed me.
    Your terrors have paralyzed me.
17 They swirl around me like floodwaters all
      day long.
    They have engulfed me completely.
18 You have taken away my companions and
      loved ones.
    Darkness is my closest friend.

## PSALM 89

*A psalm\* of Ethan the Ezrahite.*

1 I will sing of the Lord's unfailing love
      forever!
    Young and old will hear of your
      faithfulness.
2 Your unfailing love will last forever.
    Your faithfulness is as enduring as the
      heavens.

3 The Lord said, "I have made a covenant
      with David, my chosen servant.
    I have sworn this oath to him:
4 'I will establish your descendants as
      kings forever;
    they will sit on your throne from now
      until eternity.'"          *Interlude*

5 All heaven will praise your great wonders,
      Lord;
    myriads of angels will praise you for
      your faithfulness.
6 For who in all of heaven can compare
      with the Lord?
    What mightiest angel is anything like
      the Lord?
7 The highest angelic powers stand in awe
      of God.
    He is far more awesome than all who
      surround his throne.
8 O Lord God of Heaven's Armies!
    Where is there anyone as mighty as
      you, O Lord?
    You are entirely faithful.

9 You rule the oceans.
    You subdue their storm-tossed
      waves.

---

87:7 Or *will dance.* 88:TITLE Hebrew *maskil.* This may be a literary or musical term. 88:3 Hebrew *Sheol.* 88:11 Hebrew *in
Abaddon?* 89:TITLE Hebrew *maskil.* This may be a literary or musical term.

10 You crushed the great sea monster.*
  You scattered your enemies with your
    mighty arm.
11 The heavens are yours, and the earth is
    yours;
  everything in the world is yours—you
    created it all.
12 You created north and south.
  Mount Tabor and Mount Hermon
    praise your name.
13 Powerful is your arm!
  Strong is your hand!
  Your right hand is lifted high in
    glorious strength.
14 Righteousness and justice are the
    foundation of your throne.
  Unfailing love and truth walk before
    you as attendants.
15 Happy are those who hear the joyful call
    to worship,
  for they will walk in the light of your
    presence, LORD.
16 They rejoice all day long in your
    wonderful reputation.
  They exult in your righteousness.
17 You are their glorious strength.
  It pleases you to make us strong.
18 Yes, our protection comes from
    the LORD,
  and he, the Holy One of Israel, has
    given us our king.

19 Long ago you spoke in a vision to your
    faithful people.
  You said, "I have raised up a warrior.
  I have selected him from the common
    people to be king.
20 I have found my servant David.
  I have anointed him with my holy oil.
21 I will steady him with my hand;
  with my powerful arm I will make him
    strong.
22 His enemies will not defeat him,
  nor will the wicked overpower him.
23 I will beat down his adversaries before
    him
  and destroy those who hate him.
24 My faithfulness and unfailing love will be
    with him,
  and by my authority he will grow in
    power.

25 I will extend his rule over the sea,
  his dominion over the rivers.
26 And he will call out to me, 'You are my
    Father,
  my God, and the Rock of my salvation.'
27 I will make him my firstborn son,
  the mightiest king on earth.
28 I will love him and be kind to him forever;
  my covenant with him will never end.
29 I will preserve an heir for him;
  his throne will be as endless as the
    days of heaven.
30 But if his descendants forsake my
    instructions
  and fail to obey my regulations,
31 if they do not obey my decrees
  and fail to keep my commands,
32 then I will punish their sin with the rod,
  and their disobedience with beating.
33 But I will never stop loving him
  nor fail to keep my promise to him.
34 No, I will not break my covenant;
  I will not take back a single word
    I said.
35 I have sworn an oath to David,
  and in my holiness I cannot lie:
36 His dynasty will go on forever;
  his kingdom will endure as the sun.
37 It will be as eternal as the moon,
  my faithful witness in the sky!"

                                        *Interlude*

38 But now you have rejected him and cast
    him off.
  You are angry with your anointed king.
39 You have renounced your covenant with
    him;
  you have thrown his crown in the dust.
40 You have broken down the walls
    protecting him
  and ruined every fort defending him.
41 Everyone who comes along has robbed
    him,
  and he has become a joke to his
    neighbors.
42 You have strengthened his enemies
  and made them all rejoice.
43 You have made his sword useless
  and refused to help him in battle.
44 You have ended his splendor
  and overturned his throne.

**89:10** Hebrew *Rahab*, the name of a mythical sea monster that represents chaos in ancient literature.

⁴⁵ You have made him old before his time
　　and publicly disgraced him.　　*Interlude*

⁴⁶ O Lord, how long will this go on?
　　Will you hide yourself forever?
　　How long will your anger burn like
　　　fire?
⁴⁷ Remember how short my life is,
　　how empty and futile this human
　　　existence!
⁴⁸ No one can live forever; all will die.
　　No one can escape the power
　　　of the grave.*　　*Interlude*

⁴⁹ Lord, where is your unfailing love?
　　You promised it to David with a
　　　faithful pledge.
⁵⁰ Consider, Lord, how your servants are
　　　disgraced!
　　I carry in my heart the insults of so
　　　many people.
⁵¹ Your enemies have mocked me, O Lord;
　　they mock your anointed king
　　　wherever he goes.

⁵² Praise the Lord forever!
　　Amen and amen!

## BOOK FOUR (Psalms 90–106)

## PSALM 90
*A prayer of Moses, the man of God.*

¹ Lord, through all the generations
　　you have been our home!
² Before the mountains were born,
　　before you gave birth to the earth and
　　　the world,
　　from beginning to end, you are God.

³ You turn people back to dust, saying,
　　"Return to dust, you mortals!"
⁴ For you, a thousand years are as a passing
　　　day,
　　as brief as a few night hours.
⁵ You sweep people away like dreams that
　　　disappear.
　　They are like grass that springs up in
　　　the morning.
⁶ In the morning it blooms and
　　　flourishes,
　　but by evening it is dry and withered.
⁷ We wither beneath your anger;
　　we are overwhelmed by your fury.

⁸ You spread out our sins before you—
　　our secret sins—and you see them all.
⁹ We live our lives beneath your wrath,
　　ending our years with a groan.

¹⁰ Seventy years are given to us!
　　Some even live to eighty.
　But even the best years are filled with
　　　pain and trouble;
　　soon they disappear, and we fly away.
¹¹ Who can comprehend the power of your
　　　anger?
　　Your wrath is as awesome as the fear
　　　you deserve.
¹² Teach us to realize the brevity of life,
　　so that we may grow in wisdom.

¹³ O Lord, come back to us!
　　How long will you delay?
　　Take pity on your servants!
¹⁴ Satisfy us each morning with your
　　　unfailing love,
　　so we may sing for joy to the end
　　　of our lives.
¹⁵ Give us gladness in proportion to our
　　　former misery!
　　Replace the evil years with good.
¹⁶ Let us, your servants, see you work again;
　　let our children see your glory.
¹⁷ And may the Lord our God show us his
　　　approval
　　and make our efforts successful.
　　Yes, make our efforts successful!

## PSALM 91
¹ Those who live in the shelter of the Most
　　High
　　will find rest in the shadow of the
　　　Almighty.
² This I declare about the Lord:
　He alone is my refuge, my place of safety;
　　he is my God, and I trust him.
³ For he will rescue you from every trap
　　and protect you from deadly disease.
⁴ He will cover you with his feathers.
　　He will shelter you with his wings.
　　His faithful promises are your armor
　　　and protection.
⁵ Do not be afraid of the terrors of the
　　　night,
　　nor the arrow that flies in the day.

**89:48** Hebrew *of Sheol.*

6 Do not dread the disease that stalks in
  darkness,
  nor the disaster that strikes at midday.
7 Though a thousand fall at your side,
  though ten thousand are dying around
  you,
  these evils will not touch you.
8 Just open your eyes,
  and see how the wicked are punished.

9 If you make the LORD your refuge,
  if you make the Most High your shelter,
10 no evil will conquer you;
  no plague will come near your home.
11 For he will order his angels
  to protect you wherever you go.
12 They will hold you up with their hands
  so you won't even hurt your foot on a
  stone.
13 You will trample upon lions and cobras;
  you will crush fierce lions and serpents
  under your feet!

14 The LORD says, "I will rescue those who
  love me.
  I will protect those who trust in my
  name.
15 When they call on me, I will answer;
  I will be with them in trouble.
  I will rescue and honor them.
16 I will reward them with a long life
  and give them my salvation."

## PSALM 92
*A psalm. A song to be sung on the
Sabbath Day.*

1 It is good to give thanks to the LORD,
  to sing praises to the Most High.
2 It is good to proclaim your unfailing love
  in the morning,
  your faithfulness in the evening,
3 accompanied by the ten-stringed harp
  and the melody of the lyre.

4 You thrill me, LORD, with all you have
  done for me!
  I sing for joy because of what you have
  done.
5 O LORD, what great works you do!
  And how deep are your thoughts.
6 Only a simpleton would not know,
  and only a fool would not understand
  this:

7 Though the wicked sprout like weeds
  and evildoers flourish,
  they will be destroyed forever.

8 But you, O LORD, will be exalted forever.
9 Your enemies, LORD, will surely perish;
  all evildoers will be scattered.
10 But you have made me as strong as
  a wild ox.
  You have anointed me with the
  finest oil.
11 My eyes have seen the downfall of my
  enemies;
  my ears have heard the defeat of my
  wicked opponents.
12 But the godly will flourish like palm
  trees
  and grow strong like the cedars of
  Lebanon.
13 For they are transplanted to the LORD's
  own house.
  They flourish in the courts of our God.
14 Even in old age they will still produce
  fruit;
  they will remain vital and green.
15 They will declare, "The LORD is just!
  He is my rock!
  There is no evil in him!"

## PSALM 93
1 The LORD is king! He is robed in majesty.
  Indeed, the LORD is robed in majesty
  and armed with strength.

## IN the pits
READ PSALM 71:19-21

A health crisis can make us feel as if we're in
the bottom of a pit. Maybe the trials of life
already had put us in a pit, but this latest news
just pulled us down a little deeper.

It's pretty hard to claw your way up and out
of a pit, but God has a plan.

He will climb right down in the pit with you and
then pour out His love into your life until there's
so much there that it lifts you right out of that pit . . .
if you let Him in.

Serious illness is a very deep pit, but the healing
touch of God is deeper still. Invite Him into your pit.

The world stands firm
and cannot be shaken.

2 Your throne, O Lord, has stood from time
immemorial.
You yourself are from the everlasting
past.
3 The floods have risen up, O Lord.
The floods have roared like thunder;
the floods have lifted their pounding
waves.
4 But mightier than the violent raging
of the seas,
mightier than the breakers on the
shore—
the Lord above is mightier than these!
5 Your royal laws cannot be changed.
Your reign, O Lord, is holy forever and
ever.

## PSALM 94

1 O Lord, the God of vengeance,
O God of vengeance, let your glorious
justice shine forth!
2 Arise, O judge of the earth.
Give the proud what they deserve.
3 How long, O Lord?
How long will the wicked be allowed
to gloat?
4 How long will they speak with
arrogance?
How long will these evil people boast?
5 They crush your people, Lord,
hurting those you claim as your own.
6 They kill widows and foreigners
and murder orphans.
7 "The Lord isn't looking," they say,
"and besides, the God of Israel*
doesn't care."

8 Think again, you fools!
When will you finally catch on?
9 Is he deaf—the one who made your ears?
Is he blind—the one who formed your
eyes?
10 He punishes the nations—won't he also
punish you?
He knows everything—doesn't he also
know what you are doing?
11 The Lord knows people's thoughts;
he knows they are worthless!

94:7 Hebrew *of Jacob.* See note on 44:4.

12 Joyful are those you discipline, Lord,
those you teach with your
instructions.
13 You give them relief from troubled
times
until a pit is dug to capture the
wicked.
14 The Lord will not reject his people;
he will not abandon his special
possession.
15 Judgment will again be founded on
justice,
and those with virtuous hearts will
pursue it.

16 Who will protect me from the
wicked?
Who will stand up for me against
evildoers?
17 Unless the Lord had helped me,
I would soon have settled in the
silence of the grave.
18 I cried out, "I am slipping!"
but your unfailing love, O Lord,
supported me.
19 When doubts filled my mind,
your comfort gave me renewed hope
and cheer.

20 Can unjust leaders claim that God is on
their side—
leaders whose decrees permit
injustice?
21 They gang up against the righteous
and condemn the innocent to death.
22 But the Lord is my fortress;
my God is the mighty rock where
I hide.
23 God will turn the sins of evil people back
on them.
He will destroy them for their sins.
The Lord our God will destroy them.

## PSALM 95

1 Come, let us sing to the Lord!
Let us shout joyfully to the Rock of our
salvation.
2 Let us come to him with thanksgiving.
Let us sing psalms of praise to him.
3 For the Lord is a great God,
a great King above all gods.

⁴ He holds in his hands the depths of the
earth
and the mightiest mountains.
⁵ The sea belongs to him, for he made it.
His hands formed the dry land, too.

⁶ Come, let us worship and bow down.
Let us kneel before the LORD our
maker,
⁷ for he is our God.
We are the people he watches over,
the flock under his care.

If only you would listen to his voice
today!
⁸ The LORD says, "Don't harden your hearts
as Israel did at Meribah,
as they did at Massah in the
wilderness.
⁹ For there your ancestors tested and tried
my patience,
even though they saw everything I did.
¹⁰ For forty years I was angry with them,
and I said,
'They are a people whose hearts turn
away from me.
They refuse to do what I tell them.'
¹¹ So in my anger I took an oath:
'They will never enter my place of
rest.'"

## PSALM 96

¹ Sing a new song to the LORD!
Let the whole earth sing to the LORD!
² Sing to the LORD; praise his name.
Each day proclaim the good news that
he saves.
³ Publish his glorious deeds among the
nations.
Tell everyone about the amazing things
he does.
⁴ Great is the LORD! He is most worthy of
praise!
He is to be feared above all gods.
⁵ The gods of other nations are mere idols,
but the LORD made the heavens!
⁶ Honor and majesty surround him;
strength and beauty fill his sanctuary.

⁷ O nations of the world, recognize the
LORD;
recognize that the LORD is glorious and
strong.

## LASTS a long time
READ PSALM 73:25-26

We all like things that are long lasting: appliances
that keep on working, cars that outlast our car
payments, even deodorants that last all day long!

But no matter what the outcome of your current
health crisis, someday your health is going to fail
because these "tents" we inhabit are only temporary. The reality is that nothing on this earth—not
even the earth itself—was made to last forever.

But as believers in Christ, we have another
reality that will never fade away. We have a kingdom that will last forever. It's God's kingdom, and
that is why we desire Him more than anything in
this world. Your soul is the only really long-lasting
thing you have.

⁸ Give to the LORD the glory he deserves!
Bring your offering and come into his
courts.
⁹ Worship the LORD in all his holy
splendor.
Let all the earth tremble before him.
¹⁰ Tell all the nations, "The LORD reigns!"
The world stands firm and cannot be
shaken.
He will judge all peoples fairly.

¹¹ Let the heavens be glad, and the earth
rejoice!
Let the sea and everything in it shout
his praise!
¹² Let the fields and their crops burst out
with joy!
Let the trees of the forest rustle with
praise
¹³ before the LORD, for he is coming!
He is coming to judge the earth.
He will judge the world with justice,
and the nations with his truth.

## PSALM 97

¹ The LORD is king!
Let the earth rejoice!
Let the farthest coastlands be glad.
² Dark clouds surround him.
Righteousness and justice are the
foundation of his throne.
³ Fire spreads ahead of him
and burns up all his foes.

4 His lightning flashes out across the world.
 The earth sees and trembles.
5 The mountains melt like wax before the
  LORD,
 before the Lord of all the earth.
6 The heavens proclaim his righteousness;
 every nation sees his glory.
7 Those who worship idols are disgraced—
 all who brag about their worthless
  gods—
 for every god must bow to him.
8 Jerusalem* has heard and rejoiced,
 and all the towns of Judah are glad
 because of your justice, O LORD!
9 For you, O LORD, are supreme over all the
  earth;
 you are exalted far above all gods.

10 You who love the LORD, hate evil!
 He protects the lives of his godly
  people
 and rescues them from the power
  of the wicked.
11 Light shines on the godly,
 and joy on those whose hearts are right.
12 May all who are godly rejoice in the LORD
 and praise his holy name!

## PSALM 98
*A psalm.*

1 Sing a new song to the LORD,
 for he has done wonderful deeds.
 His right hand has won a mighty
  victory;
 his holy arm has shown his saving
  power!
2 The LORD has announced his victory
 and has revealed his righteousness to
  every nation!
3 He has remembered his promise to love
 and be faithful to Israel.
 The ends of the earth have seen the
  victory of our God.

4 Shout to the LORD, all the earth;
 break out in praise and sing for joy!
5 Sing your praise to the LORD with the
  harp,
 with the harp and melodious song,
6 with trumpets and the sound of the ram's
  horn.

Make a joyful symphony before the
  LORD, the King!

7 Let the sea and everything in it shout his
  praise!
 Let the earth and all living things
  join in.
8 Let the rivers clap their hands in glee!
 Let the hills sing out their songs
  of joy
9 before the LORD.
 For the LORD is coming to judge the
  earth.
 He will judge the world with justice,
 and the nations with fairness.

## PSALM 99
1 The LORD is king!
 Let the nations tremble!
 He sits on his throne between the
  cherubim.
 Let the whole earth quake!
2 The LORD sits in majesty in Jerusalem,*
 exalted above all the nations.
3 Let them praise your great and awesome
  name.
 Your name is holy!
4 Mighty King, lover of justice,
 you have established fairness.
 You have acted with justice
 and righteousness throughout Israel.*
5 Exalt the LORD our God!
 Bow low before his feet, for he
  is holy!

6 Moses and Aaron were among his priests;
 Samuel also called on his name.
 They cried to the LORD for help,
 and he answered them.
7 He spoke to Israel from the pillar
  of cloud,
 and they followed the laws and decrees
  he gave them.
8 O LORD our God, you answered them.
 You were a forgiving God to them,
 but you punished them when they
  went wrong.

9 Exalt the LORD our God,
 and worship at his holy mountain
  in Jerusalem,
 for the LORD our God is holy!

97:8 Hebrew *Zion.*   99:2 Hebrew *Zion.*   99:4 Hebrew *Jacob.* See note on 44:4.

## PSALM 100
*A psalm of thanksgiving.*

*Fact!*

1 Shout with joy to the LORD, all the earth!
2 Worship the LORD with gladness.
  Come before him, singing with joy.
3 Acknowledge that the LORD is God!
  He made us, and we are his.
  We are his people, the sheep of his
  pasture.
4 Enter his gates with thanksgiving;
  go into his courts with praise.
  Give thanks to him and praise his
  name.
5 For the LORD is good.
  His unfailing love continues forever,
  and his faithfulness continues to each
  generation.

## PSALM 101
*A psalm of David.*

1 I will sing of your love and justice, LORD.
  I will praise you with songs.
2 I will be careful to live a blameless life—
  when will you come to help me?
  I will lead a life of integrity
  in my own home.
3 I will refuse to look at
  anything vile and vulgar.
  I hate all who deal crookedly;
  I will have nothing to do with them.
4 I will reject perverse ideas
  and stay away from every evil.

5 I will not tolerate people who slander
  their neighbors.
  I will not endure conceit and pride.

6 I will search for faithful people
  to be my companions.
  Only those who are above reproach
  will be allowed to serve me.
7 I will not allow deceivers to serve in my
  house,
  and liars will not stay in my presence.
8 My daily task will be to ferret out the
  wicked
  and free the city of the LORD from
  their grip.

## PSALM 102
*A prayer of one overwhelmed with trouble,
pouring out problems before the LORD.*

1 LORD, hear my prayer!
  Listen to my plea!
2 Don't turn away from me
  in my time of distress.
  Bend down to listen,
  and answer me quickly when I call
  to you.
3 For my days disappear like smoke,
  and my bones burn like red-hot
  coals.
4 My heart is sick, withered like grass,
  and I have lost my appetite.
5 Because of my groaning,
  I am reduced to skin and bones.

# LIVING under a shadow
READ PSALMS 91:1-7; 17:8; 36:7; AND 63:7

As you live under the shadow of serious illness, we'd like to suggest that you could choose
to live under a *different* shadow. The shadow we'd like you to move under—or stay under if you're
already there—is a much bigger shadow than any disease's shadow. It's a safe, secure, protective
shadow. There's no other shadow that can eclipse this one, and when we're underneath it, we're not
in the dark; we're supernaturally in the light. It might sound strange that you can find light by being
*under* a shadow, but it's true.

While the Bible describes God as light, it also refers to Him as a shadow, protecting us in His
shade. Imagine your disease as a little, dark cloud over your head. Then picture a huge shadow
above the cloud, which makes it so bright underneath that you can barely see your little shadow-
speck. It's not just your imagination—you're under the shadow of the Almighty, where you always
can find the light.

⁶ I am like an owl in the desert,
    like a little owl in a far-off wilderness.
⁷ I lie awake,
    lonely as a solitary bird on the roof.
⁸ My enemies taunt me day after day.
    They mock and curse me.
⁹ I eat ashes for food.
    My tears run down into my drink
¹⁰ because of your anger and wrath.
    For you have picked me up and thrown
        me out.
¹¹ My life passes as swiftly as the evening
        shadows.
    I am withering away like grass.

¹² But you, O LORD, will sit on your throne
        forever.
    Your fame will endure to every
        generation.
¹³ You will arise and have mercy on
        Jerusalem*—
    and now is the time to pity her,
    now is the time you promised to help.
¹⁴ For your people love every stone in her
        walls
    and cherish even the dust in her streets.
¹⁵ Then the nations will tremble before the
        LORD.
    The kings of the earth will tremble
        before his glory.
¹⁶ For the LORD will rebuild Jerusalem.
    He will appear in his glory.
¹⁷ He will listen to the prayers of the
        destitute.
    He will not reject their pleas.

¹⁸ Let this be recorded for future
        generations,
    so that a people not yet born will
        praise the LORD.
¹⁹ Tell them the LORD looked down
        from his heavenly sanctuary.
    He looked down to earth from heaven
²⁰    to hear the groans of the prisoners,
    to release those condemned to die.
²¹ And so the LORD's fame will be
        celebrated in Zion,
    his praises in Jerusalem,
²² when multitudes gather together
    and kingdoms come to worship the
        LORD.

²³ He broke my strength in midlife,
    cutting short my days.
²⁴ But I cried to him, "O my God, who lives
        forever,
    don't take my life while I am so young!
²⁵ Long ago you laid the foundation
        of the earth
    and made the heavens with your
        hands.
²⁶ They will perish, but you remain forever;
    they will wear out like old clothing.
    You will change them like a garment
        and discard them.
²⁷ But you are always the same;
    you will live forever.
²⁸ The children of your people
    will live in security.
    Their children's children
    will thrive in your presence."

# PSALM 103
*A psalm of David.*

¹ Let all that I am praise the LORD;
    with my whole heart, I will praise his
        holy name.
² Let all that I am praise the LORD;
    may I never forget the good things
        he does for me.
³ He forgives all my sins
    and heals all my diseases.
⁴ He redeems me from death
    and crowns me with love and tender
        mercies.
⁵ He fills my life with good things.
    My youth is renewed like the eagle's!

⁶ The LORD gives righteousness
    and justice to all who are treated
        unfairly.

⁷ He revealed his character to Moses
    and his deeds to the people of Israel.
⁸ The LORD is compassionate and
        merciful,
    slow to get angry and filled with
        unfailing love.
⁹ He will not constantly accuse us,
    nor remain angry forever.
¹⁰ He does not punish us for all our sins;
    he does not deal harshly with us,
        as we deserve.

102:13 Hebrew *Zion;* also in 102:16.

<sup>11</sup> For his unfailing love toward those who
   fear him
     is as great as the height of the heavens
     above the earth.
**12**He has removed our sins as far from us
     as the east is from the west.
<sup>13</sup> The LORD is like a father to his children,
     tender and compassionate to those
     who fear him.
<sup>14</sup> For he knows how weak we are;
     he remembers we are only dust.
<sup>15</sup> Our days on earth are like grass;
     like wildflowers, we bloom and die.
<sup>16</sup> The wind blows, and we are gone—
     as though we had never been here.
<sup>17</sup> But the love of the LORD remains forever
     with those who fear him.
   His salvation extends to the children's
   children
<sup>18</sup>   of those who are faithful to his
     covenant,
     of those who obey his commandments!

<sup>19</sup> The LORD has made the heavens his
     throne;
     from there he rules over everything.

<sup>20</sup> Praise the LORD, you angels,
     you mighty ones who carry out his
     plans,
     listening for each of his commands.
<sup>21</sup> Yes, praise the LORD, you armies of angels
     who serve him and do his will!
<sup>22</sup> Praise the LORD, everything he has created,
     everything in all his kingdom.

   Let all that I am praise the LORD.

## PSALM 104
<sup>1</sup> Let all that I am praise the LORD.

   O LORD my God, how great you are!
     You are robed with honor and majesty.
<sup>2</sup>   You are dressed in a robe of light.
   You stretch out the starry curtain of the
   heavens;
<sup>3</sup>   you lay out the rafters of your home in
   the rain clouds.
   You make the clouds your chariot;
     you ride upon the wings of the wind.
<sup>4</sup> The winds are your messengers;
     flames of fire are your servants.*

<sup>5</sup> You placed the world on its foundation
     so it would never be moved.
<sup>6</sup> You clothed the earth with floods
   of water,
     water that covered even the
     mountains.
<sup>7</sup> At your command, the water fled;
     at the sound of your thunder, it hurried
     away.
<sup>8</sup> Mountains rose and valleys sank
     to the levels you decreed.
<sup>9</sup> Then you set a firm boundary for the seas,
     so they would never again cover the
     earth.

<sup>10</sup> You make springs pour water into the
     ravines,
     so streams gush down from the
     mountains.
<sup>11</sup> They provide water for all the animals,
     and the wild donkeys quench their
     thirst.
<sup>12</sup> The birds nest beside the streams
     and sing among the branches of the
     trees.
<sup>13</sup> You send rain on the mountains from
     your heavenly home,
     and you fill the earth with the fruit
     of your labor.
<sup>14</sup> You cause grass to grow for the livestock
     and plants for people to use.
   You allow them to produce food from
     the earth—
<sup>15</sup>   wine to make them glad,
   olive oil to soothe their skin,
     and bread to give them strength.
<sup>16</sup> The trees of the LORD are well cared for—
     the cedars of Lebanon that he planted.
<sup>17</sup> There the birds make their nests,
     and the storks make their homes in the
     cypresses.
<sup>18</sup> High in the mountains live the wild goats,
     and the rocks form a refuge for the
     hyraxes.*

<sup>19</sup> You made the moon to mark the seasons,
     and the sun knows when to set.
<sup>20</sup> You send the darkness, and it becomes
     night,
     when all the forest animals prowl
     about.

**104:4** Greek version reads *He sends his angels like the winds, / his servants like flames of fire.* Compare Heb 1:7. **104:18** Or *coneys,* or *rock badgers.*

21 Then the young lions roar for their prey,
  stalking the food provided by God.
22 At dawn they slink back
  into their dens to rest.
23 Then people go off to their work,
  where they labor until evening.

24 O Lord, what a variety of things you have
  made!
  In wisdom you have made them all.
  The earth is full of your creatures.
25 Here is the ocean, vast and wide,
  teeming with life of every kind,
  both large and small.
26 See the ships sailing along,
  and Leviathan,* which you made
  to play in the sea.

27 They all depend on you
  to give them food as they need it.
28 When you supply it, they gather it.
  You open your hand to feed them,
  and they are richly satisfied.
29 But if you turn away from them, they
  panic.
  When you take away their breath,
  they die and turn again to dust.
30 When you give them your breath,* life
  is created,
  and you renew the face of the earth.

31 May the glory of the Lord continue
  forever!
  The Lord takes pleasure in all he has
  made!
32 The earth trembles at his glance;
  the mountains smoke at his touch.

33 I will sing to the Lord as long as I live.
  I will praise my God to my last breath!
34 May all my thoughts be pleasing to him,
  for I rejoice in the Lord.
35 Let all sinners vanish from the face
  of the earth;
  let the wicked disappear forever.

  Let all that I am praise the Lord.

  Praise the Lord!

# PSALM 105

1 Give thanks to the Lord and proclaim his
  greatness.
  Let the whole world know what he has
  done.
2 Sing to him; yes, sing his praises.
  Tell everyone about his wonderful
  deeds.
3 Exult in his holy name;
  rejoice, you who worship the Lord.
4 Search for the Lord and for his strength;
  continually seek him.
5 Remember the wonders he has
  performed,
  his miracles, and the rulings he has
  given,
6 you children of his servant Abraham,
  you descendants of Jacob, his
  chosen ones.

7 He is the Lord our God.
  His justice is seen throughout the land.
8 He always stands by his covenant—
  the commitment he made to a
  thousand generations.
9 This is the covenant he made with
  Abraham
  and the oath he swore to Isaac.
10 He confirmed it to Jacob as a decree,
  and to the people of Israel as a never-
  ending covenant:
11 "I will give you the land of Canaan
  as your special possession."

12 He said this when they were few in
  number,
  a tiny group of strangers in Canaan.
13 They wandered from nation to nation,
  from one kingdom to another.
14 Yet he did not let anyone oppress them.
  He warned kings on their behalf:
15 "Do not touch my chosen people,
  and do not hurt my prophets."

16 He called for a famine on the land
  of Canaan,
  cutting off its food supply.
17 Then he sent someone to Egypt ahead
  of them—
  Joseph, who was sold as a slave.
18 They bruised his feet with fetters
  and placed his neck in an iron collar.
19 Until the time came to fulfill his
  dreams,*

**104:26** The identification of Leviathan is disputed, ranging from an earthly creature to a mythical sea monster in ancient literature.
**104:30** Or *When you send your Spirit.*     **105:19** Hebrew *his word.*

the LORD tested Joseph's character.
²⁰ Then Pharaoh sent for him and set him
free;
the ruler of the nation opened his
prison door.
²¹ Joseph was put in charge of all the king's
household;
he became ruler over all the king's
possessions.
²² He could instruct the king's aides as he
pleased
and teach the king's advisers.

²³ Then Israel arrived in Egypt;
Jacob lived as a foreigner in the land
of Ham.
²⁴ And the LORD multiplied the people
of Israel
until they became too mighty for their
enemies.
²⁵ Then he turned the Egyptians against the
Israelites,
and they plotted against the LORD's
servants.

²⁶ But the LORD sent his servant Moses,
along with Aaron, whom he had
chosen.
²⁷ They performed miraculous signs among
the Egyptians,
and wonders in the land of Ham.
²⁸ The LORD blanketed Egypt in darkness,
for they had defied his commands to
let his people go.
²⁹ He turned their water into blood,
poisoning all the fish.
³⁰ Then frogs overran the land
and even invaded the king's bedrooms.
³¹ When the LORD spoke, flies descended
on the Egyptians,
and gnats swarmed across Egypt.
³² He sent them hail instead of rain,
and lightning flashed over the land.
³³ He ruined their grapevines and fig trees
and shattered all the trees.
³⁴ He spoke, and hordes of locusts came—
young locusts beyond number.
³⁵ They ate up everything green in the land,
destroying all the crops in their fields.
³⁶ Then he killed the oldest son in each
Egyptian home,
the pride and joy of each family.

³⁷ The LORD brought his people out of
Egypt, loaded with silver and gold;
and not one among the tribes of Israel
even stumbled.
³⁸ Egypt was glad when they were gone,
for they feared them greatly.
³⁹ The LORD spread a cloud above them as a
covering
and gave them a great fire to light the
darkness.
⁴⁰ They asked for meat, and he sent them
quail;
he satisfied their hunger with manna—
bread from heaven.
⁴¹ He split open a rock, and water gushed
out
to form a river through the dry
wasteland.
⁴² For he remembered his sacred promise
to his servant Abraham.
⁴³ So he brought his people out of Egypt
with joy,
his chosen ones with rejoicing.
⁴⁴ He gave his people the lands of pagan
nations,
and they harvested crops that others
had planted.
⁴⁵ All this happened so they would follow
his decrees
and obey his instructions.

Praise the LORD!

## PSALM 106

¹ Praise the LORD!

Give thanks to the LORD, for he
is good!
His faithful love endures forever.
² Who can list the glorious miracles
of the LORD?
Who can ever praise him enough?
³ There is joy for those who deal justly with
others
and always do what is right.

⁴ Remember me, LORD, when you show
favor to your people;
come near and rescue me.
⁵ Let me share in the prosperity of your
chosen ones.
Let me rejoice in the joy of your
people;

let me praise you with those who are
your heritage.

6 Like our ancestors, we have sinned.
We have done wrong! We have acted
wickedly!
7 Our ancestors in Egypt
were not impressed by the LORD's
miraculous deeds.
They soon forgot his many acts of
kindness to them.
Instead, they rebelled against him at
the Red Sea.*
8 Even so, he saved them—
to defend the honor of his name
and to demonstrate his mighty power.
9 He commanded the Red Sea* to dry up.
He led Israel across the sea as if it were
a desert.
10 So he rescued them from their enemies
and redeemed them from their foes.
11 Then the water returned and covered
their enemies;
not one of them survived.
12 Then his people believed his promises.
Then they sang his praise.

13 Yet how quickly they forgot what he had
done!
They wouldn't wait for his counsel!
14 In the wilderness their desires ran wild,
testing God's patience in that dry
wasteland.
15 So he gave them what they asked for,
but he sent a plague along with it.
16 The people in the camp were jealous
of Moses
and envious of Aaron, the LORD's holy
priest.
17 Because of this, the earth opened up;
it swallowed Dathan
and buried Abiram and the other
rebels.
18 Fire fell upon their followers;
a flame consumed the wicked.

19 The people made a calf at Mount Sinai*;
they bowed before an image made of
gold.
20 They traded their glorious God
for a statue of a grass-eating bull.

21 They forgot God, their savior,
who had done such great things
in Egypt—
22 such wonderful things in the land
of Ham,
such awesome deeds at the Red Sea.
23 So he declared he would destroy them.
But Moses, his chosen one, stepped
between the LORD and the people.
He begged him to turn from his anger
and not destroy them.

24 The people refused to enter the pleasant
land,
for they wouldn't believe his promise
to care for them.
25 Instead, they grumbled in their tents
and refused to obey the LORD.
26 Therefore, he solemnly swore
that he would kill them in the
wilderness,
27 that he would scatter their descendants
among the nations,
exiling them to distant lands.

28 Then our ancestors joined in the worship
of Baal at Peor;
they even ate sacrifices offered to the
dead!
29 They angered the LORD with all these
things,
so a plague broke out among them.
30 But Phinehas had the courage to
intervene,
and the plague was stopped.
31 So he has been regarded as a righteous
man
ever since that time.

32 At Meribah, too, they angered the LORD,
causing Moses serious trouble.
33 They made Moses angry,*
and he spoke foolishly.

34 Israel failed to destroy the nations in the
land,
as the LORD had commanded them.
35 Instead, they mingled among the
pagans
and adopted their evil customs.
36 They worshiped their idols,
which led to their downfall.

106:7 Hebrew at the sea, the sea of reeds.   106:9 Hebrew sea of reeds; also in 106:22.   106:19 Hebrew at Horeb, another name for
Sinai.   106:33 Hebrew They embittered his spirit.

37 They even sacrificed their sons
  and their daughters to the demons.
38 They shed innocent blood,
  the blood of their sons and daughters.
By sacrificing them to the idols of
  Canaan,
  they polluted the land with murder.
39 They defiled themselves by their evil
  deeds,
  and their love of idols was adultery
  in the LORD's sight.

40 That is why the LORD's anger burned
  against his people,
  and he abhorred his own special
  possession.
41 He handed them over to pagan nations,
  and they were ruled by those who
  hated them.
42 Their enemies crushed them
  and brought them under their cruel
  power.
43 Again and again he rescued them,
  but they chose to rebel against him,
  and they were finally destroyed by
  their sin.
44 Even so, he pitied them in their distress
  and listened to their cries.
45 He remembered his covenant with them
  and relented because of his unfailing
  love.
46 He even caused their captors
  to treat them with kindness.

47 Save us, O LORD our God!
  Gather us back from among the
  nations,
  so we can thank your holy name
  and rejoice and praise you.

48 Praise the LORD, the God of Israel,
  who lives from everlasting to
  everlasting!
  Let all the people say, "Amen!"

  Praise the LORD!

• BOOK FIVE (Psalms 107–150)
PSALM 107
1 Give thanks to the LORD, for he is good!
  His faithful love endures forever.
2 Has the LORD redeemed you? Then
  speak out!

Tell others he has redeemed you from
  your enemies.
3 For he has gathered the exiles from many
  lands,
  from east and west,
  from north and south.

4 Some wandered in the wilderness,
  lost and homeless.
5 Hungry and thirsty,
  they nearly died.
6 "LORD, help!" they cried in their trouble,
  and he rescued them from their
  distress.
7 He led them straight to safety,
  to a city where they could live.
8 Let them praise the LORD for his great
  love
  and for the wonderful things he has
  done for them.
9 For he satisfies the thirsty
  and fills the hungry with good things.

10 Some sat in darkness and deepest
  gloom,
  imprisoned in iron chains of misery.
11 They rebelled against the words of God,
  scorning the counsel of the Most High.
12 That is why he broke them with hard
  labor;
  they fell, and no one was there to help
  them.
13 "LORD, help!" they cried in their trouble,
  and he saved them from their distress.
14 He led them from the darkness and
  deepest gloom;
  he snapped their chains.
15 Let them praise the LORD for his great
  love
  and for the wonderful things he has
  done for them.
16 For he broke down their prison gates
  of bronze;
  he cut apart their bars of iron.

17 Some were fools; they rebelled
  and suffered for their sins.
18 They couldn't stand the thought
  of food,
  and they were knocking on death's
  door.
19 "LORD, help!" they cried in their trouble,
  and he saved them from their distress.

# FACING facts

READ PSALM 100

<u>Many times we let our feelings dictate our actions.</u>
We don't do something we know we should do
because we don't *feel* like doing it. Or we do
something we know we shouldn't because it *feels*
good. Possibly you don't *feel* like praising God
today. Perhaps you don't *feel* particularly thankful.

Although this is a psalm expressing strong
emotions, they are based on facts and not feelings.
<u>Fact:</u> The LORD is God. Fact: He made us, and we
are His. <u>Fact:</u> The LORD is good. <u>Fact:</u> His unfailing
love continues forever. <u>Fact:</u> His faithfulness
continues to each generation.

As a matter of fact, you can praise Him today,
no matter what you're feeling.

<sup>20</sup> He sent out his word and healed them,
    snatching them from the door of death.
<sup>21</sup> Let them praise the LORD for his great
    love
  and for the wonderful things he has
    done for them.
<sup>22</sup> Let them offer sacrifices of thanksgiving
  and sing joyfully about his glorious acts.

<sup>23</sup> Some went off to sea in ships,
  plying the trade routes of the world.
<sup>24</sup> They, too, observed the LORD's power
    in action,
  his impressive works on the deepest
    seas.
<sup>25</sup> He spoke, and the winds rose,
  stirring up the waves.
<sup>26</sup> Their ships were tossed to the heavens
  and plunged again to the depths;
  the sailors cringed in terror.
<sup>27</sup> They reeled and staggered like
    drunkards
  and were at their wits' end.
<sup>28</sup> "LORD, help!" they cried in their trouble,
  and he saved them from their distress.
<sup>29</sup> He calmed the storm to a whisper
  and stilled the waves.
<sup>30</sup> What a blessing was that stillness
  as he brought them safely into harbor!
<sup>31</sup> Let them praise the LORD for his great
    love
  and for the wonderful things he has
    done for them.

<sup>32</sup> Let them exalt him publicly before the
    congregation
  and before the leaders of the nation.

<sup>33</sup> He changes rivers into deserts,
  and springs of water into dry, thirsty
    land.
<sup>34</sup> He turns the fruitful land into salty
    wastelands,
  because of the wickedness of those
    who live there.
<sup>35</sup> But he also turns deserts into pools
    of water,
  the dry land into springs of water.
<sup>36</sup> He brings the hungry to settle there
  and to build their cities.
<sup>37</sup> They sow their fields, plant their
    vineyards,
  and harvest their bumper crops.
<sup>38</sup> How he blesses them!
  They raise large families there,
  and their herds of livestock increase.

<sup>39</sup> When they decrease in number and
    become impoverished
  through oppression, trouble, and
    sorrow,
<sup>40</sup> the LORD pours contempt on their princes,
  causing them to wander in trackless
    wastelands.
<sup>41</sup> But he rescues the poor from trouble
  and increases their families like flocks
    of sheep.
<sup>42</sup> The godly will see these things and be
    glad,
  while the wicked are struck silent.
<sup>43</sup> Those who are wise will take all this
    to heart;
  they will see in our history the faithful
    love of the LORD.

## PSALM 108
*A song. A psalm of David.*

<sup>1</sup> My heart is confident in you, O God;
  no wonder I can sing your praises with
    all my heart!
<sup>2</sup> Wake up, lyre and harp!
  I will wake the dawn with my song.
<sup>3</sup> I will thank you, LORD, among all the
    people.
  I will sing your praises among the
    nations.

4 For your unfailing love is higher than the
heavens.
Your faithfulness reaches to the clouds.
5 Be exalted, O God, above the highest
heavens.
May your glory shine over all the earth.

6 Now rescue your beloved people.
Answer and save us by your power.
7 God has promised this by his holiness*:
"I will divide up Shechem with joy.
I will measure out the valley of Succoth.
8 Gilead is mine,
and Manasseh, too.
Ephraim, my helmet, will produce my
warriors,
and Judah, my scepter, will produce
my kings.
9 But Moab, my washbasin, will become my
servant,
and I will wipe my feet on Edom
and shout in triumph over Philistia."

10 Who will bring me into the fortified city?
Who will bring me victory over Edom?
11 Have you rejected us, O God?
Will you no longer march with our
armies?
12 Oh, please help us against our enemies,
for all human help is useless.
13 With God's help we will do mighty
things,
for he will trample down our foes.

## PSALM 109
*For the choir director: A psalm of David.*

1 O God, whom I praise,
don't stand silent and aloof
2 while the wicked slander me
and tell lies about me.
3 They surround me with hateful words
and fight against me for no reason.
4 I love them, but they try to destroy me
with accusations
even as I am praying for them!
5 They repay evil for good,
and hatred for my love.

6 They say,* "Get an evil person to turn
against him.
Send an accuser to bring him to trial.

7 When his case comes up for judgment,
let him be pronounced guilty.
Count his prayers as sins.
8 Let his years be few;
let someone else take his position.
9 May his children become fatherless,
and his wife a widow.
10 May his children wander as beggars
and be driven from their ruined
homes.
11 May creditors seize his entire estate,
and strangers take all he has earned.
12 Let no one be kind to him;
let no one pity his fatherless children.
13 May all his offspring die.
May his family name be blotted out in
a single generation.
14 May the LORD never forget the sins of his
fathers;
may his mother's sins never be erased
from the record.
15 May the LORD always remember these
sins,
and may his name disappear from
human memory.
16 For he refused all kindness to others;
he persecuted the poor and needy,
and he hounded the brokenhearted
to death.
17 He loved to curse others;
now you curse him.
He never blessed others;
now don't you bless him.
18 Cursing is as natural to him as his
clothing,
or the water he drinks,
or the rich food he eats.
19 Now may his curses return and cling to
him like clothing;
may they be tied around him like
a belt."

20 May those curses become the LORD's
punishment
for my accusers who speak evil of me.
21 But deal well with me, O Sovereign LORD,
for the sake of your own reputation!
Rescue me
because you are so faithful and good.
22 For I am poor and needy,
and my heart is full of pain.

**108:7** Or *in his sanctuary.*    **109:6** Hebrew lacks *They say.*

²³ I am fading like a shadow at dusk;
    I am brushed off like a locust.
²⁴ My knees are weak from fasting,
    and I am skin and bones.
²⁵ I am a joke to people everywhere;
    when they see me, they shake their
        heads in scorn.

²⁶ Help me, O LORD my God!
    Save me because of your unfailing love.
²⁷ Let them see that this is your doing,
    that you yourself have done it, LORD.
²⁸ Then let them curse me if they like,
    but you will bless me!
  When they attack me, they will be
        disgraced!
  But I, your servant, will go right on
        rejoicing!
²⁹ May my accusers be clothed with
        disgrace;
    may their humiliation cover them
        like a cloak.
³⁰ But I will give repeated thanks to the
        LORD,
    praising him to everyone.
³¹ For he stands beside the needy,
    ready to save them from those who
        condemn them.

## PSALM 110
*A psalm of David.*
*(God)*                    *(Jesus)*
¹ The LORD said to my Lord,
    "Sit in the place of honor at my right
        hand
  until I humble your enemies,
    making them a footstool under your
        feet."

² The LORD will extend your powerful
        kingdom from Jerusalem*;
    you will rule over your enemies.
³ When you go to war,
    your people will serve you willingly.
  You are arrayed in holy garments,
    and your strength will be renewed
        each day like the morning dew.

⁴ The LORD has taken an oath and will not
        break his vow:
  "You are a priest forever in the order
        of Melchizedek."

⁵ The Lord stands at your right hand
    to protect you.
  He will strike down many kings when
        his anger erupts.
⁶ He will punish the nations
    and fill their lands with corpses;
  he will shatter heads over the whole
        earth.
⁷ But he himself will be refreshed from
        brooks along the way.
  He will be victorious.

## PSALM 111*
¹ Praise the LORD!

  I will thank the LORD with all my heart
    as I meet with his godly people.
² How amazing are the deeds of the
        LORD!
  All who delight in him should ponder
        them.
³ Everything he does reveals his glory and
        majesty.
  His righteousness never fails.
⁴ He causes us to remember his wonderful
        works.
  How gracious and merciful is our
        LORD!
⁵ He gives food to those who fear him;
    he always remembers his covenant.
⁶ He has shown his great power to his
        people
  by giving them the lands of other
        nations.
⁷ All he does is just and good,
    and all his commandments are
        trustworthy.
⁸ They are forever true,
    to be obeyed faithfully and with
        integrity.
⁹ He has paid a full ransom for his people.
  He has guaranteed his covenant with
        them forever.
  What a holy, awe-inspiring name he
        has!
¹⁰ Fear of the LORD is the foundation
    of true wisdom.
  All who obey his commandments will
        grow in wisdom.

  Praise him forever!

---

**110:2** Hebrew *Zion*.   **111** This psalm is a Hebrew acrostic poem; after the introductory note of praise, each line begins with a successive letter of the Hebrew alphabet.

## PSALM 112*
¹ Praise the Lord!

How joyful are those who fear the Lord
and delight in obeying his commands.
² Their children will be successful
everywhere;
an entire generation of godly people
will be blessed.
³ They themselves will be wealthy,
and their good deeds will last forever.
⁴ Light shines in the darkness for the godly.
They are generous, compassionate, and
righteous.
⁵ Good comes to those who lend money
generously
and conduct their business fairly.
⁶ Such people will not be overcome by evil.
Those who are righteous will be long
remembered.
⁷ They do not fear bad news;
they confidently trust the Lord to care
for them.
⁸ They are confident and fearless
and can face their foes triumphantly.
⁹ They share freely and give generously to
those in need.
Their good deeds will be remembered
forever.
They will have influence and honor.
¹⁰ The wicked will see this and be
infuriated.
They will grind their teeth in anger;
they will slink away, their hopes
thwarted.

## PSALM 113
¹ Praise the Lord!

Yes, give praise, O servants of the Lord.
Praise the name of the Lord!
² Blessed be the name of the Lord
now and forever.
³ Everywhere—from east to west—
praise the name of the Lord.
⁴ For the Lord is high above the nations;
his glory is higher than the heavens.

⁵ Who can be compared with the Lord
our God,
who is enthroned on high?

⁶ He stoops to look down
on heaven and on earth.
⁷ He lifts the poor from the dust
and the needy from the garbage dump.
⁸ He sets them among princes,
even the princes of his own people!
⁹ He gives the childless woman a family,
making her a happy mother.

Praise the Lord!

## PSALM 114
¹ When the Israelites escaped from Egypt—
when the family of Jacob left that
foreign land—
² the land of Judah became God's sanctuary,
and Israel became his kingdom.

³ The Red Sea* saw them coming and
hurried out of their way!
The water of the Jordan River turned
away.
⁴ The mountains skipped like rams,
the hills like lambs!
⁵ What's wrong, Red Sea, that made you
hurry out of their way?
What happened, Jordan River, that you
turned away?
⁶ Why, mountains, did you skip like rams?
Why, hills, like lambs?

⁷ Tremble, O earth, at the presence of the
Lord,
at the presence of the God of Jacob.
⁸ He turned the rock into a pool of water;
yes, a spring of water flowed from solid
rock.

## PSALM 115
¹ Not to us, O Lord, not to us,
but to your name goes all the glory
for your unfailing love and faithfulness.
² Why let the nations say,
"Where is their God?"
³ Our God is in the heavens,
and he does as he wishes.
⁴ Their idols are merely things of silver
and gold,
shaped by human hands.
⁵ They have mouths but cannot speak,
and eyes but cannot see.

**112** This psalm is a Hebrew acrostic poem; after the introductory note of praise, each line begins with a successive letter of the Hebrew alphabet.    **114:3** Hebrew *the sea;* also in 114:5.

6 They have ears but cannot hear,
  and noses but cannot smell.
7 They have hands but cannot feel,
  and feet but cannot walk,
  and throats but cannot make a sound.
8 And those who make idols are just like
    them,
  as are all who trust in them.

9 O Israel, trust the LORD!
  He is your helper and your shield.
10 O priests, descendants of Aaron, trust the
    LORD!
  He is your helper and your shield.
11 All you who fear the LORD, trust the LORD!
  He is your helper and your shield.

12 The LORD remembers us and will bless us.
  He will bless the people of Israel
  and bless the priests, the descendants
    of Aaron.
13 He will bless those who fear the LORD,
  both great and lowly.

14 May the LORD richly bless
  both you and your children.
15 May you be blessed by the LORD,
  who made heaven and earth.
16 The heavens belong to the LORD,
  but he has given the earth to all
    humanity.
17 The dead cannot sing praises to the LORD,
  for they have gone into the silence
    of the grave.
18 But we can praise the LORD
  both now and forever!

  Praise the LORD!

## PSALM 116

1 I love the LORD because he hears my voice
  and my prayer for mercy.
2 Because he bends down to listen,
  I will pray as long as I have breath!
3 Death wrapped its ropes around me;
  the terrors of the grave* overtook me.
  I saw only trouble and sorrow.
4 Then I called on the name of the LORD:
  "Please, LORD, save me!"
5 How kind the LORD is! How good he is!
  So merciful, this God of ours!
6 The LORD protects those of childlike faith;
  I was facing death, and he saved me.

7 Let my soul be at rest again,
  for the LORD has been good to me.
8 He has saved me from death,
  my eyes from tears,
  my feet from stumbling.
9 And so I walk in the LORD's presence
  as I live here on earth!
10 I believed in you, so I said,
  "I am deeply troubled, LORD."
11 In my anxiety I cried out to you,
  "These people are all liars!"
12 What can I offer the LORD
  for all he has done for me?
13 I will lift up the cup of salvation
  and praise the LORD's name for
    saving me.
14 I will keep my promises to the LORD
  in the presence of all his people.

15 The LORD cares deeply
  when his loved ones die.
16 O LORD, I am your servant;
  yes, I am your servant, born into your
    household;
  you have freed me from my chains.
17 I will offer you a sacrifice of
    thanksgiving
  and call on the name of the LORD.
18 I will fulfill my vows to the LORD
  in the presence of all his people—
19 in the house of the LORD
  in the heart of Jerusalem.

  Praise the LORD!

## PSALM 117

1 Praise the LORD, all you nations.
  Praise him, all you people of the earth.
2 For he loves us with unfailing love;
  the LORD's faithfulness endures
    forever.

  Praise the LORD!

## PSALM 118

1 Give thanks to the LORD, for he is good!
  His faithful love endures forever.

2 Let all Israel repeat:
  "His faithful love endures forever."
3 Let Aaron's descendants, the priests,
    repeat:
  "His faithful love endures forever."

116:3 Hebrew *of Sheol*.

⁴ Let all who fear the LORD repeat:
   "His faithful love endures forever."

⁵ In my distress I prayed to the LORD,
   and the LORD answered me and
   set me free.
⁶ The LORD is for me, so I will have no fear.
   What can mere people do to me?
⁷ Yes, the LORD is for me; he will help me.
   I will look in triumph at those who
   hate me.
⁸ It is better to take refuge in the LORD
   than to trust in people.
⁹ It is better to take refuge in the LORD
   than to trust in princes.

¹⁰ Though hostile nations surrounded me,
   I destroyed them all with the authority
   of the LORD.
¹¹ Yes, they surrounded and attacked me,
   but I destroyed them all with the
   authority of the LORD.
¹² They swarmed around me like bees;
   they blazed against me like a crackling
   fire.
   But I destroyed them all with the
   authority of the LORD.
¹³ My enemies did their best to kill me,
   but the LORD rescued me.
¹⁴ The LORD is my strength and my song;
   he has given me victory.
¹⁵ Songs of joy and victory are sung in the
   camp of the godly.
   The strong right arm of the LORD has
   done glorious things!
¹⁶ The strong right arm of the LORD is
   raised in triumph.
   The strong right arm of the LORD has
   done glorious things!
¹⁷ I will not die; instead, I will live
   to tell what the LORD has done.
¹⁸ The LORD has punished me severely,
   but he did not let me die.

¹⁹ Open for me the gates where the
   righteous enter,
   and I will go in and thank the LORD.
²⁰ These gates lead to the presence of the
   LORD,
   and the godly enter there.

**119** This psalm is a Hebrew acrostic poem; there are twenty-two
stanzas, one for each successive letter of the Hebrew alphabet.
Each of the eight verses within each stanza begins with the
Hebrew letter named in its heading.

²¹ I thank you for answering my prayer
   and giving me victory!

²² The stone that the builders rejected
   has now become the cornerstone.
²³ This is the LORD's doing,
   and it is wonderful to see.
²⁴ This is the day the LORD has made.
   We will rejoice and be glad in it.
²⁵ Please, LORD, please save us.
   Please, LORD, please give us success.
²⁶ Bless the one who comes in the name of
   the LORD.
   We bless you from the house of the
   LORD.
²⁷ The LORD is God, shining upon us.
   Take the sacrifice and bind it with
   cords on the altar.
²⁸ You are my God, and I will praise you!
   You are my God, and I will exalt you!

²⁹ Give thanks to the LORD, for he is good!
   His faithful love endures forever.

## PSALM 119

*Aleph**

¹ Joyful are people of integrity,
   who follow the instructions of the LORD.
² Joyful are those who obey his laws
   and search for him with all their hearts.
³ They do not compromise with evil,
   and they walk only in his paths.
⁴ You have charged us
   to keep your commandments carefully.

## NO fear

READ PSALM 112:1-8

What are your phobias? Are you afraid of
snakes or bats or spiders? How about flying or
heights or small spaces? Maybe you're afraid of
needles or hospitals. Most of us in a health crisis
are afraid of getting bad news. But this psalm says
it's possible not to be that way.

How? Strangely enough, by being "fear-filled"
people. The fear that fills these people—leaving little
room for any other fear—is the fear of the Lord.
They're not afraid *of* God, but they have so much
reverence *for* God and His mighty power that they
are confident He can take care of them.

If you *know* this fear, you can have *no* other fear.

⁵ Oh, that my actions would consistently
    reflect your decrees!
⁶ Then I will not be ashamed
    when I compare my life with your
      commands.
⁷ As I learn your righteous regulations,
    I will thank you by living as I should!
⁸ I will obey your decrees.
    Please don't give up on me!

### Beth

⁹ How can a young person stay pure?
    By obeying your word.
¹⁰ I have tried hard to find you—
    don't let me wander from your
      commands.
¹¹ I have hidden your word in my heart,
    that I might not sin against you.
¹² I praise you, O LORD;
    teach me your decrees.
¹³ I have recited aloud
    all the regulations you have given us.
¹⁴ I have rejoiced in your laws
    as much as in riches.
¹⁵ I will study your commandments
    and reflect on your ways.
¹⁶ I will delight in your decrees
    and not forget your word.

### Gimel

¹⁷ Be good to your servant,
    that I may live and obey your word.
¹⁸ Open my eyes to see
    the wonderful truths in your
      instructions.
¹⁹ I am only a foreigner in the land.
    Don't hide your commands from me!
²⁰ I am always overwhelmed
    with a desire for your regulations.
²¹ You rebuke the arrogant;
    those who wander from your
      commands are cursed.
²² Don't let them scorn and insult me,
    for I have obeyed your laws.
²³ Even princes sit and speak against me,
    but I will meditate on your decrees.
²⁴ Your laws please me;
    they give me wise advice.

### Daleth

²⁵ I lie in the dust;
    revive me by your word.

119:37 Some manuscripts read *in your ways*.

²⁶ I told you my plans, and you answered.
    Now teach me your decrees.
²⁷ Help me understand the meaning of your
      commandments,
    and I will meditate on your wonderful
      deeds.
²⁸ I weep with sorrow;
    encourage me by your word.
²⁹ Keep me from lying to myself;
    give me the privilege of knowing your
      instructions.
³⁰ I have chosen to be faithful;
    I have determined to live by your
      regulations.
³¹ I cling to your laws.
    LORD, don't let me be put to shame!
³² I will pursue your commands,
    for you expand my understanding.

### He

³³ Teach me your decrees, O LORD;
    I will keep them to the end.
³⁴ Give me understanding and I will obey
      your instructions;
    I will put them into practice with all
      my heart.
³⁵ Make me walk along the path of your
      commands,
    for that is where my happiness is
      found.
³⁶ Give me an eagerness for your laws
    rather than a love for money!
³⁷ Turn my eyes from worthless things,
    and give me life through your word.*
³⁸ Reassure me of your promise,
    made to those who fear you.
³⁹ Help me abandon my shameful ways;
    for your regulations are good.
⁴⁰ I long to obey your commandments!
    Renew my life with your goodness.

### Waw

⁴¹ LORD, give me your unfailing love,
    the salvation that you promised me.
⁴² Then I can answer those who taunt me,
    for I trust in your word.
⁴³ Do not snatch your word of truth
      from me,
    for your regulations are my only hope.
⁴⁴ I will keep on obeying your instructions
      forever and ever.

⁴⁵ I will walk in freedom,
for I have devoted myself to your
commandments.
⁴⁶ I will speak to kings about your laws,
and I will not be ashamed.
⁴⁷ How I delight in your commands!
How I love them!
⁴⁸ I honor and love your commands.
I meditate on your decrees.

### Zayin

⁴⁹ Remember your promise to me;
it is my only hope.
⁵⁰ Your promise revives me;
it comforts me in all my troubles.
⁵¹ The proud hold me in utter contempt,
but I do not turn away from your
instructions.
⁵² I meditate on your age-old regulations;
O Lord, they comfort me.
⁵³ I become furious with the wicked,
because they reject your instructions.
⁵⁴ Your decrees have been the theme
of my songs
wherever I have lived.
⁵⁵ I reflect at night on who you are, O Lord;
therefore, I obey your instructions.
⁵⁶ This is how I spend my life:
obeying your commandments.

### Heth

⁵⁷ Lord, you are mine!
I promise to obey your words!
⁵⁸ With all my heart I want your blessings.
Be merciful as you promised.
⁵⁹ I pondered the direction of my life,
and I turned to follow your laws.
⁶⁰ I will hurry, without delay,
to obey your commands.
⁶¹ Evil people try to drag me into sin,
but I am firmly anchored to your
instructions.
⁶² I rise at midnight to thank you
for your just regulations.
⁶³ I am a friend to anyone who fears you—
anyone who obeys your
commandments.
⁶⁴ O Lord, your unfailing love fills the earth;
teach me your decrees.

### Teth

⁶⁵ You have done many good things for me,
Lord,

just as you promised.
⁶⁶ I believe in your commands;
now teach me good judgment and
knowledge.
⁶⁷ I used to wander off until you
disciplined me;
but now I closely follow your word.
⁶⁸ You are good and do only good;
teach me your decrees.
⁶⁹ Arrogant people smear me with lies,
but in truth I obey your
commandments with all my heart.
⁷⁰ Their hearts are dull and stupid,
but I delight in your instructions.
⁷¹ My suffering was good for me,
for it taught me to pay attention to
your decrees.
⁷² Your instructions are more valuable
to me
than millions in gold and silver.

### Yodh

⁷³ You made me; you created me.
Now give me the sense to follow your
commands.
⁷⁴ May all who fear you find in me a cause
for joy,
for I have put my hope in your word.
⁷⁵ I know, O Lord, that your regulations are
fair;
you disciplined me because I
needed it.
⁷⁶ Now let your unfailing love comfort me,
just as you promised me, your servant.
⁷⁷ Surround me with your tender mercies
so I may live,
for your instructions are my delight.
⁷⁸ Bring disgrace upon the arrogant people
who lied about me;
meanwhile, I will concentrate on your
commandments.
⁷⁹ Let me be united with all who fear you,
with those who know your laws.
⁸⁰ May I be blameless in keeping your
decrees;
then I will never be ashamed.

### Kaph

⁸¹ I am worn out waiting for your rescue,
but I have put my hope in your word.
⁸² My eyes are straining to see your
promises come true.
When will you comfort me?

83 I am shriveled like a wineskin in the
    smoke,
      but I have not forgotten to obey your
      decrees.
84 How long must I wait?
      When will you punish those who
      persecute me?
85 These arrogant people who hate your
    instructions
      have dug deep pits to trap me.
86 All your commands are trustworthy.
      Protect me from those who hunt me
      down without cause.
87 They almost finished me off,
      but I refused to abandon your
      commandments.
88 In your unfailing love, spare my life;
      then I can continue to obey your laws.

### Lamedh

89 Your eternal word, O LORD,
      stands firm in heaven.
90 Your faithfulness extends to every
    generation,
      as enduring as the earth you created.
91 Your regulations remain true to this day,
      for everything serves your plans.
92 If your instructions hadn't sustained me
    with joy,
      I would have died in my misery.
93 I will never forget your commandments,
      for by them you give me life.
94 I am yours; rescue me!
      For I have worked hard at obeying your
      commandments.
95 Though the wicked hide along the way to
    kill me,
      I will quietly keep my mind on your
      laws.
96 Even perfection has its limits,
      but your commands have no limit.

### Mem

97 Oh, how I love your instructions!
      I think about them all day long.
98 Your commands make me wiser than my
    enemies,
      for they are my constant guide.
99 Yes, I have more insight than my
    teachers,
      for I am always thinking of your laws.
100 I am even wiser than my elders,
      for I have kept your commandments.

101 I have refused to walk on any evil path,
      so that I may remain obedient to your
      word.
102 I haven't turned away from your
    regulations,
      for you have taught me well.
103 How sweet your words taste to me;
      they are sweeter than honey.
104 Your commandments give me
    understanding;
      no wonder I hate every false way
      of life.

### Nun

105 Your word is a lamp to guide my feet
    and a light for my path.
106 I've promised it once, and I'll promise
    it again:
      I will obey your righteous
      regulations.
107 I have suffered much, O LORD;
      restore my life again as you promised.
108 LORD, accept my offering of praise,
      and teach me your regulations.
109 My life constantly hangs in the balance,
      but I will not stop obeying your
      instructions.
110 The wicked have set their traps for me,
      but I will not turn from your
      commandments.
111 Your laws are my treasure;
      they are my heart's delight.
112 I am determined to keep your decrees
      to the very end.

### Samekh

113 I hate those with divided loyalties,
      but I love your instructions.
114 You are my refuge and my shield;
      your word is my source of hope.
115 Get out of my life, you evil-minded
    people,
      for I intend to obey the commands
      of my God.
116 LORD, sustain me as you promised, that
    I may live!
      Do not let my hope be crushed.
117 Sustain me, and I will be rescued;
      then I will meditate continually on
      your decrees.
118 But you have rejected all who stray from
    your decrees.
      They are only fooling themselves.

119 You skim off the wicked of the earth like scum;
    no wonder I love to obey your laws!
120 I tremble in fear of you;
    I stand in awe of your regulations.

### Ayin

121 Don't leave me to the mercy of my enemies,
    for I have done what is just and right.
122 Please guarantee a blessing for me.
    Don't let the arrogant oppress me!
123 My eyes strain to see your rescue,
    to see the truth of your promise fulfilled.
124 I am your servant; deal with me in unfailing love,
    and teach me your decrees.
125 Give discernment to me, your servant;
    then I will understand your laws.
126 LORD, it is time for you to act,
    for these evil people have violated your instructions.
127 Truly, I love your commands
    more than gold, even the finest gold.
128 Each of your commandments is right.
    That is why I hate every false way.

### Pe

129 Your laws are wonderful.
    No wonder I obey them!
130 The teaching of your word gives light,
    so even the simple can understand.
131 I pant with expectation,
    longing for your commands.
132 Come and show me your mercy,
    as you do for all who love your name.
133 Guide my steps by your word,
    so I will not be overcome by evil.
134 Ransom me from the oppression of evil people;
    then I can obey your commandments.
135 Look upon me with love;
    teach me your decrees.
136 Rivers of tears gush from my eyes
    because people disobey your instructions.

### Tsadhe

137 O LORD, you are righteous,
    and your regulations are fair.
138 Your laws are perfect

## WHEN to rejoice

READ PSALM 118:24

It's great to rejoice when you get good news as a patient or as the loved one of a patient. But you don't have to wait until then to have joy.

The psalmist isn't waiting to rejoice until the CT scan looks good. He isn't waiting to rejoice until the blood tests are normal. He isn't waiting to rejoice until his loved one is pronounced cured or in remission. No, he's rejoicing now because it's a new day and he's alive!

No matter what you've gone through or what lies ahead, will you choose joy? Each morning you awaken, you have a decision to make: to rejoice or to grumble at another day. Choose joy.

and completely trustworthy.
139 I am overwhelmed with indignation,
    for my enemies have disregarded your words.
140 Your promises have been thoroughly tested;
    that is why I love them so much.
141 I am insignificant and despised,
    but I don't forget your commandments.
142 Your justice is eternal,
    and your instructions are perfectly true.
143 As pressure and stress bear down on me,
    I find joy in your commands.
144 Your laws are always right;
    help me to understand them so I may live.

### Qoph

145 I pray with all my heart; answer me, LORD!
    I will obey your decrees.
146 I cry out to you; rescue me,
    that I may obey your laws.
147 I rise early, before the sun is up;
    I cry out for help and put my hope in your words.
148 I stay awake through the night,
    thinking about your promise.
149 In your faithful love, O LORD, hear my cry;
    let me be revived by following your regulations.
150 Lawless people are coming to attack me;
    they live far from your instructions.

151 But you are near, O LORD,
and all your commands are true.
152 I have known from my earliest days
that your laws will last forever.

### Resh

153 Look upon my suffering and rescue me,
for I have not forgotten your
instructions.
154 Argue my case; take my side!
Protect my life as you promised.
155 The wicked are far from rescue,
for they do not bother with your
decrees.
156 LORD, how great is your mercy;
let me be revived by following your
regulations.
157 Many persecute and trouble me,
yet I have not swerved from your laws.
158 Seeing these traitors makes me sick at
heart,
because they care nothing for your
word.
159 See how I love your commandments,
LORD.
Give back my life because of your
unfailing love.
160 The very essence of your words is truth;
all your just regulations will stand
forever.

### Shin

161 Powerful people harass me without cause,
but my heart trembles only at your word.
162 I rejoice in your word
like one who discovers a great treasure.
163 I hate and abhor all falsehood,
but I love your instructions.
164 I will praise you seven times a day
because all your regulations are just.
165 Those who love your instructions have
great peace
and do not stumble.
166 I long for your rescue, LORD,
so I have obeyed your commands.
167 I have obeyed your laws,
for I love them very much.
168 Yes, I obey your commandments and laws
because you know everything I do.

### Taw

169 O LORD, listen to my cry;
give me the discerning mind you
promised.

170 Listen to my prayer;
rescue me as you promised.
171 Let praise flow from my lips,
for you have taught me your decrees.
172 Let my tongue sing about your word,
for all your commands are right.
173 Give me a helping hand,
for I have chosen to follow your
commandments.
174 O LORD, I have longed for your rescue,
and your instructions are my delight.
175 Let me live so I can praise you,
and may your regulations help me.
176 I have wandered away like a lost sheep;
come and find me,
for I have not forgotten your commands.

## PSALM 120

*A song for pilgrims ascending to Jerusalem.*

1 I took my troubles to the LORD;
I cried out to him, and he answered
my prayer.
2 Rescue me, O LORD, from liars
and from all deceitful people.
3 O deceptive tongue, what will God
do to you?
How will he increase your punishment?
4 You will be pierced with sharp arrows
and burned with glowing coals.

5 How I suffer in far-off Meshech.
It pains me to live in distant Kedar.
6 I am tired of living
among people who hate peace.
7 I search for peace;
but when I speak of peace, they want
war!

## PSALM 121

*A song for pilgrims ascending to Jerusalem.*

1 I look up to the mountains—
does my help come from there?
2 My help comes from the LORD,
who made heaven and earth!

3 He will not let you stumble;
the one who watches over you will not
slumber.
4 Indeed, he who watches over Israel
never slumbers or sleeps.

5 The LORD himself watches over you!

The LORD stands beside you as your
   protective shade.
6 The sun will not harm you by day,
   nor the moon at night.

7 The LORD keeps you from all harm
   and watches over your life.
8 The LORD keeps watch over you as you
   come and go,
   both now and forever.

## PSALM 122
*A song for pilgrims ascending to Jerusalem.*
*A psalm of David.*

1 I was glad when they said to me,
   "Let us go to the house of the LORD."
2 And now here we are,
   standing inside your gates, O Jerusalem.
3 Jerusalem is a well-built city;
   its seamless walls cannot be breached.
4 All the tribes of Israel—the LORD's
   people—
   make their pilgrimage here.
   They come to give thanks to the name
   of the LORD,
   as the law requires of Israel.
5 Here stand the thrones where judgment
   is given,
   the thrones of the dynasty of David.
6 Pray for peace in Jerusalem.
   May all who love this city prosper.
7 O Jerusalem, may there be peace within
   your walls

and prosperity in your palaces.
8 For the sake of my family and friends,
   I will say,
   "May you have peace."
9 For the sake of the house of the LORD
   our God,
   I will seek what is best for you,
   O Jerusalem.

## PSALM 123
*A song for pilgrims ascending to Jerusalem.*

1 I lift my eyes to you,
   O God, enthroned in heaven.
2 We keep looking to the LORD our God for
   his mercy,
   just as servants keep their eyes on their
   master,
   as a slave girl watches her mistress for
   the slightest signal.
3 Have mercy on us, LORD, have mercy,
   for we have had our fill of contempt.
4 We have had more than our fill of the
   scoffing of the proud
   and the contempt of the arrogant.

## PSALM 124
*A song for pilgrims ascending to Jerusalem.*
*A psalm of David.*

1 What if the LORD had not been on our
   side?
   Let all Israel repeat:

# COMFORTING words
READ PSALM 119:105-112

There's no doubt that Psalms contains more comforting verses than any other book in the
Bible. But not all the words of Scripture are comforting, and not all the psalms make us feel better.

That's because when we compare our lives—our actions, words, and thoughts—to the Scriptures,
we see how many times we don't measure up to the standards God has for us. Of course, that's
assuming the Bible *is* the standard we use to measure our lives against (and not just what our friends
or neighbors are doing!).

Of the 176 verses in this psalm, only two *don't* mention a synonym for God's Word. It is clear we
are supposed to look to the Bible to guide our feet and light our paths. We definitely need to seek
comfort in it each and every day. But let's not make the mistake of not allowing God's Word at times
to convict us or challenge us or even correct us. If we want God's blessing, we need to obey His
commandments, too.

2 What if the LORD had not been on our
 side
  when people attacked us?
3 They would have swallowed us alive
  in their burning anger.
4 The waters would have engulfed us;
  a torrent would have overwhelmed us.
5 Yes, the raging waters of their fury
  would have overwhelmed our very
  lives.

6 Praise the LORD,
  who did not let their teeth tear
  us apart!
7 We escaped like a bird from a hunter's
  trap.
  The trap is broken, and we are free!
8 Our help is from the LORD,
  who made heaven and earth.

## PSALM 125
*A song for pilgrims ascending to Jerusalem.*

1 Those who trust in the LORD are as secure
  as Mount Zion;
  they will not be defeated but will
  endure forever.
2 Just as the mountains surround
  Jerusalem,
  so the LORD surrounds his people, both
  now and forever.
3 The wicked will not rule the land of the
  godly,
  for then the godly might be tempted to
  do wrong.
4 O LORD, do good to those who are good,
  whose hearts are in tune with you.
5 But banish those who turn to crooked
  ways, O LORD.
  Take them away with those who
  do evil.

  May Israel have peace!

## PSALM 126
*A song for pilgrims ascending to Jerusalem.*

1 When the LORD brought back his exiles
  to Jerusalem,*
  it was like a dream!
2 We were filled with laughter,
  and we sang for joy.
  And the other nations said,

"What amazing things the LORD has
  done for them."
3 Yes, the LORD has done amazing things
  for us!
  What joy!

4 Restore our fortunes, LORD,
  as streams renew the desert.
5 Those who plant in tears
  will harvest with shouts of joy.
6 They weep as they go to plant their seed,
  but they sing as they return with the
  harvest.

## PSALM 127
*A song for pilgrims ascending to Jerusalem.*
*A psalm of Solomon.*

1 Unless the LORD builds a house,
  the work of the builders is wasted.
  Unless the LORD protects a city,
  guarding it with sentries will do no
  good.
2 It is useless for you to work so hard
  from early morning until late at night,
  anxiously working for food to eat;
  for God gives rest to his loved ones.

3 Children are a gift from the LORD;
  they are a reward from him.
4 Children born to a young man
  are like arrows in a warrior's hands.
5 How joyful is the man whose quiver is
  full of them!
  He will not be put to shame when he
  confronts his accusers at the city
  gates.

## PSALM 128
*A song for pilgrims ascending to Jerusalem.*

1 How joyful are those who fear the LORD—
  all who follow his ways!
2 You will enjoy the fruit of your labor.
  How joyful and prosperous you
  will be!
3 Your wife will be like a fruitful grapevine,
  flourishing within your home.
  Your children will be like vigorous young
  olive trees
  as they sit around your table.
4 That is the LORD's blessing
  for those who fear him.

126:1 Hebrew *Zion.*

⁵ May the LORD continually bless you from
Zion.
May you see Jerusalem prosper as long
as you live.
⁶ May you live to enjoy your grandchildren.
May Israel have peace!

## PSALM 129

*A song for pilgrims ascending to Jerusalem.*

¹ From my earliest youth my enemies have
persecuted me.
Let all Israel repeat this:
² From my earliest youth my enemies have
persecuted me,
but they have never defeated me.
³ My back is covered with cuts,
as if a farmer had plowed long furrows.
⁴ But the LORD is good;
he has cut me free from the ropes of
the ungodly.

⁵ May all who hate Jerusalem*
be turned back in shameful defeat.
⁶ May they be as useless as grass on a
rooftop,
turning yellow when only half grown,
⁷ ignored by the harvester,
despised by the binder.
⁸ And may those who pass by
refuse to give them this blessing:
"The LORD bless you;
we bless you in the LORD's name."

## ◆ PSALM 130

*A song for pilgrims ascending to Jerusalem.*

¹ From the depths of despair, O LORD,
I call for your help.
² Hear my cry, O Lord.
Pay attention to my prayer.

³ LORD, if you kept a record of our sins,
who, O Lord, could ever survive?
⁴ But you offer forgiveness,
that we might learn to fear you.

⁵ I am counting on the LORD;
yes, I am counting on him.
I have put my hope in his word.
⁶ I long for the Lord
more than sentries long for the dawn,
yes, more than sentries long for the
dawn.

# ALWAYS on call

READ PSALM 121

A diagnosis of a serious or life-threatening illness
usually sends us scurrying in all directions to find
the help we need to cope with our situation. We
may find assistance from healthcare professionals,
from friends who have gone through something
similar, or from alternative treatments. Some of us
have looked high and low to come up with just the
right battle plan to fight our "enemy."

But don't forget the most important "weapon"
we can secure: the Lord's help. He is on call 24/7
(and you won't even wake Him up at 3 a.m.)! Not
only is He always *available*, He is always *able*. God
alone has the mighty power to watch over your life.

⁷ O Israel, hope in the LORD;
for with the LORD there is unfailing
love.
His redemption overflows.
⁸ He himself will redeem Israel
from every kind of sin.

## PSALM 131

*A song for pilgrims ascending to Jerusalem.*
*A psalm of David.*

¹ LORD, my heart is not proud;
my eyes are not haughty.
I don't concern myself with matters too
great
or too awesome for me to grasp.
² Instead, I have calmed and quieted
myself,
like a weaned child who no longer
cries for its mother's milk.
Yes, like a weaned child is my soul
within me.

³ O Israel, put your hope in the LORD—
now and always.

## PSALM 132

*A song for pilgrims ascending to Jerusalem.*

¹ LORD, remember David
and all that he suffered.
² He made a solemn promise to the LORD.
He vowed to the Mighty One of Israel,*

**129:5** Hebrew *Zion.*    **132:2** Hebrew *of Jacob;* also in 132:5. See note on 44:4.

<sup>3</sup> "I will not go home;
I will not let myself rest.
<sup>4</sup> I will not let my eyes sleep
nor close my eyelids in slumber
<sup>5</sup> until I find a place to build a house for
the Lord,
a sanctuary for the Mighty One of Israel."

<sup>6</sup> We heard that the Ark was in Ephrathah;
then we found it in the distant
countryside of Jaar.
<sup>7</sup> Let us go to the sanctuary of the Lord;
let us worship at the footstool of his
throne.
<sup>8</sup> Arise, O Lord, and enter your resting place,
along with the Ark, the symbol of your
power.
<sup>9</sup> May your priests be clothed in godliness;
may your loyal servants sing for joy.
<sup>10</sup> For the sake of your servant David,
do not reject the king you have anointed.
<sup>11</sup> The Lord swore an oath to David
with a promise he will never take back:
"I will place one of your descendants
on your throne.
<sup>12</sup> If your descendants obey the terms of my
covenant
and the laws that I teach them,
then your royal line
will continue forever and ever."

<sup>13</sup> For the Lord has chosen Jerusalem*;
he has desired it for his home.
<sup>14</sup> "This is my resting place forever," he said.
"I will live here, for this is the home
I desired.
<sup>15</sup> I will bless this city and make it prosperous;
I will satisfy its poor with food.
<sup>16</sup> I will clothe its priests with godliness;
its faithful servants will sing for joy.
<sup>17</sup> Here I will increase the power of David;
my anointed one will be a light for my
people.
<sup>18</sup> I will clothe his enemies with shame,
but he will be a glorious king."

## PSALM 133
*A song for pilgrims ascending to Jerusalem.*
*A psalm of David.*

<sup>1</sup> How wonderful and pleasant it is
when brothers live together in
harmony!

132:13 Hebrew *Zion.*    134:3 Hebrew *Zion.*

<sup>2</sup> For harmony is as precious as the
anointing oil
that was poured over Aaron's head,
that ran down his beard
and onto the border of his robe.
<sup>3</sup> Harmony is as refreshing as the dew
from Mount Hermon
that falls on the mountains of Zion.
And there the Lord has pronounced
his blessing,
even life everlasting.

## PSALM 134
*A song for pilgrims ascending to Jerusalem.*

<sup>1</sup> Oh, praise the Lord, all you servants
of the Lord,
you who serve at night in the house
of the Lord.
<sup>2</sup> Lift up holy hands in prayer,
and praise the Lord.

<sup>3</sup> May the Lord, who made heaven and
earth,
bless you from Jerusalem.*

## PSALM 135
<sup>1</sup> Praise the Lord!

Praise the name of the Lord!
Praise him, you who serve
the Lord,
<sup>2</sup> you who serve in the house of the Lord,
in the courts of the house of
our God.

<sup>3</sup> Praise the Lord, for the Lord is good;
celebrate his lovely name with music.
<sup>4</sup> For the Lord has chosen Jacob for
himself,
Israel for his own special treasure.

<sup>5</sup> I know the greatness of the Lord—
that our Lord is greater than any
other god.
<sup>6</sup> The Lord does whatever pleases him
throughout all heaven and earth,
and on the seas and in their depths.
<sup>7</sup> He causes the clouds to rise over the
whole earth.
He sends the lightning with the rain
and releases the wind from his
storehouses.

8 He destroyed the firstborn in each
  Egyptian home,
    both people and animals.
9 He performed miraculous signs and
  wonders in Egypt
    against Pharaoh and all his people.
10 He struck down great nations
    and slaughtered mighty kings—
11 Sihon king of the Amorites,
    Og king of Bashan,
    and all the kings of Canaan.
12 He gave their land as an inheritance,
    a special possession to his people Israel.

13 Your name, O LORD, endures forever;
    your fame, O LORD, is known to every
      generation.
14 For the LORD will give justice to his people
    and have compassion on his servants.

15 The idols of the nations are merely things
    of silver and gold,
      shaped by human hands.
16 They have mouths but cannot speak,
    and eyes but cannot see.
17 They have ears but cannot hear,
    and noses but cannot smell.
18 And those who make idols are just like
    them,
      as are all who trust in them.

19 O Israel, praise the LORD!
    O priests—descendants of Aaron—
      praise the LORD!
20 O Levites, praise the LORD!
    All you who fear the LORD, praise the
      LORD!
21 The LORD be praised from Zion,
    for he lives here in Jerusalem.

    Praise the LORD!

## PSALM 136

1 Give thanks to the LORD, for he is good!
    *His faithful love endures forever.*
2 Give thanks to the God of gods.
    *His faithful love endures forever.*
3 Give thanks to the Lord of lords.
    *His faithful love endures forever.*

4 Give thanks to him who alone does
    mighty miracles.
      *His faithful love endures forever.*

136:13 Hebrew *sea of reeds;* also in 136:15.

5 Give thanks to him who made the
    heavens so skillfully.
      *His faithful love endures forever.*
6 Give thanks to him who placed the earth
    among the waters.
      *His faithful love endures forever.*
7 Give thanks to him who made the
    heavenly lights—
      *His faithful love endures forever.*
8 the sun to rule the day,
      *His faithful love endures forever.*
9 and the moon and stars to rule the night.
      *His faithful love endures forever.*

10 Give thanks to him who killed the
    firstborn of Egypt.
      *His faithful love endures forever.*
11 He brought Israel out of Egypt.
      *His faithful love endures forever.*
12 He acted with a strong hand and
    powerful arm.
      *His faithful love endures forever.*
13 Give thanks to him who parted the Red
    Sea.*
      *His faithful love endures forever.*
14 He led Israel safely through,
      *His faithful love endures forever.*
15 but he hurled Pharaoh and his army into
    the Red Sea.
      *His faithful love endures forever.*
16 Give thanks to him who led his people
    through the wilderness.
      *His faithful love endures forever.*

## WHY, why, why?
READ PSALM 131

Do you know why you received the diagnosis
you did? Not *what* went wrong, but *why* it did?
Probably not. You might know you have an inherited
genetic mutation which caused the disease, but
why didn't all your relatives have it, too? And even
if you had risk factors that contributed to your
diagnosis, why doesn't everybody with those risk
factors get the same diagnosis? Why do treatments
work for some and not all? Why does one person
get cured and another doesn't?

    There are tons of questions that are simply
impossible to answer. You can spend a lot of time
asking them or you can, with a childlike heart, lean
back on the everlasting arms of Jesus.

17 Give thanks to him who struck down
   mighty kings.
                  *His faithful love endures forever.*
18 He killed powerful kings—
                  *His faithful love endures forever.*
19 Sihon king of the Amorites,
                  *His faithful love endures forever.*
20 and Og king of Bashan.
                  *His faithful love endures forever.*
21 God gave the land of these kings as an
   inheritance—
                  *His faithful love endures forever.*
22 a special possession to his servant Israel.
                  *His faithful love endures forever.*

23 He remembered us in our weakness.
                  *His faithful love endures forever.*
24 He saved us from our enemies.
                  *His faithful love endures forever.*
25 He gives food to every living thing.
                  *His faithful love endures forever.*
26 Give thanks to the God of heaven.
                  *His faithful love endures forever.*

## PSALM 137

1 Beside the rivers of Babylon, we sat and
   wept
      as we thought of Jerusalem.*
2 We put away our harps,
      hanging them on the branches of
      poplar trees.
3 For our captors demanded a song from us.
      Our tormentors insisted on a joyful
      hymn:
      "Sing us one of those songs of
      Jerusalem!"
4 But how can we sing the songs of the
   LORD
      while in a pagan land?

5 If I forget you, O Jerusalem,
      let my right hand forget how to play
      the harp.
6 May my tongue stick to the roof of my
   mouth
      if I fail to remember you,
      if I don't make Jerusalem my greatest joy.

7 O LORD, remember what the Edomites
   did
      on the day the armies of Babylon
      captured Jerusalem.

137:1 Hebrew *Zion;* also in 137:3.

"Destroy it!" they yelled.
"Level it to the ground!"
8 O Babylon, you will be destroyed.
      Happy is the one who pays you back
      for what you have done to us.
9 Happy is the one who takes your babies
      and smashes them against the rocks!

## PSALM 138
*A psalm of David.*

1 I give you thanks, O LORD, with all my
   heart;
      I will sing your praises before the gods.
2 I bow before your holy Temple as I
   worship.
   I praise your name for your unfailing
   love and faithfulness;
   for your promises are backed
      by all the honor of your name.
3 As soon as I pray, you answer me;
      you encourage me by giving me
      strength.

4 Every king in all the earth will thank you,
   LORD,
      for all of them will hear your words.
5 Yes, they will sing about the LORD's ways,
      for the glory of the LORD is very great.
6 Though the LORD is great, he cares for the
   humble,
      but he keeps his distance from the
      proud.

7 Though I am surrounded by troubles,
      you will protect me from the anger
      of my enemies.
   You reach out your hand,
      and the power of your right hand
      saves me.
8 The LORD will work out his plans for my
   life—
      for your faithful love, O LORD, endures
      forever.
      Don't abandon me, for you made me.

## PSALM 139
*For the choir director: A psalm of David.*

1 O LORD, you have examined my heart
      and know everything about me.
2 You know when I sit down or stand up.

You know my thoughts even when I'm
   far away.
3 You see me when I travel
   and when I rest at home.
   You know everything I do.
4 You know what I am going to say
   even before I say it, LORD.
5 You go before me and follow me.
   You place your hand of blessing on my
   head.
6 Such knowledge is too wonderful for me,
   too great for me to understand!

7 I can never escape from your Spirit!
   I can never get away from your
   presence!
8 If I go up to heaven, you are there;
   if I go down to the grave,* you are
   there.
9 If I ride the wings of the morning,
   if I dwell by the farthest oceans,
10 even there your hand will guide me,
   and your strength will support me.
11 I could ask the darkness to hide me
   and the light around me to become
   night—
12    but even in darkness I cannot hide
   from you.
To you the night shines as bright as day.
   Darkness and light are the same to you.

13 You made all the delicate, inner parts of
   my body
   and knit me together in my mother's
   womb.
14 Thank you for making me so wonderfully
   complex!
   Your workmanship is marvelous—how
   well I know it.
15 You watched me as I was being formed
   in utter seclusion,
   as I was woven together in the dark
   of the womb.
16 You saw me before I was born.
   Every day of my life was recorded in
   your book.
   Every moment was laid out
   before a single day had passed.

17 How precious are your thoughts about
   me,* O God.
   They cannot be numbered!

18 I can't even count them;
   they outnumber the grains of sand!
And when I wake up,
   you are still with me!

19 O God, if only you would destroy the
   wicked!
   Get out of my life, you murderers!
20 They blaspheme you;
   your enemies misuse your name.
21 O LORD, shouldn't I hate those who hate
   you?
   Shouldn't I despise those who oppose
   you?
22 Yes, I hate them with total hatred,
   for your enemies are my enemies.

23 Search me, O God, and know my heart;
   test me and know my anxious thoughts.
24 Point out anything in me that offends
   you,
   and lead me along the path of
   everlasting life.

## PSALM 140
*For the choir director: A psalm of David.*

1 O LORD, rescue me from evil people.
   Protect me from those who are violent,
2 those who plot evil in their hearts
   and stir up trouble all day long.
3 Their tongues sting like a snake;
   the venom of a viper drips from
      their lips.          *Interlude*

4 O LORD, keep me out of the hands of the
   wicked.
   Protect me from those who are violent,
   for they are plotting against me.
5 The proud have set a trap to catch me;
   they have stretched out a net;
   they have placed traps all along
      the way.          *Interlude*

6 I said to the LORD, "You are my God!"
   Listen, O LORD, to my cries for mercy!
7 O Sovereign LORD, the strong one who
   rescued me,
   you protected me on the day of battle.
8 LORD, do not let evil people have their
   way.
   Do not let their evil schemes succeed,
   or they will become proud.    *Interlude*

**139:8** Hebrew *to Sheol.*    **139:17** Or *How precious to me are your thoughts.*

# IF YOU could read my mind

READ PSALM 139:1-6

It's a good thing medical staffs can't read our minds: *Sure, I have nothing else to do but sit here and wait another hour for the doctor! Since you don't know what's wrong with me, I shouldn't have to pay for the visit, right? I hope you call your spouse back faster than you do me.*

As patients and caregivers, there are many frustrations we endure but don't verbally express. But whatever frustrations you're feeling with God, you might as well tell Him. He already knows that you don't understand how a loving God could allow this to happen. He knows you're wondering why He didn't use His awesome power to miraculously take it all away. He knows that you can't fathom how He could be in control when everything around you seems to be in chaos.

Go ahead and spill it all. He already knows, but He wants you to trust Him enough to be totally honest with Him. He can take it: His shoulders are broad enough and His love for you is strong enough.

9 Let my enemies be destroyed
   by the very evil they have planned
      for me.
10 Let burning coals fall down on their
      heads.
   Let them be thrown into the fire
   or into watery pits from which they
      can't escape.
11 Don't let liars prosper here in our land.
   Cause great disasters to fall on the
      violent.
12 But I know the LORD will help those they
      persecute;
   he will give justice to the poor.
13 Surely righteous people are praising your
      name;
   the godly will live in your presence.

• PSALM 141
*A psalm of David.*

1 O LORD, I am calling to you. Please hurry!
   Listen when I cry to you for help!
2 Accept my prayer as incense offered
      to you,
   and my upraised hands as an evening
      offering.
3 Take control of what I say, O LORD,
   and guard my lips.
4 Don't let me drift toward evil
   or take part in acts of wickedness.

Don't let me share in the delicacies
   of those who do wrong.
5 Let the godly strike me!
   It will be a kindness!
If they correct me, it is soothing medicine.
   Don't let me refuse it.

But I pray constantly
   against the wicked and their deeds.
6 When their leaders are thrown down
      from a cliff,
   the wicked will listen to my words and
      find them true.
7 Like rocks brought up by a plow,
   the bones of the wicked will lie
      scattered without burial.*

8 I look to you for help, O Sovereign LORD.
   You are my refuge; don't let them
      kill me.
9 Keep me from the traps they have set
      for me,
   from the snares of those who do wrong.
10 Let the wicked fall into their own nets,
   but let me escape.

PSALM 142
*A psalm\* of David, regarding his experience in the cave. A prayer.*

1 I cry out to the LORD;
   I plead for the LORD's mercy.

141:7 Hebrew *scattered at the mouth of Sheol.*   142:TITLE Hebrew *maskil.* This may be a literary or musical term.

2 I pour out my complaints before him
   and tell him all my troubles.
3 When I am overwhelmed,
   you alone know the way I should turn.
   Wherever I go,
   my enemies have set traps for me.
4 I look for someone to come and help me,
   but no one gives me a passing thought!
   No one will help me;
   no one cares a bit what happens to me.
5 Then I pray to you, O LORD.
   I say, "You are my place of refuge.
   You are all I really want in life.
6 Hear my cry,
   for I am very low.
   Rescue me from my persecutors,
   for they are too strong for me.
7 Bring me out of prison
   so I can thank you.
   The godly will crowd around me,
   for you are good to me."

## PSALM 143
*A psalm of David.*

1 Hear my prayer, O LORD;
   listen to my plea!
   Answer me because you are faithful
   and righteous.
2 Don't put your servant on trial,
   for no one is innocent before you.
3 My enemy has chased me.
   He has knocked me to the ground
   and forces me to live in darkness like
   those in the grave.
4 I am losing all hope;
   I am paralyzed with fear.
5 I remember the days of old.
   I ponder all your great works
   and think about what you have
   done.
6 I lift my hands to you in prayer.
   I thirst for you as parched land thirsts
   for rain.                          *Interlude*

7 Come quickly, LORD, and answer me,
   for my depression deepens.
   Don't turn away from me,
   or I will die.
8 Let me hear of your unfailing love each
   morning,
   for I am trusting you.

**144:2** Some manuscripts read *my people.*

Show me where to walk,
   for I give myself to you.
9 Rescue me from my enemies, LORD;
   I run to you to hide me.
10 Teach me to do your will,
   for you are my God.
   May your gracious Spirit lead me forward
   on a firm footing.
11 For the glory of your name, O LORD,
   preserve my life.
   Because of your faithfulness, bring me
   out of this distress.
12 In your unfailing love, silence all my
   enemies
   and destroy all my foes,
   for I am your servant.

## PSALM 144
*A psalm of David.*

1 Praise the LORD, who is my rock.
   He trains my hands for war
   and gives my fingers skill for
   battle.
2 He is my loving ally and my fortress,
   my tower of safety, my rescuer.
   He is my shield, and I take refuge
   in him.
   He makes the nations* submit to me.

3 O LORD, what are human beings that you
   should notice them,
   mere mortals that you should think
   about them?

## ME—paranoid?
READ PSALM 139:7-12

*Webster's* dictionary defines paranoia as
"irrational suspiciousness and distrustfulness of
others." After a serious diagnosis, you'll probably
be a little more paranoid about your body. Lumps,
bumps, aches, and pains that could have been
ignored before now make us very nervous.

   This psalm is a perfect paranoia prescription. It
reminds us that illness is not everywhere, but God
is. We may hide from our prognosis, but we can't
hide from God. Tomorrow shouldn't be feared
because God already is there.

   We may not know what tomorrow holds, but we
know Who holds tomorrow. And that is enough.

4 For they are like a breath of air;
   their days are like a passing shadow.

5 Open the heavens, LORD, and come
      down.
   Touch the mountains so they billow
      smoke.
6 Hurl your lightning bolts and scatter your
      enemies!
   Shoot your arrows and confuse
      them!
7 Reach down from heaven and rescue me;
   rescue me from deep waters,
   from the power of my enemies.
8 Their mouths are full of lies;
   they swear to tell the truth, but they
      lie instead.

9 I will sing a new song to you, O God!
   I will sing your praises with a ten-
      stringed harp.
10 For you grant victory to kings!
   You rescued your servant David from
      the fatal sword.
11 Save me!
   Rescue me from the power of my
      enemies.
   Their mouths are full of lies;
   they swear to tell the truth, but they
      lie instead.

12 May our sons flourish in their youth
      like well-nurtured plants.
   May our daughters be like graceful
      pillars,
   carved to beautify a palace.
13 May our barns be filled
      with crops of every kind.
   May the flocks in our fields multiply
      by the thousands,
   even tens of thousands,
14    and may our oxen be loaded down
      with produce.
   May there be no enemy breaking
      through our walls,
   no going into captivity,
   no cries of alarm in our town
      squares.
15 Yes, joyful are those who live like this!
   Joyful indeed are those whose God is
      the LORD.

PSALM 145*
*A psalm of praise of David.*

1 I will exalt you, my God and King,
   and praise your name forever
      and ever.
2 I will praise you every day;
   yes, I will praise you forever.
3 Great is the LORD! He is most worthy
      of praise!
   No one can measure his greatness.

4 Let each generation tell its children
      of your mighty acts;
   let them proclaim your power.
5 I will meditate* on your majestic,
      glorious splendor
   and your wonderful miracles.
6 Your awe-inspiring deeds will be on
      every tongue;
   I will proclaim your greatness.
7 Everyone will share the story of your
      wonderful goodness;
   they will sing with joy about your
      righteousness.

8 The LORD is merciful and
      compassionate,
   slow to get angry and filled with
      unfailing love.
9 The LORD is good to everyone.
   He showers compassion on all his
      creation.
10 All of your works will thank you,
      LORD,
   and your faithful followers will
      praise you.
11 They will speak of the glory of your
      kingdom;
   they will give examples of your
      power.
12 They will tell about your mighty
      deeds
   and about the majesty and glory of
      your reign.
13 For your kingdom is an everlasting
      kingdom.
   You rule throughout all generations.

   The LORD always keeps his
      promises;
   he is gracious in all he does.*

---

**145** This psalm is a Hebrew acrostic poem; each verse (including 13b) begins with a successive letter of the Hebrew alphabet.
**145:5** Some manuscripts read *They will speak.*    **145:13** The last two lines of 145:13 are not found in many of the ancient manuscripts.

449

<sup>14</sup> The Lord helps the fallen
    and lifts those bent beneath their
      loads.
<sup>15</sup> The eyes of all look to you in hope;
    you give them their food as they
      need it.
<sup>16</sup> When you open your hand,
    you satisfy the hunger and thirst of
      every living thing.
<sup>17</sup> The Lord is righteous in everything he
    does;
    he is filled with kindness.
<sup>18</sup> The Lord is close to all who call on him,
    yes, to all who call on him in truth.
<sup>19</sup> He grants the desires of those who fear
    him;
    he hears their cries for help and
      rescues them.
<sup>20</sup> The Lord protects all those who love him,
    but he destroys the wicked.

<sup>21</sup> I will praise the Lord,
    and may everyone on earth bless his
      holy name
    forever and ever.

## PSALM 146

<sup>1</sup> Praise the Lord!

Let all that I am praise the Lord.
<sup>2</sup>   I will praise the Lord as long as I live.
    I will sing praises to my God with my
      dying breath.

<sup>3</sup> Don't put your confidence in powerful
    people;
    there is no help for you there.
<sup>4</sup> When they breathe their last, they return
    to the earth,
    and all their plans die with them.
<sup>5</sup> But joyful are those who have the God of
    Israel* as their helper,
    whose hope is in the Lord their God.
<sup>6</sup> He made heaven and earth,
    the sea, and everything in them.
    He keeps every promise forever.
<sup>7</sup> He gives justice to the oppressed
    and food to the hungry.
    The Lord frees the prisoners.
<sup>8</sup>   The Lord opens the eyes of the blind.
    The Lord lifts up those who are weighed
      down.
    The Lord loves the godly.

## FUTURE plans
READ PSALMS 146 AND 116:2

"As long as I can, I'll keep working."
  "As long as I am able, I'll continue to travel."
  "As long as I have the strength, I'll take care
of my loved one at home."

  What promises have you made about your
future? Setting short- and long-term goals is a
fabulous idea, as they motivate us through tough
times. Still, the time may come when we are physically unable to continue on a desired course.

  These psalms give us two pledges we *always*
can keep: "I will pray as long as I have breath." And
"I will sing praises to my God with my dying breath."

  Make them your promises today.

<sup>9</sup> The Lord protects the foreigners
    among us.
    He cares for the orphans and widows,
    but he frustrates the plans of the
      wicked.

<sup>10</sup> The Lord will reign forever.
    He will be your God, O Jerusalem,*
      throughout the generations.

    Praise the Lord!

## PSALM 147
<sup>1</sup> Praise the Lord!

How good to sing praises to our God!
    How delightful and how fitting!
<sup>2</sup> The Lord is rebuilding Jerusalem
    and bringing the exiles back to Israel.
<sup>3</sup> He heals the brokenhearted
    and bandages their wounds.
<sup>4</sup> He counts the stars
    and calls them all by name.
<sup>5</sup> How great is our Lord! His power is
    absolute!
    His understanding is beyond
      comprehension!
<sup>6</sup> The Lord supports the humble,
    but he brings the wicked down into
      the dust.

<sup>7</sup> Sing out your thanks to the Lord;
    sing praises to our God with a harp.

**146:5** Hebrew *of Jacob*. See note on 44:4.    **146:10** Hebrew *Zion*.

8 He covers the heavens with clouds,
   provides rain for the earth,
   and makes the grass grow in mountain
      pastures.
9 He gives food to the wild animals
   and feeds the young ravens when they
      cry.
10 He takes no pleasure in the strength
      of a horse
   or in human might.
11 No, the Lord's delight is in those who
      fear him,
   those who put their hope in his
      unfailing love.

12 Glorify the Lord, O Jerusalem!
   Praise your God, O Zion!
13 For he has strengthened the bars
      of your gates
   and blessed your children within your
      walls.
14 He sends peace across your nation
   and satisfies your hunger with the
      finest wheat.
15 He sends his orders to the world—
   how swiftly his word flies!
16 He sends the snow like white wool;
   he scatters frost upon the ground like
      ashes.
17 He hurls the hail like stones.*
   Who can stand against his freezing
      cold?
18 Then, at his command, it all melts.
   He sends his winds, and the ice
      thaws.
19 He has revealed his words to Jacob,
   his decrees and regulations to Israel.
20 He has not done this for any other
      nation;
   they do not know his regulations.

   Praise the Lord!

## PSALM 148

1 Praise the Lord!

   Praise the Lord from the heavens!
   Praise him from the skies!
2 Praise him, all his angels!
   Praise him, all the armies of heaven!
3 Praise him, sun and moon!
   Praise him, all you twinkling stars!

4 Praise him, skies above!
   Praise him, vapors high above the
      clouds!
5 Let every created thing give praise to the
      Lord,
   for he issued his command, and they
      came into being.
6 He set them in place forever and ever.
   His decree will never be revoked.

7 Praise the Lord from the earth,
   you creatures of the ocean depths,
8 fire and hail, snow and clouds,*
   wind and weather that obey him,
9 mountains and all hills,
   fruit trees and all cedars,
10 wild animals and all livestock,
   small scurrying animals and birds,
11 kings of the earth and all people,
   rulers and judges of the earth,
12 young men and young women,
   old men and children.

13 Let them all praise the name of the
      Lord.
   For his name is very great;
   his glory towers over the earth and
      heaven!
14 He has made his people strong,
   honoring his faithful ones—
   the people of Israel who are close
      to him.

   Praise the Lord!

## PSALM 149

1 Praise the Lord!

   Sing to the Lord a new song.
   Sing his praises in the assembly of the
      faithful.

2 O Israel, rejoice in your Maker.
   O people of Jerusalem,* exult in your
      King.
3 Praise his name with dancing,
   accompanied by tambourine and harp.
4 For the Lord delights in his people;
   he crowns the humble with victory.
5 Let the faithful rejoice that he honors
      them.
   Let them sing for joy as they lie on
      their beds.

---

**147:17** Hebrew *like bread crumbs.*     **148:8** Or *mist,* or *smoke.*     **149:2** Hebrew *Zion.*

⁶ Let the praises of God be in their mouths,
    and a sharp sword in their hands—
⁷ to execute vengeance on the nations
    and punishment on the peoples,
⁸ to bind their kings with shackles
    and their leaders with iron chains,
⁹ to execute the judgment written against
    them.
  This is the glorious privilege of his
    faithful ones.

  Praise the LORD!

## PSALM 150

¹ Praise the LORD!

  Praise God in his sanctuary;
    praise him in his mighty heaven!

² Praise him for his mighty works;
    praise his unequaled greatness!
³ Praise him with a blast of the ram's
    horn;
  praise him with the lyre and
    harp!
⁴ Praise him with the tambourine and
    dancing;
  praise him with strings and
    flutes!
⁵ Praise him with a clash of cymbals;
    praise him with loud clanging
    cymbals.
⁶ Let everything that breathes sing praises
    to the LORD!

  Praise the LORD!

# ENCOURAGING a depressed loved one

The word *encourage* means to inspire or fill someone with courage, spirit, or hope. But how in the world do you encourage someone who is depressed?

To answer that difficult question, we share some thoughts from the book *New Light on Depression* by David Biebel, DMin, and Harold Koenig, MD.

"Family members, loved ones, and friends should encourage depressed persons—to get up in the morning, to go out to dinner, to go to a movie, to exercise with them, to do the things their depression is preventing them from enjoying, and to seek professional help if they are not doing so already. Once depressed people get out and start moving they often feel a lot better. Encouraging, however, is not the same as forcing, manipulating, or cajoling, nor will arguing about it help much. . . . Here, again, discernment is crucial so that your suggestions are made in the right way at the right time, to ensure the greatest likelihood that they will be accepted.

"One way to encourage your depressed friend to get out (and to get help) is to **find a good depression support group and invite your loved one to attend it with you.**"[1]

Biebel and Koenig identify four "helping patterns" they have seen Christians employ with their depressed family and friends. These are judging ("Your problem is caused by sin or lack of faith"), giving advice ("Cheer up—things could be worse!"), identification (sympathizing so much that you get sucked into the pit of depression, too), and empathy (suffering together with the person). According to the authors, "Only empathy really helps."[2]

**Empathizers deeply feel the other person's pain without making it their own.**

"The empathizer goes and gets a ladder, puts it in the pit, and climbs down to be with the depressed person until he or she is ready to climb out," the authors say. "The key difference is that the empathizer has a goal in mind—not just to feel the depressed person's pain, but to also act in a sense as a redeemer, willing to pay whatever cost there is in order for the other person to be healed.

"If you are really going to help your loved one through and beyond depression, the only way is to lay aside your rights, by choice, with the goal of serving that person's best interests until he or she emerges into the light of joy again."[3]

[1]David B. Biebel and Harold G. Koenig, *New Light on Depression: Help, Hope, and Answers for the Depressed and Those Who Love Them* (Grand Rapids, MI: Zondervan, 2004), 233. [2]Ibid., 246. [3]Ibid., 248–249.

# PROVERBS

Decisions, decisions, decisions.

Do I have the surgery now or try to put it off for a while? Should I try an investigational treatment? Do we want to travel to a big medical center or stay closer to home? Are the known risks of the drug worth the possible benefits? Is it time to get hospice care?

Serious illness brings with it a boatload of questions and a flood of essential decisions. Many, perhaps most, decisions are not black-and-white, and modern medicine often can offer only educated guesses for us. We talk to friends and family, and opinions are divided as to what our next step should be. We surf the Internet for answers, but the avalanche of information (not all of which is reliable!) may make our decision-making more muddled.

The book of Proverbs is an oasis for weary minds. It won't tell you which prescription to fill or what clinical trial to join, but its pages will give you incredible insight into life in general and human behavior in particular. Proverbs is a collection of short, wise sayings, many from the pen of King Solomon, the wisest man ever to live. They don't give us theological doctrine or prophecies but rather fundamental principles. Read them slowly and meditate on each one. Unlike much of the advice you're getting, they're not complicated—although applying these rules of conduct in our own lives sometimes can be a challenge when we're not feeling well! If you want God's guidance in your life, keep reading.

## The Purpose of Proverbs

**1** These are the proverbs of Solomon, David's son, king of Israel.

² Their purpose is to teach people wisdom
and discipline,
to help them understand the insights
of the wise.
³ Their purpose is to teach people to live
disciplined and successful lives,
to help them do what is right, just, and
fair.
⁴ These proverbs will give insight to the
simple,
knowledge and discernment to the
young.

⁵ Let the wise listen to these proverbs and
become even wiser.
Let those with understanding receive
guidance
⁶ by exploring the meaning in these
proverbs and parables,
the words of the wise and their
riddles.

⁷ Fear of the LORD is the foundation of true
knowledge,
but fools despise wisdom and
discipline.

## A Father's Exhortation: Acquire Wisdom

⁸ My child,* listen when your father
corrects you.
Don't neglect your mother's
instruction.
⁹ What you learn from them will crown
you with grace
and be a chain of honor around your
neck.

¹⁰ My child, if sinners entice you,
turn your back on them!
¹¹ They may say, "Come and join us.
Let's hide and kill someone!
Just for fun, let's ambush the
innocent!
¹² Let's swallow them alive, like the grave*;

let's swallow them whole, like those
who go down to the pit of death.
¹³ Think of the great things we'll get!
We'll fill our houses with all the stuff
we take.
¹⁴ Come, throw in your lot with us;
we'll all share the loot."

¹⁵ My child, don't go along with them!
Stay far away from their paths.
¹⁶ They rush to commit evil deeds.
They hurry to commit murder.
¹⁷ If a bird sees a trap being set,
it knows to stay away.
¹⁸ But these people set an ambush for
themselves;
they are trying to get themselves killed.
¹⁹ Such is the fate of all who are greedy
for money;
it robs them of life.

## Wisdom Shouts in the Streets

²⁰ Wisdom shouts in the streets.
She cries out in the public square.
²¹ She calls to the crowds along the main
street,
to those gathered in front of the city
gate:
²² "How long, you simpletons,
will you insist on being simpleminded?
How long will you mockers relish your
mocking?
How long will you fools hate
knowledge?
²³ Come and listen to my counsel.
I'll share my heart with you
and make you wise.

²⁴ "I called you so often, but you wouldn't
come.
I reached out to you, but you paid no
attention.
²⁵ You ignored my advice
and rejected the correction I offered.
²⁶ So I will laugh when you are in trouble!
I will mock you when disaster
overtakes you—

**1:8** Hebrew *My son;* also in 1:10, 15.   **1:12** Hebrew *like Sheol.*

²⁷ when calamity overtakes you like a storm,
   when disaster engulfs you like a
      cyclone,
   and anguish and distress overwhelm
      you.

²⁸ "When they cry for help, I will not
      answer.
   Though they anxiously search for me,
      they will not find me.
²⁹ For they hated knowledge
   and chose not to fear the Lord.
³⁰ They rejected my advice
   and paid no attention when I corrected
      them.
³¹ Therefore, they must eat the bitter fruit
      of living their own way,
   choking on their own schemes.
³² For simpletons turn away from me—
      to death.
   Fools are destroyed by their own
      complacency.
³³ But all who listen to me will live in peace,
   untroubled by fear of harm."

*The Benefits of Wisdom*

**2** ¹ My child,* listen to what I say,
      and treasure my commands.
² Tune your ears to wisdom,
   and concentrate on understanding.
³ Cry out for insight,
   and ask for understanding.
⁴ Search for them as you would for silver;
   seek them like hidden treasures.
⁵ Then you will understand what it means
      to fear the Lord,
   and you will gain knowledge of God.
⁶ For the Lord grants wisdom!
   From his mouth come knowledge and
      understanding.
⁷ He grants a treasure of common sense to
      the honest.
   He is a shield to those who walk with
      integrity.
⁸ He guards the paths of the just
   and protects those who are faithful
      to him.

⁹ Then you will understand what is right,
      just, and fair,
   and you will find the right way to go.

¹⁰ For wisdom will enter your heart,
   and knowledge will fill you with joy.
¹¹ Wise choices will watch over you.
   Understanding will keep you safe.
¹² Wisdom will save you from evil people,
   from those whose words are twisted.
¹³ These men turn from the right way
   to walk down dark paths.
¹⁴ They take pleasure in doing wrong,
   and they enjoy the twisted ways of evil.
¹⁵ Their actions are crooked,
   and their ways are wrong.

¹⁶ Wisdom will save you from the immoral
      woman,
   from the seductive words of the
      promiscuous woman.
¹⁷ She has abandoned her husband
   and ignores the covenant she made
      before God.
¹⁸ Entering her house leads to death;
   it is the road to the grave.*
¹⁹ The man who visits her is doomed.
   He will never reach the paths of life.

²⁰ Follow the steps of good men instead,
   and stay on the paths of the righteous.
²¹ For only the godly will live in the land,
   and those with integrity will remain
      in it.
²² But the wicked will be removed from the
      land,
   and the treacherous will be uprooted.

*Trusting in the Lord*

**3** ¹ My child,* never forget the things
      I have taught you.
   Store my commands in your heart.
² If you do this, you will live many years,
   and your life will be satisfying.
³ Never let loyalty and kindness leave you!
   Tie them around your neck as a
      reminder.
   Write them deep within your heart.
⁴ Then you will find favor with both God
      and people,
   and you will earn a good reputation.

⁵ Trust in the Lord with all your heart;
   do not depend on your own
      understanding.

2:1 Hebrew *My son.*    2:18 Hebrew *to the spirits of the dead.*    3:1 Hebrew *My son;* also in 3:11, 21.

6 Seek his will in all you do,
 and he will show you which path
 to take.

7 Don't be impressed with your own
 wisdom.
 Instead, fear the LORD and turn away
 from evil.
8 Then you will have healing for your body
 and strength for your bones.

9 Honor the LORD with your wealth
 and with the best part of everything
 you produce.
10 Then he will fill your barns with grain,
 and your vats will overflow with good
 wine.

11 My child, don't reject the LORD's
 discipline,
 and don't be upset when he corrects
 you.
12 For the LORD corrects those he loves,
 just as a father corrects a child in
 whom he delights.*

13 Joyful is the person who finds wisdom,
 the one who gains understanding.
14 For wisdom is more profitable than silver,
 and her wages are better than gold.
15 Wisdom is more precious than rubies;
 nothing you desire can compare with
 her.

16 She offers you long life in her right hand,
 and riches and honor in her left.
17 She will guide you down delightful paths;
 all her ways are satisfying.
18 Wisdom is a tree of life to those who
 embrace her;
 happy are those who hold her tightly.

19 By wisdom the LORD founded the earth;
 by understanding he created the
 heavens.
20 By his knowledge the deep fountains of
 the earth burst forth,
 and the dew settles beneath the night
 sky.

21 My child, don't lose sight of common
 sense and discernment.
 Hang on to them,
22 for they will refresh your soul.
 They are like jewels on a necklace.
23 They keep you safe on your way,
 and your feet will not stumble.
24 You can go to bed without fear;
 you will lie down and sleep soundly.
25 You need not be afraid of sudden
 disaster
 or the destruction that comes upon the
 wicked,
26 for the LORD is your security.
 He will keep your foot from being
 caught in a trap.

3:12 Greek version reads *And he punishes those he accepts as his children.* Compare Heb 12:6.

# GOOD fears

READ PROVERBS 1:7

Serious illnesses, especially life-threatening ones like cancer and heart disease, can strike
a chord of fear even in the bravest of us. But not all fear is bad.

The fear of being hit by a car that keeps children from running into the road is a good fear. The fear
of turning into a "pancake" that keeps people from jumping off tall buildings is another good fear to
have. These kinds of fears are lifesaving ones.

There's another lifesaving fear that's also a life-giving one. It's the fear of the Lord. It's not a fear that
God is waiting for just the right chance to zap you. Instead it's a *wow!* fear—the kind where you're just
in awe and amazement and wonder and reverence of God because of what He has done and still
can do.

It's a fear that becomes the foundation for true knowledge and wisdom in our lives. And best of all,
for those of us with uncertain futures, it's a fear that reduces all the others.

27 Do not withhold good from those who
deserve it
when it's in your power to help them.
28 If you can help your neighbor now, don't
say,
"Come back tomorrow, and then I'll
help you."

29 Don't plot harm against your neighbor,
for those who live nearby trust you.
30 Don't pick a fight without reason,
when no one has done you harm.

31 Don't envy violent people
or copy their ways.
32 Such wicked people are detestable to the
LORD,
but he offers his friendship to the
godly.

33 The LORD curses the house of the
wicked,
but he blesses the home of the upright.

34 The LORD mocks the mockers
but is gracious to the humble.*

35 The wise inherit honor,
but fools are put to shame!

## A Father's Wise Advice

**4** ¹My children,* listen when your father
corrects you.
Pay attention and learn good
judgment,
2 for I am giving you good guidance.
Don't turn away from my instructions.
3 For I, too, was once my father's son,
tenderly loved as my mother's only
child.

4 My father taught me,
"Take my words to heart.
Follow my commands, and you will
live.
5 Get wisdom; develop good judgment.
Don't forget my words or turn away
from them.
6 Don't turn your back on wisdom, for she
will protect you.
Love her, and she will guard you.
7 Getting wisdom is the wisest thing you
can do!

## PARANOIA-producing fears

READ PROVERBS 3:5-8

Once you've gotten a diagnosis of a serious illness, it's common to be rather paranoid about every new twinge. *Is something else wrong? Should I call the doctor?*

Many diseases are very "sneaky," and we're wise to remain vigilant and not let our guards down when it comes to our health. That makes us smart, not paranoid. It's the irrational fears that produce unhealthy paranoia. But once our bodies have "betrayed" us with illness, it's hard to trust them again.

The truth is that while we cannot always rely on our bodies not to let us down, we always can rely on God. Don't trust your own understanding; give Him your paranoia and receive His healing wisdom.

And whatever else you do, develop
good judgment.
8 If you prize wisdom, she will make you
great.
Embrace her, and she will honor you.
9 She will place a lovely wreath on your
head;
she will present you with a beautiful
crown."

10 My child,* listen to me and do as I say,
and you will have a long, good life.
11 I will teach you wisdom's ways
and lead you in straight paths.
12 When you walk, you won't be held
back;
when you run, you won't stumble.
13 Take hold of my instructions; don't let
them go.
Guard them, for they are the key
to life.

14 Don't do as the wicked do,
and don't follow the path of
evildoers.
15 Don't even think about it; don't go that
way.
Turn away and keep moving.
16 For evil people can't sleep until they've
done their evil deed for the day.
They can't rest until they've caused
someone to stumble.

---

**3:34** Greek version reads *The LORD opposes the proud / but favors the humble.* Compare Jas 4:6; 1 Pet 5:5.   **4:1** Hebrew *My sons.*   **4:10** Hebrew *My son;* also in 4:20.

17 They eat the food of wickedness
and drink the wine of violence!

18 The way of the righteous is like the first
gleam of dawn,
which shines ever brighter until the
full light of day.

19 But the way of the wicked is like total
darkness.
They have no idea what they are
stumbling over.

20 My child, pay attention to what I say.
Listen carefully to my words.

21 Don't lose sight of them.
Let them penetrate deep into your
heart,

22 for they bring life to those who find them,
and healing to their whole body.

23 Guard your heart above all else,
for it determines the course of your
life.

24 Avoid all perverse talk;
stay away from corrupt speech.

25 Look straight ahead,
and fix your eyes on what lies before
you.

26 Mark out a straight path for your feet;
stay on the safe path.

27 Don't get sidetracked;
keep your feet from following evil.

## Avoid Immoral Women

**5** 1 My son, pay attention to my wisdom;
listen carefully to my wise counsel.

2 Then you will show discernment,
and your lips will express what you've
learned.

3 For the lips of an immoral woman are as
sweet as honey,
and her mouth is smoother than oil.

4 But in the end she is as bitter as poison,
as dangerous as a double-edged sword.

5 Her feet go down to death;
her steps lead straight to the grave.*

6 For she cares nothing about the path
to life.
She staggers down a crooked trail and
doesn't realize it.

7 So now, my sons, listen to me.
Never stray from what I am about
to say:

8 Stay away from her!
Don't go near the door of her house!

9 If you do, you will lose your honor
and will lose to merciless people all
you have achieved.

10 Strangers will consume your wealth,
and someone else will enjoy the fruit
of your labor.

11 In the end you will groan in anguish
when disease consumes your body.

12 You will say, "How I hated discipline!
If only I had not ignored all the
warnings!

13 Oh, why didn't I listen to my teachers?
Why didn't I pay attention to my
instructors?

14 I have come to the brink of utter ruin,
and now I must face public disgrace."

15 Drink water from your own well—
share your love only with your wife.*

16 Why spill the water of your springs in the
streets,
having sex with just anyone?*

17 You should reserve it for yourselves.
Never share it with strangers.

18 Let your wife be a fountain of blessing
for you.
Rejoice in the wife of your youth.

19 She is a loving deer, a graceful doe.
Let her breasts satisfy you always.
May you always be captivated by her
love.

20 Why be captivated, my son, by an
immoral woman,
or fondle the breasts of a promiscuous
woman?

21 For the LORD sees clearly what a man
does,
examining every path he takes.

22 An evil man is held captive by his own
sins;
they are ropes that catch and hold him.

23 He will die for lack of self-control;
he will be lost because of his great
foolishness.

5:5 Hebrew *to Sheol.*   5:15 Hebrew *Drink water from your own cistern, / flowing water from your own well.*   5:16 Hebrew *Why spill your springs in the streets, / your streams in the city squares?*

*Lessons for Daily Life*

**6** ¹My child,* if you have put up security for a friend's debt
or agreed to guarantee the debt of a stranger—
² if you have trapped yourself by your agreement
and are caught by what you said—
³ follow my advice and save yourself,
for you have placed yourself at your friend's mercy.
Now swallow your pride;
go and beg to have your name erased.
⁴ Don't put it off; do it now!
Don't rest until you do.
⁵ Save yourself like a gazelle escaping from a hunter,
like a bird fleeing from a net.

⁶ Take a lesson from the ants, you lazybones.
Learn from their ways and become wise!
⁷ Though they have no prince or governor or ruler to make them work,
⁸ they labor hard all summer,
gathering food for the winter.
⁹ But you, lazybones, how long will you sleep?
When will you wake up?
¹⁰ A little extra sleep, a little more slumber,
a little folding of the hands to rest—
¹¹ then poverty will pounce on you like a bandit;
scarcity will attack you like an armed robber.

¹² What are worthless and wicked people like?
They are constant liars,
¹³ signaling their deceit with a wink of the eye,
a nudge of the foot, or the wiggle of fingers.
¹⁴ Their perverted hearts plot evil,
and they constantly stir up trouble.
¹⁵ But they will be destroyed suddenly,
broken in an instant beyond all hope of healing.

¹⁶ There are six things the LORD hates—
no, seven things he detests:
¹⁷ haughty eyes,
a lying tongue,
hands that kill the innocent,
¹⁸ a heart that plots evil,
feet that race to do wrong,
¹⁹ a false witness who pours out lies,
a person who sows discord in a family.

²⁰ My son, obey your father's commands,
and don't neglect your mother's instruction.
²¹ Keep their words always in your heart.
Tie them around your neck.
²² When you walk, their counsel will lead you.
When you sleep, they will protect you.
When you wake up, they will advise you.
²³ For their command is a lamp
and their instruction a light;
their corrective discipline
is the way to life.
²⁴ It will keep you from the immoral woman,
from the smooth tongue of a promiscuous woman.
²⁵ Don't lust for her beauty.
Don't let her coy glances seduce you.
²⁶ For a prostitute will bring you to poverty,*
but sleeping with another man's wife
will cost you your life.
²⁷ Can a man scoop a flame into his lap
and not have his clothes catch on fire?
²⁸ Can he walk on hot coals
and not blister his feet?
²⁹ So it is with the man who sleeps with another man's wife.
He who embraces her will not go unpunished.

³⁰ Excuses might be found for a thief
who steals because he is starving.
³¹ But if he is caught, he must pay back
seven times what he stole,
even if he has to sell everything in his house.
³² But the man who commits adultery is an utter fool,
for he destroys himself.
³³ He will be wounded and disgraced.
His shame will never be erased.
³⁴ For the woman's jealous husband will be furious,

**6:1** Hebrew *My son.*   **6:26** Hebrew *to a loaf of bread.*

and he will show no mercy when he
   takes revenge.
35 He will accept no compensation,
   nor be satisfied with a payoff of any
    size.

## Another Warning about Immoral Women

**7** 1Follow my advice, my son;
   always treasure my commands.
2 Obey my commands and live!
   Guard my instructions as you guard
    your own eyes.*
3 Tie them on your fingers as a reminder.
   Write them deep within your heart.

4 Love wisdom like a sister;
   make insight a beloved member of
    your family.
5 Let them protect you from an affair with
    an immoral woman,
   from listening to the flattery of a
    promiscuous woman.

6 While I was at the window of my house,
   looking through the curtain,
7 I saw some naive young men,
   and one in particular who lacked
    common sense.
8 He was crossing the street near the house
    of an immoral woman,
   strolling down the path by her house.
9 It was at twilight, in the evening,
   as deep darkness fell.
10 The woman approached him,
   seductively dressed and sly of heart.
11 She was the brash, rebellious type,
   never content to stay at home.
12 She is often in the streets and markets,
   soliciting at every corner.
13 She threw her arms around him and
    kissed him,
   and with a brazen look she said,
14 "I've just made my peace offerings
   and fulfilled my vows.
15 You're the one I was looking for!
   I came out to find you, and here you
    are!
16 My bed is spread with beautiful blankets,
   with colored sheets of Egyptian linen.
17 I've perfumed my bed
   with myrrh, aloes, and cinnamon.

18 Come, let's drink our fill of love until
    morning.
   Let's enjoy each other's caresses,
19 for my husband is not home.
   He's away on a long trip.
20 He has taken a wallet full of money with
    him
   and won't return until later this
    month.*"

21 So she seduced him with her pretty
    speech
   and enticed him with her flattery.
22 He followed her at once,
   like an ox going to the slaughter.
   He was like a stag caught in a trap,
23    awaiting the arrow that would pierce
    its heart.
   He was like a bird flying into a snare,
   little knowing it would cost him his
    life.

24 So listen to me, my sons,
   and pay attention to my words.
25 Don't let your hearts stray away toward
    her.
   Don't wander down her wayward path.
26 For she has been the ruin of many;
   many men have been her victims.
27 Her house is the road to the grave.*
   Her bedroom is the den of death.

## Wisdom Calls for a Hearing

**8** 1Listen as Wisdom calls out!
   Hear as understanding raises her
    voice!
2 On the hilltop along the road,
   she takes her stand at the crossroads.
3 By the gates at the entrance to the town,
   on the road leading in, she cries aloud,
4 "I call to you, to all of you!
   I raise my voice to all people.
5 You simple people, use good judgment.
   You foolish people, show some
    understanding.
6 Listen to me! For I have important things
    to tell you.
   Everything I say is right,
7 for I speak the truth
   and detest every kind of deception.
8 My advice is wholesome.

**7:2** Hebrew *as the pupil of your eye.*   **7:20** Hebrew *until the moon is full.*   **7:27** Hebrew *to Sheol.*

There is nothing devious or crooked
   in it.
9 My words are plain to anyone with
   understanding,
   clear to those with knowledge.
10 Choose my instruction rather than silver,
   and knowledge rather than pure gold.
11 For wisdom is far more valuable than
   rubies.
   Nothing you desire can compare
   with it.

12 "I, Wisdom, live together with good
   judgment.
   I know where to discover knowledge
   and discernment.
13 All who fear the LORD will hate evil.
   Therefore, I hate pride and arrogance,
   corruption and perverse speech.
14 Common sense and success belong
   to me.
   Insight and strength are mine.
15 Because of me, kings reign,
   and rulers make just decrees.
16 Rulers lead with my help,
   and nobles make righteous judgments.

17 "I love all who love me.
   Those who search will surely find me.
18 I have riches and honor,
   as well as enduring wealth and justice.
19 My gifts are better than gold, even the
   purest gold,
   my wages better than sterling silver!
20 I walk in righteousness,
   in paths of justice.
21 Those who love me inherit wealth.
   I will fill their treasuries.

22 "The LORD formed me from the
   beginning,
   before he created anything else.
23 I was appointed in ages past,
   at the very first, before the earth began.
24 I was born before the oceans were
   created,
   before the springs bubbled forth their
   waters.
25 Before the mountains were formed,
   before the hills, I was born—
26 before he had made the earth and fields
   and the first handfuls of soil.

8:32 Hebrew *my sons.*

27 I was there when he established the
   heavens,
   when he drew the horizon on the
   oceans.
28 I was there when he set the clouds above,
   when he established springs deep in
   the earth.
29 I was there when he set the limits of the
   seas,
   so they would not spread beyond their
   boundaries.
   And when he marked off the earth's
   foundations,
30   I was the architect at his side.
   I was his constant delight,
   rejoicing always in his presence.
31 And how happy I was with the world he
   created;
   how I rejoiced with the human
   family!

32 "And so, my children,* listen to me,
   for all who follow my ways are joyful.
33 Listen to my instruction and be wise.
   Don't ignore it.
34 Joyful are those who listen to me,
   watching for me daily at my gates,
   waiting for me outside my home!
35 For whoever finds me finds life
   and receives favor from the LORD.
36 But those who miss me injure
   themselves.
   All who hate me love death."

## JUNK food for the mind
READ PROVERBS 4:20-23

Chances are you're being a little more careful
about what you put into your body since your
diagnosis. Maybe you've made drastic changes
toward a healthier diet or maybe you're trying to
make some small eating improvements each day.

Be careful, too, about what you put into your
mind. The things that feed our minds determine
the kinds of days we're going to have. What's your
diet? Depressing stories of others with your diagnosis? Discouraging statistics off the Internet?
Anxious thoughts of what could go wrong next?

You need good food for your body and God's
Word for your mind. Don't go malnourished today.

# 9

¹Wisdom has built her house;
   she has carved its seven columns.
²She has prepared a great banquet,
   mixed the wines, and set the table.
³She has sent her servants to invite
      everyone to come.
   She calls out from the heights
      overlooking the city.
⁴"Come in with me," she urges the simple.
   To those who lack good judgment,
      she says,
⁵"Come, eat my food,
   and drink the wine I have mixed.
⁶Leave your simple ways behind, and
      begin to live;
   learn to use good judgment."

⁷Anyone who rebukes a mocker will get an
      insult in return.
   Anyone who corrects the wicked will
      get hurt.
⁸So don't bother correcting mockers;
   they will only hate you.
   But correct the wise,
   and they will love you.
⁹Instruct the wise,
   and they will be even wiser.
   Teach the righteous,
   and they will learn even more.

¹⁰Fear of the LORD is the foundation
      of wisdom.
   Knowledge of the Holy One results in
      good judgment.

¹¹Wisdom will multiply your days
   and add years to your life.
¹²If you become wise, you will be the one
      to benefit.
   If you scorn wisdom, you will be the
      one to suffer.

## Folly Calls for a Hearing

¹³The woman named Folly is brash.
   She is ignorant and doesn't know it.
¹⁴She sits in her doorway
   on the heights overlooking the city.
¹⁵She calls out to men going by
   who are minding their own business.
¹⁶"Come in with me," she urges the
      simple.

To those who lack good judgment, she
      says,
¹⁷"Stolen water is refreshing;
   food eaten in secret tastes the best!"
¹⁸But little do they know that the dead are
      there.
   Her guests are in the depths of the
      grave.*

## The Proverbs of Solomon

# 10

The proverbs of Solomon:

   A wise child* brings joy to
      a father;
   a foolish child brings grief to
      a mother.

²Tainted wealth has no lasting value,
   but right living can save your life.

³The LORD will not let the godly go hungry,
   but he refuses to satisfy the craving of
      the wicked.

⁴Lazy people are soon poor;
   hard workers get rich.

⁵A wise youth harvests in the summer,
   but one who sleeps during harvest is a
      disgrace.

⁶The godly are showered with blessings;
   the words of the wicked conceal
      violent intentions.

⁷We have happy memories of the godly,
   but the name of a wicked person rots
      away.

⁸The wise are glad to be instructed,
   but babbling fools fall flat on their
      faces.

⁹People with integrity walk safely,
   but those who follow crooked paths
      will slip and fall.

¹⁰People who wink at wrong cause
      trouble,
   but a bold reproof promotes peace.*

¹¹The words of the godly are a life-giving
      fountain;
   the words of the wicked conceal
      violent intentions.

---

9:18 Hebrew in Sheol.   10:1 Hebrew son; also in 10:1b.   10:10 As in Greek version; Hebrew reads but babbling fools fall flat on their faces.

¹² Hatred stirs up quarrels,
    but love makes up for all offenses.

¹³ Wise words come from the lips of people
    with understanding,
    but those lacking sense will be beaten
    with a rod.

¹⁴ Wise people treasure knowledge,
    but the babbling of a fool invites
    disaster.

¹⁵ The wealth of the rich is their fortress;
    the poverty of the poor is their
    destruction.

¹⁶ The earnings of the godly enhance their
    lives,
    but evil people squander their money
    on sin.

¹⁷ People who accept discipline are on the
    pathway to life,
    but those who ignore correction will go
    astray.

¹⁸ Hiding hatred makes you a liar;
    slandering others makes you a fool.

¹⁹ Too much talk leads to sin.
    Be sensible and keep your mouth shut.

²⁰ The words of the godly are like sterling
    silver;
    the heart of a fool is worthless.

²¹ The words of the godly encourage many,
    but fools are destroyed by their lack of
    common sense.

²² The blessing of the LORD makes a person
    rich,
    and he adds no sorrow with it.

²³ Doing wrong is fun for a fool,
    but living wisely brings pleasure to the
    sensible.

²⁴ The fears of the wicked will be fulfilled;
    the hopes of the godly will be granted.

²⁵ When the storms of life come, the
    wicked are whirled away,
    but the godly have a lasting
    foundation.

²⁶ Lazy people irritate their employers,
    like vinegar to the teeth or smoke in
    the eyes.

²⁷ Fear of the LORD lengthens one's life,
    but the years of the wicked are cut
    short.

²⁸ The hopes of the godly result in
    happiness,
    but the expectations of the wicked
    come to nothing.

²⁹ The way of the LORD is a stronghold to
    those with integrity,
    but it destroys the wicked.

³⁰ The godly will never be disturbed,
    but the wicked will be removed from
    the land.

³¹ The mouth of the godly person gives wise
    advice,
    but the tongue that deceives will be
    cut off.

³² The lips of the godly speak helpful
    words,
    but the mouth of the wicked speaks
    perverse words.

# 11

¹ The LORD detests the use of
    dishonest scales,
    but he delights in accurate weights.

² Pride leads to disgrace,
    but with humility comes wisdom.

³ Honesty guides good people;
    dishonesty destroys treacherous
    people.

⁴ Riches won't help on the day of judgment,
    but right living can save you from
    death.

⁵ The godly are directed by honesty;
    the wicked fall beneath their load
    of sin.

⁶ The godliness of good people rescues
    them;
    the ambition of treacherous people
    traps them.

⁷ When the wicked die, their hopes die
    with them,
    for they rely on their own feeble
    strength.

⁸ The godly are rescued from trouble,
    and it falls on the wicked instead.

9 With their words, the godless destroy
  their friends,
    but knowledge will rescue the
    righteous.

10 The whole city celebrates when the godly
   succeed;
     they shout for joy when the wicked die.

11 Upright citizens are good for a city and
   make it prosper,
     but the talk of the wicked tears
     it apart.

12 It is foolish to belittle one's neighbor;
   a sensible person keeps quiet.

13 A gossip goes around telling secrets,
   but those who are trustworthy can
   keep a confidence.

14 Without wise leadership, a nation falls;
   there is safety in having many
   advisers.

15 There's danger in putting up security for
   a stranger's debt;
     it's safer not to guarantee another
     person's debt.

16 A gracious woman gains respect,
   but ruthless men gain only wealth.

17 Your kindness will reward you,
   but your cruelty will destroy you.

18 Evil people get rich for the moment,
   but the reward of the godly will last.

19 Godly people find life;
   evil people find death.

20 The LORD detests people with crooked
   hearts,
     but he delights in those with integrity.

21 Evil people will surely be punished,
   but the children of the godly will
   go free.

22 A beautiful woman who lacks discretion
   is like a gold ring in a pig's snout.

23 The godly can look forward to a reward,
   while the wicked can expect only
   judgment.

24 Give freely and become more wealthy;
   be stingy and lose everything.

25 The generous will prosper;
   those who refresh others will
   themselves be refreshed.

26 People curse those who hoard their grain,
   but they bless the one who sells in time
   of need.

27 If you search for good, you will find favor;
   but if you search for evil, it will find
   you!

28 Trust in your money and down you go!
   But the godly flourish like leaves in
   spring.

29 Those who bring trouble on their
   families inherit the wind.
     The fool will be a servant to the wise.

30 The seeds of good deeds become a tree
   of life;
     a wise person wins friends.*

31 If the righteous are rewarded here
   on earth,
     what will happen to wicked
     sinners?*

## 12

1 To learn, you must love discipline;
  it is stupid to hate correction.

2 The LORD approves of those who are
  good,
    but he condemns those who plan
    wickedness.

3 Wickedness never brings stability,
  but the godly have deep roots.

4 A worthy wife is a crown for her husband,
  but a disgraceful woman is like cancer
  in his bones.

5 The plans of the godly are just;
  the advice of the wicked is
  treacherous.

6 The words of the wicked are like a
  murderous ambush,
    but the words of the godly
    save lives.

11:30 Or *and those who win souls are wise.*   11:31 Greek version reads *If the righteous are barely saved, / what will happen to godless sinners?* Compare 1 Pet 4:18.

7 The wicked die and disappear,
but the family of the godly stands firm.

8 A sensible person wins admiration,
but a warped mind is despised.

9 Better to be an ordinary person with a
servant
than to be self-important but have no
food.

10 The godly care for their animals,
but the wicked are always cruel.

11 A hard worker has plenty of food,
but a person who chases fantasies has
no sense.

12 Thieves are jealous of each other's loot,
but the godly are well rooted and bear
their own fruit.

13 The wicked are trapped by their own
words,
but the godly escape such trouble.

14 Wise words bring many benefits,
and hard work brings rewards.

15 Fools think their own way is right,
but the wise listen to others.

16 A fool is quick-tempered,
but a wise person stays calm when
insulted.

17 An honest witness tells the truth;
a false witness tells lies.

18 Some people make cutting remarks,
but the words of the wise bring
healing.

19 Truthful words stand the test of time,
but lies are soon exposed.

20 Deceit fills hearts that are plotting evil;
joy fills hearts that are planning peace!

21 No harm comes to the godly,
but the wicked have their fill of trouble.

22 The Lord detests lying lips,
but he delights in those who tell the
truth.

23 The wise don't make a show of their
knowledge,
but fools broadcast their foolishness.

## SOUNDS of silence
READ PROVERBS 13:3

Don't you wish some people knew when to stop talking? They ask inappropriate questions about details of your condition and tell you about people who died of the same thing you have. Their visit with you was going great until they opened their mouths!

It's all right to tell these people you don't want to hear their stories. (Ask them if the story has a happy ending and if not, politely inform them you don't want to hear it!) And if you're the relative or friend of an ill person, it's okay *not* to talk all the time. Sometimes a warm hug or a tightly clasped hand speaks more healing to us than any words you could ever say.

24 Work hard and become a leader;
be lazy and become a slave.

25 Worry weighs a person down;
an encouraging word cheers a
person up.

26 The godly give good advice to their
friends;*
the wicked lead them astray.

27 Lazy people don't even cook the game
they catch,
but the diligent make use of everything
they find.

28 The way of the godly leads to life;
that path does not lead to death.

**13** 1 A wise child accepts a parent's
discipline;*
a mocker refuses to listen to correction.

2 Wise words will win you a good meal,
but treacherous people have an
appetite for violence.

3 Those who control their tongue will have
a long life;
opening your mouth can ruin
everything.

4 Lazy people want much but get little,
but those who work hard will prosper.

12:26 Or *The godly are cautious in friendship;* or *The godly are freed from evil.* The meaning of the Hebrew is uncertain.
13:1 Hebrew *A wise son accepts his father's discipline.*

5 The godly hate lies;
    the wicked cause shame and disgrace.

6 Godliness guards the path of the
      blameless,
    but the evil are misled by sin.

7 Some who are poor pretend to be rich;
    others who are rich pretend to be poor.

8 The rich can pay a ransom for their lives,
    but the poor won't even get
      threatened.

9 The life of the godly is full of light and
      joy,
    but the light of the wicked will be
      snuffed out.

10 Pride leads to conflict;
    those who take advice are wise.

11 Wealth from get-rich-quick schemes
      quickly disappears;
    wealth from hard work grows over time.

12 Hope deferred makes the heart sick,
    but a dream fulfilled is a tree of life.

13 People who despise advice are asking for
      trouble;
    those who respect a command will
      succeed.

14 The instruction of the wise is like
      a life-giving fountain;
    those who accept it avoid the snares
      of death.

15 A person with good sense is respected;
    a treacherous person is headed for
      destruction.*

16 Wise people think before they act;
    fools don't—and even brag about their
      foolishness.

17 An unreliable messenger stumbles into
      trouble,
    but a reliable messenger brings healing.

18 If you ignore criticism, you will end in
      poverty and disgrace;
    if you accept correction, you will be
      honored.

19 It is pleasant to see dreams come true,
    but fools refuse to turn from evil to
      attain them.

20 Walk with the wise and become wise;
    associate with fools and get in trouble.

21 Trouble chases sinners,
    while blessings reward the righteous.

22 Good people leave an inheritance to their
      grandchildren,
    but the sinner's wealth passes to the
      godly.

23 A poor person's farm may produce much
      food,
    but injustice sweeps it all away.

24 Those who spare the rod of discipline
      hate their children.
    Those who love their children care
      enough to discipline them.

25 The godly eat to their hearts' content,
    but the belly of the wicked goes
      hungry.

**14** 1 A wise woman builds her home,
      but a foolish woman tears it
        down with her own hands.

2 Those who follow the right path fear the
      Lord;
    those who take the wrong path despise
      him.

3 A fool's proud talk becomes a rod that
      beats him,
    but the words of the wise keep them
      safe.

4 Without oxen a stable stays clean,
    but you need a strong ox for a large
      harvest.

5 An honest witness does not lie;
    a false witness breathes lies.

6 A mocker seeks wisdom and never finds
      it,
    but knowledge comes easily to those
      with understanding.

7 Stay away from fools,
    for you won't find knowledge on their
      lips.

8 The prudent understand where they are
      going,
    but fools deceive themselves.

13:15 As in Greek version; Hebrew reads *the way of the treacherous is lasting.*

⁹ Fools make fun of guilt,
  but the godly acknowledge it and seek
    reconciliation.

¹⁰ Each heart knows its own bitterness,
   and no one else can fully share its joy.

¹¹ The house of the wicked will be destroyed,
   but the tent of the godly will flourish.

¹² There is a path before each person that
     seems right,
   but it ends in death.

¹³ Laughter can conceal a heavy heart,
   but when the laughter ends, the grief
     remains.

¹⁴ Backsliders get what they deserve;
   good people receive their reward.

¹⁵ Only simpletons believe everything
     they're told!
   The prudent carefully consider their
     steps.

¹⁶ The wise are cautious* and avoid danger;
   fools plunge ahead with reckless
     confidence.

¹⁷ Short-tempered people do foolish things,
   and schemers are hated.

¹⁸ Simpletons are clothed with foolishness,*
   but the prudent are crowned with
     knowledge.

¹⁹ Evil people will bow before good people;
   the wicked will bow at the gates
     of the godly.

²⁰ The poor are despised even by their
     neighbors,
   while the rich have many "friends."

²¹ It is a sin to belittle one's neighbor;
   blessed are those who help the poor.

²² If you plan to do evil, you will be lost;
   if you plan to do good, you will receive
     unfailing love and faithfulness.

²³ Work brings profit,
   but mere talk leads to poverty!

²⁴ Wealth is a crown for the wise;
   the effort of fools yields only
     foolishness.

²⁵ A truthful witness saves lives,
   but a false witness is a traitor.

²⁶ Those who fear the LORD are secure;
   he will be a refuge for their children.

²⁷ Fear of the LORD is a life-giving fountain;
   it offers escape from the snares of
     death.

²⁸ A growing population is a king's glory;
   a prince without subjects has nothing.

²⁹ People with understanding control their
     anger;
   a hot temper shows great foolishness.

³⁰ A peaceful heart leads to a healthy body;
   jealousy is like cancer in the bones.

³¹ Those who oppress the poor insult their
     Maker,
   but helping the poor honors him.

³² The wicked are crushed by disaster,
   but the godly have a refuge when
     they die.

³³ Wisdom is enshrined in an
     understanding heart;
   wisdom is not* found among fools.

³⁴ Godliness makes a nation great,
   but sin is a disgrace to any people.

³⁵ A king rejoices in wise servants
   but is angry with those who disgrace
     him.

# 15

¹ A gentle answer deflects anger,
   but harsh words make tempers
     flare.

² The tongue of the wise makes knowledge
     appealing,
   but the mouth of a fool belches out
     foolishness.

³ The LORD is watching everywhere,
   keeping his eye on both the evil and
     the good.

⁴ Gentle words are a tree of life;
   a deceitful tongue crushes the spirit.

⁵ Only a fool despises a parent's* discipline;
   whoever learns from correction is
     wise.

**14:16** Hebrew *The wise fear.*   **14:18** Or *inherit foolishness.*   **14:33** As in Greek and Syriac versions; Hebrew lacks *not.*   **15:5** Hebrew
*father's.*

6 There is treasure in the house of the
godly,
but the earnings of the wicked bring
trouble.

7 The lips of the wise give good advice;
the heart of a fool has none to give.

8 The LORD detests the sacrifice of the
wicked,
but he delights in the prayers of the
upright.

9 The LORD detests the way of the wicked,
but he loves those who pursue
godliness.

10 Whoever abandons the right path will
be severely disciplined;
whoever hates correction will die.

11 Even Death and Destruction* hold no
secrets from the LORD.
How much more does he know the
human heart!

12 Mockers hate to be corrected,
so they stay away from the wise.

13 A glad heart makes a happy face;
a broken heart crushes the spirit.

14 A wise person is hungry for knowledge,
while the fool feeds on trash.

15 For the despondent, every day brings
trouble;
for the happy heart, life is a continual
feast.

16 Better to have little, with fear for the LORD,
than to have great treasure and inner
turmoil.

17 A bowl of vegetables with someone
you love
is better than steak with someone
you hate.

18 A hot-tempered person starts fights;
a cool-tempered person stops them.

19 A lazy person's way is blocked with
briers,
but the path of the upright is an open
highway.

15:11 Hebrew *Sheol and Abaddon.*  15:24 Hebrew *Sheol.*

20 Sensible children bring joy to their father;
foolish children despise their mother.

21 Foolishness brings joy to those with
no sense;
a sensible person stays on the right path.

22 Plans go wrong for lack of advice;
many advisers bring success.

23 Everyone enjoys a fitting reply;
it is wonderful to say the right thing
at the right time!

24 The path of life leads upward for the wise;
they leave the grave* behind.

25 The LORD tears down the house
of the proud,
but he protects the property of widows.

26 The LORD detests evil plans,
but he delights in pure words.

27 Greed brings grief to the whole family,
but those who hate bribes will live.

28 The heart of the godly thinks carefully
before speaking;
the mouth of the wicked overflows
with evil words.

29 The LORD is far from the wicked,
but he hears the prayers of the
righteous.

30 A cheerful look brings joy to the heart;
good news makes for good health.

31 If you listen to constructive criticism,
you will be at home among the wise.

32 If you reject discipline, you only harm
yourself;
but if you listen to correction, you
grow in understanding.

33 Fear of the LORD teaches wisdom;
humility precedes honor.

**16** 1 We can make our own plans,
but the LORD gives the right
answer.

2 People may be pure in their own eyes,
but the LORD examines their motives.

3 Commit your actions to the LORD,
and your plans will succeed.

4 The Lord has made everything for his
   own purposes,
   even the wicked for a day of disaster.

5 The Lord detests the proud;
   they will surely be punished.

6 Unfailing love and faithfulness make
   atonement for sin.
   By fearing the Lord, people avoid evil.

7 When people's lives please the Lord,
   even their enemies are at peace with
   them.

8 Better to have little, with godliness,
   than to be rich and dishonest.

9 We can make our plans,
   but the Lord determines our steps.

10 The king speaks with divine wisdom;
   he must never judge unfairly.

11 The Lord demands accurate scales and
   balances;
   he sets the standards for fairness.

12 A king detests wrongdoing,
   for his rule is built on justice.

13 The king is pleased with words from
   righteous lips;
   he loves those who speak honestly.

14 The anger of the king is a deadly
   threat;
   the wise will try to appease it.

15 When the king smiles, there is life;
   his favor refreshes like a spring rain.

16 How much better to get wisdom than
   gold,
   and good judgment than silver!

17 The path of the virtuous leads away from
   evil;
   whoever follows that path is safe.

18 Pride goes before destruction,
   and haughtiness before a fall.

19 Better to live humbly with the poor
   than to share plunder with the proud.

20 Those who listen to instruction will
   prosper;
   those who trust the Lord will be joyful.

21 The wise are known for their
   understanding,
   and pleasant words are persuasive.

22 Discretion is a life-giving fountain to
   those who possess it,
   but discipline is wasted on fools.

23 From a wise mind comes wise speech;
   the words of the wise are persuasive.

24 Kind words are like honey—
   sweet to the soul and healthy for the
   body.

25 There is a path before each person that
   seems right,
   but it ends in death.

26 It is good for workers to have an appetite;
   an empty stomach drives them on.

27 Scoundrels create trouble;
   their words are a destructive blaze.

28 A troublemaker plants seeds of strife;
   gossip separates the best of friends.

29 Violent people mislead their
   companions,
   leading them down a harmful path.

30 With narrowed eyes, people plot evil;
   with a smirk, they plan their mischief.

31 Gray hair is a crown of glory;
   it is gained by living a godly life.

## HAD a good laugh today?
READ PROVERBS 15:30 AND 17:22

Laughter is good for the body. Science is just
figuring that out, but Proverbs told us a long time
ago. Published studies show laughter has many
positive physical effects, including activating our
immune systems. It increases those "natural killer"
cells, works out our heart, drops our blood
pressure, and gives us a free diversion from life's
struggles. We all need to find ways to tickle our
funny bones: post cartoons where you can see
them; chuckle at tabloid headlines; read comical
greeting cards; hang out with funny people; and
make the most of embarrassing moments by
sharing your mishaps with good friends.
   Laughter is definitely healing medicine.

³² Better to be patient than powerful;
   better to have self-control than to
   conquer a city.

³³ We may throw the dice,*
   but the LORD determines how they fall.

# 17

¹ Better a dry crust eaten in peace
   than a house filled with
   feasting—and conflict.

² A wise servant will rule over the master's
   disgraceful son
   and will share the inheritance of the
   master's children.

³ Fire tests the purity of silver and gold,
   but the LORD tests the heart.

⁴ Wrongdoers eagerly listen to gossip;
   liars pay close attention to slander.

⁵ Those who mock the poor insult their
   Maker;
   those who rejoice at the misfortune
   of others will be punished.

⁶ Grandchildren are the crowning glory
   of the aged;
   parents* are the pride of their
   children.

⁷ Eloquent words are not fitting for a fool;
   even less are lies fitting for a ruler.

⁸ A bribe is like a lucky charm;
   whoever gives one will prosper!

⁹ Love prospers when a fault is forgiven,
   but dwelling on it separates close
   friends.

¹⁰ A single rebuke does more for a person
    of understanding
    than a hundred lashes on the back
    of a fool.

¹¹ Evil people are eager for rebellion,
    but they will be severely punished.

¹² It is safer to meet a bear robbed of her
    cubs
    than to confront a fool caught in
    foolishness.

¹³ If you repay good with evil,
    evil will never leave your house.

¹⁴ Starting a quarrel is like opening a
    floodgate,
    so stop before a dispute breaks out.

¹⁵ Acquitting the guilty and condemning
    the innocent—
    both are detestable to the LORD.

¹⁶ It is senseless to pay tuition to educate
    a fool,
    since he has no heart for learning.

¹⁷ A friend is always loyal,
    and a brother is born to help in time
    of need.

¹⁸ It's poor judgment to guarantee another
    person's debt
    or put up security for a friend.

¹⁹ Anyone who loves to quarrel loves sin;
    anyone who trusts in high walls invites
    disaster.

²⁰ The crooked heart will not prosper;
    the lying tongue tumbles into trouble.

²¹ It is painful to be the parent of a fool;
    there is no joy for the father of a rebel.

²² A cheerful heart is good medicine,
    but a broken spirit saps a person's
    strength.

²³ The wicked take secret bribes
    to pervert the course of justice.

²⁴ Sensible people keep their eyes glued
    on wisdom,
    but a fool's eyes wander to the ends
    of the earth.

²⁵ Foolish children* bring grief to their
    father
    and bitterness to the one who gave
    them birth.

²⁶ It is wrong to punish the godly for being
    good
    or to flog leaders for being honest.

²⁷ A truly wise person uses few words;
    a person with understanding is even-
    tempered.

²⁸ Even fools are thought wise when they
    keep silent;
    with their mouths shut, they seem
    intelligent.

16:33 Hebrew *We may cast lots.*   17:6 Hebrew *fathers.*   17:25 Hebrew *A foolish son.*

# 18

¹ Unfriendly people care only about themselves;
they lash out at common sense.

² Fools have no interest in understanding;
they only want to air their own opinions.

³ Doing wrong leads to disgrace,
and scandalous behavior brings contempt.

⁴ Wise words are like deep waters;
wisdom flows from the wise like a bubbling brook.

⁵ It is not right to acquit the guilty
or deny justice to the innocent.

⁶ Fools' words get them into constant quarrels;
they are asking for a beating.

⁷ The mouths of fools are their ruin;
they trap themselves with their lips.

⁸ Rumors are dainty morsels
that sink deep into one's heart.

⁹ A lazy person is as bad as
someone who destroys things.

¹⁰ The name of the LORD is a strong fortress;
the godly run to him and are safe.

¹¹ The rich think of their wealth as a strong defense;
they imagine it to be a high wall of safety.

¹² Haughtiness goes before destruction;
humility precedes honor.

¹³ Spouting off before listening to the facts
is both shameful and foolish.

¹⁴ The human spirit can endure a sick body,
but who can bear a crushed spirit?

¹⁵ Intelligent people are always ready to learn.
Their ears are open for knowledge.

¹⁶ Giving a gift can open doors;
it gives access to important people!

¹⁷ The first to speak in court sounds right—
until the cross-examination begins.

¹⁸ Flipping a coin* can end arguments;
it settles disputes between powerful opponents.

¹⁹ An offended friend is harder to win back
than a fortified city.
Arguments separate friends like a gate locked with bars.

²⁰ Wise words satisfy like a good meal;
the right words bring satisfaction.

²¹ The tongue can bring death or life;
those who love to talk will reap the consequences.

²² The man who finds a wife finds a treasure,
and he receives favor from the LORD.

²³ The poor plead for mercy;
the rich answer with insults.

²⁴ There are "friends" who destroy each other,
but a real friend sticks closer than a brother.

# 19

¹ Better to be poor and honest
than to be dishonest and a fool.

² Enthusiasm without knowledge is no good;
haste makes mistakes.

³ People ruin their lives by their own foolishness
and then are angry at the LORD.

⁴ Wealth makes many "friends";
poverty drives them all away.

⁵ A false witness will not go unpunished,
nor will a liar escape.

⁶ Many seek favors from a ruler;
everyone is the friend of a person who gives gifts!

⁷ The relatives of the poor despise them;
how much more will their friends avoid them!
Though the poor plead with them,
their friends are gone.

⁸ To acquire wisdom is to love oneself;
people who cherish understanding will prosper.

18:18 Hebrew *Casting lots.*

9 A false witness will not go unpunished,
  and a liar will be destroyed.

10 It isn't right for a fool to live in luxury
   or for a slave to rule over princes!

11 Sensible people control their temper;
   they earn respect by overlooking
   wrongs.

12 The king's anger is like a lion's roar,
   but his favor is like dew on the grass.

13 A foolish child* is a calamity to a father;
   a quarrelsome wife is as annoying as
   constant dripping.

14 Fathers can give their sons an
   inheritance of houses and wealth,
   but only the LORD can give an
   understanding wife.

15 Lazy people sleep soundly,
   but idleness leaves them hungry.

16 Keep the commandments and keep your
   life;
   despising them leads to death.

17 If you help the poor, you are lending to
   the LORD—
   and he will repay you!

18 Discipline your children while there is
   hope.
   Otherwise you will ruin their lives.

19 Hot-tempered people must pay the
   penalty.
   If you rescue them once, you will have
   to do it again.

20 Get all the advice and instruction
   you can,
   so you will be wise the rest of your life.

21 You can make many plans,
   but the LORD's purpose will prevail.

22 Loyalty makes a person attractive.
   It is better to be poor than dishonest.

23 Fear of the LORD leads to life,
   bringing security and protection
   from harm.

24 Lazy people take food in their hand
   but don't even lift it to their mouth.

25 If you punish a mocker, the
   simpleminded will learn a lesson;
   if you correct the wise, they will be all
   the wiser.

26 Children who mistreat their father or
   chase away their mother
   are an embarrassment and a public
   disgrace.

27 If you stop listening to instruction,
   my child,
   you will turn your back on knowledge.

28 A corrupt witness makes a mockery
   of justice;
   the mouth of the wicked gulps down
   evil.

29 Punishment is made for mockers,
   and the backs of fools are made to be
   beaten.

# 20

1 Wine produces mockers; alcohol
  leads to brawls.
  Those led astray by drink cannot
  be wise.

2 The king's fury is like a lion's roar;
  to rouse his anger is to risk your life.

3 Avoiding a fight is a mark of honor;
  only fools insist on quarreling.

4 Those too lazy to plow in the right
  season
  will have no food at the harvest.

5 Though good advice lies deep within
  the heart,
  a person with understanding will
  draw it out.

6 Many will say they are loyal friends,
  but who can find one who is truly
  reliable?

7 The godly walk with integrity;
  blessed are their children who follow
  them.

8 When a king sits in judgment, he
  weighs all the evidence,
  distinguishing the bad from the
  good.

19:13 Hebrew *son;* also in 19:27.

**9** Who can say, "I have cleansed my heart;
I am pure and free from sin"?

**10** False weights and unequal measures*—
the LORD detests double standards
of every kind.

**11** Even children are known by the way
they act,
whether their conduct is pure, and
whether it is right.

**12** Ears to hear and eyes to see—
both are gifts from the LORD.

**13** If you love sleep, you will end in poverty.
Keep your eyes open, and there will be
plenty to eat!

**14** The buyer haggles over the price, saying,
"It's worthless,"
then brags about getting a bargain!

**15** Wise words are more valuable
than much gold and many rubies.

**16** Get security from someone who
guarantees a stranger's debt.
Get a deposit if he does it for
foreigners.*

**17** Stolen bread tastes sweet,
but it turns to gravel in the mouth.

**18** Plans succeed through good counsel;
don't go to war without wise advice.

**19** A gossip goes around telling secrets,
so don't hang around with chatterers.

**20** If you insult your father or mother,
your light will be snuffed out in total
darkness.

**21** An inheritance obtained too early in life
is not a blessing in the end.

**22** Don't say, "I will get even for this
wrong."
Wait for the LORD to handle the
matter.

**23** The LORD detests double standards;
he is not pleased by dishonest scales.

**24** The LORD directs our steps,
so why try to understand everything
along the way?

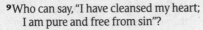

## DON'T put on a happy face
READ PROVERBS 18:14

The mind-body connection is very real—our emotions affect our hormones and even our immune systems. How we feel physically influences how we feel emotionally, but it's not the only factor. There are many people who are just fine physically, but they have a "crushed spirit." And there also are many people who have sick bodies and yet are very much at peace.

You may or may not be able to do much about your "sick body" today, but you can influence your emotions. Don't just try to put on a happy face. Be honest about your feelings with God and then ask Him to lift your crumpled spirit so that you can endure.

**25** Don't trap yourself by making a rash
promise to God
and only later counting the cost.

**26** A wise king scatters the wicked like wheat,
then runs his threshing wheel over
them.

**27** The LORD's light penetrates the human
spirit,*
exposing every hidden motive.

**28** Unfailing love and faithfulness protect
the king;
his throne is made secure through
love.

**29** The glory of the young is their strength;
the gray hair of experience is the
splendor of the old.

**30** Physical punishment cleanses away evil;*
such discipline purifies the heart.

**·21** **1** The king's heart is like a stream of
water directed by the LORD;
he guides it wherever he pleases.

**2** People may be right in their own eyes,
but the LORD examines their heart.

**3** The LORD is more pleased when we do
what is right and just
than when we offer him sacrifices.

**20:10** Hebrew *A stone and a stone, an ephah and an ephah.*   **20:16** An alternate reading in the Hebrew text is *for a promiscuous woman.*   **20:27** Or *The human spirit is the LORD's light.*   **20:30** The meaning of the Hebrew is uncertain.

<sup>4</sup> Haughty eyes, a proud heart,
and evil actions are all sin.

<sup>5</sup> Good planning and hard work lead to
prosperity,
but hasty shortcuts lead to poverty.

<sup>6</sup> Wealth created by a lying tongue
is a vanishing mist and a deadly trap.*

<sup>7</sup> The violence of the wicked sweeps them
away,
because they refuse to do what is just.

<sup>8</sup> The guilty walk a crooked path;
the innocent travel a straight road.

<sup>9</sup> It's better to live alone in the corner
of an attic
than with a quarrelsome wife in a
lovely home.

<sup>10</sup> Evil people desire evil;
their neighbors get no mercy from
them.

<sup>11</sup> If you punish a mocker, the
simpleminded become wise;
if you instruct the wise, they will be
all the wiser.

<sup>12</sup> The Righteous One* knows what is going
on in the homes of the wicked;
he will bring disaster on them.

<sup>13</sup> Those who shut their ears to the cries
of the poor
will be ignored in their own time
of need.

<sup>14</sup> A secret gift calms anger;
a bribe under the table pacifies fury.

<sup>15</sup> Justice is a joy to the godly,
but it terrifies evildoers.

<sup>16</sup> The person who strays from common
sense
will end up in the company of the
dead.

<sup>17</sup> Those who love pleasure become poor;
those who love wine and luxury will
never be rich.

<sup>18</sup> The wicked are punished in place
of the godly,
and traitors in place of the honest.

<sup>19</sup> It's better to live alone in the desert
than with a quarrelsome, complaining
wife.

<sup>20</sup> The wise have wealth and luxury,
but fools spend whatever they get.

<sup>21</sup> Whoever pursues righteousness and
unfailing love
will find life, righteousness, and honor.

<sup>22</sup> The wise conquer the city of the strong
and level the fortress in which they
trust.

<sup>23</sup> Watch your tongue and keep your mouth
shut,
and you will stay out of trouble.

<sup>24</sup> Mockers are proud and haughty;
they act with boundless arrogance.

<sup>25</sup> Despite their desires, the lazy will come
to ruin,
for their hands refuse to work.

<sup>26</sup> Some people are always greedy for more,
but the godly love to give!

<sup>27</sup> The sacrifice of an evil person is
detestable,
especially when it is offered with
wrong motives.

<sup>28</sup> A false witness will be cut off,
but a credible witness will be allowed
to speak.

<sup>29</sup> The wicked bluff their way through,
but the virtuous think before they act.

<sup>30</sup> No human wisdom or understanding
or plan
can stand against the LORD.

<sup>31</sup> The horse is prepared for the day of battle,
but the victory belongs to the LORD.

# 22
<sup>1</sup> Choose a good reputation over
great riches;
being held in high esteem is better
than silver or gold.

<sup>2</sup> The rich and poor have this in common:
The LORD made them both.

<sup>3</sup> A prudent person foresees danger and
takes precautions.

---

21:6 As in Greek version; Hebrew reads *mist for those who seek death.*   21:12 Or *The righteous man.*

The simpleton goes blindly on and
suffers the consequences.

4 True humility and fear of the LORD
lead to riches, honor, and long life.

5 Corrupt people walk a thorny,
treacherous road;
whoever values life will avoid it.

6 Direct your children onto the right path,
and when they are older, they will not
leave it.

7 Just as the rich rule the poor,
so the borrower is servant to the
lender.

8 Those who plant injustice will harvest
disaster,
and their reign of terror will come to
an end.*

9 Blessed are those who are generous,
because they feed the poor.

10 Throw out the mocker, and fighting goes,
too.
Quarrels and insults will disappear.

11 Whoever loves a pure heart and gracious
speech
will have the king as a friend.

12 The LORD preserves those with
knowledge,
but he ruins the plans of the
treacherous.

13 The lazy person claims, "There's a lion
out there!
If I go outside, I might be killed!"

14 The mouth of an immoral woman is a
dangerous trap;
those who make the LORD angry will
fall into it.

15 A youngster's heart is filled with
foolishness,
but physical discipline will drive it
far away.

16 A person who gets ahead by oppressing
the poor
or by showering gifts on the rich will
end in poverty.

### Sayings of the Wise

17 Listen to the words of the wise;
apply your heart to my instruction.

18 For it is good to keep these sayings in
your heart
and always ready on your lips.

19 I am teaching you today—yes, you—
so you will trust in the LORD.

20 I have written thirty sayings* for you,
filled with advice and knowledge.

21 In this way, you may know the truth
and take an accurate report to those
who sent you.

22 Don't rob the poor just because you can,
or exploit the needy in court.

23 For the LORD is their defender.
He will ruin anyone who ruins them.

24 Don't befriend angry people
or associate with hot-tempered
people,

25 or you will learn to be like them
and endanger your soul.

26 Don't agree to guarantee another
person's debt
or put up security for someone else.

27 If you can't pay it,
even your bed will be snatched from
under you.

28 Don't cheat your neighbor by moving the
ancient boundary markers
set up by previous generations.

29 Do you see any truly competent workers?
They will serve kings
rather than working for ordinary
people.

**23** ¹ While dining with a ruler,
pay attention to what is put
before you.

2 If you are a big eater,
put a knife to your throat;

3 don't desire all the delicacies,
for he might be trying to trick you.

4 Don't wear yourself out trying to
get rich.
Be wise enough to know when
to quit.

---

22:8 The Greek version includes an additional proverb: *God blesses a man who gives cheerfully, / but his worthless deeds will come to an end.* Compare 2 Cor 9:7.   22:20 Or *excellent sayings;* the meaning of the Hebrew is uncertain.

5 In the blink of an eye wealth disappears,
for it will sprout wings
and fly away like an eagle.

6 Don't eat with people who are stingy;
don't desire their delicacies.
7 They are always thinking about how
much it costs.*
"Eat and drink," they say, but they don't
mean it.
8 You will throw up what little you've
eaten,
and your compliments will be wasted.

9 Don't waste your breath on fools,
for they will despise the wisest advice.

10 Don't cheat your neighbor by moving the
ancient boundary markers;
don't take the land of defenseless
orphans.
11 For their Redeemer* is strong;
he himself will bring their charges
against you.

12 Commit yourself to instruction;
listen carefully to words of
knowledge.

13 Don't fail to discipline your children.
They won't die if you spank them.
14 Physical discipline
may well save them from death.*

15 My child,* if your heart is wise,
my own heart will rejoice!
16 Everything in me will celebrate
when you speak what is right.

17 Don't envy sinners,
but always continue to fear the LORD.
18 You will be rewarded for this;
your hope will not be disappointed.

19 My child, listen and be wise:
Keep your heart on the right course.
20 Do not carouse with drunkards
or feast with gluttons,
21 for they are on their way to poverty,
and too much sleep clothes them
in rags.

22 Listen to your father, who gave you life,
and don't despise your mother when
she is old.

23 Get the truth and never sell it;
also get wisdom, discipline, and good
judgment.
24 The father of godly children has cause
for joy.
What a pleasure to have children who
are wise.*
25 So give your father and mother joy!
May she who gave you birth be happy.

26 O my son, give me your heart.
May your eyes take delight in following
my ways.
27 A prostitute is a dangerous trap;
a promiscuous woman is as dangerous
as falling into a
narrow well.
28 She hides and waits like a robber,
eager to make more men unfaithful.

29 Who has anguish? Who has sorrow?
Who is always fighting? Who is always
complaining?
Who has unnecessary bruises? Who
has bloodshot eyes?
30 It is the one who spends long hours
in the taverns,
trying out new drinks.
31 Don't gaze at the wine, seeing how
red it is,
how it sparkles in the cup, how
smoothly it goes down.
32 For in the end it bites like
a poisonous snake;
it stings like a viper.
33 You will see hallucinations,
and you will say crazy things.
34 You will stagger like a sailor tossed
at sea,
clinging to a swaying mast.
35 And you will say, "They hit me, but
I didn't feel it.
I didn't even know it when they beat
me up.
When will I wake up
so I can look for another drink?"

# 24
1 Don't envy evil people
or desire their company.
2 For their hearts plot violence,
and their words always stir up trouble.

23:7 The meaning of the Hebrew is uncertain.    23:11 Or redeemer.    23:14 Hebrew from Sheol.    23:15 Hebrew My son; also in 23:19.    23:24 Hebrew to have a wise son.

³ A house is built by wisdom
and becomes strong through good
sense.
⁴ Through knowledge its rooms are filled
with all sorts of precious riches and
valuables.

⁵ The wise are mightier than the strong,*
and those with knowledge grow
stronger and stronger.
⁶ So don't go to war without wise guidance;
victory depends on having many advisers.

⁷ Wisdom is too lofty for fools.
Among leaders at the city gate, they
have nothing to say.

⁸ A person who plans evil
will get a reputation as a troublemaker.
⁹ The schemes of a fool are sinful;
everyone detests a mocker.

¹⁰ If you fail under pressure,
your strength is too small.

¹¹ Rescue those who are unjustly sentenced
to die;
save them as they stagger to their death.
¹² Don't excuse yourself by saying, "Look,
we didn't know."
For God understands all hearts, and he
sees you.
He who guards your soul knows you
knew.
He will repay all people as their actions
deserve.

¹³ My child,* eat honey, for it is good,
and the honeycomb is sweet to the
taste.
¹⁴ In the same way, wisdom is sweet
to your soul.
If you find it, you will have a bright
future,
and your hopes will not be cut short.

¹⁵ Don't wait in ambush at the home
of the godly,
and don't raid the house where the
godly live.
¹⁶ The godly may trip seven times, but they
will get up again.
But one disaster is enough to
overthrow the wicked.

¹⁷ Don't rejoice when your enemies fall;
don't be happy when they stumble.
¹⁸ For the LORD will be displeased with you
and will turn his anger away from them.

¹⁹ Don't fret because of evildoers;
don't envy the wicked.
²⁰ For evil people have no future;
the light of the wicked will be snuffed
out.

²¹ My child, fear the LORD and the king.
Don't associate with rebels,
²² for disaster will hit them suddenly.
Who knows what punishment will come
from the LORD and the king?

*More Sayings of the Wise*
²³ Here are some further sayings of the wise:

It is wrong to show favoritism when
passing judgment.
²⁴ A judge who says to the wicked, "You are
innocent,"
will be cursed by many people and
denounced by the nations.
²⁵ But it will go well for those who convict
the guilty;
rich blessings will be showered on
them.

²⁶ An honest answer
is like a kiss of friendship.

²⁷ Do your planning and prepare your fields
before building your house.

²⁸ Don't testify against your neighbors
without cause;
don't lie about them.
²⁹ And don't say, "Now I can pay them back
for what they've done to me!
I'll get even with them!"

³⁰ I walked by the field of a lazy person,
the vineyard of one with no common
sense.
³¹ I saw that it was overgrown with nettles.
It was covered with weeds,
and its walls were broken down.
³² Then, as I looked and thought about it,
I learned this lesson:
³³ A little extra sleep, a little more slumber,
a little folding of the hands to rest—

**24:5** As in Greek version; Hebrew reads *A wise man is strength.*   **24:13** Hebrew *My son;* also in 24:21.

³⁴ then poverty will pounce on you like
    a bandit;
  scarcity will attack you like an armed
    robber.

## More Proverbs of Solomon

**25** These are more proverbs of Solomon, collected by the advisers of King Hezekiah of Judah.

² It is God's privilege to conceal things
    and the king's privilege to discover
      them.

³ No one can comprehend the height of
      heaven, the depth of the earth,
    or all that goes on in the king's mind!

⁴ Remove the impurities from silver,
    and the sterling will be ready for the
      silversmith.
⁵ Remove the wicked from the king's court,
    and his reign will be made secure by
      justice.

⁶ Don't demand an audience with the king
    or push for a place among the great.
⁷ It's better to wait for an invitation to the
      head table
    than to be sent away in public disgrace.

  Just because you've seen something,
⁸   don't be in a hurry to go to court.
  For what will you do in the end
    if your neighbor deals you a shameful
      defeat?

## HEAVY hearts

READ PROVERBS 25:20

A wise person knows when to crack a joke and when not to, when to try to cheer someone up and when to just be quiet.

If you are a friend or relative of someone dealing with serious illness, don't expect that person to deal with things the way you would. It's not always your job to lighten the mood. Sometimes a person has such a "heavy heart" that "singing cheerful songs" to them would be like "pouring vinegar in a wound."

Try to gauge the person's mood and if you're not sure what's appropriate, just ask! When you do speak, make sure your words heal and don't sting.

⁹ When arguing with your neighbor,
    don't betray another person's
      secret.
¹⁰ Others may accuse you of gossip,
    and you will never regain your good
      reputation.

¹¹ Timely advice is lovely,
    like golden apples in a silver basket.

¹² To one who listens, valid criticism
    is like a gold earring or other gold
      jewelry.

¹³ Trustworthy messengers refresh like
      snow in summer.
  They revive the spirit of their
      employer.

¹⁴ A person who promises a gift but doesn't
      give it
    is like clouds and wind that bring
      no rain.

¹⁵ Patience can persuade a prince,
    and soft speech can break bones.

¹⁶ Do you like honey?
    Don't eat too much, or it will make you
      sick!

¹⁷ Don't visit your neighbors too often,
    or you will wear out your welcome.

¹⁸ Telling lies about others
    is as harmful as hitting them
      with an ax,
  wounding them with a sword,
    or shooting them with a sharp
      arrow.

¹⁹ Putting confidence in an unreliable
      person in times of trouble
    is like chewing with a broken tooth
      or walking on a lame foot.

²⁰ Singing cheerful songs to a person with
      a heavy heart
    is like taking someone's coat in cold
      weather
    or pouring vinegar in a wound.*

²¹ If your enemies are hungry, give them
      food to eat.
  If they are thirsty, give them water
      to drink.

**25:20** As in Greek version; Hebrew reads *pouring vinegar on soda.*

22 You will heap burning coals of shame on
      their heads,
   and the LORD will reward you.

23 As surely as a north wind brings rain,
   so a gossiping tongue causes anger!

24 It's better to live alone in the corner
      of an attic
   than with a quarrelsome wife in a
      lovely home.

25 Good news from far away
   is like cold water to the thirsty.

26 If the godly give in to the wicked,
   it's like polluting a fountain or
      muddying a spring.

27 It's not good to eat too much honey,
   and it's not good to seek honors for
      yourself.

28 A person without self-control
   is like a city with broken-down
      walls.

# 26

1 Honor is no more associated with
      fools
   than snow with summer or rain with
      harvest.

2 Like a fluttering sparrow or a darting
      swallow,
   an undeserved curse will not land on
      its intended victim.

3 Guide a horse with a whip, a donkey with
      a bridle,
   and a fool with a rod to his back!

4 Don't answer the foolish arguments of
      fools,
   or you will become as foolish as they
      are.

5 Be sure to answer the foolish arguments
      of fools,
   or they will become wise in their own
      estimation.

6 Trusting a fool to convey a message
   is like cutting off one's feet or drinking
      poison!

7 A proverb in the mouth of a fool
   is as useless as a paralyzed leg.

8 Honoring a fool
   is as foolish as tying a stone to a
      slingshot.

9 A proverb in the mouth of a fool
   is like a thorny branch brandished by a
      drunk.

10 An employer who hires a fool or a
      bystander
   is like an archer who shoots at random.

11 As a dog returns to its vomit,
   so a fool repeats his foolishness.

12 There is more hope for fools
   than for people who think they are
      wise.

13 The lazy person claims, "There's a lion on
      the road!
   Yes, I'm sure there's a lion out there!"

14 As a door swings back and forth on its
      hinges,
   so the lazy person turns over in bed.

15 Lazy people take food in their hand
   but don't even lift it to their mouth.

16 Lazy people consider themselves smarter
   than seven wise counselors.

17 Interfering in someone else's argument
   is as foolish as yanking a dog's ears.

18 Just as damaging
   as a madman shooting a deadly weapon
19 is someone who lies to a friend
   and then says, "I was only joking."

20 Fire goes out without wood,
   and quarrels disappear when gossip
      stops.

21 A quarrelsome person starts fights
   as easily as hot embers light charcoal
   or fire lights wood.

22 Rumors are dainty morsels
   that sink deep into one's heart.

23 Smooth* words may hide a wicked heart,
   just as a pretty glaze covers a clay pot.

24 People may cover their hatred with
      pleasant words,
   but they're deceiving you.

26:23 As in Greek version; Hebrew reads *Burning*.

25 They pretend to be kind, but don't
   believe them.
   Their hearts are full of many evils.*
26 While their hatred may be concealed
   by trickery,
   their wrongdoing will be exposed
   in public.

27 If you set a trap for others,
   you will get caught in it yourself.
   If you roll a boulder down on others,
   it will crush you instead.

28 A lying tongue hates its victims,
   and flattering words cause ruin.

# 27

1 Don't brag about tomorrow,
   since you don't know what the
   day will bring.

2 Let someone else praise you, not your
   own mouth—
   a stranger, not your own lips.

3 A stone is heavy and sand is weighty,
   but the resentment caused by a fool
   is even heavier.

4 Anger is cruel, and wrath is like
   a flood,
   but jealousy is even more dangerous.

5 An open rebuke
   is better than hidden love!

6 Wounds from a sincere friend
   are better than many kisses from an
   enemy.

7 A person who is full refuses honey,
   but even bitter food tastes sweet
   to the hungry.

8 A person who strays from home
   is like a bird that strays from its nest.

9 The heartfelt counsel of a friend
   is as sweet as perfume and incense.

10 Never abandon a friend—
   either yours or your father's.
   When disaster strikes, you won't have
   to ask your brother for assistance.
   It's better to go to a neighbor than to
   a brother who lives far away.

11 Be wise, my child,* and make my heart
   glad.
   Then I will be able to answer my
   critics.

12 A prudent person foresees danger and
   takes precautions.
   The simpleton goes blindly on and
   suffers the consequences.

13 Get security from someone who
   guarantees a stranger's debt.
   Get a deposit if he does it for
   foreigners.*

14 A loud and cheerful greeting early in the
   morning
   will be taken as a curse!

15 A quarrelsome wife is as annoying
   as constant dripping on a rainy day.
16 Stopping her complaints is like trying
   to stop the wind
   or trying to hold something with
   greased hands.

17 As iron sharpens iron,
   so a friend sharpens a friend.

18 As workers who tend a fig tree are
   allowed to eat the fruit,
   so workers who protect their
   employer's interests will be
   rewarded.

19 As a face is reflected in water,
   so the heart reflects the real
   person.

20 Just as Death and Destruction* are never
   satisfied,
   so human desire is never satisfied.

21 Fire tests the purity of silver and gold,
   but a person is tested by being
   praised.*

22 You cannot separate fools from their
   foolishness,
   even though you grind them like grain
   with mortar and pestle.

23 Know the state of your flocks,
   and put your heart into caring for your
   herds,

26:25 Hebrew *seven evils.*   27:11 Hebrew *my son.*   27:13 As in Greek and Latin versions (see also 20:16); Hebrew reads *for a promiscuous woman.*   27:20 Hebrew *Sheol and Abaddon.*   27:21 Or *by flattery.*

²⁴ for riches don't last forever,
   and the crown might not be passed to
   the next generation.
²⁵ After the hay is harvested and the new
   crop appears
   and the mountain grasses are
   gathered in,
²⁶ your sheep will provide wool for clothing,
   and your goats will provide the price
   of a field.
²⁷ And you will have enough goats' milk for
   yourself,
   your family, and your servant girls.

# 28

¹ The wicked run away when no one
   is chasing them,
   but the godly are as bold as lions.

² When there is moral rot within a nation,
   its government topples easily.
   But wise and knowledgeable leaders
   bring stability.

³ A poor person who oppresses the poor
   is like a pounding rain that destroys
   the crops.

⁴ To reject the law is to praise the wicked;
   to obey the law is to fight them.

⁵ Evil people don't understand justice,
   but those who follow the LORD
   understand completely.

⁶ Better to be poor and honest
   than to be dishonest and rich.

⁷ Young people who obey the law are wise;
   those with wild friends bring shame to
   their parents.*

⁸ Income from charging high interest rates
   will end up in the pocket of someone
   who is kind to the poor.

⁹ God detests the prayers
   of a person who ignores the law.

¹⁰ Those who lead good people along an
   evil path
   will fall into their own trap,
   but the honest will inherit good things.

¹¹ Rich people may think they are wise,
   but a poor person with discernment
   can see right through them.

¹² When the godly succeed, everyone
   is glad.
   When the wicked take charge, people
   go into hiding.

¹³ People who conceal their sins will not
   prosper,
   but if they confess and turn from them,
   they will receive mercy.

¹⁴ Blessed are those who fear to do wrong,*
   but the stubborn are headed for
   serious trouble.

¹⁵ A wicked ruler is as dangerous to the
   poor
   as a roaring lion or an attacking bear.

¹⁶ A ruler with no understanding will
   oppress his people,
   but one who hates corruption will have
   a long life.

¹⁷ A murderer's tormented conscience will
   drive him into the grave.
   Don't protect him!

¹⁸ The blameless will be rescued from harm,
   but the crooked will be suddenly
   destroyed.

¹⁹ A hard worker has plenty of food,
   but a person who chases fantasies ends
   up in poverty.

²⁰ The trustworthy person will get a rich
   reward,
   but a person who wants quick riches
   will get into trouble.

²¹ Showing partiality is never good,
   yet some will do wrong for a mere
   piece of bread.

²² Greedy people try to get rich quick
   but don't realize they're headed for
   poverty.

²³ In the end, people appreciate honest
   criticism
   far more than flattery.

²⁴ Anyone who steals from his father and
   mother
   and says, "What's wrong with that?"
   is no better than a murderer.

**28:7** Hebrew *their father.*    **28:14** Or *those who fear the LORD;* Hebrew reads *those who fear.*

25 Greed causes fighting;
    trusting the LORD leads to prosperity.

26 Those who trust their own insight are
        foolish,
    but anyone who walks in wisdom is safe.

27 Whoever gives to the poor will lack
        nothing,
    but those who close their eyes to
        poverty will be cursed.

28 When the wicked take charge, people go
        into hiding.
    When the wicked meet disaster, the
        godly flourish.

# 29

¹ Whoever stubbornly refuses to
        accept criticism
    will suddenly be destroyed beyond
        recovery.

² When the godly are in authority, the
        people rejoice.
    But when the wicked are in power, they
        groan.

³ The man who loves wisdom brings joy to
        his father,
    but if he hangs around with
        prostitutes, his wealth is wasted.

⁴ A just king gives stability to his nation,
    but one who demands bribes destroys it.

⁵ To flatter friends
    is to lay a trap for their feet.

⁶ Evil people are trapped by sin,
    but the righteous escape, shouting
        for joy.

⁷ The godly care about the rights of the
        poor;
    the wicked don't care at all.

⁸ Mockers can get a whole town agitated,
    but the wise will calm anger.

⁹ If a wise person takes a fool to court,
    there will be ranting and ridicule but
        no satisfaction.

¹⁰ The bloodthirsty hate blameless people,
    but the upright seek to help them.*

¹¹ Fools vent their anger,
    but the wise quietly hold it back.

¹² If a ruler pays attention to liars,
    all his advisers will be wicked.

¹³ The poor and the oppressor have this
        in common—
    the LORD gives sight to the eyes of both.

¹⁴ If a king judges the poor fairly,
    his throne will last forever.

¹⁵ To discipline a child produces wisdom,
    but a mother is disgraced by an
        undisciplined child.

¹⁶ When the wicked are in authority, sin
        flourishes,
    but the godly will live to see their
        downfall.

¹⁷ Discipline your children, and they will
        give you peace of mind
    and will make your heart glad.

¹⁸ When people do not accept divine
        guidance, they run wild.
    But whoever obeys the law is joyful.

¹⁹ Words alone will not discipline a servant;
    the words may be understood, but they
        are not heeded.

²⁰ There is more hope for a fool
    than for someone who speaks without
        thinking.

²¹ A servant pampered from childhood
    will become a rebel.

²² An angry person starts fights;
    a hot-tempered person commits all
        kinds of sin.

²³ Pride ends in humiliation,
    while humility brings honor.

²⁴ If you assist a thief, you only hurt
        yourself.
    You are sworn to tell the truth, but you
        dare not testify.

²⁵ Fearing people is a dangerous trap,
    but trusting the LORD means safety.

²⁶ Many seek the ruler's favor,
    but justice comes from the LORD.

29:10 Or *The bloodthirsty hate blameless people, / and they seek to kill the upright;* Hebrew reads *The bloodthirsty hate blameless people, / as for the upright, they seek their life.*

## BE ALL you can be
READ PROVERBS 27:17

We pray that as you deal with a health crisis, you're not trying to go it alone.

Whether you're the patient or the caregiver, you need support. When we try to face things alone and handle stuff all by ourselves, we can get physically and emotionally exhausted. But when we allow friends to come alongside us, they can bring out the best in us.

Do you already have those kinds of friends? If so, allow them to encourage and assist you. If not, pray for such friends. Find a support group for your disease or start a little group yourself. Get a "prayer partner" who will pray with you in person or on the phone each week. Don't know how to find a prayer partner? Ask God—He'll either show you whom to ask or tell someone to ask you! That kind of prayer support will help you become all God meant you to be. After all, that's what friends are for.

---

²⁷ The righteous despise the unjust;
　the wicked despise the godly.

*The Sayings of Agur*

**30** The sayings of Agur son of Jakeh contain this message.*

I am weary, O God;
　I am weary and worn out, O God.*
² I am too stupid to be human,
　and I lack common sense.
³ I have not mastered human wisdom,
　nor do I know the Holy One.

⁴ Who but God goes up to heaven and
　comes back down?
　Who holds the wind in his fists?
　Who wraps up the oceans in his cloak?
　Who has created the whole wide
　world?
　What is his name—and his son's name?
　Tell me if you know!

⁵ Every word of God proves true.
　He is a shield to all who come to him
　for protection.
⁶ Do not add to his words,
　or he may rebuke you and expose you
　as a liar.

⁷ O God, I beg two favors from you;
　let me have them before I die.

⁸ First, help me never to tell a lie.
　Second, give me neither poverty nor
　riches!
　Give me just enough to satisfy my
　needs.
⁹ For if I grow rich, I may deny you and say,
　"Who is the LORD?"
　And if I am too poor, I may steal and
　thus insult God's holy name.

¹⁰ Never slander a worker to the employer,
　or the person will curse you, and you
　will pay for it.

¹¹ Some people curse their father
　and do not thank their mother.
¹² They are pure in their own eyes,
　but they are filthy and unwashed.
¹³ They look proudly around,
　casting disdainful glances.
¹⁴ They have teeth like swords
　and fangs like knives.
　They devour the poor from the earth
　and the needy from among
　humanity.

¹⁵ The leech has two suckers
　that cry out, "More, more!"*

There are three things that are never
　satisfied—
　no, four that never say, "Enough!":

---

**30:1a** Or *son of Jakeh from Massa;* or *son of Jakeh, an oracle.*  **30:1b** The Hebrew can also be translated *The man declares this to Ithiel, / to Ithiel and to Ucal.*  **30:15** Hebrew *two daughters who cry out, "Give, give!"*

16 the grave,*
the barren womb,
the thirsty desert,
the blazing fire.

17 The eye that mocks a father
and despises a mother's instructions
will be plucked out by ravens of the valley
and eaten by vultures.

18 There are three things that amaze me—
no, four things that I don't understand:
19 how an eagle glides through the sky,
how a snake slithers on a rock,
how a ship navigates the ocean,
how a man loves a woman.

20 An adulterous woman consumes a man,
then wipes her mouth and says,
"What's wrong with that?"

21 There are three things that make the
earth tremble—
no, four it cannot endure:
22 a slave who becomes a king,
an overbearing fool who prospers,
23   a bitter woman who finally gets a
husband,
a servant girl who supplants her
mistress.

24 There are four things on earth that are
small but unusually wise:
25 Ants—they aren't strong,
but they store up food all summer.
26 Hyraxes*—they aren't powerful,
but they make their homes among the
rocks.
27 Locusts—they have no king,
but they march in formation.
28 Lizards—they are easy to catch,
but they are found even in kings'
palaces.

29 There are three things that walk with
stately stride—
no, four that strut about:
30 the lion, king of animals, who won't turn
aside for anything,
31   the strutting rooster,
the male goat,
a king as he leads his army.

32 If you have been a fool by being proud
or plotting evil,
cover your mouth in shame.

33 As the beating of cream yields butter
and striking the nose causes bleeding,
so stirring up anger causes quarrels.

### The Sayings of King Lemuel

**31** The sayings of King Lemuel contain
this message,* which his mother
taught him.

2 O my son, O son of my womb,
O son of my vows,
3 do not waste your strength on women,
on those who ruin kings.

4 It is not for kings, O Lemuel, to guzzle
wine.
Rulers should not crave alcohol.
5 For if they drink, they may forget the law
and not give justice to the
oppressed.
6 Alcohol is for the dying,
and wine for those in bitter distress.
7 Let them drink to forget their poverty
and remember their troubles no more.

8 Speak up for those who cannot speak for
themselves;
ensure justice for those being crushed.
9 Yes, speak up for the poor and helpless,
and see that they get justice.

### A Wife of Noble Character

10 *Who can find a virtuous and capable
wife?
She is more precious than rubies.
11 Her husband can trust her,
and she will greatly enrich his life.
12 She brings him good, not harm,
all the days of her life.

13 She finds wool and flax
and busily spins it.
14 She is like a merchant's ship,
bringing her food from afar.
15 She gets up before dawn to prepare
breakfast for her household
and plan the day's work for her
servant girls.

---

**30:16** Hebrew *Sheol*.   **30:26** Or *Coneys*, or *Rock badgers*.   **31:1** Or *of Lemuel, king of Massa*; or *of King Lemuel, an oracle*.
**31:10** Verses 10-31 comprise a Hebrew acrostic poem; each verse begins with a successive letter of the Hebrew alphabet.

<sup>16</sup> She goes to inspect a field and buys it;
    with her earnings she plants a vineyard.
<sup>17</sup> She is energetic and strong,
    a hard worker.
<sup>18</sup> She makes sure her dealings are
        profitable;
    her lamp burns late into the night.

<sup>19</sup> Her hands are busy spinning thread,
    her fingers twisting fiber.
<sup>20</sup> She extends a helping hand to the poor
    and opens her arms to the needy.
<sup>21</sup> She has no fear of winter for her
        household,
    for everyone has warm* clothes.

<sup>22</sup> She makes her own bedspreads.
    She dresses in fine linen and purple
        gowns.
<sup>23</sup> Her husband is well known at the city
        gates,
    where he sits with the other civic
        leaders.
<sup>24</sup> She makes belted linen garments
    and sashes to sell to the merchants.

<sup>25</sup> She is clothed with strength and
        dignity,
    and she laughs without fear of the
        future.
<sup>26</sup> When she speaks, her words are wise,
    and she gives instructions with
        kindness.
<sup>27</sup> She carefully watches everything in her
        household
    and suffers nothing from laziness.

<sup>28</sup> Her children stand and bless her.
    Her husband praises her:
<sup>29</sup> "There are many virtuous and capable
        women in the world,
    but you surpass them all!"

<sup>30</sup> Charm is deceptive, and beauty does not
        last;
    but a woman who fears the LORD will
        be greatly praised.
<sup>31</sup> Reward her for all she has done.
    Let her deeds publicly declare her
        praise.

**31:21** As in Greek and Latin versions; Hebrew reads *scarlet*.

# PRAY for the cure

DESPITE dedicated researchers and millions of dollars, we haven't been able to discover the cure for very many serious diseases in recent years. The government's "war on cancer" has produced some new weapons, but a cure still is a pipedream. Advances have been made in treating many of our life-threatening illnesses like heart disease and AIDS, but sure-fire cures don't exist. Doctors can make it easier to live with things like diabetes and chronic fatigue, but they can't take them away.

Perhaps one day some attackers will be conquered, but, unfortunately, new infections and viruses always seem poised to take their place. Still, **we join you in continuing to pray for the cure for your particular diagnosis.**

We're also praying you know the cure for the one terminal sickness we all have. It's both congenital (we're born with it) and inherited (from Adam and Eve who first disobeyed God).

The symptoms aren't always obvious, but they start showing up in our first toddler temper tantrum and continue to appear throughout our lives—in the self-centered things we think, say, and do, and in the good things we *fail* to think, say, or do.

The Bible explains this condition in Romans 3:23: "For everyone has sinned; we all fall short of God's glorious standard." Romans 5:12 further explains: "Adam's sin brought death, so death spread to everyone, for everyone sinned."

Sin is the diagnosis; terminal is the prognosis.

Don't kid yourself into thinking that you don't have it because you're a pretty nice person or you go to church or you were baptized as a baby. It's a sneaky condition—just like many physical diseases—and you can look fine on the outside despite being terminally ill on the inside.

However, there is a cure and you can receive it right now. It's very expensive, but the full cost has been paid for you. ("God paid a ransom to save you. . . . It was the precious blood of Christ" [1 Peter 1:18-19]). You must be willing to agree with God's diagnosis (I am a sinner) and desire to get a new prognosis (I want to accept the gift of eternal life).

**Here's how you can pray for the cure:**

*Dear God, I agree with You that I am a sinner. I want to stop living for myself and start living for You. I thank You for allowing Your Son, Jesus, to die on the cross and pay the debt I owe You. I'm asking Him to be the Forgiver of my sins and the Leader of my life. Amen.*

# LIVING as a cured person

If you just prayed for the cure of your soul, you may be wondering what happens next. You're right in thinking this prayer is not the *end* of your spiritual journey, but really the *beginning*. You're now on your way to becoming all you were meant to be.

If your physical disease were permanently cured today, what would you do? You'd be telling everyone you knew and maybe even some you didn't know! We urge you to tell someone today that you prayed for the cure of your soul. Tell someone whom you know will rejoice because you have a relationship with God and a reservation in heaven.

Then follow these steps to keep spiritually healthy:

1. Keep reading God's Word every day. Read *He Cares* and a Bible that includes the Old Testament, too. You'll discover God's amazing love for you and what He expects of those who choose to follow Him.

2. Pray to God every day—not just at mealtimes or bedtime, but converse with Him wherever you are. You can pray in your recliner or while driving your car (just keep your eyes open!). God is with you always; be sure to talk *and* listen to Him. Find a friend who shares your faith and become "prayer partners" who meet together regularly and pray for each other.

3. Worship God with others in a church near you. Labels really don't matter—just make sure it's a life-giving congregation where the people know Jesus and are making Him known.

4. Live a life that pleases God. God's Holy Spirit lives inside you now and will supernaturally empower you to live a holy life. You, of course, still will make mistakes, but as you confess them to God, He will forgive you. Check your spiritual growth progress by asking, "Am I loving God and others more this week than last?"

**You still may have problems and even sickness in your life, but your greatest problem is gone: You're no longer separated from God** and someday when you die, your soul still will live forever with Him. (You'll even get a brand-new, disease-proof body!)

Until then, live your life as a cured person.

Jesus "gave his life to free us from every kind of sin" (Titus 2:14).

# THE GIFT of knowing

HAVE YOU ever thought it's a gift to know you have a life-threatening illness? Of course, we wouldn't describe the diagnosis itself as a gift, but coming face-to-face with our own mortality can be a good thing.

After all, nobody is going to live on this planet forever, and many people will die without any warning—no time to say good-bye or get their affairs in order. So if we're all going to die, those of us diagnosed with a life-threatening disease have the gift of knowing our time *may* be closer than we thought, and we can use that time wisely.

**If you've received the gift of knowing, we suggest you put it to good use** by being prepared financially, practically, and emotionally to leave this earth.

- Make sure you have a will and your family knows where important financial papers are. If you've been the one who took care of financial matters, write out detailed instructions for whomever will take over this task.
- Make your own funeral arrangements or at least write down what your wishes are when your time does come. You'll be giving the gift of peace of mind to your family.
- If you're pretty sure you won't be here for important future dates, write cards or get small gifts to be given from you to commemorate these occasions: a graduation, a birth, a wedding, etc. It will help the recipients feel your love for them even if you're not there.
- Make certain there are no important words left unsaid. Tell (or write) your loved ones how much they mean to you. Forgive and be forgiven while there's still time. Don't leave a legacy of regret, guilt, or unresolved hurts.

"Knowing" can be a gift if you choose it to be.

# VERSE INDEX FOR MARGIN SYMBOLS

## Verses on God's Security, Peace, and Comfort

THE RAINBOW is a sign of hope first set in the sky for Noah when God promised he never again would flood the whole earth. This symbol leads you to verses about the security, peace, and comfort found in a relationship with God.

## Verses on Sin and Its Destructive Power

LIGHTNING is not a force to be ignored as it has the power to injure or even kill. The power of evil should not be taken lightly either. Sin injures and kills our spiritual life with God and this symbol shows you verses about sin and its destructive power.

## Verses on Finding Forgiveness through Jesus Christ

THE CROSS is a timeless symbol of the greatest sacrifice ever made: Jesus' death for our life. This symbol directs you to verses which explain how the Cross changed history and how anyone can find forgiveness through Jesus Christ.

## Verses on the Nature and Character of Jesus

THE PIERCED HAND reminds us that Jesus willingly allowed himself to be nailed to the cross as payment for our sins. This symbol highlights for you verses about Jesus' nature and character, which prove he really is the Son of God and our Messiah.

## WHEN GOD & CANCER MEET

Eighteen true stories of hope and healing for and about cancer survivors and their loved ones who have experienced God's miraculous touch: body, mind, and spirit. A powerful book assuring both believers and skeptics that although cancer is a very deep pit, the love of God is deeper still.

## FINDING THE LIGHT IN CANCER'S SHADOW

Hope, humor, and healing for all those living with a history of cancer, while answering the tough questions survivors often ask: Is everyone as paranoid as I am? Will life ever be normal again? What if the cancer comes back? A hope-filled book where survivors—whether cancer-free or dealing with a recurrence—can find renewed purpose and joy.

*LYNN EIB is a long-time cancer survivor and journalist, who since 1996 has been employed as a patient advocate offering emotional and spiritual support to cancer patients and their caregivers. Her Web site is www.CancerPatientAdvocate.com.*